THE ADMAN'S DILEMMA: FROM BARNUM TO TRUMP

The Adman's Dilemma is a cultural biography that explores the rise and fall of the advertising man as a figure who became effectively a licensed deceiver in the process of governing the lives of American consumers. This personage was caught up in an apparent contradiction, both compelled to deceive yet supposed to tell the truth. It was this moral condition and its consequences that made the adman so interesting to critics, novelists, and eventually filmmakers.

The biography tracks his saga from its origins in the exaggerated doings of P.T. Barnum, through the emergence of a new profession in the 1920s, the heyday of the adman's influence during the post–Second World War era, and the later rebranding of the adman as artist, until the apparent demise of the figure, symbolized by the triumph of that consummate huckster, Donald Trump.

In *The Adman's Dilemma*, author Paul Rutherford explores how people inside and outside the advertising industry have understood the conflict between artifice and authenticity. The book employs a range of fictional and nonfictional sources, including memoirs, novels, movies, TV shows, websites, and museum exhibits to suggest how the adman embodied some of the strange realities of modernity.

PAUL RUTHERFORD is professor emeritus in the Department of History at the University of Toronto. He is the author of several books published by UTP, including *When Television Was Young* (1990), *The New Icons?* (1994), *Endless Propaganda* (2000), *Weapons of Mass Persuasion* (2004), and *World Made Sexy* (2007).

The ADMAN'S DILEMMA

From BARNUM to TRUMP

PAUL RUTHERFORD

UNIVERSITY OF TORONTO PRESS
Toronto Buffalo London

© University of Toronto Press 2018
Toronto Buffalo London
utorontopress.com
Printed in Canada

ISBN 978-1-4875-0390-1 (cloth)   ISBN 978-1-4875-2298-8 (paper)

♾ Printed on acid-free, 100% post-consumer recycled paper with
vegetable-based inks.

Library and Archives Canada Cataloguing in Publication

Rutherford, Paul, 1944–, author
The adman's dilemma : From Barnum to Trump / Paul Rutherford.

Includes bibliographical references and index.
ISBN 978-1-4875-0390-1 (hardcover). – ISBN 978-1-4875-2298-8 (softcover)

1. Advertising – Social aspects.   2. Advertising – History.   3. Advertising
executives – History.   4. Advertising in popular culture.   I. Title.

HF5821.R88 2018   659.1′042   C2018-900841-5

This book has been published with the help of a grant from the
Federation for the Humanities and Social Sciences, through the
Awards to Scholarly Publications Program, using funds provided by
the Social Sciences and Humanities Research Council of Canada.

University of Toronto Press acknowledges the financial assistance to its
publishing program of the Canada Council for the Arts and the
Ontario Arts Council, an agency of the Government of Ontario.

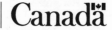

CONTENTS

ACKNOWLEDGMENTS

This biography was born in front of the television screen. The first years of watching *Mad Men*, especially the character of Don Draper, led me to ponder the complicated figure of the adman, both his skill at deception and his consequent distress, moral or otherwise. But like most academic enterprises, the completion of the biography was assisted by the efforts of other people. I received a welcome grant from the Social Sciences and Humanities Research Council of Canada which enabled me both to travel and to hire research assistants to forward the study. I would like to thank Arlene Macdonald, then a graduate student but now a professor of bioethics, who expended much effort analysing the public response to advertising and the adman at mid-century. I also thank Jodi Giesbrecht, also a doctoral candidate at the time, who explored the literature on the plight of the adwoman in the last half of the twentieth century. In addition, my research effort benefitted from the collection of materials on *Mad Men* by one of my undergraduate students, Adam Rasmi, yet another fan of that hit series. I am especially grateful to Michael Bliss, a master of biography and a long-time friend but now sadly departed, who read an earlier draft of the manuscript. He supplied a wealth of suggestions to improve the biography: in particular it was on Michael's suggestion that I added an afterword on the rise of Donald Trump. I am also very grateful to the two anonymous reviewers chosen by the University of Toronto Press. Both these individuals carefully read the manuscript and provided invaluable criticisms that served to strengthen the hypothesis, the argument, and the flow of the narrative. The system of peer evaluation may have its problems and its limits, but in my case I found the comments of these two people fair and useful, indeed most valuable. Likewise I express my appreciation for the enterprise of

Mark Thompson, an acquisitions editor at UTP, who carefully guided the manuscript through the complicated process of review and approval; to Michel Pharand, my copyeditor, who corrected my mistakes and tamed my enthusiasms; and to Barb Porter, the associate managing editor who supervised the complicated production process necessary before any academic work is published these days. Once again, I convey my gratitude to my wife, Margarita Orszag, for her understanding and patience in dealing with a husband who, although retired from the university, was often consumed by this academic project. Nor should I forget my two furry children, Rufus and Jonas, who had to accept that their human partner was not always available to look after their doggie needs.

Paul Rutherford
December 2017

THE ADMAN'S DILEMMA

Introduction
ENTER "DON DRAPER," 2007

Mad Men was one of the critical hits of the 2007/8 television year, winning a bevy of awards (though never a huge audience) for its portrayal of the life and times of the fictitious Sterling Cooper advertising agency in New York City in the 1960s. (Its audience peaked at around 4.7 million viewers for the premiere shows of seasons 5 and 6.)[1] It painted a picture of a place full of cigarettes and booze, sexual shenanigans, competition, much cynicism, and much deceit. Often the drama focused on the troubled life and times of one person, Don Draper, the highly successful creative director of Sterling Cooper, who demonstrated again and again his ability to fashion brilliant ads. In the office and at home he proved a master of deceit: actually, his whole life was something of a lie because he had stolen the name of another person. Whatever his success at the office, he found his private life empty, hollow, and he searched for some experience more real, more authentic in a series of eventually unsatisfying affairs with women.

In the next few seasons the popularity of *Mad Men* and its characters boomed, even airing outside America: it became a phenomenon that sparked all sorts of notice and commentary in the media. The show produced fan sites and fan books,[2] discussions about fashion (because the cast was so stylish) and gender (because the men were so sexist and the women so pleasing), and a new male sex symbol, Jon Hamm, who played the role of Draper.[3] The term "Mad Men" came to serve as a convenient label for a style of manhood, sometimes confident and effective, sometimes reactionary or even repressed.[4] According to Mindset Media, a market research firm, the show was especially attractive to the so-called creative class, very liberal, curious, and maybe a bit dreamy, the types who bought Apple and Audi.[5] No doubt more significant to marketers,

the *Mad Men* audience was full of upscale viewers, in their adult years
(25 to 54), earning $100,000 or more a year, thus prime consumers.[6]
Academe soon got into the act with a symposium, "The Reality of Mad
Men," at Duke University (2008) and a volume published in Blackwell's
Philosophy and Pop Culture series (2010), followed by a small collection of studies in the next five years.[7] One clever author, Dr Stephanie
Newman, a popular psychoanalyst, decided Draper and his compatriots
were emblematic of the terrible plague of narcissism that bedeviled the
populace of modern America.[8] Not everyone was pleased with the show,
of course: Daniel Mendelsohn, in the *New York Review of Books* (2011),
wrote a scathing review of the program's first four seasons. But even he
found the show had a deep fascination for viewers who were children
back in the 1960s, which in part explained why it had swarmed through
pop culture, or so he speculated.[9] By the time *Mad Men* ended, in 2015,
after seven seasons, the show was ranked along with *Sex and the City*, *The
Sopranos*, or *Breaking Bad* as one of the sensations of early twenty-first
century television.

Yet however imaginative and innovative the show – for television entertainment in America had rarely dealt with advertising as drama – *Mad
Men* spoke to its audience in a familiar tongue.[10] Its treatment of admen
and advertising reflected views that were commonplace at the mid-
century, evident in, for example, a bestseller like Frederic Wakeman's
The Hucksters (1946) or the Rock Hudson/Doris Day movie *Lover Come
Back* (1961). In fact Matthew Weiner, the showrunner, was obsessed with
authenticity, getting the right look and feel, using all manner of artefacts and texts from the period to shape scripts and acting. *Mad Men*
was a marvellous visual representation of what I have come to call "the
adman's dilemma."

At its core the adman's dilemma described a moral condition produced by the practices of deception: it referred to the sense of malaise
supposedly, and according to some authors necessarily, suffered by the
masters of deceit. The "adman" denoted a male engaged in the practice of advertising, whether as an entrepreneur, a self-employed professional, or an employee of an agency or business. That person might be
a huckster, like the patent medicine moguls of the nineteenth century,
a copywriter or an art director (often referred to now as "creatives"), an
account executive, a media buyer, an agency manager or head, a market researcher, and more recently the account planner and web devel-
oper (employed by an agency). An ad is a paid message, a distinct form
of publicity, meant to sell a product, service, industry, cause, or person

(and occasionally to un-sell a vice or a rival). People of all sorts came to treat advertising in the broad sense as a dynamic mix of art, information, entertainment, and deception: the mix varied according to the time, the brand, and the source. If it was simply a form of untruth, of deceit, it would be much less interesting – and likely less effective. The elaboration of regulations against deceptive or false advertising worked to mask the presence of artifice, at least partially, in most publicity. That certainly hamstrung efforts to regulate the deceptions, especially the exaggerations and suggestions, of advertising. Still, in time, consumers, the veterans of marketing hype, responded to the mass of publicity with their own mix of belief and disbelief. They "knew" that publicity contained much fiction. Thus the adman became in effect, though never in law – *de facto* rather than *de jure* – a kind of licensed deceiver allowed to transgress the rules of truth-telling.

Put a bit differently, the adman's dilemma signified how many writers and filmmakers came to imagine the corruption of the soul engendered by a surfeit of artifice. The dilemma was always a matter of perception. Outsiders mostly saw this as a predicament or warning that faced any persuaders who laboured in the advertising industry. Insiders were certainly aware of the perception that clearly affected their reputation and, perhaps, their sense of self-worth. But, again usually, they denied its relevance or even its existence – as long as they remained a part of the advertising community. Renegades often did explore the dimensions of the predicament, if only to explain or justify their escape from a life of moral disorder. In its basic form a story or tale about the adman's dilemma told of the young man who strove to excel at advertising, one of the central institutions of modernity, how he normally succeeded but eventually came to doubt the virtue of his existence (what's called "the liar's plight"), the moral anguish that resulted, and what he did to resolve his situation. His biography became a grand exercise in the process of self-fashioning, especially the choices made or not made to realize success or secure peace of mind. The recognition of the condition took definite shape in the two decades after the Second World War in America. A few earlier works, such as H.G. Wells's novel *Tono-Bungay* (1909) and the memoir of Helen Woodward (a prominent adwoman), had already foreshadowed the definition of this affliction. But it was a postwar series of hit novels and movies that thoroughly explored the dimensions of the angst, perhaps the most famous being Sloan Wilson's *The Man in the Gray Flannel Suit* (1955). The dilemma was both echoed and denied, occasionally finessed or (temporally) solved, in memoirs, polemics, and other discussions – in short, in works of fact as well as fiction. Furthermore that dilemma, if it evolved over time, persisted into the twenty-first century, and it affected the perception and reputation of other individuals also in the persuasion business, such as the public relations counsel or the advertising woman (the chief reason some of them appear in this biography).

The predicament facing the advertising practitioner, purportedly, grew out of a logical conundrum. The adman's dilemma meant a choice between practicing more deception or telling more truth, between seeking to persuade or just to inform, between selling and communication, between success (or at least a decent chance) and failure (the likelihood) in the marketplace. The adman's work offended against the canons of authenticity and sincerity, especially since he must plead the case of the advertiser. The more the adman told the truth of a product, the less likely he was to sell that product. The harder the adman worked to sell that product, the more likely he was to mislead – if not lie. The choice was between suffering a personal defeat or committing a moral error. What made the predicament of wider significance – and thus should enhance his plight – was the fact his moral error could have profound social consequences. That of course was the simplest and most stark formulation of the adman's dilemma, where both options had a dismal effect on the life of the individual.

The problem was rooted in the developing character of the culture, the economy, and thus of advertising. After roughly 1850, the public sphere in America was increasingly founded on a certain mode of truth-telling, better yet on an obsession with facts, whatever the actual frequency of deception. This commitment was manifest in the prominence of news and expertise, especially science, and in the ideal of objectivity. Another sign of the obsession was the trust placed in statistics, which filled the press by the late nineteenth century and were taken as an accurate representation of reality.[11] But the emphasis on truth-telling was also apparent in the workings of the public school and the university, the apparatus of the law, and the import of mass media. It attained a general currency during the course of the Progressive movement in the early twentieth century, when business and civic leaders set out to modernize America, one goal of which was to institute honesty and integrity throughout the country.[12] Such an ensemble of ideas and institutions constituted a particular "regime of truth," to borrow from the vocabulary of Michel Foucault, where certain kinds of statements were deemed true, others false or fiction, and where certain experts, such as scientists and clerics, professionals, teachers, sometimes journalists, were deemed the arbiters of truth.[13]

Nonetheless, that regime was always countered by the practical needs of commerce or, for that matter, politics. The expanding marketplace required the constant production of wants and consumers, a twin process of enticement and manufacture which soon became the task of mass advertising. Simply informing the consumer of what was available was not usually sufficient to foster the consumption and growth that the business community – indeed progress – required. The burgeoning abundance of commodities had to be transformed into particular brands, made distinctive, made appealing, via words and images so that they stood out in the competitive marketplace. The effort to shape brands and mobilize desire drove the advertising practitioner to exaggerate, to fabricate, to hide, to entertain, occasionally to lie to achieve his goal. The adman became, in effect, the chief agent of consumption, the front man of capitalism, the grand advocate of materialism, making him an obvious target of social and moral critics.

Consequently this biography of the adman explores the conversations and the tensions generated by one of the signal contradictions built into the saga of modernity: the dichotomy between the ideal of truth-telling and the practices of deception. Furthermore, the adman's dilemma had, occasionally, a more mundane importance to the character of persuasion. It could function as a kind of yoke to control or manage deception. Under certain circumstances, the dilemma might act as a social mechanism to constrain deceit and thereby to protect the integrity of the regime of truth. That required the adman should address his plight, in practice if not consciously or directly, admittedly not always a common response, even in fiction. Draper, for instance, rarely did. Recognition was only easy for renegades and outsiders. But awareness of the dilemma was more likely. Once he accepted the moral force of the dilemma, the adman or any persuader would strive to restrain the impulse or resist the direction to exaggerate or hide or fabricate, and so endeavour to tell as much of the truth as was possible, given the particulars of his situation. Normally that translated into the injunction "Don't lie" – which, of course, hardly covered the panoply of deception. Nonetheless, the mechanism worked to prevent a licensed deceiver from becoming a kind of "evil deceiver" (with apologies to Descartes) who always and only misled.

The adman's dilemma was the central motif in many of the stories about advertising and its practitioners. It was present in others, or at least its ghost was, and affected how these stories operated. But the adman's dilemma was not always acknowledged, nor was it alone in the social conversation. There were three related motifs, offshoots of the dilemma. The first was the "matrix," a web of deception spun by the adman to ensnare the consumers. This emerged in the 1920s and persisted thereafter. The awareness of the matrix spawned its own dichotomy in the rhetoric of critics and insiders, either the notion of a hapless public who always fell victim to the deceit, or of the obstinate public who resisted the adman's illusions. The second motif I will term "the ad-maker's sin," which cast him (or her) as a villain responsible for all manner of moral, social, and even political ills that America suffered. That motif flourished in the late 1950s, the 1960s, and the early 1970s, and it revived again in the social conversation just before and certainly after 2000. Linked to these two was a complex of ideas organized around the motifs of "contagion and immunity"; this complex focused on the ill effects of too much publicity, the problems of clutter as well as illusion. This complex actually appeared early in the biography of the adman (earlier than the first two motifs) and persisted throughout the period. Yet a different set of motifs, much more benign, portrayed the adman as an "innovator," a "civilizer," "industry's engine," "the businessman's ally," and "the consumer's friend," often present in the rhetoric of advertising men and women. Each amounted to a denial of the dilemma. The adman might appear at different moments as a cultural hero, even the radical or subversive, the capitalist's tool, a sad clown, or of course as a victim of the very system he served. Sometimes the adman seemed a veritable chameleon, depending on the context, the particular narrative or story.

The conversation about the adman can best be outlined through a series of questions that pertain to the work and the effects of advertising. Here my object is not just the dilemma but the overall discourse. To illustrate what was involved, I have drawn evidence of a sort from the first episode of *Mad Men*, "Smoke Gets in Your Eyes," among other texts.

How best to establish trust? The advertising man needed to somehow win the confidence of the two other parties, the client and the consumer. So the ad executive had to convince the potential sponsor that hiring his agency was the best course, one reason why tales about "the Pitch" became so common in recent stories about the adman. "Smoke Gets in Your Eyes" actually contained two such tales, one of a failure where Draper insulted a possible client, and the other of an astounding success where he wowed the client and his colleagues. Of course the more significant enterprise was to inspire trust in the broader public, to overcome the normal discount, the element of disbelief, which troubled the reception of publicity. In both cases this task involved more than demonstrating competence, although that was crucial: the adman was obliged to express the virtues of sincerity and authenticity, often taking on the guise of a truth-teller. Loads of charm was yet another virtue, one reason admen earned a reputation as very friendly guys. And Draper certainly demonstrated that ability to please a listener with flattery or dazzle – when necessary.

Where and when was deception permissible? What then were the demands of truth? The truth – of a product, a cause, a person – was a resource, a pose, and a restraint, sometimes an obstacle. Was truth negotiable? What was constant about this truth and how much was enough? Draper saved a big tobacco account when he realized that the threat of cancer did not matter when selling Lucky Strikes, given the fact no brand of cigarette could any longer make health claims.[14] What mattered was to provoke desire and establish distinction: hence his slogan "It's Toasted," which was an actual slogan employed by the client decades before. In practice the adman assumed a license to deceive – at least a bit: that was a pragmatic necessity of the craft. But what kinds, what degrees of deception were allowable (sometimes a matter determined by law)? And how was it possible to make the deception acceptable? Once the answer was to offer a "reason-why," the guise of rationality, where the adman presented the prospective user of a brand with a unique signal of its utility. Increasingly, however, the copywriter and art director – the key creatives, in the jargon of the craft – drew on the repertoire of art and entertainment to produce pleasure and mask deception. Nonetheless there lingered the presumption that Madison Avenue remained one of the chief abodes of the so-called liars' professions.

Who was the master? This question actually covered a broad spectrum of issues which reflected the prevailing ideal of the sovereign self, the autonomous individual who commanded his or her own destiny.[15] It had a particular significance where masculinity was at issue, since self-reliance and independence were often considered the marks of manliness. Typically the answer required following the money: the client who hired and approved was sovereign. This could become a matter of much distress to the adman, who was forced to submit to the sponsor's will. In the pilot, Draper, incensed that a woman had questioned his judgment, was persuaded to meet her again, over drinks, to apologize – and save the account. Sometimes the argument was made that the ordinary person, or the public in general, was sovereign, the consumer as Queen or

King, though that was more specious than credible. It was, nonetheless, a claim often advanced by the advertising agents of the 1920s and still repeated by one ad executive interviewed in the PBS documentary *The Persuaders* (2004) on the advertising industry. This claim buttressed the motif of the consumer's friend. The third possibility? That the adman was master, the one who manipulated and controlled the fate of both the client and the public. This dream of sovereignty gave rise to another notion, namely "the immaculate campaign," where the ad existed before the brand, where the advertising determined the very nature of the product. In one extreme version of this variant, the science fiction classic *The Space Merchants* (1953), advertising agencies effectively ruled the world.

What were the moral effects of deceit? The ethical problem expressed the contrast between a craft which employed deception in a society which valued truth. That could, perhaps should, produce personal angst, one of the features of the affliction I've named the adman's dilemma. How could the adman live with himself? Consequently we find fictional copywriters or account supervisors who confessed their sins or sought to escape to some other existence. Throughout the *Mad Men* series, Don Draper succumbed to such moments, though mostly he repressed any anxiety by working and playing hard, by always "moving forward," to repeat one of his favourite maxims. In the first episode he revealed his anxieties over discovery and failure when he suggested to his girlfriend he would be found out as a fraud and so trashed by his colleagues. There were actual persuaders who justified or excused their activities in a myriad of ways. P.T. Barnum mounted a life-long autobiographical project, in part, to legitimate his humbugs. And, recently, there have appeared characters who revelled in the irony of their situation, such as Nick Naylor in the movie *Thank You For Smoking* (2005), which seemed so thoroughly postmodern in its comic style (since truth was never a constant nor an absolute).

What were the social consequences of publicity? Answers to that query have been a source of pride or guilt – and horror. The evolution of a modern style of governance came to require a figure like the adman who could weave compelling stories, despite the presumption that any civilized society needed truth and trust to operate effectively. Once upon a time admen saw themselves in the vanguard of modernity, their messages deemed a force of civilization and progress. They were innovators and civilizers whose work energized the economy and enhanced life. Again in the first episode, Draper boasted to a prospective client that he and his ilk had created the ordinary concept of love, what people imagined when they spoke of being in love. But for many years, commencing in the 1920s, advertising had often served as a "folk devil" and "whipping boy" in assorted critiques.[16] That produced successive arguments organized around the motif of the ad-maker's sin. The worry about the social consequences of advertising or public relations generated a narrative of harm, stories, for example, about an excess of materialism, the subversion of democracy, the destruction of the environment, or the oppression of women. And there was another concern, this one about the perception of reality itself. What had publicity, especially endless advertising and propaganda, done to the world? In the first episode, Draper also boasted that the admen had foisted on the American public a particular vision of what happiness meant, always serving to make brands successful and so presumably to keep the economy buoyant. That was just one example of the way the adman's work had colonized the American psyche. The spectre of the matrix, a reign of false signs, came to haunt the saga of modernity. Think of Daniel Boorstin's famous polemic *The Image* (1961), although here the adman was only one of a gaggle of agents who divorced Americans from reality. What a person considered the import of publicity could determine whether the adman appeared as a villain, a victim, or even a hero.

Various narratives of understanding shaped the social conversation about the adman and advertising.[17] I will eventually elaborate six of these, listed here in their order of appearance: "the huckster's game," "the narrative of harm," "the progress myth" (and thus of justification), "a tradition of anti-advertising" (which drew on the narrative of harm), "the chronicle of struggle," and "the gospel of creativity." The various motifs mentioned previously populate these narratives. By narrative I mean a sequence of connected events occurring over time, where cause and effect are presumed, a sequence that usually has a beginning, a middle, and an end.[18] A narrative of understanding has a public and a moral character because it serves to inform how people interpret general experiences and types of individuals. It is a common resource authors, actors, and the audience can draw upon: the narrative does not generate but it does shape both the acts of creation and reception in consistent patterns. Each narrative is eventually composed of many different but related stories or tales.[19] And stories are one of the chief means we use to explain our selves and our reality. They render life intelligible, providing information and provoking affect, that is, the emotional response and the intensity of feeling of people, things like belief and disbelief, alienation or affirmation, so important to the

legitimacy of authority.[20] The actual stories, of course, might take many
shapes: perhaps a tragedy, a comedy or satire, a romance, or some mix
of these genres. Likewise, the intensity and the lesson of these stories differ. There can be a confession and a justification, sometimes
an escape, sometimes a reconciliation. The stories may, and often did,
engage a variety of other dichotomies, notably liberation versus domination, self and community, vice or virtue. And the character of the
story changed, sometimes dramatically, when the subject was a woman
who must strive for success in what was for many years a man's world.

My book does not explain how the actual advertising man worked.
I style *The Adman's Dilemma* a cultural biography: not a biography of a
"real" person, though many genuine ad executives and creatives appear
here, but of an equally "real" figure found in commentary, literature,
and entertainment.[21] This is a work in the realm of cultural history, in
both senses: as a study of representations and as a study using representations. A "figure" is a historical character who might variously be defined
as a figment of the collective imagination or as a conceptual entity, perhaps a set of stereotypes. It evolves over time in tune with the culture and
the economy. It is produced and refashioned by the social conversation,
so it is always an ongoing project. A cultural biography tells the life story
of this significant social type whose activities intrigued and disturbed the
public mind.[22] That story is not "given." You have to build the overall
trajectory out of many fragments of material, since it is concerned with
what the culture said about such a person as well as about what that
person did to or for society. There are, then, three distinct but related
dimensions to a cultural biography. First, the work must pay attention to
form, what was permissible, what was conventional in the movie or the
memoir or, say, the genre of the Hollywood romantic comedy (one of
the modes of handling the adman's dilemma).[23] Second, it must tackle
the figure as a moral being, the code of ethics, style of life, struggles and
triumphs. Consequently, the figure became a site where different kinds
of signs contest, their champions seeking to impose an interpretation or
meaning.[24] Third, it must explore the effects people argued the character's activities have had upon the host society, whether for ill or good,
and how they shaped or structured the play of power and pleasure. That
is why much of *The Adman's Dilemma* deals with how insiders and critics
perceived advertising. Such conversation constituted one way in which
society, and especially the chattering classes, pondered the problems of
their present situation. You will find a set of contrasts and contradictions built into the public understanding of the adman, these signified

(though not encompassed) by the opposition of artifice and authenticity. All the talk about the figure served as a way of exploring the scope and import of deception, the ongoing mix of truth and untruth in the lifeworld. Cultural biography incorporates not only elements of history and biography but fiction as well: it is something of a concoction, a "life and times" of actual and imagined people.

Take a close look at one set of compelling images, the sequence of shots and scenes which opened the television series *Mad Men*. The overt purpose of the sequence was to show the titles of the program, a who's who of the makers and performers. The effect of the images, however, was to deliver an ambiguous message about the strange life of the adman. At least at first, the sequence seemed, as George Dunn has explained, a visual expression of the assertion by Marx about the fate of man in modernity.[25] There were no spoken words, the only sounds a repetitive, haunting melody, taken from the instrumental version of RJD2's "A Beautiful Mine." The silhouette of a man, presumably Don Draper, stepped into a high-rise office, his black garb signifying the authority and prestige of the bourgeois male in modern times.[26] But immediately the office began to dissolve, the briefcase, the pictures on the wall, the blinds, the chair and desk, all slid through the floor. Then a shift of scene, and we saw the man in black, arms outstretched, falling downwards between huge skyscrapers on which were emblazoned an assortment of ad images and slogans suggesting glamour, love, family, indulgence, and play that he and his kind had used to seduce the American consumer. Did his fall speak of the unreality, the emptiness of such artifice? Or did the images represent the ubiquity and power of illusion? Certainly in retrospect his fall suggested flight, or the urge to escape, which would be a theme constantly repeated throughout the series, as Draper at various moments would run away from his private and work life, a signal of the adman's dilemma. But at first the fall seemed to indicate he was dropping into the abyss, unable to control or prevent his fate: that image brought to my mind Frida Kahlo's *The Suicide of Dorothy Hale* (1938/9), which memorialized the death of a woman overcome by difficulties who hurled herself from a New York high-rise. Except Kahlo's tableau of hopelessness ended with the startling image of the woman's blood-spattered corpse on the street below the Hampshire House. Instead, our man in black did not die. Moreover, the scene shifted again to a shot of the man from the back, in repose, now seated and smoking, confident and dominant, looking out on a blank screen that stood in for a world ready to be filled with his seductive imagery. The adman, so it appeared, was back in command, able to reshape his environment according to his sponsor's desires. Was he not something of a modern hero, a man ultimately in control of his own furies and the destinies of the world around him?

Organization

The book opens with a speculative essay that uses one of the novels of Herman Melville to explore the place of the deceiver in modern times. After this Prelude, the biography is then arranged in a series of grand chapters that follow the trajectory of the figure of the adman roughly from the mid-nineteenth century up to the end of the first decade of the twenty-first century. Each of the sections in these chapters focuses on one or more key texts – an autobiography or memoir, a novel, a movie, a polemic, a documentary, an interview, an exhibition, a website. Usually I have selected texts which were widely read or seen, because they had a greater impact on the social conversation. Sometimes, however, I have highlighted a work that was so novel or different that its significance trumped its lack of popularity. Often I supplement these close analyses with a briefer discussion of other artefacts. The Afterword links the biography to the most extraordinary political event of 2015–16, the rise of Donald Trump. The Moral of the Biography simply sums up why the adman's dilemma and the like matter. I have used the endnotes, in places, to incorporate additional quotations or analyses, notably from or about theory, bibliography, and history.

Prelude

THE CON MAN, THE ADMAN, AND THE TRICKSTER: HERMAN MELVILLE, *THE CONFIDENCE-MAN: HIS MASQUERADE*, 1857

The ambiguous figure of the adman had antecedents and fellows. One novel explored his origins and his ways before the figure had really appeared on the American scene. Equally important, the novel enables a brief survey of the nature and scope of deception in the broader saga of modernity.[1]

On 1 April 1857 Dix, Edwards & Co., a publisher that would shortly go bankrupt, released Herman Melville's last novel, *The Confidence-Man*.[2] The book was a difficult read, quite unlike the kind of sea adventures that had made Melville popular with readers in America and England during the previous decade. Instead *The Confidence-Man* was set on a Mississippi steamboat named the *Fidèle* running from St Louis to New Orleans on one day, from dawn to midnight on April Fool's Day. How very fitting that date: the action dealt with a series of encounters between a motley collection of passengers, some respectable and some not, and a master deceiver who was also a shape-shifter. Melville identified the novel as "a work of amusement" (180), although it would have been more appropriate to call it a work of grim satire, targeting first American life and more broadly human nature. The difficulty came with its prose style: the novel was full of metaphors, allusions, double negatives, assertions and qualifications, reversals of character and role, all of which demanded much care to decipher the author's intent and meaning. The result was full of irony. Besides, *The Confidence-Man* did not conclude, it simply ended, which led a few contemporary reviewers to assert that a sequel was in the works. The slightly sinister final comment, "That something further may follow from this Masquerade," was a reflection on the world, not about the author's intent. Melville never attempted another novel.

Reviewers on both sides of the Atlantic were often puzzled by the style and the purpose of such a work. Critics thought *The Confidence-Man* "indigestible" (*London Illustrated Times*, 25 April 1857) or "careless and rambling" (Worcester, *Massachusetts Palladium*, 22 April 1857), suffering from "a quaint, unnatural style" (*New York Dispatch*, 5 April 1857), its effect "an uncomfortable sensation of dizziness in the head" (*London Literary Gazette*, 11 April 1857). It was counted a commercial and literary disaster. Only in the last half of the twentieth century did the novel win great scholarly favour, earning a reputation as a classic of American literature. The reason was, in part, because the style and the purpose better suited the times, especially when the postmodern impulse dominated literary studies. Even so, the admiration of Melville's achievement did not produce agreement over his purpose in writing the novel nor the nature of his leading character, who might seem something of a messiah or a devil. In fact, *The Confidence-Man* was subject to especially bizarre interpretations, drawn out of the scriptures, theory, and literature.[3] Melville opened the door to such shenanigans by peppering his text with the names of such luminaries as Aristotle, Tacitus, Milton, and Shakespeare. More to the point, he had produced a thoroughly conflicted and ambiguous work that was peculiarly open to readers' own interpretations. In any case I will impose my own view, hardly original though, which sees the novel as a study in deception, a deception and even a self-deception so complete that there was no possibility of redemption.

The novel was populated with a series of different fraudsters, say a bedraggled boy selling fake safety devices or, more significantly, Charles Arnold Noble, who could talk very large indeed, a "Mississippi operator" according to one character (192). The key figure was a singular soul, whom Melville coyly suggested was something of an original, akin to Hamlet or Don Quixote, an apparently supernatural being (although never so identified), who appeared in different guises (although it was never admitted that these were avatars of one person).[4] He took pains to describe carefully the gear and style of the particular avatar: Melville made much of self-presentation – the dress, the language, the demeanour. Initially the confidence man joined the riverboat as a deaf mute who disturbed the passengers with a series of placards proclaiming the virtues of charity. Then came a grotesque, crippled African-American, "Black Guinea" he was called, seeking alms. Thereafter the confidence man was a succession of characters: a deeply disturbed merchant, John Ringman; a man in a grey coat, representing the Seminole Widow and Orphan Fund; John Truman, the agent of the Black Rapids Coal Company, who

sold stock; a herb doctor who promoted the "Omni-Balsamic Reinvigora-
tor" (72), the "Samaritan Pain Dissuader" (82), and the "Natural Bone-
setter" (92); and a man wearing a brass plate engraved with the initials of
the "Philosophical Intelligence Office" (112) which secured "boy" workers for needy farmers. Each of these men managed to extort monies
out of their dupes. But the last manifestation of the confidence man
proved the most sophisticated and stylish: the flamboyant Frank Goodman, a supposed philanthropist, who was central to events in roughly
the last half of the novel. He sought not so much funds, though he did
bilk a barber, but instead dominion, the imposition of his will upon others. As one sceptic put it early on, "Money, you think, is the sole motive
to pains and hazard, deception and deviltry, in this world. How much
money did the devil make by gulling Eve?" (33). What a silver tongue
this Goodman had. He could talk incessantly and effectively about things
philosophical and moral, all to weave a web of words in which to ensnare
his victim. After many long conversations he finally bested his fellow
fraudster, Charles Noble, who figured as one of the "foxes" while Frank
was a "wolf," to employ language Melville used elsewhere to describe the
deceivers (3–4).

   The confidence man triumphed against a cross-section of Americans:
a charitable lady, a young clergyman, a prosperous merchant, a lonely
cripple, a miser, a roughhewn Missourian, and a wily barber. Only in dispute with Egbert (a take-off on David Thoreau), a student of Mark Winsome (aka Ralph Waldo Emerson) did Frank seemingly fail, although
here the result was ambiguous. Some of these people were fully convinced of their ability to detect fraud, even though they had been vic-
timized previously. "Like one beginning to rouse himself from a dose
of chloroform treacherously given," mused Pitch, one of the victims,
"he half divines, too, that he, the philosopher, had unwittingly been
betrayed into being an unphilosophical dupe" (128). The confidence
man knew how to exploit the desires and the fears of humanity, for
health, prosperity, or security. He knew how to work on the charitable
feelings of the successful and respectable who thought it moral to aid
those in distress. He was especially adept at denigrating scepticism and
negativism. All in all, Melville's protagonist used a range of stratagems
to persuade his victims: some kind of bait, a fake acquaintanceship,
shaming, fear copy, false logic, glittering generalities, much storytelling.[5] In one encounter with the barber he employed what amounted to
hypnotism, then called mesmerism, so he was later remembered as "the
man-charmer" (234).

Above all the master deceiver in his various guises preached a gospel of confidence. He constantly called upon his listeners to trust other people. "I am Philanthropos, and love mankind," said Goodman. "And, what is more than you do, barber, I trust them" (227). His was, in other words, a gospel of authenticity, sincerity, and truth grounded on the presumed goodness of humanity, despite the dictates of prudence. Truth was constantly on his lips: the confidence man had "truth on his side," "for the voice of the people is the voice of truth" (75, 162). He railed against distrust in its many forms: "In either case," speaking here of atheism and misanthropy, "the vice consists in a want of confidence" (156). Integral to such a gospel was what a later generation would come to call positive thinking, the belief that a mind so convinced of virtue could reorder the body, realize one's fortune, perhaps remake the world. "This may be the last time of health's asking," the herb doctor told a sick person. "Work upon yourself; invoke confidence, though from ashes; rouse it; for your life, rouse it, and invoke it, I say" (78). It was all very diabolical, the deceiver posing as the truth-teller, the preacher, employing the rhetoric of truth, and sometimes what might well be true, condemning doubt and distrust as sources of every kind of evil, to seduce the reluctant listener. Which is why some scholars have managed to claim *The Confidence-Man* tells the tale of a slightly ambiguous messiah who preached a great faith in humanity, a restatement of Christianity.[6] But I think more telling was the passing comment of the London *Westminster Review* (July 1857), which published a very favourable account of the novel, "Perhaps the moral is the gullibility of the great Republic."

Melville had a deeper purpose than to extol the confidence man as the person of the time, whether seducer or saviour: he argued that the whole world was consumed by pretense, a conclusion reached by some later critics of modernity.[7] "Looks are one thing, and facts are another" (14), one character claimed early on. "What are you? What am I?," proclaimed another, the cold philosopher Mark Winsome. "Nobody knows who anybody is. The data which life furnishes, towards forming a true estimate of any being, are as insufficient to that end as in geometry one side given would be to determine the triangle" (189). In a slightly different vein, the barber pointed out that in his trade he constantly helped people deceive by putting on false appearances. Near the very end of the book, Melville repeated the famous lines of Shakespeare, although giving these a somewhat darker cast:

All the world's a stage,
And all the men and women merely players,

Who have their exits and their entrances,
And one man in his time plays many parts. (221)

Just about everyone, not only the fraudsters, was performing a particular role, sometimes more than one role, sometimes out of self-deception, in search of a personal self and social acceptance. Everywhere there were masks.[8] The self was never permanent. People were always malleable. "The devil is very sagacious," claimed the Missourian. "To judge by the event, he appears to have understood man better even than the Being who made him" (120). This fact was rather a source of bemusement than despair for Melville, at least on my reading, which is why the novel counted as a comedy.[9]

Work in the realms of philosophy and psychology has confirmed the wisdom of Melville's insights.[10] A certain amount of deception (how much is always a matter of dispute) was and remains a common attribute of life, whether human or nonhuman, and hardly confined to modern times. Deception means, simply put, the intentional effort to mislead, something common in the animal kingdom as well. According to the dark genius of philosophy, Friedrich Nietzsche, however, deception had reached its acme in the enterprises of humanity, a fact that evidently pleased him.[11] Deception could take many different forms, usually involving some mix of fabrication (promoting falsehood), manipulation (massaging the truth), or concealment (hiding reality). In each case the form of deception either evaded or worked off the truth, that which is. It is useful here to borrow the language of the psychologist Robert W. Mitchell, who outlined how deception often "parasitizes" on truth, working with the conventions and expectations of the public about telling what is.[12] The deceiver drew on prevailing schemas ("mental representations which organize and categorize regularities"), scripts (specific knowledge about how to behave in various scenarios based on past experience) and plans (information about how people achieved their goals, how one state or event became a cause for others). The most reprehensible form of deception was lying, of course, typically defined as a purposely false statement meant to deceive the victim.[13] But the lie was only the beginning of a long list of actions, using images, sounds and silences, movements, as well as words to secure compliance: secrecy; disinformation and false promises; dissimulation and evasion; mimicry, masquerade, and pretence; seduction and trickery; concealment and obfuscation; tall tales, humbug, and bullshit; flattery and hypocrisy; half-truths, exaggerations or hype, and spin; misdirection or distraction.

Supposedly everyone practises small amounts of deception of some sort regularly, both to please friends and family as well as to defend their reputations or interests, though reliable statistics are difficult to come by, especially because people do not want to admit to what are commonly deemed sins.[14] We are always likely to edit the truth, especially when talking where we need to protect or promote the self.[15] Similarly, we engage in innumerable acts of self-deception to maintain self-esteem, a sense of honour, or the will to persevere.[16] "While we say that truthfulness is good and lying is bad, the way we act suggests that that is not what we really believe," reflected the philosopher Mary Mothersill.[17] Some particularly skilled rogues, say the masters of what is called "the well-crafted lie,"[18] have earned considerable public fame: witness the nineteenth-century career of Phineas T. Barnum. One movie, *The Sting* (1973), explored this admiration for the skills and boldness of the con man: the heroes successfully executed an elaborate plot to part a villainous banker from his money. What seemed to operate in the public's mind was a brand of "utilitarianism" (to borrow from the philosophers' vocabulary), a calculus of gain or harm, for self and others, whereby people judged the merit and the severity of a deception. "They know that they can tell a lie," argued Bernard Williams, one of the most prominent moral philosophers in the late twentieth century, "as every day millions of people do, and the heavens will not fall; if the heavens were going to fall, they would have fallen already."[19] In certain areas of life, notably war, diplomacy, and politics, deception was and is rife, even considered legitimate to defend a vital public interest.[20] Just as in love, where couples engaged in mutual games of deceit: philosophers seemed especially taken by the wisdom of the opening line of Shakespeare's Sonnet 138: "When my love swears that she is made of truth, / I do believe her though I know she lies."[21] Effectively, it was difficult to find a social place where deception was largely absent: not the church, the courts, hospitals, never mind the marketplace. Everywhere small deceits meant to smooth social relations were and are a part of life. If truth-telling remained the ideal and a common action, the default in the majority of cases, or so most people believed, deception was in fact equally normal, if never so honoured.[22] There was no single norm of conduct or behaviour in the realm of communication. Nor were there absolutes, a pure truth and an impure deception, except in theory.[23]

Even so, the practice of deceit can have serious effects on both the target and the liar. One consequence of lies and other deceptions was something I will call the victim's malaise. The people Melville's confidence man persuaded expressed their chagrin, sometimes their shame, over their own foolishness in believing his lies. It was the philosophers Sisella Bok and Bernard Williams who explained this moral condition best. "Those who learn that they have been lied to in an important matter – say, the identity of their parents, the affection of their spouse, or the integrity of their government – are resentful, disappointed, and suspicious."[24] They felt wronged, their trust betrayed, their freedom undone. "The victim recognizes the barefaced lie as a pure and direct exercise of power over him, with nothing at all to be said from his point of view, and this is an archetypal cause of resentment: not just disappointment and rage, but humiliation and the recognition in the most literal sense that he has been made a fool of."[25] Truth-telling has always retained its public prestige as a social ideal, no matter what the breaches of trust over the years, which was why notorious instances of lying or deceit have usually provoked outrage. Think of the controversy over Watergate, the Iran-Contra affair, or the Iraq invasion of 2003. The commitment applied as well to less dramatic matters, such as James Frey's partial fabrication of his memoirs.[26] At its worst victims were rendered impotent, unable to act, to make choices because they could not believe whatever they were told. There was no easy way out of such a state.[27]

The moral counterpart of the victim's malaise was the liar's plight. Any kind of persuader might fall victim to a version of the liar's plight, a much more significant condition than hubris because it struck at the basis of self-image and social reputation. In the moral universe of a St Augustine or a Kant, for instance, the liar's work always harmed humanity, a self-knowledge that could never be forgotten.[28] Thus Bok followed a long line of philosophers who warned that the consistent liar ran the risk of permanently corrupting his or her soul.[29] In a discussion of the consequences of self-deception, Robert Solomon mused how "we gradually rationalize our situation, reinforce our own bad habits, and turn to blaming others, cementing ourselves not just in a matrix of fraudulent emotions but a way of life that is fraudulent as well."[30] Deceit became a habit that coarsened the moral faculties. The deceiver amounted in Bok's words to a "free rider" who exploited a common good, namely public trust, the presumption that truth-telling was in most circumstances the moral standard of conduct.[31] Besides, the habit of deception would infect other, maybe all, areas of the liar's life. Lies, pretences, evasions, concealment piled one on top of another. Was it possible for the modern liar to deceive without falling victim to self-deception, wondered Hannah Arendt? "In other words, the more successful a liar is, the more likely it is that he will fall prey to his own fabrications."[32] The constant liar isolated himself or herself from the common ruck of humanity, perhaps coming to relish the ability to fool (what Paul Ekman called "duping delight"),[33] likely evincing a contempt for the ordinary consumer or citizen. According to Harry Frankfurt, "the liar leads an existence of unutterable loneliness," trapped in a "fabricated world" and "thereby he makes it impossible for other people to be fully in touch with him."[34] Socially the known liar soon earned a reputation for dishonesty. Personally that unhappy soul suffered a loss of dignity and integrity, at some cost to self-esteem. He or she fell victim to the ways of artifice and so the self lacked that sense of authenticity deemed vital.[35] At worst the liar could lose the crucial minimum of self-respect: "nothing may seem worth doing, or if some things have value for us, we lack the will to strive for them. All desire and activity becomes empty and vain, and we sink into apathy and cynicism."[36] Perhaps so in the mundane world, but in Melville's fictional universe the con man had clearly enjoyed both the practice and the fruits of deception.

Is deceit more frequent now than in the past? There is no ready answer, though the psychologist Paul Ekman imagined that opportunities for deception were greater in modern times.[37] What is clear, however, is that deception does have a history. The particular "institutions of deceit, mystification, and concealment," in Bernard Williams's marvellous phrase, have waxed and waned, have changed or disappeared over the centuries.[38] Certain kinds of deception, of lies or masquerades, have been more prominent at particular moments: so the historian Perez Zagorin explained how religious and political persecution in early modern Europe produced a golden age of dissimulation whereby dissenters sought to escape the wrath of authority.[39] More to the point, what the historian of psychology Michael Pettit has called "an economy of uncertainty," full of "deceitful persons and deceptive things," built of railways and newspapers, produced new opportunities and sites for fraud and falsehood in late-nineteenth century America.[40] From this perspective the rise of the publicity machine constituted one of the most startling developments in the saga of modernity. Never before had there been such an elaborate, sophisticated, and extensive technology of deception (despite what the dyspeptic economist Thorstein Veblen had claimed about Catholic propaganda)[41] able to reach so many people continuously throughout the day. "And we really do live in [a] world of disinformation," observed Brooks Jackson, a journalist and author who delivered the keynote address at a 2007 conference on truth and deception.

He went on to cite one example after another of deception in diet, beauty, and health advertising – "Whole companies have been built on systematic bamboozling of the public" – before exploring at length how "the right to lie" prevailed in political advertising. Things were getting worse the more the technologies of manipulation advanced, an advance fostered by big money and cognitive research.[42] There was and remains a lot more to be said about advertising, propaganda, and public relations: such publicity was also a system of information and persuasion which people could use, often must use, to organize the activities of their daily lives. The comment made by Bok that we have learned to decode the mixed messages of ads was surely correct.[43] Nonetheless, what made the publicity machine historically so interesting was its role as the chief vehicle of deception in modern times.[44]

So Melville had described a world that was admirably suited to enter an age of advertising, one where the figure of the adman would necessarily loom large. The confidence man was not the adman, at least not automatically. Melville's protagonist did employ some instruments of propaganda, placards and pamphlets, to sell the gospel of confidence. He was no agent of another client, unless that was the devil. He certainly did not employ the media, acting more as a salesman. But the con man and the adman were cousins. Both were avatars of a single archetype: the trickster. "Was the man a trickster, it must be more for the love than the lucre," wondered that Missourian again. "Two or three dirty dollars the motive to so many nice wiles?" (129). The trickster is one of the lesser if more intriguing archetypes of world literature and art. He – usually it is a he – has won the attention of a range of scholars and intellectuals, most notably Carl Jung, who have endeavoured to pin down the attributes and the significance of this ubiquitous if ambiguous character.[45] The Greek demigods Hermes and Prometheus, the Norse mischief-maker Loki, B'rer Rabbit and the Native American coyote, the Disney character Bugs Bunny, Charlie Chaplin's Tramp, the Riddler and the Joker in the Batman stories: all have been identified as tricksters or, cautiously, as "trickster-like" or "tricksterish." Trickster types are found all over the world, in west Africa, China, or India for example. Two famed twentieth-century artists of Spain, Pablo Picasso and Salvador Dalí, seem to fit the mould. Often he is a transgressor and prankster but sometimes he is also a villain or a hero, even described as a culture hero who works a transformation of his era. Recall how Melville's confidence man has in recent times appeared as both a devil and a saviour. More generally, the archetype has an affinity with particular types of people, such as the clown, the thief, Internet hackers and "trolls," and the magician. Adding the figure of the adman to this roster so full of rogues should not occasion much surprise.

Consider the attributes ascribed to the trickster. If it is likely impossible to come up with a complete definition of such an elusive agent, still there does appear to be much agreement about his soul. "Trickster is the mythic embodiment of ambiguity and ambivalence, doubleness and duplicity, contradiction and paradox," according to Lewis Hyde, one of the most successful of his chroniclers.[46] The more rigorously academic William Hynes decided there were six characteristics common to many trickster myths: a "fundamentally ambiguous and anomalous personality," out of which flowed such other labels as deceiver and prankster, shape-shifter, transgressor, "messenger/imitator of the gods," and finally "sacred/lewd bricoleur," meaning he could fashion something novel and creative out of all kinds of existing, often mundane materials.[47] Deceit in particular seemed a speciality of many tricksters. Virtually all of these characteristics have been at one time or another attached to the figure of the adman. That, of course, is obvious in the case of deception. Likewise, the adman has proved adept at appearing in so many different guises, as friend or confidant, counsellor or advisor, businessman or artist, occasionally the voice of authority, just like Melville's confidence man. And, albeit with a bit of stretching, one could even include the "tricksterish" attribute of acting for the gods: the adman was, as critics would never tire of proclaiming, one loud voice of business.

All of which evokes the spirit of the Carnival extolled long ago by that imaginative Russian theorist Mikhail Bakhtin. Not that he wrote about the trickster. But he did see Carnival as a time and place of challenge, transgression, release, renewal, and laughter, when the lower orders, albeit briefly, broke free from the restrictions of whatever was normality. Rules and authorities were mocked. Feast replaced scarcity. Play reigned. What was grotesque was celebrated. Or so it seemed.[48] The trickster might easily appear as the agent of the carnivalesque. Similarly, the con man and the adman, though not usually other brands of persuaders. At least in some versions the trickster myths amounted to instructive entertainments which provoked laughter. That may be playful or cruel, at the expense of some victim. The pleasures of transgression evident in trickster tales expressed in one way the wider yearning for freedom from the constraints of convention, morality, authority. The tales gave vent to social tensions and – usually and in the end – affirmed social values. Now neither the public relations counsel nor the propagandist were imagined as fans of comedy, rather much more of earnestness. Advertising people did not generally see themselves as pranksters, at least not until recently, even if outsiders have sometimes treated the adman as a clown whose ways and rhetoric and rationalizations were a source of fun. But at various moments, the adman has shown a definite affinity for the carnivalesque that satirizes, upsets, and challenges. In particular he may work hard to provoke laughter if, always, to promote the sell. Thus some of the advertisements of the late nineteenth century, so too some award-winning commercials of the late twentieth century, featured extravagant and bizarre imagery, weird critters, strange fantasies, a spirit of rebellion – all manifestations of the carnivalesque.[49]

Second, the trickster was effectively an exponent of what in the American context became known as positive thinking. That creed emerged in the mid-nineteenth century, especially in the teachings of Mary Baker Eddy of Christian Science fame. It was revitalized in the twentieth century by the enormously popular works of Dale Carnegie and Norman Vincent Peale. Briefly put, positive thinking asserted the power of mind over matter, the ability of the individual to self-fashion, to transform her self and/or his environment, to realize the wildest of dreams. All that was necessary was total, passionate, unreserved belief.[50] The tricksters were often the victims of this kind of self-deception, sure they could transform the world, expressing a male version of the birthing ritual. "They are imagined not only to have stolen certain essential goods from heaven and given them to the race," claimed Hyde, "but to have gone and helped shape this world so as to make it a hospitable place for human life." Hyde went on to play with the notion that the con man was "one likely candidate for the protagonist of a reborn trickster myth" in modern America. That notion he soon discarded because, apparently, stories of the con man lacked the "sacred context" and "the ritual setting" necessary to his version of the archetype.[51] That lack was not so clear in the case of Melville's confidence man, however, who preached a gospel of hope and trust and faith that was thoroughly religious in tone. In any case the adman would soon make a cliché of the promise of transformation: only acquire the right brand to ensure good health, a new beauty, success at work, a status upgrade, and thus realize the dreams of the consumer. The spiel melded neatly with the simple tenets of positive thinking. One Left-wing critic, Barbara Ehrenreich, railed against such an ideology "that encourages us to deny reality, submit cheerfully to misfortune, and to blame ourselves for our fate."[52] In effect, she found positive thinking

to be the bane of post-2000 America: positive thinking directly rein-
forced the legitimacy of authority – really, capitalism – acting as an
instrument of social control.

Thus the adman could only be a particularly compromised trickster, rarely a free spirit, because he was harnessed to a modern strategy of governance, namely the conduct of living. It was here that the
figure of the adman played a significant role in the saga of modernity. Michel Foucault's conception of biopolitics can serve the task of
explaining the character of modern rule especially well. Modernity
meant the steady expansion of secular authority over the course and
shape of ordinary life, or so he argued. Biopolitics, a specialized form
of biopower, worked on populations, always to master "the biological
or biosociological processes characteristic of human masses."[53] This
style of rule saw elites or their agents endeavour to administer life,
how people organized their daily existence, the products they used (or
avoided), the obligations they accepted or the pleasures they enjoyed.
It drew upon purported discourses of truth, such as medicine, psychology, or the other social sciences, to justify its interventions.[54] It sought
to speed the circulation of ideas, practices, and goods through the
social body, working of course from the top down, from various head-
quarters to reach the populace at large. Biopolitics was not a form of
democracy, though nor was it inimical to that system. The technicians
of biopolitics operated by encouraging and manipulating the play of
desire, a process of seduction as well as coercion. They employed statistics, demography, and probability, all to transform people into man-
ageable publics and markets who could be governed. They established
norms of conduct, sometimes backed up by law or regulation (as, for
instance, in the case of alcohol consumption). They elaborated "technologies of the self," another of Foucault's happy phrases, whereby
people could do, willingly, as they ought: that form of guidance lay
at the core of the liberalism which became so widespread in Europe
and America.[55] Biopolitics soon proved an effective means of administering the growing citizenries of Europe and America, and elsewhere,
from a distance, meaning from one central location. Foucault was most
intrigued by the spread of public health, the rise of insurance, the
efforts to control sexuality, the attempt to encourage productivity, and
such like measures. He paid little attention to publicity beyond a few
comments on campaigns of education. But, in fact, advertising developed into a formidable brand of biopolitics, especially during the early
twentieth century, when admen sought to manufacture wants and sell

all manner of goods to a national market of middle-class families in America. They fashioned designs for living of a kind Foucault saw as a key signal of modernity.[56]

There is, finally, one last similarity between trickster and adman. The trickster, however immoral, always acts in a context where questions of right and wrong are central. Perhaps that is why the trickster myth seems to exercise a particular fascination for people of all sorts: we can see in his activities the contours and predicaments of our life. The moral dilemma the figure of the adman evokes revolves around the issue of truth and deception. The adman served as an exception in a society supposedly resting on the virtues of truth, trust, sincerity, authenticity, and integrity. He enjoyed what the novelist Margaret Atwood called "the pleasures of fabulation":[57] he had a license of sorts to voice something other than the truth. The character, at times, took on the aspect of a liminal figure in the saga of modernity, drawing here on the ideas of the anthropologist Victor Turner.[58] He (and Turner's theory was cast in masculine terms)[59] existed between other stable states. Let me extrapolate from Turner's argument. What was the figure of the adman between? Reality and fantasy, truth and illusion, authenticity and artifice, fact and fiction, art and commerce. Turner noted the element of play in liminality, the generative aspect, how it brought change, but also produced ambiguity and paradox – including the polluting function that disturbed the goal of social purity. Sometimes the figure of the adman seemed caught in a double bind, trapped by conflicting moral and commercial imperatives. Sometimes the adman did consciously become a modern prankster, outside normal convention, playing with self and society. And sometimes the public relations counsel or the political consultant appeared as the trickster's more sinister variant, a Svengali who manipulated and controlled all the actors from behind the stage. Speaking very generally, then, the figure of the adman symbolized a great divide and a consequent tension between the official commitment to truth-telling, social and personal, and the common practice of deception, which of course was one of the subjects Melville had explored in *The Confidence-Man*.

Hence the ongoing fascination with the adman, a fascination which sometimes bordered on revulsion. "It is well-known, of course, that a cavalier attitude toward truth is more or less endemic within the ranks of publicists and politicians, breeds whose exemplars characteristically luxuriate in the production of bullshit, of lies, and of whatever other modes

of fraudulence and fakery they are able to devise."[60] That sneer came
from the noted philosopher Harry Frankfurt in his popular work *On
Truth* (2006). In an earlier polemic, he referred to "exquisitely sophisticated craftsmen" in the realms of advertising, politics, and public relations who – "with the help of advanced and demanding techniques of
market research, of public opinion polling, of psychological testing, and
so forth" – endlessly generated enormous quantities of bullshit, the target of his obloquy.[61] Ad-makers, propagandists, public relations counsels: these were the specialists of deception who directed the publicity
machine. They employed the whole panoply of instruments, from lies
to spin, concealment to exaggeration, to sell the goods and ideas of corporate America, governments and parties, and other elite bodies. The
sociologist Michael Schudson called brand advertising "the art form of
bad faith: it features messages that both its creators and its audiences
know to be false and it honors values they know to be empty."[62] In short,
observers often did regard Madison Avenue as the chief home of the
professional deceiver.

"Deception is essential to our well-being and, in some form or other,
to all of our endeavours."[63] That declaration appeared towards the
end of a long discussion on the inevitability and the necessity of both
deception and self-deception in *Born Liars* (2011), a popular book of
investigation and explanation by Ian Leslie, a British author. Deceit was
and always had been a part of human nature apparently, the practice a
result of living together in groups of people. If telling the truth was so
central to society and the individual, deception was nonetheless part of
the modern condition, rife throughout the mundane existence and the
institutional life of all societies. The argument was erudite and intriguing, full of anecdotes, and grounded in psychology and philosophy plus
bits and pieces from biology and history and the other social sciences
and humanities. But what counted here was not so much the merit of
what Leslie said as who he was. Leslie was a freelance journalist, and a
previous author, who had worked for leading media outlets such as the
Guardian and the BBC. But he also had a second career in advertising.
He had been employed by both JWT and TBWA Chiat Day, two leading
agencies. He identified himself as a "brand strategist" who specialized
in marketing brands in what he called "the brave new digital world."[64]
In short, Leslie was an adman. His book actually said very little about
either advertising or consumerism, except to suggest that the deceits of
advertising were often beneficial. He equated advertising with fiction,
where the target knew to suspend disbelief.[65] But justifying publicity or

marketing was hardly his aim. Propounding a new ethics of conduct was. *Born Liars* seemed to embody the perspective on life which prevailed in the circles of advertising. Leslie had universalized his experience, or so it might appear. The adman was now telling us what the modern world was really like. And deception was central to his conception of its workings.

1

THE HUCKSTER'S GAME

"I'm an advertising man."

"An advertising man!" The worldly wise salesman did not conceal his disfavor. Mr. Lord attempted to picture the important part that advertising already had in business and the big rôle it was destined to play. The salesman lost his temper and exclaimed:

"It's a cheap business! You'll never get any straight concern interested in it. Why, you fellows are no better than 'Mike' McDonald or 'Al' Hankins" [two notorious Chicago gamblers].

– Anecdote of the 1880s[1]

The epithet of the huckster has always haunted the men and women involved in the persuasion industries. That fact speaks to the lasting effect of the first narrative of understanding, the huckster's game. The huckster refers variously to a person, usually deemed to have a mercenary soul, who sells shoddy goods in an aggressive or sensational fashion. The reason the epithet stuck to the figure of the adman lies in the origins and the early development of the publicity system. The first persuader, P.T. Barnum, and his infamous successors, the patent medicine moguls, were entrepreneurs, merchants with a product, who employed publicity to sell their wares directly to a mass of customers. Their antics and their success captivated the public imagination much more so than the more mundane doings of the first advertising agents, most of whom were space-buyers who placed but rarely prepared ads prior to roughly 1880. In practice these hucksters pioneered many of the techniques of modern advertising, such as reason-why and scare copy, storytelling, emotional appeals, even the erotic and ironic sells. But they were often condemned as the masters of deceit and fraud, a series of con men who preyed upon the hapless public. Their very success raised serious doubts about the moral character of modernity, or at least of America. The roguish stereotype of the huckster was fixed to the name of the adman by a series of novels in the first three decades of the twentieth century. That taint of notoriety would forever stain the stories of the persuaders, however much later generations of advertising practitioners after 1910 would strive to escape their past and earn respect.

1. Barnum's Folly: *The Life of P.T. Barnum, Written by Himself,* 1855

"If we could enter, with anything like a feeling of zest, into the relations of this excessively shameless book, we should be inclined to treat its publication as the most daring hoax which the author has yet perpetrated upon the public," declared the anonymous reviewer in *Blackwood's Edinburgh Magazine,* a British periodical. "But it has inspired us with nothing but sensations of disgust for the frauds which it narrates, amazement at its audacity, loathing for its hypocrisy, abhorrence for the moral obliquity which it betrays, and sincere pity for the wretched man who compiled it. He has left nothing for his worst enemy to do; for he has fairly gibbeted himself."[2] What occasioned this extraordinary outburst was one of the publishing sensations of the day, the much-hyped appearance of an autobiography of the notorious American showman, Phineas Taylor Barnum. And *Blackwood's* was not alone. Many reviewers, notably in Great Britain but also in America, were shocked by the effrontery of this "inveterate sinner" who had foisted his saga upon the publics of America and Britain.[3]

The affliction, what I have called the adman's dilemma, first arose in the course of P.T. Barnum's autobiographical project. Which may seem strange: Phineas T. is best remembered as nineteenth-century America's most brilliant showman, especially as the maestro of the Barnum and Bailey circus, and one of the chief founders of the country's brand of mass entertainment. His story certainly fascinated his contemporaries, and his exploits continued to intrigue popular authors and eventually scholars to the present day. Observers could readily imagine how he might thrive in present-day America, a master of, say, trash television, someone combining the talents of a Disney and a Trump.[4]

But he was not only a showman. Just as important, the same Barnum was and is rightly celebrated (and sometimes condemned) as the "uber-huckster" of that century, a man whose skill at advertising his wares swiftly became legendary.[5] He was known in his day as "the very prince of

humbug" (a term he applied to himself), at his death called "the king of
advertising" by a French newspaper, and remembered much later as "the
Shakespeare of advertising."[6] One of the leading advertising creatives of
the late twentieth century, Jerry Della Femina, enthused about Barnum's
mastery of the craft, his pioneering discoveries about advertising, the fact
he could teach modern ad-makers a thing or two.[7] No wonder: for Barnum's assorted enterprises always floated on a sea of publicity, so much
so that loud, repeated, and voluminous advertising made his shows not
just appealing but sensational.[8] He was especially adept at concocting fictions about the discovery and the nature of his exhibits.[9] Thus Barnum
was the first actual embodiment of the modern adman in America, the
person whose practices and justifications generated the initial wave of
social conversation about that cultural figure.[10] Then and later, his name
was synonymous with the successful practice of deception.[11] Less well
known, however, was the fact that Barnum also suffered some of the discontents that would always shadow the figure of the adman.

P.T. Barnum (1810–91) had an extraordinary career, full of adventures
and hoaxes and sensations – and occasional disasters. He won notoriety
in the mid-1830s over the grotesque Joice Heth affair: he fashioned a
touring exhibition of this aged African-American woman whom he presented as the 161-year-old ex-nurse of the father of the country, George
Washington.[12] In 1841 he acquired the American Museum in New York
City, which he stocked with all manner of objects meant to excite and
inform the public. He was especially skilled at finding and promoting
living curiosities, anomalous or extraordinary bodies, such as giants,
fat people, a bearded lady, even Chang and Eng, the famed "Siamese
twins" (they were actually Chinese). His first great hit, though, was the
so-called Feejee Mermaid, an ugly concoction of monkey head and fish
body that he advertised with wildly imaginative images of a beautiful
sea maiden, a display that apparently brought hordes of people into his
Museum. Shortly afterwards, he exhibited and then toured "General
Tom Thumb," a young dwarf whom he trained to play various comic
roles as self-important adults, eventually taking the tour off to England
(where he provided some special showings for Queen Victoria) and then
into western Europe. In 1850 he won much praise, and made a small
fortune, by bringing to America Jenny Lind, aka the "Swedish Nightin-
gale," to sing throughout the country: his publicity not only fashioned
her as a great singer of operatic pieces (she was relatively unknown in
America before his campaign) but as one of the finest examples of pious
womanhood in the world. Although a risky speculation devastated his

finances in 1856 (some critics thought this a just retribution for his sins), much work and touring soon brought a return to prosperity. Unfortunately his expanded and now famous Museum burned down twice (fire caused Barnum much hardship: his garish estate, Iranistan, also called "Humbug Palace," burned in 1857, and as did his New York showplace the Hippotheatron in 1872). The second Museum disaster in 1868 led to a brief retirement.

That could not last. He was too full of energy, or so he later claimed. In the early 1870s and thereafter until his death, he returned to the business of entertainment with a travelling circus (he had experimented with a tour of exotic animals twenty years earlier) that became, as it was so loudly advertised, "The Greatest Show on Earth." He and his associates transformed the circus into mass spectacle: they offered all kinds of performances, pioneered the three-ring show, displayed exotic peoples from the far corners of the world, collected and hyped captivating animals (notably the "Jumbo mania" built around a huge elephant), and used the rails to transport their circus swiftly from place to place, making the extravagant show a national phenomenon. His last exploit occurred in 1889 when he and Bailey (who actually initiated the plan) took the circus across the Atlantic to perform at the London Olympia (where, once again, Queen Victoria witnessed a Barnum show). Soon after, he died very wealthy and much honoured, the showman as hero to some, the "children's friend" to many more.[13]

Barnum would have been pleased by all the fine words his passing occasioned. Throughout most of his long life, he proved inordinately conscious, obsessed even, with his reputation and his fame. He lectured and wrote a lot and about many things; getting money was a favourite topic, the virtues of Christianity and politics, the glory of America – he even published a children's book. But what he wrote about most of all was himself. His first effusion came in 1841, appearing in serial form in a New York newspaper: a semi-fictionalized celebration of the Joice Heth affair, *The Adventures of an Adventurer*, by "Barnaby Diddledum," where he bragged loudly about how he had deceived everyone, not just the masses but learned folk as well.[14] Here was a clear example of duping delight, where the deceiver shamelessly announced how he relished his exploits. Almost fifteen years later, after he had rocketed to fame and notoriety, he published his first formal autobiography, *The Life of P.T. Barnum*, clearly a bid for respectability as well as immortality. That did not satisfy either. Consequently in 1869 he wrote the even longer *Struggles and Triumphs: Forty Years' Recollections of P.T. Barnum*, where he extensively revised the

earlier *Life* and added much new material to justify his claims to public favour. Nor was this the end of the project. Thereafter he appended
regular additions to newly republished versions of the autobiography,
which was eventually available free to patrons who attended his circuses.
In 1889, just before his death, he offered a revision of *Struggles and Tri-*
umphs, now encompassing sixty years of experiences. And his wife added
a final last chapter following his death, which meant that, unlike nearly
all autobiographies, Barnum's really did achieve closure! Altogether it
is estimated that well over a million copies of these many editions circulated in late nineteenth-century America, making his life narrative
second only to the New Testament in some accounts.[15]

The most interesting text remains the 1855 *Life*, because of what Barnum revealed and what critics said. Indeed, none of his other editions
provoked anything like the notice or comment that greeted the appearance of *The Life*. The moment of telling seemed especially propitious:
only forty-five, he was already well off and well known, apparently financially secure, his American Museum a landmark in New York City, and his
fame as a promoter established across the Republic and in Europe. What
he hoped was not only to cash in on his notoriety (supposedly selling
the publishing rights for $15,000, a considerable sum then) but to reach
an enormous number of Americans, something like five million people,
he once mused.[16] Naturally he advertised vigorously his new "exhibit"
of the singular and unusual. He circulated the news of the forthcoming
autobiography to a host of newspaper editors. He likely sponsored the
publication of a hoax memoir, *The Autobiography of Petite Bunkham*, full
of satire, to spark interest.[17] His *Life* actually came out in mid-December
1854 (even if dated 1855), and soon ads appeared in newspapers replete
with complimentary quotations about this "Wonder Book."[18] "Let the
reviewers say what they will, people will read it," thought the *Savannah*
Republican. "It is sweeping over the Union like a tempest," exaggerated
the *Merchant's Ledger*. "It is in every man's hands, from the mechanic's
to the millionaire's." Well, not quite: in the end *The Life* sold 160,000
copies, a respectable total, yes, but hardly proof of an overwhelming
popular enthusiasm. As well it appeared in three different editions in
London, and was translated and published in France, Germany, Sweden,
and Holland.[19]

The legitimacy of autobiography depends on a kind of contract,
whereby the author assures readers of his or her sincerity and authenticity, sufficient to ensure those readers have purchased a true story
by the one person who really knows what happened.[20] The particular

difficulty Barnum faced was his justified reputation as a charlatan. How could you trust the word of the self-declared prince of humbugs? What Barnum promised in the brief Preface was "a true history" of his adventures and enterprises, including his infamous "humbugs."[21] Customers could expect a mix of fun and fact as well as some confessions, which might strike certain readers as "injudicious" (iv). The advertising supplemented and elaborated on such promises, the press acting as an impartial authority here. The promotion assured them, "The genius of humbug has made a clean breast to his readers" (*Rochester Democrat*). Supposedly, "if one wants fun, more innocent mirth, of the richest kind, here it is" (*Rome Excelsior*). But there was even more delight in store. "It gives the reader an insight into the ways of the world," enthused the *Utica Herald*. The book was a veritable manual of success, far better than, say, a gift of $5,000 to carry a young man through to comfort and security in life, at least according to the *Albany Knickerbocker*. "To help a business man; to furnish him with driving, go-ahead ideas; to open his mind and fill it with sound, practical business thoughts that will insure him a large and rapid fortune, Barnum's Autobiography is the very thing."[22]

What readers actually got were four hundred pages of anecdotes, digressions, confessions, brags, justifications, illustrations, and maxims, all of them organized in a roughly chronological order that covered the upbringing, the struggles and setbacks, and the eventual triumphs and notoriety of the showman. Barnum employed a friendly, conversational tone throughout, forthright and bold, seemingly honest, rarely apologetic or remorseful, and occasionally gleeful or a bit contrite. The showman's imperative – that you must first entertain – ran throughout the life narrative, and especially in the first half of the autobiography: he did fill *The Life* with amusing tales about his own pranks and adventures, sometimes adding those of other people, including family members. The focus was naturally on his public life, although he was often candid, or seemed so, about his motives, his anxieties, his failures, as well as his successes. He did feature explanations of his humbugs (more on this later), sufficient to give readers some appreciation of the ways of artifice. He even told stories about when and how he was conned by others, where Barnum himself became the victim of deceit. He said little about his marriage and family (his wife hardly figured in *The Life*), nor did he speak of his intimate self, his body or its yearnings, except to mention illness or exhaustion, but of course such an absence was common in nineteenth-century autobiography. What was unusual was his dedication: "To the Universal Yankee Nation, of which I am proud to be one." There was no such nation, not then. The term "Yankee" was a regional designation, confined to the inhabitants of the northern states of the Republic, especially New England. If this was a marketing ploy, the dedication was likely to irritate Southerners, who were locked in an ongoing struggle for political supremacy with their Yankee brethren. But the dedication did indicate one of the identities Barnum wished to appropriate: energetic, aggressive, egocentric, innovative, ambitious, clever, plain-spoken, practical, ingenious – more amoral than immoral? – a man on the move, a man who was thoroughly modern, not tied to tradition and the past.

Some scholars have concluded that Barnum actually set out to write a counter-autobiography, perhaps a parody of Benjamin Franklin's work, which was then the gold standard of this genre. *The Life* became a textual form of the American Museum, his story really a collection of exotic and amusing exhibits.[23] Or it emerged as both an instance of and a satire on the mythology of the self-made man and the rise of mass culture.[24] Another scholar decided *The Life*, indeed the whole of Barnum's autobiographical project, blurred the line between the hoax and reality, that it mocked as well as claimed respectability, that it revealed the American dream as no more than a gigantic con game.[25] Yet a fourth talked of "autobiographical masquerade," the "inauthentic self," "dishonest truthfulness," how *The Life* cycled between "deception and exposé," which gave the autobiography a strangely postmodern cast![26]

Not on my reading. I do not believe that Barnum attempted any kind of Franklin parody, at least not consciously.[27] Instead he extolled the ideal of the self-made man, that era's version of the sovereign self, who possessed the will to succeed and the boldness to act, whatever the struggle or adversity such might entail. It all amounted to a celebration of self-fashioning, in some ways a rags-to-riches story. And he adopted the pose of the truth-teller who was willing to bear his soul to his fellow men. Yet the range of quizzical comment suggests that *The Life* was and remains a puzzling text which somehow never fulfilled the autobiographical contract. The reason? *The Life* expressed the predicament that afflicted the character of an adman who was caught between the worlds of artifice and authenticity. I find *The Life* a largely honest, if failed, effort at autobiography, where the narrator could not successfully negotiate the divide between two contradictory ways of life. The particular nature of this dichotomy reflected the social conditions of antebellum America, of course. *The Life* was a contested site where the "carnivalesque" and the "Victorian" struggled for supremacy. One anonymous reviewer in

The New Englander (v. 13, February 1855, 158) detected exactly this clash, only to condemn the former and praise the latter.

Recall that the term "carnivalesque" derives from the work of Mikhail Bakhtin, where it denotes a time and a place of laughter, of mockery, of reversals, trickery and transgressions, of appetite and bodily pleasures that can only be an affront to the normal or regular society of the bourgeois. Some years ago, the historian Jackson Lears gave the term a special significance in his book *Fables of Abundance,* arguing that the tradition of the carnivalesque played a vital role in the prehistory of modern advertising in America.[28] Barnum made much of his upbringing as a prankster – yet another variant of the trickster archetype – devoted to all manner of practical jokes: "I was born and raised in an atmosphere of merriment" (105). He acquired a deep distrust of the hypocrite and the puritan, any moral elite who sought to police and censor, to prohibit the fun of ordinary folk. At the moment of his birth, his grandfather, "decidedly a wag" (10), played a trick on him, bequeathing a worthless tract of land: young Barnum grew up thinking himself a landowner, only to discover later what a horror this fabled Ivy Island was when he finally visited the site. Joking around, masquerade, and telling tall tales: all were necessary to entering the male brotherhood in his hometown of Bethel, Connecticut, where young and old men constantly played tricks on each other and on the innocent. Such early influences were confirmed by his apprenticeship in the task of selling assorted goods, especially lottery tickets and hats, where chicanery was also the norm. Buyers and sellers, "each party expected to be cheated, if it was possible," Barnum said of the hat business (99). He took great pleasure in being sharper and more imaginative than his confreres and competitors. The carnivalesque was a realm where deceit was a virtue. And it was here that Barnum learned the arts of deception. Even in this official autobiography he sometimes expressed the pleasures of duping delight.

The litany of Barnum's humbugs, his confessions and brags, were the highlights of *The Life,* of course. He explained, sometimes frankly, often coyly, how he had consistently used publicity to entice and to dupe the public. First Barnum concocted an intriguing story about the exhibit, freely mixing fact and fiction, akin to the tall tale, which might be used in ads, offered for sale on site in a booklet, or told as part of the actual presentation. The Heth story, for instance, emphasized her age (backed up with a bogus document of authenticity), her religiosity (she loved hymns), and the patriotic dimension of her life (the nurse of George Washington). Then Barnum worked the press: he bought ads, planted stories, cultivated editors and reporters, always to build and maintain the interest and the curiosity of the public. Thus he created the "Jenny Lind" mania that supposedly swept through the United States. "I had put innumerable means and appliances into operation for the further-ance of my object, and little did the public see of the hand that indi-rectly pulled at their heart-strings, preparatory to a relaxation of their purse-strings," he admitted; "and these means and appliances were con-tinued and enlarged throughout the whole of that triumphal musical campaign" (315). Finally he assembled a package of posters, pictures, and the like to fuel the public excitement. For the exhibit of the Feejee Mermaid, "I was industriously at work (though of course privately) in getting up wood-cuts and transparencies, as well as a pamphlet, proving the authenticity of mermaids, all in anticipation of the speedy exhibition of Dr. Griffin's specimen" (236).

No wonder that Barnum practised virtually every kind of deception. He did admit to the occasional outright lie. He increased the age of Tom Thumb from five to eleven to ensure he really was seen as a dwarf. Or he claimed that his "Woolly Horse" – purportedly no less than an amalgam of "the Elephant, Deer, Horse, Buffalo, Camel, and Sheep" (350) – had actually been captured by the famous explorer Colonel John C. Frémont during his adventures in the American West. He could wildly exagger-ate: the illustrations of the Feejee Mermaid suggested visitors would see a bare-breasted beauty. Hardly any of his major exhibits were without some component of distortion: even he admitted to some chagrin over a much hyped model of Niagara Falls, complete with "real water," that was actually very "small potatoes," the falls just "eighteen inches high" (226). He could pretend as well: thus he or a compatriot, a supposed visitor of the Heth exhibit, placed a letter in a newspaper which charged that Heth was merely an automaton, a ploy that successfully renewed public curiosity. He loved half-truths: his Swiss Bell-Ringers were actually from Lancashire, England, which Barnum did not think sufficiently exotic. He might misdirect and conceal: he publicized a free exhibit of newly captured buffalo (they were not) when in fact people had to pay to be ferried across to where they could see the sad collection of beasts (and the fake buffalo hunt). He was forever ready to use "soft soap" – as he put it, "the faculty to please and flatter the public so judiciously as not to have them suspect your intention" (286) – maybe an appeal to the visi-tor's intelligence, to win sympathy or provoke curiosity.

Barnum relished the notoriety his humbugs generated. Occasionally he inserted an anecdote that spoke of the admiration of the public. How

the wealthy of New York greeted him so heartily after his first foray overseas with General Tom Thumb. How ordinary folk went to the American
Museum not only to see the wonders there but hoping to spot Barnum himself. He recounted a story of a ticket-seller talking about the merit of a lecture Barnum had delivered on the philosophy of humbug. "'But it makes
no difference whether it was good or not,' continued the ticket-seller, 'the
people will go to see old Barnum. First he humbugs them, and then they
pay to hear him tell how he did it! I believe if he should swindle a man out
of twenty dollars, the man would give a quarter to hear him tell about it'"
(375). Barnum was a celebrity, his name synonymous with trickery. The
practical joker had triumphed despite the forces of virtue and hypocrisy.

The record of tales and pranks (though not of deceptions) thinned out
as Barnum succeeded as a businessman. Increasingly *The Life* celebrated
the social and moral conventions of the Victorian order. He admitted to
a yearning for respectability and security. He spoke warmly, if briefly, of
the joys of marriage and family. He declared his devotion to Christianity.
"In all my journeys as 'a showman,' the Bible has been my companion,
and I have repeatedly read it attentively, from beginning to end" (247).
He gave up alcohol, becoming a temperance lecturer. He sermonized
on the necessity of morality. "The rogue, the man of rough passions,
the drunkard, are not to be envied even at the best, and a conscience
hardened in sin is the most sorrowful thing that we can think of" (189).
He filled his story with the statistics of success, the hordes who visit his
Museum and shows, the many places he displayed his exhibits, the scale
of his enterprises, and above all the receipts these enterprises earned. He
noted his acquaintance with other worthy souls, including a clergyman
(usually the bane of any prankster) and of course royalty, and recounted
the praise of his enterprises that appeared in the press. He took great
pride in describing at length how the grand tour of Jenny Lind brought
a unique species of cleansed and civilizing entertainment to America. He
could not resist some mention of his extravagant mansion "Iranistan," a
kind of "Oriental Villa" borrowed from a place he had seen in Brighton,
England. Yet he inveighed against excessive materialism. "Money should
in no sense be made the standard of respectability or honor. We should
never worship 'golden calves'" (274). He offered some rules of business
success: thrift, perseverance, sobriety, self-reliance, hard work, and, yes,
honesty and integrity – and always advertise. The final sentence of *The
Life* signified his conversion to the bourgeois verities of the day: "I am at
home, in the bosom of my family; and 'home' and 'family' are the highest and most expressive symbols of the kingdom of heaven" (404).

How then could he justify all his deceptions? Barnum never said, not in his autobiographies or interviews, that "there's a sucker born every minute," although one can well understand why that expression of contempt stuck to his name.[29] Witness his comment regarding the public's response to the "Woolly Horse" humbug: "They could have swallowed any thing, and like a good genius, I threw them, not a 'bone,' but a regular tit-bit, a bon-bon and they swallowed it at a single gulp!" (350). Indeed, he suggested that the public liked to be duped: "the public appears disposed to be amused even when they are conscious of being deceived" (171). They did so because all the staging and packaging enhanced the delight as well as exercised the faculty of judgment, where the onlooker might evaluate the worth of the delusion. Which meant, if you can believe his testimony, that no one suffered from the victim's malaise, because everyone enjoyed the cleverness of the lie. The scale and variety of his exhibits gave him the permission to practice a modicum of deceit. "I should hope that a little 'clap-trap' occasionally, in the way of transparencies, flags, exaggerated pictures, and puffing advertisements, might find an offset in a wilderness of wonderful, instructive, and amusing realities," he wrote in defence of his Museum. "Indeed I cannot doubt that the sort of 'clap-trap' here referred to, is allowable, and that the public like a little of it mixed up with the great realities which I provide" (225). The thing was, people got value for their money, whether they paid to visit the Museum or to see one of his spectaculars. Here, then, was the first intimation of what would become a common justification of the adman as a licensed deceiver who offered the public a kind of service, a form of deception, necessary to their happiness.

That was not enough to satisfy his Victorian side, however. At the end of *The Life*, Barnum's tone became a trifle belligerent. He claimed that he was in fact "a public benefactor, to an extent seldom paralleled in the histories of professed and professional philanthropists." For the trouble with America was "a severe and drudging practicalness" which neglected the kind of wholesome entertainment that enriched the lives of foreign lands. "The consequence is, that with the most universal diffusion of the means of happiness ever known among any people, we are unhappy." What Barnum did – yes, to his profit – was to rectify this lamentable lack. His museum gave the public a marvellous array of pleasures that also worked to instruct "the masses" about animal life. The Jenny Lind extravaganza elevated and refined the musical taste of "the cultivated and the wealthy" and "the middling classes." This instead of "the intemperance and kindred vices" that once afflicted all. So, ultimately, how could anyone hold the publicity against him? Even "the moralist or the Christian" ought to be satisfied (399–400).

Early responses to *The Life* were often favourable. Readers agreed the book was highly amusing. They found merit in his story of struggle and success. They could excuse his humbugs and his brags. "We rather like this trumpeting ourselves," declared one sanguine soul.[30] But in the end Barnum's hope was dashed: the "moralist" was deeply offended. His book certainly got noticed by the literary press. The *New York Times* devoted two reviews to *The Life*, the second (16 December 1854) much more critical than the first (12 December 1854). The attack of the *London Times* extended over three issues of the newspaper (30 December 1854, as well as 5 and 12 January 1855). W.H. Hurlbut's essay on two contrasting types, "Barnum's and Greeley's Biographies," in the *Christian Examiner* (March 1855) ran to twenty pages, "from the meaner to the manlier Yankee."[31] The Reverend T.M. Eddy provided a second unhappy "Christian" response to Barnum of seven pages in *The Ladies' Repository* (3 March 1855). Severn Teackle Wallis expressed the South's disdain in another long joint review, "Barnum and Mrs. Stowe," in the Baltimore magazine *The Metropolitan* (April 1855), which twinned Barnum with another *bête noire*.[32] Although the literary periodical *The Knickerbocker*, a Northern magazine, initially (January 1855) offered a generally favourable notice, a few months later (March 1855) it carried a much more negative joint essay, "Town and Rural Humbugs," on Barnum and Thoreau, full of sarcasm directed towards the philosophies of these very different souls.[33] There were briefer reviews of Barnum alone, but still thoughtful and also critical, in *The New Englander* (February 1855) and *Harper's New Monthly Magazine* (March 1855). Neither compared in virulence and disdain to the trio of lengthy diatribes that appeared in the United Kingdom: fully nineteen pages long in *Tait's Edinburgh Magazine* (February 1855), the fifteen-page "Revelations of a Showman" in *Blackwood's Edinburgh Magazine* (February 1855), and the eleven-page "Barnum" in *Fraser's Magazine for Town and Country* (February 1855), where the anonymous reviewers had the space to reflect on Barnum's work as a symptom of moral decay. Many of the choice bits in these and other reviews (such as the *Blackwood's* denunciation quoted earlier) were reprinted, sometimes with additional comments, in newspapers and periodicals in the United States. Thus *The Economist*'s brief dissection of Barnum appeared in *Littel's The Living Age* (17 March 1855). Barnum's autobiography had provoked wordy outbursts and much outrage from the self-appointed guardians of public ethics, the typical role of book reviewers then, in Britain and America.

The tone and emphasis of these reviews differed. Not all were ferocious. But the themes and even much of the language of the moral explosion were similar. "Every thoughtful and self-respecting man is insulted by the pompous publication of the story, because it implies the public will read it with pleasure" (*Harper's*). *The Life* was deemed unacceptable, a thoroughly repellent book, something which should never have been written, nor published, or even read. "Such books are getting to be common in our literature, and it is time that they were stopped."[34] Life narratives were supposed to constitute lessons in self-improvement, public achievement, and moral triumph for the edification of young and old alike. But *The Life* dealt in matters far better left concealed, in swindles, cunning, vulgarity, charlatanry, and deceit: "a living libel upon all that is manly in humanity" (*Tate's*). Perhaps it was yet another of Barnum's hoaxes, full of more lies? Of all the humbugs, "this history of his life is the grossest and the most flagrant" (*London Times*). It served as an "advertisement" (*Christian Examiner* and *The Ladies' Repository*) of the man himself, the perverse effort of a blackguard to boost his public notoriety. *The Life* was not a true confession by a man overcome by remorse; instead, it was the loud brag by a man who craved adulation for his success at duping the public. "We must all know, and all admire him," the *London Times* asserted in a moment of irony. The result was a species of "moral poison" (*Fraser's*), a manual for scoundrels, bound to be a "bad influence" (*Knickerbocker*), which could only produce "infinite mischief" (*New York Times*). "As if the example of a success notoriously based on such shameful resources were not sufficiently pernicious," intoned *Fraser's*, consumed with a sense of moral horror, "this 'prince of humbugs,' as he rejoices to style himself, records for the edification of mankind a system of imposture, which has already found many followers, and will, no doubt, engender a prolific race of imitators, less able perhaps, but probably even less scrupulous, than their great prototype." Here was the grand affront: books were supposed to have a moral utility but *The Life* could only foster evil. "What is the use of being honest if the doings of Mr. P.T. Barnum are to be endorsed with the world's approval?" (*London Times*).

Barnum was both pitied and condemned. No doubt some of the blame for his conduct in life was owed to his upbringing. "The child was the father to the man" (*London Times*).[35] The reviewers had little but contempt for the carnivalesque ways of Bethel and Connecticut. His youth was surrounded with the ills of prankster culture, "knavish tricks and clownish nonsense" (*The Metropolitan*). Was his uncle not a practical joker, "perhaps the most despicable and detestable variety of the human species?" (*Christian Examiner*). Then he was further schooled in immorality, in cunning and deceit, because of the abysmal practices of local business in that benighted land. But the point was that Barnum had thrived, he had become a lord of misrule in the carnivalesque realm, surpassing all others, moved only by a desire to make money by preying on human gullibility.[36] The reviewers saw Barnum's Victorian declarations about probity and religion as no more than cant, evidence of hypocrisy or self-deception. "Fear God and cheat your neighbor – is Barnum's moral" (*The Metropolitan*). What was particularly insulting was his claim that he should be seen as a public benefactor. More accurately, he represented a "Yankee Lazarillo de Tormes" (*London Times*) or "Cagliostro" (*The Economist*), the enemy of all that was worthwhile.[37]

Much of the attention focused on the humbugs of what the *New York Times* called "the stupendous and magnificent master of deception." Here it was Barnum the persuader who excited the moralist because his actions had so offended against the cult of truth.

"His life and history ignore the central importance of truth." (*The Ladies' Repository*)

"The original fault – the untruth – remains and cannot be done away with by any subsequent act." (*The New Englander*)

"He can discern no distinction between truth and falsehood, save as either tends to swell his amount of personal profits." (*Blackwood's*)

Versions of the story of Joice Heth, the Feejee Mermaid, Tom Thumb, the Woolly Horse, and even the Jenny Lind mania were recounted over and over again, nearly always with comments on Barnum's shamelessness, his predatory zeal, or his contempt for the public. Running through such descriptions was an almost visceral distaste for the figure of the adman. Barnum had concocted a "vulgar machinery" (*Knickerbocker*) designed to dupe the public, no less than "a system of organized deception" (*Fraser's*) that generated a "manufactured enthusiasm" (*London Times*) among the masses. Not surprisingly such views led some critics to lament or denounce the spreading influence of advertising. After all, Barnum was only "the most accomplished known practitioner" of "that modern art of 'puff'" (*London Times*). He and his kind exploited "the inexhaustible store of credulity in the public reservoirs" (*Blackwood's*). Thus the critics introduced a notion that would become commonplace in the social conversation about the adman, namely the idea of the hapless public. "The multitude believe and buy. In fact, they believe and buy more than they ever did before ... We swallow the camels of Brandreth and the mermaids of Barnum"[38] (*Christian Examiner*). Art, literature, and especially the press were cheapened and debauched by the triumph of such exuberant "puffery." Early on, during the Joice Heth humbug, Barnum had discovered how easy it was to convert the press into "an immense organ of deception" (*Fraser's*). Even the grand tour of Jenny Lind, for all its musical excellence, was tainted. The authentic and the genuine were disappearing from our lives: instead, "sham and shiftiness everywhere" (*Fraser's*). The adman could not but corrupt, or so it seemed. Momentarily breaking ranks with its compatriots, *Blackwood's* wondered whether *The Life* might actually do some good by exposing the nefarious games of the huckster.

More ominous, Barnum emerged as the exemplar of a corrupt America. That theme was most pronounced in the polemics of the British reviewers, where you could detect a definite glee over the fact that *The Life* demonstrated how sordid was the condition of the Republic – albeit mixed with a certain fear the contagion might spread to a purer Britain. In the United States, seemingly, it was better to be "accounted" a "clever rascal" than an "honest man" (*Blackwood's*). But the complaint over Yankee shame was also echoed in Southern commentary and occasionally present in the anxieties of Northern critics as well. Barnum's sins were all too representative of American ways. Consider how widespread was the worship of "the almighty dollar" (*Fraser's*) or the fascination with success. "Success may render almost anything tolerable to us" (*The Metropolitan*). "And Barnum is the embodiment and impersonation [*sic*] of success" (*New York Times*). Where else was there so much evidence of low cunning and blatant fraud? All of which led *The Economist* to wonder whether so damaged a society as the United States could possibly hold together once all the free land was occupied. An eccentric view perhaps, but *The Economist* and other critics gave voice to what would become another common theme: that America was the true abode of the adman. The Republic was no less than "the chosen land of quackery" where all manner of hucksters could thrive. "Our elastic institutions give ample scope and verge enough to the most audacious of humbugs" (*Christian Examiner*). Barnum really was the epitome of the shrewd Yankee.

Evident in such rhetoric was the beginnings of a particular complex of ideas about the adman and advertising which I will call "contagion and immunity." That linked to one of the imperatives of a further stream of biopolitics which sought to ensure the purity, however defined, of the social body.[39] The concern translated into an effort to keep whatever was deemed alien or harmful out of the community, whether by banishing the toxin or by strengthening the forces of resistance. The proponents of that complex in this case feared publicity might act as a virus to infect the social body with delusion and deceit. Puffery of all kinds threatened to undermine the regime of truth. Often this argument presumed ordinary folk lacked the will or the ability to resist the seductions of the adman. Thus they sought some means to protect or immunize the hapless public against what they imagined was a disease of untruth. The worry about contagion would provoke at various times a demand to censor advertising, whether to restrict the amount of posters in the cities and towns or to prohibit the appearance of the most specious ads in newspapers. In this case the critics thought of *The Life* as an evil form of publicity, especially injurious to the moral health of youth. The critics were acting as the voice of the victim's malaise to condemn Barnum the deceiver. Condemnation was not sufficient, however, at least not for the most outraged moralists. Immunity required, here, suppression, the removal of the autobiography from bookstores and libraries.

Barnum was sufficiently aware of the moral explosion to be disturbed. He came to recognize he was a victim of the liar's plight, even though he thought the charge of lying unfair. He even tried to respond by registering his dissent in *The Trumpet and Universalist Magazine*, which had quoted large portions of *Blackwood's* diatribe:

> [I]n the faithful narrative of my show-business I have not attempted to justify my stretching of the cords of morality (for this would be indefensible), and any appearance of rejoicing in the success of some of my schemes which may have been considered questionable must be ascribed in a good measure, or a bad measure, to my inborn and life-long love of a practical joke and my professional life as a Showman. It is not a vindication but a fact, that men as politicians, sectarians, and lawyers frequently do what they would *not* do as *men*; and the same I suppose is true generally of caterers for public amusement. I do not defend what I here speak of, but I think it is hardly fair to make fish of a lawyer and flesh of a showman.[40]

That amounted to a masked defence of the practice of deception as a necessity of his occupation as a showman, if not as the prototype of the adman. But such a response did not deal with his reputation problem, something he recognized in a letter to a friend in 1865. "For 30 years I have *striven* to *do good*, but (foolishly) stuck my worst side outside, until half the Christian community got to believe that I wore horns & hoofs."[41]

All of which suggests Barnum was also suffering from a classic case of self-deception, at least when he wrote *The Life*. That condition meant its victim refused to spell out the truth of his or her circumstances – or, as one scholar preferred, "to engage with the world."[42] He believed not just that he was a good man, meaning a respectable and honoured entrepreneur, but that his life was a model of how to succeed in America. He was aware that he had transgressed the moral code of his times. But what he paid attention to, what he expected others to recognize, was his struggles and achievements, his commitment to virtue, the pleasures he had brought people, and in particular his effort to civilize the country: the Jenny Lind enterprise. He did not pay attention to the moral implications or consequences of his humbugs. Others did. The fact was that "the moralist or the Christian," to use Barnum's own language, could not countenance his recourse to deception to achieve wealth and notoriety, especially not when he might be taken as a representative American. In any case Barnum's plight, his self-deception, was to prove a common enough feature in the stories of the modern persuader such that it would re-occur in later expressions of the adman's dilemma.

Once Barnum had overcome his financial difficulties and made a second fortune, he set about rectifying the ill effects of *The Life*. In 1866 he published *Humbugs of the World*, where he exposed all manner of deceptions visited on a suffering humanity in times past and recent.[43] Presumably this lengthy text served to prove that Barnum was on the side of virtue, ready to identify and reveal any dangerous hoax. But there was more. Early on in the book, he proclaimed his devotion to the cult of truth, and his disdain for the sceptic who doubted the existence or substance of honour, honesty, and authenticity. He offered up a much more congenial definition of humbug: it consisted "in putting on glittering appearances – outside show – novel expedients, by which to suddenly arrest public attention, and attract the public eye and ear." Later, he added an especially suggestive description of the nature of advertising: "Advertising is to a genuine article what manure is to land – it largely increases the product." The purpose of such claims was to render harmless the kind of deception he practised, to suggest it was an always legitimate tool of doing business right. Perhaps as well he hoped to shift the practice of advertising from the realm of vulgarity to the realm of respectability.[44] No less than the merchant or the manufacturer, the adman was an entrepreneur, not to be confused with the hoaxers Barnum had so zealously exposed.

Then he corrected the folly of his earlier autobiographical venture. He acted as the instrument of the most outraged critics to banish his own work. He acquired the plates to *The Life*, which he destroyed to ensure that no more copies of this mistake were circulated to incite the fury of the moralist.[45] That was hardly an endorsement of the charge of contagion, however. In the replacement, *Struggles and Triumphs* (1869), he wrote another, more elaborate explanation of his past conduct as a promoter and adman:

> It was the world's way then, as it is now, to excite the community with flaming posters, promising almost everything for next to nothing. I confess that I took no pains to set my enterprising fellow-citizens a better example. I fell in with the world's way; and if my "puffing" was more persistent, my advertising more audacious, my posters more glaring, my pictures more exaggerated, my flags more patriotic and my transparencies more brilliant than they would have been under the management of my neighbours, it was not because I had less scruple than they, but more energy, far more ingenuity, and a better foundation for such promises. In all this, if I cannot be justified, I at least find palliation in the fact that I presented a wilderness of wonderful, instructive and amusing realities [repeating a phrase from his earlier *Life*] of such evident and marked merit that I have yet to learn of a single instance where a visitor went away from the Museum complaining that he had been defrauded of his money. Surely this is an offset to any eccentricities to which I may have resorted to make my establishment widely known.[46]

Modernity, the way of the world, had dictated his actions: it was the only way to succeed. This excused, though it did not justify, how he played out the role of the deceiver. In any case, now he made much more of his efforts to provide all Americans with wholesome, moral entertainment, suitable to the whole family. Elsewhere in the book, Barnum even had the gall to declare "that the maxim of Dr. Franklin can never fail to be true, that 'honesty is the best policy.'"[47] He had travelled far away from that other maxim of frankness, much more evident in *The Life*. He had rehabilitated himself.

History has proved far more sympathetic to Barnum, even his claim that he was a "public benefactor," than his antebellum critics. The obituary of the *London Times* labelled Barnum's last great spectacular in that city "the comedy of the harmless deceiver and the willingly deceived."[48] In *The Fabulous Showman* (1959) the popular author Irving Wallace cast

Barnum in the role of a liberator who worked to free America from the dour, grey legacy of a puritan tyranny.[49] That was an exaggeration, since the puritan legacy was hardly so potent a force in Barnum's day, though the moral distrust of amusement did hobble the growth of "wholesome" entertainment for a time. Some years later the social historian Neil Harris coined the term "operational aesthetic" to describe and justify Barnum's form of deception: he provided stories and displays which invited people to test, discover, and debate the truth, making a sort of intellectual game that enriched people's lives.[50] More recently the historian James Cook placed Barnum among a collection of other masters of "artful deception," "playful frauds," and "dubious authenticity" who pioneered the pleasures of mass culture in the nineteenth century.[51] Walter McDougall, yet another American historian, in *Throes of Democracy* (2008), a survey of American society in Barnum's day, argued that the Republic was a nation of hustlers, full of pretense and self-deception, key reasons for the astounding success of the United States because these "vices" enabled innovation.[52] Barnum featured here as one such innovator, "a peddler of pretense" who found "a huge market" for his wares.[53] That amounted to a reversal of the charge once directed against *The Life*. Barnum now embodied the dynamism of a United States as it expanded across a continent. The man who was damned as a symptom of moral decay had become a sign of national vigour.

All of which revalued this huckster's story. Barnum appeared as an artist whose mixing of fact and fiction, illusion and reality, served the cause of wonder. Imagination trumped authenticity. The perspective implicitly denied the imperative of truth: it presumed that deception was endemic and even necessary. Thereby Barnum was recruited into yet another company of moderns who worked to undo the so-called disenchantment of the world. The huckster as artist made "delights that do not delude," that activated the powers of reasoning to enable the public to better negotiate "the conflicting meanings of modernity."[54] He was "a public benefactor," a culture hero in a renovated drama of modernity. Here we find an honoured type of trickster who really did make life better via transgression.

Not that everyone was or is convinced by such reflections. The crucial issue was not necessarily the deceptions Barnum practised, even should a reader accept his claim they were harmless in their way, but the very methods of deception that he pioneered. The early chronicler of advertising, Frank Presbrey, hardly a critic of publicity, laid some of the blame for a surge of deception in the late nineteenth century on Barnum's shoulders: his example could be baneful.[55] (That was a bit unfair, no doubt: the later deceivers were more than just Barnum's children.) Irving Wallace, one of his champions, had doubts, given the trajectory of modern advertising.[56] A present-day reading of *The Life* by Charles Baxter, both a novelist and an academic, went much further in its condemnation of the huckster.[57] Baxter compared *The Life* to Walt Whitman's *Leaves of Grass*, which had also appeared in 1855. "With the poet you get the love of mankind and an indifference to riches; with the showman, you get the money in a world of trickery." They represented the two poles of life in mid-nineteenth-century America. Barnum became the source of original sin: he was none other than the pioneer of the attitudes and ways that would come to haunt and curse the United States. His autobiography served as guide to the habits of the adman. "Barnum points to something sacred in advertising – its ability to turn appearances into reality." How? By the vigorous use of "false superlatives and inflated rhetoric," by constant repetition until your message achieved "traction." "Truth value is always trumped by hype, and hype in turn is fuelled by controversy." That was how you could sell anything, whether freaks, superstars, or politicians. "In a world ruled by advertising and by the con men who construct the game and plant the shills, even a war (no, especially a war) can be sold to the public through flimflam." Such a line of argument echoed the moral explosion which greeted the publication of *The Life* back in 1855.

The morale of this huckster's story remained deeply ambiguous. Not for Barnum perhaps. Initially he had tried to confront his dilemma: hence *The Life*. That failed to please. The book satisfied neither his need for social legitimacy nor moral absolution. Later he finessed his dilemma through an adroit process of suppression, denial, and redefinition. That worked for him. But his story left behind unanswered questions. Was the value of truth non-negotiable? What level of deception was permissible? Ultimately the understanding of Barnum depended not only on his own conduct and his own confessions, but on what followed afterwards – and what commentators judged the effects of publicity on the course of modernity.

2. The Fake Healers: Samuel Hopkins Adams, *The Great American Fraud*, 1907

"Gullible America will spend this year some seventy-five millions of dollars in the purchase of patent medicines. In consideration of this sum," declared the righteous journalist, "it will swallow huge quantities of alcohol, an appalling amount of opiates and narcotics, a wide assortment of varied drugs ranging from powerful and dangerous heart depressants to insidious liver stimulants; and, far in excess of all other ingredients, undiluted fraud. For fraud, exploited by the skillfulest of advertising bunco men, is the basis of the trade."[58] That was the opening salvo of a series of reports on "the nostrum evil" and "quacks" written by Samuel Hopkins Adams and first published by *Collier's*, commencing in October 1905. The sensational series was collected and republished in various editions under the auspices of the American Medical Association and under the same title, *The Great American Fraud*.[59] There, Adams produced what constituted the first complete example of the narrative of harm, and a precursor to the motif of the ad-maker's sin, where the admen figured as villains and their publicity a major threat to the well-being of the nation.[60] His purpose was to foster "an aroused public sentiment" (68) that would drive the press and the politicians to safeguard public health.

The Great American Fraud was only one of the hucksters' stories inspired by the rise of the patent medicine industry. In many ways the healers or "nostrum makers," as they were known in contemporary parlance, were near perfect hucksters: they hawked what were widely considered to be dubious or shoddy goods to a needy and credulous public. Their success had required advertising on a grand scale, or what Adams simply labelled fraud. In various ways these hucksters confronted the problems endemic to the craft, especially the need to establish trust and to practice deception. Which was why their stories, or more precisely the stories about them, also amounted to an exploration of the new prominence of the advertising expert in the saga of modernity. None of them left behind a memoir or autobiography: we have nothing equivalent to Barnum's *Life*. Instead we have a diverse series of texts, some factual and some fictional, some contemporary and some later, that together fashioned the social conversation about this expression of the figure of the adman.

Adams's fury was nothing new. Off and on doctors, pharmacists, and journalists had raged against the patent medicine evil decades before Adams wrote his exposé. The variety, number, and popularity of proprietary remedies had grown mightily throughout the previous century, especially in the years after the Civil War.[61] One witness told a Congressional committee in 1906 that there were an estimated 50,000 nostrums "made and sold in the United States."[62]

Critics put much of the blame on the ignorance and credulity of the public itself, and Adams would play that theme as well. But there were

other reasons, notably the sad state of medicine and the republican temper of Americans. Doctors were often scarce and expensive, their practices frightening and their cures uncertain, especially where women's
ailments were concerned. People rightly feared the surgeon's knife and
the penchant for "the heroic therapy" (bloodletting, calomel, and blis-
tering), although that waned towards the end of the century.[63] Besides,
many Americans espoused the virtues of self-reliance and self-help: they
distrusted professionals and they sought the means to remedy their own
ills. A wide assortment of entrepreneurs rushed to meet that desire,
offering a bewildering variety of remedies which might contain herbs,
alcohol, narcotics, or even minute doses of poison but promising to cure
a host of ills, and do so cheaply and easily. The patent medicine industry
boomed after 1870 because the proliferation of newspapers provided
these healers an instrument to tout their wares to enormous numbers of
people. Some of the entrepreneurs made fortunes.[64]

Publicity – massive, repeated, and continuous advertising – was the
key to success, not only to fix the brand in the public mind but to fend
off the competition. Advertising had to do it all, recalled the renowned
copywriter Claude C. Hopkins later, one reason why "the greatest advertising men of my day were schooled in the medicine field."[65] By the end
of the century, some of the major firms in the industry were mounting
million-dollar ad campaigns each year. Much of the regular business of
advertising agencies involved the placement, and sometimes the preparation, of patent medicine ads in newspapers across the country. Newspapers and magazines also earned a steady and welcome stream of income
from all the nostrums offered for sale in their columns. And the entrepreneurs not only employed the press to reach sufferers. There were
sandwich men and advertising wagons in the cities, travelling medicine
shows in the countryside, health pamphlets and booklets replete with
testimonials, special almanacs, form letters to sick folk, handbills and
posters, outdoor ads – brand names and slogans of some of the remedies
were even painted on rocks and barns! America had already entered the
era of ad clutter.

The criticism of the patent medicine business escalated rapidly in the
new century. Many doctors and pharmacists, it was true, dealt in nostrums, recommending and selling favourite remedies to patients and clients. But others, whether out of self-interest or a concern for the public's
health, called for new laws to force the healers to reveal the contents
of their remedies. The American Medical Association certainly was hostile to much of the trade. One government scientist, Harvey Washington

Wiley, chief of the Bureau of Chemistry, Department of Agriculture, had already launched a campaign to cleanse America's foods and drugs. The widely read *Ladies' Home Journal*, run by the energetic Edward Bok, had banished nostrum ads from his magazine and set out to expose their deceptions as well as the menace of the remedies.[66] Some politicians in state legislatures worked to force the disclosure of ingredients to alert the public to what they were consuming. It was more than enough to upset the Proprietary Association of America (sometimes the Proprietary Medicine Manufacturers and Dealers Association) who regularly took steps to protect the trade of their members from the harassment of governments, legislatures, and the press.

Then the industry became the target of the muckrakers, one of the vehicles of the Progressive movement. The muckraking era was a brief but noisy episode in the history of American journalism. It lasted no more than a decade (1902–12), its heyday really limited to a few years in and around 1905, after which the critical urge fell victim to business pressure and, perhaps, public weariness. Typically the "muckraker" – named by President Theodore Roosevelt, and he was not being complimentary – was a crusading journalist, moved by some reforming zeal, who set out to document the ills and the corruption that marred America's industrial order.[67] These muckrakers were attached to such popular magazines as *McClure's Magazine*, *Ladies' Home Journal*, *Collier's*, *Cosmopolitan*, or *Everybody's Magazine*, which had recently captivated middle-class audiences in cities big and small. There was an almost evangelical flavour, a deep sense of moral outrage, to the exposés of Ida M. Tarbell (Standard Oil), Upton Sinclair (*The Jungle*, a 1906 novel that dealt with the meatpacking industry), Ray Stannard Baker (on the plight of labour), Lincoln Steffens (urban corruption), and David Graham Phillips (corruption in the Senate), to name some of the most prominent. The muckrakers took up the stance of the passionate investigator reporting on actual conditions, filling their revelations of evil with facts and names. Their purpose was to awaken public anger sufficient to producing a wave of reform that would purge and purify. And, initially, they were very successful, their reports causing much excitement, selling many copies of the magazines, and provoking political action.

The new assault on patent medicines actually began in 1904, when Edward Bok of the *Ladies' Home Journal* hired the lawyer Mark Sullivan (1874–1952) to explore the machinations of the nostrum manufacturers. His most famous exploit was to demonstrate that the ads for Lydia Pinkham's Vegetable Compound, a popular remedy for female ills, were something of a lie. They suggested that Lydia Pinkham, touted as a wise and benevolent grandmother, would respond sympathetically to the written pleas of any woman sufferer. In fact, as Sullivan revealed in 1905, she had been dead for twenty years, which he proved with a photograph of her tombstone juxtaposed to an ad supposedly showing Lydia "in her laboratory."[68] He also prepared an exposé of the ways in which the Proprietary Association worked to discipline both the press and the politicians. That report never appeared in the *Journal*, however. Although impressed, Bok deemed it too long and too legalistic for his magazine. Bok sold the article to Norman Hapgood, editor of *Collier's*, who had already mounted his own investigation of the patent medicine industry. Hapgood had got into a dispute with the famous Democrat William Jennings Bryan when *Collier's* criticized Bryan for carrying a full page ad for Liquozone in his *Commoner*, Bryan's weekly paper. The exaggerated response of Bryan and Liquozone to what was intended as a mocking comment inspired Hapgood to go further.

Hapgood's instrument was the thirty-four-year-old Samuel Hopkins Adams (1871–1958), then a freelance journalist.[69] Adams was the son of a minister, which might explain some of his moral fervour. He had gone to college, then worked for nine years at the New York *Sun* mostly on the crime beat, before joining *McClure's*, the hotbed of muckraking, where he served as an ad manager before becoming a writer again. Adams had developed an interest in public health, writing about tuberculosis, which led one of his compatriots at *McClure's*, Ray Stannard Baker, to suggest he pursue the topic of patent medicines. S.S. McClure was not especially interested in the topic but he recommended Adams to Hapgood, and that began the investigation. Adams employed what were already the standard techniques of the mass press to produce the truths of journalism. He collected some of the nostrums and the advertisements, he sent samples of the remedies off to laboratories to discover their contents, he interviewed a few of the healers, and he got in touch with Dr Wiley and other like-minded critics. Adams found a young physician who had worked in the business of healing before quitting, supposedly in disgust, who could provide an eye-witness account of what actually went on. Adams also explored who wrote testimonials for the remedies and whether these were valid, what exactly had happened to the people on record as cured by one remedy or healer or another. (Purportedly he was briefly the target of a blackmail threat aimed at halting his activities.)[70] All this sleuthing took about five months. Meanwhile Hapgood prepared *Collier's* readers with hints of what was to come.

The series debuted on 7 October 1905. It was the major item that week.[71] The first, introductory article was topped by a marvellous graphic, a background of nostrum bottles around which snakes were entwined and in front a hooded skull, blank eyes staring out at the reader, all under the title "THE GREAT AMERICAN FRAUD." Throughout *Collier's* made excellent use of illustrations and photographs to enliven and reiterate Adams's revelations. The first series of six reports focusing on "the nostrum evil" ran until 17 February 1906, and included the additional report (but no byline) by Mark Sullivan. This was the series that caused the most excitement and upset, and not just among the public. The Proprietary Association could do little to stem the tide. Politicians and journalists were now exercised. The series led in part to the passage of a Pure Food and Drug Act in 1906 which required correct labelling of what was in a remedy.[72] A second series, "Quacks and Quackery," about healers who operated through the mails, appeared as four reports between 14 July and 22 September 1906. That assault caused much less interest, though its findings were summarized in the *Literary Digest*. In any case a now-galvanized AMA collected both series, and some additional articles, including summaries of material from the *Ladies Home Journal*, in one booklet. This had sold an estimated 150,000 copies by 1912, and double or triple that amount was likely in circulation.[73] It was definitely a success.

Fraud was a grand mix of fact, opinion, and judgment. Adams presented readers with a mass of data about these hucksters, their brands, the advertising, the assorted drugs, the consequences, and the victims. He filled his account with names, altogether 264 "concerns and individuals," he claimed in an afterword (147). Sometimes he enlivened his polemic with sarcasm, a dose of bitter humour provoked by the success of the con. The prevailing discourse of truth was science, not say the traditional knowledge or Indian lore or Oriental wisdom which the healers sometimes evoked: Adams time and again made reference to what the laboratory knew about a drug to demonstrate harm. But the series drew its vigour from a moral passion. Adams was tracking evil and exposing greed. He used a slew of epithets to characterize the various healers – charlatans, fakers, bunko men, swindlers, monsters, ghouls, scavengers, leeches, even murderers: some hucksters were more vile than others, apparently. His moral passion was easily translated into a civic passion. He made use of the rhetoric of shame, damning the public authorities for their failure to act against this menace. How could politicians and editors allow the persistence of such a social cancer in America? How could they submit to the dictates of the Proprietary Association? Evident throughout was a distinct undertone, call it a gender bias: the acceptance of the hucksters' deceit offended the code of masculinity, the sense of honour and the imperative to protect which should characterize the behaviour of the American male.

Adams adopted the pose of the explorer. There was a mythological cast to his foray, the hero venturing into hell to do battle with demons on behalf of the community. For what he described was a bizarre netherworld of strange characters, weird brands, and dark magic, a topsy-turvy place where the rules of logic no longer held sway. Hence this comment on the carnivalesque property of the huckster's domain:

> Study the medicine advertising in your morning paper, and you will find yourself in a veritable goblin-realm of fakery, peopled with monstrous myths. Here is an amulet in the form of an electric belt, warranted to restore youth and vigor to the senile; yonder a magic ring or mysterious inhaler, or a bewitched foot-plaster which will draw the pangs of rheumatism from the tortured body "or your money back"; and again some beneficent wizard in St. Louis promises with a secret philtre to charm away deadly cancer, while in the next column a firm of magi in Denver proposes confidently to exorcise the demon of incurable consumption without ever seeing the patient. Is it credible that a supposedly civilized nation should accept such stuff as gospel?" (55)

His series proceeded through the various realms and circles of this netherworld to reveal the twin hierarchies of evil. The initial nostrum series first surveyed Peruna and like remedies saturated with alcohol, and then Liquozone and the so-called germicides that could never cure anything; third and more sinister came "the subtle poisons" – the specific target here was Orangeine, which contained some narcotic that enslaved and degenerated; last and worst were the brands that preyed on the incurables, people suffering from tuberculosis, cancer, or epilepsy. The quack series dealt successively with "the sure-fire cure school" that advertised cures for any disease; "the miracle workers" who drew on fake science or even the Bible; "the specialist humbug" who took on the guise of a medical expert; and, worst of all, "the scavengers" who promised a cure for the drug habit but actually just supplied their victims with another dose. Presiding over this netherworld was the Proprietary Association, no less than a parliament of villains, who worked to protect both realms from any outside interference.[74]

Adams estimated the total value of the patent medicine industry at $250 million (9). What it supplied, however, was a bogus product, either harmless fakes or dangerous potions. He drew little distinction between the ordinary nostrums and the supposed "ethical" remedies that reported their contents.[75] None of the remedies had any real value. Most cures for minor ills would occur naturally. The trouble was that many remedies might well delay that cure or, worse, increase the sickness. They were always an obstacle to good health, especially those concoctions that were full of alcohol or contained cocaine or opiates or such substances as prussic or sulfuric acid, strychnine, or acetanilide, a particular favourite at the time. Some of these brands offered people an apparently respectable way of drinking booze: "Hostetter's Bitters contain, according to an official state analysis, 44 per cent. of alcohol; Lydia Pinkham appeals to suffering womanhood with 20 per cent. of alcohol; Hood's Sarsaparilla cures 'that tired feeling' with 18 per cent.; Burdock's Blood Bitters, with 25 per cent.; Ayer's Sarsaparilla, with 26 per cent., and Paine's Celery Compound, with 21 per cent." (21). The industry fostered addiction, its best customers the "repeaters" who were never cured and so were always willing to pay for some new elixir. A small but especially vile circle of quacks who promised to cure impotence were actually engaged in blackmail: they threatened to expose the unfortunate man to his neighbours or employer if he should stop buying the fake remedy.

Adams sprinkled his account with references to the notion of the hapless public. He found it difficult to understand that people could be so easily fooled. One remedy, the "Slocum Consumption Cure is a fake and a fraud so ludicrous that its continued existence is a brilliant commentary on human credulousness" (50). But that case was only an extreme example of the general problem. "Ignorance and credulous hope make the market for most proprietary remedies" (32). The cause of the mass delusion had to lie in deception, in the effects of the mass advertising which exploited the hopes and fears of a gullible public. "For printers' ink is the very life-blood of the noxious trade. Take from the nostrum vendors the means by which they influence the millions, and there will pass to the limbo of pricked bubbles a fraud whose flagrancy and impudence are of minor import compared to the cold-hearted greed with which it grinds out its profits from the sufferings of duped and eternally hopeful ignorance" (69). No wonder that the largest expense on the healer's ledger was for advertising, as much as 50 per cent of their total expenditures, far greater than the cost of manufacture. Sullivan estimated that at least five of the major concerns paid out around $1 million a year to newspapers to tout their nostrums (124).

What Adams detailed was the fact that these hucksters had solved some of the problems of persuasion attendant on the adman's dilemma, though of course he did not put such an unhappy triumph in these words. First of all, he made abundantly clear how the healers established that necessary modicum of trust. Many of them employed titles and credentials: there was a Dr Oren Oneal, Dr G.M. Curry, Prof. F.T. McIntyre, Prof. T.J. Adkin, the Rev. W.N. Ritchie, all claiming professional or moral standing to impress the credulous. Some of these fakers actually offered medical books: Dr W.O. Coffee, who ran an eye-and-ear clinic, plagiarized the illustrations from a reputable source to justify his supposed "Absorption Treatment" (103). Others would recount their connections with a medical society or their work with various hospitals or businesses, few of which were true: Dr G.M. Curry, who claimed to cure cancer, was one such inveterate sinner.[76] D.M. Bye, yet another supposed doctor, had even funded his own church, and many another huckster would employ religious imagery and rhetoric to mask his swindles. Even more traded on the prestige of science, exploiting whatever was popular – the language of medicine or a new discovery – to convince: Adams recalled how twenty years ago, "Radam's Microbe Killer filled the public prints with blazonry [*sic*] of its lethal virtues" (23). Then they would adopt the pose of the friend, a public benefactor who worked so hard to free people from sickness and ill-health. Here was an early instance of the motif of the consumer's friend. That required, however contradictory it might seem, a rhetoric of anti-professionalism, the claim that the doctors did not know or that official medicine was dangerous, thus appealing to the republican spirit of the population. You could cure yourself, with a little help from your friends, whatever the experts said. Often, you could supposedly get your money back (though Adams believed few people tried) should you not be completely satisfied.[77]

Nonetheless, the chief instruments the healers used to win trust were the testimonial and the endorsement.[78] The larger concerns claimed thousands and thousands of testimonials from cured folk, ordinary women and men who had once suffered some ailment but now gratefully acknowledged that the medicine had wrought a transformation. These constituted a democratic testament to the potency of their nostrums, no matter what the critics, most especially the doctors and scientists, might assert. Not medical science, then, but common sense: that was the proof of efficacy. It was an excellent way of meeting any claim of a victim's malaise, since users were so pleased. The testimonials, or rather the best of them, the hucksters published in their advertisements and in their medical books. Analysing one of these compendia, Pierce's *World's Dispensary Medical Book*, Adams concluded that most testimonials were genuine but rarely honest. A few came from accomplished writers, another collection from public men, but the vast majority were from the ignorant if not illiterate. "The ignorant drug-taker, returning to health from some disease which he has overcome by the natural resistant powers of his body, dips his pen in gratitude and writes his testimonial" (4). The trouble was that too many of the testimonials were solicited, especially those from public men. The hucksters hired "hunters" to approach, say, naval officers, congressmen, senators, hospitals, and the like to endorse a product. Even more testimonials were edited to ensure they served their purpose, meaning the huckster's agents rewrote the letters to make clear the virtues of the brand. And many testimonials were just simply dated, that is, the testimonial referred to a cure which had eventually proven false. Thus Doan's Kidney Pills "ran an advertisement in a Southern city embodying a letter from a resident of that city who had been dead nearly a year. Cause of death, kidney disease" (65). In fact a testimonial from one Mary Adams for Dr Richards' Dyspepsia Tablets ran in the same issue of a newspaper that carried her obituary, her death the result of "dropsy" (162)!

If the testimonials were the grand means of defence, observed Adams, then newspaper ads were the chosen weapon of aggression. Here he found no limit to the deception: such ads were full of exaggerations, lies, half-truths, evasion, masquerade, distortion, and misdirection. Not that they were all alike: far from it. The imagination of the healers was boundless. Even so-called specifics made wild promises of curing an extraordinary range of ills: "Just as to Peruna all ills are catarrh, so to Liquozone every disease is a germ disease" (28). Liquozone's rhetoric was full of "pseudo-scientific charlatanry" about what its magical ingredients might remedy (25). The powders of Orangeine "pretend to cure asthma, biliousness, headaches, colds, catarrh and grip (dose: powder every four hours during the day for a week! – a pretty fair start on the Orangeine habit), diarrhoea, hay fever, insomnia, influenza, neuralgia, seasickness and sciatica" (33). Pond's Extract employed scare copy to market the potion during a meningitis epidemic in New York; in the same way, Peruna exploited a yellow fever emergency in New Orleans. Duffy's Pure Malt Whiskey advertised endorsements from three "distinguished divines and temperance workers" who were anything but.

Dr King's New Discovery for Consumption ("IT STRIKES TERROR TO THE DOCTORS"), "the only sure cure for consumption in the world," was in reality "a pretty diabolical concoction" of morphine and chloroform (45–6). In Adams's telling, the healers had seemingly avoided the troubles of the adman's dilemma: since the truth would threaten profits, they had wholeheartedly embraced deception, thereby accepting the state of moral error.

These hucksters had also solved the sovereignty problem, much to the chagrin of both Adams and Sullivan. Few seemed willing and no one seemed able to hinder the healers' activities. *Fraud* portrayed the victory of the healers as a series of betrayals. All too many politicians turned a blind eye to the poisoning of America, and some actively worked on behalf of the pernicious industry. Many a physician, who should have known better, actually recommended one or another remedy to a needy patient. Adams told the story of a Pennsylvania merchant who took Antikamnia, a potion loaded with acetanilide, to cure insomnia on his doctor's advice. The result? He soon sickened, lost weight, his skin turning "dusky" and his blood "a deep chocolate color," and eventually he entered "a state of stupor" (38–9).

But the muckrakers saved most of their moral fury to lambaste the press. Why? That was not only out of a sense of professional offence: the outrage reflected their liberal sympathies. The press was supposed to be an instrument of truth, the vehicle of fact, not lies. It was supposed to combat moral error, not contribute to that error. Or, to use the language of social theory, newspapers were required to act as one of the chief buttresses of the regime of truth. "Relying so wholly on the press to undo evil," wrote Sullivan, "how shall we deal with that evil with which the press itself has been seduced into captivity?" (123). Adams and Sullivan believed that neither the nostrum evil nor the explosion of quackery could persist without the connivance of the press. Yet the press had been bought off by the profusion of advertising revenue generated by the patent medicine industry. "Mr. Hearst's papers alone reap a harvest of more than half a million dollars per annum from this source," wrote Adams (55). Even medical and religious papers carried the fraudulent ads. Just as bad, newspapers had submitted to the practice of the so-called red clause (so named because it was typed in red) in ad contracts warning that all advertising would be withdrawn from a newspaper should its state legislature pass any act inimical to the industry. Some such clauses even prohibited newspapers from publishing any material that might upset the healers. The *Cleveland Press* lost $18,000 in ad revenue in forty-eight

hours after assaulting the "drug trust" (139). Witness the sad result in
Massachusetts, where the legislature had discussed the issue of patent
medicines in 1905: Sullivan reported on the near "universal silence" of
the press which failed to cover the debate over a proposed bill (124).
Worse yet, some unspecified newspapers actually editorialized against
the effort to compel the healers to label the contents of their medicines.
He went on to detail what seemed a conspiracy of the Proprietary Association where the healers had discussed at one of their meetings just how
to impose their will upon the nation's press. Who then were the masters?
Here were all the signs of an organized and unregulated tyranny.

Neither Adams nor Sullivan reported any evidence that the healers
were troubled by moral qualms or doubts about their nefarious trade.
There were few signs of the liar's plight here. Yes, when questioned
about one claim or another in their advertising, these hucksters might
backtrack, thereby admitting some exaggeration. But otherwise they
were obdurate. Sullivan's article, for instance, copied a letter to a newspaper editor by Frank Cheney (proprietor of Hall's Catarrh Cure, the
creator of the "red clause," and president of the Proprietary Association), where he defended the "red clause" as sound business practice,
not an assault on the freedom of the press. Adams conducted an extensive interview with Dr Samuel B. Hartman, the maker of Peruna, then
the most popular nostrum on the market.[79] He stated the rationale for
his cure-all simply, referring here to the American public: "They see my
advertising. They read the testimonials. They are convinced. They have
faith in Peruna. It gives them a gentle stimulant and so they get well"
(4). The implication? Hartman believed that he was offering a suffering
humanity a great boon.

Adams did not wonder whether Hartman or any of his ilk were themselves suffering from self-deception. Instead, he and Sullivan deemed
these hucksters blatant liars. (Adams singled out one of Hartman's lies
about the consequences of using Peruna.)[80] The muckrakers' critique
rested on the presumption that the healers were neither authentic nor
sincere.[81] Consequently their deception was a conspiracy against truth,
and a conspiracy which had produced untold suffering and death. The
whole business was a case of modernity gone wrong, a perversion of the
imperatives of any regime of biopolitics. Instead of health and purity,
two of the goals of such a regime, the commerce in patent medicines
produced sickness and death. It corrupted politics and the press and so
endangered the moral health of the nation. It was a kind of misrule, or,
to borrow from Foucault's lexicon, a form of "thanatopolitics," the very

reverse of what should prevail.[82] *The Great American Fraud* was one of the most stark and hostile portrayals of the figure of the adman to appear in the American experience. Twenty years later, the judgment of evil was revitalized by the charges and popularity of a later bestseller, Arthur Kallet and F.J. Schlink's *100,000,000 Guinea Pigs: Dangers in Everyday Foods, Drugs, and Cosmetics* (1934). The judgment would persist in the social conversation for many years to come.[83]

3. The New Napoleon: H.G. Wells, *Tono-Bungay*, 1909

Adams's diatribe spent little time actually exploring the life stories of any of the nostrum sellers. That was left to fiction. Adams himself fashioned one such character in a novel he wrote called *The Clarion* (1914), about a journalist. The British writer William Locke produced another with his *Septimus* (1909). But H.G. Wells wrote the best story. It was a far more sophisticated and complicated piece of work than the other novels and before long was counted a classic of English literature on both sides of the Atlantic. *Tono-Bungay* was styled as a fictional autobiography of the nephew of a huckster who rose very high but fell fast and hard. The huckster sported the exotic name Ponderevo and his product was a patent medicine called Tono-Bungay.

Wells expressed the adman's dilemma in the form of a dialogue, and he employed three different characters to voice its complicated dimensions: Edward Ponderevo, his nephew George, and his artist friend Ewart. There was much else in the novel, not the least George's various failed romances, that does not concern us here, though the result was to make the whole story a lengthy ramble. *Tono-Bungay* was "a condition of England" novel, meaning that Wells used his characters and their stories to reflect on the plight of English society. What troubled Wells the socialist was not the slow death of a traditional England of hierarchy and order, but the rise of a hectic and hollow society of commerce, full of waste and fakery and inequality. The extraordinary rise of the tonic Tono-Bungay (which has been deciphered as "ton o' bunk eh")[84] registered the fatal flaws of this new England. In short, where Adams had deemed the nostrum business evidence of modernity gone wrong, Wells argued more forcefully that the making of Tono-Bungay was a harbinger of a modernity about to triumph.[85]

Edward Ponderevo was the driving force throughout much of the novel. He was no ordinary man: congenial and sociable, almost lovable in some ways, he was "always imaginative, erratic, inconsistent, recklessly

inexact" (259), but also full of energy and desire, the desire to triumph,
to win fame and fortune. He was, so his nephew once reflected, a devotee and a victim of the cult of Napoleon, meaning his ambition knew
no bounds. He idealized America as a land of zip and enterprise, the
place "where things hum" (68). America meant modernity, the site of a
triumphant capitalism. Initially a provincial pharmacist, trapped so he
thought in a country backwater, Edward soon escaped stagnation and
moved to London, where he invented the idea of Tono-Bungay, "a Real
Live Thing" (133) that only required effort and advertising to assure success. This tonic he vigorously promoted across the nation using a simple
but arresting slogan, the image of "a genially nude giant" (128), an earnest style of rhetoric, in short much "lies and clamour" (149). Edward
designed the ads himself. And before long they were everywhere, since
the Ponderevos poured their earnings back into more advertising.
Edward followed up his success by inventing new versions of the nostrum,
buying up other patent medicines, and expanding into the marketing of
household goods. Soon he moved into finance and speculation. All the
while he had increased his spending, eventually lavishing money on the
renovation of a country estate. Then it all collapsed, the illusions and the
fakery punctured by press scrutiny, Edward ironically a victim of another
kind of the publicity that had made him so famous.

Supposedly Edward had no qualms about the merits of Tono-Bungay
and the style of his advertising, or at least none he would admit. But his
rationalizations leave the impression he recognized that some people
would find his enterprise dubious. "It's the sort of thing everybody does.
After all, there's no harm in the stuff – and it may do a lot of good – giving people confidence, f'rinstance, against an epidemic." The purpose
of the advertising was to put "Faith" into the populace. He was selling
hope to a needy population in search of answers to the conundrum of
health, thus acting as the consumer's friend. It was akin to Christian Science, he claimed, a case of mind over matter, a brand of positive thinking, echoing a not unusual proposition. "Everybody who does a large
advertised trade is selling something common on the strength of saying
it's uncommon." It was just "the modern way" to be so emphatic (135).
The virtue of advertising was to energize commerce, to make trade, to
bring employment to the people. In short, Edward would never see that
Tono-Bungay was a swindle, that his wild claims about its efficacy were
no more than outright deception. Which was why his rise symbolized
the triumph of illusion that so troubled Wells about modern England.
"There he stands in my memory," George said of Edward, "the symbol of

this age for me, the man of luck and advertisement, the current master of the world" (271). The huckster and his ilk were taking charge of the nation's destinies.

It was Edward's nephew who felt the full force of the adman's dilemma. George Ponderevo recognized the fraud, even though he joined his uncle because the enterprise promised money (so he could win his lady love) as well as excitement. He played the role of the business manager in the Tono-Bungay enterprise: he organized the production and distribution of the tonic which ensured Edward's advertising brilliance would generate profit. A younger man, and a bit of a prig, George spoke as the moralist who from the beginning believed that "the sale of Tono-Bungay was a thoroughly dishonest proceeding." He thought the nostrum at best "a mischievous trash ... likely to become a bad habit and train people in the habitual use of stronger tonics, and insidiously dangerous to people with defective kidneys" (137). But what really disturbed his moral sense was the advertising: it was full of lies, vulgar and excessive, rubbish for fools. He was horrified by the stunning success that his Uncle, and he too, enjoyed from the practice of deceit. "I cannot claim that a single one of the great businesses we organized added any real value to human life at all," he lamented. "Several, like Tono-Bungay, were unmitigated frauds by any honest standard, the giving of nothing coated in advertisements for money" (220). George was a victim of the liar's plight. In the end, sick of "all this damned rascality," he had to escape the "laborious cheating" to engage in "something solid" (203).

That "something solid" he sought turned out to be technological, initially the making of an aeroplane. George spoke not as the representative of an old England but as an acolyte of Science (a word often capitalized in his account). He could not resist an ode to his god:

> She is reality, the one reality I have found in this strange disorder of existence. She will not sulk with you nor misunderstand you nor cheat you of your reward upon some petty doubt. You cannot change her by advertisement or clamour, not stifle her in vulgarities. Things grow under your hands when you serve her, things that are permanent as nothing else is permanent in the whole life of man. That I think is the peculiar satisfaction of science and its enduring reward. (277)

Here in the realm of science reigned George's conception of the truth, pure and transparent, a truth that could dissolve all the deceptions of commerce. To the figure of the adman Wells countered that of the scientist. It was an updated, an Edwardian version of that earlier cult of truth which had informed Barnum's critics, equally absolute and uncompromising. There was a terrible irony about such a credo, however, at least according to the Wells of this novel. Science did not necessarily assure humanity much more hope than commerce. For George ended his autobiography, still mouthing the virtues of Science and Truth, when piloting a destroyer, an instrument of war, he had designed and sold to some foreign power!

Ewart offered the most unusual take on the character of the persuader. He had only a small part in the novel – Wells calls him Bob in one place, Sydney in another. Ewart was George's school chum, later his compatriot in various London jaunts, who became a sculptor of sorts, before disappearing from the scene. But early on in the saga of Tono-Bungay, he visited the establishment of the Ponderevos, where he argued the case for advertising as art. Ewart spoke as one artist to another. Truth was not at issue, nor deception. Advertising was likely to revolutionize the world, he claimed, because it transformed ordinary commodities into valued goods. The modern merchant found "something that isn't worth anything – or something that isn't particularly worth anything, and he makes it worth something" (159). Like the sculptor, the adman took a lump of undistinguished material and fashioned it into a lasting monument for himself and others. "You turn water – into Tono-Bungay" (160). (Edward, naturally, harrumphed at that effusion.) Anyway what the adman really sold was salvation. Nobody wanted to be what he was but what he dreamed of: "What we want to be is something perpetually young and beautiful – young Joves, young Joves, Ponderevo – pursuing coy half-willing nymphs through everlasting forests ..." (158). The huckster was the poet who crafted the stories of enchantment, leading people into the promised land.

Thus Wells wrote a brief exposition of what would become the gospel of creativity, that narrative of understanding in which the adman emerged as a culture hero. Wells had also registered a denial, however. Ewart's exuberance, his grandiloquence, were a sign of irony. He was actually playing the role of the cynic: he was mocking the Ponderevos, especially an uncertain Edward who admired the rhetoric but distrusted the tone. So advertising was not art. The adman was no more than a false prophet. Edward Ponderevo might well be the personification of modernity, but that was the problem. His creativity was a threat to the moral health of the country, if not the physical health of the population. This huckster was a dangerous rogue whose activities endangered the very progress of the land.

4. Stories of Magic and Mischief: Huckster Fictions 1906–1931

In 1928 Earnest Elmo Calkins, one of the pioneers of modern advertising, opened his book of essays, entitled *Business the Civilizer*, with a lament. The image of advertising and the adman all too prevalent in recent literature was deeply misleading: he cited (though not always accurately) a range of American and British authors who had besmirched the reputation of the new profession.[86] They left the impression that advertising was little more than an exercise in fraud, a gigantic con game which exploited the gullibility of the public and hindered the progress of industry. The advertising practitioner appeared as a huckster ready to use any form of deceit to sell his goods, however shoddy. This was all the more distressing because ever since 1900, and especially in the 1920s, the persuasion industries had boomed, advertising agencies had become an important social as well as economic institution, and the advertising agents had taken on airs as the instruments of modern progress.

In fact neither advertising nor the adman were prominent subjects in the spate of so-called economic novels that had emerged in America after 1865. According to David Zimmerman, most of the hundreds of such novels that appeared between the end of the Civil War and the beginning of the First World War "fall within recognizable subgenres: the economic reform novel (which encompasses labor jeremiads, Populist polemics, and utopian lectures), the success tale (which includes rags-to-riches stories, Wall Street romances, and novels about financial titans), and consumer fiction, the sentimental and narrative formulas for which evolved over the latter half of the nineteenth century."[87] Advertising might figure in a few of these and other stories. In one of Mark Twain's bestsellers, *A Connecticut Yankee in King Arthur's Court* (1889), advertising was a tool the exile Hank Morgan used to fool the locals, subvert authority, and modernize a backward land. Much later, advertising was one of the pursuits of the young Eugene Witla, Theodore Dreiser's hero in *The "Genius"* (1915), always to win affluence, though at the cost of his artistic talent, indeed of his authenticity. And in a different vein, advertising was a major source of the banality, the superficiality that saturated the small-city America of Sinclair Lewis in his bestseller *Babbitt* (1922). George F. Babbitt was a realtor, admittedly a relative of the adman because he also promoted his wares (and he did write some ads), but his experience of advertising was largely as a consumer and a victim.[88]

Nonetheless, there was a small group of what I will call "huckster fictions" in the twenty-five years after 1905 that focused directly on publicity, and sometimes on the adman himself. None of these really fit into any of Zimmerman's categories. They were part of the comic tradition in America, those tall tales, farces, and gentle satires that poked fun at the foibles and features of modern life. Although overall they did treat advertising as a discourse of untruth, and so commented on the problems of persuasion, there were only a few signs of the motif of the adman's dilemma, certainly by comparison with the adman fictions of a later generation.

The first of these huckster fictions, the first adman novel in fact, was Ellis Parker Butler's *Perkins of Portland* (1906), actually a collection of short stories which had initially appeared separately in trade and popular magazines.[89] Butler's hero was the great Perkins, purportedly the brightest star in the business, "the father, mother, and grandparent of modern advertising."[90] The resulting tall tales chronicled his largely successful efforts to sell patent medicines, guinea pigs, canned cheese, a new subdivision, a sensational novel, and ad space on automobiles and even in a play. Perkins employed a host of techniques, such as saturation publicity, fake testimonials, brand extension, and press notices, all of which would remain commonplace in the repertoire of advertising. If any one writer deserves the credit for launching the adman as a character in American literature, it is surely Butler. His version was congenial, neither sinister nor troubled.

Samuel Hopkins Adams also wrote a novel, called *The Clarion* (1914), in which a key figure was Dr L. André Surtaine, a wealthy maker of proprietary medicines. Adams's novel was really about a young man, the son of the fake healer, who set out to reform journalism. Unlike *Fraud*, this book was no great success, though in the end it sold about 37,000 copies and was even made into a movie. In 1915 Edwin Lefèvre, eventually well known for his stories about Wall Street, published his novel *H.R.*, a satire of New York life, about the rise of one Hendrik Rutgers who organized the sandwich men (also known as human billboards) into a powerful force in the economic and public life of the city.[91] Lefèvre maintained a constant tone of mockery: of the rich and poor, of New York, business and the press, women as a species, the socialists, the suffragettes, the church, etc.[92] A year earlier, Roi Cooper Megrue and William Hackett, two accomplished playwrights, had delivered what proved a modest hit called *It Pays to Advertise*, which ran on Broadway for almost a year at George M. Cohan's Theatre. The production had a didactic purpose: the authors incorporated into the play a whole series of statistics to demonstrate just how important advertising had become.[93] The actual story, both fast-moving and witty, explored the ways young Rodney Martin and his agent the adman Ambrose Peale used advertising to launch a new brand of soap. The play was novelized a year later, not so successfully, by Samuel Field and turned into a silent movie in 1919.[94] More importantly, in 1931 Paramount released *It Pays to Advertise*, directed by Frank Tuttle and featuring a young Carole Lombard (before she became famous).[95] Less popular was Aaron Hoffman's play *Nothing But Lies* (1918), one of the first farces of agency life, which centred on the shenanigans of the adman George Washington Cross, an inveterate liar.[96]

By contrast, Christopher Morley's short comedy *The Story of Sugar Cubes* (1922) was about the misadventure of a new product launch, derailed by conflicting romances, via a series of letters, reports, and essays, a variant on the epistolary novel.[97] And William Woodward's *Bunk* (1923) followed the progress of Michael Webb, purportedly a character in an unwritten novel, who could undo deception, albeit sometimes at the expense of the client's life. Woodward thereby added the word "debunk" to the American lexicon.[98] Hollywood produced a few more additions to this roster, notably *His Picture in the Papers* (1916), starring Douglas Fairbanks, and the famous *Safety Last* (1923), a Harold Lloyd comedy, both silent movies that featured young men who employed publicity to promote their romantic ambitions. More substantial was *The Virgin Queene* (1928), a novel by Harford Powel, Jr, a sometime advertising practitioner, based in part on the example of his acquaintance, the much acclaimed ad executive Bruce Barton.[99] Here the motif of the adman's dilemma did appear: Powel's accomplished protagonist, Barnham Dunn (note the nod to Barnum), experienced a burnout. He tried to escape the world of advertising by fleeing to the English countryside, only to discover that he could never escape the life of deception, nor the fame of a successful deception. The first and last lines of this comedy of manners were the same: the lead for an ad. That signified how he had gone full circle.

These fictions shaped a uniform picture of the huckster and his world. First of all, none, not even the young protagonists, were outsiders. All were white American males, mostly Anglo-Americans so it would seem, thus part of the privileged circle of the prevailing gender and ethnic codes of the time. Jews, women, and black Americans were absent from their ranks. Just as, where romance played a part, the hucksters were determinedly heterosexual. Rodney Martin (*It Pays to Advertise*), Hendrik Rutgers (*H.R.*), George Washington Cross (*Nothing But Lies*), Pete Prindle (*His Picture in the Papers*) all employed their skills to win the heart of a woman. None were effete, none evinced the supposed style of the homosexual, not even the apparently asexual Perkins or the burned-out

Dunn (*The Virgin Queene*). These men were (or had been) go-getters, "live-wires" in the jargon of the times, full of enthusiasm and energy. Perkins was always a font of new ideas on how to make money. "What I wanted was excitement, – an adventure, – and I knew that if I could find Perkins, I could have both," claimed his partner. "A scheme is a business adventure, and Perkins was the greatest schemer in or out of Chicago" (95).[100] Obstacles, setbacks did not deter him. Like Perkins, the eagerness of Ambrose Peale (*It Pays to Advertise*) proved highly infectious: this adman managed to overcome the doubts of Rodney and eventually the reluctance of his father Cyrus, making them converts to the creed of advertising. H.R.'s love interest aptly described him as "this masterful man, who was resourceful, original, undeterred by conventions, indifferent to the niceties of life, unafraid of public opinion as of social ostracism" (75). Similarly, the highly personable adman George Cross was the instigator of a host of schemes that drove the action of the play. One Dr Gray, the psychology director of an agency in Morley's *The Story of Ginger Cubes*, was deemed "a whirlwind" (10). The two rich men's sons, Rodney Martin and Pete Prindle, shook off the laziness bred by their comfortable circumstances to become, in the end, highly successful admen. After some months of rest and recovery, Dunn became a furious writer of a simulacrum of a Shakespearean play ("The Virgin Queene" of the novel's title) and at the end he was back in the saddle as a copywriter. In short, these men were thoroughly "modern" and masculine, embodying the virtues of energy, competitiveness, persistence, and imagination, presumably virtues that no moralist would find unfortunate.

One proficiency that set these hucksters apart from their fellow men was their talent for persuasion. They were noted for their social skills, their ability to communicate and to feign friendliness. "I may remark that, since Perkins has become famous," noted William Brown, his partner, "every advertising agent has copied his cheerful manner of speech, so that the ad. man who does not greet you with a smile no longer exists" (17). Perkins became famous because he demonstrated a capacity to boom any kind of product. "He could do anything, could Perkins" (119). Peale had a similar talent: "There was something hypnotic and persuasive about him when he got started" (novel: 83). Despite his youth, H.R. seemed able to hypnotize people with his promises and claims. "To some he was a humbug, to others a crank; to some a genius, to a few a dangerous demagogue" (86). Barnham Dunn embodied the copywriter at his best, the master of compelling words, able to produce highly successful appeals for all manner of trivial goods. He was "not merely a preacher of uplift, but its own most bracing example" (8). The huckster was a kind of mesmerist who excelled in a world where the media was so important and publicity was king. Rhetoric had long been a manly art much admired (and its excess sometimes condemned). What made the figure of the adman so interesting was his purported ability to command attention and to persuade in a modern environment dominated by mass communications. "In such communities" – meaning wherever news rules, where it had become "a sacred commandment" – "success is necessarily a matter of skilful publicity" (37), wrote Lefèvre; meaning, of course, advertising, stunts, spectacle, and public relations.

Another attribute contributed to the success of these hucksters: they were full of self-confidence. Pete Prindle and Rodney Martin were convinced they could do the near impossible – win public attention, parental accolades, and their sweethearts – once they decided to work hard. Perkins was forever promising unlimited riches. "In ten years we can buy Manhattan Island for our town-seat and Chicago for our country-seat" (7), he told his prospective associate when trying to sell the first advertising scheme. H.R. had a sudden vision that once he quit his job as a lowly bank clerk, he could become rich, win fame and power, and secure the hand of the bank president's daughter. From a rational standpoint, then, they were suffering from a bad case of self-deception. Their intelligence, their knowledge should have told them the rules of logic meant almost certain failure. Instead, the hucksters were actually the beneficiaries of self-deception. It gave them the determination to triumph – whatever the odds.

It is what the hucksters did with the manly virtues that might cause upset. Effectively they had, or rather they claimed, a license to lie that allowed them to transgress the official code of truth-telling. Consider the case of George Washington Cross. "I never know when to believe you," declared his partner Nigh, the older adman (10). Nigh's son Allan, who played the roles of both critic and fool in the drama, was sure that Cross could never be believed: "If falsehood is the root, it has reached its full growth in George Washington Cross. His whole life, his business, everything about him is lies – lies – nothing but lies!" (18). "He always tells the truth," claimed the stenographer Lorna (18). "When it is something he knows people would like to hear" (19). Nor did Cross deny the merit of these charges. He admitted he was "a cheerful liar" (21). But the point was that Cross was not self-interested. "I'll never tell a malicious lie, a mean or cowardly one" (22). He only lied because he cared about others. He lied "cheerfully, gladly, for the sake of those around me. If I can't tell people something to make them happy, I keep my mouth shut. I just can't help saying things to make people feel good" (21). In author Hoffman's view, what justified his hero's persistent deception was his priority of care and his determination not to harm. He was really a moral liar, if such a creature were possible. Most certainly he didn't anguish over the liar's plight, except for a time when it threatened his romance with Ann Nigh, a supposed "truth fiend" (58), and a second fool in Hoffman's play.

George Washington Cross is an extreme case, admittedly. But deception is rife in the other fictions. H.R. expressed his contempt for the truth: "*Truth*! Pshaw! Can you imagine that combination of four consonants and one vowel serving as a political platform or included in any live concern's instructions to salesmen? Never! No, sir" (89). Although Dr Surtaine eventually gave up making nostrums, the old rogue did not retire from the business of deception as such. Instead, he took up a new, presumably more "genteel endeavour" (KL [Kindle Location] 6325), the manufacture and marketing of Cerebread, a nerve and brain food backed up with all sorts of testimonials from European physicians. That was Adams's way of marking the adman, the inveterate huckster who always had some new scam to sell to the public. After masking the truth, pretending "The Virgin Queene" he wrote was an unknown play by Shakespeare himself, Dunn learned that he could not undo the deception: nobody would believe his confession. And in some occult fashion the claim may have been authentic: author Powel suggested that when Dunn wrote he was actually infused with the spirit of Shakespeare, that he was merely the conduit for the master's final gift to humanity. In *It Pays to Advertise*, the father Cyrus Martin and his secretary Mary Grayson reach an agreement to fool Rodney Martin into believing that Mary loves Rodney (which eventually proves to be true), all to get Rodney to become an achiever. That is only the beginning of an escalating series of deceptions. Cyrus deceives himself and blames Mary for the fiasco of their conspiracy, and later Mary deceives Cyrus when crafting the deal to buy out "13 Soap," Rodney's company. Rodney and Ambrose, often with Mary's help, try to bamboozle a series of people – even more in the movie than in the play. "All's fair in love and business," declared Ambrose Peale (play: 71). The details do not matter; rather, the fact is that truth-telling was the exception, not the rule here. In the America of these fictions, life was inundated with sham, pretence, lies, evasions, hypocrisy; in Woodward's words, it was full of "bunk." It was a topsy-turvy, carnivalesque realm where fraud and farce reigned supreme.

What set these fictions apart from many others where deceit was hardly unusual, however, was that the habit and practices of deception were raised to the stature of an ideology: they became advertising. Advertising was the key to modern business, the sure-fire way to make gargantuan profits. In this fashion the fictions seemed to justify that guilty pleasure of duping delight. Butler established the frame when he crafted Perkins as a veritable pope of advertising. "Perkins is the advertising man. Advertising is not his speciality. It is his life; it is his science" (68). Little wonder he came out with all sorts of outlandish pronouncements. To wit: "The ad. makes the world go round." Or again: "The ad. is the biggest thing on earth. It sways nations. It wins hearts. It rules destiny. People cry for ads" (124, 125). Likewise the character of Ambrose Peale, whether in the play, novel, or movie: this fast-talking enthusiast for advertising had a personal mission to convert any and all listeners to the wisdom of branding and publicity. "It can do anything but keep you from coming into the world or going out of it" (novel: 160–1). When Cyrus finally succumbs to Peale's spiel (the rhyming name was intentional), repeating his slogans and brags, Mary rightly announces, "You've got religion" (novel: 333). Adams's Dr Surtaine poured all his efforts into advertising, caring little about the product. He was extremely proud of his "Old Lame-Boy," the image of "a man half-bent over, with his hand to his back and a lamentable expression on his face" (KL 513). In *The Story of Ginger Cubes*, Christopher Morley outlined a variation on this theme with his portrayal of George Gray of the "Gray Matter Advertising Agency." Gray sent to one of the principals a series of pleas and proposals filled with babble about public service, the necessity of a "Big Idea," the need to encourage "consumer-benevolence," and the merits of the "Institutional-Advertising" his agency practised (29–31). This adman was a bishop in the church of advertising, his preaching full of "tripe" (27) and "bunk" (36), as two critics declaimed.

The most extraordinary device, however, was something I will call the "immaculate deception."[101] Perkins initiated this when he decided to launch his cure-all for pain. All he had was a catchy name and a slogan: "Perkins's Patent Porous Plaster/Makes all pains and aches fly faster" (5). He had no actual product. "Bother the plaster! The ad.'s all right, and that's the main thing. Give me a good ad., and I'll sell lead bullets for liver pills" (4). He planned to use massive advertising to foster a demand and then sell the trademark to some established patent-medicine company. Yes, the campaign did generate an extraordinary demand, but Perkins could not sell the trademark; so he cobbled together a product out of fly paper, renamed the brand, and sold it around the world. Similarly, Rodney Martin and Ambrose Peale set out to challenge the soap trust by mounting a campaign for a high-priced product named "13 Soap." Peale explained the brilliance of this Big Idea: "The 13 Soap – it's great – it's got imagination – Soap – a fact – 13, unlucky – unlucky for what? Why, dirt. Imagination, superstition, humor. Cleanliness, soap – all associated in one phrase. Plus buncombe, good old bunk for the pinheads – the most expensive soap in the world" (novel: 165). Of course, they had no actual product. Instead, they employed massive advertising to establish the brand and stoke the demand sufficient to get the established players in the business to buy them out. Which is eventually what Cyrus Martin did. The immaculate deception relied wholly on the inspired use of words, images, and lots of publicity to sell. Only the advertising counted. There was no authenticity, just a simulacrum created by the signs alone. The immaculate deception expressed the grand dream of the adman, where he worked his commercial magic irrespective of the messy material dimension of an actual product or client. Such an appealing dream would persist, appearing again in later stories such as the Doris Day and Rock Hudson hit *Lover Come Back* (1961). This was the trickster at his best.

Occasionally characters in these huckster fictions voiced the emerging maxims of anti-advertising – "this lying business" (Hoffman 12) – that might upset an insider. In the movie, when Cyrus Martin called "fraud" the repackaging of his product as "13 Soap," Rodney merely replied, "that's advertising." Hoffman presented the adman's son, Allan Nigh, as the vehement critic of the industry. "It is a wholesale exploitation of the masses," he told his bemused listeners. "You lure the wage-earner to waste his substance upon medicine that won't cure; food that won't digest; soft drinks that ruin their stomachs; hard drinks that ruin their brains" (8). Suffering a dose of the adman's dilemma, a tired Barnham Dunn called his trade "slavery – very remunerative, very much admired slavery, but slavery just the same" (9). Words failed him "when I compare my early ambition with my present performance" (12): he had devoted his considerable literary talents to selling the doubtful goods of others, all for "a mess of pottage, and … the pottage had turned out to be confoundedly indigestible" (30). Similarly, Allan Nigh yearned to be free of his connection with the adworld. "Let me get out of this business and lead an *honest* life," he loudly proclaimed (8).

Even so, the prime target was not the adman or advertising but the hapless public. The huckster fictions introduced to American literature that myth of a passive or submissive populace, one that would, of course, persist throughout the social conversation about advertising.[102] The authors made reference time and again to the gullibility of the consumer, at home and sometimes in the world at large. "You all remember Stoneley's account of meeting a tribe of natives in the wilds of Africa wearing nothing but Perkins's Paper Porous Plasters," mused his associate, "and recall the celebrated words of Rodriguez Velos, second understudy to the Premier of Spain, 'America is like Perkins's Paper Porous Plasters – a thing not to be sat on'" (11). According to Peale, "ninety-seven per cent. of the people are sheep and you can get 'em all by advertising" (novel: 89). Suckers were everywhere, declared Nigh senior in *Nothing But Lies*: "I can't help it if there is one born every minute" (9). The burden of such quips was that the moral blame lay with the American people who foolishly believed the messages. They were responsible for the success of advertising. Anita Loos, who wrote the intertitles for *His Picture in the Papers*, warned viewers right at the start of the movie: "Publicity at any price has become the predominant passion of the American people." What in the end these fictions satirized was the credulity of high and low in America. The rule of business, of life, was *caveat emptor*: if you were fleeced, then you were at fault. But recognize that this critique of America's marketplace was not especially sharp: in all cases, the authors decided the adman's deceptions and the public's gullibility had produced results that caused no serious harm. In the end, even that supposed truth fiend, Ann Nigh, came around: "What are a few lies if you can help those around you?" (85). The huckster might be a rascal and a rogue; he was not yet a Svengali.

The picture of the adman that emerged in the huckster fictions embodied a perverted version of the pragmatism which flourished in America in the first decades of the twentieth century. That philosophy of life emphasized the agency of people, their ability to determine the course of events. It well-suited the mood of the times, the particular mix of anxiety and exuberance, the determination to remake America, whether according to corporate or Progressive designs.[103] Pragmatism had been elaborated by William James, a Harvard philosopher and celebrity, in a series of 1907 lectures which recapitulated ideas that he and his friends, Charles Peirce and John Dewey, had formulated and propagated over the past four decades.[104] In his sixth lecture James focused on the issue of truth. What he emphasized was the notion that truth was not so much a property or an absolute, but an instrument that best served to realize some particular purpose. "'The true,' to put it very briefly, is only the expedient in the way of our thinking," he claimed (KL 1529). Truth had to be useful, and that was proved by experience. "Truth is MADE, just as health, wealth and strength are made, in the course of experience" (KL 1501–2). Which meant that truth was flexible rather than fixed, something which could and would change because the acts of people determined their reality. "Truth HAPPENS to an idea. It BECOMES true, is MADE true by events" (KL 1379–80).

Probably James would have been aghast at the suggestion that his conception of truth could somehow explain, even justify, the deceptions of the huckster.[105] (Neither the words "advertising" nor "huckster" appeared in his lectures.) But Perkins of Portland and Hendrik Rutgers were pragmatic men of destiny who made their own "truths" and, in the process, a bit of reality. Similarly, the admen Ambrose Peale and George Washington Cross employed lies to bring about a kind of "truth." "Our account of truth is an account of truths in the plural, of processes of leading, realized in rebus," asserted James, "and having only this quality in common, that they PAY" (KL 1497–8). Calkins assigned the currency of the shibboleth "it pays to advertise" to the popularity of the Megrue and Hackett play (3). But Butler put that same phrase in the mouth of the great Perkins much earlier (94). The huckster fictions had exaggerated the apparently widespread belief in the magical powers of the adman to make new "truths." "By Jimminy," declared Peale towards the end of *It Pays to Advertise*, "then all the things we told your father the other day are true" (novel: 310). Such were the surprises of pragmatism – and advertising.

The huckster's game was not quite the ramshackle narrative it might appear. At its core was a fundamental presumption: someone, a prankster, the fake healer, an advertising agent, set out to fool the gullible public to make a profit. Above all, the huckster was an example of the calculating self, a risk-taker who succeeded because he understood "human nature," especially the weaknesses and the emotions of people. The advertising he used was cast as a discourse of fraud. The public was found wanting, its commitment to rationality feeble. The resulting stories could take a variety of shapes, however. One might amount to a chronicle of shame, as in the case of the moral assault on Barnum. Another, even more sinister, might emphasize peril, becoming itself part of a narrative of harm, which was the thrust of Adam's muckraking effort. Yet a third could beguile readers as a comedy, really a sort of tall tale, true of many of the huckster fictions. Here at least the huckster appeared almost admirable or at least excusable, such as Butler's Perkins the Great. In every form the stories usually spoke to the moral condition of the times, where the huckster's success was a sign or a warning of disorder. Barnum (though not in his own mind), Ponderevo, or Peale were all agents of misrule whose deceptions succeeded because the public lacked the intelligence or the will to find the truth. The affliction of the adman's dilemma was present in the social conversation, but the motif was neither fully articulated, nor was it prevalent. Likewise, the motif of the ad-maker's sin was implicit in the works of the critics of Barnum and explicit in the exposé of Adams. The narrative of the huckster's game might wane in later years when the adman proper came to dominate the stage. But it left behind a legacy of contempt, reflected in two of the claims aired by characters in the series *Mad Men*:

Roy Hazelitt: "Madison Avenue? What a gas. Perpetuating the lie. How do you sleep at night? ... You hucksters in your tower created the religion of mass consumption." (*Mad Men*, "Babylon" 1:6)[106]

Don Draper's Stepfather (or rather his imagined ghost): "You're a bum, you know that ... What do you do? What do you make? You grow bullshit." (*Mad Men*, "Seven Twenty Three" 3:7)

2
THE RISE OF THE ADVERTISING AGENT

The advertising man, the genius of America, is usually young, good-looking, sartorially perfect, with sleek hair and parti-colored shoes. Consciousness of the eminence of his position in American business has made him as complacent as Douglas Fairbanks. He does not conceal his awareness of the fact that he is the cornerstone of the most respectable American institutions ... For it is democracy that has made him a God.

– S.N. Behrman, 1919[1]

Just after the war ended, the playwright S.N. Behrman, in a light-hearted essay, asserted, "'Publicity' is the reigning philosophy, the magic conjuring word."[2] In 1923 the British visitor Hilaire Belloc declared that "the essential mark of the American social spirit" was "publicity: the spirit of the market-place."[3] Less than a decade later a French visitor, the much more critical Georges Duhamel, lamented how publicity had taken command, especially at night, creating "a *charivari* of light, a riot, a battle, a triumph of disharmony and disorder" to intimidate and befuddle the mind.[4] This kind of discovery of a wave of publicity, whether called a riot, an invasion, clutter, or an ad swarm, would become a perennial of social comment in and about America. A writer in every generation found that the volume of promotional noise was greater than ever before. These rediscoveries amounted to a recognition of the imperialism of advertising, the way it constantly sought to colonize more and more public and private spaces.

Certainly advertising had boomed in the thirty years between the turn of the century and the onset of the Depression. By one estimate total advertising volume went from roughly $500 million in all media in 1900 to $3.4 billion in 1929.[5] That was because corporate America embraced publicity as a regular and crucial instrument of marketing and propaganda. People, women in particular, and in the big cities, were trained to become consumers of advertising and of goods.[6] Much of the business of advertising was masterminded by a profusion of agencies staffed by a variety of specialists such as copywriters and art directors, account executives, media buyers, and research experts – all of whom were counted as advertising men and women.[7] The US Census found 40,000 advertising agents and salesmen in 1930 (but 57,000 hucksters and peddlers).[8] A *Who's Who in Advertising* for 1931 contained bios of 5,000 admen (and 126 women), not complete though because it missed a host of leading practitioners.[9] These ad-makers were joined by a smaller collection of what were called by the end of the 1920s public relations counsels, also men, also serving mostly corporate America. The boom in publicity provoked a cultural response: a new series of stories that reflected the phenomenon of mass advertising and the figure of the adman who was variously characterized as a professional, a hero, and a villain.

1. The House of Truth: George Creel, *How We Advertised America*, 1920

The regime of truth which came to prevail in modern times was always a contested system because, despite the prominence of the sciences or the obsession with facts, there were rival discourses, notably religion, with claims to universal application, and especially on matters of ethical conduct.[10] In any case, following Foucault, what counted was the production of truth, the elaboration of "the ensemble of rules according to which the true and the false are separated and specific effects of power attached to the true."[11] Truth and power were intimately linked.[12] Institutions such as the universities, the media, the churches, the bureaucracies, and the courts constituted the machinery of truth.[13] In particular there were "truth games" ongoing in the public sphere, where contestants struggled to assert their claims to determine what were the relevant facts or the appropriate values or the right designs for living.[14] These generated a series of issues or questions about truth-tellers: "Who is able to tell the truth? What are the moral, the ethical, and the spiritual conditions which entitle someone to present himself as, and to be considered as, a truth-teller? About what topics is it important to tell the truth?"[15] In such circumstances it was vital to arrive on the "official" lists of truth-tellers – like, say, the scientist on physics or the cleric on morality – to acquire the credibility to be able to exercise influence over behaviour. We shall see how this elusive goal continually shaped the biography of the adman.

Soon after 1900 advertising practitioners sought to add their names to the list of truth-tellers who advised Americans on the proper conduct of life. Success would have denied or at least masked the adman's dilemma, and before it was fully identified. The impulse behind that project was both commercial and professional. Industry leaders and spokesmen assumed that establishing the veracity of advertising would enhance the effectiveness of advertisements as tools of persuasion. In the same way, the reform-minded among their ranks saw this goal as essential to transforming advertising into a profession such as medicine or law. The project necessitated an assault on the huckster, the elimination of what was considered fraudulent advertising because its presence undermined both the burgeoning industry and the nascent profession. Thus was born the "truth-in-advertising" campaign.[16]

In 1905 the newly formed Associated Advertising Clubs of America (later of the World, still later the American Advertising Federation) took up the cause of truth. The AACA was an industry group, its members including not just advertising agents but the representatives of publishers and advertisers, a cluster interested in, as one leader argued, "cleaning its own house."[17] In practice the cause involved mighty gusts of rhetoric about the need for truth, the promulgation of codes of conduct, eventually (in 1911) the publication of a model statute aimed at banning fraudulent advertising, and the organization of vigilance committees (later known as Better Business Bureaus) to police the performance of advertisers. In 1912 the advertising clubs replaced their old slogan, "The world branded with publicity," with a new claim, "The world stamped with truth," symbolized by "a circular seal with 'Truth' inscribed on a globe."[18] The project mixed both self-regulation and government regulation, especially after the creation in 1914 of the Federal Trade Commission, which took an increasing interest in the field of publicity. The truth-in-advertising campaign would continue into the 1920s and even the 1930s, focussed especially on patent medicines, oil stock boosting, tipster sheets, bucket shops and boiler rooms, as well as promoters of inventions, land and mining sales, securities, and cemetery plots. What the campaign avoided was an assault on the swelling volumes of corporate and national advertising, the source of so many lucrative billings.

America's entry into the First World War provided what appeared to be a golden opportunity to enhance the legitimacy of advertising and the reputation of the industry as a source of truth. Two years after the end of the Great War, a once-prominent war bureaucrat produced a book which celebrated the virtues and the exploits, and above all the patriotism, of all kinds of persuaders. It signalled, among much else, the arrival on the public scene of a new kind of professional, an expert in persuasion, and a member of a new cadre of specialists that seemed crucial to the advance of modernity. The author was George Creel (1876–1953), the ex-head of the Committee on Public Information, or CPI (1917–19), which had functioned as America's chief agency of propaganda. Back in April 1917, when the United States joined the war, the government feared that it might soon face severe social unrest because of the signifi-cant divisions fostered by sectional feelings, class animosity (especially the militancy of labour), and ethnic differences (which really meant too many "untrustworthy" foreign immigrants, especially from Germany and its allies). President Woodrow Wilson and his team determined the coun-try needed a new instrument to swiftly dispel doubt and dissent and to mobilize war enthusiasm – hence the CPI. That agency steadily took on more and more tasks, including the management of the press, and even the massive effort to sell America's war to allies and to the enemy. The apparent success of its propaganda campaigns, which impressed politi-cians, businessmen, and advertising people alike, had a major impact on the course of both advertising and public relations in the postwar years.[19]

Then in his early forties, Creel was an ebullient, energetic, and aggres-sive journalist, a zealot more than a bit thin-skinned, too caustic for the civil service, at least in normal times, but he did have the great virtue of passionate loyalty to the Democrats and to Wilson. He had been a muck-raker in the prewar decade, full of moral fervour, writing for and editing newspapers, espousing a variety of Progressive reforms – he was suspi-cious of big business – and even helping to prepare an exposé of child labour, though never achieving the stature or significance of the work of, say, Samuel Hopkins Adams. Early on Creel had proved a great fan of Wilson, purportedly urging him to run for President in 1906. Creel worked hard for a Democratic victory in both 1912 and 1916, writing *Wilson and the Issues* (1916) to support Wilson's bid for a second term. Initially he turned down the offer of a position in Washington, express-ing a personal distaste for bureaucracy. The war emergency transformed the situation, however: Creel was eager to serve his President and his country in such a crisis. He even hoped to advance the success of his liberal aims, as did so many pro-war Progressives, though ultimately that would prove impossible.

How We Advertised America was billed as a popular account of the mis-sion, the staff, and the work of the CPI at home and abroad.[20] It was not particularly popular. It certainly was a record. The book was 466

pages long, divided into three uneven parts, the longest on the domestic scene, the next on the foreign section of the CPI, the shortest on
demobilization – all this plus an appendix. It proved an often dreary catalogue of people and their activities: Creel took the opportunity to survey the work of all of the major divisions of the agency, and by the end
of the war there were many. But he had two other purposes. One was
to settle old scores, to answer back to all the lies, slander, and criticism
he and the CPI had received, an obsession which reflected his sensitive
soul. The tome sometimes became an extended whine over the mistreat-
ment he had suffered because of the opposition and the carping of both
Congress and the press. The other purpose was to praise the personnel
associated with the CPI. He was especially generous in his comments on
the virtues of his superiors – notably Wilson of course – and of his subordinates. He had been blessed, so it seemed, with men of consummate
skill and moral vigour, the kind of patriots that ensured the success of
the agency's work.

That story of success was the overarching theme of Creel's book. He
touted the urgency of the problems facing Wilson: first the wide variety
of enemy aliens, pacifists and isolationists, labour militants and socialists
who doubted or opposed the war, and later the fury of nativists or Ameri-
canizers, the militarists and the conservatives who sought to punish and
repress legitimate dissent. Creel also painted a picture of a massive German system of propaganda, extensive throughout the world, operating
in the United States, and extravagantly funded – thus building up the
image of a formidable enemy. Creel argued that the CPI was a peculiarly
American innovation, better than the systems of censorship and propaganda adopted by the European allies, and much more effective. The
CPI had found the right methods to take command of public opinion
to unite the citizenry (or at least the vast majority of Americans) behind
Wilson's vision of a war for democracy. In short, the agency built consensus at home. Almost as important, the CPI changed world opinion as
well, making a misunderstood America into one of the most popular of
nations. Both conclusions included a hefty dose of exaggeration.

The key was the CPI's commitments to voluntarism, publicity, and to
fact. Here Creel was clearly beholding to the liberal verities about public
discourse that were commonplace among prewar Progressives. Progressives preferred public compliance to government rules, sought to educate rather than coerce, and emphasized the appeal to facts and reason
instead of emotion. The intent was to provide the individual with the
correct information sufficient to persuade a public deemed rational of

the merits of the war policies. Creel meant no irony when, in another context, he referred to the CPI as the "House of Truth."[21]

In no degree was the Committee an agency of censorship, a machinery of concealment or repression. Its emphasis throughout was on the open and the positive. At no point did it seek or exercise authorities under those war laws that limited the freedom of speech and press. In all things, from first to last, without halt or change, it was a plain publicity proposition, a vast enterprise in salesmanship, the world's greatest adventure in advertising. (4, Creel's emphasis)

The CPI worked with newspapers to prevent the publication of information that might aid the enemy. It strove to avoid any attempt to suppress debate and dissent. "In no other belligerent nation was there such absolute frankness with respect to every detail of the national war endeavor" (6). And in fact whatever censorship and suppression did occur was carried out mostly by others, notably the Attorney General and the Postmaster General, though Creel did serve on a censorship board. Instead the CPI elaborated an extraordinary apparatus of publicity, lovingly detailed by Creel: it sponsored ads of all kinds, photographs and films, posters and billboards, window-cards, pamphlets, exhibitions and expositions, speakers, lectures and slides, conferences, cartoons, a daily newspaper, syndicated press features, foreign language material, even used radio and letters, and arranged visits overseas and in America. The most unusual initiative was the creation of the Four Minute Men (a whole chapter was devoted to this division): these were local notables, volunteers all but carefully selected, scattered across the country, who were fed a series of speaking points so that they could deliver brief talks in movie theatres, grange halls, churches, even lumber camps and Indian reservations, wherever crowds gathered. The overall aim was to surround the citizen with a mass of material that fostered not only compliance but enthusiasm, whether on behalf of the war effort in general or to support some particular initiative such as the various Liberty Bond campaigns. In so many ways the CPI's pro-war campaigns expressed that mode of governance called biopolitics, where the official views of the governors were circulated as widely as possible, in this case to establish or affirm war patriotism as a discourse of truth.

It was these bond campaigns in particular which critics and later historians believed gave the lie to Creel's claim of a "House of Truth." Now he made much of the determination to present only the facts of the case, never to hide the unpleasant or to demonize the enemy or to incite the passions. "One of the chief bitternesses against the Committee on Public Information was that it did not preach a gospel of hate," he proudly asserted (443). Perhaps initially the CPI did strive to report and inform fairly. But the many pamphlets and books the CPI produced and circulated were never dispassionate explanations of events. The bias was more pronounced as time passed because the CPI responded to the escalating hysteria of the war enthusiasts. The sin of manipulation was even more apparent in the kinds of images the CPI sponsored, notably the poster campaigns for the Liberty Loan campaigns. The agency fashioned idealized portrayals of American types – soldiers, mothers, liberty herself, brutal images of the "Hun" and sad depictions of the victims of his brutality. (None of these images, some of which became famous, were reproduced in *How We Advertised America*, although the book sported numerous photographs of leading personnel.) Creel's committee had come to deal as much in symbols as in facts. And it was the excellence and the apparent impact of this brand of publicity which so impressed outsiders later – and distressed critics then, notably liberals. Thus John Dewey, once hopeful the war would renew the Progressive cause, lamented that the crisis had spawned "a 'cult of irrationality' fed by 'an insidious and skilled effort … to detach the volume of passionate energy from its original end'."[22] That Creel could never admit.

Throughout his account, Creel emphasized system and structure, the planning, the techniques, the variety of media and appeals, and the use of experts and specialists to produce the right kind of public opinion. He pointed out that one of the first tasks of the Committee was to bring order to the confusion and chaos, the duplication and the waste of the propaganda work in Washington. He carefully explained the way he and his agency responded swiftly to the government's needs or outside initiatives, proof of the ability to make the right decision on demand. He made much of the CPI's frugality, offering up a series of budgets which showed the committee only consumed a modest amount of public funds and often managed to generate monies from, for example, the sale of its films. He claimed the Committee even turned over $2 million to the Treasury (428). Above all, he showed that he had worked hard to recruit all kinds of talented people to serve the cause.

The experts and the specialists Creel brought to Washington were in peacetime journalists, writers, illustrators, artists, professors, advertising men, public relations personnel – all producers of culture. Among them were veteran muckrakers such as Samuel Hopkins Adams and Ida Tarbell, the accomplished writer Arthur Bullard, the famed illustrator and cartoonist Charles Dana Gibson, and the historian and dean Guy Stanton Ford. The Division of Advertising was chaired by William H. Johns, then head of the George Batten agency and of the newly formed American Association of Advertising Agencies. He was joined by a few advertising heavyweights who had been in charge of such industry organizations as the Associated Advertising Clubs of the World and the Association of National Advertisers. Creel also attracted youth, in particular Bruce Barton and Edward Bernays who in the next decade would become prominent persuaders, Barton as the consummate advertising agent and Bernays as the master of public relations. It was this collection of persuaders who mounted what Creel depicted as a rational and total advertising effort that supposedly conformed to the verities of the Progressive movement.

Altogether Creel and his people, mostly men, belonged to "the professional-managerial class" (or PMC), a rapidly expanding stratum or class fragment in urban America. The category was first named by Barbara and John Ehrenreich, two academics and radical activists.[23] This gathering constituted a loose collection of specialists who worked outside the stratum of small merchants, self-employed professionals, and prosperous farmers, the core of the so-called old middle class, even if the PMC might fit within the upper levels of the middle classes.[24] These new professionals and managers existed between capital and labour: in Marxist parlance (appropriate because the category grew out of Marxian discourse) they were not rulers or workers in the usual sense, nor members of the petite bourgeoisie. They did not own the means of production but their function in the social division of labour was, often, to control or assist the operations of the processes of production. They might best be classified as salaried mental workers, usually paid by big business or government or universities, to serve and direct large-scale organizations.[25] What these managers and professionals had, or claimed to have, was cultural capital, knowledge, and expertise, often first acquired by a college or university education, which established their social and economic value. The PMC itself was not altogether new. It might include lawyers, doctors, and engineers, especially those on salary or contract to a business or government; these had begun to appear in the late nineteenth century. But it encompassed as well corporate managers who were much more recent, in numbers at least, dating back in America to the rapid growth of corporations between 1895 and 1905. It also counted the multiplying ranks of technical experts, even scientists, who could design and supervise the increasingly complicated machinery of modern life in the

new twentieth century. The producers of culture were just one component of the PMC, again fairly recent in any quantity, who worked in and
around the rapidly expanding mass media of communications to fashion
news, entertainment, and advertising, and who staffed the burgeoning
educational and welfare institutions that sought to train, succour, or manage the population. The Ehrenreichs provided a chart summarizing the
growth of selected occupations which indicated that the PMC constituted
about 175,000 individuals in 1900, nearly 750,000 in 1920, and just over a
million by 1930.[26] That still did not amount to a large proportion (some
3.1 per cent) of the nonfarm labour force of nearly 38.4 million in 1930.[27]

Potentially the PMC were rivals of both capital and labour. Experts of
one kind or another, they were supposed to deal in truth. Professionals
in particular asserted a moral superiority based upon their knowledge,
a sense of social responsibility, and a disinterested attitude. Managers
similarly espoused ideals of order, rationality, efficiency, economy, and
harmony which purportedly rendered them better suited to master-
ing the means of production than the actual capitalists.[28] Both groups
demanded of society a certain respect, a higher status, and a degree of
autonomy, as well as comfort and affluence. There was a streak of anti-
commercialism embedded in the make-up of the professional ethos
that might – and in the 1920s and 1930s occasionally did – generate
a kind of advisory mentality. According to the Ehrenreichs, the PMC
were great champions of the Progressive effort to modernize America,
which could bring the professional into conflict with the excesses of
business rule. But in practice the PMC usually lined up with capital to
administer labour, even if that authority was less harsh or even more
humane than the already legendary rule of the tycoons and robber bar-
ons of an earlier moment. Effectively, the Ehrenreichs assigned to the
PMC the primary task of social reproduction, that is, the maintenance of
the culture and class relationships of the capitalist order. Furthermore,
the very desire for respectability and affluence rendered professionals
and managers prone to fears of falling in status and/or selling out their
integrity. Michael Augspurger, a literary scholar, has argued that the ability to exploit such anxieties accounted for the extraordinary success of
Sinclair Lewis's novels – *Babbitt, Arrowsmith,* and *Dodsworth* – in the 1920s.
Lewis had spoken to a stratum fearful it was losing its autonomy and its
distinction to the ever-advancing commercial ethos.[29]

All of which sheds light on the hopes and plight of the adman. In
some ways the advertising agents and publicists existed on the margins
of the gathering of professionals and managers. The advertising agents

were emphatically new men, since the copywriter and the art director were not common in the agency until the first decade of the twentieth century. Although there were press agents before the war, the public relations counsel was not really born until the early 1920s, when Edward Bernays coined that label. Unlike law or medicine, the advertising men, if university educated, were non-credentialed: they did not belong to a widely accepted profession that exercised control over its marketplace as well as the character and the conduct of its members. They were not even able to determine the style and content of the advertising courses which had emerged in journalism and business programs in colleges and universities after 1900.[30] More like engineers, the advertising men and the publicity agents were heavily dependent on capital for their livelihood. Clearly they were engaged in a brand of social reproduction. Some admen identified much more with their clients than their fellows, who were always also their business competitors, one reason why forging any kind of professional solidarity proved so difficult. And they created nothing but words and images considered by many outsiders of dubious merit; hence the reputation of the adman as a tout and deceiver that found expression in huckster fiction. Not even businessmen trusted the adman to act honestly, it seemed. Little wonder that such a situation engendered anxiety and insecurity.

The war had represented a chance for the advertising agent to demonstrate both his civic utility and moral worth. In 1918 William D'Arcy, involved in the work of the CPI and then president of the Associated Advertising Clubs of the World, told his fellows at the annual meeting how the wartime achievements of the industry were so grand that advertising had demonstrated both its "vital power" and its "greater service."[31] He even equated its significance to the nation to that of Congress. Certainly Creel was impressed. Prior to the war, he claimed "advertising was regarded as a business, not a profession, and the majority looked upon the advertising agent with suspicion, even when he was not viewed frankly as a plausible pirate belonging to the same school of endeavor as the édition-de-luxe book canvasser" (157). In his time as a Progressive journalist, he went on record to stigmatize the practice of corporate publicity as a threat to the health of the democracy. But the sterling efforts of his propagandists showed otherwise. The second Liberty Loan campaign "afforded justification, for recognition of advertising as a real profession, and to include it as an honorable and integral part of the war-machinery of government" (157–8). The very enthusiasm, the patriotism of the advertising agents, was signal proof of their dignity and respectability.

2. Philosophers of Persuasion: The Works of Claude Hopkins, E.E. Calkins, and Edward Bernays, 1910s and 1920s

Ever since 1900, practitioners, journalists, and even a few academics had produced a large range of books and essays that presented a radically different appreciation of the figure of the adman than apparent in the huckster fictions. He became, in the most exuberant of these positive treatments, something of a hero of America's saga of modernity, one of a select group of men who had forwarded the progress of business and the country.[32] These works took the form of textbooks, commentaries, and memoirs published to feed the interests of the rapidly growing industry of advertising, the business community, and the public at large.[33] The genre peaked in the 1920s when, as the home economics expert Christine Frederick put it, Americans recognized that they lived "in a vast whirligig of advertising, to be sure ..."[34] A key purpose was to champion persuasion, and most especially advertising and the adman, to its practitioners, to business, and to the public. The apologists were especially eager, and anxious, to demonstrate that publicity work now constituted a profession not only as respectable as law and medicine, but offering a service vital to the success of business and the happiness of the public. The trouble was that the advertising agent, even to his fans, seemed an anomalous figure who operated in the realms of both culture and economics, realms which though always entangled in practice were normally treated as distinct and separate.[35] Perhaps in response apologists fashioned a series of related motifs that positioned the adman as a civilizer, the businessman's ally, industry's engine, and the consumer's friend. Thus were born stories of justification to further legitimize both the industry and the profession.

The whole of this genre will serve only as background and context here. I will focus chiefly on the works of two of the most prominent copywriters of the era, Claude Hopkins (1866–1932) and Earnest Elmo Calkins (1868–1964), as well as the books written by Edward Bernays (1891–1995), sometimes inaccurately called "the father of public relations." These men acted as the philosophers of the persuasion industries because they produced stories of explanation and justification. In the end Bernays' views would prove the most controversial, and his personal notoriety the most lasting, though in the 1920s Hopkins and Calkins enjoyed a higher status in the publicity system. Each of these men belonged to the "professional-managerial class" but only Bernays thoroughly embodied the supposed ethos of that social fragment. Together they elaborated a narrative of progress which placed the figure of the adman at the centre of the saga of modernity.

The ad-makers, of course, were renowned as storytellers. Writing good, effective copy, words that moved people to buy, was commonly considered the most celebrated and mysterious achievement of the advertising agent.[36] More to the point, the works of these two advertising men were popular at the time, and the fame of Hopkins's writings lasted well beyond his own lifetime. Moreover, Hopkins and Calkins embodied rival approaches to advertising, respectively the "hard sell" and the "soft sell." There is some evidence that they had little respect for each other's work, both the ads and the books.[37] Thus the fact that at bottom they shared so many presumptions about advertising and the adman makes the juxtaposition all the more intriguing.

Hopkins boasted that in one glorious year he earned the astronomical sum of $185,000 from commissions paid by his agency Lord & Thomas.[38] That was evidence of his achievement in an occupation notorious for its money obsession, and was well-remembered later in reports of his prowess. (A source of the interest in advertising was the widespread belief that admen earned very large salaries, more so than their compatriots in better established professions.) Hopkins was born to a firmly religious family of clergymen and journalists (his father ran a newspaper) in a small town in Michigan, where he was briefly a lay preacher. He did not go to a regular college, and he would always doubt the virtues of any university training. Nor did he long remain in preaching, apparently because he rebelled against the "fanaticism" (his word) of his Scotch Presbyterian upbringing, although he certainly did retain a dogmatic cast of mind as well as a fervent devotion to the work ethic. His advertising career started in the early 1890s at the Bissell Carpet Sweeper Company, where he was credited with initiating some highly effective marketing strategies.[39] He made a fortune some years later by promoting the infamous remedy Liquozone (in which he had a financial interest), although he was absolved of any fraud by the muckracker Samuel Hopkins Adams.[40] Then, at age 41, he joined Lord & Thomas, a rising Chicago agency, where he reached the pinnacle of his fame as the star copywriter, producing campaigns for Palmolive Soap, Quaker cereals, Pepsodent toothpaste, and a raft of other national brands. Hopkins excelled at writing robust, repetitive, seemingly logical copy, usually with a catchy slogan, which presented consumers with a compelling reason-why, or as a later generation of ad-makers termed it, a "unique selling proposition," to buy the brand in question.[41] His campaigns were never pretty and they could

be very wordy, but they were unquestionably effective, or so contemporaries judged. With good reason Tim Wu much later labels him a modern alchemist because of his ability to turn dross – beans, toothpaste,
etc. – into sales gold.[42] Hopkins proved a master of what Wu has called
"demand engineering," where the advertising demonstrated how a product could solve an ordinary problem of life, sometimes a problem (like
bad breath or plaque) hitherto unrecognized.[43] He and owner Albert D.
Lasker turned Lord & Thomas into one of the leading agencies in America, sometimes the top agency by overall billings.[44] When Lasker left to
serve in Washington, Hopkins was placed in charge which, he lamented,
meant that his annual income from copywriting was much reduced.[45]
But he was no happier when Lasker returned, and he retired from Lord
& Thomas, likely in 1924, though he continued to do some copywriting.[46] Hopkins had worked almost continuously, and worked very hard,
since he first entered advertising in the early 1890s. Work, writing copy,
and making money were his form of play.

Only towards the end of this hectic life did he find the time to reflect
and write about his experiences. In 1923, while still at Lord & Thomas,
he wrote *Scientific Advertising*, in which he vigorously expressed his views
about the proper character of advertising (for which Lasker apparently
compensated him with a cheque for $10,000).[47] He filled the slim book,
slightly over one hundred pages, with precepts and guidelines about how
to advertise effectively. Four years later, now retired, he published, first
in serial form, *My Life in Advertising*, a kind of autobiography that was
meant as a "business story," full of accounts of success – and not a little
bluster – "to offer helpful suggestions to those who will follow me."[48] At
the end of *My Life* he lumped together in one chapter "something about
my private life, my idiosyncrasies, habits, and desires";[49] but in fact his
arrogance and convictions shone through in all the chapters. Together
these books, especially *Scientific Advertising*, became industry classics, referenced by such later masters of the craft as Rosser Reeves and David
Ogilvy, and was added to lists of "must reads" for prospective advertising
agents. In 2011 both books were released in one Kindle edition, further
evidence that they have retained their currency.

Earnest Elmo Calkins also earned a lot of money. But what he highlighted in one of his autobiographies was the fact that he had received
in 1926 the first gold medal of the Harvard Advertising Awards bestowed
on an individual for his creative endeavours and high standards.[50] That
spoke to another obsession of the adman, namely the yearning for recognition, which would eventually spawn a host of different award systems.

(The trouble was virtually nobody in the general public knew who wrote
the ads, however clever: the forward to a book by Theodore MacManus,
the master of car advertising, called him "the most eminent member" of
his profession, sometimes considered "the greatest advertising man," but
admitted he was "almost unknown to the outside world.")[51] Calkins was
born into a professional family in a small town in Illinois. What shaped
his youth and the course of his life was a disability: a bout of measles
at age six in addition to an inherited trait produced an increasing loss
of hearing – over time, Calkins became, as he liked to put it, a "deafened" person who found solace in a world of books, printing, maps, and
eventually art. Instead of baseball and other boyish pursuits, things that
demanded a social facility, he consumed Milton, Ruskin, and all kinds of
literature, which gave him a fund of knowledge that would prove invaluable in later life. He did managed to graduate from college, but he had
considerable difficulty finding suitable employment until he ended up
writing copy for the Charles Austin Bates agency in New York. Here he
found his métier: "Like a monk in his cell, I worked out my economic
salvation oblivious of the world outside."[52] Here too, he found a complimentary soul, Ralph Holden, a self-confident, sociable business type, and
in 1902 they established Calkins & Holden, widely acclaimed as one of
the first modern agencies, meaning they offered clients a full service of
research, copy, art, and ad placement. In particular Calkins emphasized
the importance of design and art – his agency boasted an art department
that became a model for rivals – to capture the eye and excite the interest of readers.[53] They worked on campaigns for Force cereal (the "Sunny
Jim" jingles), the Lackawanna railway (the "Phoebe Snow" character),
Arrow collars, Pierce-Arrow cars, many magazine promotions, even
Thomas Edison's laboratory. These campaigns used copy, art, and design
to encourage a more emotional attachment to a brand than reason-
why. Unlike Hopkins, who preferred to promote mass brands, Calkins's
approach served better to sell upscale products to a middle-class market.
Calkins and Holden were the pioneers of image advertising, where the
purpose was to establish the personality of a brand in the mind of the
consumer, to build good-will rather than produce immediate sales. Or, as
Wu put it, this technique of brand building amounted to "the engineering of reputation," an investment in the future where success promised
lasting profits.[54] Calkins & Holden never made it to the top of the agency
rankings (it was the fourteenth agency by billings in the USA in 1927).[55]
But the agency was much esteemed as one of the creative powerhouses
of the era. Calkins retired from the agency in 1931, both because of

Holden's death (in 1926) and because of the arrival of radio advertising, which his deafness meant he could never master.

Calkins wrote much more about advertising than did Hopkins. Early on, he and Holden published one of the first advertising textbooks entitled *Modern Advertising* (1905, and re-released in 1916). Calkins alone revised and updated the textbook under the title *The Business of Advertising* (1915), which he followed with yet another primer, *The Advertising Man* (1922) in a vocational series designed to tell prospective young men and women about the nature and the requirements of the profession. In a different vein, he offered a collection of his essays for assorted periodicals under the title *Business the Civilizer* (1928), which ought to have been called, given its content, "Advertising the Civilizer." Indeed, Calkins was noted for his literate and opinionated commentaries on advertising, business, and life, notably "Beauty the New Business Tool" (1927) and "What Consumer Engineering Really Is" (1932). Meanwhile, he had already published an autobiography, *"Louder Please!"* (1924), that was chiefly meant to be "the story of a deafened man, and not a history of advertising" (174). Over twenty years later, he provided a revised and updated version called *"And Hearing Not"* (1946), incorporating more material on his experiences in advertising.[56]

Virtually all the stories of justification admitted that advertising had once had an odious reputation as "a yell and a lie" because of the reign of the circus promoter and the fake healers.[57] In his lengthy history of advertising, otherwise a celebration meant to demonstrate its longevity, Frank Presbrey devoted a few pages to lamenting the outrages that had marred the record in the late nineteenth and early twentieth century.[58] By comparison, Calkins regretted "the prostitution of advertising" when swindlers of all sorts, but especially the healers "so cynical and cold-blooded," employed its power to harm the public.[59] Even Hopkins, who had earned a fortune promoting one nostrum, now admitted that he no longer approved of this "evil," nor would he ever practice this particular "class of advertising."[60] The whole experience had hindered the growth of respectable advertising and stained the occupation itself – businessmen were disgusted with such a shoddy trade.[61]

No one wanted to dwell on the sad past. The admission was twinned with fulsome tales of reform and improvement that had purportedly transformed the practices of advertising. That was one of the lessons conveyed in the first of the adman memoirs, this published by George Rowell (1906) who had laboured to make his craft a legitimate business.[62] The next generation of advertising men had an additional mission: to represent advertising as a science. Obviously the purpose was to appropriate the prestige attached to the name, and in particular to counter any lingering assumption among businessmen that advertising amounted to a waste of money. What was deemed a science, of course, was also deemed a discourse of truth. By "science" writers meant a body of laws and a system of analysis which could order an otherwise incoherent reality.[63] Here the nascent profession all too easily fell victim to wish-fulfilment, if not self-deception. Unlike in Rowell's day, the work of the agent was no longer merely the placement of ads but the preparation of these ads, the writing of copy and the selection of images which would move the public to buy the brand. But this shifted the ad-maker's work into the intangible and mysterious realm of culture, which provoked a yearning for guidelines, rules, even laws that would ensure that the well-informed agent always used the right words and images. Nearly all the writers thought they had found the answers. The novel discipline of psychology promised an understanding of the mind and human nature, the golden key to persuasion first elaborated by W.D. Scott in his *The Psychology of Advertising* (1908).[64] A more extensive list of textbooks, written by teachers and practitioners, revealed just how to go about promoting any product, though of course their "rules" did not always agree.[65] One renowned but conceited soul, albeit in a chapter purportedly written by another, sought to brand his own set of rules as the MacManus "method" or "way" of advertising.[66] And not without reason: Theodore MacManus, a proponent of the soft sell, had written one of the most acclaimed ads of the era, a secular sermon called "The Penalty of Leadership" (1915) for Cadillac, which employed suggestion and association to enhance the status of the automobile.

The unnamed target of the MacManus way was Hopkins's own definition of scientific advertising. Hopkins claimed that advertising, in the right hands, was an applied science grounded in psychology and experience. "It is based on fixed principles and is reasonably exact," he wrote. "The causes and effects have been analyzed until they are well understood. The correct methods of procedure have been proved and established. We know what is most effective, and we act on basic laws."[67] That was because of the efforts of the major advertising agencies, which now orchestrated most national brand name campaigns. They researched the company, the product, the consumer, and above all the advertising. Hopkins's model was the mail-order advertisement, which was in fact the successor to the patent-medicine ads of an earlier day. What counted was plain speaking, simple (never literary) and sincere (never carnivalesque) and clear (never pretentious or fancy), the offer of a coupon or the like, something concrete, all to provoke an action by the consumer. "If fine writing is effective in any way it is a detriment. It suggests an effort to sell," he warned. "And every effort to sell creates corresponding resistance. Salesmanship-in-print is exactly the same as salesmanship-in-person. Style is a handicap. Anything that takes attention from the subject reduces the impression."[68] He extolled the virtues of keyed advertising, where one could link a response to a particular style of ad, just to see what words or images worked best to move sales. In effect the advertising agent turned America into a gigantic laboratory in which he tested appeals to ensure both economy and efficiency, the biggest impact for the least expense. Advertising need no longer be a gamble or a risk to any businessman.

Calkins seemed less sure, and certainly less dogmatic, than Hopkins. He placed a higher value on imagination and aesthetics, "and creation cannot be done along such hard and fast lines" as work in other businesses.[69] In *"Louder Please!"*, for example, he told how he had drawn on his knowledge of fables and parables, as well as his recollections of small-town life, to craft his early advertisements. He included in his autobiographies stories of his failures as well as successes. He and Holden admitted "no human being can really foretell the actual results of any advertising that was ever planned."[70] He observed that what advertising really did was to produce "a favorable state of mind toward the advertiser's goods," a proposition very different from Hopkins's focus on sales.[71] But, even so, he argued that successful advertising rested on statistical research, a disciplined creativity, and an understanding of the laws of human nature. "Advertising is an experimental science just as is medicine, or, for that matter, just as is law."[72] The priority of good design, Calkins's particular concern, demanded a knowledge of art, including the innovations of modern art. A concern for "beauty" was a hard-headed business imperative as well as an exercise of aesthetic sensibilities.[73] The successful advertising man was "the one who solves the problems" of marketing, whatever they may be.[74] In short, business could rest assured that advertising was essential to a victory in the marketplace.

Hopkins and Calkins also agreed that advertising was, or was fast becoming, a discourse of truth. Now Calkins found distasteful the excessive rhetoric of the truth-in-advertising campaign, this "uplift movement," akin to "the virtuous unction of Sunday-school evangelists."[75] But he fully endorsed the efforts of advertising agencies and publishers to cleanse advertising of lies. He extolled the moral virtues of honesty and sincerity, especially the latter. "Absolute belief in the article to be advertised on the part of the man preparing the advertising is necessary," Calkins argued. "Advertising to be successful must be sincere and truthful. There are no exceptions to this rule."[76] In a similar vein Hopkins emphasized the importance of believability, one reason any claims in an ad had to be specific. "People recognize a certain license in selling talk as they do in poetry," he reasoned. But exaggeration they would discount. Facts brought conviction. "People do not expect an advertiser to lie," asserted Hopkins. "They know that he can't lie in the best mediums. The growing respect for advertising has largely come through a growing regard for its truth."[77] Here was a sign that the adman's dilemma, even if unnamed and unrecognized as such, could play the role of a social mechanism to restrain the enthusiasms of the advertising agent.

According to one of their rivals, Theodore MacManus, the fundamental difference between advertising, or at least his style of promotion, and propaganda lay in the commitment to honesty: propaganda was based on "untruth" or "partial truth." He made the claim that the ad columns now "elicit a larger measure of faith and confidence than does the editorial page."[78] He and others might admit there were still problems, remnants of the bad old days: hence Roy Durstine, a partner in BDO, lamented the prevalence of the paid testimonial in the 1920s.[79] Such lapses would disappear as the young profession matured. But almost none of these men were prepared to recognize that exaggeration, half-truths, diversion, pretence, distortion, all the varied forms of deception, were an inevitable dimension of the advertising business.[80] Hopkins blithely included in his autobiography a case where he successfully faked the farewell of an automobile to boost sales, even though he knew its designer R.E. Olds had no intention of retiring.[81] He did not see his action as a kind of deceit. Moreover, the agents argued vigorously that accuracy was a necessity to ensure effective and successful advertising: "Truth Is a Mighty Advertising Technique," pronounced Calkins.[82] (Calkins also warned his "deafened" compatriots against pretence, the habit of pretending to hear, because that common practice only made them seem "slow, thick-headed, stupid persons.")[83] Clearly Hopkins, who claimed to represent the consumer, not the client (yet more evidence of self-deception?), believed his success rested on his ability to tell simple truths to the public in ways that made advertising a legitimate form of information about commodities.[84] A public celebration of deception would have expressed a cynicism that ill-suited the mood of sanctimonious idealism prevalent in the 1920s.

The advertising agent was reconfigured as a marketing expert, a business counsel, an applied scientist, a consumer engineer, even a truth-
teller. What else? Some apologists implied, though they never stated
this explicitly, that the adman was also a redeemer. That was rooted in a
sense of power. There was a kind of double-think at work here. Nobody
claimed that advertising could work miracles. Hopkins doubted that
it could alter the established habits of the public.[85] Calkins doubted
whether advertising could ever counter "a waning fashion or create a
new one."[86] Even so, Hopkins touted the "almost unlimited scope" of
advertising to generate sales, demonstrated by the enormous range of
commercial successes.[87] Notoriously, Hopkins asserted, "People are like
sheep": they followed the crowd, they sought "happiness, safety, beauty,
and content. Then show them the way."[88] Similarly, Calkins argued that
a massive dose of advertising could make a public already "so standard-
ized, so herd-minded" "interested in anything."[89] That explained why it
had such an impact on ordinary life. "Advertising modifies the course of
a people's daily thoughts, gives them new words, new phrases, new ideas,
new fashions, new prejudices and new customs," he wrote. "In the same
way it obliterates old sets of words and phrases, fashions and customs. It
may be doubted if any other one force, the school, the church and the
press excepted, has so great an influence as advertising."[90] In the prose
of other writers such arguments morphed into the claim that advertising was a public service, like the news. The adman provided the kind of
information the consumer needed to live properly. The adman worked
to cheapen the price of goods. The adman energized the economy.
The adman was an agent of public welfare. And so on. It was such assertions which affirmed the claim the advertising agent was the consumer's
friend.[91]

Hopkins was never much interested in just where advertising had led
the American public – or at least he did not comment on the social
or cultural effects of the adman's rule. Others did. Occasionally, they
recognized the link between advertising and materialism.[92] But these
agents were much more enamoured of the notion that advertising
had fuelled the amazing progress of American society. In effect they
championed a species of biopolitics in which the adman had fostered
the rapid acceptance of all sorts of innovations to make living easier,
more comfortable, and healthier. Frank Presbrey quoted approvingly the
accolade of a prominent journalist that the advertising agents were the
true "revolutionists" of the age.[93] Calkins, in particular, elaborated this
maxim, especially in *Business the Civilizer*. "Advertising is a machine for

making it easier to live the way we live now" (19). It had made possible the selling of the enormous output of mass production; it had educated consumers so that they could enjoy the wealth of new goods; it had worked to promote the tools which relieved the drudgery of housework for the wives of America. Its style and ubiquity had fostered the improvement of business behaviour, what he called "Living Up to Advertising" (40). Which was why he could assert that "advertising is in many ways a sort of public service that is perhaps at least as beneficial to the public as it is to the advertiser" (25–6). He asked readers to consider what might happen should advertising disappear: his essay "A World Without Selling – Time, A.D. 2004" (58–75) imagined a backward dystopia where Americans lived a drab life of hardship and poverty because industry's engine, the work of the adman, had been banished.[94] Such views were sanctified by an address President Calvin Coolidge gave to the American Association of Advertising Clubs in 1926: not only were advertising men the apostles of modernity, they were the agents of civilization who fostered the desires which energized people to excel and innovate.[95] The adman was, along with the entrepreneur of course, the male progenitor of a dynamic new world.

Years later, after much further propaganda by the advertising industry, the claim that advertising fostered progress, and the motif of the adman as civilizer, became objects of mockery in a popular novel, Eric Hodgins's *Blandings' Way* (1950), a Book of the Month Club selection. Hodgins put the progress myth in the awkward rhetoric of Sir Zooanian Dree, an Indian visitor, supposedly a notable statesman, attending a party among a gaggle of pseudo-intellectuals. A hitherto silent guest of honour, he surprised the party by suddenly proclaiming that American advertising was the hope of the world. "'In my countree,' said Sir Zooanian, in his soft, slurring voice, 'thee greatest need is thee cultivation of wants. If my people could be made to want more they would at last bestir themselves to have more. American oddvertising and oddvertising methods are making now a small beginning, very small but a beginning, in thee cities. Ah yes'" (105). The people at the party were stunned by the outburst, some ready to endorse the claim because of its exotic source, although the spiel only made the chief protagonist, the copywriter Blandings, very uneasy, especially when he realized the Indian was convinced Blandings's slogan for a brand of laxatives had been a stroke of genius. In any case, the moment was shattered when Dree later admitted he was no longer a premier or a politician: he had been defeated some years earlier. Now he was an employee of J. Walter Thompson India and was in the USA on a refresher course. How disappointing, how crass: the wise man was revealed as no more than an adman whose proclamation was the same self-serving nonsense that had become hackneyed in America.

The fantasy of social rebirth was not the only masculine expression of gendered and class thinking evident in these stories of justification. That attribute also ran through the commentary on the character of the ideal agent. The point was to establish how advertising was a most fitting occupation for the bourgeois male, especially anyone hoping to join "the professional-managerial class."[96] The assorted textbooks were full of lists of the qualities necessary for success: organization, curiosity, imagination, originality, honesty, optimism, enthusiasm, energy, and sociability were recurring virtues.[97] The new recruit needed a knowledge of human nature, a business sense, a touch of the romantic and the pragmatic, and a willingness to work hard. Calkins placed great faith in the influx of new men, college-educated men, virtuous and sophisticated, as the means by which the profession would reach greater heights of fame and significance.[98] By contrast, Hopkins remained suspicious of college men or literary types, too interested in applause rather than sales, and instead emphasized that the proper role model was no less than the salesman and the proper training ground "the school of real business."[99] In his manual *The Advertising Man*, Calkins similarly extolled the advantages of actual experience: a year at a country paper, a year behind a store counter, a year as a travelling salesman. Furthermore, both drew on martial analogies to underline the manliness of their profession. "Napoleon himself is the fairest prototype of the advertising man," wrote Calkins and Holden. "His work and his methods were different, but the elemental qualities are the same."[100] "Advertising is much like war, minus the venom," claimed Hopkins. "Or much, if you prefer, like a game of chess. We are usually out to capture others' citadels or garner others' trade."[101] Both men, albeit in different ways, emphasized that the ideal adman was above all a rational and calculating self who could thereby best serve the needs of business and the consumer.[102] It was here that they embodied the masculine dream of the sovereign ego, the self who was always in command of his destiny and his environment. The fact that this ill-suited the profession, where power lay ultimately with the client – in other words with business – was at least for the moment set aside.[103]

In reality the last of the three philosophers, Edward Bernays, faced the most difficult task of justification. Corporate advertising was well established by 1920. Public relations was not. Its legitimacy was questioned even in some parts of the adworld. Public relations had grown out of press agentry in the years after 1900, when corporations hired pioneers like Ivy Lee to manage their dealings with the news media and the public. Bernays had started a bit later. He was full of contradictions: a very small man physically, he boasted a big personality; he was foreign-born but American-educated, Jewish but not religious, of bourgeois background yet progressive in spirit – his father a grain exporter, his uncle none other than Sigmund Freud. Bernays was always a bit of an outsider and decidedly unconventional. Out of college in 1912, almost by accident he took up work publicizing stage plays and eventually celebrities, notably Enrico Caruso, who toured the US in 1917. When war came, Bernays eagerly sought and found employment with the Committee on Public Information, moved both by patriotism and insecurity, so it seemed: he would always seek acceptance and approval. Success there (mostly – at the end he upset Creel) led him to launch his own publicity business after the war, much assisted by his new wife Doris, a silent partner. Bernays soon proved a brilliant publicist, particularly skilled at winning over and servicing business clients such as the formidable George Washington Hill, the tobacco tycoon.

Bernays was a master at manipulating the news, and it was for Hill that he scored one of his most spectacular stunts in 1929. Hill, the owner of the leading cigarette brand Lucky Strike, wanted to break the taboo against women smoking in public. Bernays organized the "torches of freedom" march in New York on Easter Sunday: fashionable young women joined the parade, smoked in public, and declared their liberation. This feminist event, however fake, won the attention of newspapers across the country and catalysed further challenges of the taboo. It was deemed a striking success, proof publicity could undo old customs. This and earlier triumphs Bernays constantly publicized: he was a consummate self-promoter, a braggart, not above embellishing a story to hype his role. By the end of the decade, Bernays had gained a roster of corporate clients and was charging them a hefty annual retainer fee. In the Depression year of 1931, he apparently earned nearly $100,000, of which 60 per cent was profit.[104]

Bernays loved to speak and to write, much like Barnum, another master of ballyhoo, and for much the same reasons: to promote himself and to reinforce his significance. During the 1920s he wrote two books, the first *Crystallizing Public Opinion* (1923), which became one of the initial classics in the field of public relations, and the second *Propaganda* (1928), a good deal more controversial, even sinister, because it sought to rehabilitate an instrument widely seen as anti-democratic.[105] The declared

purpose in both cases was to educate the literate public and the elites as
well as to establish public relations as a social science and as a profession,
related to but distinct from advertising. The unspoken purpose was vin-
dication, respectability, and recognition – for Bernays himself.

Like the other philosophers, Bernays wrote against the sad record of
the past, in his case the press agents who loudly and falsely publicized
some person or play, and the wartime propagandists who exaggerated
and lied, always to manipulate the newspapers and the public. But,
again, Bernays did not dwell on the problem. He sought to fashion a
novel appreciation of the role of persuasion in the governance of the
country. For public opinion had become a crucial factor in the affairs of
corporations, institutions, and governments – the old rubric "the public
be damned" no longer applied. Here was the conundrum. According to
Bernays – and he drew upon the thoughts of such luminaries as Gustave
Le Bon, William Trotter, and Walter Lippmann – the practice of democracy suffered from what could become a fatal flaw: the irrational public. Bernays, very much the social engineer, sported his own discourse
of truth – the necessity of biopolitics – in his case psychology. He was
the first of the persuaders to thoroughly endorse the notion of "Freud's
brain," meaning the proposition that the ordinary person was ruled by
emotion, custom, passion, and the unconscious, but not much by reason.
He focused his attention on the crowd or the herd not the individual:
society was composed of a series of groups divided by race and creed and
other loyalties into factious entities. The mind of the people was chock
full of stereotypes, prejudices, symbols, and clichés. The group mind,
apparently, was hobbled by inertia, unwilling to learn from experience
and so change its ideas. "The average citizen is the world's most efficient
censor. His own mind is the greatest barrier between him and the facts,"
argued Bernays. "His own 'logic-proof compartments,' his own absolut-
ism are the obstacles which prevent him from seeing in terms of experience and thought rather than in terms of group reaction" (CPO 122).
Here was a counter to that notion of the "hapless public" that satirists
and critics talked about; Bernays imagined an "obstinate public" which
must be led. Fortunately America was blessed by leaders and experts who
were rational beings, who could direct modernity – implicitly Bernays
presumed a meritocracy. He believed the only recourse was the rule by
elites, or what he grandly called "the intelligent few" (P 31), who took
on the task of moulding public opinion to suit the demands of progress.
The persuaders were instruments, perhaps members, of this necessary
"invisible government" (P 9).

Bernays had to demonstrate just how the counsel on public relations, a term he claimed he had coined, could "organize chaos," a favourite phrase of his. He opened *Crystallizing Public Opinion* by recounting stories of success, presumably drawn from his own experience, where the counsel (never specified but likely Bernays) had aided commercial enterprises, government bodies, even a foreign government, that of Lithuania, then seeking recognition. He proceeded to explain the techniques necessary to winning public attention and, especially, to persuading the opinion leaders of this obstinate public. Naturally he emphasized research: first to identify the important groups of opinion and then to establish their views, altogether a work of classification and surveillance preparatory to any task of governance. Bernays urged gaining the support of existing associations and setting up single-purpose front organizations. That required recruiting socialites, celebrities, business leaders, or experts – "the intelligent few" perhaps? – who could advance the cause and circulate messages. But the key was the media. What was needed was some kind of stunt, like his later "torches of freedom," which generated news and excited the press. All of this activity was carefully scripted to ensure a consistent message went out which worked with ideas and symbols already present in the mind of the people. "Human nature is readily subject to modification," he reasoned (CPO 150). The counsel had to seduce, to work with desire or fear, to harness the instincts of the public. "Human desires are the steam that makes the social machine work" (P 52). "The public relations counsel sometimes uses the current stereotypes, sometimes combats them and sometimes creates new ones" (CPO 162). He warned that the businessman and the advertising agent "must not discard entirely the methods of Barnum in reaching the public" (P 84). The counsel strove to break through the clutter of ads and news with a novel message that would circulate widely through the media. So public relations worked as another channel of persuasion, although the counsel might employ advertisements. Indeed, Bernays urged using all means of communications, including direct mail, radio, and movies, even word-of-mouth, an especially prescient observation. Of course in the 1920s the chief task was to capture the front pages of the newspapers, so the counsel not only purveyed but actually made news. In all Bernays had elaborated a blueprint for any biopolitical project. He was not focused on how a corporation might overcome the ill effects of some scandal or mistake. Rather, he saw the counsel as a person who could regularly exercise control over the beliefs and behaviour of ordinary people, over the course of life, and thus redeem democracy.

"Modern propaganda is a consistent, enduring effort to create or shape events, to influence the relations of the public to an enterprise, idea, or group" (P 25).

What was the character of this new hero of modernity? Like the advertising men, Bernays expended much effort in fashioning a professional identity. And to some degree his counsel of public relations shared attributes with the ideal adman. Strange as it may seem, he sometimes styled his version of the persuader a broker or mediator who acted on behalf of both the public and the elite. That made the counsel almost a representative of the public, much like the ideal adman, who informed authority of the concerns of the people. On occasion Bernays also took the lawyer as a model: the counsel served "to advise his client and to litigate his causes for him." This advocate pleads the client's case before "the court of public opinion" (CPO 50). Always he (at that time it was necessarily a man, despite his wife's actual influence) was an impartial and objective social scientist, someone who must know the public, its dreams, its beliefs, its best interests. "The training of the public relations counsel permits him to step out of his own group to look at a particular problem with the eyes of an impartial observer and to utilize his knowledge of the individual and the group mind to project his client's point of view" (CPO 122). Naturally the counsel must be an ethical persuader, someone who would never take on a client or a cause inimical to the best interests of the public. He must "avoid the propagation of unsocial or otherwise harmful movements or ideas" (CPO 215). Likewise the counsel had a duty to be candid. He was a truth-teller who would never stoop to deceive. Such injunctions were either a case of hypocrisy or self-deception, of course: in practice, for example, Bernays normally masked the name of the client who funded the public relations campaign. Although aware early on about the health risks associated with smoking, nonetheless he worked for the American Tobacco Company, Hill's firm, to entrench the smoking habit, especially among women.[106] The fact was that Bernays sought to engineer the consumer and the citizen in the interests of his client. Deception was as much part of his science as it had been of the huckster's game.

The claims of these three philosophers illustrate a dispute about the nature of persuasion that would persist among apologists and critics of advertising throughout the twentieth century, although the intensity of that dispute would wax and wane over the decades. It was rooted in the understanding of human nature, and more particularly of the mind of the ordinary American.[107] One view preferred to see that person as rational, someone who could be persuaded by fact, argument, and logic. It presumed the priority of the conscious mind, rather than the subconscious or the unconscious. It drew on old liberal notions of the bourgeois male who supposedly valued rationality as well as debate: here John Stuart Mill comes to mind, as does Jürgen Habermas.[108] This led to what has been called the information processing model, where the persuader employs some kind of reason-why argument to gain attention, provoke interest, engage desire, and so inspire action.[109] Top advertising men such as Albert Lasker, Claude Hopkins, and later Rosser Reeves, and to a degree David Ogilvy, espoused the merits of the model. Towards the end of the century it was revitalized by the ironic sell or the postmodern style associated with the Wieden & Kennedy agency, among others, and assessed in such novels as Alex Shakar's *The Savage Girl* (2001) and Jonathan Dee's *Palladio* (2002), where the consumer is positioned as a knowing subject. The figure of the adman, consequently, became a kind of educator who brought a sort of knowledge to the consumer.

The alternate views, however, emphasized emotion more than reason. They emerged in the immediate pre–First World War era as a result of the growing influence of psychology – notably the works of W.D. Scott – on the design of advertising. After the war its force would be strengthened by the influence of behaviourism – and here John B. Watson, a psychologist hired by J. Walter Thompson, would be crucial – and even more by the rise of psychoanalysis and the spreading popularity of the ideas of Sigmund Freud.[110] Bernays was one such believer. From these perspectives the ordinary American was considered primarily a feeling creature, often irrational, moved by emotion, where the subconscious or the unconscious reigned over much of his or her life. Such presumptions gave birth to what I will call the psychological tradition of persuasion, where information was much less significant than stimulus.[111] The persuader needed to employ images and symbols to awaken desire and to program the public. Later adherents of this tradition would include market researchers such as Ernest Dichter and Clotaire Rapaille, advertising men such as Bill Bernbach or George Lois, and a raft of fictional characters. The figure of the adman, as a result, appeared more as a seducer or enchanter than as a reporter or educator. It was this perception that would fuel in the 1920s, and similarly refuel much later, in the 1950s and 2000s, the outcries of critics who saw the adman threatening the rule of reason and the psychic health of the citizenry.[112]

In practice, of course, the actual advertising or propaganda often mixed words and images, reason-why and emotion, to sell a brand or an idea. That was certainly true of the work of Calkins. In addition, what was lost in this dispute was the persistence of deception. Both models of persuasion were prone to deception in all its various forms, although that form might differ. For example, it was easier to suggest with images that God somehow blessed a brand than to actually say this. The words used in scare copy could readily exaggerate the peril of infection or the prospect of transformation. Just because you assumed the buyer was rational did not mean you thought her smart. Often it was just the opposite. Whatever the strategy, whether to highlight information or to entertain, the fact that advertising and propaganda necessitated some form of deception persisted, if often unrecognized or excused as puffery or poetic license.

Besides, no matter how copious or loud the rhetoric of insiders, the character of advertising was such that it was rarely accorded the status of a discourse of truth by outsiders. So compact and so concentrated, an ad could never amount to a complete statement of the merits and defects of a brand. The adman might only ever speak part of the truth, his focus being on the product or brand itself, not on the product in context, its rivals or its exclusions, let alone the possible social consequences of consumption. Corporate and advocacy ads were not that different here: they promoted one enterprise or one cause. Industry-wide campaigns touting a particular commodity, say beef, were similarly limited because they usually neglected competing goods or services. The apparent exception of comparative advertising wasn't – that novelty, which emerged in America after the 1960s, lent itself to further deception since it worked to hype the virtues of the client's brand, one reason it was sometimes referred to as "knocking copy." The political advertising that became so prominent in American elections in the age of television was always prone to half-truth and exaggeration, especially when these served to slam a rival candidate. The wise consumer or citizen soon learned the necessity of researching a variety of sources of information about alternatives before making a significant purchase or casting a vote.

3. The Adman's Jesus: Bruce Barton, *The Man Nobody Knows*, 1925

The celebration of the adman reached its apogee in a peculiar way. In the mid-1920s Bruce Barton (1886–1967), one of the stars of the adworld, produced a publishing sensation entitled *The Man Nobody Knows: A Discovery of the Real Jesus.*[113] It had first appeared in serial form in the *Woman's Home Companion*, edited by a friend of the author (and it was later serialized in the Hearst chain of newspapers). The book was heavily promoted by Barton and his agency, then BDO, as well as by the publisher Bobbs-Merrill, prominently displayed in stores near the Bible, and soon endorsed by businessmen and some clergymen. The book sold around 250,000 copies in a year and a half, and it ranked no. 4 in 1925 and no. 1 in 1926 on the nation's nonfiction bestseller lists. It continued to sell thereafter: an estimated half a million copies had been printed by 1944.[114] Barton followed this success with other books on the Bible, religion, and St Paul. But none matched the success of his Jesus book.

Barton's book was not quite a biography. He claimed all he intended was "to paint a portrait" (11). It was more a collection of related essays about Christ's life, especially the last three years of his life, which together constituted a work of popular philosophy. *The Man* was well-crafted and well-written in a style that was easy to digest. It mixed references to the Gospels and to contemporary or historical people such as Henry Ford and Abraham Lincoln. Barton employed the authority of Biblical narratives to buttress his claims, but glossed their messages to suit his arguments. *The Man* appeared to have three main purposes. The first was to tout Christ as a manly redeemer, which located the book in a tradition of biographical treatments that emphasized the masculinity of Jesus.[115] Jesus emerged as a kind of action hero, akin, say, to Douglas Fairbanks: strong, muscular, healthy, handsome, and commanding – quite unlike the image of the sissy that Barton claimed was all too prevalent in Sunday Schools. The second aim was to promote Jesus as a champion of play and plenty, rather than a puritan, a kind of understanding that suited advertising's definition of the ideal consumer.[116] This Jesus was a sociable man, never a dismal or forbidding sort, one who enjoyed both the outdoors life and a good time, the kind of man with whom you might want to go off fishing or enjoy a banquet. The third purpose was to depict Jesus as "The Founder of Modern Business" (the title of one chapter) who had created a long-lasting organization that would eventually conquer the Roman world. This Jesus boasted superlative executive abilities: he had a vision, he knew how to recruit and train disciples, how to inspire the crowd, to best rivals, and to transcend any obstacles (even the crucifixion served his aims). Most importantly, Jesus had espoused a gospel of service to humanity which, in Barton's mind, was or should be the inspiration of corporate America. *The Man* was also a manual of good conduct. Barton used the life of Christ to preach how people, especially how men and businessmen, ought to behave at work and in society.

The skillful way Barton demonstrated the human and masculine character of Jesus, plus his modernizing of Christian morality, were likely the chief sources of *The Man*'s popularity with the public. A collection of letters to Barton and his publisher demonstrated how thankful men and women were for a Christ they could admire as well as like.[117] Few of the fans showed much interest in the business side of Barton's Christ.[118] One historian, Erin Smith, concluded that Barton's books (not just *The Man*) filled "a vacuum of advice," much as did advertisements, in the life of Americans troubled by the ways of modernity and the waning of traditional authority.[119] Barton's manly Christ was a friend and confidant, a coach and adviser, who offered useful guides to daily living.

By contrast, intellectuals, both secular and religious, were much more critical of the book. Their commentary focused largely on the apparent sanctification of business in *The Man*. In fact there was a touch of sycophancy (not unusual in the writings of ad-makers then) in Barton's treatment of the "big men" of corporate America.[120] Most of the substantial reviews in newspapers, magazines, and the occasional book displayed a deep distaste – "a feeling almost of revulsion" in the words of one critic – for the portrait of Jesus as CEO.[121] The *Commonweal* writer found *The Man* so full of "indelicate claptrap" and "poisonous nonsense" that it could only be considered profane.[122] In some measure Barton's book suffered because of the impact of an earlier bestseller, Sinclair Lewis's *Babbitt* (1922), about a real estate promoter, a novel which had skewered the moral blindness of the all-too-ordinary businessman. The fact that Barton used his work to extol the virtues of modern salesmanship made some critics believe he had turned Jesus into a glorified Babbitt.[123] But even more readers worried that Jesus had become just another "Brother Rotarian" (that sneer from the noted culture critic Gilbert Seldes)[124] whose teachings were reduced to an insipid gospel of service. "Here is an attempt to claim the authority of Jesus for the pseudo-morality which underlies modern business enterprise," lamented Reinhold Niebuhr, then a young, brilliant, and liberal theologian.[125] The Left-wing intellectual James Rorty thought Barton had created a "grotesque ad-man Christ" in his own image who might then "serve as a kind of robot reception clerk for the front office of Big Business."[126] Even one of his colleagues, Theodore MacManus, spoke out against the excessive religiosity of *The Man* and the way Barton cast Jesus "as a supersalesman and the prototype of all Rotarians."[127]

The opinions of later cultural historians could be equally dismissive: "evasive" and "fatuous," an "unintentionally hilarious book," something that "truly did cry out for satirization."[128] Richard Fried, Barton's biographer, deemed *The Man* "so feathery a book" that it likely could not bear too much close analysis.[129] But because of its popularity the book was also considered emblematic of the dominion of capitalism in the America of the 1920s. If so, Barton's view of business was very particular, an expression of the views of his profession rather than of big business, never mind of commerce in general. A number of historians have noted how *The Man* actually promoted a grandiose origin myth for advertising in which Jesus was the original and the ideal adman.[130] In short, Barton's work counted as yet another story of justification mounted by the new professionals.

In its uncomplimentary review of *The Man*, the *New York Times* (10 May 1925) called Barton "one of the high priests of modern advertising." That was a particularly fitting description. Barton was a preacher's son – not in itself unusual, since many of this generation of advertising men had a cleric in their family backgrounds. Barton senior was a prominent Congregational pastor in Boston and later Oak Park, Illinois, a scholar of some note in his own right, whose views and advice helped to shape the portrayal of a manly Christ in his son's book. Bruce had thought of following in his father's footsteps, and in 1914 he did publish *A Young Man's Jesus* to help his fellow strivers. But after college he had moved into journalism and eventually advertising. He was successful in both pursuits, especially in advertising, where he became the master copywriter at BDO, the agency he and two partners formed in 1919. During the 1920s that agency won fame as the maker of corporate image campaigns, notably for General Motors and General Electric, in which Barton promoted the idea of a corporate "soul" and a gospel of corporate service. He perfected a style of magazine advertisements, really abbreviated advertorials full of uplift, well described as "business sermonettes."[131] Meanwhile he won notice as a writer and as a lecturer, always working on behalf of the moral progress of business, advertising, and life. His views informed the address President Coolidge gave in 1926 on the responsibilities and achievements of the profession. In 1927 Barton himself delivered a revealing lecture entitled "The Creed of an Advertising Man" to a convention of ad-makers: there, he declared his great sense of pride to be working in advertising, "the voice of business," because "in the larger development of business and the gradual evolution of its ideals lies the best hope of the world."[132] In fact, or rather in private, Barton did have doubts about the worth of his profession because it fostered so much of the waste endemic to competition.[133] That was one reason, and there were others, why a later scholar, the marketing expert

Stephen Brown, might call him "a complete hypocrite."[134] But publicly he was the single most prominent spokesman of advertising, very much its high priest, especially after the publication of *The Man*.

Barton concentrated much of the treatment of Jesus as adman in two of the seven chapters of the book, "His Method" and "His Advertisements," although the claim was occasionally apparent elsewhere. The second chapter opened with a brief reflection on why his particular take fitted a retelling of the drama of the Son of God. Because Jesus was "many sided" (124), different people – a doctor, a preacher, a communist, a lawyer – were bound to see a different Christ. (Both Niebuhr and Seldes thought much the same – every author produced their own Christ – though they also believed Barton had stretched the truth beyond the bounds of credibility.) He, Barton, was an advertising agent and so his Jesus would be the perfect realization of the adman. Recognize that from the agent's perspective, God was the client, Jesus was his instrument. Should Jesus come to America now, Barton enthused, he would be active selling his message in the press, the modern marketplace.[135] What Barton saw was a history of Creation devoted to advertising. "The first four words ever uttered, 'Let there be light,' constitute its charter" (125). Nature was made full of plumage and blossoms that advertised their owners' wares. The very evening stars served as a gigantic billboard announcing "There is a Cause: A God" (125). It was statements like these that provoked charges of distortion. But they embodied a fundamental belief about life. "He came as close as anyone will to achieving a philosophy of advertising," argued the journalist Alistair Cooke on Barton's death, "because he saw the whole of human history as an exercise in persuasion."[136]

John Ramage, a scholar of rhetoric, has noted how a fundamental contradiction about human nature ran through *The Man*.[137] On the one hand Barton himself and his Jesus appealed to the good side of humanity. At one point Barton paused to explain that the success of God's "experiment" on earth depended on "the help of men" who "wholeheartedly" committed themselves to the work of making life better and happier (179–80). Clearly Barton believed that some men, notably the "big men" of commerce and politics, had done so. Yet elsewhere his view of ordinary people was much darker. Here he seemed to subscribe to the notion of an "obstinate public." Time and again the multitudes appeared in Barton's story as credulous and demanding, even cowardly, and sometimes cruel. At the end the crowd, or rather the "rabble" (219), abandoned Jesus to his fate at the hands of the vengeful authorities. Ramage suggested the contradiction reflected the confusion advertising men felt when they sought to understand the minds of consumers. By the 1920s the idea that the American public was basically irrational, ruled more by emotion or the unconscious, had taken hold of many writers in the trade journals of the advertising industry. This worked to enhance the stature of the business executives and their persuaders who saw clearly just what was necessary, who strove to lead people down the right road. (*The Man*, according to Niebuhr, was part of "a frantic effort" by business "to preserve its moral self-respect" by investing the life of Jesus "with the 'success' ideals which it so passionately cherishes.") [138]

Barton argued that Jesus had faced a major marketing problem in the last three years of his life. Barton modelled his conception of the racial and religious situation in Palestine on the supposed character of the marketplace in America in the mid-1920s. Jesus had a Big Idea, simple, forceful, and revolutionary: that there was only one just and good God, indeed a happy God. Barton had no time for elaborate doctrines or differences of creed, nor did he think Christ did. He had the "most daring of all" missions: to preach the Gospels to all humanity (89). "He called upon men to throw away fear, disregard the limitations of their mortality, and claim the Lord of Creation as Father. It is the basis of all revolt, all democracy" (96). Jesus had to create the demand for his Big Idea in a setting already cluttered with so many gods and religions. And he had to persuade not just men and women or the high and the low, but Jews and Samaritans and eventually Romans and Greeks, in a world full of ignorance, prejudice, and deceit, where the authorities – notably the Pharisees and the scribes and the Romans, all of whom figured as enemies in Barton's drama – were first suspicious and then hostile. Christianity "conquered not because there was any *demand* for another religion but because Jesus knew how, and taught his followers how to catch the attention of the indifferent, and translate a great spiritual conception into terms of practical self-concern" (104). Although of course Barton did not so describe the Jesus mission, it was framed as an exercise in biopolitics where he sought to organize the conduct of life of an extended population, even if in this case it was an exercise that ran counter to the supposed will of both religious and secular authorities. Its greatest advantage, obviously, was that it could boast a discourse of truth without equal, or so Barton might argue, that gave Christ's project a vigour and momentum that were extraordinary.

What Christ knew was the technology of publicity. According to Barton, Jesus had an instinctive – or was it divine? – command of the very science of advertising Barton's colleagues touted. "Surely no one will consider us lacking in reverence if we say that every one of the 'principles of modern salesmanship' on which business men so much pride themselves, are brilliantly exemplified in Jesus' talk and work" (104). (In fact James Dwyer thought this "burlesque of the life of Jesus Christ" was thoroughly irreverent.)[139] Barton's Christ was a master of spectacle, of playing to the crowd. "He was advertised by his service, not by his sermons" (136). His cleansing of the hallowed Temple in Jerusalem – proof, by the way, of his vigour and strength – announced to authorities and ordinary folk the arrival of an adamant Son of God.[140] Just as the miracles, the various cures, or the feeding of the multitudes: Barton even imagined the headlines in a fictional *Capernaum News* to show how healing a sufferer demonstrated Christ's divinity and his revolution to the citizenry. Jesus, so it seemed, practised a (largely) non-violent species of the propaganda of the deed where actions were designed to produce a political effect in the minds of the crowd. He created the kind of news that excited passions. Those people who witnessed his miracles gave testimonials to others about his rebellion and his love. (By contrast the reviewer in the *New York Times* claimed Jesus told those he healed not to reveal the cure, evidence Jesus was not at all like the modern advertiser.)

Barton's Jesus was a man of few words, but his words were always so well-chosen, so effective. He knew how to capture the attention of listeners immediately, which after all was the first purpose of any advertisement. Of Jesus's encounter with a Samaritan woman at Jacob's Well, Barton declared, "Dramatic, isn't it – a single sentence achieving triumph, arousing interest and exciting desire" (99). But where Jesus the adman excelled was as the storyteller who fashioned tales that illustrated the force of some moral instruction. The parables were "the most powerful advertisements" (107) ever produced, and the parable of the Good Samaritan was "the greatest advertisement of all time" (143). Barton devoted fifteen pages to an explanation of how the parables exemplified "all the principles on which advertising text books are written." Individually they were marvels of condensed and simple prose, always crisp and graphic, full of specifics not generalities, which conveyed "a message so clear that even the dullest can not escape it" (143). Altogether they embodied that cardinal principle of successful advertising, namely "the necessity for repetition" (154). For the thoughts of Jesus, however revolutionary, were few in number but the subject of one parable after another – "*many* stories, *many* advertisements, but the same big Idea" (156).

The last key ingredient of Christ's advertising was sincerity, which the advertising agents of the day claimed was essential to their task. "Sincerity glistened like sunshine through every sentence he uttered" (151). When he cleansed the Temple, Barton enthused, "There was, in his eyes, a flaming moral purpose" (37). Yet *The Man* was full of examples where Jesus employed techniques that smacked of deception. He presented himself as the friend of all sorts of people. He spoke in the language of the farmer or the fisher where necessary to win listeners. He evaded instead of answered – "Jesus seldom argued" (112) – and responded to interrogators with a cryptic remark or another question, "one of the best weapons in the whole armory of persuasion" (111). He told even his disciples what seemed like half-truths because they lacked the capacity to understand the whole truth. ("The final conference with the disciples is presented as a kind of 'pep' talk," reasoned a dyspeptic James Rorty, "similar to those by which, during the late New Era, the salesmen of South American bonds were nerved to go forth and gather in the savings of widows and orphans.")[141] But Jesus could never be charged with deception because he really was the Son of God. His sincerity was the result of his authenticity: "What he was and what he said were one and the same thing" (151). He always spoke the Truth. The case of Jesus realized an otherwise unattainable ideal of transparency. Christ's advertising was, by definition, what could be called immaculate persuasion, untainted by any deception. That was why he was ultimately the perfected version of the figure of the adman. (Such a portrait, lamented Gilbert Seldes, destroyed "all traces of austerity, even of nobility," producing a Christ for "a vulgar age.")[142]

Barton himself eventually recognized that he had fashioned a Jesus that was too much in his own idealized image. He was stung by the criticisms of his book, despite its popular success. He concluded that the problem lay in the fulsome references to advertising. In the late 1930s, when he and the publisher pondered the wisdom of a new edition, he thought of removing that material, only to be dissuaded by the publisher. But for a new release in 1956 he did the necessary rewrite, or rather excision. The stories of the manly redeemer and Christ the entrepreneur remained. So too did the gospel of service where commercial success depended upon a commitment to bettering humanity. But this second version of *The Man* made no attempt to present Jesus as adman or to justify his service and parables as advertisements. The social conversation had shifted since the 1920s, the reputation of advertising was now once again too tarnished, the original claims an obstacle to the future success of *The Man.* It was a wise marketing ploy. The revamped book sold well, even appearing in digital form after the turn of the century.[143]

4. Anti-Advertising: James Rorty, *Our Master's Voice: Advertising,* 1934

The stream of contempt that greeted Barton's Jesus indicated that the adman's narrative of justification, the stories of service and redemption, had not convinced many intellectuals. "Advertising is a queer cross between a black art and a swindle," mused Walter Pitkin, a popular philosopher, in 1932.[144] That *bon mot* signalled a view of advertising as degraded speech and art, for some writers a cultural ill, common among critics, novelists, and artists. The view was rooted in a long-standing suspicion of both business and consumption, which in turn reflected the import of republican civics and puritan morality.[145] The disdain might draw on the memory of Barnum's exploits or the exposés of the fake healers. But increasingly it was nurtured by an emerging narrative of anti-advertising, yet another response to the publicity boom, and one which also drew on the values associated with "the professional-managerial class." Although a number of writers contributed to this narrative, the works of Thorstein Veblen, Stuart Chase, Helen Woodward, and James Rorty stand out because of their originality. If the particulars of each of their stories differed, nonetheless they all questioned the legitimacy of advertising, describing it as a discourse of untruth, full of deception. That perception cast the figure of the adman in the role of a false prophet.

The credo took shape initially in the works of the iconoclast Thorstein Veblen (1857–1929). Although the books of this pioneering economist were not widely read, his ideas exercised considerable influence over a generation of public intellectuals, especially those on the Left.[146] Veblen's comments on advertising, which he sometimes lumped into "salesmanship" and "sales-publicity," were scattered across his later works. His most concentrated treatment came in one chapter, "Manufactures and Salesmanship," in *Absentee Ownership* (1923), where he included an extended appendix which ironically celebrated the Propaganda of the Faith mounted by the Roman Catholic church as the acme of successful advertising.[147] Veblen treated advertising as one instrument that business (and he was very critical of owners) used to "sabotage" the apparatus of production and endanger the health of society: it was a waste, it maintained or increased the price of commodities, it debauched the press, it preyed on human weaknesses, especially fear and shame, and it fostered an excess of needless consumption. It was always an incitement to consume, to live beyond one's means, a charge that would reoccur many times in the critique of advertising, even among those who lacked Veblen's animus towards the consumer society. But above all advertising was mendacious, the production of "systematized illusions" designed to construct consumers, a heinous example of "the art of 'putting it over'": its watchword was "the old Latin formula *Suppressio veri, suggestio falsi.*"[148] He said little about the actual "publicity engineers," who were now trained in "the fabrication of customers," except in passing to suggest they were both morally and mentally deficient.[149] Apparently Veblen thought that advertising agents were little more than dupes and tools of a predatory business class. But his strictures were not likely to disturb the peace of mind of any advertising executive or copywriter because they were little known outside of the intellectual community.

It was Stuart Chase (1888–1985) who successfully explored the new web of deception.[150] Chase was an accountant by training but an engineer at heart. After some experience in public service, where he was fired because he exposed the failure of regulation to restrain the exorbitant profits meat-packers garnered during the war, Chase devoted himself to reforming the character of the American economy.[151] He soon became a prolific writer who won a degree of popular fame with two books, first with *The Tragedy of Waste* (1925) and even more with *Your Money's Worth* (1927), co-written with the engineer F.J. Schlink. The latter polemic was a selection of the recently founded Book of the Month Club and a best-seller sold in multiple editions, and so generated considerable attention.

Although clearly influenced by the work of Veblen, Chase was much more interested in the practices and results of advertising than was his mentor. He looked upon advertising as a mix of poetry and deception: "magic rather than information is the goal of modern salesmanship."[152] He was well aware of how the industry had employed the findings of psychology to fashion a series of appeals – to the desires for wealth, fame, acceptance, sexiness, power, or health – sufficient to captivate any American. He warned that "the modern advertiser has developed a technique of artificial stimulation that would make Cleopatra blush."[153] The increasing volume and variety of advertising, where the key was unending repetition, had produced a kind of Wonderland, a chaotic yet charming place, full of simulacra. "It creates a dream world," he mused: "smiling faces, shining teeth, schoolgirl complexions, cornless feet, perfect fitting union suits ..."[154] The result was an unending pressure on the hapless consumer to "buy, buy, buy."[155] We might like to live for a while in this dream land: it was "stimulating, colorful, romantic," almost as much

fun as "going to the movies."[156] The trouble was that the dream world
served only to distance us from reality, to mask the truth about what
was available and what was useful. "We are all Alices in a Wonderland of
conflicting claims, bright promises, fancy packages, soaring words, and
almost impenetrable ignorance."[157] The argument constituted the first
extended treatment of the idea of a matrix constructed by advertising
which served to dupe and dominate the public. Chase's views expressed
the same fear of contagion that had moved the earlier collection of
critics who had attacked Barnum's *Life* and, beyond this biography, the
whole system of publicity in the mid-nineteenth century.

Likewise, Chase hoped to erect a defence, to immunize the public
against the contagion of advertising. His scheme of immunity, however,
was a good deal more ingenious than mere censorship. Chase hoped to
undo the ill effects of the web of deceit and dreams through the workings of a host of commissions and laboratories, mostly state-funded, that
would deliver the facts about brands to educate the consumer. On the
one side was science, which promised truth, and on the other advertising, or as he sometimes termed it "quackery," which offered only fraud
and falsity. Let the expert, trained and objective, speak. In short, Chase
proposed to discipline, if not banish, the figure of the adman who would
be replaced by a true consumer engineer, devoted first and foremost to
the public good, not private profit. The intent was to submit the marketplace to the dictates of the regime of truth, so that provable, verifiable
information about commodities would determine the buying decision.
Assessment and comparison would eliminate that structural defect of
advertising, namely its sole focus on the merits of one brand. Chase and
Schlink established the non-profit Consumers' Research to begin the
enormous task of education necessary to achieving such a lofty goal.

Aware they might be charged with an animus against business, Chase
and Schlink included a slightly specious claim that they had no quarrel with advertising done properly.[158] Advertising men were not fooled.
Industry spokesmen such as Calkins, Durstine, and Barton were well
aware that *Your Money's Worth* and Chase's earlier book were attacks on
their profession, and they responded accordingly to protect their narrative of justification.[159] They might admit Chase was well-meaning and sincere – Durstine was especially patronizing. They might agree that some
kinds of advertising, like patent medicine ads, were dubious – but things
were improving. Lies and deception were largely banished from the ads
of national brands which thus served the needs of consumers. Chase's
books were full of half-truths, they neglected the good of advertising, his

arguments much too selective, thought Barton, who damned this muck-raking mentality which sought sensation rather than recounted fact. All of the advertising men, and Calkins in particular, repeated versions of the progress myth, positioning advertising as the engine of modernity. And they chided Chase for wanting to return to an earlier America of home production and generic brands.[160] These apologists were clearly irked by the notion that the expert should replace the adman as the consumers' friend.

In fact Chase had not really talked about the advertising agent at any length. In *The Tragedy of Waste*, Calkins noted disparagingly, Chase had drawn upon the experience of H.G. Wells's Ponderevo as one of his "authorities."[161] In *Your Money's Worth*, Chase and Schlink quoted exten-sively from a most unusual memoir by Helen Woodward (1882–c.1960) to demonstrate how the typical copywriter worked with "a sort of cynical passion" to entice rather than inform the consumer about the necessity for a brand.[162] That was a wise choice: *Through Many Windows* (1926) was a far more intriguing and a much more witty and engaging auto-biography than any penned by an advertising man. Active for almost twenty years as a copywriter, selling books, soap, or foods, Woodward had become one of the very few acclaimed women in the profession before she retired in 1924.[163] Indeed, because of her book she emerged as the first example of the renegade, a type of considerable importance in the biography of the adman: the renegade was an ex-persuader who in a work of fact or fiction spoke out against advertising, the adman, and the industry. The testimony of the renegades, what they said about their past profession, would prove a crucial influence on the way the social conversation evolved.

Woodward had initially found in advertising an occupation where her imagination and her talents allowed her to excel, and to have a lot of fun taking risks and seeking novelty. But in time she began to have serious doubts about the worth of all her endeavours. Partly that was because she saw agency life, once full of creative excitement and disorder, disciplined by the rigour of the business-minded and the misleading gospel of ser-vice, by the professionalizing zeal of the new wave of advertising men. Just as important, however, were her worries about the flawed nature of the consumer society and her sympathies for socialism, which made her critical of business rule. She concluded that advertising must invari-ably involve deception, if not self-deception. Individually the ad workers might be both likeable and honest, certainly as honest in their dealings with their compatriots in the office as any other workers. But the work required he or she push the virtues of consumption on the public, no matter the moral cost. "To be a really good copywriter requires a passion for converting the other fellow, even if it is something you don't believe in yourself."[164] You had to glamorize the mundane, make the ordinary extraordinary. There could be neither sincerity nor authenticity. The result was a sense of disgust: she could not abide the brand once the job was done. No wonder so many creatives suffered burn-out by the time they reached forty. "The realization came to me with a slow shock that I was nothing, we were nothing," she claimed. "We were feathers all of us, blown about by winds which we neither understood nor controlled."[165] *Through Many Windows* could not be counted a thorough-going attack on advertising. The memoir was too ambivalent, her story characterized by both satisfaction and alienation. The ethical unease she reported was symptomatic of one aspect of the adman's dilemma and her memoir a forerunner of the chronicles of struggle that emerged after 1945. But it clearly illustrated the hollowness of the narrative of justification pushed by so many advertising men.[166]

Woodward's views impressed because of her experience. The much more radical James Rorty (1890–1973) had also worked as a copywriter in New York and San Francisco, notably at BBDO in the late 1920s. In his case this did not produce any sense of satisfaction: he lamented how circumstance had forced a return to "my advertising vomit, prodding my fair white soul up and down Madison Avenue and offering it for sale to the highest bidder."[167] Just as important were his politics: he had become a freelance journalist, poet, and author loosely attached to the New York circle of Left-wing intellectuals.[168] For a time he worked as a writer in the consumer movement launched by Chase and Schlink to educate the public and to counter advertising. But Rorty was no liberal (although in his own book he would thank the duo for their assistance and their critique). Moreover, he was a "Red," in the parlance of the day, whose ideology combined large doses of Veblen and Marx. At various moments in the 1920s and 1930s, he was linked to one communist faction or another (and subsequently purged), ending up in the Trotskyite camp. He hoped the Depression would provoke a revolution in America; but he feared the economic misery would more likely foster a fascist dictatorship. Rorty as renegade was the most original and radical voice in the emerging tradition of anti-advertising.

In 1934 Rorty published his magnum opus, *Our Master's Voice: Advertising*, which in retrospect was a vehicle for a compelling narrative of harm where the motif of the ad-maker's sin was manifest. Yes, it was an unwieldy compendium, almost 400 pages long, that mixed memoirs, fact and fiction, journalism and satire, analysis and polemic, sometimes witty, sometimes bitter, occasionally turgid, often sophisticated. The mark of Veblen, especially that theorist's disdain for business and consumption, was obvious. The book was dedicated to Veblen and to those others who might speed the "burial of the ad-man's pseudoculture."[169] If less apparent, the shadow of Marx showed up when Rorty dealt with class and class conflict. Although focused on advertising and agents, the text rambled, sometimes losing coherence, because Rorty roamed over past and present, the state of the media, or the plight of social science. One section on magazines was mostly the work of his wife, the activist Winifred Raushenbush, and an associate. Surprisingly the Depression was not central: *Our Master's Voice* was more about the adworld of the 1920s. In some ways it was meant as an answer to Barton's credo, not just his Jesus book but his other writings as well – references to Barton appear in various places, in addition to one chapter where Rorty dissected *The Man Nobody Knows*.

Rorty was writing at a moment when it seemed possible that the newly emerged consumer movement might generate a successful effort to actually tame the deceptions of advertising. That was the Tugwell bill, either the "unfair," the "Red," or the "late lamented" bill, depending on who was speaking. This piece of intended legislation – named after assistant secretary of agriculture Rexford Tugwell, a member of Franklin Delano Roosevelt's brains trust – sought to update the Pure Food and Drug Act of 1906, which had resulted, in part, from the furor over patent medicine advertising. The bill dealt with the advertising of food, drugs, and cosmetics. It specifically defined as deceptive any advertisement, whether by ambiguity or inference, that fashioned a false or misleading impression of the brand. Such a formula struck at the core of advertising, always to some degree a discourse of untruth. As Rorty correctly pointed out, "'ambiguity and inference' is the stock-in-trade of the advertising copywriter" (359). Passage of such a bill would have created a precedent that threatened the very character and the influence of the overall publicity system. This was clearly Rorty's hope: that passage would undermine if not quite undo the psychic harm advertising had committed on the American public. The Tugwell bill did not survive, of course, as the drug and the advertising industries mounted an effective campaign to defang and eventually suppress it. The advertising men even employed the techniques of public relations to upgrade the image of advertising, though to little avail. But the fact remained that the hopes of Rorty and other critics and sceptics of advertising were permanently dashed.[170]

As so often happened when the subject was advertising, Rorty gave his argument a biopolitical spin. This was a battle over the very character of national life, or more specifically over the purity of the culture. Rorty fashioned his own story of decline, in which an "organic" culture of small-scale enterprises and civic values had been superseded by an acquisitive culture, or rather a parasitic "pseudoculture," false to the core and already decadent. The "pseudoculture" privileged money, greed, waste, and emulation. "All advertising is obviously special pleading," (19) "directed at the consumer by vested property interests, concerning the material, moral and spiritual content of the Good Life" (16). Its purpose, as Veblen had suggested, was to create a particular mentality of acquisition among the public, thereby to produce consumers who were subject to irrational appeals (based on fear, sex, and emulation) that worked against their own objective class interests. "It has taught them how to live, what things to be afraid of, what to be proud of, how to be beautiful, how to be loved, how to be envied, how to be successful" (32–3). It was an example of how culture could undo economics, how images and rhetoric could forestall the birth of a proletarian consciousness. Rorty's version of the web of deception suffused not only the advertising columns of the press but all of the media, including radio and cinema, and had recently spread into the schools as well. In an interesting reversal of Barton's dogma, Rorty lamented that "the ad-man's religion is today the prevailing American religion" (285). Behind it all lay the fact of business rule, where corporate America worked to amass profit and dominate politics. In effect Rorty presumed the force of what would later be called hegemony theory, where the ruling class employed language and culture to control what was defined as normal, to suppress dissent and ensure compliance, and thus to build or maintain legitimacy.[171] Like Chase before him, with his notion of a dream world, Rorty's "pseudoculture" was another version of the matrix, that web of deception and illusion.

Rorty expended some time exploring the whole apparatus of advertising. He argued cogently that the apparatus was no unfortunate excrescence on the capitalist body but a vital and integral part of the new order. He likened the publicity machine to "a grotesque, smirking gargoyle" (32) set atop the structure of business. "The ad-man had become the first lieutenant of the new Caesars of America's commercial imperium not merely on the economic front but also on the cultural front" (320). The agencies were full of talented folk, many of whom thought they were engaged in art or in missionary work. That was hypocritical. They worked to turn consumers, especially women, into neurotics and slaves.

Rorty pointed to the tension that existed among the various kinds of advertising agents: the account executive, the copywriter and artist, the research director, all scrambling for their share of the rewards. Their work was hectic, demanding, and lucrative, but always insecure and ultimately unsatisfying. They were caught up in an "endless chain of selling" (36), selling their ideas to their colleagues, a client, and to the public. Rorty portrayed the advertising agency as a cultural factory, or as he preferred a "mill," subject to a ferocious kind of discipline.

But what was most striking about *Our Master's Voice* was Rorty's reflections on the adman as a social and moral type. It was in these passages that he elaborated in detail, for the first time, the dimensions of the adman's dilemma. Early on, he described at some length how the soul-destroying character of ad-making constructed a grotesque kind of person, caught up in the destructive embrace of the liar's plight:

> Your ad-man is merely the particular kind of eccentric cog which the machinery of a competitive acquisitive society required at a particular moment of its evolution. He is, on the average, much more intelligent than the average business man, much more sophisticated, even much more socially minded. But in moving day after day the little cams and gears that he has to move, he inevitably empties himself of human qualities. His daily traffic in half-truths and outright deceptions is subtly and cumulatively degrading. No man can give his days to barbarous frivolity and live. And ad-men don't live. They become dull, resigned, hopeless. Or they become daemonic fantasts and sadists. They are, in a sense, the intellectuals, the male hetæræ of our American commercial culture. Merciful nature makes some of them into hale, pink-fleshed, speech-making morons. Others become gray-faced cynics and are burned out at forty. Some "unlearn hope" and jump out of high windows. Others become extreme political and social radicals, either secretly while they are in the business, or openly, after they have left it. (19)

Rorty, in effect, had played the gender card: he had unmanned his onetime colleagues. Here he called them male prostitutes. Elsewhere he called them "parasites and unconscious saboteurs" (208) or "tortured eunuchs" (219). He asked one fictional advertising man whether he recognized he was "a charlatan, a cheat and a liar," no more than "a degraded clown costumed in the burlesque tatters of fake science, fake art, and fake education" (343). He ruminated over the almost feminine quality of "your died-in-the-wool ad-man." He was always "enceinte with big ideas, or nursing their infant helplessness" which meant that in his delicate condition he could not be held responsible for his opinions or actions. "Hence the ad-man's morning sickness, his tell-tale fits of dizziness after lunch, his periods of lachrymose sentimentality, his sleepless vigils after hours, his indifference to considerations of elementary logic – the charming hysteria, in general, of his high-strung temperament" (44). Unlike a real man, self-reliant and independent, the adman was no more than the well-paid tool of his corporate masters. The point was that Rorty denied that cult of masculinity, here the mastery of science and creativity and service, which underpinned the narrative of justification touted by the philosophers of persuasion. The adman was not really a person like other males but rather "the subhuman or pseudohuman product of an inhuman culture" (332).

Little wonder Rorty ended *Our Master's Voice* on a sinister note. The admen, those self-appointed but false prophets of modernity, would be at the forefront of any fascist takeover in the United States. Americans might soon have their own homegrown Goebbels.[172] At another level Rorty's polemic was an indictment of the so-called new men who had filled the corridors of ad agencies – and beyond that an indictment of "the professional-managerial class" that, whatever the rhetoric, had proved so subservient in his mind to the masters of capital.

Our Master's Voice was a splendid failure. On merit alone it deserved both a wide readership and a considered debate. It received neither, selling roughly 3,000 copies, according to Stephen Fox.[173] Some portion of those copies apparently reached ad-makers – "amid cries of 'Foul!'" according to *Time* (21 May 1934) – who were understandably disturbed. But otherwise the book was soon forgotten, at least in the immediate social conversation. Did the fact that *Our Master's Voice* was deemed Red – critics often spoke of "Comrade Rorty" – account for its neglect? Perhaps. But in addition, the book was not sufficiently well-crafted to reach a general audience: the work was hard to digest, it lacked sensational details about actual personalities or specific sins, it rambled on and repeated itself too much to capture the imagination. America would have to wait more than two decades before another furious exposé of the machinations of the adman, this one by Vance Packard, won the attention of the public.[174]

That failure was not because the adman's stories of justification had taken command of the social conversation. Far from it. The Depression was hardly conducive to popular support for any stories which celebrated the authority of business and publicity. The highly successful film version of Noel Coward's play *Design for Living* (1933), produced and directed by Ernst Lubitsch and rewritten by Ben Hecht, although chiefly about a ménage-à-trois, featured one of the first portrayals of the adman as a successful but obsequious sleaze: Max Plunkett.[175] The same year, *100,000,000 Guinea Pigs* by F.J. Schlink and Arthur Kallet, where advertising and thus the agent worked to promote the poisoning of America, proved a bestseller. Similarly the massive popularity of *Ballyhoo*, a new satirical magazine, that consistently lampooned advertising campaigns, supposedly reaching at one point a circulation of nearly two million copies, demonstrated that many readers were convinced advertising was always prone to deception.[176] "If you will go back in your mind," the trade journalist C.B. Larrabee warned advertising men in 1934, "you will remember that there has always been a good-natured skepticism toward advertising, but today this skepticism is based on studies and some pretty logical arguments by opponents of advertising."[177] In 1937 Gallup surveys discovered an extraordinary 88 per cent of those polled supported the proposal to ban "misleading food, cosmetic, and drug advertising."[178] The narrative of anti-advertising enjoyed much currency among the public, leaving the adman stigmatized as a deceiver, whether that meant a rogue or a villain.

But where was the groundswell of support to tame advertising? It never arose. There is contradiction, even paradox, here. If the public found advertising problematic, that public seemingly accepted its ubiquity. The limits that beset the public distaste for advertising were signalled by popular fiction in the years after the Second World War.[179] In 1947 Herman Wouk published his first novel, *Aurora Dawn*, a Book of the Month Club selection but not a top seller, which amounted to a moral comedy about the corrupting effects of the publicity system.[180] One of the characters was Michael Wilde, a painter, who played the role of the outraged intellectual – and thus the hater of advertising. It was Wilde who delivered a celebrated oration against advertising. "Advertising blasts everything that is good and beautiful in this land with a horrid spreading mildew. It has tarnished creation" (KL 1718). Nothing could be worse, so it seemed. The adman did the devil's work; he acted as the evil deceiver, always just to sell. How demeaning. Yet at the end of the novel Wilde chose fortune and comfort over sacrifice and purity: he married the daughter of the soap magnate whose promotions fuelled the advertising and thus the corruption. Wilde sold out. He chose hypocrisy. For all the sound and fury, his credo of anti-advertising lacked much moral substance. He accepted the way things were – the ubiquity of advertising was natural, part of a world where business and money reigned. In a later gloss on this novel, dated 1956, the now-famous Wouk allowed that his purpose was never reform but simply "to raise a laugh against some of its abuses, which are not so much monstrous or evil as just plain silly, and unworthy of an adult civilization" (KL 71).[181]

The publicity system was both tolerated and discounted after the rise of the advertising agent and the emergence of public relations. A survey of ninety-two magazine articles on advertising published between 1900 and 1940, mostly in specialized or elite publications, found a rough balance between supportive and critical commentary.[182] Advertising was a vehicle of untruth as well as a source of information that nonetheless had acquired, if not quite legitimacy, then acceptance. Why? Because the adman played out a role as an instrument of a particular species of biopolitics, the construction of a consumer society, where he fostered the circulation of goods that reshaped the lives of middle-class Americans in ways approved and sponsored by the elites and welcomed by the affluent. He might also claim he was guided by an appealing credo, in this case what was called "the American Way of Life," which was endlessly touted in his rhetoric.[183] But he, like much of "the professional-managerial class," served the interests of capital first and foremost, usually enthusiastically.

Underlying the apparent disconnect, of course, was the fundamental distinction between artifice and authenticity, between the ubiquity of deception and the ideal of truth-telling. Culture feeds on contradiction, at least innovation and explanation do. The dichotomy laid the foundation for two postwar narratives of understanding about the figure of the adman.

3

THE CHRONICLE OF STRUGGLE

In the public mind the advertising business is firmly established as a grey-flannel world of three-Gibson lunches, three-button jackets, unabashed throat slicing and zany argot ("Let's smear some of this on the cat and see if she licks it off").
– *Time*, 12 October 1962

The supposed existence of a sad but persistent state of moral angst throughout the land was elaborated in a long article in *Time* (31 March 1961), "The Anatomy of Anxiety," where the cover featured a reproduction of Edvard Munch's famous painting *The Scream*. Apparently America was overcome by guilt and fear, fears of "a loss of identity," of isolation, of "helplessness," of "nothingness," and guilt over the failure to act, to correct, to redeem. That was particularly acute in the fields of "advertising, communications and entertainment." Although *Time* did not just single out the adman as a victim, his anxiety over his ability "to write a novel or to know all about the atom" – admittedly a bizarre group of failures – were signs of the despair. The anonymous writer was heavily influenced by the popularity at the time of psychoanalysis, citing such stars as Rollo May, Otto Rank, Alfred Adler, Karen Horney, Erich Fromm, and Harry Stack Sullivan, in addition to Freud of course. He or she ascribed this age of anxiety to a collapse of faith, an excess of freedom and change, assorted forms of repression, even the workings of the Oedipus complex. But at bottom the writer found "the ultimate cause of anxiety in the U.S." rooted in the force of "pragmatism," which as earlier writers detected was the prevailing philosophy of the adman. It was this credo that vitiated the concept of truth and rendered the search for truth impossible. "Few things could produce more anxiety in

people who either believe in, or want to believe in, a moral order." In
the roughly twenty-five years between the end of the war and 1970, the
adman's dilemma seemed at its most intense, at least from the perspective of the social conversation.

1. The Peculiar Tribe: Martin Mayer, *Madison Avenue, USA*, 1958

Time devoted more attention to persuasion and to advertising practitioners in these years, and notably in the decade between the mid-1950s
and the mid-1960s, than it had before or would later.[1] That presumably
was both a sign and a cause of the importance of the figure of the
adman in the social conversation. The historian Lizabeth Cohen has
argued cogently that after 1945 the American state and business and
labour consciously constructed a "consumers' republic." That meant
"an economy, culture, and politics built around the promises of mass
consumption, both in terms of material life and the more idealistic
goals of greater freedom, democracy, and equality."[2] The adman was a
key player in the economic and cultural dimensions of this elite project
because of his presumed ability to persuade the public. At the time
one leading historian, David Potter, pointed out how modern advertising was and remained a particularly American institution because it
both expressed and served that outstanding attribute of the country, its
abundance of material goods.[3] In the new era of television and affluence, the gross advertising billings ballooned nearly fivefold during
the 1950s, going from $1.3 billion in 1950 to $6 billion in 1960, then
to $10.5 billion in 1970, largely to speed the consumption of a swell-
ing host of brands.[4] Likewise, the public relations industry boomed:
big business established and enlarged PR departments, ad agencies
organized special PR units, and independent firms sprung up in New
York and elsewhere to ensure that the corporate message was privileged in the mass media. The counsel of the adman was sought when
a client planned a new initiative. Sometimes advertising agents were
even involved in the design of new products or the refashioning of old
brands: for example, in 1954 Philip Morris signed with the Chicago-
based Leo Burnett agency, and then worked with them to relaunch the
Marlboro brand as a men's cigarette.[5] The adman could be, or could
easily imagine himself to be, the confidant of the owner or the top
manager of his business clients. Certainly ad-makers were deemed the
crucial specialists in the marketing mix. In short, postwar America saw
the golden age of Madison Avenue.

But there remained problems around the persistent habit of deception. Over the years, *Time* kept a watch on the trickery and dishonesty
that was endemic on Madison Avenue.[6] In particular it reported how the
Federal Trade Commission went after some of the industry leaders, such
as Ted Bates & Co. and Foote, Cone & Belding. "Sincerity," "authenticity," and "truth": all were for sale. Not even advertising men and women
could believe in the ethics of their profession: according to a poll that
Time cited, less than one in ten thought his fellows honest.[7] A onetime
leader in the advertising game, Chester Bowles, who had since moved
into politics and government, dismissed his past as something of a mistake. "There's a phoniness that runs through a lot of it," he said, according to *Time* (21 April 1961). "In advertising, things are exaggerated."
Even David Ogilvy, then the most celebrated of admen, admitted in a
Time report (20 October 1961) that the most telling criticism was "on the
grounds that advertising corrupts public taste, and makes lying respectable." All of which was why, as a *Time* cover story (12 October 1962) put
it, advertising men were "so nervous over charges that Madison Avenue
is somehow corrupting the standards of Main Street."

Now *Time*, at least when it mattered, came to the defence of the advertising man, repeating a mild version of the progress myth articulated
decades earlier by Calkins and Barton. In the previously mentioned
cover story, the magazine blandly concluded it "unlikely that the public
will ever be suborned out of its unemotional recognition of the adman
for what he is: a highly effective salesman without whose efforts the world
would be a far more primitive and less pleasant place." What was more
interesting, however, was how in this and other stories the magazine presumed the figure of the adman constituted a particular kind of being,
both very modern and very American. Its writers also believed that the
public had acquired a sense of just who and what the life of this adman
was: competitive, insecure, cutthroat even, extravagant, often exciting,
full of alcohol, and sex-obsessed. "Moviegoers have a clear impression
of the nature of life on Madison Avenue: it is a combination of Sydney
Greenstreet bullying Clark Gable in *The Hucksters* and Rock Hudson
seducing Doris Day in *Lover Come Back*."

Time argued that this view was not really correct, never mind complete. Already one author had tried to set the public right. In 1958 a
young but experienced journalist published what soon proved a successful account of the advertising industry. Martin Mayer (b. 1928), a writer
for the magazine *Esquire*, had published a study of Wall Street and would
later produce a series of books on, for example, schools, bankers, lawyers

and judges, and television. But, if at last count he had thirty-five non-fiction works to his credit, *Madison Avenue, USA* arguably remains his most famous study and certainly has become one of the classics of the literature on advertising.[8]

Mayer wrote as a reporter, not a critic. His intention was not to expose but to explore an industry and a profession that intrigued many Americans. He based his account on a wide range of interviews with advertising agents. "In the cliché of the trade, an advertising agency is nothing but people" (74). He immediately distinguished his views from those of apologists and critics who, he claimed, exaggerated the import of advertising. Two of "its worst nuisances," he thought, were "the advertising man's apparently insatiable need for self-justification and the advertising critic's apparently unceasing attacks on the business for its alleged fraud, deceit and 'hidden persuasion'" (317). Instead he argued that advertising could only have a limited, commercial effect by adding a value to a particular brand, which if the campaign worked might thereby advance in the marketplace. "Advertising is essentially a surface phenomenon, a wind that can stir still water ... When the wind blows with the tide, it seems to create an elemental motion; when it blows against the tide, it blows in vain" (311). His book amounted to a denial of the charge that the adman exercised any sort of authority over American life.

This thesis, however, was not argued at length. Mayer was much more interested in people and process. Throughout he scattered names, paying special attention to the luminaries, each with his own distinct approach to selling, such as Rosser Reeves (reason-why), David Ogilvy (brand image), Norman B. Norman (the unconscious sell or empathy), or Bill Bernbach (entertainment, meaning creativity and humour). Effectively, then, he made clear how the adworld remained divided between adherents of the information processing school and the psychological tradition.

Mayer devoted considerable space to elaborating the routine of work at the advertising agency. He carefully delineated the assorted roles of the various kinds of admen, the copywriter, of course, but also the art director, the account executive, the media buyer, and the market researcher. He emphasized how the key to success was the discovery of the "Big Idea" necessary to establishing the look and feel and the message of a campaign. He explored in one chapter what had been the most recent spectacular campaign, the effort by the leading agency Foote, Cone & Belding to promote Ford's new Edsel. Only later was it clear how the launch was a complete disaster, something he admitted in his revised introduction, and supposedly good evidence of his thesis. (It was the information in this chapter which most intrigued John Kenneth Galbraith when he favourably reviewed Mayer's book: the proof, as he put it, that "Adam and Eve wouldn't bite" despite the best efforts of Madison Avenue.)[9] In another chapter he focused on market research, paying particular attention to two powerhouses, the so-called mad genius Ernest Dichter (a progenitor of motivational research) and the more prosaic Alfred Politz (the king of statistics). It was, all in all, a masterful portrait of a highly competitive, always extravagant, creative industry where intelligence, innovation, and aesthetic sensibility were in great demand.

The most interesting aspect of the book, at least from the standpoint of cultural anthropology, was the way Mayer depicted the character and life of what amounted to a newly prominent tribe of Americans. The admen belonged to "the professional-managerial class," of course, which by this time was firmly ensconced in corporate America – and growing rapidly.[10] Except this breed was not quite like other men (and women) in the PMC, not really a normal businessman or manager or a professional, hardly just a worker, though they shared some of the attributes of all four. He recognized that advertising had a distinct reputation as "glamorous, financially rewarding, and somehow not quite honest" (28). Mayer's portrait was much more detailed, but not very different, though he did make clear how the ad-makers were the masters of self-fashioning.

The advertising men, observed Mayer, gathered in particular places. Notably they worked on Madison Avenue, where the agencies and the media were located, a part of New York they had effectively created in the country's imagination where, of course, the street was now iconic if not notorious. While the buildings were just nondescript modern on the outside, he found that each of the leading agencies had designed offices which expressed a unique or special quality, since appearance was so important in advertising: the feeling of a bank (Young & Rubicam), a movie set (McCann-Erickson), lots of grey tones (fitting Grey Advertising), a sense of elegance (J. Walter Thompson), a touch of psychology (Norman, Craig & Kummel). The advertising men dined, and dined well, in a series of classy nearby restaurants, all too many enjoying the high life of good food, splashy entertainment, and assorted pleasures on lavish expense accounts. The account executive, in particular, had earned much envy because his need to entertain clients on the company's account meant he could enjoy cost-free the life of a playboy: great food, much booze, night life, and "girls." The successful practitioners commuting into the city daily and living in the Westchester suburbs, made the advertising men "among the leaders of the great middle-class migration out of New York City" (13) in the postwar era. Likely this was all a bit exaggerated, but it conveyed the impression that the adworld was a real place in and around the great metropolis.

The advertising men had a particular style of work and life, often characterized by contrasts and even contradiction. Already these supposed experts in communication were known for their arcane jargon, a special adman's lingo, although Mayer gave only a few examples (one opened his account).[11] They dressed well but never too boldly – again appearance was a priority – in a fashion he described as "colourful conservatism" (12–13). Many enjoyed the thrill of the game, the excitement of producing a successful sell to the millions, except the downside was anonymity, never being able to claim any public credit for their achievements. The successful were extremely well-paid, far better than most other employees, one fortunate soul (Senator William Benton) purportedly earning three or four hundred thousand dollars by age thirty-five. (Certainly advertising personnel were high earners, reported *Time* [12 October 1962], "about 50% more than a man with similar assets can command in engineering or electronics.") The allure of fast money and many perks purportedly attracted much young talent. But these also burnt out more quickly, either leaving the industry or dying off (at 58), ten years before the national average, according to Mayer.[12] Madison Avenue was known as "ulcer gulch" for good reason: the adman's "work subjects him every day to the worst kind of commercial, social and psychological insecurity" (27). Advertising men were infamous for suffering all sorts of mental and physical disorders, such as nervous breakdowns, cardiac arrest, and perennial gastrointestinal problems. One cause was stress: ad work was hard and demanding, with long hours, many crises, much competition, and above all a lot of insecurity. "In the agencies, especially, at the heart of advertising, endless confusions of purpose, functions, organization and status create a nervous, overworked and overstimulated internal society," wrote Mayer (324). That meant the agent was prone to bouts of anxiety: the constant need for novelty, the ever-present fear of losing a big client, the worry a campaign would not win approval or would not work, the fear of rivals inside and outside the agency, the perennial search for more pay and more status.[13] However lucrative the prospects, being an adman was never easy. It required working in a community, wrote Mayer, characterized by a "strange blend of assertion and obedience, prosperity and insecurity, flamboyance and timidity" (323–4).

At the root of the trouble was deception, although Mayer dealt with this issue gingerly. Towards the end of his study, he seemed to let the adman off the hook for any acts of dishonesty. "The truth or falsity of advertising values is a matter of individual opinion, not a subject for objective analysis" (319). That comment was specific to the issue of added value, how advertising produced a brand image whose authenticity apparently did not matter in a marketplace where only belief really counted. This was in contrast to his dismissal of the public relations counsel who worked in the shadows "to direct and if necessary distort" the news (304). One was visible and obvious, the other hidden and sinister. Apparently Meyer as a journalist saw the other kind of persuader, the expert in public relations, as a threat to the press and his profession. The adman supplemented and supported the media, supposedly putting him on the side of the public good. In effect, and for the first time, a major author had recognized the social permission given the adman to deceive, to fashion a useful fiction that did no harm to the republic. That signalled the beginning of the era of the licensed deceiver, never wholly accepted, always controversial, but perhaps inevitable thanks to the ubiquity of advertising.

But the adman was never completely exonerated. Elsewhere Mayer proclaimed that "the vices of advertising" were "flattery, boastfulness, scorn and servility" (324). There was an affliction, an unfortunate moral condition, rooted in the adman's dilemma, troubling this community. His complaints cast a shadow on the practice of masculinity on Madison Avenue. Not that Mayer put it this way. He condemned the advertising man for his insincerity, the constant toadying to clients and the "so degrading" practice of always using the clients' brands (325). That last was especially demeaning because it seemed to signal the imperative of servility. And he singled out the top agency BBDO because it periodically lectured its staff about this imperative. (The agency posted signs proclaiming, "Confucius say, Advertising men who use product advertised by rival agency should draw paycheck from rival agency" [325].) Mayer also disdained the way agencies condemned their competitors in an unseemly scramble for new business. "Advertising men who denounce their rivals as incompetent fakers should not be surprised at the public belief that advertising is full of incompetent fakers" (326). In the same way, he discounted a large part of the research the agencies in the 1950s promoted to win new clients as "self-serving and essentially dishonest" (281). The adworld needed a major infusion of professionalism, he concluded, to make it more respectable, more ethical, and (although he never used the term) more manly. Mayer had rediscovered that often-noted problem with the adman: how the necessary subservience to external masters had bred a persona that clashed with the ideal of the sovereign self.

2. Stories of Angst: Frederic Wakeman, *The Hucksters*, 1946 and 1947

Overall, Mayer's criticism was fairly muted, which was why his book did not disturb too many practitioners. In the *Saturday Review* (29 March 1958) Sylvester Weaver, the former head of NBC and a self-declared professional advertising man (thus an insider) hailed the book "as a most knowledgeable, fascinating, and fair exposition of much of our world." But many other writers, some of whom had worked in advertising, were convinced of the essential immorality of the advertising business, though whether that made the adman himself a victim or a villain was a matter of debate. Their fiction trumped Mayer's fact.

These persuader fictions, mostly adman novels and movies, could be very different in tone and style from their huckster predecessors. True, the practice of deception was central to both kinds of fictions. But the huckster variety had been light-hearted comedies, where the adman was a rogue, his world was satirized, and the American public mocked. That style persisted in the form of Hollywood's romantic comedies where the denizens and the foibles of the adworld remained objects of humour. Many of the other persuader fictions, however, were serious, normally dramas in which the protagonist was beset by career and moral difficulties. The persuader fictions of both varieties, comedy or drama, were often vehicles for a new narrative of understanding, the chronicle of struggle, at the heart of which was the motif of the adman's dilemma. What had been evident in James Rorty's polemic back in the 1930s, his dark view of the state of the adman, was now emphasized in fiction. The birth and the popularity of that narrative spoke not only to the heightened postwar significance of advertising but to the anxieties fostered by the exuberant materialism of the emerging consumers' republic. I refer to the worries occasioned by the obsession with things, the lack of authenticity, the triumph of self-indulgence, the corruptions of luxury, the allure of glamour, and the prevalence of envy, many of which have been assessed by the historian Daniel Horowitz in his *The Anxieties of Affluence*.[14] Collectively the persuader fictions were one entry in a literature of moral protest.

The cycle began with the work of one renegade, in retrospect the single most significant renegade in this biography of the adman because of the influence of his fiction. In 1946 a sensational new novel had placed the figure of the adman near the centre of the American experience. That year saw the publication of Frederic Wakeman's bestseller *The Hucksters*, a social melodrama that exposed the linked worlds of advertising and radio.[15] The novel combined sin and cynicism, confession and revelation, romance and even tragedy, as well as social criticism and moral affirmation. What made the novel unusual was its focus on the way commerce had taken command of radio at the expense of quality, diversity, and innovation. Wakeman was already a published author. More to the point, he had been an advertising man at Lord & Thomas and its successor Foote, Cone & Belding, where he apparently had worked on the design of radio programs. Supposedly he knew of what he wrote, of the strange tribe of people who presided over the marketplace and the culture of America: here was the truth of experience. Later, during a radio discussion, in response to an advertising man's criticism, he told listeners that yes, indeed, he had told it like it was.[16]

The book was eagerly anticipated and not only by the inhabitants of Madison Avenue and the radio industry. The publisher Rinehart stoked the fires with heavy promotion, including, ironically, radio commercials, one of Wakeman's chief targets of obloquy. The Book of the Month Club endorsed the novel as a choice selection for its middlebrow audience, at the time a virtual guarantee of a big sale. Newspaper critics soon proclaimed it a must read, just for the revelations, even those reviewers who found the romantic interludes a bit tedious. The book did sell around 750,000 copies, becoming one of the top ten novels of the year. The movie rights were purchased by Metro-Goldwyn-Mayer for a reported $200,000. The studio employed one of its veteran directors, Jack Conway, to craft a new vehicle for its star Clark Gable and to introduce Deborah Kerr to American audiences. The result appearing a year later was not such a great success, neither with movie-goers nor critics, perhaps because the screenwriters cleansed the story of sex and some of its controversy, while heightening the element of romance. Yet the movie did earn a fair-sized audience and a profit. One later survey of the impact of the story learned that 13 per cent of some 3,500 adults read the book and 19 per cent saw the movie: the result was to reinforce and sharpen the negative views people had of advertising and radio.[17] In particular Wakeman revitalized the pejorative term "huckster," once meaning a small-time merchant dealing in shoddy goods, but now permanently attached to the figure of the adman.[18] Years later Fairfax Cone, an esteemed advertising man, blamed the continued late-night showing of the movie on television for the persistent and lamentable "picture of advertising and advertising people in the United States."[19]

The Hucksters explored how one man struggled to find himself, and especially to protect and assert his masculinity, in an unfriendly world and time, right near the end of the war. Vic Norman (played by Gable), the chief protagonist, was a thirty-five year old advertising man, no longer young but not yet middle-aged, still handsome, his looks and charms very appealing to women, a man who was definitely on the make after his service at the (fictitious) Office of War Information.[20] He got a high-paying job with the New York ad agency Kimberly & Maag, which boasted one very lucrative account: Beautee soap, a heavy radio advertiser and thus the sponsor of much popular entertainment. The trouble was that the account came with its own built-in ogre, the vulgar and sadistic client Evan Llewelyn Evans, who was modelled on the actual businessman George Washington Hill, the much-feared and much-maligned head of American Tobacco. (Evans was played superbly by Sidney Greenstreet in the movie.) Evans took inordinate pride in his mastery of advertising and of men, and had reduced the agency co-owner Mr Kimberly – or "Kim" (he never had a first name) – to a quivering mass of nerves kept functioning by drink, pills, much sex (with his wife and with whores), and of course a lot of money. Initially Norman managed to please Evans without losing his soul, as he was not ready to worship at the altar of Mammon. Much of the novel focused on his skillful handling of the radio business, where he laboured to fashion hits that worked best as vehicles for commercials. But Norman fell in love with Kay Dorrance, the refined wife of an absent soldier (in the movie version Deborah Kerr is a war widow), and that set the stage for Vic's downfall. Now he wanted both money and security to ensure his future with Kay. He succumbed to "the Fear" that Evans instilled in all subordinates: the certainty that they would lose their jobs if they did not do everything possible to satisfy the whims of the old man. Once he realized what had happened, that he had become something he loathed, the servile adman, Norman promptly rebelled. In the novel he resigned his job, turning down the promise of an agency partnership. He telephoned to say good-bye to Kay and her so-adorable children. Thus he affirmed his manhood, and took the moral course, by rejecting the corruptions of both advertising and illicit love. In the movie he not only told off Evans but poured a carafe of water over his head. Then he joined his war widow Kay in her car. Once again Norman had affirmed his manhood. Once again he had chosen a course dictated by the credo of the sovereign self.

Wakeman left his protagonist Vic Norman bereft of money, job, and woman, making this adman's story something of a tragedy in which the hero has to give up the American dream to ensure his manhood. Telling the truth meant failure as an adman. That was too much sadness for Hollywood and Clark Gable, apparently. In Conway's version of the story, the widowed Kay convinced Vic not only that they should marry now, but that he should "sell things you believe in – and sell them with dignity and taste." In effect the adman's dilemma was denied: you could tell the truth, at least of a product you admired. Romance was the answer, not money. As a consequence, advertising itself was not a problem, since the adman need only renounce deception to satisfy the ethical imperative. This happy and implausible ending was the most obvious sign of how MGM had taken the sting out of Wakeman's novel – and of his take on advertising.

Wakeman put some of his more trenchant comments on advertising in the mouths and actions of Evan Llewelyn Evans who, for some readers and viewers, was actually the most memorable character in this adman novel. Evans seemed a throwback to the days of the patent medicine moguls, even if his product was soap, not a cure-all. Despite the fact he was one of the bosses, he was also "the General MacArthur of the ad game" (21) who had his own credo of advertising and showmanship. He wanted his advertising simple, repetitive, and everywhere, his radio loud and obvious and commonplace. It was Evans who claimed that all was artifice. "There's no damn difference between soaps. Except for perfume and color, soap is soap ... But the difference, you see, is in the selling and advertising" (23). It was Evans who evinced the most thorough contempt for the public. "All you professional advertising men are scared to death of raping the public; I say the public likes it, if you got the know-how to make 'em relax and enjoy it" (24). It was Evans who showed Norman just how advertising needed to make its mark: Evans hawked and spat on the boardroom table to demonstrate the sort of action that made a message memorable, what would ensure people remembered the brand.[21] MGM left this scene in the movie.

Throughout the novel, Wakeman made Norman a confessing animal ready to tell everyone, and especially his lady love, about the sins of his trade and of himself. Vic seemed a self-professed cynic, one of the so-called moderns who lacked a belief in the virtue of anything outside of himself, and maybe not even that. Yet he certainly acted as if he believed in self-fashioning, seizing every opportunity to craft the persona of an aggressive, witty, and imaginative player. This was one "cold-blooded sonofabitch" (86), as an admirer put it, who didn't give a damn. Vic bragged to Kay about how he was waging "my private war against the world. Rather successfully too. But believing in nothing, up to and including myself" (270–1). Advertising was his route to easy money. "I don't like to work, so I work for one reason. To make money" (11). But he hated advertising, even though he was very good at the charm and the fakery it required. "The men you have to serve. The things you have to do. It makes my flesh creep" (42). And he loathed commercial radio, even though he was one of the people who ensured the lamentable quality of popular entertainment. "Somehow or other I have a disdain for the kind of cheap, sensational mass advertising appeals it takes to sell goods. Just as I feel a kind of contempt for what you have to put on radio to get a lot of people to listen to your program" (130). Wakeman's adman was very much the consummate deceiver who practised all kinds of deception, including outright lies, to persuade a client, a performer, or the hapless public. "We're all a bunch of hustlers and connivers in this business ..." (7); "We don't steal, probably because it's bad for business, but we sure as hell do everything else for clients" (88). The unreformed Norman seemed especially proud of his studied sincerity, the way he could dress and speak so as to convince everyone of his version of the truth. It was, he concluded with a certain bitter irony, the key to his success. Yet still he suffered doubts about the morality of his conduct and the emptiness of his life. He yearned for authenticity, some way of connecting with the real world of values and people. He wanted to be settled somewhere, and when he acquired an apartment he tried to furnish it with antiques. That search for authenticity was why he felt so passionate about Kay and her family, who together embodied the traditional virtues of love, purpose, and happiness. The romance transformed this cynic and rogue into a moral creature who in the end had to reject a career and a lifestyle that were so patently false.

The common tone of praise for the novel was set by an early review in the entertainment weekly *Variety* (22 May 1946): *The Hucksters* was "a lulu," which "packs a terrific wallop," "one of the treats of the season," "the most provocative treatment to date on the ad agency business." The novel struck the right note, since it not only knocked advertising – never popular – but it also slammed the dismal state of radio. That encouraged critics to express their own animus. The reviewer in the *Washington Post* (2 June 1946) took the opportunity to lash out at the ubiquitous radio commercial, "these snippets of dementia," most of which were "an insult to the intelligence, a disgusting display of banality, spurious enthusiasm and shabby commercialism." Wakeman's book was variously described as "Hogarthian" (*New York Times*, 26 May 1946), Hemingwayesque (*Harper's Magazine*, 1 August 1946), and "the 'Uncle Tom's Cabin' of the radio world" (*New York Times*, 30 June 1946). Constance Curtis, writing in the New York *Amsterdam News* (20 July 1946), an African-American weekly, thought *The Hucksters* important because "it gave the American public the opportunity to see the manner in which they are continuously rooked into buying" through unending repetition, the constant dinning of brand names, to hype the most ordinary of products. And, according to the veteran cultural critic Gilbert Seldes, reading the novel one gets "the sickening sense that vulgar and stupid men are deciding, by their own standards, what radio programs shall be."[22] The novel was a loud wake-up call to the public about the debauching of American culture.

The portrayal of the adman as the consummate deceiver especially captivated the imagination of critics. The novel's take on the adman's dilemma and its consequences seemed so intriguing and so fitting. Russell Maloney, the first *New York Times* (26 May 1946) reviewer, found *The Hucksters* "a wonderful, brawling tale" because it detailed "the incredible doings of incredible people," a strange group of corruptors. Harrison Smith, writing in the *Saturday Review* (24 May 1946), noted how the adworld was "filled with pushing, greedy people, bored with their own cleverness and their wisecracks." A second review in the *New York Times* (27 May 1946), by Orville Prescott, neatly summarized the immoral appeal of the adman's peculiar lifestyle: "All those beautiful and complacent women, all those exhilarating daily crises, the sense of power, the ever-rising tide of money and what it could buy, antiques, liquor, black-market steaks and black-market reservations on the Super-Chief [transcontinental railway], celebrity, psychoanalytic treatments and ulcers." That kind of abundance did seem to encapsulate the American dream of lush prosperity. But the costs were high. "Somewhere deep down they despise the shoddiness in what they are creating," claimed Harrison Smith; "they want to make money in heaps and get out fast before they are destroyed by the easy anodynes of drink, psychiatrists, and cold sex." Kimberly, so Prescott added, was reduced to "a loose-living hypochondriac, a slave to Benzedrine and alcohol and especially the personal slave of Evan Llewellyn Evans." And Vic Norman, no matter how expert he was at deception, "hated the flattery, sycophancy, duplicity, throat-cutting, back-stabbing, stupidity, depravity and waste of ability on unworthy ends of his profession." All of which served to underline the necessary lesson of this story. The moral of Wakeman's novel was obvious to Charles Poore, yet another of the reviewers in the *New York Times* (30 June 1946): "What is a man profited if he should gain the whole world and lose his own soul?"

The critics were understandably much less impressed by the romance and by Norman's renunciation. Neither were believable. That was why the book could never be considered serious literature. The best part of Wakeman's story was concentrated in the first one hundred pages or so, where he reported how things were – when he seemed the truth-teller – before he detailed the romance with Kay. Harrison Smith noted how the novel presented "an odd paradox. It seems to be completely sincere and believable as long as it is confined to insincere and fantastic people." "Mr. Wakeman's people are excellent when they are roasting the daylights out of what he calls the 'sincere' set," claimed Charles Poore, referring here to the false types who polluted the ad and radio worlds; "when they grow sincere themselves, it's all pretty embarrassing." According to Gilbert Seldes, Vic "falls in love with an exalted and boring woman who needs satirizing almost as much as radio does." Prescott argued the romance was no more than "an ineptly described and unconvincingly motivated love affair. The lyrical raptures of the participants may be exact reporting, but they sound pretty silly in print. And the combination of physical indulgence with soulful talk and noble renunciation is synthetic and pretentious." Vic's sudden repentance led one anonymous critic to question whether such martyrdom, such nobility really suited the portrayal of the adman created in the previous three hundred pages of the novel.[23] That was the point: the critics doubt the possibility of any moral transformation of such a villain. The figure of the adman worked best only when he embodied the sins of deception and cynicism. That ensured his responsibility for the materialism and the crassness that marred American life.

The success of *The Hucksters* launched a cycle of persuader fictions, forty-five novels and twenty-nine movies altogether, that featured some kind of adman or publicist, a cycle which lasted until the early 1970s (see Table 3.1).[24] At roughly the same time as *The Hucksters,* three other writers offered adman novels, among them *Aurora Dawn* (1947), the first work by Herman Wouk, who would become a bestselling author in later years. In one year alone, 1958, eight novels were published. Most of the movies came in clusters in 1956–7, 1959–65, and finally in 1967–70. They seemed to suit the mood of the times, if one can credit the insights of C. Wright Mills and other social critics. Mills found the American middle classes at mid-century afflicted by a bevy of neuroses.[25] David Riesman (*The Lonely Crowd,* 1950) and William H. Whyte, Jr (*The Organization Man,* 1956)

Table 3.1 The Persuader Fictions (1946–72). The items are arranged by clusters and in five year chunks of time, except for the last collection. The individual novels are listed by author, title, and date, the movies by director, title, and date. An asterisk indicates the item is featured in this chapter or elsewhere in the biography.

Date	Novels	Movies
1946–50	*Frederic Wakeman, *The Hucksters* 1946	
	Fielden Farrington, *The Big Noise* 1946	
	*Eric Hodgins, *Mr. Blandings Builds His Dream House* 1946	
	Arkady Leokum, *Please Send Me Absolutely Free* 1946	
	*Herman Wouk, *Aurora Dawn* 1947	*Jack Conway, *The Hucksters* 1947
	Abraham Bernstein, *Home Is the Hunted* 1947	S. Sylvan Simon, *Her Husband's Affairs* 1947
	Charles Yale Harrison, *Nobody's Fool* (Public Relations) 1948	H.C. Potter, *Mr. Blandings Builds His Dream House* 1948
		Frank Capra, *State of the Union* (Publicity) 1948
	Robert Hardy Andrews, *Legend of a Lady: The Story of Rita Martin* 1949	Joseph L. Mankiewicz, *A Letter to Three Wives* 1949
	*Eric Hodgins, *Blandings' Way* 1950	
1951–5	Jeremy Kirk, *The Build-Up Boys* (Public Relations) 1951	
	*Frederik Pohl and C.M. Kornbluth, *The Space Merchants* 1952 (as a serial)	
	Shepherd Mead, *How to Succeed in Business Without Really Trying* 1952	
	Robert Alan Aurthur, *The Glorification of Al Toolum* (A TV play as well) 1953	
	Howard Browne, *Thin Air* 1954	George Cukor, *It Should Happen to You* 1954
	Robert Bruce, *Tina: The Story of a Hellcat* 1954	
	Alfred Eichler, *Death of an Adman* 1954	
	Murray Leinster, *Operation: Outer Space* 1954	
	Ian Gordon, *The Whip Hand* 1954	
	Matthew Peters, *The Joys She Chose* 1954	
	Shepherd Mead, *The Big Ball of Wax: A Story of Tomorrow's Happy World* 1954	
	Samm Sinclair Baker, *One Touch of Blood* 1955	
	*Sloan Wilson, *The Man in the Gray Flannel Suit* (Public Relations) 1955	
	Al Morgan, *The Great Man* (Publicity) 1955	
1956–60	Gerald Green, *The Last Angry Man* 1956	*Nunnally Johnson, *The Man in the Gray Flannel Suit* (Public Relations) 1956

(Continued)

Table 3.1 The Persuader Fictions (1946–72) *(Continued)*

Date	Novels	Movies
	Samm Sinclair Baker, *Murder – Most Dry* 1956	José Ferrer, *The Great Man* (Publicity) 1956
	John G. Schneider, *The Golden Kazoo* (Politics) 1956	Frank Tashlin, *The Girl Can't Help It* (Press Agent) 1956
	George Panetta, *Viva Madison Avenue* 1957	Elia Kazan, *A Face in the Crowd* (Publicity) 1957
	Ernest Lehman, *Sweet Smell of Success, and Other Stories* (Publicity) 1957	Alexander Mackendrick, *Sweet Smell of Success* (Publicity) 1957
	Morton Freedgood, *The Wall-to-Wall Trap* (Publicity) 1957	Frank Tashlin, *Will Success Spoil Rock Hunter?* 1957
	Robert L. Forman, *The Hot Half Hour* 1958	Charles Walters, *Don't Go Near the Water* (Public Relations) 1957
	James Kelly, *The Insider* 1958	
	Harold Livingston, *The Detroiters* 1958	
	Shepherd Mead, *The Admen* 1958	
	Edward Stephens, *A Twist of Lemon* 1958	
	J. Harvey Howells, *The Big Company Look* 1958	
	Middleton Kiefer, *Pax* (Public Relations & Publicity) 1958	
	Robert Van Riper, *A Really Sincere Guy* (Public Relations) 1958	Charles Walters, *Ask Any Girl* (Market Research) 1959
		Alfred Hitchcock, *North by Northwest* 1959
1961–5		*Delbert Man, *Lover Come Back* (comedy) 1961
		H. Bruce Humberstone, *Madison Avenue* (based on *The Build-Up Boys*) 1962
		Blake Edwards, *Days of Wine and Roses* (Initially 1958 TV play by J.P. Miller) 1962
		Norman Jewison, *The Thrill of It All* 1963
	John Leonard, *The Naked Martini* 1964	David Swift, *Good Neighbour Sam* 1964
	Beverley Gasner, *Nina Upstairs* 1964	Arthur Hiller, *The Americanization of Emily* 1964
	Allen Dodd, *The Job Hunter* 1965	Jack Donohue, *Marriage on the Rocks* 1965
		John Boorman, *Catch Us If You Can* (UK) 1965
1966–72	*Elia Kazan, *The Arrangement* 1967	David Swift, *How to Succeed in Business Without Really Trying* (also a novel and play) 1967

Table 3.1 The Persuader Fictions (1946–72) *(Continued)*

Date	Novels	Movies
		Michael Winner, *I'll Never Forget What's'isname* (UK) 1967
		*Robert Downey Sr, *Putney Swope* 1969
		*Elia Kazan, *The Arrangement* 1969
	Edward Hannibal, *Chocolate Days, Popsicle Weeks* 1970	Jim Clark, *Every Home Should Have One* (UK) 1970
	Jack Dillon, *The Advertising Man* 1972	Michael Ritchie, *The Candidate* (Politics) 1972
	Helen Van Slyke, *All Visitors Must Be Announced* 1972	
	Irving Wallace, *The Word* (Public Relations) 1972	

likewise found the professionals and the managers in a disturbed state. The persuader fictions, consequently, were very much caught up in that social mood of anxiety probed by *Time* some years later. The possibility such angst might contain a fair dose of pretense was no obstacle to its exploitation by writers and movie-makers.

These fictions varied widely in character, style, and circumstance. As many of the novels were written by advertising men, they, like Wakeman's book, could boast the truth of experience. Once again, it was the renegade who explored the character of the adman's dilemma, whatever the beliefs (or fury) of his onetime colleagues. Shepherd Mead, a long-time employee of Benton & Bowles advertising agency, wrote three novels in different genres in the 1950s; his first, *How to Succeed in Business Without Really Trying* (1952), was a hit as a novel, play, and musical. Most novels had an advertising man or woman as their protagonist, but many fictions, especially among the movies, might deal with other types, such as public relations counsels or celebrities born of publicity. A few fictions dealt with politics to show how advertising and publicity served to corrupt democracy, in particular John G. Schneider's novel *The Golden Kazoo* (1956) and Michael Ritchie's movie *The Candidate* (1972).[26] More dealt with broadcasting, now especially television, which became so much an aspect of American life after the war. Three of the novels were also part of the wave of science fiction that took off in the 1950s, the best of these *The Space Merchants* (1953) by Frederik Pohl and C.M. Kornbluth, which became a minor classic of the genre:

the authors imagined a future world roiled by social turmoil because ruled by predatory ad agencies. A couple of fictions were mysteries and thrillers, notably Alfred Hitchcock's *North by Northwest* (1959), where the adman struggled to extricate himself from another, more perilous world full of deception. Some of the most popular movies, for example *Lover Come Back* (1961), were romantic comedies where love eventually triumphed. A small group of novels claimed to "tell it like it is," such as Robert Forman's *The Hot Half Hour* (1958), about what became the infamous TV quiz shows of the late 1950s, or Shepherd Mead's *The Admen* (1958), which chronicled the struggles of agency life, spiced with some illicit romance. Others indulged in broad satire, the best of which was Robert Downey Sr's *Putney Swope* (1969), about an African-American takeover of an advertising agency, which became a cult favourite. A few fictions achieved considerable popularity, notably Sloan Wilson's *The Man in the Gray Flannel Suit* (1955), selling nearly 100,000 copies in that year, and the ensuing movie by Nunnally Johnson (1956), starring Gregory Peck in peak form.[27] The last entry in the cycle, Irving Wallace's *The Word* (1972), about a public relations man, was like the first, Wakeman's novel, a bestseller. None of the novels, however, could claim to be great, and none achieved a status in English literature comparable to that of H.G. Wells's *Tono-Bungay*. By contrast, some of the movies, especially the Johnson and Hitchcock efforts, would later be ranked as significant examples of the art of cinema of the 1950s.

Although the theme of cultural and social criticism was present in many of these works, it was generally modest and often muted, sometimes even treated ironically.[28] In a later preface to his book, Herman Wouk thought a crusade against the "amalgam of sketchy amusement and hard-eyed selling" of the broadcasting world seemed "faintly ridiculous."[29] Instead, the persuader fictions dealt more often in moral angst, where the figure of the adman had to confront the problems of self-deception and deception that supposedly plagued work in the publicity system. There was a definite formula, as two noted cultural critics, John Kenneth Galbraith and A.C. Spectorsky, pointed out in their reviews written at the peak of the persuader cycle in the mid-1950s. According to Galbraith, the hero was always a conflicted soul, both a star adman and a deep cynic driven by money yet equally troubled by a conscience "which tells him that he is engaged in a conspiracy against the American people." As there was "no moral way" to make so much money, "he must mislead the American people on caries [tooth decay] and calories and louse up their radio and television shows."[30] Spectorsky referred to the adman fictions as "cautionary immorality plays" that featured "Horatio Alger upside down," since the protagonists had to lie their way to the top before undergoing a change of heart. According to Spectorsky, once on top this "dehumanized and lethal loner" rejected the imperative of deception to escape, whether to "operate ethically" or "to secede from the rat race" as a "gentleman farmer" or "successful writer." Sex often played a contradictory part, both as a prize of success and a way to escape.[31]

I will focus on three different stories where the angst was intense. The first, *Blandings' Way* (1950), fell into the camp of sophisticated comedy, spiced with elements of drama. Eric Hodgins, the author, had served briefly as an advertising salesman and later as a manager in the magazine business, notably at *Fortune* and Time Inc. His first novel was *Mr. Blandings Builds His Dream Home* (1946), a marvellous spoof of the troubles of a well-off city man, employed at an advertising agency, when he acquires and renovates his country home. The novel proved very popular and was turned into a successful movie (1948) starring Cary Grant and Myrna Loy. *Blandings' Way* continued the saga of the adman's rural troubles, until finally he and a grateful family fled back to Manhattan; but it also explored in much greater depth the worries of the adman. Although a Book of the Month Club selection, the sequel did not achieve the first novel's fame, even though it was a fine piece of satire that effectively chronicled one man's struggle to discover meaning and purpose in his life. A few years later, Galbraith, in his generally scathing review of the persuader novels, called *Blandings' Way* "by far the best story ever told of life in an advertising agency."[32]

Once an aspiring writer who had chosen advertising to make good money, the protagonist Jim Blandings was now a highly successful copywriter who nonetheless wanted to escape the evasions, half-truths, and outright lies – often told for trivial or unnecessary products such as hair restorers, whiskey, or constipation remedies – that consumed his existence at the ad agency.[33] At times he experienced moments of extreme self-doubt and self-loathing, when he worried that he was no more than an incompetent or useless fool. "I cannot bear to think of the success of my deceits," he once reflected.[34] Clearly this was a man afflicted by the adman's dilemma, and especially a version of the liar's plight. A self-proclaimed liberal, he desperately wanted to believe in some grand cause and to contribute to some great scheme. The humour came in the details of how he struggled with himself and others to make a difference. What he discovered to his horror was that the practice of

deception was embedded in his life: it ran through everything he said
and did – to acquaintances and friends, to his wife and family, even to
himself – despite his supposed yearning for honesty, integrity, substance.
Furthermore, he learned that he was a failure at any other kind of
work – this after investing time and money running a country newspaper – except at advertising, where he proved again his mastery at writing
copy. In the end, he gave up his experiment, accepted his destiny (as
he put it), and returned to the city, big money, and advertising, all of
which is reminiscent of the fate of Barnham Dunn in *The Virgin Queene*
some two decades earlier. *Blandings' Way*, consequently, is a story of
defeat – perhaps the reason it was never as popular as the earlier
novel – in which the adman overcomes his angst by recognizing his
limitations and accepting his reality. One lesson of this story, though,
was that the "curious type of creation" that was advertising was no more
flawed than most other pursuits Americans had taken up.[35] Once again
the justification of deception lay in its success.

Sloan Wilson's *The Man in the Gray Flannel Suit* (1955) and its successful 1956 movie adaptation had much more conventional endings. Both
were enormously popular, and the phrase "the man in the gray flannel
suit" was added to the language as a signifier of the Madison Avenue
type, even though it was about public relations rather than advertising
per se. Wilson's story was very much a drama. There were many sides to
the story: whether the hero Tom Rath would tell his wife how he had
fathered an illegitimate child during the war (he did); whether he would
be able to inherit his grandmother's house menaced by a lying caretaker
(yes, in the end); and whether he would be compelled to sacrifice his
family to the insatiable needs of the corporate world (no, that fate he
avoided). Tom, goaded by his wife, sought a higher salary by taking on
the job of selling a broadcasting czar to an audience of doctors, and
eventually to America, as the leader in a campaign for mental health.
He swiftly discovered that the corporate world was full of duplicity, that
advancement, even survival, depended on his willingness to submit and
conform, to play the game. At one moment he seemed ready to be a yes-
man, to tell (and thus deceive) his boss that a planned keynote speech
was fine – if that is what the boss wanted to hear. Fortunately his wife
urged him to have the guts to speak the truth – once again the persuader's masculinity was at stake. So he acted out the role of the truth-
teller: he argued that the speech was dreadful because it amounted to
phony adspeak that could only alienate the audience and defeat its purpose. This brand of straight talk, apparently alien to Madison Avenue,

impressed the boss. "The public doesn't like fakers, and neither do I," proclaimed the network executive.[36] And what was the message of the story? That truth and virtue could triumph. "Let this be a lesson to me," decided Tom. "Sometimes things really do turn out all right" (KL 2950).[37] More to the point, the story celebrated the power of romance and family to defeat the forces of deception. Tom Rath had chosen authenticity over artifice and was rewarded – unlike Vic Norman.

The other intriguing aspect of *The Man in the Gray Flannel Suit* was the way it conflated the character of adman and public relations expert, or alternately fashioned a single image of the plight of the persuader in corporate America. The novel generalized the adman's dilemma. Years later, in 1983, Sloan Wilson commented on the way readers had redefined the meaning of his story:

> To my surprise, my novel, which I had regarded as largely autobiographical, was taken by some serious thinkers as a protest against conformity and the rigors of suburban life. (KL 3805–6)

> Somehow my hero, Tom Rath, was taken to be a typical advertising man, though in the book he had worked on a charitable foundation for mental health established by the president of a big broadcasting company. Intellectuals, hippies and flower children began to consider him not a protester against conformity, but an arch example of it, the squarest guy in the world. He was attacked as a proponent of materialism, bad thinking or no thinking at all ... (KL 3813–15)

But this was hardly a misreading. Wilson had melded the multiple worlds of persuasion throughout. In a milieu dominated by what Rath called "the slick advertising guys" (KL 2600), it was all too easy to conform to the routines of the persuasion game. When he returned from the war, "all I could see was a lot of bright young men in gray flannel suits rushing around New York in a frantic parade to nowhere" (KL 3735). Once an upset Rath had imagined he could easily manage the fakery of advertising. "I'll write copy telling people to eat more corn flakes and smoke more and more cigarettes and buy more refrigerators and automobiles, until they explode with happiness" (KL 2262). Or again he lamented how the rat race, the social pressure to succeed, unmanned him. "How smoothly one becomes, not a cheat, exactly, not really a liar, just a man who'll say anything for pay" (KL 2548). Rath was one angry man, his name chosen by Wilson to signal such a state, angry because he

was trapped in the adman's dilemma, where the seductive goal of affluence imperiled his moral health. Nonetheless, he eventually showed that
the conundrum of the adman's dilemma could be overcome by an act of
courage, a manly act: he told the truth and he was rewarded.

Appearing near the end of this cycle of persuader fictions, Elia
Kazan's *The Arrangement* (1967) and 1969 film adaptation offered the
most extreme story of moral angst. Kazan, a famed movie director, was
very much the outsider: he had never worked in advertising. Nonetheless, his story was labelled semi-autobiographical because it dealt with
the offspring of an immigrant, so like other entries it carried the truth
of experience. "I feel what it contains is the truth," he asserted later; "it
was, one way or another, lived through by me, and I put it down as truth-
fully as I could."[38] The novel, although very long and often rambling, was
an unquestioned popular success, becoming the number-one bestseller
in 1967, albeit with a decidedly mixed response from critics.[39] Despite a
collection of talented actors (notably Kirk Douglas, Deborah Kerr, and
Faye Dunaway) and some marvellous scenes and mischievous dialogue,
the film was a failure, too much an incoherent synopsis of the novel to
win kudos from critics or movie-goers.[40]

But in print or on film the story was certainly powerful. It chronicled
the troubles of a man undergoing a nervous breakdown. Kazan's protagonist, Eddie Anderson, another war veteran, was apparently on top of
the world, a man who had it all. After roughly twenty years, he reigned
as the star copywriter at the Williams and MacElroy agency in Los Angeles, and was the mastermind behind an especially specious tobacco
campaign for Zyphyr, the *clean* cigarette. He boasted a grand salary, he
owned three cars, a fine, ultramodern home, complete with swimming
pool and part-time servants, he was married to an elegant and loving
and forgiving wife, and he had a bevy of obliging women to satisfy his
sexual needs. And yet he was neither happy nor satisfied. Instead, he was
a divided self: one persona was Eddie Anderson, the successful adman
and thus master of deception; a second was Evans Arness, a successful
magazine writer who excelled in exposés (thus a kind of truth-teller);
and a repressed third was Evangelos Arness (really Topouzouglou), the
eldest son of a Greek-American rug merchant, who he both loved and
hated and who he had to escape to succeed. More to the point, Eddie
loathed advertising because he must constantly lie, whether to impress
his boss or his colleagues or to move a client's goods. That was brought
home to him when he started an affair with Gwen, also at the agency, a
free spirit who forced him to recognize how demeaning and distasteful

were his ad work and his phony life. Compelled to give up Gwen to save his marriage, he eventually lost control over his demons, tried and failed to commit suicide, and began a lengthy journey of self-discovery, where he progressively rejected the life and the pleasures and the things that had once defined his existence.

At one point Eddie concluded that all was deception, which seems to happen to fictional characters suffering the liar's plight. "I began to think of all appearances, including that of things – of clothes, cars, food packages, public buildings, in fact just about everything that hit my eyes – as false fronts, as techniques of advertising," he later admitted. "I began to think of our entire civilization as poses and attitudes, masks and simulacra."[41] He had, in short, a Melville moment, reminiscent of the kind of insights that had peppered *The Confidence-Man*. But it was Eddie's oh-so-cynical boss who explained how advertising served the "arrangement" that underlay society. "How long do you think this world of ours would last if anyone told the truth? We live by the grace of an unspoken agreement not to speak the truth to each other," argued Finnegan. "If anyone in business spoke the truth, who'd buy goods, for one thing? It's our lies – well-intentioned always, that keep this world of ours together" (303). That constituted a justification of the adman as a licensed deceiver whose activities were a crucial source of the social cement modernity required. But the cost was too high. Eddie wanted to be sincere, honest, and truthful in all his doings, to become the anti-adman. He hoped "to do one small good thing before I die" (405), as he said in both the novel and the movie. What happened was a kind of redemption brought on by much struggle, the death of his father, and above all the love of Gwen. He found a modicum of peace and comfort as a free soul, liberated from the thralldom of deception – and affluence. Once again the extraordinary power of romance overwhelmed the falsity of the world at large.

Later Kazan pointed out both the rationale for and appeal of persuader fictions. Some critics had panned his decision to set the story in the world of advertising. Yes, he agreed, it might well be cliché. But it was also so apt for America. "It typifies the split between what we profess and what we are." The advertising industry was "the epitome of this business civilization." And working in that industry had definite moral costs. "Everyone feels some degradation, some violation of self, when they spend their lives selling."[42] Beginning with the saga of Vic Norman, these fictions often took the form of confessions which, to repeat the counsel of Michel Foucault, had long ago become one of the chief means the West had fashioned to produce truth.[43] Confession is a special ritual of discourse that involves both self-examination and avowal, where the speaking subject is also the object of the assertion. Hodgins's Blandings constantly explored his own thoughts and behaviour to determine who and what he was. Confession operates in a particular nexus of power and knowledge that designates someone – an authority, a partner, an observer – as the crucial listener who must judge, console, forgive, or perhaps punish. Kazan's Anderson/Arness was forever speaking to a person, whether Gwen, his wife, his boss, his father, old friends, a judge, even to himself. According to Foucault, confession offers the speaking subject absolution, "it exonerates, redeems, and purifies him; it unburdens him of his wrongs, liberates him, and promises him salvation."[44] Wilson's Rath emerged a happier man at peace with his wife and his life, sure of his moral health. Confession offers the listener truth, authenticity, and understanding about life and the world. The persuader fictions made abundantly clear the downside of too zealous a pursuit of the American dream.

The confessional model produced, as Foucault put it, "a literature ordered according to the infinite task of extracting from the depths of oneself, in between the words, a truth which the very form of the confession holds out like a shimmering mirage."[45] Such a literature might please the masses, but the banality of these fictions easily upset the sophisticated. The reviewer in *Time* (10 November 1958), for instance, found tiresome all these "Drumbeatniks," the admen and the like who brooded over their moral state. Spectorsky concluded that the novels were just too "slick" and "glib," so they could be no more than "a reasonable facsimile of art."[46] But the final complaint must be left to Galbraith. "It is my general thesis," he wrote, a bit tongue-in-cheek perhaps, "that novels about Madison Avenue are at least as great a potential menace to our culture as the industry they undertake to expose."[47]

3. The Adwoman's Plight: Delbert Mann, *Lover Come Back*, 1961

The predicament facing the adwoman was in some ways worse than that troubling her brother. The adworld was defined as a masculine domain, which meant she must always be something of an alien. Here too writers and filmmakers found sufficient angst to produce interesting fictions.[48]

Late in 1961 Universal Studios released a new romantic comedy entitled *Lover Come Back* that would soon become one of the top-grossing movies then showing in the USA. The script was written by two professionals, Stanley Shapiro and Paul Henning, and the film was directed by yet another veteran, Delbert Mann, and featured two established stars, Doris Day and

Rock Hudson. This hit was in many respects a reprise of an earlier Day-Hudson sensation, *Pillow Talk* (1959), also co-written by Shapiro. The title had been used for previous movies about romantic troubles in 1931 and 1946. Both *Pillow Talk* and *Lover Come Back* belong to a short-lived Hollywood subgenre of the late 1950s and early 1960s called the "sex comedy," which boasted all sorts of witty innuendo and some erotic display to tease and to evoke the play of libido at a time when sexual mores were rapidly liberalizing. What set *Lover* apart was that it was also part of the ongoing cycle of persuader fictions. Some reviewers even concluded that it offered, in the words of one *New York Times* critic (9 February 1962), a "pasting of advertising": "It's enough to make a fellow never want to believe another ad."

The movie's portrayal of the advertising industry was not especially critical, however. The industry's authority was presumed. Madison Avenue, so the announcer claimed, was the place where were born the ideas "that decide what we, the public, will eat, drink, drive and smoke, and how we will dress, sleep, shave and smell." The ad-makers were shown working away in the high rises of New York, in clean, well-appointed, and nicely ordered offices that spoke of affluence and success. The adman and especially the adwoman were dressed up in fine clothes (not really Mayer's "colourful conservative" garb) that simultaneously announced their taste, status, and success: Doris Day, in particular, appeared in a range of enticing high-fashion garments. They lived in very pleasant apartments full of the amenities and accoutrements of the good life. Out on the town, they enjoyed the easy ways of the expense account to cover the costs of fine dining and entertaining. The movie left the impression that advertising was the route to a prosperous and glamourous way of life.

In fact *Lover* was not so much about advertising itself as about the competition and the romance of two account executives, Jerry Webster (Rock Hudson) and Carol Templeton (Doris Day), employed by rival agencies. Around this complicated romance, the movie enacted a variant on the adman's dilemma, one that explored the plight of women in advertising. Webster acted out the classic role of the huckster: he was a rogue and trickster who used all kinds of deceit to achieve his nefarious ends. "He's a man of the world. He's smooth, he's competent, he's experienced, he's a real man," said Jerry of himself – but as part of a deception when he faked another person and persona. Webster was the epitome of deception, and certainly not a man suffering from the liar's plight but instead one who relished the delights of deceit. Early in the movie he won a new client by seducing him with a few choice lies and much booze, song, and women – a veritable "Roman orgy." Later he successfully advertised something called VIP, which required that he hire a chemist to invent the product: the adman's version of immaculate conception, where the ad generated the brand. His television commercials were little marvels of exaggeration, bluff, and evasion. The campaign could become "the most convincing demonstration of the power of advertising ever conceived," Jerry told his doubting boss, the emasculated Peter Ramsey (played by Tony Randall); "You have sold a product that doesn't exist." The effort was inspired by an attempt to deceive, first another woman (causing Jerry some difficulties), then Carol herself, and eventually the Advertising Council, a fictitious moral guardian of the supposed ethics of the business. (Such a body did exist but did not police advertising.)

No less important, Jerry was also a playboy (we see him first arriving at work in a car driven by a stylish and sexy woman), eager to make a new sexual conquest, and Carol soon became his next target. That required another kind of advertising campaign. He assumed the guise of the chemist Dr Linus Tyler, playing him as a caring and honest man – and a virgin troubled by fears of impotence and in need of sexual comforting.[49] His masquerade, his pretense and promise, almost won Carol's heart – until she learned the truth. Eventually, Jerry did manage to get her into a hasty marriage and into bed after both had consumed too much of the newly developed VIP, an intoxicating candy – what the country "long needed: a good ten-cent drunk," according to its inventor. The escapade worked an unbelievable transformation in Jerry's nature: he suddenly became a moral creature worried about Carol's well-being. Such was the power of romance, a commentary on the role of love in persuader fictions. The escapade also made Carol pregnant. The movie ended with a contrite Jerry successfully pleading the virtues of marriage to a reluctant but entrapped Carol, then lying on a stretcher on her way to the birthing room. Perhaps unintentionally, *Lover* celebrated the ways of deception, how the adman could make his own reality.

The more unusual character, however, was Carol Templeton. The adwoman as a type had already appeared in persuader novels: as the thoughtful copywriter Susan Harlow in Helen Woodward's *Queen's in the Parlor* (1933), the publicity director Elisabeth Dennings and the fashion copywriter Gloria Hancock in Ruth Willock's *5:30 to Midnight* (1941), and the advertising executive Rita Martin in Robert Hardy Andrews's *Legend of a Lady* (1949) (see Table 3.2). But not in a hit movie, at least not as a major figure until *Lover Come Back*. Furthermore, Carol was an account executive, when in fact most of the women actually employed in advertising were confined to the ranks of secretaries and copywriters.

Table 3.2 The Adwoman's Plight. The table lists a variety of texts where a female persuader appears prominently in works written between the memoirs of Woodward and Mary Wells Lawrence, both of which are discussed in this book.

Memoirs	Novels	Movies
Helen Woodward, *Through Many Windows* 1926		
	Helen Woodward, *Queen's in the Parlor* 1933	
	Maysie Grieg, *Heart Appeal* 1934	
	E. Evalyn Grumbine, *Patsy Breaks Into Advertising* 1939	
	Ruth Willock, *5:30 to Midnight* 1941	
	Helen Haberman, *How About Tomorrow Morning?* 1945	
	Robert Hardy Andrews, *Legend of a Lady: The Story of Rita Martin* 1949	Joseph L. Mankiewicz, *A Letter to Three Wives* 1949
Bernice Fitz-Gibbon, *Macy's, Gimbels, and Me* 1951		
	Matthew Peters, *The Joys She Chose* 1954	George Kukor, *It Should Happen to You* 1954
		Delbert Mann, *Lover Come Back* 1961
		Norman Jewison, *The Thrill of It All!* 1963
	Beverley Gasner, *Nina Upstairs* 1964	
Shirley Polykoff, *Does She ... Or Doesn't She?: And How She Did It* 1975		
	Jane Trahey, *Thursdays 'til 9* 1980	
	Anne Tolstoi Wallach, *Women's Work: A Novel* 1981	
		Stan Dragoti, *Mr. Mom* 1983
Jane Maas, *Adventures of an Advertising Woman* 1986		
		Glenn Gordon Caron, *Picture Perfect* 1997
	Matt Beaumont, *e: A Novel* 2000	Nancy Myers, *What Women Want* 2000
	Alex Shakar, *The Savage Girl* 2001	James Mangold, *Kate & Leopold* 2001
Mary Wells Lawrence, *A Big Life in Advertising* 2002		Dylan Kidd, *Roger Dodger* 2002

Now the portrayal of Carol was not a particularly happy one. On the one hand she was shown as a hard-working professional: independent, imaginative, talented, and aggressive, able to direct a team of specialists in the intelligent design of a new campaign. She was also, at least initially, a person of considerable integrity, an exponent of the ethical side of advertising, who was revolted by Jerry Webster's deceptions and duplicity. That led her into a battle to bring Webster to justice before the court of the Advertising Council. She soon learned she also had to fight the sexism of males, both her boss and the men on the council, who were amenable to the way Jerry used sex and the woman's body to win friends. When she thought she might beat Webster and capture the VIP account, she admitted, "There's nothing I won't do to get this account." Truth was not enough. In the process of wooing the fake Dr Tyler, she proved willing to employ the same kind of bribes and ploys – paying for clothes and dinners, even going to a striptease show – that Webster would use. In the end it seemed the adwoman was no less willing to play the game of seduction than the adman.

Unfortunately there was another side to Carol's character. The adwoman suffered because of her gender. She proved something of an intruder in the profession. "I love the creative challenge of advertising," she told the fake Dr Tyler. "It's the social challenge that presents a bit of a problem." She couldn't drink because she couldn't hold her alcohol, making entertaining clients difficult. That was one sign of her inadequacy in a line of work where alcohol was the inevitable lubricant of doing business. Worse yet, she was soon revealed as a repressed soul, both a prude and a puritan, who had suppressed her feminine nature to succeed in the business world. She struggled to control her emotions – and sometimes she failed. Although physically attractive, Carol seemed embarked on a life that denied sex, and thus love. She found the mantra "sex sells" revolting. She called Webster "that depraved monster" because of his playboy style. ("His whole career has been built on one idea – sex," she declared.) Jerry of course teased her about her sexual inexperience and inadequacy as a woman. She wasn't married, he quipped, because "a husband would be competition. There's only room for one man in the family." She was unwomanly, a view confirmed by her female assistant Millie, who rejoiced when Carol dressed for a day of golf with the fake Dr Tyler ("Hallelujah! Today, you are a woman"). Later, as the phony Dr Tyler, Jerry exploited these weaknesses and vulnerabilities to trap her in his web of deception. He created the fake persona of an honourable and dedicated man who, like Carol, lacked sexual experience. Carol became a victim of self-deception: she wanted to believe so much in Jerry's fabrications that she almost sacrificed her virtue to save his male psyche. "You're so cultured, so refined," she told the fake Dr Tyler. In a private aside to herself, she proclaimed, "A woman instinctively senses when a man can be trusted." That scene occurred at an aquarium, where an especially rapacious fish avidly consumed its prey, a visual symbol that Jerry would soon "get" Carol. In fact she never saw through Jerry's lies. It was another man, her boss, who told her the sad truth, when firing her for being such a dope. It was all a comment both on the power of self-deception and on the foolishness of a supposedly accomplished woman. In the end, Carol learned that biology really was destiny: the pregnancy and coming birth meant she had to submit to the pleas of a now reformed Jerry. But the visual here, a helpless woman on a stretcher wheeled away by male orderlies, betokened her necessary submission to social convention. She had to surrender her independence. Is it any wonder some later critics found *Lover Come Back* tainted with a stain of misogyny?[50]

One could well read this movie as a further example of how Hollywood in the years after the Second World War imagined the downfall of the career woman.[51] But the persuader novels, whether written by women or men, had also doubted the viability of the advertising woman. She was caught in a double bind, the victim not only of the industry but of her gender as well. The supposed logic of femininity made impossible the success of the self-fashioning that was the special skill of the adman. The doubled self of the adwoman – her public persona as energetic, creative, autonomous, and controlled, but her repressed private being as emotional and nurturing and moral – was an inherently unstable hybrid. She could not successfully deny her nature. Helen Woodward's adwoman Susan Harlow eventually escaped advertising for a life in the home. Maysie Grieg's heroine in *Heart Appeal* (1934) was only ensured happiness when she realized how wrong was her fierce commitment to independence and thus her avoidance of romance – although she hoped to mix work and marriage, to stay in advertising with her man in their own agency. By contrast, the once triumphant Rita Martin in Robert Andrews's novel *Legend of a Lady* (1949) suffered an emotional breakdown that drove her out of advertising into the arms of a man: that submission became her salvation. Romance for the adman expressed his desire for authenticity, the rediscovery of something sincere and substantial and true. Romance for the adwoman expressed her recognition that she was a woman first, that advertising was never enough to satisfy her soul.

These notions persisted long after the appearance of *Lover Come Back*. The provocatively named Domina Drexler (dominatrix anyone?) in Anne Tolstoi Wallach's novel *Women's Work* (1981) was a talented creative director, cursed by a doubled self, who constantly struggled against the presumptions and restrictions of a male-dominated adworld. "Domina felt as if she didn't belong in her body. As if she were a spirit watching her real self go through the motions of living" (305).[52] She only escaped her sense of alienation when she shed her pose of unfeeling rationality to rebel vociferously against her male masters. Caroline, the successful adwoman in the movie *Mr. Mom* (1983), had to fend off the unwanted advances of a male boss – and soothe the injured pride of a stay-at-home husband. In the romantic comedy *Kate & Leopold* (2001), featuring Meg Ryan and Hugh Jackman, Kate was presented as a market researcher who had suppressed her femininity to advance her career, even dressing in a mannish fashion, although still subject to the harassment of a lusty male boss. Eventually she chose to reject her career and its phoniness to find true love with an English duke who had travelled through time from the late nineteenth century. That was her way out of the adwoman's version of the dilemma.

In most of these stories, especially the comedies, one source of difficulty was the moral nature of women that made them ill-suited to the demands of advertising. Helen Woodward's heroine Susan Harlow in *Queen's in the Parlor* (1933) railed against her fate: "Why do I have to be in this damnable business anyway – lying all the time – all lies – lying twenty-four hours a day" (81). But not always. Carolyn Rhodes, a character in E. Evalyn Grumbine's *Patsy Breaks Into Advertising* (1939), argued the opposite. She thought women were necessary to advertising because they represented their gender, the life of the home and the family, the imperative of shopping, all of which was so important to the consumer society.[53] Domina Drexler presumed that women were actually better suited to advertising because their training ensured a facility for deceit. "She'd always felt advertising was marvelous work for women," mused Drexler. "We learn young how to manipulate, coax, push without seeming to. Clients, who pay the bills and want action, are like all men, used to being obeyed. We treat our clients like old-fashioned husbands and fathers, and it works perfectly. And we know how to juggle everything, the way women know" (219). Just like any male huckster, Kate Mosley, the adwoman in *Picture Perfect* (1997), designed a series of lies about her marital intentions to sell her virtues to the top brass of her agency. That she recanted in the end was only evidence that the adwoman faced the same difficulties posed by deception as any male colleague.

What had changed was revealed by the story of the hit movie *What Women Want* (2000), yet another romantic comedy, starring Mel Gibson and Helen Hunt, but directed by a woman, Nancy Meyers. It became the highest-grossing movie directed by a woman in the USA up to that time.[54] The movie was, in some ways, reminiscent of *Lover Come Back*, as it also dealt with the rivalry and romance of an adman and an adwoman, except they were creatives rather than account executives. Once the star at his agency, Nick Marshall suddenly found himself superseded by a new hire, Darcy Macguire, and he set out to sabotage her. Like Jerry Webster, Nick was the huckster, the playboy, the chauvinist who, as a result of a freak accident, discovered he could read the minds of women, including that of his female boss. So empowered, Nick easily outplayed Darcy, who lost her job which, as discussed earlier, suggests that the adwoman was never so good at the game of deception as her male compatriot. At the same time Nick's telepathy bred both an empathy for women and an attachment to Darcy, which in turn inspired a change in his behaviour. At one point, he asserted women were so much more moral than men, that the adwomen would never stoop to the dirty tricks he had used, reflecting the assumption that gender did rule behaviour. Like Carol Templeton before her, Darcy Macguire was the consummate professional, a woman hired because she was a master of persuasion able to communicate effectively with other women. But she did not lose her integrity or fall into the trap of self-deception, as had Carol. The only reason Darcy failed was because Nick stole her ideas to secure his triumph. At the end of the movie, when Nick had confessed his sins, she regained her job – and promptly fired Nick! But this is a comedy, so Darcy also admitted her love for the transformed Nick: she rescued him from his past of deceit, becoming, as Nick put it, "My hero." Once again romance produced the triumph of authenticity over artifice. More to the point, Darcy got it all: the job, the man, her independence, and her success. The adwoman's plight was solved, at least in this story. Except, of course, that she got it all because of Nick's efforts: at first his deception and later his honesty. He remained central.

4. A Story of Triumph: David Ogilvy, *Confessions of an Advertising Man*, 1963

The stories or tales of angst chronicling struggle normally have some happy resolution. But there is one stellar work – fact rather than fiction, supposedly – by a successful insider in which the struggle and angst end in triumph and a deep sense of self-satisfaction. In this ending, the adman's dilemma – or its ghost, because the motif was in the background – was apparently denied. The memoir was a riposte to all the calumnies about advertising popularized by renegades.

In 1982 Richard Heffner introduced an interview with advertising executive David Ogilvy in a very clever fashion.[55] Heffner was the host of an American televised public affairs show called *Open Mind* on the PBS network. Heffner noted that once upon a time, back when he began broadcasting in the mid-1950s, advertising had been a hot topic, especially among intellectuals. At that time the figure of the adman occupied centre stage as a noted villain. But today that interest and concern, "the regret that there will always be an adman," had largely disappeared, or so he thought. Outside of the discussion of political advertising, the issue of advertising was apparently of small moment in the social conversation. Heffner set out to remedy this absence somewhat by speaking with the most celebrated of advertising men in America, David Ogilvy. It was an inspired choice, for it was Ogilvy, more than any other person, who had worked so successfully to rehabilitate, or should one say "habilitate," the figure of the adman in American life.

That star status might seem surprising. After all, David Ogilvy (1911–99) was not even an American; he was a "Brit" who had arrived as an adult in the United States, where he gained his expertise researching consumers with George Gallup. He had only opened his agency, Ogilvy Benson & Mather, in some ways an extension of an existing British agency, back in 1948. But Ogilvy had achieved much fame as one of the creative wizards on Madison Avenue during the 1950s. He had masterminded a collection of very publicized campaigns for brands such as Hathaway shirts, Schweppes soft drinks, and Rolls-Royce. He won attention as the proponent of the so-called brand image school of advertising, noted in Martin Mayer's 1958 classic, where the adman worked to build a particular and lasting personality for the product. Most important, Ogilvy mounted an effective campaign of self-promotion to advertise both his agency and himself to the industry, to business, and to the press. By the early 1960s, OBM had become one of the leading agencies in New York, claiming total billings of $55 million. During its rise, Ogilvy crafted a most unusual but certainly appealing trade and public persona: nothing less than a British gentleman, almost an aristocrat of advertising, eventually earning the soubriquet "the king of Madison Avenue."[56] It proved one of the most effective examples of self-fashioning in the many stories of the ad-makers.

Ogilvy cemented his celebrity status with the astounding success of his memoirs, *Confessions of an Advertising Man*, published in 1963. The book spent five months on the bestseller lists, went through six printings in six months, and eventually sold well over a million copies. Moreover, it won the acclaim of his colleagues. Not since the days of Barnum had there been such a popular work of autobiography in the realm of American persuasion.

Confessions was promoted as a book of compelling honesty. One of the blurbs on one paperback edition neatly expressed its overt character and its supposed appeal: "a masterpiece of calculating candor ... entertaining, literate and thought-provoking."[57] Other promises proclaimed that it was "the most honest work you've ever read," that Ogilvy "hides nothing" and reveals all manner of secrets. Actually, the book was imbued with the spirit of the theatre: Ogilvy treated the pages as a kind of stage on which he performed as a series of characters to entertain and educate his audience. The author was pictured on the cover of one edition as a seasoned philosopher, seated in a large chair, clad in a tweed jacket, and smoking a pipe. "I spend my life speaking well of products in advertisements," he claimed early in his memoirs; "I hope that you get as much pleasure out of buying them as I get out of advertising them" (9).[58] There was no sign of self-loathing here.

But there was contradiction and exaggeration. Much later, Jane Maas, another ad-maker and author, claimed that Ogilvy had admitted his confessions were, like most such works, "really a thinly disguised business presentation."[59] Despite the title, the book was not really an admission of past sins, but rather a boast of past triumphs. Whatever his peculiarities, the Ogilvy detailed here was never a villain who required absolution. He emerged as an energetic, innovative entrepreneur who had realized the promise of the American success ethic. *Confessions* was only a partial memoir of sorts, hardly a complete recounting of Ogilvy's career or exploits. It was also a manual, full of lists of dos and don'ts, meant to tell any reader what was the right way to conduct the business of advertising. (Ogilvy was notorious for his passion for rules: a man he wanted to hire told Ogilvy he could not take the job because "You have 284,000 rules against the kind of advertising I do.")[60] One reason the book would prove popular with a later generation of ad-makers was exactly that property, the way it served as a primer in the lore of advertising. Furthermore, *Confessions* had elements of polemic, exposé, and apologia as well as the story of struggle. Ogilvy sometimes took readers backstage, though less to appreciate what admen actually did as to proclaim what admen should do. Altogether it made for an engaging mix of fact, opinion, and story-telling.

If he did not seek absolution for himself, he certainly sought, if not for-giveness, then at least understanding for his profession. That required some commentary on advertising itself, and here Ogilvy positioned him-self as a reformer. He scattered brief references to the low repute of advertising people, the British disdain for the adman, the American busi-nessman's dislike of advertising, and the public's upset over the volume of promotional noise. He admitted some sympathy with the charge that all too much advertising was "a vulgar bore" (200), dull and bland and loud. He wanted to abolish billboards, political advertising, and the clut-ter of television ads, he suggested in passing. Packard, Galbraith, and Toynbee, the most famous critics, all received some attention, as did a few others in a final chapter on anti-advertising. But so too did some even more famous souls, such as Franklin D. Roosevelt and Winston Churchill, who had spoken up for advertising. He even managed to find a Russian, Anastas Mikoyan, the long-time communist politician, who defended advertising Soviet-style. On the whole, Ogilvy's justification of advertising amounted to a mild restatement of the by-now hackneyed progress myth, first propounded back in the early decades of the twen-tieth century. He rejected those critics, and he seemed to be thinking of Galbraith, who disapproved of affluence. Theirs was the discredited way of the elitist and the puritan.

Ogilvy also asserted, though never really proved, that the talents and skills of successful advertising men were unfortunately unrecognized. Evi-dence of that was the lack of advertising men appointed to top posts in government, especially by comparison with journalists, lawyers, even pro-fessors. "Senior advertising men are better equipped to define problems and opportunities; to set up short-range and long-range goals; to meas-ure results; to lead large executive forces; to make lucid presentations to committees; and to operate within the disciplines of a budget," Ogilvy declared. "Observation of my elders and betters in other advertising agen-cies leads me to believe that many of them are more objective, better organized, more vigorous, and harder-working than their opposite num-bers in legal practice, teaching, banking, and journalism" (39). Thus the neglect of the advertising executive was a loss to the nation. More to the point, the figure of the adman deserved as much respect for his virtues as a leader as did any other recognized professional.

Ogilvy's more effective ploy, however, was to confront and refute the prevailing stereotype of the adman as huckster or hidden persuader. His initial course was to demystify ad work by emphasizing how the agency was akin to any other bastion of creative endeavour. The first chapter of *Confessions* recounted his experiences as a chef at the prewar Hotel Majestic in Paris, purportedly a most famous kitchen run by a fearsome but inspiring master, one Monsieur Pitard, noted for his amazing cuisine. Ogilvy entitled this chapter "How to Manage an Advertising Agency," since he claimed that he had learned the basics of leadership at the feet of this chef, especially the need for one formidable boss (such as Pitard, such as Ogilvy himself) to rule the organization. Out he came with a list of ten kinds of behaviour he admired (at the top, a willingness to work hard) and eight behaviours he expected of himself (at the top, being fair and firm). The crucial element, as he put it, of "a research laboratory, a magazine, an architect's office, a great kitchen" (11), or an ad agency was its ability to recruit and manage creative people. Naturally Ogilvy numbered himself among this camp. He explained how such types were typically "high strung, brilliant, eccentric nonconformists" (19) who thus were both unconventional and innovative. He quoted one academic expert who expressed Ogilvy's own prejudices: "Creative people are especially observant, and they value accurate observation (telling themselves the truth) more than other people do" (24). Furthermore, they boasted a greater brain capacity, a deeper connection with their unconscious, and a talent for synthesis. Ogilvy thus aligned the figure of the adman with the scientist, the artist, and, of course, the master chef. In effect he argued that the much-maligned ad-makers actually belonged to a superior brand of humanity who saw more deeply into life than ordinary people.

But advertising agents were not mere dreamers. Sometimes Ogilvy reversed course. He made no apologies for the fact that the prime duty of the adman was to sell his clients' products. Just the opposite. He explained how much he enjoyed the hunt for new clients, how he anguished over the Pitch, how he suffered when a client departed, and above all how he relished making money. In his view the life of the agency was structured by a chain of selling, the same notion put forward earlier by James Rorty: the adman was forever promoting his ideas to his fellows, to clients, and to the public. This was equally crucial: here he aligned ad-makers with the needs of business, not art or entertainment. Ogilvy fiercely criticized advertising agents who emphasized creativity over commerce, who sought awards rather than sales. "It is the professional duty of the advertising agent to conceal his artifice" (112). After extolling the creative personality in earlier chapters, he later condemned the popularity of the word "creativity" in the profession. What Ogilvy employed to tame the creative impulse was the discipline of research. "I have my own dogma," he admitted, "and it springs from observing the behavior of human beings, as recorded by Dr. Gallup, Dr. Starch, and the mail-order experts" (151). Like Claude Hopkins, one of his self-proclaimed mentors, Ogilvy believed that advertising was a science where research and experience had demonstrated the correct ways to advertise different categories of products. Running through his lists was a determination to "get it right," to find the best "look and feel," as if ensuring that a headline with the correct number of words might overcome the chaos of the sell. His insistence was not phony. Such certainty was fundamental to his sense of identity: it established that the adman was, or could be, a man of knowledge, a wielder of truths, who offered clients the assurance that he had mastered the phenomenon of selling. But if that claim were to strike a reader as too far-fetched, then Ogilvy fell back on the position that the adman was as much a businessman, and just as profit-minded, as his clients.

One aspect of the adman's work that Ogilvy devoted much time explaining was the Pitch, or as he called it the "Presentation." The Pitch was really the most important event in the chain of selling. Here the agency presented its proposals for an advertising campaign to a new or existing client.

> Like a midwife, I make my living bringing new babies into the world, except that mine are new advertising campaigns. Once or twice a week I go into our Delivery Room and preside over what is known as a Presentation. These awesome ceremonies are attended by six or seven of my henchmen and notables from the client's official family. The atmosphere is electric. The client knows that he is going to be asked to approve a campaign which will cost millions. The agency has invested much time and treasure in preparing its offering. (85)

The Pitch was bound to involve an abundance of artifice. The exercise, if something of a ritual, became a contest, where questions of truth and the practice of deception were both present. It was sometimes thought of as theatre: the conference room became a stage where assorted admen did whatever they could to persuade the audience, in this case the sponsor who would fund their style of advertising. But it was also a game, since the admen presented and the company men responded, asking questions or making suggestions, all to discover whether a particular kind of artifice was worthwhile. Little wonder the Pitch could embody the complications of the adman's dilemma: the presenters might declare their sincerity and their honesty, but truth was always a problem and a limitation, since they had to produce a brand story which excited, no matter what the character of the product.

Such an event was really an exercise of power which required thorough preparation, rehearsal, and scripting to ensure the client was persuaded. Ogilvy never admitted that the Pitch was a contest of wills, as was the case when Vic Norman and Evan Llewellyn Evans clashed over the design of a new campaign in *The Hucksters*. The proposal had to be backed up with copious amounts of facts about the market and the customers, though Ogilvy recognized some chairmen did not like statistics. The agency's Plans Board, full of experienced souls, first vetted the campaign. The prospective client was researched to produce the necessary psychological profile of this new buyer. One spokesman, often Ogilvy, prevailed so as to maintain a united front and to impress the client that the agency's executive was engaged. The end result might be a compromise: Ogilvy emphasized the need to find an agreement between client and agency – to be flexible. However, sometimes things could go horribly wrong. Once he presented after lunch to Sam Bronfman of Seagram, who promptly fell asleep, woke up in a foul mood, and rejected what had taken several months to prepare. In any case, the Pitch was where the ad executive proved his worth. "You will never become a senior account executive unless you learn to make *good presentations*," he warned (180). The Pitch was the ultimate arena for the adman.

Ogilvy extolled the virtues of his own patented mode of address: the well-mannered sell. That was based upon an abiding respect for the intelligence of the consuming public. "The consumer isn't a moron; she is your wife" (119), a comment that proved the most famous aphorism in a book replete with such statements. The claim expressed Ogilvy's conviction that the consumer was a rational being who responded best to fact and logic. He implicitly rejected the notion of "Freud's brain." The adman worked not to manipulate but to educate. He must always operate within the bounds of good taste, never offending or upsetting or exploiting. He should seek to charm, never to shout or clown. However bold or unusual his campaigns, they had to offer the consumer a sound reason-why she should buy the wares he promoted: "advertising serves a useful purpose *when it is used to give information about new products*" (185). Ogilvy was a great advocate of narrative, constructing a compelling story that would tell the public clearly, if at some length (Ogilvy like wordy ads), just why the brand was superior to its rivals. He asserted that one of his most famous campaigns, the ads he wrote for Rolls-Royce, gave consumers "nothing but facts" (119). He expressed distaste for what he termed "the *belles lettres* school of advertising" (138), where "purple prose" and "bombast" (139) masked rather than revealed the true meaning of things. Here Ogilvy sought legitimacy by drawing on the plain speech tradition so celebrated in American culture, at least that culture influenced by the civic ideology of republicanism. The tradition extolled the virtues of transparency, where words signified exactly and accurately a reality. The speaker "told it like it was," free of illusion, so the listener could readily comprehend the message. It was a utopian dream that nonetheless conditioned the understanding of both politics and the marketplace. The ideal of plain speech, of course, had long ago been evoked to denounce puffery of all sorts, including advertising.[61] But it had also been appropriated by advertising agents who sought to make their spiels credible. Ogilvy was only updating a rhetorical ploy put forward earlier by Claude Hopkins, among others. But it was nonetheless a clever way of asserting that the adman was actually a truth-teller.

Similarly, Ogilvy confronted the slur that the adman was little more than the hired gun of the capitalist – or worse, the prostitute, in James Rorty's diatribe. A rhetoric of manliness ran through Ogilvy's memoirs. Following convention, he crafted an image of advertising as a highly competitive and risky enterprise where security was an impossible dream. Unlike the lawyer or doctor, the agency manager travelled "on the edge of a precipice" (73) because he could so easily lose his accounts. Ogilvy vigorously expressed the virtues of self-reliance and self-confidence, even, it seemed, a species of self-deception that might enable the newcomer or the young to strive for success. Consequently he had always vigorously touted his own merits. "Gentle reader, if you are shocked by these confessions of self-advertisement," Ogilvy explained, "I can only plead that if I had behaved in a more professional way, it would have taken me twenty years to arrive. I had neither the time nor the money to wait. I was poor, unknown, and in a hurry" (42). Once he had arrived, he emphasized the virtues of independence. No longer was he willing to mount a speculative presentation to win a new client. Never would he hire an employee simply on the say-so of an existing client. Always he avoided the big account – he mentioned the ill-fated Edsel – whose demands and whose fate might overwhelm the agency. "I have never wanted to get an account so big that I could not afford to lose it. The day you do that, you commit yourself to living with fear. Frightened agencies lose the courage to give candid advice; once you lose that you become a lackey" (58). He boasted he had resigned accounts where the client became a dictator or the demands made the account unprofitable. "Come to think of it, we have resigned three times as many clients as we have been fired by. I will not allow my staff to be bullied by tyrants, and I will not run a campaign dictated by a client unless I believe in its basic soundness" (81). Ogilvy had the gall to include a chapter, full of stories and rules, which demonstrated how to be a good client! Ogilvy's adman was a good approximation of that sovereign self much valued in the histories of American and modern individualism.[62]

The most intriguing feature of *Confessions*, however, was its insistence on the moral imperative of truth. This is where you can discern the effects of the adman's dilemma, how it could operate to guide the behaviour of the persuader. It almost seemed as if Ogilvy set out to replay Benjamin Franklin, the great American autobiographer and moralist, whose Poor Richard famously declared "honesty is the best policy."[63] That theme found expression in different ways. Fatal to the morale of an agency, apparently, was a leader who engaged in "acts of unprincipled opportunism" (23). The one essential quality in advertising, Ogilvy proclaimed, was not brains or imagination – though both were vital – but "intellectual honesty" (21). Elsewhere he added "candor" and "objectivity" (181). He urged honest dealings with clients, a readiness to admit one's mistakes and to tell the client when he was wrong or his brand flawed. The adman had to be sincere in his belief in the worth of the brands he promoted: "professional detachment" (60) might work in law or medicine, but never in advertising. He strongly supported the common practice that insisted agency personnel use their clients' products, itself a sign of authenticity. Thus he wore Hathaway shirts, drove a Rolls-Royce, filled it with Shell gasoline, ate Pepperidge Farm toast, drank Puerto Rican rum with Schweppes – all his clients' brands. Besides, he warned, "it is flagrantly dishonest for an advertising agent to urge consumers to buy a product which he would not allow his wife to buy" (83). Most importantly, the task of the adman was neither to lie nor deceive, and not just to "tell the truth, but make the truth fascinating" (134). The liar would soon be found out, at the cost of his own reputation, his client's, and advertising in general. Now Ogilvy did admit to the occasional bit of deception, as when he made a claim that was dubious, even a bit phony. But his only sin was of omission. "I must confess that I am continuously guilty of *suppressio veri*." For which he believed common sense gave him license. "Surely it is asking too much to expect the advertiser to describe the shortcomings of his product? One must be forgiven for putting one's best foot forward" (195). Once more the figure of the adman requested permission to deceive, but only a bit.

The whole argument was specious. The most famous headline Ogilvy ever penned, and of which he was inordinately fond, was for Rolls-Royce: "At Sixty Miles an Hour the Loudest Noise in the New Rolls-Royce comes from the electric clock." That was highly unlikely, more an exaggeration than a proven or provable fact, given all the conditions under which even a Rolls might be driven. Interestingly, the fictional ad executive Finnegan, meaning Elia Kazan in the novel *The Arrangement*, suggested that Ogilvy really couldn't be serious about the accuracy of his slogan.[64] But his *Confessions* showed otherwise: he was deadly serious, and this was Ogilvy's version of a fact. There were other, similar instances of what seem in retrospect a wilful blindness to reality. Ogilvy touted the truth of his Visit USA campaign, where he told Europeans that a week's expenses need only amount to £35. He claimed that figure "was arrived at after careful verification" (55). Thus, one copywriter checked into a New York hotel where satisfactory rooms were available at $6 a night! You might well ask just what was deemed satisfactory, if the room was sufficient for a family, or whether that family could afford to eat as well as sleep. Critics apparently did charge that the £35 was ridiculously low. But Ogilvy quoted in rebuttal one German financial paper which praised this "very *truthful* campaign" (57). At bottom what trumped any criticism were the spectacular results: eight months into the campaign French, British, and German visits to the USA had increased by roughly a quarter to a fifth over previous totals. "The proof of the pudding was in the eating," he recalled (57). Again, truth was a very flexible property and could include a certain amount of fiction – as long as that fiction proved effective. Did that mean Ogilvy was either deluded or suffering from a nasty case of self-deception when he presented himself as a truth-teller? Not quite: Ogilvy adhered, in practice, to a utilitarian brand of ethics where consequences mattered, a moral stance that has often enjoyed much support among scholars and the public. Ogilvy revealed he was a pragmatist, akin to the very hucksters celebrated and derided in the early decades of the century.

Had Ogilvy solved the adman's dilemma? Partly – when that dilemma was deemed an affliction. So he and his colleagues might well conclude. Perhaps that is one more reason for the book's success. Recall that the dilemma was a matter of perception. The *Confessions* was a story of achievement, of confidence, of satisfaction. Instead of the deceiver, the

adman (or at least this adman) was more of a truth-teller. Instead of
a seducer, he was a teacher. Instead of a charlatan, he was an expert,
someone a client could trust. Not just a hireling, he was also an entrepreneur. He had joined the owner class, which effectively lifted him out
of the PMC and, ironically, away from the majority of agents who would
remain employees. Ogilvy might admit to some difficult moments, especially the anxiety of the Pitch, worrying that his British accent might
damage the agency's case. He might emphasize the persistent sense of
insecurity which bedevilled his profession. But there was none of the
guilt that troubled some of the fictional admen or adwomen. Furthermore, the *Confessions* neatly finessed the ambiguous or hybrid status of
the figure of the adman: he was both a dreamer and a technician whose
utility to business and society drew upon his contrasting skills. Ogilvy had
effectively updated the mythos first propounded by writers such as Barton, Hopkins, and Calkins. The adman was indeed a biopolitical figure
who worked to build the wants that fostered the good life. "Dear old John
Burns, the father of the Labor movement in England, used to say that the
tragedy of the working class was the poverty of their desires. I make no
apology for inciting the working class to desire less Spartan lives" (196).
There was proof of the adman's import in the saga of modernity – and in
the building of the affluent society.

In later years Ogilvy's connection with advertising changed dramatically. His agency thrived, not as a creative hot shop, but as an established
mainline company. Nor did Ogilvy retain his stature as a wizard, perhaps
because he was more a man of words than images, and television was the
big advertising story of the 1960s. Others took his place in the adworld
as great innovators. He resigned as chairman of Ogilvy & Mather in 1973
and left the United States to retire to an estate in France, from whence
he still endeavoured to direct agency affairs. But he did not alter his
views about advertising substantially, although his years in Europe seem
to have sharpened his disenchantment with the practices of America's
commercial television system. During the course of the interview with
Heffner, Ogilvy made much the same kind of points as he had made
earlier about the disappearance of the huckster, the well-mannered sell,
his distaste for clutter and political advertising, and his objection to puritans. In his new manual *Ogilvy on Advertising* (1983) he also reflected
on how wrong-headed was the continued low repute of advertising, and
thus of the adman, both of which he deemed mostly honest and forthright. "Few of us admen lie awake nights feeling guilty about the way we
earn our living," he wrote. Opinionated, engaging, and full of lists and

aphorisms, that manual proved popular, as had his *Confessions*. Not so
his attempts at a renovated autobiography, first *Blood, Brains and Beer*
(1978) and an updated version, *David Ogilvy: An Auto-biography* (1997),
which his own biographer judged a "flop." Little matter: his *Confessions*
was counted a classic in the list of must-read books of the profession fifty
years after its initial publication. Ogilvy's fame as The Compleat Adman
remained assured.

Only for a generation would the adman appear so significant as a key
character in the ongoing saga of modernity and the management of
business. Nonetheless, the chronicle of struggle would prove a persistent narrative about the adman, the adwoman, and persuaders in general throughout the rest of the century and beyond. Ogilvy's *Confessions*
alone could not dispel its appeal. His book had demonstrated how an
awareness of the adman's dilemma could work to constrain the inevitable recourse to deception. Ogilvy's well-mannered sell, his devotion to
reason-why, his warnings against dishonesty: all were indications of how
the spectre of this dilemma served as a social mechanism to protect the
regime of truth. But the clash between the attendant moral discipline of
the mechanism and the directions to exaggerate and fabricate mandated
by the industry was a burden some admen, at least in fiction, found too
difficult to bear. The narrative captured what seemed the essence of that
ambiguous and conflicted figure. And it suited the widespread notion
that modernity had produced a serious unsettling of the self. Obviously
the figure of the adman fitted well into this modern drama.

4

A WORRISOME DOMINION

Mitch, you're a youngster, only star class a short time. But you've got power. Five words from you, and in a matter of weeks or months half a million consumers will find their lives completely changed. And you know the old saying. Power ennobles. Absolute power ennobles absolutely.

– Fowler Schocken in The Space Merchants, 1953[1]

Fowler Schocken was an adman supremo in a science fiction novel by Frederik Pohl (who had worked as a copywriter, and thus a renegade of sorts) and Cyril Kornbluth. "Mitch" was Mitchel Courtney, a star class "copysmith," one of Schocken's bright boys. Both men were privileged beings living in a future America where ad agencies were now the wealthiest and most influential firms in the republic. The resulting dystopia was imagined as a rigid hierarchical society where a small elite, sometimes called "executives," enjoyed the good life and reigned over a huge mass of "consumers," who suffered much deprivation, trash products, and hard labour. Businesses waged a brutal warfare to gain control of industries and economies – the immediate goal was a whole planet: a virgin Venus. But what made *The Space Merchants* stand out was its depiction of how advertising had become a loosely regulated and highly aggressive instrument of governance. Schocken's comment, only a reversal of the famed assertion by Lord Acton, was meant to celebrate the sense of command enjoyed by the copywriters of the future. These admen were firm believers in "Freud's brain" (and the novel did employ a bit of the vocabulary of psychoanalysis), people who long ago had tossed away the appeal to reason. Now they used a barrage of inescapable ads, constant repetition, evocative language and images, sex and death messages, and various tools of biological control to program the unconscious of consumers, or as Schocken put it, to redesign "a world's folkways to meet the needs of commerce."[2] They had spiked common products, such as cigarettes or a coffee substitute, with addictive substances to further enslave this hapless public. Over-population and hyper-consumerism threatened to exhaust the earth's resources, so the main opposition came from a movement of "Consies" or "Conservationists," who were the target of constant repression. Here was a nightmare of advertising as a technology fashioned by a totalitarian regime of biopolitics which foresaw the complaints of a later generation of environmentalists regarding the ill-effects of promotion and persuasion. *The Space Merchants* proved a critical success and, purportedly, sold well in many languages.[3] The book was very much an action novel of the standard type, and its ending, where Mitch and the forces of decency triumphed, was a bit lame. Presumably what worked was the social satire, because that certainly exploited common fears. The underlying reason for the book's success was the prevalence in the postwar years of another set of stories, about the dominion of advertising, linked to the popularity of a revived wave of anti-advertising. It was this narrative of harm that emphasized the social and economic centrality of the adman in the making of modern America, or at least the making of its ills.

1. The New Narrative of Harm: Vance Packard, *The Hidden Persuaders*, 1957; *The Status Seekers*, 1959; and *The Waste Makers*, 1960

"I cannot think of any circumstance in which advertising would not be an evil."[4] That observation is attributed to Arnold J. Toynbee, one of the most famous historians in the anglophone world, and especially in the United States, during the postwar era. Toynbee was celebrated because of his superb history of world civilizations which, despite its erudition, sold widely, at least in its abridged editions. Perhaps he never actually said this. But the sentiment of disgust expressed here certainly coincides with Toynbee's thoughts on the modern world. In 1961 at Williamsburg, Virginia, he vigorously condemned the machinations of Madison Avenue.

> In the Western world of our day, the tempter's role, which in St. Francis' personal history was played by the saint's father, is being played, toward our society as a whole, by everything we sum up under the name of Madison Avenue and all that this label stands for. A considerable part of our ability, energy, time, and material resources is being spent today on inducing us

to do hard labour in order to find the money for buying material goods that we should never have dreamed of wanting if we had been left to ourselves. The first assault on the cupidity that is in every one of us is made by Madison Avenue by finesse. The strategy is to try to captivate us without allowing us to be aware of what is being done to us. If this sly approach does not do the trick, Madison Avenue has further psychological weapons in its armory. If all else fails, it will resort to sheer bullying, and it will carry this, if necessary, to the third degree. Now this is the inner adversary with whom we heave [*sic*] to contend. And, just because he assails us from within, he is more formidable than any external opponent. And often we externalize our opponent when he is really within us. *I would suggest that the destiny of our Western civilization turns on the issue of our struggle with all that Madison Avenue stands for more than it turns on the issue of our struggle with communism.*[5] (my italics)

Toynbee went on to declare that advertising was both un-Christian and un-American. Christ would have rejected "this skillfully engineered besetting temptation." So too would the Founding Fathers, since "disposing of the maximum quantity of consumer goods was not the purpose of the American Revolution. What is more, it is not the true end of man."[6]

These comments certainly captured the attention of pundits inside the media and the adworld, especially that blast about the destiny of the West. Although extreme, Toynbee's outburst signified the new surge of anti-advertising that had already seriously challenged the legitimacy of persuasion and specifically the advertising industry because it assumed the unfortunate dominion of the adman. The revival may have emerged later, in the realm of polemic rather than of fiction. But the revival swiftly proved exceptionally vigorous – and popular. It had something to do with the extraordinary advance of commercial television, which had conquered American homes in the 1950s. According to Erik Barnouw, the historian of American broadcasting, by 1957 already forty million homes, 85 per cent of the total homes in the USA, were viewing an average of five hours of TV every day.[7] That had meant a substantial increase in the amount of promotional noise in the domestic space and thus in the private life of Americans. It was much harder to avoid the commercials in an ongoing TV show than the ads in the pages of a newspaper or magazine, or even on the radio, because the television engaged the senses of both sight and sound.[8]

But the revival of anti-advertising had more to do with the success of the effort to build what Lizabeth Cohen called "the consumers' republic."

And success it was: she has pointed out how the United States entered a boom time of prosperity after the war like never before.[9] The exercise of power almost invariably provokes some form of resistance, however.[10] This biopolitical project designed to organize American life around the practice of mass consumption threatened the values of people, and most especially members of the intelligentsia, on both the Left and the Right, who found the materialism of the era both offensive and dangerous. Some portion of their criticism focused on Madison Avenue, the source of so much of the propaganda that conditioned and celebrated the kind of American Cohen has labelled the "purchaser as citizen," whose satisfaction of personal wants purportedly benefitted the nation.[11]

This second wave of anti-advertising, as Toynbee's comments revealed, was emphatically moralistic in character and tone. The political critique of advertising as the voice of capitalism, evident earlier in the works of Helen Woodward and especially James Rorty, had receded somewhat, though it had certainly not disappeared in the rhetoric of all critics (witness the case of Herbert Marcuse, author of *One-Dimensional Man*, a 1964 polemic). The old concern about truth and deception remained, of course: that was a hardy perennial. The affliction of the adman's dilemma remained largely in the background rather than at the forefront of these texts, however, because the focus was more on advertising than on its personnel. The greater concern was now over just what Madison Avenue was doing to the individual souls and the culture of Americans, an alarm Rorty had raised in the thirties. It rested on the widespread assumption that the advertising men had refined or developed new techniques of mind-control rooted in the social sciences, and in particular in psychoanalysis. Two motifs, offshoots of the adman's dilemma, became prominent during this second wave of anti-advertising. Critics took up again the notion of the matrix, that web of deception which surrounded the hapless public and which originated on Madison Avenue. More importantly, these writers elaborated the motif of the ad-maker's sin, something previously apparent in some criticism (for instance in the work of Chase and Schlink) and most pronounced in Rorty's *Our Master's Voice*, but now pervading the social conversation. The ad-maker's sin held the advertising practitioner responsible for the assortment of social and moral ills critics believed the consumers' republic suffered. For a time this new narrative of harm appeared likely to prevail in the social conversation.

The first entry was an initially obscure work called *The Mechanical Bride* (1951) by a Canadian professor of English, Marshall McLuhan.[12] At the time McLuhan could be counted one of those angry highbrows who seemed so vocal in intellectual circles in North America, and who railed against the vulgarity and debauchery of mass culture. McLuhan was also something of a Freudian, or at least he adopted the right pose and some of the language to psychoanalyse the United States. He did this chiefly by using magazine advertisements to unpack what his subtitle called the "Folklore of Industrial Man," a novel technique which enabled him to explore imaginatively the assorted myths, dreams, and habits of what he recognized was a consumer society. The adman was one of the villains of this tragedy: McLuhan presumed a duopoly of Madison Avenue and Hollywood which poured streams of "illusion and falsehood" (vi) into the supine minds of Americans. "Gouging away at the surface of public sales resistance, the ad men are constantly breaking through into *Alice in Wonderland* territory behind the looking glass which is the world of subrational impulse and appetites" (97). Never before, apparently, had people been subjected to such a massive campaign of commercial education. In the course of his often bizarre collection of exhibits – there were fifty-nine chapters with titles such as "Love-Goddess Assembly Line" or "The Tough as Narcissus" – he touched upon all sorts of subjects, such as the erotic sell, planned obsolescence, programming the unconscious, the matrix, the dream world, even the rule of the market researcher (a particularly amoral creature) that would exercise later critics. For the moment, though, *The Mechanical Bride* was largely neglected, selling only a few copies.[13] Later, however, when McLuhan earned so much fame as the guru of the TV age, the book would receive much more attention, despite the fact that its author had turned away from his initial mix of highbrow anger and Freudian presumption.[14]

David Potter's *People of Plenty* (1954) was a far different work, although both innovative and imaginative. Potter was much more the regular scholar, a noted historian and something of a conservative from a Southern background. He had set out to explain the singularity of the American character because of the effects of economic abundance, a material condition he argued had determined the nature of the national experience. The one key institution of that abundance was advertising, a subject he dealt with at length in a chapter. He noted in passing that the villainy of the adman had been "a favourite theme for a full quorum of modern satirists, cynics, and Jeremiahs" (167). But Potter was only interested in the way advertising had conditioned the culture, especially the shift from the emphasis on production to consumption. "It dominates the media, it has vast power in the shaping of popular standards, and it is really one of the very limited group of institutions which exercise social control" (167).

Unfortunately, unlike, say, the school or the church, the advertising agency had no redeeming social purpose, no moral imperative to improve humanity. That, he observed, was why its influence caused so much concern. He regretted that advertising worked always to advance materialism, to create wants and often to stimulate the sentiments of envy and emulation (here reflecting Veblen). But his most interesting critique focused on the way advertising had taken control of the mass media (outside of books and movies), which harked back to the exposé of Samuel Hopkins Adams fifty years earlier. Newspapers, magazines, and broadcasting had become vehicles primarily geared to attracting an audience, "not to engage the mind" (182), but to sell the eyes and ears of people to advertisers. The result was to fabricate a mass culture that was too full of pap (not a word he used though) and conformity and too lacking in controversy and difference. Altogether the dominion of Madison Avenue operated "to make the individual like what he gets – to enforce already existing attitudes, to diminish the range and variety of choices, and, in terms of abundance, to exalt the materialistic virtues of consumption" (188). Potter clearly feared that the unchecked influence of advertising had perverted America.[15]

By contrast the young journalist Walter Goodman did focus on the strange attitudes and ways of the adman in his exposé *The Clowns of Commerce* (1957). Here he collected a range of loosely connected essays, some of which had appeared in national magazines in previous years, all of which were highly opinioned but mostly lightweight. Absent was much discussion of actual ad-makers, perhaps to avoid legal problems, so the admen emerged as a bizarre breed of humanity lacking any moral substance. It was, he mused, "a profession that has so little in common with the elemental concerns of humanity" (30). It was also a profession beset by angst, and here Goodman echoed the messages of the persuader fictions: the adman was engaged in a "relentless war with his client, his public, his product and himself" (274). Running through Goodman's commentary was a sense of the absurdity and triviality of brands, such silly things that required so much time, energy, and talent to build and maintain. Deception always reigned, anything might be claimed of a brand, when the imperative was to sell. Anyway the adman was portrayed as an agent of corruption whose work served to degrade the language, business, politics, consumption, television, and thus life itself. "The adman's influence only begins in his actual advertisements; like a fetid stream, it seeps from its pages in the magazine, its spot on television to cloud the surrounding waters" (236). The admen "almost single-handed" had made conspicuous consumption "an obsolete vice," instead now an enduring characteristic of American life (236). Goodman's book excited some people in the advertising community. But it had only a small presence in the social conversation, in no way comparable to Mayer's more substantial and specific *Madison Avenue, USA*, and one that did not last, perhaps because it was in press when a blockbuster, *The Hidden Persuaders*, came out.[16]

Vance Packard (1914–96), another journalist, mounted the first popular assault on advertising and the adman, outside of the realm of fiction anyway, in the postwar era. It was the equivalent of *The Hucksters*, if a decade later. At the end of the 1950s, Packard produced a remarkable trilogy of bestsellers, each of which focused on the problems of abundance and affluence. The books were full of detail, stronger on diagnosis than cure, and lacking much theory which, after all, might bore rather than excite the mass of readers Packard sought. They contained a good deal of shock, anecdotes that startled or frightened, a dose of moral outrage over the state of modern America, especially the machinations of authority, and the occasional soothing comment to forestall despair. It was rare that a social critic had so successfully exploited the anxieties of the times. *The Hidden Persuaders* (1957), his first and most successful effort, stood at the top of the bestseller lists for roughly a year. And its success lasted: the book went through forty-five editions and had sold about three million copies by 1975. *The Status Seekers* (1959) stood atop the lists for four months, and stayed on the lists for a year. *The Waste Makers* (1960), the most radical of the critiques, only managed a few weeks at the top but registered on the lists for six months. Packard became one of the most widely read nonfiction writers in America – and the appearance of foreign editions expanded his audience, especially in Britain and Europe. These works added phrases to the American language, notably "the hidden persuaders," which served as much as the earlier term "the hucksters" as a label for ad-makers, public relations counsels, and marketers. Packard not only became very prosperous – it is estimated that he earned $180,000 from *The Hidden Persuaders* in its first year – but he also became a minor celebrity who gave lectures, appeared on television, wrote magazine articles, won awards, and received admiring letters (plus a few negative ones) from fans. That launched him on a long career as one of America's small collection of popular social critics, although his later work never attained the fame and notoriety of his initial trilogy. When he died in 1996, he was best remembered for these early polemics.[17]

Packard was a liberal and a moralist who drew inspiration from an idealized vision of a rural and small-town America that now existed only in an imagined past. He espoused a brand of individualism that distrusted the power that various elites – business, politicians, admen, experts – exercised over the common man and woman. His judgment of the ills of the consumers' republic reflected a sometimes all too visible nostalgia for the moral and social virtues, and the people, of an earlier America. Yet that nostalgia signified a bedrock of beliefs that served as his ideology. His chief biographer Daniel Horowitz claimed he was a believer in a producer ethic (as against a consumer ethic) that emphasized authenticity, the simple life, hard work, civic responsibility, personal independence, self-restraint, widespread property ownership, and the distrust of the big and the distant. More succinctly, the historian Jackson Lears called Packard a champion of "plain living and plain speech,"[18] making him akin to those moralists who had taken Barnum to task so long ago. (Even though, when he succeeded, as some critics groused, he lived very well indeed.)

Packard came by his nostalgia honestly. He had grown up on a farm and then in a university town, when his father took on a job at the research and teaching farms of a college. At Penn State he acquired a taste for both journalism and social science, earning a BA and later a Master's degree at the Columbia Graduate School of Journalism. Soon after he entered the world of big-city media, eventually becoming an accomplished writer for magazines. There he learned about the ways and significance of advertising, and chafed against the restraints its supposedly pernicious influence imposed on his writing. Like many a journalist he came to share the common animus towards the huckster and his ways – the adman was always something of a rival to the reporter.

In 1956 the collapse of the *American Magazine*, his main employer, forced Packard to go fully freelance. He needed a popular work – even better: a bestseller – to avoid financial disaster. He picked a topic on advertising that he had first tackled for a piece commissioned by *Reader's Digest*. That had never been published, at least in part so he suspected because the magazine was then seeking advertisers. *The Hidden Persuaders* proved the most sensational of the trilogy because it exploited the fears of brainwashing (though he never used that term) that seemed so widespread in the Cold War atmosphere of the 1950s. Packard focused his attention on the rise of motivational research, or MR, an effort to apply the lessons of social science, and especially psychoanalysis, to the selling of goods, purportedly by programming the unconscious. A 1958 cover of the paperback, for instance, was full of leading questions: "What makes us buy, believe – and even vote – the way we do?"; "Why men think of a mistress when they see a convertible in a show window?"; or "Why women in supermarkets are attracted to items wrapped in red?" A British edition of the same year outlined a man's face, putting a red dot between his eyes, which became the target of a large, stylized, zigzag, black arrow, all to suggest the assault on the mind. A later Canadian cover featured a ripe red apple attached to a fish hook and line to signify the seduction of the innocent, or was it the ignorant, in a variant on the Adam and Eve myth. Each of these images announced the book as an exposé of some sinister conspiracy at work in the modern world.

MR was only the most recent expression of a project to apply the techniques of psychology to understand how to get consumers to respond to ads. That project had begun back at the beginning of the century when Walter Dill Scott and other scholars produced their studies of psychology and marketing. Packard paid no attention to this history. He argued that the postwar boom had produced so much abundance that advertising had to find a new way to compel Americans to consume much more than they needed. He focused on the postwar efforts of men like Ernest Dichter and Louis Cheskin, both of whom figured prominently in *The Hidden Persuaders*, to sell to corporations and advertising agencies their services as marketing experts who knew how to stimulate consumers. He relied heavily upon the testimony of these self-promoters and their willing clients (like Weiss and Geller, otherwise a small Chicago agency) to fill his book with all manner of bizarre anecdotes. He regaled readers with stories of tests to see what kind of "crazy" person (paranoid, sadist, etc.) heavy drinkers preferred to be, or how menstruation determined the buying moods of women, or what was "the sensuality and sexual connotations of pens" (97).[19] Many of these stories were trivial or just plain silly, but some were a good deal more sinister, such as when Packard explained how the admen and their MR experts had targeted girls to ensure they became good consumers. Further, he argued that MR had spread into public relations and even politics, notably the 1956 national elections, where it was used by partisans to discipline the electorate. Perhaps most frightening was the prospect of its future sophistication: he imagined that, say, by 2000, the "biophysicists" would have created "biocontrol," where the populace was somehow wired up so that electrical signals could determine "mental processes, emotional reactions, and sense perceptions" (220–1). There was something a bit contradictory about all this piling on of examples: clearly Packard was both fascinated

and repelled by the ingenuity of the motivational researchers. At one
level the book might be read as a guide to the wacky behaviours of family, friends, and neighbours: was that avid gardener really searching for
a pregnancy substitute and did that smelly man really take pride in his
body odour? At another level Packard's book became a manual of MR, a
kind of advertisement for this fad, something Ernest Dichter recognized
when he wrote a "Dear Vance" letter to Packard in 1958.[20] The fact was
that Packard exaggerated the popularity of MR in advertising circles,
where it always remained controversial and contested.

In Packard's telling, MR was an amalgam of Freud and Pavlov plus
a dash of Riesman.[21] What he variously called "motivation analysts,"
"depth boys," "symbol manipulators," and "professional persuaders,"
thereby incorporating market researchers and advertising personnel,
were engaged in expensive efforts to speak directly to the unconscious
of Americans. He itemized the various tools, mostly drawn from psychoanalysis and psychology, that were used to plumb this subconscious: the
depth interviews, projective tests such as Rorschach or TAT (Thematic
Apperception Test), storytelling or psychodrama, lie detector tests,
hypnosis, and "subthreshold experiments" (later called subliminal persuasion).[22] What he thought was so dangerous was that the resulting messages were masked, or rather "hidden," from the logical centres of the
mind. The advertising men did this by exploiting the power of images,
colours, symbols, and such to communicate directly to what a Freudian
might call the id. These hidden messages sought to exploit the appetites and flaws of humanity, people's fears of loss or embarrassment, the
sin of envy, the sex drive, the yearning for indulgence, and so on. They
intended to establish triggers that would lead the dazed woman in the
supermarket or the awestruck man in the showroom to buy – irrespective
of need or value. "Typically they see us as bundles of daydreams, misty
hidden yearnings, guilt complexes, irrational emotional blockages. We
are image lovers given to impulsive and compulsive acts. We annoy them
with our seemingly senseless quirks, but we please them with our growing docility in responding to their manipulation of symbols that stir us
to action" (34). All of which Packard saw as an attack on rationality. The
overall effect of this new advertising was to encourage the irrational and
the impulsive in human nature, to demean humanity. Much of MR, he
added, "seems to represent regress rather than progress for man in his
long struggle to become a rational and self-guiding being" (34). He concluded his polemic with a chapter entitled "The Question of Morality,"
where he asked in a series of leading questions about how any of these

efforts to manipulate the public could be considered right. What especially disturbed Packard, what seemed so completely immoral, was the insidious invasion of "the privacy of our minds" (240). He concluded his book by declaring the sanctity of the individual soul, the need to protect the right to privacy.

Two years later *The Status Seekers* debunked what Packard saw as the prevailing myths of classlessness and upward mobility as mass delusions. He drew heavily on the work of sociologists to draw portraits of class divisions, and to a lesser extent the differences of race and religion, which separated Americans into distinct communities and strata. Since Americans were no longer able to rise in the increasingly rigid class hierarchy, they or at least a significant number of status-seekers strove to buy their way upward. He found Americans caught up in a frenzy of emulation à la Veblen, seeking to enhance their status by consuming wildly and, so he felt, needlessly. It was yet another instance of artifice over authenticity, keeping up appearances. Once again, the adman was to blame, at least in part. Packard called the admen "merchants of discontent" because they worked to exploit the "upgrading urge" (182).[23] They endeavoured first of all to stoke the fires of status anxiety. Then they strove to persuade people that acquiring that fashionable set of living room furniture or "a new swept-wing Dodge" (185) would demonstrate their social superiority. The problem was not just that such campaigns were false promises: Packard, no more than Veblen or Chase before him, could never accept the virtues of conspicuous consumption. The problem was also that such deception must ultimately provoke social unrest, especially in the event of a depression, when the status-seekers found their supposed social achievements were hollow – and their personal insolvency real. He even concluded his critique of the adman by quoting the peculiar outburst of an actual ad-maker, who had claimed that advertising "has done more to cause the social unrest of the Twentieth Century than any other single factor" (188).

The assault on the advertising was actually more extensive and intense in the final polemic. *The Waste Makers* was by far the most radical of Packard's commentary on the consumer society because he reinterpreted modern America, and again in ways similar to Wells and Veblen and Chase before him, as a society of waste; in short, a dystopia. To his mind what other commentators might call abundance Packard thought too easily became glut. The problem was that economic growth could only continue under the present system if the public was somehow compelled to consume to excess. "The way to end glut was to produce gluttons" (43).

The tragic answer was "planned obsolescence" and above all the "obsolescence of desirability." Too much of the corporate world had purposefully
shed the priority of utility to fashion shoddy goods that soon broke down,
a betrayal of that producer ethic Packard espoused. Businesses used the
imperative of style, changes in fashion, and the tyranny of the new to convince the public to discard whatever they owned as quickly as possible in
order to buy the latest goods. The result was increased personal debt and
public poverty, the rise of business oligarchies, air and water pollution,
the exhaustion of resources, the trashing of the countryside, and dependence on foreign sources of raw materials. This line of argument could
enable Bill McKibben, a later Green sympathizer, to count *The Waste Makers* as prescient and Packard as an environmentalist *avant la lettre*.[24]

Despite what logic might suggest, Packard once again blamed the
admen much more than the business chiefs for the prodigality of the
era. Admen, he argued, had become the masters of the economy and
the culture of America:

> As advertising men have found themselves with more and more billions
> of dollars at their command, they have moved into a role of considera-
> ble power in influencing the behaviour of the entire populace. They have
> become to a very large extent masters of the nation's economic destiny,
> and perhaps the nation's most influential taste makers. They have become
> dictators of the content of many if not most radio and television programs,
> judges with life-and-death power over many periodicals, and at least co-
> designers of many products being offered to the public. (228)

Packard even cited David Potter to justify the claim that advertising had
emerged as a major social and moral institution in the past generation.
The trouble was that the adman's rule did not serve to improve human
nature. Instead the admen had fashioned "the all-pervading smog of commercialism in American life" (319), in other words a matrix from which
there was no escape. Rarely before had the public been bombarded by so
much promotional noise, "a fairly constant siege of hard sells, soft sells,
funny sells, sly sells" (217). Pity the hapless public: "Millions of consumers are manipulated, razzle-dazzled, indoctrinated, mood-conditioned,
and flimflammed" (250). But what so disturbed Packard was that the
admen acted in effect as ideologues, and here he argued a case that
recalled James Rorty's attack on the adman's pseudoculture. Admen not
only designed campaigns to sell specific brands, Packard asserted.
They were, above all, conscious agents of materialism who manufactured

"a love for possessions and a zest for finding momentary pleasures. They sought to encourage Americans to break out of their old-fashioned inhibitions and to learn to live it up" (164). The aim was to banish any lingering puritanism, to boom hedonism, and to foster new wants, all to ensure the persistence of consumption and growth. It was the work of admen as immoral advocates that threatened to debauch the American soul. Here was a full-blown diatribe against the ad-maker's sin.

Yet at moments in his trilogy Packard excused or even exonerated the adman and advertising. In *The Hidden Persuaders*, for example, he admitted that a majority of admen and other promoters "still do a straightforward job and accept us as rational citizens (whether we are or not)" (36). He recognized that advertising contributed to both the prosperity and to the enchanting, the colour, of American life. In *The Waste Makers*, he even suggested that he intended "no villains in this book" (23) because most Americans were wastrels at heart. Perhaps Packard hoped thereby to avoid criticism that he was too one-sided or biased? But the sincerity of these declarations seemed doubtful given the overall thrust of the trilogy. Whatever restraints an awareness of the adman's dilemma might impose on the conduct of the ordinary advertising practitioner, and in times past, now had little effect on the ways of the MR wizards. Packard had resurrected the old fear of the evil deceiver who employed artifice and seduction to mislead and manipulate. Like Rorty before him, though much more successfully, Packard had portrayed the adman as the master of deception and the corruptor of American life. *The Hidden Persuaders* argued that the newest breed of admen had unfortunately learned how to fashion tools that so deceived the mind that the faculty of reason was damaged or even denied. They might claim that they sought to find out what the consumer wanted; but in reality they were determined to program the consumer's unconscious. *The Status Seekers* and even more *The Waste Makers* claimed that the adman's dominion had perverted the course of American civilization by promoting materialism, the obsession with consumption, and a society of waste. It was all a betrayal of the promise of America.

Such a charge, of course, was not new. Much of what Packard argued about clutter, the matrix, artifice, materialism, and even "psychological marketing" (*Hidden Persuaders* 211) had been "discovered" as it were by an earlier generation of scolds and critics. (Goodman as well wrote on MR and especially about Ernest Dichter.) Packard had managed to write up these claims in a fashion that was easy to read and, apparently, convincing to many people. But what he contributed to the mix of anti-advertising was the evidence that the advertising man had refined a more compelling brand of deception than ever before. Previously it might be presumed that an individual could discount the lies or counter the half-truths or exaggerations, or challenge the masquerades of the hucksters, even if he or she could not altogether evade the plethora of ads. All that was required was an aware and sceptical public, able to detect the con. But now Packard had seemingly exposed a sinister and masked conspiracy to establish an unrecognized dominion over the thoughts, senses, and actions of individuals. The new breed of admen had moved beyond the lie. "You" could not escape the efforts of these hidden persuaders. They had science on their side, most especially the tools of psychoanalysis. Their messages entered the subconscious in ways that the ego could not readily discern. They influenced behaviour, even compelled certain acts, over which the conscious mind had little control. They deceived the ego, which assumed it exercised its own will. The true horror of the conspiracy was that "you" would never know "it" had succeeded. The individual could not know she or he was a victim. Once it was claimed that there was no place to hide from all the clutter; now Packard suggested it was becoming impossible to resist the power of the adman. That was an assertion of dominion.[25]

Overall, the scholarly community was not much impressed by the analysis and the tone of the trilogy, according to Daniel Horowitz.[26] But some public intellectuals did listen. A.C. Spectorsky, for one, found *The Hidden Persuaders* fascinating and frightening.[27] The Williamsburg address of Professor Toynbee seemed to bear the marks of Packard's revelations about the nefarious activities of the adman. True, only one other writer, Samm Sinclair Baker, followed up with a detailed critique of the adman's immoral ways. Baker was an ex-adman and mystery novelist, not an academic but a renegade, whose *The Permissible Lie* (1968) charged his onetime colleagues with constantly practicing deceit by recording "only those 'facts' that praise the product and ignoring reality that includes negative facts," making advertising a species of "*untruth*."[28] More to the point a wider range of authors, some academics, did launch assaults on advertising, where the adman appeared as some kind of villain, which proved far more innovative and popular than Baker's revelations. What was especially striking was both how divergent were the politics and how common the moral outrage of all these critiques when they contemplated the ad-maker's sin.

First came a liberal screed (of sorts): John Kenneth Galbraith's enormously successful book *The Affluent Society* (1958), which spent roughly thirty weeks on the *New York Times* bestseller lists. In a new twist of the hackneyed charge of excessive materialism, Galbraith presented an America suffering from "private opulence and public squalor," where social needs were sacrificed to satisfy individual wants (191).[29] Such a tragic imbalance, he surmised, was a result of celebrating private goods over, say, education, parks, roads, clean air and water, and similar public goods. People wanted low taxes to ensure they could use wages to spend lavishly on satisfying their own and their families' desires. Advertising played a crucial role through what Galbraith called "the dependence effect." For the supposed wants were neither natural nor genuine. They were designed by business to ensure production and eliminate risk. He wrote about the "synthesis of wants," the "manufacturing of demand," and the process of "want formation" (127), all attributes of the effort to construct the consumers' republic. He thought advertising worked to fan the fires of emulation (there was more than a hint of Veblen here), to compel people to acquire more and more products. He lamented how "every corner of the public psyche is canvassed by some of the nation's most talented citizens to see if the desire for some merchantable product can be cultivated" (194). The adman manufactured a never-ending wave of desire that drove the consumer boom to the great advantage of capitalism, if not to the public or America. Madison Avenue, as one critic asserted, now represented the same "hosts of Lucifer" who had tempted a long-suffering humanity in times past.[30] He and other commentators soon charged Galbraith with both an elitist intent and a puritanical zeal that sought to regulate life. Not without cause: Galbraith obviously thought many of the wants of his fellow citizens were frivolous and their purchases a source of waste, not comfort. But the burden of Galbraith's animus against Madison Avenue was the way its messages served to deceive the American public about the definition of the good life. Its success suggested that some considerable segment of the reading public suffered a sense of guilt over how the consumer society allocated resources to privilege the fortunate at the expense of the commonweal.[31]

Next came a bestseller by the historian Daniel Boorstin, *The Image* (1961), more of a conservative diatribe against "the menace of unreality," itself the product of deception, illusion, and untruth, now afflicting American life (240).[32] "The shadow outsells the substance," he intoned in one of his many asides. "The shadow has become the substance" (133). His was a story of cultural despair and moral decline occasioned, so it seemed, by the advance of mass communications, of which advertising was only one agency. Now Boorstin thought the problem lay with a flaw in the American character. "If there is a crime of deception being

committed in America today, each of us is the principal, and all others
are only accessories" (260). That condition of moral error attendant on
the adman's dilemma was now universalized – everyone was afflicted.
If anything, he blamed the "whole American tradition of pragmatism,"
from Benjamin Franklin on, for "a consuming interest in the appearances of things" (212). He specifically objected to the search for actual
villains: Madison Avenue might be a common "whipping boy" but the
advertising men were merely one of the "acolytes of the image" (204), "at
most our collaborators, helping us make illusions for ourselves" (205).
Even so, persuasion and the adman in Boorstin's saga of modernity did
play a major role in the degradation of the American psyche. *The Guardian* (1 March 2004) recalled *The Image* as "a brilliant and original essay
about the black arts and corrupting influences of advertising and public relations." Boorstin cited the case of P.T. Barnum as the first advertiser to discover "how much the public enjoyed being deceived" (209).
He devoted a lot of space to the claim that "the rise of advertising has
brought a social redefinition of the very notion of truth" (289), "from an
emphasis on 'truth' to an emphasis on 'credibility'" (212). "God makes
our dreams come true," he mused. "Skillful advertising men bring us our
illusions, then make them seem true" (212). They had befuddled "us"
with what he termed "their peculiar truths" (213). And yet "we" enjoyed
it all, "we" were fascinated not just by the deception but by "the stage
machinery, the process of fabricating and projecting the image" (194).
In effect Boorstin had located deception and self-deception at the core
of modernity.

Not that his book was always read that way. Much later the media
theorist Douglas Rushkoff argued, in a new preface to *The Image*, that
Boorstin had identified the key innovation of Madison Avenue in the
postwar world: how the adman fashioned a mythical landscape of brands
to master our conscious and unconscious understandings of life.[33] Perhaps so, except as in the case of Galbraith before him, Boorstin's work
was more an assertion than a proof of the way advertising had worked. It
captivated audiences then and later because it presented anew that idea
of an overarching matrix which distanced the public from reality and
experience and conditioned it to accept the rule of elites. "We" were lost
in a fake world of simulation.[34] Advertising, if not alone, had made "us"
that way.

The same kind of assumption about the adman's dominion underlay the third strike against Madison Avenue, Betty Friedan's *The Feminine Mystique* (1963). Here the guiding ideology was neither liberal nor

conservative but feminist. Once again the core problem was rooted in the effects of deception: in a later introduction, Friedan emphasized how she and the women she knew had been "living a lie," one perpetuated by men, by experts, by the media, and by institutions.[35] That lie was "the feminine mystique" which served to imprison women in the home as wives and mothers whose yearnings for creativity and significance were satisfied by the false promises of consumption. Friedan explicitly denied that this was the result of some sort of economic or male conspiracy against women. But, as in the case of Packard's or Boorstin's denials, the thrust of her argument suggested otherwise. She pointed out how educators, psychoanalysts, magazine editors, social scientists and others had fashioned and propagated this ideology of subordination. In a chapter entitled "The Sexual Sell" (which in the light of later linguistic developments might better be called "the gendered sell"), Friedan identified the persuaders, in particular the market researcher, as key villains who had used flattery and threat to discipline and oppress women to suit the needs of capitalism and patriarchy.[36] They certainly seemed to be moved by a kind of malevolence: here the force of misogyny had triumphed over whatever limits on deception the mechanism of the adman's dilemma might impose on Madison Avenue. "The manipulators and their clients in American business can hardly be accused of creating the feminine mystique," she declared. "But they are the most powerful of its perpetrators; it is their millions which blanket the land with pervasive images, flattering the American housewife, diverting her guilt and disguising her growing sense of emptiness" (228). Madison Avenue was at the centre of a massive postwar propaganda campaign "to give women 'prestige' as housewives" (255). She ransacked the records of motivational research to show how time and again women were sold a pack of illusions, the myth of "happiness through things" (219), to assuage their ambitions or protect their looks or advance their status. "How skillfully they divert her need for achievement into sexual phantasies which promise her eternal youth, dulling her sense of passing time" (228–9). Perhaps the worst crime was how "our girls" had been indoctrinated by commercials, advertisements, and magazines – "we sacrifice our girls to the feminine mystique" (231). The popularity of Friedan's book ensured that the adman would often be viewed as the evil deceiver during the rise of the so-called second wave of feminism in the late 1960s and early 1970s.

Like Galbraith and Boorstin before her, Friedan did not actually assess the advertising campaigns she condemned. None of the grand critiques of advertising, not even Packard's, devoted much attention to the actual practices of advertising. A number of other writers, however, did probe how advertising had become a peculiar and sinister language of domination and deception. The esteemed Aldous Huxley in *Brave New World Revisited* (1958) warned how the admen used "verbal or pictorial symbols" and even music to condition the mind of the public. "Orpheus has entered into an alliance with Pavlov – the power of sound with the conditioned reflex."[37] Although little interested in advertising per se, the radical Herbert Marcuse, perhaps the most famous of that strange crew of Freudo-Marxists and a major philosopher of the New Left, did explore publicity in *One-Dimensional Man* (1964) as one prominent expression of the compacted, authoritarian style of discourse which had served to close down discussion and encourage submission.[38] In his case, mind you, the motif of the ad-maker's sin was harnessed to a condemnation of the ruling classes of the consumers' republic, particularly the capitalist elite. Similarly the English Marxist art critic John Berger in *Ways of Seeing* (1972), a famed book and a BBC documentary, explored how advertising men had appropriated the devices fashioned during the centuries-old tradition of oil painting to design a language of images, or manufactured sights, resting on the technology of colour photography, to program the mind. "One may remember or forget these messages but briefly one takes them in," he exclaimed, "and for a moment they stimulate the imagination by way of either memory or expectation."[39] What they did was to add glamour to brands and what they encouraged was envy, a besetting social sin in the affluent West. A bit later another feminist did what Friedan had not: Jean Kilbourne collected and analysed the images admen used to stereotype, and thus harm, women as juvenile, sexy, irrational, submissive, and the like. First in a series of illustrated lectures and then in an oft-shown documentary, *Killing Us Softly* (1979), she indicated how advertising constituted a language of patriarchy which demeaned and supposedly disciplined its victims.[40]

Yet the most successful and outlandish of these exposés were two sometimes (unintentionally) funny bestsellers by Wilson Bryan Key, *Subliminal Seduction* (1973) and *Media Sexploitation* (1977).[41] Together with yet a third effort, *The Clam-Plate Orgy* (1980), Key's exposés sold around a million copies.[42] After roughly a decade this great promoter, an American but in the early 1970s a journalism professor residing in Canada, had earned much money and lasting notoriety by revealing "the truth" about subliminal persuasion, that is, signs and stimuli which were unrecognized by the conscious or logical centres of the brain.[43] He built upon an earlier scare in the late 1950s, briefly referenced by Packard, to argue that subliminal messages, generally in the form of embedded words or images, were now swarming throughout the media, infecting not just ads but news, movies, record covers, just about everything – "There is literally no escape" (SS: 81). He filled his books with statistics and pseudoscientific commentary, drawing on celebrities such as McLuhan, Freud, even once on Marcuse, to pretend his was a scholarly work. Key presumed everyone had a dynamic unconscious which missed nothing, and an unconscious which was especially prone to remembering signs that were salacious or forbidden or frightening. This enabled the hidden persuader "to ruthlessly exploit the desires, needs, fears, or anxieties which function uncontrollably within each human being" (SS: 8). "Madison Avenue account executives actually brag about planting subs [subliminal messages] which, they claim, no one will be able to find" (MS: 165). Key "proved" his wacky case by offering close readings of ads where he "found" raunchy or profane words, erect penises and moist vaginas, as well as death symbols. A gin ad might be full of SEX embeds or phallic symbols, the ice cubes hiding messages that only an eager subconscious could easily see – though a trained viewer might be able to detect some of the elusive signs. Somehow all this "dirty" stuff worked to enhance the appeal of the brand, creating a lasting, "strong emotional relationship" (SS: 29) between a brand and a drive like sex or death. Key had proposed that the adman (among others) had refined a new way to deceive the always-hapless public by exploiting a human vulnerability, namely a technique to directly and invisibly communicate with an irrational unconscious that usually ruled behaviour. He thought this massive assault on the rational mind was unhinging North America, creating mass neuroses and psychoses that threatened the mental health of the population. Whether many people believed such nonsense was immaterial, since the books offered entertainment and guidance: North Americans discovered a new parlour game, a test of one's imagination, that required they decode magazine ads in search of the hidden embeds.[44]

However eccentric Key's views, his books did express two themes often present in this wave of anti-advertising. The first was a kind of cultural and moral despair about the state of America. Key occasionally proclaimed that an excess of self-indulgence afflicted the United States, even worrying that his country was "trapped in a rapidly accelerating spiral toward self-annihilation" (MS: 215). Certainly Packard was not the only critic who evinced a nostalgia for an earlier or more innocent America. Potter felt America had suffered a moral decline just as advertising became so potent an authority. The original subtitle of Boorstin's polemic had been *What Happened to the American Dream*, which embodied the sense of loss, his belief that America had fallen from grace, which had pervaded *The Image*. Galbraith's argument sported a kind of rural disdain (albeit with a puritanical touch) for the values of the urban and affluent society. Friedan's assault was directed in part at the consumer ethic whose imposition had vitiated the promise of the supposed emancipation of women earlier in the century. The point is that all these critics thought the postwar celebration of mass consumption, the worship of things, demonstrated the onset of a sad and dangerous reign of materialism that subverted some just moral order.

Since advertising was deemed one of the main culprits, the adman and his associates could only be the villains in this story of decline. That presumption highlights the second theme of conspiracy. Key left no doubt there was a conspiracy, even if he seemed a bit confused over exactly who were the conspirators – the advertising agencies, the government, maybe just the CIA and the FBI, big business, even social scientists – and when they began to work their dark magic: was it just after the war or in the past fifteen years? Before him, Marshall McLuhan, Walter Goodman, and Samm Sinclair Baker had in a similar fashion put much blame on admen for the corruption of America's soul, though the last two also saw these admen as victims of the very system of advertising. Goodman and Baker, perhaps as a result, imagined that the affliction of the adman's dilemma upset the spirit of advertising people. Most of the other critics carefully avoided declaring there was any actual conspiracy. Galbraith mocked this cast of mind in his marvellous review of persuader fiction. But the figure of the adman still embodied the forces of deception that plagued America. Packard, Huxley, and Friedan damned market researchers because they had fashioned tools of stimulation that were so patently evil. Kilbourne actually stigmatized advertisers, presumably admen and their clients, as "America's real pornographers" because she thought their practice of the erotic sell could be "hard core."[45] Both Galbraith and Boorstin found in Madison Avenue a powerful cause of the dystopia they feared America was becoming. Clearly so did Toynbee. The point here is that the adman, whether knowingly or not, was engaged in a conspiracy against a virtuous America.

Both of these themes were reworked in the last popular expression of the harm narrative, Christopher Lasch's *The Culture of Narcissism* (1979).[46] Once more, the book proved a bestseller (although it only stayed in the top ranks for seven weeks), its fame no doubt enhanced when Lasch was invited to Camp David to advise President Carter over what became his notorious "Crisis of Confidence" speech in July of 1979.[47] Lasch was another noted historian, but also, again, a moral and social critic who in his case drew upon Freudian ideas of human nature. And, as before, the discussion of advertising (mostly in chapter 4) was only one part of a larger hypothesis, in this instance about the breakdown of the family and the rise of a disordered self, about an America where a new pathology of narcissism afflicted masses of people. What worried Lasch was a loss of authenticity, of genuine forms of love or community, despite all the rhetoric about self-fulfilment.

Even so, he appeared to sum up so much of what had been said before about consumption and advertising: his suspicions of affluence recalled Galbraith, his strictures on public language sounded a bit like Marcuse, his upset over the power of images drew on Boorstin, his worry about envy evoked the concerns of Berger. Lasch mixed conservative and radical views, questioning for example both feminism and capitalism. He referenced two French critics of modernity, Jacques Ellul on propaganda and Guy Debord on the society of the spectacle, to support his belief that dystopia was nigh.[48] Lasch railed against "the propaganda of commodities" (a term actually employed much earlier by the radical sociologist C. Wright Mills) because that celebrated possessions and encouraged alienation, diverting the citizens from significant political action. Deception was so rampant that the line between truth and falsehood was hopelessly blurred. "Truth has given way to credibility, facts to statements that sound authoritative without conveying any authoritative information" (74). He thought advertising promoted a false liberation of women and children, "only to subject them to the new paternalism of the advertising industry, the industrial corporation, and the state" (74). He lamented that psychiatry had become "the handmaiden of advertising" (164) to better discipline its victims. He presumed, like Toynbee, that Madison Avenue was the great authority that had shaped the sad moral state of the nation:

In a simpler time, advertising merely called attention to the product and extolled its advantages. Now it manufactures a product of its own: the consumer, perpetually unsatisfied, restless, anxious, and bored. Advertising serves not so much to advertise products as to promote consumption as a way of life. It "educates" the masses into an unappeasable appetite not only for goods but for new experiences and personal fulfilment. It upholds consumption as the answer to the age-old discontents of loneliness, sickness, weariness, lack of sexual satisfaction; at the same time it creates new forms

of discontent peculiar to the modern age. It plays seductively on the malaise
of industrial civilization. (72)

Whatever the originality of the rest of his hypothesis, very little of his
critique of Madison Avenue would have struck a consistent reader of the
screeds of anti-advertising as novel. Nor would that hypothetical reader
have learned much about the actual practices of the advertising industry:
like so many of the critics, Lasch had eschewed any analysis of specifics
to indulge in grand generalizations. But perhaps the very familiarity of
Lasch's argument attested to how embedded such views had become in
the social conversation.

Disdain for the adman dominated the intellectual terrain. Hardly any
outsiders had a good word for Madison Avenue. There was eventually
one exception: Jerry Kirkpatrick, a professor of business, wrote the only
sustained answer to this second wave of anti-advertising. His *In Defence of
Advertising* (1994) was a singular work of advocacy based on Ayn Rand's
philosophy of Objectivism and the economic thought of Ludwig von
Mises.[49] He did consider advertising a beneficent force, resting his argument on a version of the old progress myth. But much of his polemic
was devoted to charting the ignorance or stupidity of the assorted foes
of advertising, few of whom actually appeared in his text (outside of Galbraith and Key), especially their collective lack of a proper understanding of philosophy and economics. He had little to say about the figure of
the adman, other than to generalize occasionally about the ways or aims
of marketers. Such an eccentric work had no apparent impact on the
social conversation, other than as a curiosity.[50] The adman had to look to
his fellows for any succour.

2. Stories of Justification: The Ad-Makers' Polemics and Memoirs, 1944–1975

Ogilvy was not alone in writing his memoirs in 1963. Many other advertising or marketing types, some women but more often men, wrote books
meant, at least in part, to justify advertising and the adman to the public.
Here they countered the charges explicit in the motifs of the adman's
dilemma and the ad-maker's sin. Here they elaborated variants of the
motifs of the businessman's ally and of the consumer's friend to render
their profession reputable. At times they drew upon the widespread currency of the virtues of the planned consumers' republic to strengthen
their case. In all, these books constituted works of rationalization that

sought to explain, advocate, defend, validate, and condone. They drew upon, as it were, the inheritance of the adman: the notions, the axioms, and the claims made by Hopkins, Calkins, and the many other apologists and champions from the 1910s and 1920s.

Some of these books took the form of surveys and polemics. One popular introduction, *This Fascinating Advertising Business* (1947), employed the motif of industry's engine, and in an imaginative fashion, to establish just how crucial the adman was to the American economy:

> Instead of calling this a behind-the-scenes view, we might say the book provides a look under the hood of a big motor truck, representing American business, of which advertising is the electrical system. Certainly advertising supplies the spark that makes the whole machine run. Often it is also the self-starter. Advertising provides the lights that enable folks to see the machine, as well as helping those inside to steer a straight course. In its ability to retain the good will of present customers and to add new ones, advertising is both the storage battery and the generator of business.
>
> And who can deny that it is the *horn?*[51]

Ogilvy's onetime brother in law and long-time rival, Rosser Reeves, one of the most prominent of copywriters and executives at the Ted Bates agency in the postwar era, wrote a bestseller entitled *Reality in Advertising* (1961) that, like Hopkins's work nearly four decades earlier, trumpeted the science of advertising as the key to economic success. Ernest Dichter, the infamous wizard of commercial psychology, strove to answer critics like Packard and Galbraith in *The Strategy of Desire* (1960), where he touted promotion, publicity, and especially his version of motivational research (MR), as the tools necessary to make America and the world a much better place.

Perhaps the strangest of these efforts, though, was a collection of essays with the intriguing title *The Huckster's Revenge* (1959) and subtitled "The Truth About Life on Madison Avenue," by the retired advertising executive Fred Manchee. The front cover sported the image of a businessman with sword and a metal helmet preparing to do battle. Purportedly "the huckster's revenge" was also the title of a successful polemic Manchee had already written – except he hadn't, the polemic was just imagined, likewise its success, both serving as a useful (if slightly deceptive) ploy to bring together what he had actually compiled. The essays were full of anecdotes, reflections, and maxims inspired by his thirty years at the famous BBDO agency (once dubbed "Bunco, Bull,

Deceit and Obfuscation" by no less than Harry S. Truman, as Manchee admitted).[52] These were provoked, so he claimed in his brief biographical entry, by the fact the ad business had become "the butt of so much ridicule and unfair criticism in recent years." (Although he took issue with both Packard and Galbraith, Manchee was especially exercised by Walter Goodman's *The Clowns of Commerce*.) The blurb on the front cover promised instead that "The Huckster's Revenge depicts the sunny side of advertising and documents its truth." That it tried to do, though the result was more banal than stimulating, particularly because he filled his pages with encomiums to colleagues. Apparently virtually everyone in advertising, of both genders, was honest, hard-working, congenial, friendly, understanding – even the wives. Manchee's quips were so mild they could hardly exact any revenge on the culprits that caused his sense of grievance. *The Huckster's Revenge* served more as a sign of the dissatisfaction of advertising people with the prevailing stereotypes of admen and advertising in the social conversation.

But most of the advertising writers and executives who chose to respond employed some version of life-writing, either autobiography or memoirs. That began when James Webb Young, a noted copywriter and later executive with J. Walter Thompson, published a collection of his columns from *Advertising Age*, a major industry magazine, as *The Diary of an Adman* (1944). Subtitled "The War Years June 1, 1942–December 31 1943," the *Diary* tracked Young's doings and musings over an eighteen-month period. They fashioned the impression of a humane, thoughtful, and creative soul who relished his work but who also sought relief on his country estate, an impression which apparently pleased his fellow advertising confrères. Soon afterwards, Earnest Elmo Calkins, by now thoroughly retired, re-launched his earlier autobiography (with revisions and additions) as *"and hearing not – ": Annals of an Adman* (1946). Then came *Adventures in Advertising* (1948) by another heavyweight, John Orr Young, who had co-founded the Young & Rubicam agency back in the 1920s. Young was an escapee who had left advertising for public relations many years earlier. He was not a renegade, though: his account of the adworld was suitably favourable. Over the next twenty-five years a diverse group of writers chronicled stories of triumph: the advertising woman Bernice Fitz-Gibbon (1951), the author John Gunther in a biography of the legendary ad executive Albert D. Lasker (1960), two damaged ex-admen Milton Biow (1964) and Jim Ellis (1968), the direct-mail wizard Maxwell Sackheim (1970) and the ad agency executive Fairfax Cone (1969), and two legendary creatives, Draper Daniels (1974) and Shirley

Polykoff (1975), much later the purported models for Don Draper and Peggy Olsen in the TV drama *Mad Men*.[53] Even the polemics by Dichter and Reeves drew heavily on their own experiences to fashion arguments about the realities and the promise of persuasion.

On the surface these memoirs etc. seemed to conform to the standard conventions of the genres of life-writing. They were full of tales of past battles, of strivings and successes and achievements, of building a business and of building America. Sometimes the apologists made reference to what had swiftly become a classic of advertising advocacy, Neil Borden's *The Economic Effects of Advertising* (1942), a thoroughly academic work which however cautious its claims was widely interpreted as proving the social and economic benefits of advertising.[54] They tied their stories of individual triumph to the wider sagas of business, of modernity, and of the nation and even democracy. Like Ogilvy, the apologists linked the mission of advertising to a self-serving variant of the myth of progress, where the admen worked to bring about the utopia of a consumer society. Gunther concluded, twice, of Lasker that "he helped revolutionize the marketing of goods and contributed substantially to the increase in the American standard of living that distinguished the first half of the twentieth century" (14). Perhaps most exuberant, though, was the outburst of Bernice Fitz-Gibbon: "What's more, despite its many maligners, advertising is the noblest pursuit of all. Sure it is. Our free-enterprise system hangs on the creation of wants, and on satisfying these wants. Advertising keeps the wheels of industry turning. When you can do good for the nation's economy and at the same time do well for yourself, that's the perfect life work" (14). Dichter went a step further when he counted the adman and the market researcher as the key makers of a future paradise of wonderful goods and happy people. That was the ultimate promise of motivational research.

Memoirs, autobiographies, even some biographies lay claim to a particular form of truth, where the text becomes testimony, the result of witnessing. The first two genres rest upon what's been called "the autobiographical pact," in which the author affirms to the reader that the story is about a real person and his or her actual experiences.[55] Their force rests on the authenticity of memories and records. But the testimony usually amounts as well to a form of special pleading where the storytelling asserts the personal significance and the moral probity of the subject. Life writings represent a series of "rhetorical acts" that seek to vindicate or justify as well as to explain and dispute.[56] Much may be hidden: reading Milton Biow's autobiography, for example, would not reveal how a financial scandal effectively destroyed his once-prominent agency.[57] And the argument can swiftly become tendentious: Jim Ellis used the last chapter of his memoirs to settle old scores, since he saw himself as the victim of a coup that forced him out of the presidency of the Kudner agency. The adman chronicles, moreover, posed a particular difficulty because the personage in question had been so closely identified with the practices of deception, recalling the plight of Barnum. Thus the notice of Fairfax Cone's very sober memoirs published by *Kirkus Reviews* (13 November 1969), often the source of tame comments, wondered whether anyone outside the industry would be willing to believe his devotion to high ethics. In short, the stories of triumphs (and some failures) written by advertising people necessarily laboured under a deficit of credibility due to the currency of the huckster stereotypes their life writings endeavoured to counter.

All of the works, polemics as well as memoirs, sought to combat in one way or another what they deemed was the false view of advertising and of the ad-maker. It was all a conspiracy by outsiders, perhaps the cultural elite, who just didn't know what advertising was. Apologists blamed an assortment of villains: New Deal zealots (James Webb Young), professors and teachers (Harry Lewis Bird), some unspecified "thought leaders" (Woodrow Wirsig), the "ivory tower" (Fairfax Cone), and always novelists and Hollywood.[58] "As I well know, if you want to write a best seller about the advertising business," lamented Jim Ellis, "the surest way is to turn the spotlight on one little corner of the business, in which case you can portray it as a racket or a rat race – a racket in which you 'succeed without really trying' or hypnotize people into buying things by the black art of using 'hidden persuaders' – or a rat race conducted by harassed hucksters, flirting with ulcers and coronaries, busily cutting each others' throats in the canyons of Madison Avenue" (11). Often the apologists charged the critics of advertising with elitism, seeing them as highbrows who wanted to lord over the American people. Apparently this intelligentsia just did not recognize the legitimacy of the desires of the public for the good life. Thus the apologists wrapped themselves in the garb of democracy: anti-advertising became a conspiracy against the common man.

The apologists might share some of the complaints of the critics. "It is true that, for romance, advertising has tended to rate brassières and dentifrices above charm and wit," lamented John Orr Young in a discussion of materialism. "It is true that fear psychology is still too liberally used to sell many things that should not be sold that way. It is true that a great deal of subtlety is used to extend appetites for things for which appetites should not be whetted" (124). Walter Weir in his *Truth in Advertising and Other Heresies* (1963) sympathized with those who objected to so much clutter, since he thought too many ads in print and on television were "monstrous inanities" and "bores" (167). Cone was indignant over the flood of what he thought were irrelevant and insulting ads on television. But the apologists were not prepared to give any credence to the charges of a Galbraith or a Packard that advertising programmed the public. "They are imputing to their 'ad-man' an occult, evil power of legerdemain and persuasion," charged an outraged Fred Manchee (viii). A number of writers made reference to the failure of the Edsel campaigns of the late 1950s, when heavy advertising by Ford failed to convince the public to purchase the new automobile. There was proof that advertising could not rule an unwilling public. It was Rosser Reeves, however, who most vigorously rebutted the claims that advertising manipulated or debauched the public, especially the notion that Madison Avenue had forced people to buy things or sponsored materialism. "Advertising men have no such Svengali power" (140). He mocked the idea of a gullible or simple-minded public, "a thick substratum of cement heads" who didn't know what they wanted. He thought both Galbraith's idea of the dependence effect and Packard's fears about motivational research were nonsense. *"Advertising does not synthesize desires. Desires instead synthesize advertising"* (141). Advertising only had power when it worked with existing desires to realize what people felt they needed or wanted. The true role of advertising was "to get business away from his competitors" (150). That was its importance to economics and to America. Indeed, "advertising is the voice of competition – the voice of free enterprise, in a free world" (152).

Likewise, the apologists denied the charges that the adworld was filled with clowns and rogues, unrepentant hedonists who enjoyed the high life thanks to ample expense accounts. Often they insisted that advertising, like any other business or profession, was full of ordinary folk subject to the normal pressures and desires of living in America. James Webb Young told readers he hoped his use of the term "adman" "connotes all the Diary pretends to be: just the plain account of a shirt sleeve worker, with a decent pride in his medium" (46). Neither in advertising nor in public relations, recalled John Orr Young, "have I found the boudoir adventurers and the alcoholics that Wakeman, for example, pictured in *The Hucksters*" – only hardworking, "fairly plain folk, given to an earnest pursuit of their specialities" (viii). Yes, admen might have a great capacity for fun – but they were usually as serious and committed a group as lawyers or doctors or any of the other professions.

The two women who wrote autobiographies questioned the stereotype of a special adwoman's plight circulated by persuader fictions. They did not deny the importance of gender. Both Bernice Fitz-Gibbon and Shirley Polykoff noted and regretted that advertising was chiefly a male domain. They hoped their stories would act as a guide and a manual, even an exhortation to young women to enter advertising. Fitz-Gibbon, who had been so successful in retail advertising, argued that copywriting was a "natural" occupation for women because they were masters of the domestic field, trained shoppers, and, above all, materialistic (which she regarded as a virtue). "After all, advertising is selling things. And it's the girls who are thing-minded" (281). Both had to struggle with the dichotomy of home and workplace. At home, Polykoff recalled, she had to minimize her career – and accept a lower salary so as not to threaten her husband's ego – while at work she had to pretend that she did not have a family which might claim her time and energy. But neither autobiography evinced any feminist streak, any complaint about how they were treated as women in this male domain.[59] Instead, they chronicled the triumph of two women who found in advertising a place to express their selves and realize their ambitions. "Looking back over a half century of my life in advertising (of course, I started in the cradle), I realize that in so many ways I have been a winner," wrote Polykoff. "Let me count the ways: I've achieved goals beyond those I set for myself; I've enjoyed the challenge of my work and have never been bored" (128).

Sometimes the apologists seemed to accept the notion of angst, that advertising was an unusually demanding and insecure occupation full of stress. That was certainly how John Orr Young recalled his early years at Young & Rubicam: just too full of excitement and anxiety, which provoked both depression and ill-health. "Agency people are continuously perched on the edge of anxiety," mused Fairfax Cone. "Will their recommendations be accepted or rejected out of hand? If they are rejected will the agency be given another chance, or will the advertiser turn to an eager competing agency?" (72). James Webb Young talked of the need for an escape, taking a sabbatical or finding a hobby – such as, presumably, his country estate. Apparently even his wife thought persuasion just wasn't "something 'real'" (167). Similarly, Ernest Dichter presumed the adworld suffered from an overdose of artificiality. "The increasing eagerness of advertising executives, for instance, to buy farms and take up cattle raising or apple growing on the side," reasoned Dichter, "is an

instinctive rebellion against a restricted existence" (271). John Gunther
saw Albert Lasker, for all his success, as a conflicted soul, often troubled
by doubts about his activities, even by a sense of guilt. By contrast both
Shirley Polykoff and Bernice Fitz-Gibbon seemed oblivious to this problem of angst, quite unlike that earlier adwoman afflicted with worries
and doubts, Helen Woodward. And although he admitted some of his
fellows suffered much anxiety, Draper Daniels claimed he had avoided
the ulcers and filled his memoirs with light-hearted yarns about people, their shenanigans and their campaigns, writing more in the comic
mode. Just as important, nearly all the writers paid attention to the joys
of advertising, the pleasures of working in such a creative enterprise.
James Webb Young inaugurated that theme when he spoke about the
highs he enjoyed while working furiously and effectively to prepare copy:
"Nothing like it" (116). Gunther claimed that for all his troubles Lasker
enjoyed "a rich, full, fruitful, and variegated career" (2). Manchee filled
his account with stories of people passionate about their work and convinced of its worth. At times it seemed these ad writers wanted to have
it all ways, to present their occupation as fulfilling and difficult, even
glamourous.

Nor did the apologists always agree on just what kind of creature the
adman really was. James Webb Young decided he must be a practising
social scientist, a specialist in human nature. Bird and Biow thought him
a natural showman. Cone denied advertising was either entertainment
or show business, proclaiming instead of his fellow executives that "a
more forthright group of businessmen would have been hard to find"
(171). But Rosser Reeves lamented that most advertising men were "still
necromancers at heart. They do believe in ghosts. They listen to voodoo
drums, whisper magic incarnations, and mix, in their potions, eye of
newt and toe of frog" (153). In reality, he suggested, they should realize
they were essentially salesmen, who needed to understand the science
of selling, and never artists, here repeating a maxim made famous by
Claude Hopkins a generation earlier.

That kind of confusion carried over into the way these apologists
approached the issue of deception. True, the most common conceit
remained the definition of the persuader as a truth-teller, albeit of a special kind. For a new edition of *Crystallizing Public Opinion* (1961), Edward
Bernays prepared a lengthy introduction that told the story of publicity
throughout the ages, starting in classical Greece. Bernays sought to link
public relations to the Enlightenment project where publicity ensured
transparency, the foundation of good government in the polity and

the economy. Even Woodrow Wilson got recruited: purportedly he had declared, back in 1912, "publicity is one of the purifying elements of politics."[60] Bernays outlined a renovated version of the progress myth where the persuader served the advent and maintenance of democracy. Writers as different as Bird, Fitz-Gibbon, Manchee, Cone, Weir, and Reeves all extolled the virtues of truth and denounced the persistence of dishonesty, suggesting that (as before, as always) the ethical practices of advertising were improving. According to Fitz-Gibbon, "advertising's standards of integrity are as high as or higher than those in banking or medicine" (296). "No one can afford to disregard or offend against truth or human sensibility," argued Weir. "And the sooner we come to that conclusion the better the advertising we can and will create" (49). Cone spoke out against both outright lies and especially half-truths, what he called "the weasel – a flaw in the promise that makes the proposition fuzzy" (6). "If it is true, you can say it," asserted Reeves. "If it is false, you cannot say it" (65). The bold claim was a bit strange coming from the mastermind of the Ted Bates agency, which had recently earned noto-riety for questionable and deceptive advertising. These injunctions, the commandment "never lie," bespoke the way the adman's dilemma acted as social mechanism to limit the practice of deception, at least in the realm of rhetoric.

But there were signs that the facade had begun to crack a bit. John Orr Young displayed real admiration for the wiles and ways of the huck-ster common years before, "a man of mighty words and foxy stratagems" (6), "a sort of honest dishonest man. He dearly loved to cheat the cus-tomer and he was free to admit it" (7). That was a safe enough aberration because the type was supposedly consigned to the past. Maxwell Sack-heim admitted that the ad stories he concocted many years ago to sell *Power of Will*, a manual on success, were "to some extent the products of my imagination" (77). Draper Daniels took pride recounting a successful campaign for a light Schlitz brew where the slogan was carefully crafted to mislead the not-too-bright drinker. "Real gusto in a great light beer" translated into "real guts in a great light beer" (247). Similarly Milton Biow outlined how his agency's campaign for Philip Morris purportedly fooled smokers about the non-existent soothing properties of the ciga-rette by touting the fact that its tobacco mix lacked an irritating ingredi-ent. Biow also explained how he had mislead a client into believing the idea behind a campaign was his own. "Try this strategy some time and see how it works. You're doing it for your client's good. That should clear your conscience" (34). Shirley Polykoff announced she had to undergo a process of self-hypnosis to convince herself of the compelling virtues of a brand before she could write effective copy. "If I can't convince myself, then I can't convince anyone else either" (73). Such comments recognized that deception and self-deception played at least some role in the arts of publicity. But none of these musings were intended to advocate outright lies or to justify some kind of duping delight.

Only Dichter, ever the iconoclast, was not at all concerned whether the adman deceived or not. This bad boy of the marketing business espoused an eccentric and at times contradictory philosophy of life based upon his understanding of psychoanalysis and his work in the exotic domain of motivational research. More than any other adman author, Dichter sought to identify the adman not just as the businessman's ally or the consumer's friend, but as the maker of the consumers' republic. First off, he argued that the one constant in the universe was unending flux: "change is the only permanent thing in life" (268). It followed that progress obeyed a higher law which encompassed all of humanity. Dichter's vision was strangely Victorian in character: "Human progress is the conquest of the animal within us" (13). The alternative was social and national decline – or perhaps communism. What really counted was conditioning people to accept, rather than fear, change. "Throughout this book, I have tried to stress the fact that growth and progress are the only possible goals of life" (282). Second, Dichter believed the whole of society was caught up in a web of self-deception, "the illusion of rationality" (115) which led people to kid themselves that they understood why they made any decision. Now in his Freudian guise, Dichter argued that all human conduct was rooted in the irrational ways of the unconscious, and most certainly when the consumer decided what to buy. Emotion reigned over logic. Combining these assumptions and the instruments of persuasion became central to the persistence of the American dream. "The techniques of selling, advertising, public relations, and motivational research are directly applicable, not only to commercial problems but also to those of a wider and more socially oriented purpose" (25). The overall goal of advertising was to foster "creative discontent" rather than "contentment" (15). The enemies of progress were satisfaction and puritanism: he urged the celebration of materialism where the public constantly sought new experiences and new pleasures. "Such an expansive life can be considered ethical not only from the point of view of the individual but also from that of society" (16).

Ernest Dichter had no doubt about the morality of the adman's rule. He deemed that rule a moral necessity. Elsewhere, especially in a dictionary of objects he published a few years later, Dichter distilled the knowledge he generated through years of MR research to explain how to sell almost everything to a programmed public.[61] Here he made clear his vision of a fragmented mass public where the consumers were actually clusters of people shaped by differences of experience, age, gender, education, or psyche that could be motivated using the right tools and appeals, especially by working on their desires. That put him at the forefront of the drive for what Lizabeth Cohen deemed a crucial instrument of the consumers' republic, "the paradigm of the market segment."[62] Dr Dichter espoused an elitism as pronounced as that of the critics, where people like this fine doctor determined what the public needed and launched campaigns to foster their compliance. It was for their own good, and for the nation's good, an extreme version of that motif of the consumer's friend. Dichter's brand of biopolitics clashed dramatically with Galbraith's: Dichter thought private affluence the key to social progress. But, like Galbraith or Packard, he fancied his style of rule was as firmly moral as they believed was their call to rebellion. As the *Kirkus Reviews* (9 September 1960) pointed out, whether the gospel according to Dichter was good or not, "a lot depends on who does the persuading." Dichter had turned the ad-maker's sin into the ad-maker's virtue: the adman became the necessary agent who would eliminate the unfortunate puritanical habits inherited from the past that prevented the progress of the future.

Dichter's "strategy of desire" was outlandish. It was also outrageous. Dichter had laughed off the worries over brainwashing by urging authorities to take up the psychological weapons designed by MR to remake the world. Rosser Reeves, for one, would have none of this nonsense: Reeves thought MR just mumbo-jumbo designed to seduce the ignorant. Although he did not mention Dichter by name, he did denounce "The Freudian Hoax" as well as the myth of the hidden persuader. Reeves's colleagues might be less contemptuous or less severe. But in any case they were not interested in arguing anew the cause of the adman as messiah in some updated version of Bruce Barton's bestseller. They seemed afraid to give any credence to a grand statement of the potentials of publicity. They presented advertising as no more than a legitimate and necessary tool of business, hardly an instrument of social or moral rule then. Reading their accounts it seemed as if the spectre of the adman's dilemma did act like a mechanism of restraint to constrain deceit, no matter that a modicum of deception might be licensed. Sometimes they liked to appear as businessmen themselves, meaning hard-headed and savvy entrepreneurs, and sometimes as professionals, men and women of high standards, who sold expertise to their clients. Underlying such claims was a yearning for a stable and reputable identity, free of the ambiguities and sins attached to their occupation in times past. Occasionally they even pretended they acted as representatives of the consuming public. Witness John Orr Young's variant on this old saw: "Well, my idea of public relations is simply that of representing the public at the management, or policy level" (132). And sometimes they shed the pose of modesty (though Reeves and Ogilvy never pretended as much) to boldly assert their significance. Towards the end of *Adventures in Advertising,* Young produced a weird set of calculations whereby he could argue that some $48.8 million had been spent on advertising his copy over the years, which itself had generated $480 million in total marketing, which must have produced "several *billions* in sales" (198). That surely established his credentials as the businessman's ally. On a different note, Shirley Polykoff recounted how she had received letters from grateful women inspired by her famous Clairol campaigns: "one could begin to feel like a do-gooder" (39). That certainly made the case for her as the consumer's friend. All of which underwrote a common and satisfying conceit, that there would always be a need for the persuader, visible or hidden.[63]

3. The Public Speaks: R.A. Bauer and Stephen Greyser, *Advertising in America: The Consumer View,* 1968

Both the apologists and their critics had often made claims about what the American public thought about the persuasion industries, whether people believed the ads, how much they liked or disliked all that selling. Apologists, of course, mostly imagined this public was both sovereign and friendly, sometimes even eager to read ads; critics, and many a humourist, portrayed consumers as a hapless public easily bamboozled or manipulated by the adman. The rise of polling, especially after 1940, produced what seemed more certain evidence of how Americans viewed the industry, the ads, and the effects of advertising. The findings of these surveys, however, were ambiguous: they revealed that the public was able to endorse both the adman's narrative of progress and the critic's narrative of harm. In retrospect that apparent contradiction was the most significant result of the most elaborate survey of public opinion published in the postwar period, Bauer and Greyser's scholarly work entitled *Advertising in America* (1968).[64]

The 473-page tome was no bestseller, not even in academic circles. It was the child of an alliance between the American Association of Advertising

Agencies, a national trade association, and Harvard University's Graduate School of Business Administration, evidence of the linkage between the worlds of business and social science that became a topic of much concern in the late 1960s. The 4As, as it was called, had grown increasingly worried about the impact of all the anti-advertising rhetoric so common in the late 1950s and early 1960s.. They commissioned a study of American views by the Opinion Research Corporation to furnish members with information to inform a future public relations campaign in defence of advertising. They collaborated with two professors of the business school, which had always cultivated a close relationship with the corporate world. Twice before Harvard's business professors had produced important works on advertising: Ralph Hower's history of the Ayer's agency (1939 and 1949) and Neil Borden's famous *The Economic Effects of Advertising* (1942).[65] Stephen Greyser, then a junior faculty member, taught advertising at the school. Raymond Bauer was a well-known professor who had already published two major articles in which he questioned the wisdom of anti-advertising.[66] Two "research practitioners" from advertising agencies also served as representatives of the 4As during the preparation of the study. The book proclaimed its objectivity of course, but the project and its personnel were clearly sympathetic to the views of the advertising industry.

The research strategy was both extensive and sophisticated. Home interviews were conducted with 1,846 people who were asked their views on the saliency of advertising (how important the issue was to their lives), the overall phenomenon, and particular aspects of advertising. The sample was deliberately biased towards upscale individuals, this to ensure the survey captured the college-educated, presumably the most critical demographic, although the results were weighted to ensure no subgroup was over-represented in the results. The responses to some specific statement were measured on a five-point Likert scale: generally agree, partially agree, can't say, partially disagree, and generally disagree. In addition some views were sampled twice, as a positive and a negative (both "advertising is essential" and "advertising is not essential"), the findings then melded to produce composite figures. Most of the original group, 1,536 in fact, then participated in a counting exercise where they noted particular ads that they found annoying, enjoyable, informative, or offensive in a half day period. That led to a second interview to discover why people had noted certain ads and why they had classified these the way they did. There was even a second counting exercise where a small group only documented every fifth ad they came across. All of this endeavour generated a considerable amount of data, along with lots of supplementary statements from the respondents, about the institution, the content, and the effects of advertising.

The professors concluded that things were not nearly as bad as some advertising people had feared. True enough, the public believed the adman exercised an authority over life.[67] You could find evidence that some people were influenced by the motif of the ad-maker's sin. But you could also find support for the motif of the consumer's friend. There wasn't much evidence of any generalized kind of victim malaise among the respondents, though possibly that was because the survey didn't explore this matter directly. But people were certainly wary, having experienced too many ads that exaggerated or misled. Despite a lot of ritualized griping about ads and in particular commercials, most Americans did not believe advertising was an especially important issue in their lives or in the social conversation, at any rate not compared to religion, the federal government, or education. (Even professional sports ranked slightly higher than advertising.)[68] The actual counting revealed that people only noticed a small portion of the ads they were exposed to in the course of a day, and only responded to, meaning liked or disliked, a fraction of those.[69] The public, the authors presumed, was neither hapless nor compliant but aware, even obstinate, able to judge and resist the seductions of an ad.[70] Bernays might be right about obstinacy, but wrong about the lack of reason. Witness this collection of edited comments from some of the subjects:

"I appreciate it. I read all the ads I can find, watch commercials; I am interested in them" (92)

"I approve of advertising because if I need something I use advertising – that is my way of communication with new things" (93)

"I think some advertising is quite excellent, but some is not; I have seen commercials that make me *not* want to buy the product" (93)

"It's immaterial to me. It has not helped or hindered me one way or another" (93)

"I don't like false advertising – should have plenty in stock when they advertise it's available ... Too much advertising becomes like a broken record" (93)

"Their claims are far out and wild" (93)

Perhaps most importantly, Bauer and Greyser decided there was "a reservoir of good will" towards advertising, far larger than any "reservoir of generalized ill will" (95). Most of the respondents readily admitted the economic legitimacy of advertising since it was deemed essential to the proper workings of the marketplace, encouraged the development of better products, and raised the standard of living, all claims apparent in the industry's long-standing narrative of progress. As one respondent put it, "it is a must," and another, "It's a part of American business" (92). In his remarkable introduction, Ithiel de Sola Pool, a prominent MIT social scientist, declared that the perception that advertising was a necessary evil was not widespread.[71] Most women actually enjoyed ads, apparently. "To eliminate advertising would be to eliminate one of the pleasures, as well as one of the guides, of the American public" (xi).

Where the respondents dissented, or rather agreed with critics, was over the social and moral roles of advertising. People expressed much irritation with the volume, the repetition, the silliness, and the interruptions of advertising: it really was something of "an environmental pollutant" (135). One reason people deemed some advertisements "offensive" – for alcohol, cigarettes, some medicines, and female undergarments, for example – was chiefly (50 per cent) out of a "moral concern" that the product shouldn't be advertised or the ad itself was "bad for children" (223). There was in the comments of some respondents a definite disdain for the practice of selling. First, significant numbers agreed (wholly or partially) that advertising persuaded people to buy what they didn't need (73 per cent), thus ensuring the adman was seen as the chief promoter of the materialism that supposedly bedevilled American life. Second, many respondents charged advertising with often deceiving because it did not provide "a true picture of the product" (60 per cent), making the adman also an agent of untruth. Third, a sizeable proportion decided advertising commonly "insults the intelligence of the average consumer" (43 per cent), an affront in a democratic polity.[72] All of which would seem to lead to the conclusion that many people believed that the institution of advertising sometimes harmed society, that the adman too often subverted the moral order.

Even the authors recognized that this mix of opinion demonstrated Americans had a complicated view of advertising – and hence of the figure of the adman – despite their claim that so many viewed it favourably. In fact, on the evidence Bauer and Greyser supplied, the public view was a lot more contradictory and ambiguous, at times incoherent, than they seemed willing to admit. Less than half of the respondents (41 per cent) had a favourable view of advertising, almost as many a decidedly mixed feeling (34 per cent), and the rest were indifferent (8 per cent) or even unfavourable (14 per cent) to it. If almost nine in ten of the subjects agreed advertising was essential in one sample, then almost three in ten agreed it wasn't in another.[73] Large numbers of respondents seemed uneasy about offering a clear or decided opinion on some of the questions: 48 per cent admitted they could neither wholly assent to nor dispute the proposition that "advertising results in lower prices," and 45 per cent were similarly ambiguous when faced by the claim that "advertising results in higher prices" (461–2). When they actually categorized ads, the distribution was equally mixed: annoying (23 per cent), enjoyable (36 per cent), informative (36 per cent), and offensive (5 per cent).[74] Both the most enjoyable and the most irritating ads appeared on television, closely followed by radio, a sign of some kind of love/hate relationship with broadcasting. People said they objected to ads and commercials more because they were intrusive or insulting than because they were untruthful or offensive. But Bauer and Greyser thought the fear of deceit might underlie these views, even if not always cited.

Advertising in America included a summary of polls about attitudes towards advertising taken between the late 1930s and the early 1960s. These attitudes, Bauer and Greyser observed, seemed remarkably consistent and stable, the findings similar to the 4As survey and even a recent British survey. Perhaps so; but the anomalies were also consistent. Time and again respondents agreed that the adman's code of conduct was actually improving. But always large numbers, sometimes a majority, thought the ads they saw were misleading. Although most respondents in the 4As survey might think advertising was full of exaggeration, if not lies, still a majority believed that the adman's practices had improved over the past decade. There was a disconnect here, which Bauer and Greyser put down to changing "standards of judgement" (105) – an improbable observation.

Later surveys would clarify aspects of this confusing picture. It seemed the public was actually composed of clusters defined not by class or gender but by outlook: in one study, the authors talked about "the ambivalents, the skeptics, and the hostiles" who had very different attitudes towards advertising.[75] Bauer and Greyser had themselves found a small group of 15 per cent of respondents convinced that advertising was in desperate need of reform. By contrast, they found that black Americans were noticeably more favourable to the institution of advertising than whites. In addition, people drew a distinction between their personal use and the social impact of advertising.[76] "The major reason Americans

offer as to why people approve of advertising is its *informational* role,"
claimed Bauer and Greyser, "the fact that it tells about products and
services, their prices, and where to get them" (333). Later polls showed
that advertising was considered a sort of discounted speech, something
you could not wholly trust: there was ample evidence that Americans
approached ads with a mixture of belief and disbelief. They recognized
that "truth in advertising" was always a dubious property, given the pressure to exaggerate, if not lie. But they thought they could glean useful
information, and sometimes a bit of pleasure, from the blend of fact,
fancy, and fiction that was advertising.[77] What they wanted most in Bauer
and Greyser's day, supposedly, was a larger component of information.
Later, more respondents might opt for a larger dose of entertainment.

Bauer and Greyser clearly doubted that advertising enjoyed the degree
of influence over the life of America that critics might presume. So, in
practice, did much of the public. Except when it came to others. The
investigation found evidence of that complex of ideas I have called contagion and immunity, particularly the worry about infection. The people
at risk were their neighbours and their children. Americans feared the
impact of advertising on values, its subversion of truth and its temptation of the weak. Later surveys, for example, discovered that the public,
despite what the industry might say, believed that subliminal advertising was both too common and too effective.[78] Other studies indicated
that support for advertising waned over time, and that new social sins,
like stereotyping, caused increasing concern. The default position in the
1960s and later was to presume that the adman was both a seducer and
a deceiver.

It was, all in all, a peculiar form of dominion that the adman supposedly
exercised over the life of America. Critics blamed that rule for all manner of sins, of course, though their case rested more on speculation and
assertion than on proof. Sometimes it seemed the critic exempted most
ad-makers, damning only a few or the system of advertising or the nature
of America itself. The rule was both denied and affirmed by advertising people, who wanted social credit but feared social blame. It became
a commonplace assumption among the public, except it was also presumed that the rule worked not on the rational self. Such contradictions spoke to the reality not of hegemony, but of biopolitics, where a
specialized group of experts endeavoured to determine the conduct of
one important aspect of living, the practice of consumption, despite the
doubts and the disdain of the target population. Yes, to channel Foucault,

the purpose might be an administered economy in which goods moved rapidly from industry to the home; but the reality was otherwise, one in which many new goods failed and people often resisted the wiles of the adman. The notorious failure of the Edsel was signal evidence of that resistance. The public accepted the inevitability of the adman, and of his deceits, but lamented the volume, the loudness, the repetition, and the vulgarity of his advertising, though individuals might enjoy some of the messages and find others useful. Most important consumers filtered out a lot of the ads to which they were exposed. The actual making of the consumers' republic required a panoply of techniques such as government initiatives, laws and regulations, subsidies and tax policy, as well as the designs of marketing. Advertising was only one part of the mix. For all the noise, the worrisome dominion of Madison Avenue was much more myth than reality, a myth useful to critique the prevalence of materialism or of mass culture, especially among highbrows. The case points to the way a biopolitical enterprise could provoke both fear and resistance – and yet win acceptance.

5
THE GOSPEL OF CREATIVITY

Bill Bernbach stopped selling dreams and started selling the truth – wrapped in wit.
— Andrew Cracknell, 2011[1]

Flippancy was one cornerstone of the creative revolution; honesty was another.
— Jane Maas, 2012[2]

Slowly, and only partially, the figure of the adman was recast in the social conversation, both in fact and in fiction, during the decades after 1960. Initially the public relations counsel was little affected. But the adman, more and more the "ad-maker" because of the increasing entry of women into the ranks of the industry, was almost born anew. The adman was soon best labelled a "creative," a term which encompassed the copywriter and the art director. Of course the old version of the advertising man as a businessman or a professional, the once-celebrated account executive and the always-necessary manager: these never disappeared. Nor did advertising's version of the scientist, the market researcher, who in the shape of the account planner in the 1990s and beyond became increasingly important.[3] But in the refashioned agencies of the late twentieth and the early twenty-first centuries, the crucial dyad of copywriter and art director was put at the centre of the advertising complex, most especially in the realms of rhetoric and imagery. And the creative was deemed most akin to the artist, a personage, according to the romantic tradition, imbued with imagination who sought the original and the striking. There was precedent: the copywriter had constituted, at least since the 1890s, one of the more recognized types of advertising practitioners, although his colleague the art director was less often singled out. But now the stature of both jobs as "creatives" was raised above all other contenders. "The creatives are the ones who lay the golden eggs," claimed Peter Mead, then Joint Chairman of AMV BBDO, a British agency; "the account executives are the ones who have to go out and sell them."[4] What was called creativity soon became an imperative and an obligation, almost moral in force, which worked to justify the craft and the industry of advertising. That put the craft on the ground floor of a creativity boom which would sweep through Anglo-American society in a frantic search to celebrate and regularize the making of novel and useful ideas to solve a myriad of social problems.[5] Thus advertising entered its third age, the adman seeking (if not always with great success) to escape the revitalized stigma of the huckster.

1. Bernbach the Redeemer: "Adman's Adman," *Time*, 31 March 1958

In modern culture there was another realm of untruth which nonetheless overlapped with that which is and that which is not: the arts and letters, broadly defined to include painting, literature, drama, and its more vulgar offspring, mass entertainment. The realm of fiction grew massively during the nineteenth and especially the twentieth centuries. The flourishing of the arts and letters constituted the most obvious signal of a confusion about the exact divide between what is and is not. Fiction was not truth, except that one long-standing tradition of understanding in the arts claimed that paintings, plays, and novels may speak a truth about the human condition which the rigorous methods of science could never capture.[6] Fiction was not duplicity because users knew it did not correspond to reality, except that the arts did employ the techniques of deception, so they amounted to a kind of permissible lie.[7] Oscar Wilde penned a famous defence of lying as a manifestation of the liberated imagination which drove art ever forward: his target was the infection of realism which, he argued, had perverted the arts in the cause of truth.[8] Similarly, Nietzsche proclaimed, "We have art lest we perish of the truth": he too regarded the lie, more broadly untruth, as the source of a "life-advancing" and "life-preserving" force.[9] Nietzsche's proclamation reflected a notion that enjoyed wide currency in intellectual and popular circles, namely that the artist was a cultural hero who created novel meanings of life for the general mass of humanity.[10] Put another way, the artist worked to re-enchant a world suffering the dismal effects of too much modernity.

This kind of reasoning offered the adman a redefinition as an artist, particularly as a master of irony who imagined something dramatic or provocative, often in an amusing fashion, which "everyone" knew was neither true nor false.[11] Admittedly that was more of a stretch for public relations counsels or propagandists who typically had to adopt the pretence of the truth-teller. By contrast, admen could – and eventually some did, notably after the 1960s – glory in their own gospel of creativity which made of advertising a lesser form of art. It was a kind of truth claim that at least some portion of the American public would come to appreciate, if not always or all the time. It was also a method of realizing that quest for authenticity that drove the modern self: the artist was a fortunate soul who might achieve self-discovery, effect self-fashioning, and enjoy self-indulgence by pursuing the honoured cultural activity of imagining. At least the claim countered the puritanical thrust of a regime of truth, that element of moral disdain and moral command, for instance, that the reviewer David Bazelon had found so upsetting in Sisella Bok's work.[12] At best the claim might resolve the adman's dilemma. Artifice and authenticity were no longer at odds. Artifice or at least successful artifice became, no matter the apparent paradox, the instrument of authenticity.[13]

One man had pointed the way forward for the profession, or so it was argued. In a moment of timely exuberance, at the end of a century, when people were supposedly caught up in a mood of reflection, *Advertising Age* (29 March 1999), now the industry's premier journal, declared William Bernbach (1911–82) the most influential ad-maker of the twentieth century. That was no surprise: Bill Bernbach had already achieved the honoured status – and not only in the United States – as the grand redeemer, the genius who had led the so-called Creative Revolution which re-founded advertising.

By the end of the century the advertising community had acquired a sense of history and, more to the point, a pantheon of stars to buttress a sense of its significance. P.T. Barnum, the first successful adman, remained an ambiguous figure. Few would deny his stature, but he was no good model. His dubious reputation, his skill at deception, his supposed contempt for the public ("There's a sucker born every minute"), all this had tarnished his legacy.[14] Barnum was someone that the advertising people of the early and mid-twentieth century who strove for respectability as professionals and business types preferred to consign to the unfortunate past. That ill-repute had lingered on even as the community changed its declared ethos. Other later advertising men had won some lasting favour in industry circles, such as J.W. Thompson or Albert Lasker, who became leaders of top agencies and were thus remembered as builders of a new business. Then there were the stellar copywriters

Claude Hopkins, he of "scientific advertising," and Raymond Rubicam, a champion of creativity, both of whom were honoured for their mastery of the arts of persuasion. In the postwar era the two most prominent names were Rosser Reeves, a successor to Hopkins, and David Ogilvy, the great self-promoter, both earning great fame outside the industry as geniuses of advertising. Recall that both wrote bestsellers.

But none of these names, in the end, could match the acclaim, even the reverence, attached to Bernbach in the community of advertising people. In the beginning he was an outsider, a New Yorker, yes, but a Jew in a business then dominated by Anglo-Americans and suffused with mild anti-Semitism. Later commentators often noted how he lacked the looks and the style of the stereotypical adman, always remaining a decidedly ordinary man on the surface. He had gone to college, graduating from New York University with a degree in commercial science in that dismal year of the Depression, 1933. In a few years he managed to find employment in advertising as a copywriter, first at William H. Weintraub Inc. and later Grey Advertising (where he became a vice-president of art and copy), both designated "Jewish" agencies, which meant they had only a restricted list of clients. In 1949, however, he, a colleague, and a friend joined forces to launch their own initially "Jewish" agency, Doyle Dane Bernbach (although Ned Doyle was in fact an "Irish" account man). Bernbach masterminded the creative side of what was called either DDB or, strangely, just "Doyle Dane." During the next decade or so, DDB became ever more famous on Madison Avenue because of its imaginative campaigns for Ohrbach's (a low-cost department store), Levy's Rye Bread, El Al Airlines, and soon a wider range of clients including Polaroid, Avis, even American Airlines, but especially Volkswagen. The success marketing the VW Beetle, once dubbed the "Nazi car," made this "Jewish" agency especially famous. By the early 1960s "Doyle Dane" was widely regarded as the most exciting and creative agency in America, superseding Ogilvy & Mather. That reputation swiftly brought the kind of business success that was the golden measure of achievement in the adworld: by 1970, DDB (not in the top ten in 1960) was ranked the third largest agency in the country, with billings of nearly $325 million.[15]

Bernbach had elaborated a new philosophy and fashioned a new style of advertising that suited the taste of consumers and the needs of clients in the era of sixties affluence. In the process, he had trained a new generation of copywriters and art directors, hiring a range of young Americans from different ethnic backgrounds, notably Jews and Italians, and women as well as men, making DDB seem unlike the other leading agencies where Anglos predominated. He freed these "creatives," as they were now called, from the thralldom of the account executives and the plans boards, so the teams of copywriters and art directors could produce original and compelling art. They not only won ad awards, that other measure of achievement, but also soon broke free to set up their own creative "boutiques" (initially a term of contempt, soon an accolade), which carried on the good work Bernbach and DDB had launched. Very soon the established agencies began to follow suit, hiring new talent to match what DDB and the boutiques could offer clients. This, in essence, was the Creative Revolution, and Bernbach was its acclaimed leader.[16]

Bernbach began to win this acclaim as a revolutionary late in the 1950s. A brief report in *Time* (31 March 1958), suggestively entitled "Adman's Adman," neatly outlined what would remain the chief components of the Bernbach story.[17] The report began by citing the success of his agency, how it was "the fastest-growing ad agency on Madison Avenue." The shop he had created, DDB, was purportedly very different from its rivals on Madison Avenue. Bernbach emphasized not market and consumer research – the pride of the established agencies – but creativity, the search for the "great idea" which would move people. That often privileged the visual over the verbal, finding a simple but striking image, "a specific selling point that got across a message without a lot of talk." He broke with the long-standing tradition of emphasizing words, sometimes called the editorial-style advertisement, to showcase a picture of some sort, which was a more European practice, though the author of the *Time* report did not mention its origins. The result was a wave of clever and unusual ads which became "the talk of the town," or at least that part of New York enamoured of Madison Avenue.

> He made an obscure New York bread one of the city's best known with ads showing nibbled slices and the message, "New York is eating it up." Among the agency's other memorable copy: a plug for Israel's El Al airline's new, faster Britannia plane service, with a picture of the Atlantic Ocean one-fifth torn away ("Starting Dec. 23, the Atlantic Ocean will be 20% smaller"); its challenging ads for Ancient Age bourbon ("If you can find a better bourbon, buy it"); a Max Factor lipstick ad showing the Colosseum and a pair of fiery eyes staring from a Roman Senator's bust ("Any man will come to life when you wear Roman Pink").

No less startling was the fact that Bernbach broke with the resurgent huckster stereotype which had conditioned the public's understanding of the adman in the 1950s. He was no cynic, like the account executives that populated the persuader fictions of that decade. Nor was he a victim of the adman's dilemma and its attendant ills. Instead of subservience to the client's wishes, where an Evan Llewelyn Evans (to borrow Frederic Wakeman's fictional tyrant) determined the ad and the campaign, DDB demanded independence, the right "to run the ad account as it sees fit." Just as important, Bernbach eschewed the high life of lavish entertainments and much booze and fine clothes which a Jerry Webster (borrowing here the adman villain of *Lover Come Back*) so enjoyed. "I'm probably the only agency president who lives in Brooklyn," Bernbach argued, apparently a sure sign of a plain man leading a modest life. All of which was why, as Maxwell Dane boasted, Bernbach and his partners "don't have to be afraid of our clients." The fact that similar kinds of statements turned up in Martin Mayer's bestseller (also in 1958) would suggest that Bernbach's persona as an anti-huckster was as cultivated as, say, David Ogilvy's reputation as an aristocrat of advertising.[18]

Thereafter *Time* did not pay much attention to Bernbach or DDB. He was not featured on the famous 1962 cover of the issue that explored in depth the advertising industry, though he was mentioned in the actual story. *Time* did, however, refer to the "Bernbach Syndrome" (23 April 1965) as the "most successful" and "widely imitated" selling technique of the times. Five years later (16 February 1970), it called him the "ad world's most influential innovator" in an essay that touted Bernbach's claim that "honesty sells." Perhaps more gratifying was a cover story in *Newsweek* (18 August 1969), "Advertising's Creative Revolution," where Bernbach was able to assert that DDB had really begun "the revolution toward creativity in advertising," though he had to share the limelight with his rival David Ogilvy. A few years later, his agency had single billing in a special exhibition entitled "An Advocate Art: The Communication Advertising of Doyle Dane Bernbach" at the Parsons School of Design in New York.[19] He also received the praise of two younger advertising men, both self-declared innovators, Jerry Della Femina and George Lois, who in their memoirs (1970 and 1972, respectively) identified Bernbach as their mentor, the man who had remade advertising.[20]

But it was really after his death in 1982 that Bill Bernbach became something of a saint in advertising circles. In 1984 the advertising journalist Larry Dobrow published a celebration of sixties' advertising, a kind of art book displaying examples of that decade's originality, which featured Bernbach as the founder and driving force of the Creative Revolution. A few years later Bob Levenson, a colleague, friend, and well-known creative director, issued another art book of sorts, this one replete with ads from the glory days of DDB. He called the effort *Bill Bernbach's Book*, the book the man himself would have written if he had had the time, and filled the work with commentary and anecdotes as well as quotations from Bernbach that served to accentuate the tone of worship. Later authors mostly added to what was fast becoming a legend. Mary Wells Lawrence, perhaps the most famous advertising woman of her time, praised Bernbach in her own 2002 memoirs. More to the point she later told yet another author (who was writing about the famed Volkswagen campaign) of her years working under Bernbach, "There was something volcanic, something unsettling going on; it was a little like being in the company of Mao or Che or the young Fidel." Lee Clow, another noted creative, this time originally an art director, recalled that Bernbach "managed to change the business forever." "His work transformed the New York advertising scene and soon sent ripples throughout the country." Similarly, the British chronicler Andrew Cracknell, a onetime copywriter, assigned Bernbach a "monumental place in history," quoting approvingly from a *Harper's Magazine* obituary in which the writer claimed Bernbach "probably had a greater impact on American culture than any of the distinguished writers and artists who have appeared in the pages of *Harper's* during the past 133 years." Even a scholarly account of the sixties advertising scene, by journalist and historian Thomas Frank, celebrated Bernbach as a revolutionary, "Madison Avenue's answer to Vance Packard," a man who critiqued consumerism and transformed advertising, making him a social critic of some considerable stature. "Bernbach was the first adman to embrace the mass society critique, to appeal directly to the powerful but unmentionable public fears of conformity, of manipulation, of fraud, and of powerlessness, and to sell products by so doing." Remembering Bernbach seemed to encourage hyperbole among all sorts of chroniclers. Was it any wonder that in 2014, DDB Worldwide still featured on its website a seven-page collection of quotations from the great man?[21]

Bernbach's stellar reputation rested upon a widespread caricature of postwar advertising as dull and phony. In fact much of the advertising in print and television did conform to the so-called information processing model where the adman made some grand claim, like Rosser Reeves's famous USP, about the virtues of the brand, and made that claim repeatedly to ensure the message was drilled into the mind of the hapless consumer. Such a practice filled the air with lots of promotional noise: it was a time of earnest enthusiasm and much pretension, when everything supposedly worked well – just as promised. But in retrospect commentators saw too much fantasy, the prevalence of tired clichés, the dominion of "advertisingese," a kind of false speech. After the decade, fifties' advertising, especially on television, seemed full of exaggeration and lies, a massive exercise in deception meant to convince Americans they lived in a consumer paradise full of perfect goods. It all amounted to a perversion of the information processing model: although the industry claimed the consumer was a rational buyer, it treated her as both dumb and gullible.[22]

Bernbach's style was far different. It rested, so legend went, on a new philosophy of advertising at odds with the prevailing rules of the game. "Advertising is fundamentally persuasion," according to one of Bernbach's most-quoted maxims, "and persuasion happens to be not a science, but an art." He simply did not believe that anyone had or could design a formula or a science à la Reeves or Ogilvy for effective advertising. ("Rules are what the artist breaks; the memorable never emerged from a formula.") Like his fellows, Bernbach emphasized the need to capture attention. ("If your advertising goes unnoticed, everything else is academic.") But this priority required a concern with aesthetics – originality, boldness, wit – to produce a pleasing ad which might entertain. ("It's not just what you say that stirs people. It's the way that you say it.") More importantly, Bernbach broke away from the information-processing model to assert the priority of emotions. ("You've got to say it in such a way that people will feel it in their gut. Because if they don't feel it, nothing will happen.") He specifically urged "warm, human persuasion" rather than "cold arithmetic," one reason the Bernbach style featured a lot of humour, something other greats like Hopkins, Reeves, and even Ogilvy disparaged. Bernbach never denied the virtues of conveying information. Logic, however, was not enough. ("The fragile structure of logic fades and disappears against the emotional onslaught of the hushed tone, a dramatic pause, and the soaring excitement of a verbal crescendo.") He proclaimed time and again the necessity to engage the passions of the consumer. ("At the heart of an effective creative philosophy is the belief that nothing is so powerful as an insight into human nature, what compulsions drive a man, what instincts dominate his action, even though his language so often camouflages what really motivates him.") Which was why the adman, like any communicator, must be an artist first. ("The real giants have always been poets, men who jumped from facts into the realm of imagination and ideas.")[23] Bernbach had opted for a mode of persuasion that emphasized the need to produce

the right feelings in the audience, an approach which foreshadowed an
understanding of the human mind fashioned some decades later by neu-
roscientists such as Antonio Damasio or Joseph LeDoux.[24] In some ways,
Bernbach's philosophy seems closer to that of Ernest Dichter than of
other advertising men, although Bernbach never espoused the creed of
motivational research.

There was another vital dimension to the Bernbach philosophy: a
devotion to truth-telling. "The big thing," he told *Time* (16 February
1970), "is recognizing that honesty sells. There is no reason why honesty
cannot be combined with the skills of persuasion." Again like his fellows,
he asserted that the adman must be sincere should he wish to convince
the consumer. ("You've got to believe in your product ... you've got to
believe in your work. Only a deep belief will generate the vitality and
energy that give life to your work.") But the adman must also make the
truth interesting, if he hoped to persuade. He must fashion an honest ad
that conveys a sense of authenticity. It was the degree of success enjoyed
by DDB in this regard that constantly impressed later writers: Mary Wells
Lawrence, for example, recalled that what Bernbach always wanted was
to create ads which were "honest and candid, smarter and more interesting." She and many others thought the finest example of the Bernbach style was the much-acclaimed Volkswagen Beetle campaigns that
Bernbach's agency masterminded from the late 1950s to the mid-1970s.
Jerry Della Femina said of the so-called Lemon ad, where the company
admitted some cars might suffer defects, "It was the first time anyone
ever told the truth in print." Dominik Imseng actually suggested another
example, entitled "Think Small," was really "an anti-ad" – "it cut through
the clutter of advertising itself, standing out in a way no other ad had
done before, or has done since."[25]

Bernbach himself made much of the role of the truth-teller in his
response to the strictures of the moralist Arnold Toynbee, for whom
advertising could only be a species of deception. Bernbach demurred,
citing the example of the Volkswagen campaign. "For the past two years
we have run advertising for Volkswagen cars with the purpose of persuading Americans that simplicity, craftsmanship and low price were available
to them in an automobile," he told the readers of *Printers' Ink.* "These
were ads that conveyed facts simply and honestly to the consumer. They
seemed to sell the country on filling their automotive needs modestly
and with good taste."[26] DDB was not selling something phony, not selling false dreams, but selling the truth.[27] Supposedly, if you accepted this
argument, Bernbach, like Barton or Ogilvy before him, had avoided or

solved the adman's dilemma, depending on how you cast his philosophy. There was no dilemma because there was no deception. Nor, as a consequence, was there any ad-maker's sin or a dangerous matrix.

Was Bernbach a redeemer? Had he achieved what had hitherto seemed impossible, to make advertising into a discourse of truth? The short answer, of course, was no. The Volkswagen campaigns, especially the print ads, did avoid the fantasy imagery prevalent in Detroit auto ads, employing stark photographs (instead of fancy illustrations), negatives as well as positives, references to gas mileage and insurance and even breakdowns, to craft an image of the Beetle as an inexpensive and utilitarian vehicle. In practice, even if this was never recognized, the Bernbach style did submit the ad message to that discipline of the adman's dilemma as a social mechanism where the injunction "never lie" worked to limit deceit. Still, DDB dealt first and foremost in artifice, employing the tools of hype, diversion, half-truth, and similar techniques of deception to promote the brands of its clients. Some of the most famous commercials of the Volkswagen campaigns – for example "Snow Plow" or "Keeping Up with the Kremplers" – were exercises in fiction that conveyed, albeit very cleverly, an exaggerated impression of the durability and the frugality of the Volkswagen Beetle.[28] Not surprisingly the print ads failed to mention what one later observer called "the Beetle's awful safety record."[29] But the myth of the redeemer, the exponent of originality and honesty and authenticity who pioneered a new kind of publicity suited to the needs and tastes of the times: that myth was of lasting significance to the adworld.

2. The Reign of the Innovators: The Memoirs of Jerry Della Femina (1970), George Lois (1972), and Mary Wells Lawrence (2002)

What had emerged in all this hagiography was an effort among insiders, the actual practitioners, to change the conversation about the figure of the adman. Thus was born the idea of the innovator, a type increasingly celebrated in the rhetoric of the craft. The term could designate a maverick, someone who broke with the orthodoxy of the day. It could mean a creative wizard who fashioned an imaginative campaign that launched a new brand or revitalized an old one. It might signify the pioneer and the trendsetter who set advertising on a new course. It did indicate an artist whose work served to enchant the worlds of consumption. Such a person played out the role of the modern magician or sorcerer, since he attached meanings and inducements to the world of objects.[30] The key was that this person introduced something new, a visual technique or a turn of phrase or a sound effect, something singular, although soon emulated by his or her fellows. The "new" might seem a modest innovation to an outsider, but to insiders that was creativity.

Bill Bernbach remained the patron saint of this novel breed of adman. But the title of maverick, for instance, better suited others active in the 1960s and 1970s. Consider first that peculiar California phenomenon, Howard Luck Gossage (1917–69), remembered as the "Socrates of San Francisco," who came closest to the archetype of the trickster.[31] He achieved some prominence in the sixties thanks to the unusual campaigns he wrote (with Gossage as copywriter) for Fina Gas, Qantas Air, the Sierra Club, *Scientific American*, and Irish Distillers, and for sponsoring the introduction of the Canadian scholar Marshall McLuhan to the United States. Some of his essays were later collected in a book published by his fans in the 1980s, long after his death.[32] There he actually called himself a "maverick" (162), fittingly so because he was very much a moralist critical of the ways of his fellows.

In fact the book was decidedly odd, more an exponent of anti-advertising than any other work by a practicing advertising man. He was almost a renegade, except that he never "escaped" the craft. He ragged his colleagues for their arrogance, willfulness, and even duplicity; he objected to ordinary advertising because it was not only dull but ubiquitous; he lamented the influence of the adman over the content of the media; and he worried about the way ads incited an excess of consumption. His writings conveyed a mild version of the motif of the ad-maker's sin, a man who wondered out loud, "Is advertising worth saving?" Gossage was a proponent of interactive advertising, the use of direct response, contests, provocation and stunts, some stimulus to get the public involved. "An ad ideally ought to be like one end of an interesting conversation. First we say something, then you make some sort of a response ... Then, next time, we either amplify our remarks based on your assumed response or say something new; and so on" (138). Most importantly, Gossage, as a good trickster, wanted to have fun, to entertain and sometimes startle, often to make the consumer laugh. He hoped people would welcome advertising into their homes. This unusual man actually had few clients for his modest agency, and he won little recognition among the powerhouse agencies of Chicago and New York – but the memory of what he did and said persisted in local circles for years afterwards. Occasionally he was imagined as the founder of a unique or divergent tradition of west coast advertising represented in agencies such as Chiat Day (later TBWA/Chiat/Day), Goodby Silverstein & Partners, or Wieden & Kennedy (later Wieden+Kennedy). Perhaps it would be wiser to count Gossage as a forerunner of the style of promotion which emerged once the internet had matured.

Far better known, however, were three very talented New York innovators, who in the eyes of the industry and the media carried forward the Creative Revolution begun by Bill Bernbach. We begin with two men: copywriter Jerry Della Femina (b. 1936) and art director George Lois (b. 1931). Worried by the consequences of the Creative Revolution, that "King" of Madison Avenue, David Ogilvy, claimed on one public occasion, "I say the lunatics have taken over the asylum!" (4).[33] Della Femina and Lois were among those lunatics.

Both men wrote engaging memoirs of the advertising scene in the 1960s. Della Famina's *From Those Wonderful Folk Who Gave You Pearl Harbor* (1970) was certainly the most popular of the two books, soon becoming a classic along with Ogilvy's *Confessions of an Advertising Man*[34] Like Ogilvy, Della Famina was eager to promulgate rules about the craft, except that his rules, and even more so his tone, were definitely unlike those of *Confessions.* The book's title communicated that fact. Purportedly, on his first day at the mainstream Ted Bates agency, he had dropped this line about Pearl Harbor in a discussion of Panasonic, a Japanese client (113). Listeners might be shocked, and readers later amused, but Della Femina was proud – that made it abundantly clear he was a maverick. The message of *Those Wonderful Folk* was that no matter how serious advertising was or might be, it must always remain a source of humour as well.

Della Femina was very much the newcomer, an Italian-American from a working-class family who hardly fitted the Anglo and bourgeois style of the established advertising community. He had worked at a series of agencies, mainline and boutique, as a copywriter during the 1960s before starting his own shop with Ron Travisano in 1967. In his best-seller he described an advertising industry in crisis because of a clash of generations and styles. That was caused, so it seemed, by the ongoing Creative Revolution. The arrival of a host of young people, mostly men, non-Anglos, particularly Italian and Jewish Americans, usually more attuned to popular and even street culture, had produced something like a civil war between the established agencies and the newer shops, as well as within the older agencies when management hired "crazies" like Della Femina to stay relevant. That, he argued, only added to the angst, the miasma of fear, which an earlier set of works had identified as an abiding sin of the profession. Della Femina, for one, scoffed at all the existing rules and conventions: the old agencies were staid and dull, "very banklike, and very sleepy" (23), which was why clients more and more sought advertising men and agencies in tune with the times. He portrayed a work life full of booze, drugs, sex, and all sorts of shenanigans designed, supposedly, to release the creative juices. Wildness was now the key to, and the signal of, creative brilliance. Ever the prankster, Della Femina's last words were "advertising is the most fun you can have with your clothes on" (270).

Whatever his differences with old-fashioned advertising people, this maverick was still a devotee of artifice. He was effusive in his praise of Bill Bernbach and especially his Volkswagen campaign, because of its authenticity, honesty, and substance. But, much like his predecessors, Della Femina was the victim of doublethink, or self-deception. There is one particularly telling anecdote in his account of the struggles of his own agency. Early on, they were on the verge of collapse because they had too few clients and too many expenses. What to do? Why, hold a grand Christmas party, invite hordes of people, especially prospective clients, and spend lavishly, all to create the impression the new agency was a resounding success. It worked: clients started coming in the day after the party. "Part of this business – a big part of it – is illusion. Illusion is very important; it makes the potential clients aware of who the hell you are" (267). What Della Femina proposed was the need to fashion a brand of deception that was more credible because more contemporary – and more fun. He did seem very much one of Barnum's children.

So too did George Lois. The son of Greek immigrants, a child of the Bronx, always with a chip on his shoulder, he became an art director working for a time at DDB before setting out in 1960 to found his own agency and moving yet again, in 1967, to set up a new creative boutique. *George, Be Careful* (1972) celebrated the iconoclast, the "bad boy" in all his glory.[35] Lois also self-identified as a maverick (231) and recognized Della Femina as "my fellow Madison Avenue crazy man" (134). Lois spoke of "the Creative Hundred," "a hundred creative nonconformists with common roots and a separate language from the oily mainstream of American advertising" (226). He too emphasized the themes of struggle and resistance: his book title expressed the admonition he never obeyed: Lois always sought risk, excitement, sensation. He took pleasure recounting how his wild behaviour excited and irritated others. He had little respect for regular advertising, here sounding a bit like Gossage: "Most advertising is hot, stale, recycled air. Smog" (227). What he valued was flamboyance, the theatrical. His boldest effort was the "When You Got It, Flaunt It" campaign for Braniff airways, notorious because it was so happily boastful. His most original work was a series of magazine covers he designed for *Esquire* – Sunny Liston as a black Santa Claus, Mohammad Ali as the tormented Saint Sebastian, Lieutenant Calley surrounded by Asian children. "They outraged the mighty, they angered advertisers and they irritated readers – but they visualized America's changes and needled our hypocrisies. And nobody ever diddled with my work" (145). Throughout the memoir Lois emphasized his fierce streak of independence, how unwilling he was to submit to any outside interference, whether a fellow ad-maker or a client. Any attempt to defile his work could bring violence. Nor would he suffer indifference. Once he had to discipline the whiskey baron Samuel Bronfman, then sleeping during a presentation. "But I wasn't about to play the foot-shuffling adman who swallows his pride and does a jig for a dozing client. So I whacked the table and Bronfman quit snoozing" (86). Lois saw himself as an artist whose work spoke truths that demanded respect.

The most extraordinary and unusual member of this triumvirate of innovators, however, was a woman. Mary Wells (b. 1928), later Wells Lawrence, became in a very short time a legend as the first woman to conquer Madison Avenue. Starting at McCann-Erickson, she apprenticed as a copywriter in the creative milieu of DDB during the late 1950s and early 1960s, before winning kudos for her singular ideas at Jack Tinker & Partners. She was especially noted for applying a fashion aesthetic to the planes and staff of Braniff, purportedly a campaign that revitalized the airline – after which she married its chief executive. When she hit the glass ceiling – she was denied the presidency she thought her due – she broke free to launch her own agency, Wells Rich Greene, in 1966.[36] "I wanted a heroic agency, I dared everybody to be bold, to be thrilling and I dared our clients to be bold and thrilling," she recalled in her memoirs[37] (46). WRG soon won clients (among them American Motors cars and Benson & Hedges cigarettes) and awards (for the popular "Plop, Plop, Fizz, Fizz" campaign for Alka-Seltzer, for example) to emerge as the hottest of the creative boutiques, earning $100 million in annual billings by 1971.[38] A reviewer in *Time* later referred to her as "the godmother of a style of advertising that was witty, irreverent and anti-authority."[39] Wells soon became the first female CEO of a company listed on the New York Stock Exchange, and by the mid-1970s was earning a salary of $300,000, making her the highest-paid female executive in advertising.[40] Both Della Femina and Lois paid homage to this "queen of the advertising world," expressing their admiration for her creative genius.[41] At one point in 1975, Bill Bernbach seriously contemplated a merger of DDB and WGR.

No wonder she became an inspiration to ambitious women. "I want to be like Mary" was the cry, or so it was reported.[42]

Eventually her star waned, of course, and by the 1980s the agency was no longer very hot. Tired and perhaps jaded, twice a victim of cancer, she (and her partners) sold WRG in 1990, and Mary Wells retired from advertising.[43] Twelve years later she published her autobiography, *A Big Life in Advertising* (2002), supposedly to set the record straight. Her purpose, as one critic noted, was to build, or maybe rebuild, her brand in the way David Ogilvy had used his *Confessions* many years ago.[44] Her publisher even organized a national book tour where she gave media interviews and talked big about a return to save an adworld gone boring. But the autobiography did not enjoy a great deal of success. Critics noted that it seemed more a long chat than a thoughtful reflection, its anecdotes a bit too polished to be always credible; in the end, the book suffered from an "overwhelming shallowness."[45]

Nonetheless, *A Big Life* presented the opinions of one of the most accomplished of innovators, all the more interesting because she was a woman. Here Wells variously described herself as an alchemist, an actress, and a storyteller. She even claimed a certain psychic talent, an ability to receive visions that would shape her life – and advertising. That did not quite make her a truth-teller, though. "Advertising, in any form, is about telling stories that captivate readers or viewers and persuade them to buy products" (70). The story worked to transform the brand and even the user, hence the alchemy of advertising. But above all she applied the analogy of the theatre to the ad business: she wrote of "theatricalizing life with dreams" (8). "My way of running an agency was as if it was a motion-picture company with a lot of productions happening at one time" (46). All of which made her an exponent of "White-lie advertising" (140), where dreams and theatrics served to hype the brand. She accepted the necessity of a kind of self-deception about the merits of a product, which she called "self-hypnosis" (30), to ensure advertising carried conviction. The ad-maker presented the product as it should be, in its ideal form, not necessarily as it was. She or he was a sort of magician who enriched and enchanted, who brought things to life.

Like the other innovators, what she relished, so she claimed, was not the money but the pleasure – a career was about "following your bliss, expressing your creative self" (270). But she also admitted the exhilaration of power: "From the first minute I loved the challenge of motivating 500 people I couldn't see, and who couldn't see me." (176). There was more than a bit of the Svengali in her reflections. Above all, she proudly emphasized that she had invented herself. "No one invented a life and handed it to me" (166). She consciously adhered to that grand myth of self-fashioning which seemed both so American and so appropriate to the ad-maker.

Which may also signal the reason she avoided becoming a victim of her gender. Wells was aware of the difficulties a woman faced in the adworld. But she was no feminist (as Gloria Steinem pointed out in a nasty sneer).[46] Rather, despite her fame as a spectacularly successful woman, she consciously thought and acted like a man. She denied that men ever conspired against her. She admired the hard work, the persistence, the risk-taking, and the sacrifices she assumed was the lot of the successful CEO. She set out to emulate this hero, to enjoy, as her book title proclaimed, "a big life." "I was willing to accept the guilt of not giving enough of myself to almost anybody, just as businessmen were used to doing. I wanted a big life," she wrote in response to Steinem. "I worked as a man worked. I didn't preach it, I did it. I simply acted as I saw others in business act – at the time, they happened to be, primarily, men. In my corner of the universe, America, I found them welcoming and helpful, I liked them and I just accepted their culture" (164). Put another way, Mary Wells embraced the masculine ethos of the adman's gospel of creativity. Being an innovator didn't mean challenging the fundamentals of the persuasion industries.

In different ways, the last two innovators, Lois and Wells, saw themselves as artists who crafted original and striking work. Neither of them seemed troubled by either the spectre or the affliction of the adman's dilemma (nor was Della Femina, though he was more prankster than artist). They were devotees of imagination who employed artifice to fashion a new kind of truth. They were sincere. Della Femina similarly believed he and his fellow mavericks were talking to the public in a way and a language that was "real" and authentic, unlike the dated earnestness of the mainline agencies.[47] Lois in particular considered his art both truthful and avant-garde, something desperately necessary to combat the hypocrisies of America. Unlike the generation of ad-makers in the 1920s, or their postwar successors, who strove to list themselves as truth-tellers in the prevailing regime of truth, these innovators felt they had fashioned a kind of advertising that escaped the complications posed by the traditional opposition of artifice and authenticity. Their fictions supposedly enjoyed the same kind of authority and conviction that was attached to all forms of art.

3. Advertising Becomes Art: Kirk Varnedoe and Adam Gopnik, *High &*
Low, MoMA 1990–1991 and Doug Pray, *Art & Copy*, 2009

The advertising men (and women) might imagine their works amounted
to art. Did anyone else? One answer came in 1990. In the autumn of that
year, the esteemed Museum of Modern Art in New York City presented
a spectacular exhibition entitled *High & Low: Modern Art and Popular
Culture*, that later travelled to Chicago and then Los Angeles. What was
called in the jargon of the museum trade a theme or thesis exhibition,
expressing a particular argument as well as a complicated narrative, *High
& Low* cast a long shadow, partly because its kind was not soon repeated.
The show and the book, an extraordinary exhibition catalogue, were the
joint work of the co-curators Kirk Varnedoe (1946–2003), the museum's
director of painting and sculpture, and Adam Gopnik (b. 1956), editor
and art critic at *The New Yorker*. In addition there was a collection of essays
entitled *Modern Art and Popular Culture: Readings in High and Low*.

The exhibition was well remembered years later as both significant and
contentious: the catalyst of a great debate, a "landmark" and "amazing,"
"a kind of watershed," and, most intriguing, a "fascinating disaster."[48] The
purpose of the exhibition was revisionist: to demonstrate how modern
art and popular culture had always been locked together in an embrace
which generated all sorts of inspiration among artists and other innovators. The emphasis was on the artists, some 250 of their works on display,
to indicate how aspects of the Low provoked or shaped the masterpieces
of modern art. The curators were selective: they focused only on painting and sculpture, first in Paris and then New York, as instances of the
High, and on newspapers, caricature, comics, graffiti, and advertising
in the popular arts. In the exhibition catalogue Varnedoe was the chief
author of "Words," "Graffiti," and "Advertising," Gopnik of "Caricature,"
"Comics," and "Contemporary Reflections"; they co-wrote the introduction and the final "Coda." Among the popular arts, they paid the most
attention to publicity in its various forms: words and images, product
catalogues, packaging, window display, and advertisements. Varnedoe's
chapter on advertising and art consumed roughly one-third of the exhibition's catalogue, signalling its crucial importance in their version of
the saga of modernity. And the topic of advertising turned up in other
chapters, notably in "Words" and "Contemporary Reflections."

The exhibition did receive a modicum of praise, some from heavyweights in the art world. Arthur C. Danto, the noted philosopher of art,
called *High & Low* "a remarkable and valuable" endeavour in his essay

in *The Nation* (26 November 1990). The redoubtable Robert Hughes, the art critic of *Time*, was less positive but certainly sympathetic, leaving the impression that *High & Low* was a noble failure. And he specifically exempted the very scholarly exhibition catalogue, which he deemed "the indispensable text" (*Time*, 22 October 1990), so full of wisdom and enthusiasm about both modern art and popular culture. In fact even severe critics of the show often thought that book was impressive.

The most immediate effect, however, was a firestorm of criticism, a load of abuse so extreme, so full of fury and vitriol, that Varnedoe and MoMA would shy away from any similar show thereafter. The troubles began well before the exhibition opened, when some progressive critics, gathered around the magazine *October*, planned a counter exhibition which later became just a counter symposium. The storm commenced with an outburst in the *New York Times* (5 October 1990), two days before the exhibition opened to the public. There the art critic Roberta Smith declared *High & Low*, at best, "the wrong exhibition in the wrong place at the wrong time," one that told a story "crushingly familiar, superficial and one-sided." The exhibition was too timid, too selective, too arrogant: it excluded too much (especially the best of contemporary art), it slighted the popular arts, and it reaffirmed the tired MoMA view of modern art. Critics on the Left were angered because MoMA had once again denigrated popular culture – just why were the comics or graffiti "Low"? Art Spiegelman produced a marvellous cartoon that spoofed the supposedly reactionary views of the curators. Critics on the right were equally upset because they believed MoMA had sanctified trash – those same comics and graffiti – not to mention advertising. At the time and later, commentators railed against omissions (where was photography or pornography?), the lack of theory or any effort to tackle issues of power, the impoverished treatment of the popular arts or the inability of an exhibition to make a clear argument. Even Arthur Danto feared the show itself lacked the means to effectively convey information about the rationale for many of the displays to the public. The mix of mounted art, vitrines full of bits of popular culture, and wall texts could not work, especially when compared to the exhibition's catalogue. Altogether *High & Low* was condemned as both too traditional and woefully postmodern, as elitist and populist, but always as disappointing: an art history experiment gone wrong.[49] Nonetheless, the public seemed genuinely pleased with the show, if attendance figures are any indication: the *New York Times* (3 December 1990) reported the exhibition drew around 2,000 people a day at first, rising to 2,500 or 2,700 in later weeks. These totals might not be as large as those at a recent Warhol retrospective (some 4,000 a day) or a Picasso and Braque exhibition (3,500 a day), but they surely gratified the battered organizers, as did no doubt the more measured response of the press later in both Chicago and Los Angeles.

In retrospect a chastened Varnedoe thought the very title an unfortunate incitement to such violence. He told *Newsweek* (10 October 1990) that if MoMA had used a moniker like "City Life: Modern Art and Urban Experience," the response would have been more restrained. There were, of course, many possible explanations. The art world around 1990 was much upset by disputes over postmodern theory and feminist advocacy, by the display of "arresting images" such as those of Robert Mapplethorpe, by the attacks of Senator Jesse Helms who sought to censor.[50] More particularly, critics on the Left had targeted MoMA because it seemed to slight the contemporary artists of recent times, such as Jeff Koons or Barbara Kruger or Cindy Sherman, who drew heavily on popular culture. Critics on the Right wondered whether the newly minted Varnedoe (an art history scholar and a MacArthur Fellow appointed director in 1988) could be trusted to protect the heritage of the country's premier institution of modern art. His new book, *A Fine Disregard* (1990), had the temerity to employ a rugby analogy to interpret modern art. Varnedoe worried observers of all stripes because he had become something of a celebrity, even appearing in an ad for a local, upscale clothing store (the proceeds going to charity).[51] *High & Low* was the first major show fully under his aegis.

The exhibition challenged the prevailing narrative of modern art articulated years ago by such public intellectuals as Clement Greenberg and Dwight Macdonald.[52] Briefly put, this narrative presumed not just a dichotomy and a hierarchy but an irreconcilable opposition between High and Low, between the fine arts and mass culture, or sometimes the avant-garde and kitsch. This narrative was itself linked to a more general theory of mass society, where supposedly materialism and conformity reigned over American civilization. Mass culture might feed off the High, certainly degrading the fine arts to manufacture products that were commercial and, well, false. (The narrative might easily blend with the tradition of anti-advertising in the imagination of other anxious highbrows: witness Marshall McLuhan's *The Mechanical Bride*.) The avant-garde could only preserve its purity and élan by remaining separate and above the ruck of humanity. All that was truly creative in this highbrow fable flourished in the closely guarded gardens of the High. But Varnedoe and Gopnik used the analogy of the wheel to argue that

High and the Low really constituted one artistic universe. There was no necessary enmity, no irreconcilable opposition, despite the persistence of distinctions and difference. As Varnedoe quipped in the book, you cannot separate "the vanguard from the vulgar" – there had always been fruitful crossovers (63).[53] That revision could only displease critics who cherished hierarchy and complexity, as well as their rivals who denied there was any validity to the talk of distinction and superiority. Much later, on reflection, at least some of the critics, for example Rosalind Krauss, a noted professor of art history, came to appreciate the virtues of the exhibition and the book.[54] Varnedoe's claim about the title being inflammatory had merit.

The show and the book treated advertising extensively and carefully, usually avoiding the moral judgments so commonplace in the tradition of anti-advertising.[55] Both followed the familiar MoMA narrative of art, one that dealt largely with the Parisian scene starting in the late nine-teenth century and switching to the New York scene in the post-1945 era, though with a few forays into other sites, such as Bolshevik Russia or 1950s England. Inevitably the book offered a more complete, elaborate, and understandable story.

Consider first the show. A documentary entitled *Art in an Age of Mass Culture* (1991) featured a walk-through of the exhibition with Varnedoe and Gopnik.[56] It began with a large kiosk full of replicas of late-nineteenth century Parisian newspaper pages, news, and ads, before offering a survey of Cubist works by Picasso and Braque. Roughly one of the two floors used for *High & Low* focused directly on advertising and art. That involved mostly pictures on walls, sometimes documentary photographs as well, and ads and the like in vitrines, with explanatory texts to tie both collections together. Clearly the emphasis was on the art, lots of paintings and some sculptures all effectively arranged to allow a careful appreciation. There was one big ad image: Bibendum, Michelin's famous tire man. The image was located in a room devoted – so the wall text announced – to "The 'Spectacle' of Billboards," where the most prominent offering, again, was the art. There was also a special display window to the outside (and inside) of the museum, a kind of ad for the exhibition, where were presented various items by Claes Oldenburg, who in the early 1960s had created an installation called *Store*. The larg-est picture was James Rosenquist's *F-111* (1964–5), which mixed images of consumption and war, in a room of its own so that a visitor would feel enclosed by the elaborate and extended collage. The photographs of Parisian placards, the pages of catalogues, the assorted ads: all these were clearly supplementary to the art, and sometimes seemed a bit lost among the glories of modern and contemporary art, except that the presentation and the wall text endeavoured to make clear their importance and their innovation. Understanding the relationship between High and Low, however, was much easier in the documentary because of the lucid explanations of the curators.

Varnedoe's lengthy chapter on advertising and art was a superb piece, beautifully written, well researched, amply illustrated, and much more comprehensive than the show itself. The essay paid the most attention to such masters of modern art as Georges Seurat, Pablo Picasso, Francis Picabia, Max Ernst, Fernand Léger, René Magritte, Richard Hamilton, Jasper Johns, and Andy Warhol. A number of the artists represented, such as Aleksandr Rodchenko and Kurt Schwitters, or the better known Magritte and Warhol, had also at some point in their lives played out the role of the adman. (Strangely missing was Salvador Dalí, who in America in the 1940s was profitably involved in crafting advertising images.) Varnedoe noted how these men borrowed typographic formats, slogans, techniques of simplification or enlargement, and common images and arrangements from the practices of publicity. He briefly surveyed the evolving look of advertising as well, especially the appropriation of words and images and arrangements from modern art. He cited the claim of an advertising man at Young & Rubicam in 1954 who observed that a large proportion of the ads in any one issue of *Life* bore "the influence of Miró, Mondrian, and the Bauhaus" (315). More generally, Varnedoe explored the increasing influence of psychology, the so-called Europeanization of Madison Avenue (when the emphasis shifted from words to images), the postwar sophistication of consumerism and the rush to exploit symbolism. (But missing here was any serious treatment of the most important postwar phenomenon: the rise of television advertising.)[57] At one point Varnedoe reinterpreted the gospel of creativity as a fulsome embrace of the theory and practices of modernism.

Altogether *High & Low* offered museum-goers an art that was familiar and an advertising imagery that was novel. Varnedoe and Gopnik relied on the technique of juxtaposition, selecting and comparing particular examples to drive home their message about the linkages between art and advertising. They might find two artists, such as Picabia and Léger, who drew on similar sources of advertising to fashion different images, which thereby confirmed the old idea of genius (that the imagination of the individual was crucial) and the newer concept of the embrace of fine and popular art.[58] The plan was to generate "conversations" among the artists, the objects, and the viewers, about the intricacies of the "wheel" of art and life. Similarly Varnedoe in his chapter took great pains to show how each leading artist sported a very personal response to the ubiquity of publicity. Seurat found in the poster ads of Jules Chéret, however giddy and commercial, a kind of energy and fluidity he emulated in works such as *Le Chahut* (1889–90) and *The Circus* (1890–1). Although a socialist, Léger relished advertising because of its capacity to convey so much so quickly. Living in a still recovering Britain, Richard Hamilton was struck by the lush appeal and the cheap glamour of postwar American ad imagery, and these attributes he captured in his art. Rosenquist, at one time a painter of billboards, was both fascinated and repulsed by the apparent force of advertising. In his "Contemporary Reflections," Gopnik noted how Barbara Kruger, a champion of anti-advertising, nonetheless appropriated the typographical and visual devices of advertising to produce tableaux meant to subvert the regime of stimulation and consumerism. There was no one way the avant-garde responded or borrowed.

Varnedoe's writings, in particular, conveyed a new appreciation of the figure of the adman in the making of modern culture. True, this was more implied or suggested than stated outright. What so impressed Rodchenko with the work of the adman, thought Varnedoe, was the way it foretold the coming of "a coherent new public language, more arresting and efficient than any before it" (57). Later, when exploring Seurat's upbeat versions of the ad poster, he noted how they expressed "staged artificialities that are both enervating and energizing, madly false and cloying, yet wholly alive with a specifically modern vitality" (241). They might, like the ads, embody a kind of duplicity but also a spirit in tune with one version of modernity, "hard, electric, and mechanical" (241). In fact in one of his discussions of Rosenquist's *F-111*, Varnedoe referred to the "vocabulary of advertising, the great shaper of consciousness and fabricator of myth in the Western nations in our century" (231). Less often, however, Varnedoe noted the work of American advertising men such as E.E. Calkins, David Ogilvy, Rosser Reeves, or Bill Bernbach. He presented such men as the equivalent to the grand artists, that is, innovators whose concepts and styles determined the evolution of their discipline. Bernbach appeared in the guise of a creative genius who designed "imaginative campaigns that called attention to their cleverness as they violated conventional wisdom" (316). His rival Ogilvy also received kudos because his ploy of the Hathaway shirt man, who sported an eye patch, prefigured the Marlboro man and other symbolic characters that conjured up associations and emotions to promote a brand.

In such comments resided the notion of the adman as a licensed deceiver. The virtues of his creativity (for no women were listed here) sanctioned his deceptions.

Varnedoe's writing and the exhibition itself effectively raised the stature of the adman as a creative soul, not the least because the source was MoMA, that bastion of High art. Nor was *High & Low* the only sign of a change of status. At roughly the same time, from 31 October 1990 to 25 February 1991, the Centre Georges Pompidou in Paris presented *Art & Pub*. The Centre, a cultural complex, housed the Musée National d'Art Moderne, an equivalent to America's MoMA. The exhibition was a much more extensive and detailed exploration of the exchanges and embrace of art and advertising over the course of the previous century. The burden of this story, though, was much the same: that both were forms of creative expression which served to enrich the culture of modernity.[59]

Those two exhibitions were signal events, watersheds perhaps. But there were more indications that the adman had achieved fame as a creative powerhouse. Consider the appearance of large format, glossy, illustrated books with titles such as *The Best of Ad Campaigns!* (1988), *The Art of Persuasion: A History of Advertising Photography* (1988), and *Advertising in America: The First 200 Years* (1990), the last two under the imprint of Harry N. Abrams Inc., the famed publisher of art books.[60] Before and after came specialist museums, such as London's Museum of Brands, Packaging and Advertising (1984, relaunched 2005), a privately owned institution; the Advertising Museum Tokyo (2002), sponsored by the Dentsu ad agency; the Musée de la Publicité in Paris (initially 1978, reorganized 1999), part of a larger grouping devoted to the Arts Décoratifs; and the graphics and advertising section of the Victoria and Albert Museum in London (2002).[61] In October 2011, for example, the Musée des Arts Décoratifs presented *Sagmeister: Another Exhibit about Promotion and Sales Material*, along with an illustrated book in French and English. Stefan Sagmeister (b. 1962) is a well-known graphic designer, based in New York, who had done work (as he boasted in his book) selling culture, corporations, his friends, and even "Myself." The exhibit showed his designs, posters, ads, packages, covers, and other promotional materials. He was celebrated in a gallery as if engaged in an aesthetic pursuit: the adman was ranked among the community of contemporary artists.[62]

It was the documentary filmmaker Doug Pray, however, who in 2009 used the storyline of the innovator so effectively to justify advertising as a virtuous form of creativity. The documentary received a decent exposure across the country, including one airing on PBS, assorted awards, and much critical notice. This gorgeous piece of propaganda was sponsored by The One Club, a New York based non-profit devoted to excellence in advertising, which organized award shows and maintained a creative hall of fame. *Art & Copy* sought to show how a small collection of artistic entrepreneurs had enriched the world with their colourful and imaginative creations over the past several decades, though especially in the last third of the twentieth century. It carried extended interviews with the ad-makers – variously identified in the publicity for the film as "visionaries" or "heroes" – who elaborated their philosophies and discussed their work.[63] The focus, of course, was on male copywriters and art directors: yes, Bill Bernbach and George Lois (still going strong as a loudmouthed maverick), but added to the roster of innovators were Dan Wieden and David Kennedy, Lee Clow and Hal Riney, Jeff Goodby and Rich Silverstein, names known in the trade but hardly to the general public. (The documentary mirrored The One Club's own creative hall of fame, which was stuffed with males.)[64] The only females of any note were Phyllis Robinson, a key creative in the fashioning of the DDB style, and of course Mary Wells Lawrence. The messages of these interviews were bolstered by statistics on the significance of advertising, pictures of the creative workplaces of the assorted "geniuses," words and images that linked ad-making to communication and to art, and above all samples of the ads, these creative masterpieces – which, the documentary emphasized, were so unlike the dreary mass of advertising. In one of his own spiels, Doug Pray claimed *Art & Copy* was about the brilliant 2 per cent of advertising, not the 98 per cent that so bored the public.[65] These masterpieces, it appeared, broke through the matrix, that web of deception sponsored by the rest of the marketing.

Perhaps the most intriguing attribute of the documentary was its presumption (how often the notion arose!) that these stars had largely solved the adman's dilemma. Similarly, they had escaped the burden of the ad-maker's sin. In objective terms – income, education, labour, status – the men still belonged to the "professional-managerial class," like their predecessors in the 1950s or the 1920s. Not that they suffered any of the troubles of too much debt or loss of autonomy or a declining sense of significance or pleasure which supposedly afflicted elements of this "class."[66] The assorted stars appeared so satisfied, so pleased with themselves: they enjoyed freedom, status, money, and a sense of significance. They dressed as they liked, their work was full of play, and they produced what they wanted. Above all, the admen perceived themselves as artists outside the class system. "They are both subversives and establishmentarians, salesmen and entertainers," correctly noted Kenneth Turan, the film critic of the Los Angeles *Times* (11 September 2009), "people who believe they are in the most exciting business on Earth." Much was made of the claim that their personal experience determined the character of their advertising: George Lois was a street kid and, as a result, his work provoked; while Hal Riney's unfortunate childhood led him to highlight the emotions he had missed. Much was also made of their rebellion against the conventions of advertising and business: these guys went their own way, they were agents of change. The art they fashioned had consequences: they were cultural producers whose slogans and images shaped popular culture. The role of business seemed to slip into the background. Thus it was George Lois who had "made" Tommy Hilfiger. It was Wieden & Kennedy who had turned Nike into a megahit. It was the art of these innovators that made capitalism, not vice versa. And they had achieved all this with public-pleasing campaigns like "Got Milk?" or "Just Do It."

A glance at the reviews at Amazon.com shows that many writers were impressed. One articulate fan thought the documentary redeemed the industry because it showed how the work of these stars connected "us with something artful and truthful."[67] Viewers actively engaged in ad-making sometimes found the documentary positively inspirational. No wonder: one may speculate that to adpeople *Art & Copy* neatly finessed the strictures of anti-advertising. The subjects, like the other innovators before them, admitted that all too much publicity was specious or boring and perhaps toxic, a kind of intellectual and emotional pollution. But what they produced was better labelled entertainment, a happy marriage of commerce and art, as well as information. It was fun for the advertising man, the client, and the consumer – supposedly. The more creativity ruled, the more the mavericks challenged the status quo, the better for the public and business. This line of reasoning fitted well the contours of a neoliberal order where the star entrepreneurs were esteemed as agents of progress. Their very success served to justify an admittedly flawed system, in this case a system of promotion and publicity.

The narrative had also spread abroad. During the 1960s, the Toronto ad executive Jerry Goodis earned both fame and notoriety in industry and media circles as a Canadian version of Bill Bernbach – and his agency, Goodis Goldberg Soren, became the hottest in the business. His later memoir, suggestively entitled *Have I Ever Lied to You Before?* (1972), touted the way he challenged convention, and he even scolded the industry (one reason he won notoriety was because the press often loved to quote his *bon mots*). A later documentary by the National Film Board of Canada (1976) similarly celebrated his status as a maverick. At much the same time, a series of young newcomers in London worked to transform the earnest and often staid character of British advertising. Their success was chronicled much later in a BBC documentary entitled *The Rise and Fall of the Ad Man* (2009), which surveyed the story of the creative geniuses over the span of three decades, up to the early 1990s. Supposedly by the eighties the adman was looked upon as something of a shaman by many prominent leaders in business and politics in the City. In this story, though, the innovators, and in particular Saatchi & Saatchi, reached too far, disturbed the establishment, and were soon reined in. The most unusual variant of the innovator storyline was a Chilean movie entitled *No* (2012). That semi-fictional story celebrated the initiative of an adman who crafted a positive, upbeat campaign to mobilise, successfully, the pro-democracy forces in the 1988 referendum that caused the downfall of Augusto Pinochet. Few texts (though Barton's life of Jesus was of this kind) had so effectively imagined the adman as a public saint.[68]

4. The Creative Process: Michael J. Arlen, *Thirty Seconds*, 1980

The presumption that advertising was art, that the adman was an innovator, had to rest on an understanding of just how the adman worked, whether he really was creative in any meaningful fashion. In fiction the adman's brand of creativity had long been the butt of humour, evident in the first cycle of huckster fictions. Consider just one example from a later comedy, the eureka moment of the adman played by Cary Grant in the movie *Mr. Blandings Builds His Dream Home* (1948).[69] Jim Blandings, a copywriter, had tried throughout the movie to come up with a slogan for a brand of ham called Wham. He had failed ... until, right at the end of this comedy, he overheard his African-American maid tell his children, "If you ain't eatin' Wham, you ain't eatin' ham." Blandings was visibly struck by the brilliance of this insight. He knew it was gold. So he appropriated the declaration and the next scene shows the slogan, with an illustrated version of the maid's jovial face, gracing a full page in a magazine. The viewer might count him a fool or a knave who had recourse to such plagiarism. Or the viewer might recognize Blandings as perspicuous, a sociologist of sorts whose practiced grasp of popular culture made him aware of the magical words that would sell the brand to the mass audience. That viewer might also see the achievement as decidedly modest, even picayune, an exercise in trivia. In any case the answer to Blandings's problem had arrived in a flash. He had found his "Big Idea" for the campaign, the goal of all admen.

Helen Woodward in *It's an Art* (1938), even more Frederic Wakeman in *The Hucksters* (1946), characterized what the adman practiced as a degraded kind of creativity because it involved such effort to produce something so banal. That presumption certainly ran through the persuader fictions, both in a comedy such as *Lover Come Back* (1962) and a drama such as Elia Kazan's *The Arrangement* (1967 and 1969). By contrast, Rosser Reeves, ever the braggart, writing in *Reality in Advertising* (1961), declared that "the raw conception of a U.S.P. is the advertising man at his apogee, and it involves creativity of the highest order" (67). Reeves's unique selling proposition (USP) was the grand feature of a brand, something its publicity could claim was unique. Finding it, the key to reason-why advertising, was essential.[70]

There were many variations on the story of discovery. In his *Diary of an Adman* (1944), James Webb Young reported how he had once woken up at three in the morning with "a full-fledged idea for one client's next campaign" (118). The "three rhyming words," the crucial slogan for a hangover cure, just "came into Mr. Blandings's head" in Eric Hodgins's later novel *Blandings' Way* (1950), and Jim "uttered them aloud in a trance-like voice" (309–10). It was common to argue that the hidden workings of the unconscious generated the solution. In his *Confessions of an Advertising Man* (1963), David Ogilvy admitted to "keeping open the telephone line to my unconscious" to ensure he wrote copy that was both innovative and imaginative (28). Such comments enhanced the mystery and the romance of the adman's enterprise.[71]

Inevitably, before long, copywriters sought the formula for creative success, some practical method that any decent ad writer or illustrator could employ to ensure they found an idea which was both novel and useful. The aforementioned James Webb Young (1886–1973), a copywriter at the leading agency J. Walter Thompson, wrote *A Technique for Producing Ideas* in 1940, apparently after giving some lectures to advertising students at the School of Business of the University of Chicago the previous year. This short work, slightly over fifty pages, proved so successful that it was republished many times over, in different languages, with a new edition appearing in 2003. Bernbach himself wrote the introduction to a 1965 edition. *A Technique* was far more influential than his *Diary of an Adman*. In it, Young postulated a five-step process of information-gathering, mastication and then incubation, a eureka moment, and finally elaboration and refining. In a revealing analogy he compared his cognitive tool to the workings of Henry Ford's assembly line, meaning it could be "learned and controlled" (KL 65). Anyone, not necessarily a really talented soul, could triumph if only he or she worked hard and followed the rules.[72]

A compatriot, Alex F. Osborn (1888–1966), came up with the technique of brainstorming which, for a time, especially in the 1950s and the 1960s, captured the fancy of some executives in the industry and soon spread to the wider business community. Osborn was a prominent member of the advertising community, one of the original founders of BBDO in 1928. Ten years later, legend has it that Osborn "saved" the agency by applying his technique of brainstorming to the problem of generating campaign ideas. After the war, he became a best-selling author, writing two famed works, *Your Creative Power* (1948) and *Applied Imagination* (1953), which went through many editions. Both volumes dealt broadly with the phenomenon of creativity, emphasizing, as in the case of Young's work, how anyone properly motivated and trained might excel. Both, especially the latter, discussed Osborn's version of groupthink. To "brainstorm," he wrote once, "means using the brain to storm a creative problem – and do so in commando fashion, with each stormer attacking the same objective."[73] It required the organization of a small, carefully selected group (Osborn spoke of the wisdom of recruiting some adwomen), tasked to deal with a specific problem, who jointly generated a mass of new ideas. None of these ideas were subject to judgment or criticism at this session: the whole purpose was to produce novelty and quantity. Participants were urged to be imaginative and free-wheeling, to use such techniques as addition and subtraction, to substitute or reverse, always to combine, employing the old ideas to build the new. Osborn did once tie brainstorming back to a Hindu practice. But his version was akin to the doctrine of positive thinking so appealing to the mentality of the adman. You had to banish doubt, self-criticism, judgment, anything negative. Only later were the new ideas thus generated subjected to discussion and evaluation in order to fashion a really useful creative solution. In the last decade or so his life, Osborn largely escaped from advertising to emerge as a leading guru of creativity boasting his very own institute.[74]

The practice of brainstorming persisted in advertising circles after 1970 as one way to produce a host of ideas. But it was replaced in the community's rhetoric as the key tool by the popularity of Bernbach's supposed innovation, the creative dyad of copywriter and art director.[75] This alliance of opposites, often compared to a marriage, was later deemed – for example, by George Lois – as the instrument that fashioned the brilliance and flamboyance of the Creative Revolution of the 1960s.[76] It amounted to a dethroning of the copywriter, who had once reigned as the top creative, and the rise of the art director, befitting the new import of the image in the age of television. It undermined the authority of the account executive and even the plans boards and similar groups which had vetted the creatives' endeavours. Instead, the two individuals were given a joint brief to work out a series of possibilities and proposals that must meet the approval of the creative director – and, as always, the client. Much later, an accomplished executive, Nina DiSesa, recalled fondly the dynamic duo she had once formed with a male art director:

> In fact, there couldn't have been two more dissimilar people than Frank and me in the history of advertising: He was hip; I was not. He was a loose cannon; I was wrapped as tight as a drum. It was obvious that Frank liked to have fun; I preferred to worry. He was a shameless womanizer who thought Spandex was a natural fabric, like cotton; I despised and distrusted Spandex. He already had a stellar creative reputation at Y&R; I was still trying to prove myself as a creative force. The most challenging difference was that I was a well-rounded creative person with a healthy right brain (creativity, intuition) and a fully functioning left brain (champion of logical thinking and adult behavior). Frank's left hemisphere had atrophied. He was left-brain-dead.[77]

Apparently because they were so different, they fashioned great ads together, gaining such a reputation that the agency bosses used their talents to solve all kinds of knotty creative problems. DiSesa's account, like others, emphasized how the twosome worked as a kind of aesthetic assemblage, a melding of disparate talents and sensibilities, to throw out words and images that excited and stimulated. It was intense, even passionate, sometimes fun, often hard work, but marvellously effective as a grand creative device.[78] But the successful team was more a matter of personality and chance than any set of techniques. We were back to the old notions of magic and serendipity.

The impact of such celebrations, however, was always countered by much more critical treatments of the gospel of creativity, albeit by outsiders who imagined or actually probed how the adman worked. "A hilarious, hugely entertaining look at the advertising industry": this praise appeared in the Penguin edition of Michael J. Arlen's bestseller *Thirty Seconds* (1980), a work that originated as a two-part article in the *New Yorker*.[79] The book was that and much more. It was an extended study, running to 211 pages, of the making of a television commercial entitled

"Tap Dancing" for AT&T's long-distance lines. It became a classic exploration of the meanings and the actual workings of creativity in the world of the adman.

The son of a noted novelist, Michael J. Arlen (b. 1930) was a journalist and the television critic of *The New Yorker*. He was particularly known as the author of *Living Room War* (1969), on television's coverage of the Vietnam War, and *Passage to Ararat* (1975), a semi-autobiographical account of his Armenian heritage. *Thirty Seconds* was his take on the way a ubiquitous form of art was actually fashioned. Since its release, the same or a similar topic has caught the fancy of many other observers and writers. Two of the best journalistic treatments are Randall Rothenberg's exploration of the making of a Subaru campaign, and especially a commercial, in *Where the Suckers Moon* (1994), and the section on the birth and death of the Song airline launch in the PBS special *The Persuaders* (2004). In fiction, there were novels such as Jonathan Dee's *Palladio* (2002) and Alex Shakar's *The Savage Girl* (2002), the satires *e* (2000) and *e²* (2009) by Matt Beaumont, as well as a series of movies such as *Crazy People* (1990) and *What Women Want* (2000). Then there is the ever-growing number of scholarly pieces, mostly articles but also the occasional book, often by British scholars, studies of the creative departments and ad-making routines in advertising agencies. I will assess Arlen's pioneering work in the light of some of these later efforts.

The purpose of the AT&T/Ayer project was to change the public attitude towards long-distance phoning. In the words of Jerry Pfiffner, the leader of the Creative Group, long distance was burdened with some guilt, a bit of fear – the late-night "bad-news phone call" – and the reputation as costly. The new campaign sought to dispel the "*negative, uncasual* quality" and "emphasize the *casual, positive* aspect: long-distance is fun, it's easy, it's cheap." The basic approach was soft sell, an emotional appeal, hopefully not "sentimental" but "upbeat" (12–13). "The thing about these phone ads is that what we're really doing is selling emotion," asserted another member of the team (98). Arlen joined the process of designing the campaign well after it had started, a year before. Already the theme and style had been set, key personnel hired to produce the commercials, some locations set up. He did expend some effort outlining what had gone before, particularly the amount of work involved in the selection of the final design for the campaign. But Arlen focused on the actual making of only one of the commercials, a "vignette" ad composed of a sequence of happy scenes of assorted people phoning each other.

Arlen's book was not only about process but also about people. Or rather it studied the creative process by focusing on the diverse collection of participants – what a later scholar referred to as a "motley crew"[80] – who somehow contributed to the finished AT&T commercial, "Tap Dancing." That meant the agency personnel from N.W. Ayer, creatives and account managers, the client representatives, the film director and his team, the performers, and the associated editors and specialists recruited to add the music and massage the sound and film. Arlen's research seemed mostly an extended series of interviews. "Arlen is primarily an eavesdropper," noted one reviewer, "briefly profiling the actors, setting the scene and then letting the dialog of the principal players drive the action."[81] Certainly *Thirty Seconds* was full of descriptions of the host of individuals, how they dressed, what they did, what they reasoned, buttressed and spiced by an abundance of quotations. Except for the occasional comment, Arlen largely stayed in the background. All of his subjects were named, and most were quoted, which gave *Thirty Seconds* the character of an intimate portrait of a peculiar set of aesthetic technicians.

In that regard it was similar to the bestseller written by Martin Mayer in the late 1950s: Arlen had explored a kind of tribe, largely middle-class, who could claim a special mission, an intriguing workstyle, even a singular lingo. Like Mayer's sample, Arlen's was full of brothers-in-arms. They had worked together on past projects: they constituted a network of experts who knew each other's work and trusted each other's abilities. The leading players, outside of the performers, were overwhelmingly male, a sign of how little had changed even as late as 1979 (when the action occurred). Later scholars have pointed out that usually the top creatives in America and elsewhere were and are men. Women may have entered the ranks of the industry in large numbers but men often remained in command of the actual process of creation.[82] It was this very fact which gave force to Nina DiSesa's memoir *Seducing the Boy's Club* (2008): how other women could emulate her success, whether to deal with the masculine ethos or to smash through the glass ceiling. "I discovered a place that was drunk on testosterone," wrote DiSesa when she took over as a creative director at JWT Chicago in 1991. "There was a lot of old-school, Chicago ad-guy posturing for positions of power, and male chauvinism permeated the halls – a residue from the previous leadership."[83] She also recalled how men used humour to belittle and intimidate, at least in some of the organizations where she served. Academics agreed, making comments about a locker room spirit or calling creative departments boyland.[84] Women were by no means excluded but the feminine was definitely not welcomed in this masculine domain. No wonder DiSesa's manual on managing men advocated not challenge and resistance but "the art of S&M (Seduction and Manipulation)," the better to capitalize on what she thought was the vigour and strengths of masculinity.

Arlen did find another kind of divide, marked by clothes, between the business types who appeared in suits and the creatives who were clad in more casual outfits. At one meeting Phil Shyposh, the AT&T ad manager, wore "a handsome, conservative gabardine suit," while Fred McClafferty, the Ayer supervisor of the Long Lines account, and George Eversman, a senior vice-president, wore "sedate well-tailored gray plaid suits" (63). By contrast, on another occasion, Arlen noted that Jerry Pfiffner, a senior vice-president creative as well as group leader, turned up "wearing his standard costume of sports shirt and Levi's – always real, no-nonsense Levi's." Steve Horn, the film director, arrived in "a loose and lineny outfit of beige shirt and beige slacks, very cool and flowing and somewhat pukka-sahib" (160). Such "uniforms of art and business" (63) signified a potential clash, though in Arlen's case there was mostly harmony. But not always: copywriters and art directors were notorious for their distrust of outsiders, the client representatives and the account supervisors, who might tamper with the creative work.[85] DiSesa claimed she sometimes blew up when she thought the account man did not respect her mastery of the art, though she also tried to involve him in the design process. In the larger agencies the creatives were located in separate quarters, say, on their own floors, where they could be as feisty and zany as they wished, or so it was imagined, away from the oversight of the straight-laced business types. Matt Beaumont made the crazy antics of the creatives the core of his two satires of the London ad scene.

It was impossible to identify one auteur, one person who was the author of the commercial. The process of designing the campaign had begun the previous year, when a creative group of fifteen tossed around hundreds of different approaches, themes, and slogans. That had involved much hard work of the sort outlined in Young's and Osborn's manuals. Jerry Pfiffner claimed he had come up with what became the basic theme embodied in the slogan "Reach Out and Touch Someone." But once the shoot began, the key person was unquestionably the director Steve Horn, recruited because of his past success in realizing emotional briefs. Horn and his team worked through the details of the ad – but not alone, since Pfiffner and his associates were always on site to offer advice.

Furthermore what gave "Tap Dancing" its cohesion and its emotional charge was, at least in part, the music, arranged by someone else, and the sound mix, the work of yet one more specialist. And what fashioned the finished product out of the raw material, some ten thousand feet of processed film, was the work of the film editor, Howie Lazarus. "Howie's work on 'Tap Dancing,' while no more authorial than Steve Horn's or Jerry Pfiffner's, is in certain ways no less authorial," wrote Arlen (178–9). Right at the end of the process, J. Walter Cannon, vice-president public relations at AT&T and the man who gave final approval, told the creatives after viewing the spot, "Just try to lighten up on the red" (201). The actual process of ad-making was very far from the model of the artist or even movie production, where the director was deemed the auteur. The creatives, at least in this instance, had to share credit with many others. The ad-making amounted to an industrial process where a special assemblage of talent and authority both constructed and negotiated the final result. Randall Rothenberg's later description of the making of one Subaru commercial, though full of more conflict, likewise emphasized the shared nature of this kind of aesthetic project.[86] But there were exceptions: *The Persuaders* left the impression that Song's campaign was the brainchild of one wizard, Andy Spade, the co-founder of the fashion enterprise Kate Spade.

Three aspects of the process stood out in Arlen's account. The first was that the creativity of the adman was distinctly limited, even constrained, and not just by what had been done before. The participants treated creativity as a set of magic ingredients to be added to the mix to heighten the emotional charge. Technique was highly valued. Steve Horn claimed his signature style was telephoto, whatever that meant. Bill Eaton, the musical arranger, asserted his work was "*close* to popular, of course, but it's not the same as popular" (41). The existence of a schedule, of deadlines, operated constantly to force the process into familiar channels because that was what everyone knew and understood, despite the rhetoric about innovation. In fact, as the sociologist Sean Nixon pointed out in a later study, creativity meant not innovation so much as modification, where the creative worked in an established genre to find some minor novelty in a "familiar constellation of meaning."[87] Ad-making was constantly subject to fads and fashions, as the creatives copied the techniques and ploys that had worked before. At one level Howie Lazarus recognized this. He told Arlen how in the 1960s "the most popular technique was shooting into the sun" to achieve "that bleached-out, high-lit effect, very striking" (181). Ten years later, the basic technique had become the vignette commercial, which allowed a lot of information and stimulus to be packed into a short compass; this was partly a consequence of the shift from sixty-second to thirty-second spots. "Tap Dancing" thus conformed to the prevailing model for the emotional ad.

The second aspect of the process was the joint commitment to artifice, and thus the easy acceptance of the practices of deception. The creatives and the producer were always searching for the right look when shooting the various scenes that made up "Tap Dancing." Does the cowboy in the rodeo bit appear real? Do the soldiers in a scene set in a barracks say Army? What props, what furnishings make a place appear to be a hockey locker room or the apartment of a young African-American woman or a barber shop? Typical of the small deceptions was the recourse to "Billy's rain." A yoga scenario required some rain. A smattering of "*regular* rain" would not do since that just would not film properly. Instead the rain machine came out to deliver the appropriate amounts of "course spray" and "fine spray" on the correct windows (92–3). Steve Horn recalled how one effort to fake the casual in a Miller Lite beer commercial took hours and hours to capture just the right pool shot. Linda Swenson, one of the actors, told a marvellous story about doing a spot for McDonald's. She had to take a few bites out of a hamburger. But something always went wrong and the shoot just continued. The trouble was that every burger was "stone cold," because that way they stayed together, and "coated with grease" so they photographed better. "By the end of the day, I reckoned I'd chomped away on fifty stone-cold, greasy hamburgers, flashing this big happy smile each time, and, I'm telling you, that may not be Shakespeare but it sure was acting" (84). The result was neither quite fiction nor reality. It was an idealized or typified portrayal of happy people, stereotypes all, who were acting out some American drama of connection in settings that would be known and familiar to a national television audience. The adman sought verisimilitude, the seemingly true, not authenticity.

The third aspect was the apparent seriousness of the whole endeavour, a quality which turned the story into a comedy of sorts. That was not always the case in such treatments. Augusten Burroughs, a onetime creative, presented himself as both a cynic and a prankster on and off a shoot in his memoirs *Dry* (2003). But Arlen's people were very much professional. Only one of the participants, an actor, expressed any strong distaste for such commercial work. His colleague, the same Linda Swenson, asserted, "I love the work" (83). Certainly this motley crew appeared to approach the task with both sincerity and even some enthusiasm. They obsessed over the most trivial of details. They argued over all sorts of tactics. Arlen peppered his book with the earnest *bon mots* of assorted players.

"So, strategy-wise, we started with a kind of two-faced objective: the casual thing and the people-outside-the-family thing." (13)

"I like the concept, but does it work structurewise?" (117)

"Not really real, but more real than commercial." (158)

"I think it's strong. But let's make sure we go wide and tight and then freeze on the smile." (187)

"You have to reach back into the recesses of your mind and find music that's really sincere." (189)

That kind of lingo convinced the anonymous reviewer in *Kirkus Reviews* (30 April 1980) that the admen were "crass, jargon-spouting creeps of the most laughable sort." That was far too harsh. More just was the judgment of Matt Seidel in *The Millions* (2 February 2015): "Each participant demonstrates a sincerity about his or her calling that is as touching as it is risible."

By the time Arlen reached the launch of "Tap Dancing" on the *Johnny Carson Show*, the critic in the *Christian Science Monitor* (9 June 1980) concluded that "the reader is nearly in awe of the amount of talent, and, presumably, intelligence that, over a period of two years, has been poured into these 30 seconds." But this critic felt a bit let down. "A never posed but implicit question in *Thirty Seconds* is the rationale – even the morality – of such resources being devoted to a project that might strike many as an empty endeavor." The point Arlen had made, however, was that neither morality nor sense had much to do in a world where art was wedded to commerce.

It was likely that eventually a movie would satirize the creative process by emphasizing the insanity of the whole endeavour, characterizing the copywriters and the art directors as mad souls. Recall that charge during the years of the Creative Revolution: the lunatics have taken over the asylum? Well in *Crazy People* (1990) they certainly took over the advertising agency. But there was a problem: the movie was bad and it failed at the box office. Purportedly it did not even earn back its cost when shown in movie theatres. Vincent Canby, the movie critic of the *New York Times* (11 April 1990), called the effort "a humorless satire of the advertising world." It only deserves notice here because the story told expressed an extreme view of who the adman really was and how he operated.

Crazy People had two veterans in starring roles, Dudley Moore as the adman Emory Leeson and Darryl Hannah as the troubled Kathy Burgess, the inmate of a sanatorium. Their performances were decent – Moore in particular was a justly acclaimed comic actor. The flaw was in the design of the movie, the way it attempted to combine social satire and romantic comedy. The noted reviewer Roger Ebert aptly captured this mistake when he imagined how some wacky censor, his fictitious "Movie Police," had dictated the addition of a "love story," a "lot of lovable, huggable goofballs," and a "heart-warming romantic conclusion" to make "a cynical satire about advertising" conform to the formula of the romantic comedy.[88] The movie started well and often had good moments, but it increasingly fell apart as the romance between Leeson and Burgess took hold of the plot.

Leeson began as an experienced creative who suffered a mental, or at least spiritual, breakdown, a result of the liar's plight. He worked in what was a hard-boiled agency surrounded by cynics who were always out to manipulate the public. "Let's face it, Steve," Leeson told a colleague, "you and I lie for a living." In one mad burst of energy, he had produced a series of supposedly honest ads for well-known brands: "a dozen new ad campaigns for everything from Volvo ('Boxy but good') to United Airlines ('Most of our passengers get there alive')."[89] His aghast colleague Steve had Leeson committed to a psychiatric institution to rest and recover. Clearly Leeson was a victim of the adman's dilemma: he could no longer lie, and when he told the truth, then he was deemed mad and lost his job, at least until he "recovered."

The bizarre ads were accidentally sent out and published in magazines across the country. A jaded public loved them. Sales took off. Drucker, the agency boss, portrayed as a nasty and greedy sleaze in a suit, tried to take over this novel style of "truth in advertising." Meanwhile, Leeson recruited other inmates to design blunt, often bawdy ads which touted some attribute of a brand that people thought authentic. Neither the agency honchos nor the clients could really understand their appeal. But here was a form of advertising that conformed to the plain speech tradition where the adman expressed an opinion that was both sincere and honest. In the process the inmates improved, acquiring self-esteem and a certain confidence because they had become proven artists.

So was the only honest adman really some kind of "mad man"? An innovator, yes, but a demented one? Ebert noted how the inmates turned out to be "natural-born advertising geniuses, of course. (One of the basic Movie Police Laws is that crazy people are always saner than the rest of us.)" They acted a bit zany and talked a bit strange, the kind of image of creatives at work already familiar to readers and viewers since the Creative Revolution. They came up with their winning ideas through some mysterious serendipity, presumably the result of their disordered state. Their slogans, if sincere, carried the stigma of lunacy. Nonetheless they worked. These "mad men" were more adept than the professionals. Because they were already deranged, their moral senses confused, they could not suffer from the adman's dilemma. One might admire the spunk and ingenuity of the inmates, or pity their condition and their lot in life. The viewer was not likely to respect them or their new profession. *Crazy People* made a mockery of the gospel of creativity.

But it was only a feeble satire, lacking much bite. Most of the imaginary ads were only honest about the specious style of the sales pitch – the inclusion of sex, for example – not the "truth" of the product. As more than one critic noted, the movie actually testified to the power of the very form of persuasion it ostensibly mocked. "At the preview I attended, people exploded into laughter every time one of Moore's ads came on," reported the critic in *Entertainment Weekly* (20 April 1990). "Yet what they were getting off on was the clever effectiveness of the ads; they were sharing in Moore's huckster triumph. *Crazy People*'s blunt-edged satire may be aimed at Madison Avenue, but it ends up skewering a nation that is starting to think like Madison Avenue. The movie wants you to giggle and say, 'Yup, we sure are saps, aren't we?'" That was reminiscent of the days of Barnum, when the public supposedly relished the recognition of a clever deception.

5. Limits: Robert Downey Sr, *Putney Swope*, 1969; Jonathan Dee, "But Is It Advertising," 1999, and *Palladio*, 2002; Jason Reitman, *Thank You for Smoking*, 2006

The positive tenets of the narrative, its themes of publicity as art, advertising as enchantment, the adman as innovator, never triumphed in the wider social conversation. Just the opposite. There emerged a whole series of counter stories and tails that mocked or disputed these tenets. Most of these were in the realm of fiction. Some of the most pointed were movies, particularly comedies: *I'll Never Forget What's'isname*

(UK, 1967), *How to Succeed in Business Without Really Trying* (1967), *Putney Swope* (1969), *Nothing in Common* (1986), obviously *Crazy People* (1990), *How to Get Ahead in Advertising* (UK, 1989), *Picture Perfect* (1997), *One Night Stand* (1997), *What Women Want* (2000), *Sweet November* (2001), *Kate & Leopold* (2001), *How to Lose a Guy in 10 Days* (2003), and *Thank You for Smoking* (2006).[90] They left the impression that, despite all the rhetoric, the advertising game was just that: a pursuit full of competition, duplicity, and insecurity where the demands of art were subordinated to the practice of deception. I will look at only three of these stories: two movies and one critique and novel by a single author.

Early on the myth of the redeemer was viciously ridiculed by Robert Downey Sr's *Putney Swope* (1969), a so-called underground movie that presumed the adman's dilemma persisted even in the new era of creativity. The young filmmaker Downey was no renegade, though he had shot some experimental commercials and sat in on some meetings at an ad agency. The movie was very low-budget and starred largely unknown actors. It was shot in black and white, though with colour inserts – for the commercials. It seemed rough and unfinished, a "surreal, anarchic comedy" in the words of a later critic.[91] The movie expressed the mood of irreverence associated with the then popular counterculture of young America. The satire, also called "The Truth and Soul Movie," mocked a wide range of different targets, from black militants to white business-men; but most especially it savaged the advertising man. Much later, in 2006, a DVD release of what was by then a cult favourite carried the so-appropriate caption "Up Madison Ave."

Putney Swope, among other things, was about the failure of a revolutionary project to transform advertising into a discourse of truth and authenticity. The abortive revolution had begun with an accident. Elias Sr, the founder and chairman of the ad agency, died at the meeting of his executive board, right after making a proclamation about the need for "creative foreplay" to capture consumers. (With his body lying on the boardroom table, his greedy colleagues swiftly removed the man's wallet and jewellery.) The remaining directors thought to avoid selecting one of their rivals by voting instead for the African-American Putney Swope, presuming he could never win. He did. Swope swiftly took command, fired nearly all the white admen and hired mostly African-Americans, in particular a group of black militants. He proclaimed he would not advertise such harmful products as alcohol, cigarettes, and war toys. He insisted on complete creative freedom: no interference from the white businessmen. He called upon his creative team, indeed any employee, to fashion ads that told the truth about the product, however harsh that might be: consequently a life insurance ad showed how a poor soul lost an arm and a leg to pay the premiums. Everyone, the copywriters and other employees, awestruck businessmen and fascinated consumers, the hysterical media, even the president of the United States (played by a dwarf), got excited at this novelty.

But Swope was something of a phony. Once in charge, he acted like a despot. He demanded his clients pay upfront $1 million in cash, the money stored in a huge glass aquarium, guarded by black cowboys. He stole ideas from other admen. He fired those who displeased or disagreed with him. He hired an armed bodyguard, albeit an incompetent one. He dressed up as both a black militant and as a Castro clone. He surrounded himself with black hucksters no less venal than their white predecessors. Then he began to "sell out," to approve ads that were as trashy and degrading as any produced by the mainstream agencies. And the movie showed a series of these efforts, including a lengthy commercial for an airline that was really an example of softcore pornography. Another character, the bizarre "A-rab," called Putney a "jive nigger," meaning apparently a bullshitter. Near the end, he told his creative team he had reneged, that he would accept ads for harmful products, purportedly to test their moral fibre, only to find that they were willing to follow his lead. In disgust, suffering a version of the liar's plight perhaps, he decided to end the project, to escape – but with $8 million of the fees collected from business clients. The rest of that money was burned when the A-rab threw a Molotov cocktail into the pile because he was not supposed to get any of this swag. That was how the movie ended: with a burned-out aquarium. So much for the effort to transform something as flawed as advertising. *Putney Swope* mocked the whole reform enterprise as fatuous nonsense.[92]

One of the later counter-stories drew on the legacy of the now often-discredited critique of mass culture, and thus on the distinction between the High and the Low.[93] Initially the novelist Jonathan Dee (b. 1962) reworked that storyline in a fascinating essay entitled "But Is It Advertising?" for *Harper's Magazine* (January 1999). The piece was ostensibly about the 1998 Clio Awards, the best-known annual awards ceremony of the American advertising industry. And he did discuss what happened and what he saw, which was a host of ads and commercials. The point of his essay was to determine just what sort of art form, better yet artifice, advertising really was. Dee's essay was subtitled "Capitalist realism at the Clio Awards," a nod to sociologist Michael Schudson, who had coined the term in his analysis *Advertising: The Uneasy Persuasion* (1984).[94] Obviously Schudson had derived the label from the tradition of Socialist Realism, notorious in the art world because of its submission to the dictates of Stalin's communist regime of the 1930s. Each form of sponsored art might celebrate a different goal: the Soviet version idealized production, the American version consumption. But they also shared many features, especially in the way they depicted, or simplified or typified, reality. More to the point, advertising was full of characters rather than individuals – say, the typical housewife or the playboy – and full of abstracted scenarios of life, about the present but oriented to the promise of a better future. "The central value of American capitalist realism remains, for all its staggering refinement, as old as Marx: the fetishism of commodities," wrote Dee. "Capitalist realism amounts to an insistent portrait of the world as a garden of consumption in which any need – no matter how antimaterial, how intimate, or how social – can be satisfied by buying the right things."

But Dee went beyond this charge. He agreed that the "aesthetic Berlin Wall" between High and Low had crumbled. The trouble was that this event set free the corrupted aesthetic of advertising to pollute all forms of creative expression with its practices, whether popular music or contemporary art. He recounted a series of examples where pop musicians had sold their songs to ad agencies, where film directors used their talents to make commercials, how authors such as William Burroughs (for Nike) or Douglas Coupland (for Absolut vodka) had become touts, how movies such as *Independence Day* (1996) resembled commercials, how highbrow artists such as Damien Hirst or Jeff Koons actually mirrored the work of the admen. This was more the trashing of art than the enchantment of life.

Dee placed deception at the core of its aesthetic enterprise. "The men and women who make ads are not hucksters," he argued; "they are artists with nothing to say, and they have found their form." He did not deny the appeal of some of the television commercials, for example Apple's "Think Different" campaign, where the company-appropriated genius was "so perversely compelling." But he made use of a concept the literary critic and sometime novelist George Steiner had taken from physics: "anti-language, that which is transcendentally annihilating of truth and meaning," in Steiner's words. Dee recognized how advertising had recently evolved away from talking about the product or the user to sell values or express moral homilies or to tout ideals. He cited how Apple Computer employed a photo of Gandhi, how Heineken Beer urged "Seek the Truth," and how Kellogg's possessed "Simple is Good." Advertising appropriated and changed the context, and hollowed out the meaning, always to hype the commodity. "The real condition of advertising speech is not falsehood as much as a kind of truthlessness." Dee was especially exercised because so many of the Clios struck an ironic pose, using humour to mock sincerity. He was also upset by the way the adman possessed dissent and rebellion – again, Apple's "Think Different" campaign – to sell mundane goods. The consequence of advertising's influence was to undermine the foundations of authenticity. "The real violence, though, lies not in the ways in which these messages are forced upon us," he concluded, "but in the notion they embody that words can be made to mean anything, which is hard to distinguish from the idea that words mean nothing." Arthur Danto had famously claimed that art was above all "embodied meanings," while Varnedoe and Gopnik favoured the notion of work characterized by "originality and intensity" (16). Dee thought the contemporary commercials, like much of what was called contemporary art, faked it all too effectively for the cultural health of America. Advertising was a dangerous kind of faux art.

Dee exaggerated, wildly in places, especially because his choice of examples – or of horrors, as he presumed – was so selective. The commercials shown at the Clios were hardly representative of the whole corpus of advertising. The award-winners were among the most imaginative and expensive, the most artistic ads the agencies produced.[95] Far more ads, particularly in print or on the radio, if also deceptive, aspired to become news, not art. But his polemic did serve to prick the balloon of self-esteem any admen might enjoy over their new status as maestros of creativity. He took obvious relish in recalling the debacle of 1991 when the Clios ceremony fell apart due to bankruptcy and mismanagement, and the audience rushed on the stage to grab the statuettes themselves. "In a ceremony promising the rigorous judgment of aesthetic success, the prizes wind up being distributed randomly – symbols of excellence, stripped of their relation to that which they symbolize," Dee declared. "They should give out the Clios that way every year." That would signify how the admen were suffering from a terminal case of self-deception.

This animus infused Dee's later novel *Palladio*. "'Don't you get tired,' he said, 'of all the lying?'" (133).[96] That question was posed by one adman, Mal Osbourne, to another, John Wheelwright, both characters in *Palladio*. It was yet another variant on a query and a statement that kept reoccurring in the biography of the adman. Wakeman posed it in *The Hucksters*. Emory Leeson, the adman in *Crazy People*, had said something similar. Here, in Dee's novel, the question was never answered, not directly. But John's later actions "said" yes, effectively he did. Dee's novel was a complicated and ambitious study of psychology, morality, and circumstance in modern America, where much of the plot revolved around the supposed nature of both contemporary art and contemporary advertising. But *Palladio* combined the styles of a novel of ideas and the tragic romance into one social melodrama. The impressive work, sometimes acclaimed but not a bestseller, was subject to a number of different readings.[97] My approach emphasizes the ways *Palladio* elaborated the discontents of deception, especially in the realm of advertising. The novel illustrated, if in an unusual fashion, how the triumph of creativity had not dispelled but merely refined the adman's dilemma of old.

Although full of a range of intriguing personages – a cynical copywriter, a feisty filmmaker, two aging radical professors, and so on – the novel featured three main protagonists. The first was the congenial, perceptive, but insecure John Wheelwright, a youthful art director upset with the petty corruptions of his work. The second was the lovely, clever, but always alienated Molly Howe, initially a youngster who grew up during the course of the novel. Never herself creative, for she had no real occupation, she became the source of disruption in the social equation. The third personality, the most intriguing and mysterious, was the accomplished and imaginative but dictatorial Mal (Malcolm) Osbourne, an older creative and an executive. It was Mal (was it only an accident that the name connoted the bad or the flawed?) who was the great, and a bit crazed, visionary who planned a new kind of marketing institution called Palladio. Furthermore, Mal's rhetoric – his conversations, a recruiting letter, a speech – served as the main vehicles for Dee's critique of the gospel of creativity.

The novel was actually a collection of linked tales divided into three unequal parts. The long opening section oscillated back and forth between the tale of Molly growing up, and her romantic entanglements, this over the span of roughly a decade, and the tale of John, once Molly's old flame, who left his New York job (and relationship) to join Mal as the administrator of what became Palladio. The second part took the form of John's diary, where he described the troubled intimacies of the threesome and the fiery destruction of Palladio. The last part, the shortest section, recounted the fate of the various damaged souls of the melodrama, a retreat into self-deception and stunted lives. Dee interspersed among these separate tales a series of cryptic fragments of ad speak, art talk, and media commentary under the label "*MESSAGE*," presumably bits of the ongoing social conversation.[98] The ending left the impression that

America, despite the Palladio experiment, remained a culture mired in bullshit and humbug.

Dee actually included a tale of the horrible Pitch early in the novel. The Doucette casual wear account, worth $35 million in billings, so important to Canning Leigh + Osbourne, was going up for review. That caused a sense of dread among the creatives, as the loss of the account would likely mean firings. Mal was supposed to oversee the creative work the agency would put forward at the Pitch. He did not, nor did he approve what was done. The agency staffers arrived at the Pitch not knowing what was to come. Mal proposed a more radical version of the controversial Benetton campaign of the 1990s (though he did not admit this), free of any corporate logo, full of transgression and social consciousness, all to generate publicity and buzz. Doucette would become a new Renaissance patron of the avant-garde arts. The client was horrified by that prospect. The agency staffers were equally shocked – "deranged, but brilliant" (85), one commented.[99] The account went elsewhere, and the agency broke up, Mal leaving the partnership. Here was another instance of the adman's dilemma, where the persuader endeavoured to fashion a truthful art to avoid the normal deceptions, only to face the rejections of the client and his colleagues.

The novel existed squarely in the established tradition of anti-advertising. Mal was on record as a devout hater of advertising: "I want to kill it" (79). Why this animus? "Advertising is the beast," he once proclaimed, presumably making it the source of all ills, an endorsement of the motif of the ad-maker's sin (227). "The language of advertising is the language of American life: American art, American politics, American media, American law, American business" (117). Here, in a letter meant to recruit ad people, Mal explained how the Creative Revolution of the 1960s had failed, how the Bernbach promise of redemption was betrayed. Back in 1973, the year he joined DDB, Mal thought advertising was an integral part of "a movement to restore the idea of truth in language, of plain speaking – a kind of democratic speech to set against the totalitarian language of the times" (115). But, sad to say, over the next thirty years the effort to foster plain speech, honesty, and truth had succumbed to a wave of irony, assiduously nourished by admen everywhere:

> Our society propagates no values outside of the peculiar sort of self-knowledge implied in the wry smile of irony, the way we remove ourselves from ourselves in order to be insulated from the terrible emptiness of the way we live now. That wry smile mocks self-knowledge, mocks the idea of right and wrong, mocks the notion that art is worth making at all. (116)

Mal's diatribe was a restatement of Dee's earlier charge that advertising constituted an anti-language, a lot of noise saying nothing which sapped signs, words, and images of their meaning. Instead of truth, the ad-maker was wedded to deception, the creative impulse devoted to fashioning messages "about envy, ... about sex, about lust, about instant gratification" solely to move product (227).

Arguably Dee showed elsewhere in Palladio that irony, however wicked, was never about nothing. Roman Gagliardi, John's partner at the New York agency, designed a massively cynical campaign for the Beef Council. The point was to imply that the client knew the risks of beef. The ads would simply evade the health anxieties of the public. "'Six burgers a week. That's all we ask'" (119). The campaign was thus about appetite, not about nothing. Mal's diatribe boasted its own dose of hype.

Mal's vision was both utopian and bizarre. Palladio was his name for a unique art institute-cum-advertising agency that briefly flourished, becoming extraordinarily famous and ultimately notorious. According to reviewers (since Dee did not explain), the title "Palladio" referred to "palladium," a protective image in Greco-Roman times, or to the Italian architect Andrea Palladio, whose classicism influenced design in the early American republic. In any case Palladio was a place, ruled by Mal, run by John, and funded by corporate clients, where an elite group of creatives, some ad-makers but mostly artists, were free to produce original and intense work. That work, initially, was circulated to a mass audience through the apparatus of the publicity system, on billboards, in magazines, and so on – except that the art was never to be tainted with any commercial message or client logo. Moreover, the client must use other means, perhaps a listing of credits elsewhere, to associate the firm with the new art. Corporate America would sponsor the success of a new avant-garde which might thus enchant not only the world of consumption but the lifeworld itself. And succeed the Palladio project did at first, as a media sensation and as a sales technique. Best of all, the process effectively reversed the normal mode of advertising, where the ad-maker remained anonymous and the client's name ubiquitous. Dee had imagined a unique solution to the problem of recognition, or the lack thereof, which had long upset the profession. Seemingly, Palladio had realized that old dream of the sovereign ego, where the ad-maker had total control of his or her work, in fact might concoct the immaculate campaign free of any brand.

But, in the end, Palladio did not work that way. (Like *Putney Swope*, *Palladio* was about a failed revolution.) True, Mal and John kept the clients at bay. But the final word on what was deemed art now resided with Mal. He refused the effort of Ellen Sizemore, a hotshot creative (and John's bedmate at Palladio) because one of her creations appropriated a passage by Jack Kerouac. No work bearing the stamp of Palladio could "filch value": "No looting, no sampling, no colonizing the past" (297). That had been the nasty practice of admen for years. Everything at Palladio must be original – an imperative that expressed Dee's view that art must bring something new into the world. Understandably, Ellen was not amused. "What is this, Year One? What is he, fucking Pol Pot or something?" She soon escaped back to New York. And Mal's diktat provoked a short-lived rebellion among the other creatives.

The second problem was more fundamental. If the clients were kept at bay, Capital was not. One ferocious critic labelled Palladio "the absolute epicenter of corruption" because it went well beyond the typical sin of the sellout (259). The creatives were effectively "brainwashed. They don't even know what it is they've been brought here to do" (259). One of the professors behind another source of opposition called "CultureTrust" (modelled on the Adbusters foundation) went one step further, when John tried to buy their submission:

> Dissent is the art. And crushing dissent, Johnny, in case you haven't twigged to this yet, is the business that you're in. Swallowing it, bastardizing it, defanging it, eliminating it. The reason you think our art's meaning wouldn't change if we sold it to you is that you don't think it means anything anyway. Art comes from somewhere. It has provenance. Changing that provenance changes the art. Denying that provenance denies the art. (329)

The touted purity and independence of Palladio was no more than an illusion, only another form of self-deception. The experiment was in fact just an updated reformulation of the old claim that advertising was art in the service of commerce.

What brought down Palladio, however, was the flawed character of the gospel of creativity. The stunning novelty of the experiment, all the media attention, swiftly fueled celebrity. Mal was one person who became a star: his hubris was so great he publically declared, at one awards ceremony, that he had "killed" advertising (227). But the artists at Palladio also shared in the fame, one in particular called Jean-Claude Milo, a reclusive star, passionate, antisocial, committed only to his work. His results at first produced excitement. Though not an adman, he shared a fear that purportedly disturbed copywriters and art directors, namely that the energies of creativity would be exhausted. He kept striving for a more extreme and a more intense experience, which led into the dead-end of performance art. This struck clients as peculiar, since his work was never to be seen outside Palladio, making it almost an un-ad. But Milo's celebrity was sufficient that all manner of marketing big-wigs gathered for the unveiling, a most bizarre kind of Pitch. What happened was that Milo took the final step – call it a self-sacrifice perhaps, certainly a suicide – consuming himself and eventually much of the building in an orchestrated conflagration. No one had guided Milo; Mal was absent, John was preoccupied, the two men who could have forestalled the idiotic expression of a creativity gone mad. The upshot was a brief media frenzy of speculation and condemnation that marked the end of the experiment.

Dee let one cynical adman, Roman Gagliardi, reflect the glee the "real" practitioners felt over this failure. For he had been much disturbed by the initial success of Palladio. "It made him feel alienated, profoundly so, though from what, he wasn't sure," Roman mused. "He just didn't want to live in a world that took people like Mal Osbourne seriously" (355). The frenzy over the conflagration – MoMA, it was rumoured, had offered a million dollars for the "snuff film" of the Milo affair – proved otherwise. As yet another copywriter exclaimed, "Hey, who says irony is dead?" (354). There was, in the end, a definite limit to how far the gospel of creativity might transform the ad world or enchant the real world.[100]

In fact what it did was fill that world with untruth, or so yet a third probe of the ways of the persuader presumed. "My job requires a certain … moral flexibility." That comment might well apply to the job description of the adman. The admission, however, was made by a colleague of sorts, the lobbyist Nick Naylor, a character played brilliantly by Aaron Eckhart in the comedy drama *Thank You for Smoking*. Naylor was really a public relations counsel of the Bernays lineage, although one critic identified him as an "ad exec," and not without cause.[101]

Thank You for Smoking was a work of genial satire, based on a book by Christopher Buckley and directed by Jason Reitman (b. 1977), who had experience in television advertising. It won more favour with critics than the public, although the movie certainly pulled in a goodly sum at the box office.[102] Just about every interest represented was satirized: Big Tobacco and the anti-smoking movement, government and business, Hollywood and the press, teachers. That was one reason a few reviewers were unhappy, because the movie didn't pick a side, presumably that of anti-smoking.[103] Instead, the target was the so-called practice of spin which had spread through America.

At the beginning Nick Naylor labelled himself one of the most "truly despised" people in the country. He was the public voice of Big Tobacco, perhaps the most vilified business in the USA, damned for causing the deaths of hundreds of thousands of people each year. He was the vice-president of the Academy of Tobacco Studies, a front organization funded by tobacco firms to defend smoking and ward off attacks by any legitimate means, including fake science, legal action, and propaganda. The last was Nick's specialty: he was a skilled talker, a master of the art of rhetoric. "That's the beauty of argument," he told his son, "if you argue correctly you're never wrong." We first met him on a televised talk show where he managed to score by suggesting Big Tobacco was actually the friend of a "cancer boy," a customer, whereas the anti-smoking advocate really wanted him to die. But Nick was also a separated father, the sometime guardian of his devoted son Joey, who had reached an age when he was inquisitive about his dad's occupation. Nick not only had to explain – he took Joey on business trips – but guide his son in the ways of moral conduct. That might seem an improbable task for a person mired in deception.

Nick's enemy was Senator Finistirre of Vermont who planned to dishonor cigarettes by mandating the printing of a skull-and-crossbones image on each package of cigarettes. Nick proposed to offset this bad publicity by using product placements in Hollywood movies: as in the early days of talkies, the lead actors ought to be depicted visibly relishing a cigarette, particularly in a scene full of sex and sensuality. He even went off to Hollywood to contact a facilitator, who arranged to place such an ad in a future science fiction film starring two leading actors, Catherine Zeta-Jones and Brad Pitt. The purpose was to make smoking enticing once again, as in the days of Lauren Bacall and Humphrey Bogart.

Nick's forte, however, was to sow doubt and confusion. This he shared with the other members of the MOD (merchants of death) Squad, a woman lobbying for the alcohol industry and a man speaking for the firearms interests, who met each week for lunch to share stories and insights. Nick might question a speaker's credentials or argue that evidence of harm was not complete or stifle criticism by proposing a $50 million anti-teen smoking campaign. The one action which caused him some moral difficulty was bribing a dying ex-Marlboro Man to ensure his silence, though that too he managed to do. He countered any assault by his own charge, thus suggesting that the skull-and-crossbones ought to go first on Vermont's cheese because of the cholesterol menace, a blow to the Senator. Always he urged the wisdom of personal responsibility and freedom of choice, shifting the ground of the debate from health to liberty. He worked to deceive via diversion, bluff, pretense, half-truth, dissimulation, distortion, sometimes bullshit, or just plain concealment.

What was most remarkable, and most engaging, was his lack of self-deception, unusual in the stories of and about the persuaders, especially the adman. He obviously did not suffer the effects of the adman's dilemma, even if the movie sometimes left the impression he should. Nick knew he was a deceiver, though he likely would have preferred the term "spin doctor." Or perhaps "advocate," because he occasionally made reference to the analogy of the lawyer: it seemed every cause or interest deserved a voice in the social conversation. He was asked on a couple of occasions why he worked as a lobbyist. Once, slyly, he answered, "Population control." On another occasion he claimed money, as like everyone he had to pay the mortgage. But the most honest answer was pleasure: he was so skilled at deception that he took pride in what he could achieve. Nick was a character who might be justly charged with that sin of "duping delight," as he was in a newspaper exposé by a reporter-cum-bedmate that nearly ruined him. In the end he cut free from Big Tobacco, just before it began to surrender to all the lawsuits, to establish his own public relations consultancy to assist unloved, troubled, and of course wealthy corporations, such as the logging industry, Big Oil, or cell phone manufactures, these last being clients who were worried by charges of brain damage. He also succeeded in fashioning his son in his own image: a master of argument who espoused the creed of personal responsibility. It is all a bit reminiscent of that singular character the confidence-man, fathered by Herman Melville, discussed at the beginning of this biography. One reviewer decided, "thankfully Reitman (son of director Ivan) steers clear of cheesiness by never showing him completely transform[ed] from cretin to hero. He is always the man we love to hate."[104]

However lovable, what Nick dispensed was neither enlightenment nor enchantment but obfuscation. He was another kind of falsifier, more pernicious because more perceptive and more able than most of his breed. This charge was more common in treatments of persuaders other than the figure of the adman. The sin was elaborated in one such denunciation entitled *Toxic Sludge Is Good for You* (1995), an exposé of the public relations industry.[105] Adam Curtis, the British documentary filmmaker, in his most noted work *The Century of the Self* (2002), found in Edward Bernays the most notorious of the persuaders who sought to stupefy the public. Some years later Jason Reitman directed a much more popular film called *Up in the Air* (2009), starring George Clooney as a kind of salesman of death (figuratively speaking) who sold the virtues of termination to employees caught in the horror of a corporate downsizing. The theme of obfuscation was widespread in the new millennium, where it might serve to dishonour the persuasion industries.

6. Ubiquity: Morgan Spurlock, *POM Wonderful Presents: The Greatest Movie Ever Sold*, 2011

The denial of enchantment, of advertising enriching art or life, was evident in a peculiar documentary directed and starring Morgan Spurlock. What the adman delivered, according to Spurlock, was a ubiquity of selling, a mass of clutter that now filled the whole waking world – the only escape in America, as Ralph Nader put it, was to sleep. Morgan Spurlock (b. 1970) is a noted independent filmmaker who achieved considerable fame when he wrote *Super Size Me* (2004), an exposé of the ill effects of the fast food industry, and especially McDonald's, on the health of Americans. That documentary recounted the sad results of his own experience of eating only McDonald's food for one month: major weight gain, puffiness, liver troubles, and depression. Spurlock had fashioned here the mix of self-experiment or self-sacrifice, humour, and revelation that became the trademarks of his documentary style. The documentary proved a significant public relations embarrassment to the industry. The popular success of his tale of woe is often credited with bringing some changes to the menus of McDonald's and similar franchises.

Spurlock was provoked to launch an investigation into the ubiquity of selling when he was shocked by an especially blatant instance of product placement in his favourite television drama of the moment. The upshot was another "joke doc," as one wag declared, with the cumbersome title *POM Wonderful Presents: The Greatest Movie Ever Sold*.[106] The film explored issues of authenticity and truth crucial to the question of enchantment. The title announced its strange character: POM Wonderful, a fruit-drink company, had committed to paying $1 million for the special billing. Spurlock fashioned a film about product placement, marketing, and advertising that was to be fully funded by product placement, marketing, and advertising – and he then boasted about that fact.

Once more Spurlock immersed himself in the events he recounted. Right at the beginning, he set the scene by arguing and showing how the decline of the television commercial – the result of TiVo and the internet – had pushed advertisers to put their messages everywhere, even in urinals, to reach consumers. Thereafter the film covered his efforts to make the documentary from beginning to end. These included his pitches to admen and prospective clients to find sponsors, meetings and interviews with specialists and critics about the process (some occurring at sponsors' sites), negotiations over co-promotion deals, and a plethora of ads, not only product placements but actual commercials. Some of the most edifying and humorous moments came when he interviewed a range of people: other filmmakers such as J.J. Abrams and Quentin Tarantino, critics such as Noam Chomsky and Ralph Nader, and assorted veterans of advertising such as Bob Garfield, then retired from his post at *Advertising Age*. Spurlock was horrified when it was suggested he had pioneered a new class of documentary, saturated with selling, that others might adopt, since the field of documentary filmmaking was largely free of ads. What he intended, he claimed, was "transparency," making clear the whole process, the personnel, the companies, the methods involved in the practice of product placement, or as some people in Hollywood called it, "brand integration." That was why some reviewers concluded *The Greatest Movie* was the most "meta" of all documentaries: subject and object were one.

The first obstacle Spurlock faced was the suspicion, if not the hostility, of the marketing and business communities. He had a reputation as a foe of commerce because of *Super Size Me*. The suspicion was deserved: *The Greatest Movie* had an undertone of mild anti-commercialism, not least because it mocked the assorted absurdities of selling. Spurlock sought some expert guidance to counter the impression of enmity and to establish his possible appeal. Early on, he paid a visit to a firm, Olson Zaltman, which claimed the ability to discover just what your brand personality was. That furnished one of the most amusing segments of the documentary, where he was interviewed at length about his past, his attitudes, his views on life. It was determined that Spurlock had a contradictory brand, both "playful" and "mindful," which meant he had to seek support from prospective clients who valued, among other things, taking risks. In a later commentary on the experience (on the DVD release of the documentary), Spurlock suggested the finding was if not useful, then at least predictive, because he did win support from risk-takers. Not that Spurlock placed much stock in such silliness, and he agreed with a musician who found talk of "your" brand "cheesy," somehow demeaning. The segment nonetheless furnished the first evidence of one of the conclusions of the investigation: how a series of individuals and companies boasting an arcane knowledge and the requisite vocabulary had become so well established in the realm of marketing. Much later, Spurlock had a similar and equally bewildering experience at Buyology, a neuromarketing firm, that tested what stimuli – fear, craving, sex – might elicit action, which was important in shaping the trailer for *The Greatest Movie*. This was all reminiscent of the old conceit of the adman, albeit dressed up in new clothes. Advertising here appeared as a science as well as an art – that presumption of a hybrid form again – where experts, notably market researchers, could claim they had fashioned sure-fire instruments of selling. That was no more convincing now than in the days of Claude Hopkins or Ernest Dichter, both of whom assured clients they had nearly all the answers. Spurlock was more bewildered or disturbed, but always amused, than he was convinced. As before, the claims of certainty were mostly a mix of myth and self-deception, but still a useful fiction to generate employment.

The advertising practitioners were especially wary of Spurlock. He showed in the film some samples of his attempts to persuade representatives of various advertising agencies. One group wondered what his angle would be, presumably whether he would condemn advertising and criticize the advertisers. Understandably, after so many decades of bad press, the ad-maker was not about to welcome yet another so-called exposé. Where was the profit in associating with a dubious outsider like Spurlock? Another group of admen did appear ready to help – while the camera was filming; once they were off record, however, they, like all the others, said no. It was an unintended but telling sign of the presumed prevalence of duplicity in the ad world. The general consensus was: "We want nothing to do with your movie." The one exception was Richard Kirshenbaum, already a friend of Spurlock, and his partner Jon Bond, two veteran admen, who thought his project sounded like fun and agreed to offer advice and assistance. Friendship overcame fear.

Spurlock needed all the help he could get in approaching business. At this moment he mutated into an adman of sorts. When asked specifically by Kirshenbaum how far he would go to win sponsors, he replied, "Whatever it takes." Later he admitted (in his DVD commentary) to some nine months of searching for sponsors, making some 500 to 600 cold calls to drum up prospects. The big corporations, such as Volkswagen, Apple, Coke, and of course McDonald's, all turned him down. The breakthrough came when Kirshenbaum persuaded an existing client, Ban deodorant, to hear his Pitch. The success Spurlock had in convincing Ban to join up as a sponsor established him as "brand friendly," which then opened doors to other prospects. Viewers of the documentary then saw Spurlock working hard to sell his vision, complete with the promise of fair dealing and much advertising, first to Sheetz, a fast food chain, and later to POM Wonderful. He even turned up with storyboards to convince the owners and their executives. He made an obviously inflated claim, "I love Sheetz," to impress one group – which promptly recognized this example of "shameless marketing." In the case of POM he promised not only top billing and a commercial, but also that he would only drink POM on air and blur out the image of any other drinks. That succeeded. Later, his Pitch for the proposed commercial, where he put forward three jokey spots, failed completely and so POM executives dictated the style and content of the ad. But in the end his efforts paid off: in addition to Ban and POM he got Mini Cooper, Jet Blue, Hyatt, Amy's Kitchen (frozen pizzas), Merrell shoes, Aruba Tourism, even a strange shampoo, Mane 'n Tale, for both animals and humans: roughly twenty brands in all. The success produced a series of contracts where he made commitments – and he sought legal advice to determine the extent and the limits of compliance. The most important, of course, was a promise not to disparage any brand. The treatment had to be positive.

The promises and the commitments led to moments of angst – signs of an "existential crisis" were apparently a trademark of his style[107] – when Spurlock worried on screen whether he was selling out. In a way he was afflicted by the adman's dilemma because whatever he did, play the truth-teller or play the promoter, would mean a kind of failure, whether moral or financial or professional. What he feared was the loss of artistic integrity because the sponsors could determine so much of what was said and shown. The key was to ensure, as director J.J. Abrams put it, "storytelling, not story-selling." Here, probably unintentionally, Spurlock mirrored a worry that was often expressed in stories, more fiction than fact, about the adman. Both Noam Chomsky and Ralph Nader warned Spurlock of the perils of co-optation. He even consulted a bunch of "men on the street" about what constituted a sellout. "A sell-out is someone that has no honor and does something just for money and doesn't take anything else into consideration," said one. Another suggested the key was whether "you" the filmmaker did better – presumably realizing "your" purposes – than the sponsors: if so you were just buying in. And that became the tagline or slogan: "He's not selling out, he's buying in." Here was the philosophy of Donald Trump, briefly interviewed as the greatest celebrity spokesperson. In fact the two actual admen, Kirshenbaum and Bond, were full of glee, sure that by admitting he was selling out, Spurlock wasn't. "It's genius," according to Bond, in a dubious endorsement of the virtues of confession. On screen, near the end, TV host Jimmy Kimmel called Spurlock "a shameless whore," and Spurlock said "yes,"

with a smile and a chuckle. Certainty the hype and the product placement in *The Greatest Movie* were often so blatant that they became both
absurd and ironic. In one instance, while conducting an interview with a
critic of any form of brand integration, this in a Jet Blue terminal, Spurlock filled the screen with pointers, labels, and a warning that the viewer
was being sold assorted brands. In the credits Spurlock announced that
none of the sponsors, not even POM, received final approval of the finished documentary. Apparently buying in had moral legitimacy.

Even so, a few critics noted that before the completion of the film,
POM got in trouble with the government over its health claims. There
was no mention of this in the documentary. That made Spurlock a pur-
veyor of false or at least deceptive advertising. Later he seemed to admit it
would have been wise to include in the film some reference to the case.[108]

Consequently the practice of product placement lacked virtue because
of the self-evident absence of sincerity, on the part of the filmmaker or
the adman, whether in the documentary or in general. The practice was
no more laudable on the grounds of honesty. Spurlock asked Nader, "Is
there such a thing as truth in advertising?" "Yes," replied Nader. "Advertisements that say they're lying are telling the truth." Some of the "man
on the street" interviews evinced a more nuanced or less self-assured
view, namely that there was honest advertising, that a modicum of truth
was necessary, that this truth was always glossed, hyped or slanted to
achieve the sell. In effect they recognized how the adman's dilemma (as
a social mechanism) worked to restrain, but never to banish, deception.
Spurlock himself, while munching on one of Amy's pizzas, wondered
aloud, "can you trust what regular people say?" He then told a story of
how he had sought to deceive his son when Nemo the goldfish died – he
had rushed to the pet store to buy what was Nemo 2. He didn't know how
long the deception would hold. The point was that the deceit in advertising was no more than an extension of the dishonesty that was commonplace in ordinary life. But such a fact hardly served to support any claim
that the reign of the adman had enriched the world.

The Greatest Movie went a step further to disprove the notion. Spurlock
made a special trip to São Paulo, Brazil's largest city and one of the most
populous metropolises in the world – where, by the way, he showed how
he was so well treated in the local Hyatt hotel. The purpose was to pub-
licize a place where advertising had been banished from the visual surround by a "Clean City Law." Some years earlier, the mayor, guided by his
director of urban planning (and both were interviewed), had instituted
a ban to dispel all "visual pollution" that made it impossible to actually

see the city. The move, initially controversial, supposedly now garnered the support of 90 per cent of the populace. Retailers had accepted and adjusted, or so they said in interviews. People on the street expressed their approval: "Everything is much clearer." Spurlock found the ad-free landscape amazing, and in the DVD commentary expressed the wish that some American city might try a similar experiment. But the actual before-and-after scenes of São Paolo told a different story, as one reviewer noted. "The place is posited as kind of reclaimed paradise, a chance for overexerted eyes to relax and enjoy real beauty, a conclusion that ignores how its rows of blank buildings also look dingy and boring."[109] The only exception was the shots of street art, of graffiti, which enhanced the otherwise dreary cityscape. What happened next in the documentary was a welcome return to the colour and variety of American billboards. Spurlock did not draw from his foray to São Paolo the plausible judgment that the absence of advertising must be replaced by some form of public art to ensure that a big city was visually exciting.

The Greatest Movie received a lot of attention from the film community. Reviewers were generally favourable, and certainly amused. But however clever and imaginative the documentary, the apparent argument appeared (to some) shallow, lacking the evidence to surprise a knowledgeable viewer or to effectively condemn advertising.[110] In fact, Spurlock's work is much more complicated and sophisticated than the reviewers seemed willing to credit. He really had fashioned an unusual and substantial investigation that served to render the familiar, the accepted, into something noticeable. The viewing public, however, was not particularly impressed, at least if the box office figures were a sign of interest. According to Box Office Mojo, the film generated only $638,476 in domestic sales, not nearly enough to cover a production budget estimated at $1.8 million.[111] It is possible that product placement did not in the end pay for the documentary, since some of the money was tied to performance achievements. There could be many reasons why *The Greatest Movie* failed to cause the popular excitement of, say, *Super Size Me*. But one reason was that many people simply accepted, and often discounted, the plethora of advertisements that surrounded their daily routine.

Spurlock's documentary could not provide a final answer to whether advertising or the adman served to enchant or pollute the world. Any conclusion was likely to remain subjective, a problem similar to the difficulty raised whenever the question of art, especially of what is art, arose. However irritating or distracting, the clutter of ads was arguably preferable to the bare walls and absent billboards of a Soviet city or a reformed

São Paulo. In fact advertising caused much less fuss than graffiti, a common rival that was more authentic perhaps but also more controversial, and often condemned because it supposedly defiled public spaces. That might not be the case in the countryside, where even an adman like David Ogilvy (in his famous *Confessions*) thought billboards disturbed the beauties of Nature. At a minimum, the adman was an artist whose fictions and deceptions did serve to enliven, at least in the city if not elsewhere. But also at a minimum, the adman's work cluttered and disfigured, it usurped spaces that might serve other artistic purposes. And in the case of product placement, advertising served better "story-selling" than "storytelling."

After all the discussion and the rhetoric, the broader social conversation hadn't changed much since the emergence of the gospel of creativity. Consider again Doug Pray's *Art & Copy*. Critics on the web and in the media were far from pleased with this exercise in myth-making. One blogger felt the documentary was too much a vehicle for the "self-mythologizing" of the various stars. Other reviewers agreed Doug Pray had let the admen off much to easily, so they might "present themselves as geniuses and rebels with a bigger agenda." Jennifer Merin called *Art & Copy* a "docuvertisement" for advertising, however "slick and stylish," with only "select moments of truth and clarity." It seemed Pray had fashioned an argument that was just too unbalanced. "There's a big difference between inviting a little sympathy for the devil and nominating Satan for sainthood," mused Nathan Rabin. "*Art & Copy* is mightily diverting, for those who don't mind being sold a slick bill of goods." These responses were obviously conditioned by the tradition of anti-advertising and the narrative of harm which critics did not think Pray and his subjects had effectively trumped. The hard moral questions had been avoided, they reasoned. "It would be nice, though, if he [Pray] pushed his subjects a little harder when they say – as several do – that they had to fight to convince their clients and peers that the best advertising is based on big, simple ideas and powerful emotions," wrote the reviewer in the *New York Times* (20 August 2009). "Are they alarmed that their approach has permeated the culture, from art to journalism to politics? No one seems to be." Or again, this rhetorical question: "And do you, rebel/artist/advertising billionaire, feel complicit in creating this consumer madness?" asked one scold. "This massive spider web where we're sold stuff from the time we open our eyes to the time we close them?"[112] However great the storyline of the maverick and the innovator, all the talk about creativity and enlightenment might please ad-makers, but it still did not altogether convince the chattering classes. The same conundrums remained: artifice over authenticity, deception versus truth, fakery not sincerity, service but rarely sovereignty. It should not surprise, then, that the shadow of Vance Packard continued to haunt the stories told about the power of the adman.

6
A TYRANNY OF SIGNS

Advertising, in the minds of its practitioners, is a controlling science. *Perception is reality*, the admen and -women confidently declare; there is no truth outside consumers' beliefs, the convictions that advertising's technicians are trained to create.
                                                                    – Randall Rothenberg, 1994[1]

We made you want anything that anyone willing to pay us wanted you to want. We were hired guns of the human soul. We pulled the strings on the people across the land and by god they got to their feet and they danced for us.
                                                                    – Joshua Ferris, 2007[2]

What advertising had done was "to seep out beyond its proper sphere and take over the culture." That was the claim of Mark Crispin Miller, identified as the Director of Media Studies at Johns Hopkins University. He appeared in an NBC primetime documentary entitled *Sex, Buys & Advertising* on 31 July 1990.[3] The documentary opened by asserting that America had experienced an advertising explosion during the 1980s. "Everybody's doing it," the host Deborah Norville asserted: that declaration was a signal of marketing's moment, the feeling or fear that advertising and promotion in general were now pre-eminent, that they had infiltrated or surpassed news and entertainment. (Accordingly, a couple of economists some years later estimated that about one-quarter of America's GDP was devoted to persuasion, very broadly defined.)[4] The documentary attempted to sample the various dimensions of the ad swarm: a coming Estée Lauder campaign, the rush of celebrity ads, the Nike campaigns, a Pitch for a new account, specialized advertising of various kinds, research on consumers and youth, the regulation of industry practices, and the problem of fraudulent advertising.

It was full of bits and pieces of television commercials, mostly recent, as well as a range of talking heads, a model, the actor Michael J. Fox, officials, professors, and so on, some of them, like Miller, critical, but others industry types, admen mainly, who explained or justified. Running through the documentary, however, was the presumption that advertising was definitely a discourse of power. One crucial point reiterated a few times was the fact that admen believed emotion, not logic, was the key to making a successful selling effort, a belief in line with the thrust of brain and mind studies.[5] Miller clearly worried about the advertising effect, as did Dr Carol Moog, a psychologist, also briefly featured. When ads populated the visual surround, when advertising took over the culture, then what? Well, Norville noted the signs of a consumer revolt, which by this time was a tired cliché roughly seventy years old. But she concluded that advertising was here to stay, and declared it was the responsibility of consumers, especially parents, to ensure that the advertising effect was disciplined.[6]

During the next two and a half decades, and especially as the World Wide Web matured, America experienced an acceleration and an extension of the ad swarm. Advertising appeared in more and more spaces – increased product placement in movies, commercials in public schools, the rise of brand stores, messages on building facades, on sidewalks and in parking lots, on fruit, even in urinals. The most dramatic invasion occurred in a new space, the internet. Although once touted as a domain free of selling, the internet and its offshoot the World Wide Web eventually succumbed to the marketing imperative. By 2016 the digital ad spend, at an estimated $72.09 billion, surpassed the monies spent on television for the first time.[7] Initially the blight took the form of email ads, or spam, selling an assortment of usually shoddy goods, and infamously a collection of penis enhancers. But before long websites were polluted by a host of so-called banner ads and pop-ups, increasingly videos, touting all manner of products. At the same time the fact that online activity could be traced and recorded enabled what Tim Wu, an accomplished and many-sided law professor, has called "the attention merchants" – Google, Facebook, and the like – to capture information about the tastes and interests of a mass of individual consumers which was then sold to advertisers.[8] People seemed willing to share such information in return for all the free stuff search machines and social media offered. This sparked a boom in targeted advertising, where ads tailored to, say, a cruise-lover followed her wherever she went on the web, which could seem like a new kind of stalking.[9] Another change, this on traditional as well as online media, was the spread of stealth marketing, where the ads were embedded in the program, or where the program itself, news or entertainment, was sponsored by an advertiser. This approach could defeat the work of TiVo or ad blockers that forestalled more obvious forms of advertising. More to the point, stealth marketing fashioned a new kind of unconscious sell that evaded the cognitive defenses of consumers, or so Mara Einstein claimed.[10] Twenty-five years later, Miller's fear that advertising had taken over the culture, at least the popular culture, seemed even more correct.[11]

Consequently, *Sex, Buys & Advertising* was only the beginning of a series of probes of marketing's moment, the advertising effect, and the changing role of persuaders generally in a period when digital technologies and soon the internet were rapidly altering the communications scene. What these also charted, moreover, was the slow decline in the significance of the advertising man, though not necessarily the intensity of his dilemma, over the course of the next twenty-five years.

1. Stories of the Matrix: Barry Levinson, *Wag the Dog*, 1997

It was a peculiar movie that, a few years later, showed how the scope and the power of the persuader had expanded in the new era of marketing's moment. It imagined a public sphere where selling and spin were so pervasive that truth was no longer a possibility. But it also suggested that the figure of the adman was passé.

On screen came a version of an old saying, apparently an American phrase dating back to the nineteenth century: "Why does a dog wag its tail? Because a dog is smarter than its tail. If the tail were smarter, the tail would wag the dog." The actual meaning was a trifle ambiguous, but the saying usually suggested a situation where a part, indeed a small part, dominated the whole of something.[12] That saying opened a dark political satire entitled *Wag the Dog*, first shown late in 1997. The movie followed the increasingly bizarre efforts of two accomplished rogues who launched and sold a fake war to save an incumbent president threatened by a sex scandal. That kind of serious comedy was never common in the output of Hollywood. But *Wag the Dog* proved surprisingly popular and even long-lasting, despite the fact it was a low-budget film (estimated cost $15 million) that was shot quickly, in only twenty-nine days. In roughly five months it generated over forty million dollars at the box office in the United States.[13] The success had something to do with the onset of the Clinton/Lewinsky sex scandal early the following year, and a bit later the military escapades that President Clinton authorized against Sudan, Afghanistan, and later Iraq. All this made the movie eerily prophetic. It rejuvenated the old saying, making "wag the dog" a useful tool of analysis in the press commentary on the Washington scene. And it persisted in the public memory well into the new century as a classic statement about the threat news manipulation posed to the workings of democracy in a digital age. It signalled how the nature of persuasion had been transformed by technology.

The more obvious reason for the movie's success, however, was its superb quality as both satire and performance. Janet Maslin (*New York Times*, 26 December 1997) talked of "the film's ring of truth," while Roger Ebert (2 January 1998) found the movie "absurd and convincing at the same time."[14] *Wag the Dog* was very much a collaborative project involving top professionals in the movie business. It began life as a novel by Larry Beinhart entitled *American Hero* (1993), which suggested the Gulf War was a kind of pageant fabricated to ensure the re-election of President George H.W. Bush. The movie rights were purchased by Tribeca Productions, a company founded by actor Robert De Niro and producer Jane Rosenthal. Later the veteran director Barry Levinson (b. 1942) took an interest not in the novel or the script so much as the idea of the fraud. Levinson later revealed his disquiet with the influence of television and the sinister potential of digital technology. He engaged the equally accomplished playwright David Mamet to refashion the story. Together they worked to effect a satire that might capture the craziness as well as the danger they found in the nexus of media and politics. Levinson then persuaded two leading actors, De Niro and Dustin Hoffman, to play the key roles in the resulting script of, respectively, Conrad Brean the spin doctor and Stanley Motss the Hollywood producer. They were joined by other noted performers: actor Woody Harrelson, singer Willie Nelson, and the comedian Denis Leary, as well as the relative newcomer Anne Heche, who played a youthful and all-too-serious White House assistant, Winifred Ames. The result was full of energy, wit, and absurdity, yet welded into a coherent tale about the dominion of the simulacrum in the public sphere of America.[15]

Brean and Motss were relatives of the adman, postmodern variants of that figure. They created images, words and music, news and entertainment, designed to sell as if they were ads, except that their sponsor was hidden. Brean was the more mysterious of the twosome: he never responded to the question about what exactly he did for the president, nor was his past ever revealed. (Levinson later admitted, "He's someone we don't define.")[16] But his forte was crisis management, hence his nickname Mr Fix-It. The president (whose face was never shown) had told his team to contact Brean when news of the charge he had molested a teenage girl in the White House was about to be revealed – on the very eve of an election. Brean was a mix of public relations counsel and political tactician who understood how to manufacture news. He immediately assumed command of the White House staff, turning the press people into mere ciphers who spoke what he wanted. He was completely amoral, not at all interested in the truth of the molestation charge or how justice could best be served, but only seeking to divert the attention of media and public to ensure the scandal did not damage the president's re-election bid. He was concerned not with what the news meant but with what it did, not with reality but with appearances. He soon dreamed up the ploy of a war with Albania, a place few Americans knew much about, which made it ideal as an enemy because then the necessary images of conflict could be readily fabricated. He set out to find the people who might produce a persuasive deception. Time and again, he proved a master of rhetoric who could persuade just about anyone – the awestruck Ames, a dubious Motss, an arrogant CIA man – of the merit of his arguments.

The crucial partner Brean persuaded was Stanley Motss, a veteran Hollywood producer who yearned for a unique challenge – and wanted credit, something he felt his industry denied producers (there was, it was mentioned, no Oscar for a producer). Motss was the showman – his character "very much that of a P.T. Barnum," in the words of Jane Rosenthal who was listed as one of the movie's co-producers.[17] Motss was no more ethical than Brean, though he was honest and forthright in his dealings with his fellow conspirators. He was also vain, confident, excessive, imaginative, and ingenious – much like Barnum. It was Motss who hired the team of specialists who could orchestrate the whole spectacle. It was Motss who dreamed up the signs and sounds of what became act 1 and act 2 and eventually the finale of the war, first the fictional invasion of Albania to forestall nuclear terrorism, later the effort to bring back a fake American hero, William Schumann or "old shoe," trapped in Albania, and finally the grand state funeral for this dead hero. Most importantly, he never flagged: he surmounted all obstacles, even when the CIA declared the war at an end or the purported hero (well played as a deranged criminal by Woody Harrelson) got shot trying to rape a woman. "The war isn't over until I say it's over," he once boasted, despite the depressed spirits of the others. His one weakness was his desire for fame. "I'm prouder of this than anything I ever did in my life," he declared. Brean had warned him he could never tell anyone about his show or his success, but should instead accept an ambassador's post. When Motss threatened to tell all, to get credit, Brean had him executed – offstage, where he was the "victim" of a heart attack.

Wag the Dog was about the web of deception that surrounded the American public. Levinson and Mamet determined that crucial segments of the movie were to be shown occurring on a television screen because this was the prime source of the view of "reality" – in effect a hyperreality – consumed by this public. Much time was devoted to displaying how Brean, Motss, and his team designed the frauds, both their discussions and their apparatus. One lengthy segment detailed the fabrication of a video news release where a young, abused Albanian girl purportedly fled a terrorist assault on her village. Viewers were taken into the studio to see the preparation of the actor, the filming of her flight, and, most striking of all, the digital magic which put a village behind her, a bridge underneath her, and a cat in her arms (in fact she was carrying a bag of chips!). Under the guidance of Motss and Brean, the Willie Nelson character concocted a war anthem and various other songs to accompany the visuals. Another character, called the Fad King, played by Denis Leary, designed merchandising tie-ins for war-themed shoes, burgers, and a memorial, all to captivate the public and generate money. In conversation, Brean suggested that simulation had become the rule of politics in the United States. He left the impression that the fad for yellow ribbons during the Iran hostage crisis, or was it the Gulf War, was a put up job. (In *Wag the Dog* it was old shoes slung into trees and over wires, a reference to the fake hero Schumann imprisoned behind enemy lines.) He suggested Reagan's people had concocted the invasion of Grenada in 1983 to divert attention from the recent massacre of marines in Beirut. He claimed he had been present when filmmakers staged one of the classic images of the Gulf War, a supposed precision strike that sent a bomb down a chimney.

In short the truth was something manufactured by the practices of deception. There was no longer any independent measure of what actually happened. Asked whether some claim really was correct, he replied, "How the fuck do we know?" In response to a denial, he stated, "Of course there's a war. I'm watching it on television." All that was remembered of past wars, he announced, were the images and slogans designed by the experts of propaganda. The irony was that in such a bizarre world, the greatest sin was actually telling the truth, for the deception must never be exposed. "Nobody can tell this story – ever," asserted Brean. That was why Motss had to die.

What led to Motss's fatal mistake was his fury when he saw on television some supposed experts claim that the forthcoming victory of the president was a consequence of political advertising. Throughout the movie Levinson and Mamet placed bits of campaign commercials about which Motss expressed contempt: "fucking amateurs," he once called the unseen advertising people. The ads were so corny, so staged, so traditional they could only provoke disgust over such a feeble effort to persuade. The message here was that the old way of winning elections was no match for the new ways of fabricating news and entertainment. The adman was no longer in the vanguard of the persuasion industries.

There were plenty of signals of contempt for the gullibility of the media and the public as well. Just feed the news people pictures, sensations, and scoops, always to suit their deadlines, and they would effectively do your bidding. Early on, Brean promoted a denial that the president's absence from Washington had anything to do with the B-3 bomber (which did not exist), knowing that denial would excite the media to tout the opposite. The plight of the hapless citizenry was now acute. There was no one to tell them the truth anymore. They were so irrational, emotional, and ignorant, so trusting, that they were easily duped. In one scene Motss had to convince a recalcitrant president to deliver a particular speech about, among other things, the hero left behind. As a result Motss delivered the speech himself in the oval office to a test audience of White House secretaries. So moved were they that they left the room in tears – and the president submitted. In another scenario, a purported photo of prisoner Schumann conveyed in Morse code the command "Courage Mum" and produced a wave of patriotic sentiment. Of course the fraud worked. The media turned away from the sex scandal and the public forgot its existence in the war hysteria. Even the opposing candidate found no purchase to break the illusion.

The deceivers had triumphed. They were licensed by the unwillingness of the media and the public to see through the illusions. According to Dee Dee Myers, onetime White House press secretary (1993–4), what the movie revealed was that the whole process was a joke: spin was everywhere and seeing could not be, or should not be, believing.[18] Many of the difficulties attendant on the adman's dilemma were solved in this fictional universe. The persuaders did not need to build public trust: that was a part of the system of television, news, and even entertainment. Nor did they have to worry much about truth because their web of deception determined what in fact *was* truth. Here was Baudrillard's syndrome: reality replaced by hyperreality. Only the persuaders were not quite sovereign: the president had set the goal, he interfered in the project occasionally, though only trivially, making Brean and Motss the masters of the grand deception. In this weird universe there was some accuracy, a certain rightness, to one of Motss's final boasts: "It's the best work I've ever done in my life. Because it's so honest." The joy, the sense of fun and achievement, was reminiscent of the sentiments of the rogues who had populated the huckster fictions in the first decades of the twentieth century. Nonetheless, like any good satire, *Wag the Dog* might be fun but its message was serious. It was a plea for scepticism and a celebration of cynicism meant to provoke a recognition of a hidden "truth" about political life.

Except it was not so hidden or unrecognized. *Wag the Dog* was one entry in a series of texts which I call the stories of the matrix, a reference to *The Matrix* (1999), one of the more innovative and successful blockbusters of the time. The movie posited a dystopic future where humanity lived a false existence because people's minds were dominated by illusions manufactured to perpetuate the rule of machines. This was merely the extreme expression of a common anxiety often found in the social conversation. Assorted authors, documentary filmmakers, and a few movie directors were concerned, or at least feigned concern, about the way so much of the people's experience of reality was always mediated by a network of intermediaries in the media. That was part of the postmodern angst: it was a lesson about the power of simulacra a person might acquire by reading the fashionable French theorist Jean Baudrillard.[19] His work, in fact, was briefly referenced in one shot in *The Matrix*, though so quickly that only the cognoscenti might notice it.

More to the point, the stories of the matrix gave voice to that problem of truth in the contemporary world so much associated (albeit in different ways) with the 1980s writings of such prominent French theorists as Baudrillard, Michel Foucault, and Jean-François Lyotard. Perhaps most provocative and controversial was Baudrillard's later work, *The Gulf War Did Not Take Place* (1991), initially a series of essays for the press, where he gave substance to the fear that the war was a fiction concocted to fool the public, its truth only existing on the screens of the world, a signifier of a fictitious signified. The postmodern angst reflected a belief that truth was no longer knowable except as a social construct dependent on the subject position of the speakers.

In America the authors first on the scene expressed this angst in diverse and multiple ways. Neil Postman worried about the predominance of show business – an entertainment imperative, in all forms of public discourse, especially because of the bias of television – in his widely acclaimed polemic *Amusing Ourselves to Death* (1985). The Left historian Stuart Ewen, in *All Consuming Images* (1988), focused on the way a plethora of commercial images, akin here to Baudrillard's project, had gained ascendancy over life and discourse. The following year, Bill Moyers, a noted broadcast journalist, gave much wider circulation to such alarm when he hosted a documentary entitled *Consuming Images* (1989), where Ewen, Postman, and similar worriers were given airtime to criticize the matrix. Two of these, Herbert Schiller and Mark Crispin Miller, were especially exercised by the apparent ubiquity of advertising imagery, and both produced substantial books that detailed their fears of the power of commercialism: Miller's *Boxed In: The Culture of Television* (1988) and Schiller's *Culture, Inc.: The Corporate Takeover of Public Expression* (1989).

The most influential work, however, came out of the Left advocacy of the noted radical social critic and famed linguistics scholar Noam Chomsky: Edward S. Herman and Noam Chomsky, *Manufacturing Consent: The Political Economy of the Mass Media* (1988). Here they documented the so-called propaganda model of journalism in which the news media functioned as the instrument of the corporate and political elite, most especially in their coverage of world affairs. Four years later, some of the claims in the book, already notorious in press circles, were transformed by Mark Achbar and Peter Wintonick, two Canadian filmmakers, into a highly successful documentary called *Manufacturing Consent: Noam Chomsky & the Media* (1992), which also charted and celebrated Chomsky's life as a radical. These works, among many others, served to fix two related notions in the social conversation, namely the charge of media betrayal, whereby journalism had become inimical to reasoned and democratic discussion, and the spectre of a surge of propaganda that worked to indoctrinate the public to perpetuate the dominion of the ruling elites. Both of these notions were evident in the intellectual mix of *Wag the Dog*.

Still, the movie owed more to another stream of opinion which would flourish after 2000. That one focused on the apparent perversion of politics by the practice of various forms of news management, not just propaganda but what was called "spin": the bias or frame of fact and opinion, together an amalgam of advertising and public relations carried out by political operatives – like Brean. The first popular expression harked back to a well-remembered movie *The Candidate* (1972), starring Robert Redford as the novice Bill McKay who became a cipher for the operative Marvin Lucas (played by Peter Boyle). Less successful was Sydney Lumet's exploration of the machinations of the operative Pete St John

(Richard Gere) in *Power* (1986): this film left the impression that a skilled and unscrupulous character could package nearly any kind of nincompoop so he could win office. But the particular inspiration for the style, perhaps even the dialogue, of *Wag the Dog* was a documentary entitled *The War Room* (1993) directed by Chris Hegedus and D.A. Pennebaker. The film focused on the efforts of George Stephanopoulos, communications director, and James Carville, the key tactician, to convince the electorate to choose Bill Clinton as president in the 1992 campaign. The two had allowed the filmmakers limited access to their actions and discussions over the course of the campaign, which gave viewers a backstage look at the process of selling a candidate, managing the news, and overcoming crisis. Although not widely released, the documentary was much acclaimed and certainly influential. Partly as a result of such publicity, James Carville emerged as a celebrity, certainly not a villain, who had sincerely and effectively carried out the kind of political work essential in a media-saturated arena.

That consequence affected the perception of agency, the capacity to act, and hence the perception of the adman and his compatriots. In effect *Wag the Dog* and similar stories presumed that the affliction and the yoke of the adman's dilemma was waning. Underlying the postmodern angst was the alarm that the condition or process of hyperreality, where the simulacrum determined what was true, had entered a state of autopoiesis, which meant it had become a system that maintained, regulated, and reproduced itself no matter what the actions of individuals. One of the complaints directed against Foucault and other poststructuralists was their anti-humanism, the way the subject became just an object shaped by relations of power in their theories. At one point in his commentary on *Wag the Dog*, Levinson claimed the thoroughly administered politics he had elaborated was a closed system, without villains or heroes, not good versus evil, merely "the way it has to function."[20] He noted how Brean and Motss displayed "no sense of morality," other than completing the job. "Selling has become everything," he lamented, another complaint about the system, not the individual. All the digital magic that could fabricate the simulacrum he found frightening, a comment which hinted at a species of technological determinism. The unseen masters of the matrix now had the tools to fabricate reality easily and effectively on a daily basis. The agency of the protagonists was limited, perhaps vitiated, by the compulsions and demands of the system, meaning the institutions of the media and politics as well as the news process. But such a view also worked against any moral judgment of the goals and actions of the persuaders. That was not a view which would prevail in the social conversation.

2. Capitalism's "Cultural Turn": Naomi Klein, *No Logo*, 2000

During the 1990s the tradition of anti-advertising slowly revived, linked to the expression of postmodern angst. The Adbusters Media Foundation, launched in Vancouver in 1989, would become one of the centres of agitation in succeeding years, especially as the champion of culture jamming (notably the public mocking and defacing of ads). It soon fashioned anti-consumption advocacy ads, few of which the television outlets would show, published a magazine called *Adbusters* full of criticism and parodies or "subvertising," and promoted Buy Nothing Day, an annual rite of protest.[21] A small group of critical documentaries came at the end of the decade. Harold Boihem's *The Ad and the Ego* (1997) aimed to show how advertising had built a total environment, a matrix, which trapped the hapless individual, despite that individual's belief that he or she was immune. A clever and witty documentary entitled *Affluenza* (1997), shortly followed by *Escape from Affluenza* (1998), took a few swipes at advertising in the struggle to free America from the social disease of materialism. Sut Jhally, a communications professor and a radical, author of a study of advertising, fashioned a particularly apocalyptic documentary entitled *Advertising & the End of the World* (1997) that rehearsed again the old narrative of harm. In his book *Breaking Up America* (1997), Joseph Turow, also a communications professor, blamed the creatives and the ad executives for targeting clusters of consumers by income, gender, age, ethnicity, and similar social divides, a strategy which threatened to fragment and polarize the public. In 1999 the noted feminist advocate and lecturer Jean Kilbourne published *Deadly Persuasion*, where she explained, according to her subtitle, "Why Women and Girls Must Fight the Addictive Powers of Advertising." Not all the works were critical, of course: James B. Twitchell, an English professor, wrote *Adcult USA* (1996), which was largely sympathetic, although its subtitle, "The Triumph of Advertising in American Culture," also spoke of power. None of these initiatives provoked any great stir in the social conversation, however, even if they signalled a deepening interest in the impacts of advertising.

A change occurred with the new millennium. Late in 1999 Naomi Klein (b. 1970), a young Canadian journalist, produced a startlingly new exposé about the ill effects of advertising and marketing called *No Logo*. That book would soon prove a major international bestseller, as significant, wrote one scholar, as the works of Stuart Chase or Vance Packard.[22] It has been estimated that *No Logo* sold over a million copies and was translated into many languages, reaching a vast audience outside the anglophone world. Klein reiterated her views in interviews and lectures, at least once to a corporate gathering, in a collection of essays (2002), in a documentary (2003), and eventually in a reissued tenth anniversary edition of *No Logo*.[23] No doubt, as was claimed later, the book had benefited from serendipity: *No Logo* appeared soon after the WTO protests in Seattle which had captured so much public attention. Klein's polemic served to explain why there was a deep sense of outrage among the activists of the so-called anti-globalization movement. Luck aside, however, the book had real merit.

Remarkably, *No Logo* was Klein's first book. She had left the University of Toronto, degree unfinished, in the early 1990s, eventually to work as a columnist for the Toronto *Star*, the city's largest daily newspaper and one that boasted a mildly liberal and populist orientation. There she found the space and the time to research what she argued was a revolution in the dynamics of global capitalism that threatened social justice, democracy, and both identity and authenticity in the contemporary world. *No Logo* was an unusual book: long and complicated, it was part academic treatise and part memoir, a polemic full of fact and argument, vigorous and imaginative, reminiscent of the style of James Rorty's unsung anti-advertising screed *Our Master's Voice* (1934).[24] Like Rorty, Klein wrote well, indeed very well; her prose was engaging, bold, full of wit, thoughtful but committed: the voice of an activist. The hardback *No Logo* even appeared in anarchist colours, with a deep, nearly solid black cover plus some red (and white) lettering, suggesting a similar radical fervour. While Rorty was an ex-copywriter, Klein was a self-declared ex-mall rat, a member of the consuming masses. *No Logo* was not about the adman per se (whereas *Our Master's Voice* often was), although ad executives and creatives (including Rorty) certainly figured as experts and villains in the text. It focused more on the marketing industry broadly defined and upon its corporate clients, and, most importantly, on what Klein labelled "superbrands."

Or, to be more precise, it was about capitalism's "cultural turn," the ways in which leading corporations sought to capture the culture of the world by promoting the empire of the brand.[25] Klein had divided her argument into four grand sections: "No Space," "No Choice," "No Jobs," and "No Logo." The first two focused on the history of brand mania and the new marketing offensive, the third on the way the imperative of brand production in the "First World" fostered sweatshops in the "Third World," and the last on the rise and character of a new social movement, often dubbed "anti-globalization," directed against this "branded world." Juliet Schor, a leading scholar on the topic of affluence, emphasized how Klein avoided the production side bias that afflicted many works on the Left.[26] Klein's skillful linkage of promotion, consumption, production, and protest, always enlivened with some telling stories, was one of the great strengths of her investigation. What she had to say about marketing, however, was her most crucial contribution to the biography of the adman.

Klein posited the emergence of a great divide within the ranks of corporate America during the 1980s and into the 1990s. One stream of businesses, best represented by the giant retailer Walmart, sought profit by emphasizing price – sales, discounts, promotions – which appealed to Americans in search of a deal. That strategy seemed to triumph on the so-called Marlboro Friday in April 1993, when Philip Morris dramatically cut the price of its Marlboro cigarettes, the world's favourite, to meet the challenge of bargain competitors (12). Some observers decided that the "death" of a prestige brand such as Marlboro meant the end of the power of brand names and a blow to the commercial significance of advertising.

Far from it, for what prevailed in the rest of the decade was a new wave of brand imperialism. This too was rooted in the 1980s, when management theorists (Klein was particularly taken by the views of Tom Peters) and some corporate leaders came to proclaim the significance of brand equity, meaning the value added to a product or enterprise by the popular significance of its name. Here too there was "a defining moment," this in 1988, "when Philip Morris purchased Kraft for $12.6 billion – six times what the company was worth on paper" (7). Even more importantly, a collection of prominent corporations emphasized the promotion of their unique "brand vision" and their distinctive logo above everything else (23). As exemplars of this strategy, Klein named Tommy Hilfiger, Absolut Vodka, The Body Shop, Disney, Starbucks, even Microsoft, but most especially Nike. Nike had generated huge profits after the recession of the early 1990s by contracting out production to cheap suppliers in the less-developed world and by lavishing funds on advertising and other forms of marketing, notably expensive commercials, sponsored events, product placements, and brand stores. Crucial to the success of this strategy was the expansion of the commercial sphere. These enterprises sought to invade all manner of public and private spaces:

always the home, the workplace, play sites, the school – even washrooms. The logos spread everywhere. "No space has been left unbranded" (73). Here was a new version of the matrix.

Worse yet, the marketers had appropriated social and moral values, or at least tried to. That charge made *No Logo* an extended study of governance. Over time, apparently, the very meaning of a brand had changed or, better yet, had grown into something extraordinary. In the beginning, and for many years afterwards, the brand was chiefly a name, not much more than a trademark attached to a product which signified reliability and quality. But recently the brand had broken free from any one product to become a signifier of a value, a lifestyle, a community, an ethos attached to the company and all its products. "Branding, in its truest and most advanced incarnations, is about corporate transcendence" (41). In the book and later in an interview, where she talked of brands selling "a kind of pseudo-spirituality – a sense of belonging," Klein suggested the brand builders were attempting to fill a real void caused by the decline of traditional institutions and the state's retreat from the community.[27] She never effectively substantiated this intriguing suggestion. In any case, she did show how Nike claimed to epitomize the spirit of fitness and sport; Starbucks was not just a coffeehouse but a meeting place, the embodiment of community; The Body Shop was about environmentalism and feminism; Disney expressed the "wholesome" values of family harmony and a traditional America; Virgin was always the "rebel" brand and Tommy Hilfiger was always "cool." In fact Hilfiger had lots of rivals outside the clothing business because many enterprises in the nineties sought to capture that elusive quality of "cool" and thereby the youth market. Nike was especially adept at using striking commercials, superstars, and branded stores and events to establish its "swoosh" as the sign of "cool." This and similar corporations were now the "superbrands." In her introduction to the tenth anniversary edition of *No Logo*, Klein added that the technique she sometimes called "spiritual branding" had spread into politics: thus the Obama brand, so full of style, boasted a narrative and an ideal that was able to claim wide popularity, but unfortunately lacked substance, meaning a real determination to reform American democracy and life.[28]

Both price competition and brand mania had served to benefit the adman. Worries that the advertising industry had lost its importance in the workings of the marketplace – evident in a 1991 sequel by Martin Mayer to his bestseller *Madison Avenue, USA* (1958) – were soon mitigated by statistics.[29] Klein noted in one chart early in the book (11) how the total ad spend in the United States had exploded after 1991 by over 50 per cent to nearly $200 billion by 2000. (In fact she underestimated the growth rate: later figures put it at 85 per cent and the total near $250 billion, or a whopping 2.5 per cent of the GDP, higher than at any time since the 1920s and early 1930s.)[30] Increasingly the adman came to consider himself a "brand steward," an expert who did not sell a product or mount a campaign but worked to identify, articulate, and nurture "the corporate soul" (43). Advertising expenditures were an investment in the future of the brand, irrespective of immediate sales. "Savvy ad agencies have all moved away from the idea that they are flogging a product made by someone else, and have come to think of themselves instead as brand factories, hammering out what is of true value: the idea, the lifestyle, the attitude," she argued. "Brand builders are the new primary producers in our so-called knowledge economy" (195–6). No longer "the pitchman," the adman was now "the philosopher-king of commercial culture," borrowing here from the rhetoric of Randall Rothenberg (7).[31] This was why creativity was such a watchword of the ad business, for the superbrands were "forever on the prowl for creative new ways to build and strengthen their brand images" (26). Klein noted, with some disgust, how a few agencies – Wieden & Kennedy stood out – sought to appropriate all signs of dissent or protest to sell a brand. "Masters at pitting the individual against various incarnations of mass-market bogey-men, Wieden & Kennedy sold cars to people who hated car ads, shoes to people who loathed image, soft drinks to the Prozac Nation and, most of all, ads to people who were 'not a target market'" (304–5). Implicit was a distaste for such deception and yet a recognition of such cleverness. Once again the figure of the adman provoked ambivalence, even in such a vocal critic.

Underlying Klein's analysis was the presumption that the superbrands were potent sources of identity and meaning sufficient to determining the actions of people in all walks of life. The corporations were taking over the culture: they captivated, they censored, they restricted choice. That was an old charge, of course, if now dressed in new clothes. What she thought of as "brand bullies," such as Mattel or Disney, used copyright and other laws to prevent criticism or parodies of their brands. The beer and clothing corporations that sponsored rock concerts increasingly shaped these to hype the brand, turning the performers into hired guns. Walmart refused to carry material, records or magazines that might clash with the carefully cultivated family image of the chain. Starbucks sought to eliminate all competition by a form of "brand bombing" (129) that filled an area with outlets. Disney's Celebration village in Florida was a totally controlled space and one that excluded billboards: here people were "leading the first branded lives" (158). She claimed Tommy Hilfiger worked effectively to exploit "the hip-hop aesthetic" among the poor and the affluent. "Like so much of cool hunting, Hilfiger's marketing journey feeds off the alienation at the heart of America's race relations: selling white youth on their fetishization of black style, and black youth on their fetishization of white wealth" (76).

But the great irony of the wave of "spiritual branding" was to make this version of the corporate rule vulnerable to upset. Klein the activist was also very much Klein the optimist. She believed that the appropriation of the values of play or tolerance or feminism could both provoke a backlash and offer avenues for counterattack. In the last section of *No Logo* she carefully discussed, and sometimes critiqued, instances of culture jamming, efforts to reclaim the streets, consumer boycotts, the way McDonald's use of the courts against two activists backfired, and how Nike and Shell had been forced to respond when protests captured media attention.

> By attempting to enclose our shared culture in sanitized and controlled brand cocoons, these corporations have themselves created the surge of opposition described in this book. By thirstily absorbing social critiques and political movements as sources of brand "meaning," they have radicalized that opposition still further. By abandoning their traditional role as direct, secure employers to pursue their branding dreams, they have lost the loyalty that once protected them from citizen rage. And by pounding the message of self-sufficiency into a generation of workers, they have inadvertently empowered their critics to express that rage without fear. (441–2)

Even a decade later, after 9/11 had derailed the anti-corporate movement, Klein still found cause to expect an assault on corporate governance. Some of the superbrands had waned, some were in crisis. The Obama experience might educate and excite a move to fashion the real thing, a political transformation. Above all the adpeople and the marketers had found and exploited a longing "for social change, for public space, for greater equality and diversity" which the superbrands could never satisfy.[32] Social movements just might succeed.

In a retrospective essay ten years later, Russell Belk, a noted scholar of marketing, reasoned that Naomi Klein had become a global brand in her own right.[33] (She admitted as much, though claiming she tried to be "a really crap one.")[34] By and large *No Logo* received a favourable reception from public intellectuals, if the wide assortment of reviews are a fair indication. Her book was soon labelled as the Bible or even the *Das Kapital* of the anti-globalization movement. Clearly she had managed to capture some of the anxieties and concerns evident in the social conversation at the turn of the century. The point was, as Belk put it, "no other book has been as widely read or has stimulated as much discussion" on the topic of the global economy. "Klein's depiction of the expanding universe of brands is graphic, literate and level-headed," claimed Tom Mertes in the *New Left Review* (July 2000). "This is the best panorama of contemporary commodification we now have." That was the key: Klein's analysis of the brandscape of modern life. The reason she won fame was because she had fashioned an updated narrative of understanding. In her later, much darker polemic on modern capitalism, *The Shock Doctrine* (2008), Klein wrote about the cardinal importance of a "story" that would explain the underlying structure of the lived experience. Only in that way could people understand what was happening and resist the machinations of the elite.[35] That "story" she had supplied. The fact that this narrative of harm was also a bit of a fable, its claims sometimes exaggerated or specious, was no obstacle to its appeal.

Not that she lacked critics. One anonymous anarchist in *Red and Black Revolution* (Summer 2001), though willing to admit *No Logo* was an "interesting book" and a "good introduction," found the utility of the work "severely limited" because Klein argued advertising was the problem when the real enemy was capitalism. Similarly, Mertes, if even more impressed, believed what was missing was a good dose of "political economy" to demonstrate that the root of the problem was not "brandmasters" but some unspecified capitalist core, presumably banks and big energy. On the other hand, *The Economist* (November 2002) unwisely carried an inane review of *Fences & Windows* that charged her with, of all sins, adolescence, since she so hopelessly misunderstood capitalism. In *The Rebel Sell* (2004) Joseph Heath and Andrew Potter, two fellow Canadians, argued she was just another victim of "the countercultural idea," which they blamed as the source of social ills and of the Left's disarray.[36] In fact even reviewers otherwise impressed by Klein's overall argument variously criticized her grasp of history or economics, her limited selection of examples, her neglect of the high-tech industry and of Wall Street, a too-American focus, an overly romantic appreciation of the activists, and a mistaken evaluation of the extent of corporate authority.[37]

What was missing was any mention that Klein had effectively miscast the overall phenomenon of advertising. She had concentrated her attention, understandably, on the "coolest" dimension of advertising: the promotions of the superbrands. Certainly the most celebrated television and cinema commercials of the late 1980s and 1990s, honoured in industry award festivals the world over, were fashioned to sell Nike, Apple, Absolut Vodka, Coca-Cola or Pepsi, Chanel, British Airways, Budweiser or Heineken, to name only a few brand builders. But many more print as well as broadcast ads were designed to sell product rather than build brand. And that was particularly true of non-media advertising, such as catalogues and other forms of direct mail: no more than 60 per cent of the ad spend went to newspapers, magazines, radio, and television. Reason-why ads that offered the consumer some fact – low price, large quantity, better taste, improved performance, durability – remained commonplace. That was especially true of retail outlets such as supermarkets, car dealers, and Walmart. It also applied to high-tech industries such as telephone or computer companies. One of the top advertisers in America, Procter & Gamble, a master of product advertising, was completely missing from the index of *No Logo*. Besides, corporations like IBM or AT&T might launch campaigns to promote the brand, a product, and/or the corporate image. Randall Rothenberg showed as much in his detailed account of the campaigns that Wieden & Kennedy designed for Subaru in the early 1990s. Advertising was a much more diverse phenomenon than *No Logo* recognized.

Just as importantly, advertising had always served as a tool of branding. Klein's potted history masked this fact. Recall the efforts of the patent medicine sellers or the arguments of Hopkins and Calkins. Department stores at the turn of the century had created special environments organized around a season or a theme, where shoppers were surrounded by stimulation and simulation in ways similar to the branded stores of Nike, Disney, and so on.[38] These department stores also garnered much publicity and favour by sponsoring such community events as the Santa Claus parade. In the 1920s Bruce Barton had made his name as an adman who could find and promote the soul of a corporation, the equivalent of the corporate epiphanies Klein described. The ad agencies for companies such as Coca-Cola or Philip Morris or Pepsi-Cola in the 1950s and 1960s were accomplished brand builders and brand stewards. The marketing surge Klein charted was merely another chapter in a much longer epic. Capitalism's "cultural turn" had first occurred long ago, back in the 1890s or earlier.[39]

Similarly, the reviewers failed to recognize that the burden of her critique was not really new. She specifically distanced herself from past "anti-marketing spasms" and academic criticisms (1930s activists excepted) because they were largely "unthreatening." What she especially objected to was the sole focus on "the content and techniques of advertising" as well as the contempt of academic critics for the "seemingly clueless people" who succumbed to persuasion (303). Although true to a degree, this bold claim was misleading because the brief description was incomplete. The tradition of anti-advertising had always assumed the adman had his sights set on ruling the culture. Back in the 1930s Rorty had worried about the way business and the adman propagated a pseudoculture inimical to America's health, democracy, and progress. A generation later Arnold Toynbee would have agreed. More recently the historian Jackson Lears had shown how the fables of advertising served to refashion America's culture, and cultural critic Thomas Frank had explored how advertising people had co-opted the counter-culture in the 1960s.[40] Similarly, in two stellar histories of advertising, Roland Marchand had demonstrated how the adman effectively refined a near ideology of the brand and a concept of the corporate soul even before the Second World War.[41] Other scholars had charted the way the adman had taken command of images, especially in the era of television.[42] Of course the way Klein ignored much of what had gone before, the lessons and legacies of history, was not at all uncommon in the social conversation: critics and apologists usually showed little knowledge of history. That's one reason there has seemed so much repetition in the rhetoric surrounding the adman's dilemma.

One might also claim, a bit unfairly perhaps, that she also failed to take account of the future. Writing when she did, before the turn of the century, she did not foresee the major changes in advertising, marketing, and persuasion generally wrought by the World Wide Web, the birth of social media, and the spread of mobile technologies. But in this too she was not especially unusual: neither did most people.

Klein's insight was to explain the extraordinary advertising and marketing assault of the 1990s by tying it to a further sophistication of the techniques and doctrine of branding. She managed to make sinister the very logos that populated the life of so many Americans, in particular her own cohort. She wrote with passion because she had been the dupe of marketing, just as so many other young people apparently saw themselves. It seemed at times that her fury grew out of a bad case of the victim's malaise: as someone deceived so often, she now felt obligated to strike back. She brought home the power of advertising to shape our perceptions of reality, or rather she appeared to demonstrate such an authority. No less importantly, she explored how people could resist and counter that authority. "There is a jujitsu logic to mobilization against the magnetism of the logo," claimed Tom Mertes, "that Klein explains very well." Thus she updated the tradition of anti-advertising for yet another age and generation. "The argument was arrogant, paranoid and wrong," lamented Martin Wolf of the *Financial Times*. "But it was also an intellectual coup."[43] Klein had harnessed the energies awakened by postmodern angst to a new crusade to liberate everyone from corporate domination.

3. The Spectre of Svengali: William Gibson, The "Blue Ant" or "Bigend" Trilogy, 2003–2010

Consider this list of professional persuaders, both real and fictional: Mal Osbourne and Hubertus Bigend, ad executives; Chas Lacouture and Clotaire Rapaille, marketing gurus; Nick Marshall, an experienced copywriter, and Alex Bogusky, a creative director; Edward Bernays (as a historical character), Nick Naylor, and Arthur Isaiah Gardner, public relations counsels; Lee Atwater (as a historical character), Karl Rove, and James Carville, political consultants. All were featured in the social conversation during the first decade of the new millennium. The first three were protagonists in novels, as was Gardner. Marshall and Naylor were characters in popular movies, both comedies. Bernays was one of the founders of public relations back in the 1920s, and the three political consultants (two Republican and the other a progressive) were featured in documentaries.[44] Bogusky was much discussed in the press as a wizard who had revitalized aging brands prior to his retirement from advertising in 2010, when he claimed he moved into social advocacy.[45] What made these men special was their actual or imagined notoriety as masters of the arts and sciences of persuasion. They had influence, power even; the ability to change life, or so it seemed.

The most interesting of these men was the unlikely named Hubertus Bigend, a Belgian-born adman operating mostly in London but active across the globe. He seemed to realize that elusive goal of the sovereign self, and thus to escape that most intractable aspect of the adman's dilemma: subservience. More to the point, he was a new kind of persuader suited to the demands of the digital revolution. Bigend was the creation of the already celebrated science fiction writer William Gibson (b. 1948), an American living in Vancouver, famous for coining the word and the concept of "cyberspace." He published three widely reviewed and well-read novels during the decade: *Pattern Recognition* (2003), *Spook Country* (2007), and *Zero History* (2010), all of which appeared on the *New York Times* bestseller list.[46] Each of the books dealt with the present, more precisely the year prior to publication, although they took on the guise of science fiction. This accidental trilogy (it was never intended as such) constituted an exploration of the bizarre world fashioned by 9/11 and its aftermath: "They're novels of what I like to call 'the turn of the century,'" Gibson declared in one of the many interviews he gave about the project.

The novels belonged to the genre of thrillers, involving a puzzle, a quest, and some action. There was a flavour of the Bond saga about the trilogy, the result of much globe-trotting, strange technologies, bits of derring-do, and direct references to that hero.[47] But each take on the so-called present differed. Begun before 9/11, *Pattern Recognition* focused on the world of brands and marketing, written (so it seemed) under the influence of Naomi Klein's *No Logo*. *Spook Country* emphasized the issue of security and the spreading apparatus of surveillance, complete with a strange array of rogue government agents, ex-Cuban Soviet-trained criminals, and some super-effective onetime spies who were now self-declared and very moral pranksters. *Zero History* was suffused with the objects and signs of militarism, albeit linked to questions of commerce, fashion, and, once again, brands.

Altogether the trilogy presumed a world overwhelmed by a web of information and deception, stuffed with simulacra, a place where hyper-reality reigned – all of which is why critics sometimes called this a dystopia, although Gibson said he did not write it as such.[48] Gibson crammed his stories with references to laptops, the internet, CCTV, GPS, data mining, online video, the darknet, mobile devices, drones, augmented reality, all the paraphernalia that had shaped or penetrated the lifeworld in the new millennium. There was so much Apple gear in the last novel, *Zero History*, that one reviewer charged Gibson with a kind of product placement.[49] What redeemed the world was a persistent hunger for authenticity, expressed through a distrust of artifice, the rejection of brands, a taste for art, and the celebration of creativity. In the end the heroes, in all cases women, the coolhunter Cayce Pollard in *Pattern Recognition* and the ex-rock musician-now-journalist Hollis Henry in the other two novels, avoided disaster and found satisfaction in a world temporarily stabilized.

Bigend was no hero. But neither was he a villain. Only in *Zero History* was he a major protagonist. Yet he was a presence throughout the novels, as was his agency Blue Ant, which explained why the trilogy acquired its name. That was not intended: initially Gibson thought Bigend would play only a minor part in his story; instead he became crucial. "It was like I didn't need to invent him," claimed Gibson. "He just kind of expanded exponentially from his entry point, and then I rolled with that, and his world kept getting bigger and bigger."[50] He sometimes appeared as a deity initiating and controlling people and things in a time and places so conditioned by marketing's moment and the digital revolution.[51]

The character and career of Bigend were revealed little by little over the course of the trilogy, although even at the end he remained a man of much mystery. The sketch of his origins, though, was fairly clear: he was a product of privilege. In *Spook Country*, we learn that he was born in 1967, the only child of the marriage of a wealthy Belgian industrialist and a Belgian sculptor. His mother Phaedra had links to the Situationist International, a movement that mixed surrealism and Marxism to foster a rebellion against what its mentor Guy Debord famously called "the society of the spectacle." (None of which is spelled out in the book, however.) We are left with the suggestion that this link explained his sensitivity to the realm of signs and simulacra. His education, we were told earlier in *Pattern Recognition*, began in an exclusive British boarding school and ended in Harvard. He dabbled a while in Hollywood, lived for a time in Brazil, and then launched Blue Ant in Europe – already a man attuned to the global perspective of the era. When we first met him, he was already an advertising mogul, celebrated in the press as a successful innovator. He was also one of the ultra-rich, for whom money was never a problem, which of course made him a very rare kind of adman.

Occasionally Gibson commented on his unusual and striking physical presence, his body, and his tastes. He was a handsome man, appealing to women, who at first looked "like Tom Cruise on a diet of virgins' blood and truffled chocolates" (PR 6). Gibson later made a point of signalling his predatorial cast by noting how plentiful and prominent were his teeth. His disconcerting smile, consequently, made him seem "a version of Tom Cruise with too many teeth, and longer, but still very white" (PR 57). When older, he acquired an aura of power that was not at all like Tom Cruise. "He somehow managed always to give her the impression, seeing him again, that he'd grown visibly larger, though without gaining any particular weight," thought Hollis Henry. "Up close, he always seemed too full of blood, by several extra quarts at least. Rosy as a pig. Warmer than a normal person" (ZH 19). Furthermore he had taken to wearing a signature outfit, a suit of International Klein Blue, an especially intense colour designed by a French artist that served to unsettle other people. Everywhere he went he commanded attention and space,

people and things. "He has a kind of dire gravity" warned the unnamed
Cayce Pollard. "You need to get further away. I know" (ZH 337). All these
references led one academic to conclude that Bigend was no less than a
modern Dracula, a kind of vampire, always full of appetite.[52]

Bigend once declared himself "a bohemian" (ZH 22) – a style inherited from his mother – which freed him from the greed for money. "My
passion is marketing, advertising, media strategy" (PR 65). His mission
seemed innocuous: "I want to make the public aware of something they
don't quite yet know that they know – or have them feel that way" (PR
63). He liked to present himself as a "lateral-thinking imp of the perverse, thirty-something boy genius, seeker after truth (or at least func-
tionality) in the markets of this young century" (PR 66). He posed as
a philosopher, given to making all kinds of statements about marketing's moment: that more creativity went into selling than producing (PR
67), that the public was driven by irrational urges (PR 69), that people
bought narratives not products (ZH 21), that everything reflected something else (PR 68), that the world was now constituted by mass communications (SC 137). Such claims were hardly novel, of course: Bigend was
simply parroting the clichés of postmodernism.[53] He admitted to a fervent curiosity, a determination to investigate "anomalous phenomena,"
the "very peculiar things that people do, often secretly" (SC 139), so as
to craft a better way of selling. "Intelligence, Hollis, is advertising turned
inside out" (SC 139). Which was why he funded Cayce Pollard to hunt
down the source of a mysterious video released in pieces and popular
on the internet. Similarly, he hired Hollis Henry to discover what it was
about an elusive container travelling the high seas that excited spooks
and, in a second quest, the person who designed a highly successful
secret brand of clothes.

His "core tenet," Bigend boasted, was "that all truly viable advertising addresses that older, deeper mind, beyond language and logic" (PR
69). Blue Ant "from the beginning billed itself as a high-speed, low-drag
life-form in an advertising ecology of lumbering herbivores" (PR 6)
and was later called "the first viral agency" (SC 146). "We aren't just an
advertising agency," mused Bigend. "We do brand vision transmission,
trend forecasting, vendor management, youth market recon, strategic
planning in general" (ZH 21). What he sought was all kinds of data,
especially on things novel or innovative that he might exploit to sell.
He was, however, still concerned with creativity: he even set up "some
weird new entity" that targeted and assisted creatives (ZH 396). He set
out to license one of the big hits of Hollis's group to fuel the popular

appeal of a commercial for a Chinese car. Among his various marketing achievements, this derived from the Pollard hunt, was the design
of a "viral pitchman platform" (SC 139) embedded in old movies, all to
sell shoes. "That's fucking horrible," exclaimed Henry (SC 139); "Something ghastly," asserted Pollard (ZH 335). They did not understand. It
was Bigend's effort to fashion a simulacrum of art to appropriate the
appeal of authenticity.

Hollis called him "a monstrously intelligent giant baby" (SC 207), but
akin to "some peculiar force of nature," like a rogue wave (ZH 346). He
could be charming, but he did not inspire much trust. He had no dis-
cernible sense of ethics. Not once did he seem bothered by the dilemma
or the liar's plight. Deception did not provoke any discontent in this
adman. He justified hiring a "vicious lying cunt" with the quip, "we are
in the business of advertising, after all" (PR 203). According to one
observer, "he's utterly amoral in the service of his own curiosity" (SC
207). He was willing to surrender one of his employees to an enemy, an
employee in whom he had invested much time and money to remake,
because that seemed the only way to protect his prize project. What was
so dangerous was his ability to persuade other people to do his bidding.
"There was something amorphous, foglike, about his will," reasoned
Cayce Pollard. "It spread out around you, tenuous, almost invisible; you
found yourself moving, mysteriously, in directions other than your own"
(PC 68). Likewise the claim of his later victim, Hollis: "There was no way,
she knew, to tell an entity like Bigend that you wanted nothing to do with
him. That would simply bring you more firmly to his attention" (ZH 18).
Bigend was apparently irresistible.

He was much more than just an ordinary marketer, of course. What
moved Bigend was his desire to know and to rule. "An overly wealthy,
dangerously curious fiddler with the world's hidden architectures,"
Hollis decided (ZH 18). Not that he always succeeded in his persistent
efforts to micromanage. Both Cayce and Hollis managed to preserve
some measure of integrity and autonomy. In *Zero History* Bigend even suffered a palace revolt at Blue Ant, which threatened to derail his schemes.
Yet in the end Bigend triumphed. There were lots of omens of his victory
in London's public relations community, some sort of "hive-mind thing."
"PR people dreaming of Bigend. Imagining they see his face on coins"
(ZH 234). There were intimations that he and a partner had managed to
own most of Iceland because of the bank scandal that overwhelmed the
country. More to the point, his most grandiose project, to determine the
immediate future of all market transactions (called "Finding the order

flow"), came to fruition. The consequence, apparently, was to negate the market, to make it "no longer real," to fashion another simulacrum (ZH 401). Bigend became a sovereign in his own right, which meant he had solved one problem attached to the adman's dilemma.

Reviewers had fun trying to identify what sort of man Bigend was. In a commentary on *Spook Country*, Anthony Byrt at the *New Statesman* (23 August 2007) called him "an accentless Machiavellian fixer with unnervingly white teeth." Even more imaginative was James Purdon's description in *The Guardian* (12 September 2010): "a sinister Belgian marketing mogul who reads like a cross between Charles Saatchi and Doctor Mabuse." But in fact Bigend took on the guise of a Svengali, an enchanter particularly suited to the postmodern times. The first Svengali was the grand villain in the best-selling novel *Trilby* (1894) by the English author George du Maurier. The novel had proved a massive hit on both sides of the Atlantic. Although the plot was much more about the supposed bohemian life in mid-century Paris, and Svengali was only present in a few (albeit crucial) passages, nonetheless he was by far the most memorable of the characters and his name passed into popular mythology. He was presented as a musician, a hypnotist, a deceiver, and a Jew, both unpleasant and aggressive: there was a definite streak of anti-Semitism in his portrayal. Svengali cast a spell over a young woman who then became a singing sensation in Europe, remaining under his total command until he fell sick and died, which ended her subjugation, her career, and soon her life. The epithet Svengali came to describe a person, usually a man, who thoroughly dominated another, by means of some form of mental control, often someone creative and a woman, to realize some nefarious purpose.[54] The stereotype had a particular resonance for the adman because of its association with persuasion and deception. It fit Bigend even more because of his ability to win over women, however reluctant and suspicious, who were both imaginative and innovative.

There were earlier characters in fiction who might suit the comparison. One of the first was J. Ward Moorehouse, a public relations counsel in John Dos Passos's epic trilogy *U.S.A.* Mostly present in the first volume, *42nd Parallel* (1930), Moorehouse evolved from a poor but clever boy into an oily character, apparently sincere but invariably sinister, who prepared various forms of publicity to defend the wealthy and the powerful, from big business to warmongers to patent medicines, endangered by the agitation of labour leaders, social reformers, socialists, and other "cranks." Moorehouse was very much an exemplar of the corruption that tainted the discourse and practices of American democracy, according to the then-radical Dos Passos. In real life one possible Svengali was the Freudian doctor-turned-market researcher Ernest Dichter, the notorious champion of motivational research during the 1950s and 1960s. His studies explained how a succession of firms might work on the collective id of consumers to get them to repeatedly buy goods of all kinds. Of course Dichter was never independent; he was always a client of business. But like Moorehouse he was purportedly engaged in a kind of mass hypnosis.[55]

Despite these antecedents, the spectre of the Svengali was most appropriate in marketing's moment. It provided a human face to a system of publicity which was so ubiquitous and sometimes so distressing. It fitted the taste for conspiracies, the suspicion that villains were at work beneath the surface of affairs and life to secure some profit, a presumption evident in Gibson's trilogy. And its link to hypnosis suited the presumption the admen and other persuaders employed emotion, not logic, techniques which foiled the conscious mind to program the unwary. At his worst the Svengali was deemed fundamentally amoral, never troubled by the affliction I have called the adman's dilemma. Any and all forms of deception, from the lie to the masquerade, were tools he might employ to realize his Machiavellian purpose. The failings, the shams of democracy could be easily ascribed to the activities of a Lee Atwater, a Karl Rove, or even the principals of Greenberg Carville Schrum.[56] Clotaire Rapaille, clearly a successor to Dichter, was shown in the PBS documentary *The Persuaders* (2004) as a man who had won the patronage of big business with his spiel about the irrationality of the public, much along the lines of Bigend, in fact.[57] (Rapaille talked more of the reptilian brain, whereas Gibson's Bigend emphasized the "mammalian mind" (PC 69).) The cynical ex-philosophy professor Chas Lacouture in Alex Shakar's satire *The Savage Girl* (2001) worked to sell the jaded public of his city on the virtues of an absurd non-product, namely diet water, a bizarre send-up of the consumer society. The ways the adman seemed to pray on women could be mocked in the character of the macho Nick Marshall, played by Mel Gibson, in the sophisticated comedy *What Women Want* (2000), in which a freak accident gave him the ability to read women's minds so that he could design ads to program their shopping. That kind of surveillance might count as a bizarre comment on the wisdom of Bigend's dictum about the centrality of intelligence in the practice of advertising. By contrast, the equally sophisticated but earnestly serious BBC documentary *The Century of the Self* (2002), by Adam Curtis, found in Edward Bernays one source of the deformations that had afflicted the life and politics of

Britain and America during the preceding century. Bernays had supposedly fashioned the various tools of persuasion to enable the elite, primarily businessmen and politicians, to effectively hypnotize the mass public,
hence to tame democracy and foster the consumer society.[58] One of the
admen, Alex Bogusky, eventually sought redemption for his past sins by
taking up the cause of social advocacy.

Bernays and most of the other persuaders were sinister. But Bigend as
Svengali was actually more ambiguous.[59] Or at least that was the intent,
if we can believe the comments Gibson made in various interviews. After
the project ended, Gibson told CNN, "I originally assumed he was just a
standard walk-on evil figurehead, but the other characters started falling
into a weird kind of love-hate with him, and I suppose I did, too. I don't
always believe his explanation of our world, and I doubt he does either,
but he's definitely been a delight to work with."[60] Another interviewer
asked Gibson whether he thought there were any Bigends around, "scan-
ning the world with a heightened perception of these larger trends that
interweave marketing and fashion and technology and enormous revenue streams?" Gibson doubted their existence – "but I sort of wish there
were."[61] Perhaps "they" were necessary to bringing order into the chaotic
world Gibson had imagined.

In fact Bigend was not unique. There were real world analogues. One
of the reviewers had mentioned Charles Saatchi (b.1943), a renowned
ad executive who in the eighties and early nineties had excited the business world when he and his brother endeavoured to make their agency
a total marketing enterprise, only to fall victim to hard times and, supposedly, hubris. Saatchi, it should be noted, was also a great patron of
contemporary art, notably Damien Hirst and Marc Quinn. But the more
obvious analogue was the amazingly successful persuader-cum-entrepreneur
Martin Sorrell (b. 1945). Sorrell might lack the flamboyance of Hubertus
Bigend, or for that matter Charles Saatchi. Nor was he an obvious
candidate for the role of a Svengali. But he had fashioned a massive
marketing and communications empire in the conglomerate WPP that
by 2016 encompassed old-fashioned agency brands such as J. Walter
Thompson and Ogilvy & Mather and new-style entities such as GroupM
(media investment management), Hill&Knowlton Strategies (public
relations and public affairs), and BtoD Group (branding and identity).
In particular, he was attuned to the digital revolution and the import
of data: he claimed, notoriously, that he was much more in the data
business than in advertising, at least the advertising of the past.[62] It was
eerily reminiscent of Bigend's comment about the central importance of

intelligence, although Bigend was fascinated by secrets and Sorrell was focused on big numbers.[63] The point is that Gibson, whether intentionally or not, had crafted an image of a new kind of adman very different from the creative geniuses of the previous generation but superbly suited to handling the complexities of communications and finances in the era of digital technology.

4. Contagion and Immunity: PBS, *The Persuaders* Website, 2004+

Cayce Pollard, the hero of *Pattern Recognition*, had a peculiar affliction – let's call it logophobia – which was linked to her talent as a coolhunter. Agencies like Blue Ant employed her to test the worth of potential brand or corporate logos, how in effect these would sell to the public. But the downside of this ability, more magical than logical, was an acute sensitivity to the presence of logos on products, either in advertising or anywhere in her immediate environment. This amounted, as Gibson put it, to an "allergy, a morbid and sometimes violent reactivity to the semiotics of the marketplace" (PR 2). It was a special instance of the victim's malaise, where the sufferer had a physical reaction to untruth and deception. It had first emerged at age six, when she suffered "a phobic reaction" (PR 34) to the presence of Bibendum, the famed Michelin Man, one of the earliest of the powerful logos of the twentieth century. The intensity of the reaction varied widely. She got sick if the signs of Tommy Hilfiger's fashion were nearby, likely because these were so phony, so lacking in authenticity, at least by the standards of critics like Naomi Klein.[64] She was made uneasy by the presence of Zippo lighters in a California-style Vietnamese restaurant. But Japanese logos did not disturb her. Nor did most national logos – with the exception of the iconography of Nazi Germany. In short, her psyche had preferences, likes and dislikes of a sort. She enjoyed some immunity. But she could experience an emotional and physical collapse if exposed to some especially potent symbol. That was the reason she tried to live a *No Logo* life, where all the brand markers were removed from her clothes and the detritus of advertising banned from her domestic space. Advertising had power over her, a kind of involuntary influence, because it was her psyche and her body, not her rational self, that reacted. She found that she could only forestall an attack by consciously repeating a nonsense mantra that created a partial psychic defence.

Gibson had imagined an extreme version of a condition that was common among the public: a contradictory response to advertising and marketing that mixed likes and dislikes, belief and disbelief, pleasure and distress. This contradiction rested on the presence of a particular complex of ideas that revolved around the concepts of contagion and immunity, both of which were locked into a personalized response to the phenomenon of biopolitics. Although evident previously – in fact, in Barnum's time – this complex was much influenced by the recognition of marketing's moment and the presence of postmodern angst, which shaped the perception of the power of advertising in the social conversation.[65] It drew heavily upon other stories, at least those critical of advertising; in other words, on the narrative of harm and the related tradition of anti-advertising. But it was distinct because contagion and immunity presumed that a cure of the social or the political body was possible. My argument is not that this complex prevailed in the social conversation. The complex existed beneath that conversation and constituted a kind of grid which could structure what was usually cast in the form of moral outrage.

I will sketch and assess the assorted tales evident in the material at the website of the PBS program *Frontline* devoted to the documentary *The Persuaders* (2004), a study of the marketing industry. The purpose of the website was explicitly educational: *Frontline* was the premier vehicle for the public broadcaster's in-depth investigation of the present, and its findings were meant to assist teachers and advance learning. The material included the documentary itself, which was available online, a transcript, a teacher's guide, some summary and analysis, supplemental essays or articles, extended interviews with key participants, snippets of press reviews, links to other relevant websites, and, most importantly, the published response of viewers. The site, posted on 9 November 2004, was still on the web over a decade later, in December 2015.[66] At some point, however, some of the links had lapsed and viewer responses were closed.[67] The documentary and the website proved popular. One sign of their success was the frequency of citation, the fact it was soon integrated into college and university courses which focused on mass communications and the media. The documentary served as the stimulus; the rhetoric of contagion and immunity was a response evident in the public commentary.

The Persuaders was the work of a particular team: filmmakers Barak Goodman and Rachel Dretzin and media theorist Douglas Rushkoff, the co-writer (with Goodman) and the on-screen narrator. They had initially collaborated on an earlier *Frontline* documentary called *The Merchants of Cool* (2001), which had detailed the marketing assault on America's teens. At 90 minutes long, *The Persuaders* was a lengthy extension and expansion that investigated the contours of marketing's moment in the broader society and in the nation's politics.[68] It was aired one week after the successful re-election of George W. Bush as president, which might account for the sour attitude of some disgruntled correspondents to its report on politics. It proved a sophisticated mix of many examples of advertising, sometimes a kaleidoscope of images and a cacophony of sounds, a lot of talking heads, and the intelligent storytelling and commentary of Rushkoff. The main chunk of the documentary dealt broadly with advertising and promotion in society and the economy before focusing on the ways in which marketing had colonized the realm of politics. One series of segments sampled the progress of Song, a discount airline launched by Delta and aimed at women. Throughout, participants reflected on the habits and capacities of the public, although as was normal in such productions ordinary Americans were present only as objects, not subjects. Nonetheless the documentary did convey a mix of views from ad-makers, marketers, and market researchers as well as their critics and other observers. That signalled the continued dominion of the male: of the ten main participants, Naomi Klein was the only woman and of the twenty-one others interviewed only three were women. The key persuaders were Andy Spade, a brand consultant, Kevin Roberts, then CEO of Saatchi and Saatchi Worldwide, and two market researchers, Douglas Atkin and Clotaire Rapaille, as well as one political pollster, the Republican Frank Luntz. The most sensational segments were the interviews with Rapaille, a child psychologist turned marketing guru who had impressed corporate America, and with Luntz, a populist who had mastered the art of deception by testing and choosing the right words. The key critics, aside from Klein, were two familiar academics, Mark Crispin Miller and, more briefly, Stuart Ewen, both often on record about the harm of advertising, whose complaints were balanced here by the views of Bob Garfield, a noted columnist for the leading industry paper *Advertising Age*.

The bias of the documentary was discernably "progressive," meaning it expressed a deep sense of alarm about what the so-called persuasion industries might be doing to the culture and the public. It avoided advocacy, of course, since the aim was to inform and to provoke discussion. There were some comic moments, perhaps unintentional, inspired by Roberts' enthusiasms, his claim that some brands like Cheerios had attained the status of "lovemarks," or Rapaille's bizarre proclamations about codes and meanings, such as the "fact" that cheese in America was "dead" matter stored in a morgue, namely the fridge. There were also some sinister revelations, notably the existence of Axciom Corporation, which maintained a massive database of information on individual Americans that could be mined to fashion new selling or partisan efforts. *The Persuaders* argued the unfortunate emergence of a "clutter crisis" brought on by the escalating volume and the ubiquity of advertising and promotion in the past two decades; in other words, by the recent arrival of marketing's moment. The effort to break through the clutter to engage consumers only served to exacerbate the crisis by producing yet more promotional noise. Even so, the advertising executive and the market researcher had found what they thought were new techniques involving constant surveillance and constant promotion.

These reflected the presumption that emotion would nearly always trump reason, a reiteration of that old notion of "Freud's brain," where the id or the unconscious reigned over the actions of the individual. Roberts talked about "loyalty beyond reason," Rapaille of the domination of "the reptilian brain," Atkin of the cultish quality of brand loyalties. Luntz believed it was all "gut," that the emotional charge of any stimulus, any word, was much more significant than its surface meaning. All such declarations denigrated the old notion of the rational person, even the economic man, who carefully and logically evaluated the merits of a buying – or voting – decision. The talk of the moment might claim that power lay with the individual – Roberts was especially voluble about the empowered consumer, and Garfield denied the existence of a "Svengali spell" – but the reality, according to the documentary, was decidedly the opposite: consumers and citizens were subject to constant manipulation to activate their "hot buttons," irrespective of their feeble rational abilities. One conclusion was that demagoguery and demographics combined to fragment America into a collection of separate and hostile factions à la Joseph Turow, though he was not mentioned. The upshot was a worry that America, and especially its democracy, was seriously menaced by the new modes of marketing.

Much of the rest of the website accentuated the theme of alarm. The teaching guide suggested asking students to compare Luntz's emphasis on how voters felt about Thomas Jefferson's claim that an "informed citizenry" was a requirement of democracy. One of the embedded articles raised the spectre of a further wave of manipulation produced by the sophistication of neuromarketing, then a novelty. Rachel Dretzin, in a "producer's chat," worried about the effects of all the marketing on the psyches of her children. The press snippets called the report "chilling," "frightening," "scary." The extended interview with Miller was especially gloomy. There was, to his mind, no longer an "outside" to clutter: we lived in "a universe of propaganda"; in other words, the matrix ruled.

Which meant apparently the asphyxiation of the culture and the death of authenticity.

The messages about just who was to blame for the present state of affairs, whether the public or the adman, were unintentionally contradictory and confusing, however. That old notion of the hapless public, the pawn of hidden persuaders, persisted in the rhetoric of the critics. But even Klein suggested that, ironically, consumers were accidentally responsible because, over time, they developed immunities to marketing that required ever more massive and imaginative campaigns.[69] Frank Luntz presented himself as the truth-teller, a champion of the plain speech tradition who told the public the facts in a language they could understand.[70] Kevin Roberts styled himself as the friend, the cheerleader of the empowered consumer whose ads were "true, authentic, open" so as to connect and engage her. Clotaire Rapaille blamed no one except the reptilian brain that apparently wanted the SUV, whatever the cost to the environment. At one point Rushkoff claimed that despite a library of studies "nobody really knows" what ads work, when, and on whom. Right at the end of his exploration of the landscape of marketing, Ruskoff concluded that everyone was to blame for the ad swarm and the clutter crisis. "Marketers find a way so deep inside each one of us that it no longer feels like persuasion at all," thinking perhaps of Rapaille's spiel. "Maybe we are in control. Once the market becomes the lens through which we choose to see the world, then there's no 'us' and 'them' anymore. We're all persuaders." The final word was left to Stuart Ewen: "The secret of it all, the secret of all persuasion, is to induce the person to persuade himself."

The responses from visitors to the website included a range of opinions. There were two sources of input. The first was listed as a "producer's chat," where the day after the broadcast twenty-five people sent in questions that were answered by Rachel Dretzin. Much more revealing, however, was the "join the discussion" section, where over 130 visitors left their comments on the documentary and the problem. It is, of course, impossible to construct a complete profile of this group of correspondents, some of whom were anonymous, others who used pseudonyms.[71] One segment was made up of people engaged in marketing, then or in the past; another collection self-identified as students. But there were all sorts of men and women, some clearly teachers or mothers, most not claiming any vocation or affiliation, some on the Right and more on the Left, though the politics of most remained a mystery. The correspondents occasionally made reference to other writers, such as Marshall McLuhan, Vance Packard, and, notably, George Orwell (but not, interestingly, Wilson Bryan Key, whose bogy of subliminal seduction was largely passé). They also referenced assorted works of fiction: one writer recalled M.T. Anderson's *Feed* (2002), a dystopian novel in which marketers enjoyed a direct line to the networked brains of most Americans. A couple of correspondents displayed an ironic sense of pleasure in this world of clutter, enjoying the game of decoding all the signals sent their way. A few seemed to adhere to that older narrative of understanding, the progress myth, where the adman and advertising served to foster abundance.[72] A few doubted that advertising had much effect on the culture.[73] More seemed to despair over the prospect of a new wave of manipulation. One individual simply admitted his ambivalence: he subscribed to both *Communication Arts*, because he was a graphic designer, and *Adbusters*, because he was also "an alarmed citizen."[74]

Despite such diversity, however, many more correspondents evinced moral outrage over the effrontery and the activities of the new breed of persuaders. Such people were especially exercised by the clutter crisis. "Orson Cummings" railed against "the ubiquity of advertising; it drives me up the wall daily." "I absolutely DESPISE the onslaught of advertising sources," stated "Randy Davis," "that aggressively invade and intrude on a person's being in all forms." "Elizabeth Votaw Loux" yearned for a respite, a week without advertising. "Juanita Genco" hoped the crisis would reach "a critical mass where none of it affects anyone anymore and the smartest decision a company can make is not to advertise." Call this loose collection the moralists. They clearly were suffering from the victim's malaise. What follows looks more closely at their litany of complaints. I have sampled generously from their commentaries to convey the special flavour of this outlook. But treat their views as indicative of a particular stance, not representative of the American public.

Rushkoff's suggestion that "we're all persuaders" was now speedily rejected. Moralists blasted marketers like Spade, Rapaille, and Luntz as con men or Svengalis whose practices threatened the integrity of culture and democracy. "John McDonnell" railed against "the flim flam artists" who had perverted a style of advertising that focused on reason-why, its proper purpose to inform about a product or service. "Jason Smith," himself an adman, proclaimed, "the self-indulgent pap that snake oil salesmen like Spade foist upon advertisers represents the worst kind of creative egotism this business has to offer." "Adrian White" denounced the "sociopathic ad agency creeps subverting democracy with subtle brainwashing techniques." "Walter Vargas" lamented "the likes of

Clotaire Rapaille, who do nothing more than play head games with the public." Upset by the word play of Luntz and his clients, "James Hinde" concluded, "Theirs is a profoundly cynical and destructive enterprise." Such characters could never merit acceptance. "Any person who is trying to confuse an issue, invoke fear, hide information, manipulate me, etc. is proving to me that they are my enemy, not my friend," wrote one anonymous correspondent. This is only a cross-section of the many outbursts against what appeared to the moralists as a new generation of deceivers.

Nor did these correspondents accept the argument that advertising was just a weak force. The angry and upset writers resurrected the old narrative of harm. They found plentiful evidence of the ad-maker's sin. First and foremost was the charge that advertising fostered affluenza, the disease of excessive consumption which in turn generated a materialism that imperiled the American soul. "I can not believe that through psychology, anthropology, sociology and other ologys advertisers are luring us into buying products not necessary to meet our basic needs," argued one anonymous correspondent. "Now products are symbols of status, wealth, power, fashion etc. We are being programmed into feeling that products, material things, are necessary to feel good about ourselves. It is crazy that we allow this to happen." Some moralists, here in a question to Dretzin, feared the sad effects on the minds of children. "The increased corporate savvy in marketing to children is distressing to me. Children have lost their connection to the earth and to their childhood as they get caught up in aggressive consumerism, at home, in the school, on the playground." There were even the occasional echoes of "our master's voice," harking back to James Rorty's polemic. "In fact, everything discussed in this program is driven by Wall Street – stock price is everything to corporate America," stated "David Nelson." "It dictates what the media tells us (or doesn't), and even dictates policies in Washington." Then there was the charge that democracy was threatened, if not undone, by the new wave of surveillance and propaganda. According to "Bob Fiddler," "the improving sciences of research, segmentation and persuasion, have made a farce of the electoral process, which is now operated by cynics at the command of zealots." Perhaps thinking of the recently concluded general election, one anonymous writer reasoned that people would find themselves subject to "covert manipulation" which negated will and agency. "People will think they are voting their hearts when in fact they will be voting in a manipulated way. America has become very polarized on many issues and I wonder if some of these techniques are a factor." One Canadian viewer, "Mario Bonneville," concluded this was all very Orwellian. In *Nineteen Eighty-Four* it was "War is peace" but in 2004 it was "Climate changes" (instead of the scary global warming) and the "War on terror" (instead of the war on Iraq), examples of people "thinking in a prefabricated way."

Slightly more novel was the impulse to blame the postmodern condition, or at least the angst, on the persuaders. What "Jason Greenberg" deemed "a vicious cycle of media and advertising" had turned the culture into a closed system where illusion reigned. "It's a giant echo chamber in which everyone is trapped; we can't break through the clutter because no one can tell the clutter from reality." More specifically "Rene Gonzalves" claimed the new marketing was destroying authenticity. "The danger I see is when the natural meanings that we would naturally find in our everyday products and services gets highjacked and mutated into "designer meanings" which probably don't even exist, e.g., a "Song" day or a "Starbucks community danish." All the talk about lovemarks and cults did not convince these sceptics: the communities that brands might build, say, the Saturn fan club mentioned in the documentary, were ersatz, pathetic substitutes for the real thing. The upshot was to imperil the psychic health of the country. "Rather than trying to reach out to our better natures or educate us about alternatives," lamented an anonymous writer, "marketing of this kind seeks to strengthen the very forces that tend to disrupt society and lead to more severe mental distress."

Moralists might now be willing to allow the traditional adman to hype the utility or value of a product. But the turn to emotion appeared an illegitimate effort to undermine rationality. The move into politics endangered a realm of life deemed more sacred than the profane domain of the marketplace. "It is one thing to get people shopping," reasoned "Hendrik Sadi," "but it is another thing when you influence policy makers and deceive voters by catchy, clever sounding phrases that hide the truth." The new marketing appeared as a contagion that could all too easily corrupt the hapless public. That judgment reflected a deep fear of the prevalence of what Michael Pettit has termed "the deceivable self," a mind that was vulnerable to the kind of infection the new persuaders purveyed.[75] It was not just the impressionable youth that was at risk, although some correspondents did specifically worry about the targeting of children and teens. "As I sat in my house watching this insanity, I only thought 'people can't see behind this to what it all really means?'" wrote "John Bauer" in a suggestive commentary. "Then it hits me that most people don't have the intellect to comprehend the idea that they're not promoting family values when you buy their product, but just getting you to buy their product. I find it all very sad, and a proof ever more that we're a nation of morons." All too many moralists did not believe their fellow citizens had the capacity to resist. According to "T. Perry," "The messages may not work well with informed folks like those who wrote letters, but for the average American it is not really that difficult to 'induce the person to persuade himself.'"

The presumption of contagion evoked a related series of wrongs, such as corruption, subversion, debasement, or degradation. The moralist felt something had been lost, some virtue impaired. "Sadly," warned "David Nelson," "the make-believe world of consumerism will be the downfall of our society in America." "Marketing is the hallmark of American tackiness," wrote "Kathy Handyside." "It disgusts me." "I find the entire premise as well as the practice of market persuasion vile and insulting," wrote "Randy Davis." Its practices demeaned the individual and the society, a cause for shame rather than celebration. "To me, the most frightening reality behind all of this marketing philosophy/practice is that the people behind it seem to be perfectly happy with the fact that they are attempting to manipulate people at their most vulnerable point," according to "Joe Montanaro." "Regardless of whether or not these tactics work or will work in the future seems insignificant compared to the impulse of the powerful to control the powerless at any cost."

By contrast these moralists did articulate an opposing credo of immunity. That might take the form of a vigorous assertion that he or she only responded to the facts, to evidence of price, quality, and utility. According to "Kathy Handyside," the "ONLY thing that gets me to buy something is quality at an affordable price." Or as "David Upton" put it, "As an individual, I make my own decisions, purchase my goods, and buy my gas (except Exxon, because I do hold a grudge) based on service, quality, and economy." Which was the point: such correspondents announced their commitment to reason. As "Lea Pounds" put it, "consumers have a responsibility too – thinking. We're not mindless captives of the evil marketer's whims. We have the capacity – and responsibility – to seek out information and think for ourselves." Such a moralist implicitly rejected the idea of "Freud's brain" and its contemporary variants that extolled the import of the emotions. Rationality amounted to a mode of protection that ensured an immunity to the siren songs of the new persuaders. "I love the Bud ads, but I do not drink Bud," added "David Upton." "I will never buy car insurance from a company with a gecko as a spokesman, and I will chase any pollster off my property if they knock on my door thinking they know enough about me to show a personalized video."

Some of these correspondents urged the need for media literacy programs in schools to instil a mode of protection in the susceptible youth. "Ken Franklin," an employee of *Consumer Reports*, touted the magazine's virtues as a source of "the unvarnished truth." Another urged the wisdom of lying when approached by a market researcher. More moralists hoped exposés, such as they deemed *The Persuaders* to be, might awaken people to the perils of manipulation. *"The Persuaders* is like the special glasses which allowed a few to see the controls and remain free," thought "Roger Hoffman," referring here to the mode of protection employed in the scifi movie *They Live* (1988) to defeat subliminal commands. "Spread it around." That suggested a touching faith in the power of fact and argument to bring about redemption, a faith which contradicted the worry about the prevalence of the deceivable self.

Such assertions spoke the language of biopolitics. The moralists were moved to protect and even purify the social body and the body politic. One person asked Dretzin: "How can we get the marketers out of the political system? Luntz is one scary guy." Others favoured the return of reason-why advertising or, more radically, the return to a simpler life, where possessions were not so central. The moralist understood the new marketing as a perverse brand of biopolitics. "It seems to me the goal of market research and messaging is to numb us into compliance," wrote "Michele Matthews," "and to prey on human weaknesses rather than enhance our strengths as a people and consumers." Recall the three key terms of this philosophy: circulation, desire, and freedom. Contagion was obviously a perversion of circulation: the persuaders sought to mobilize a compliant public to accelerate the purchase of goods or to boom the popularity (or notoriety) of a candidate, no matter what the moral or social cost. They worked directly on the play of desire, seeking a mode of seduction – "the emotional hot buttons" (in Dretzin's words) – that was little different from coercion. That too was deemed perverse. And the persuaders vitiated freedom, leaving the deceivable soul a mere pawn in the hands of the elite. All the time, mused "Ingrid Chilberg," she had imagined herself free and independent. Instead, she found "my very cortex was being reconnoitered and analyzed for the best methods to manipulate me. My poor lizard brain was comfy on a rock in the sun, basking in the innocence it took for granted." Humorous perhaps, but yet another perversion of something deemed invaluable. "Consumers aren't really "empowered" or have more "choices," charged "Kim Dearborn." "Rather, consumers are being conditioned to become enslaved to materialism." The marketers aimed to dominate, not to liberate, the public. Implicit was the fear that the contagion they fueled would eventually infect irreversibly both the social body and the body politic, producing more and more zombie consumers and zombie citizens who were ruled by emotion.

The generally hostile response to the persuaders indicated that the perception of the adman's dilemma persisted, whatever ad people might say about their benign purposes. One aspect of that dilemma centred on the issue of trust. Admen had always sought some kind of license to buttress their modes of persuasion. That was necessary to ensuring at least a degree of credibility, if only among the deceivable public. But the obverse was the deceitful self, and many ordinary Americans still thought the adman all too easily fit that bill, most especially when he pursued a course which threatened to unseat reason. The fact that Rapaille could so easily con the lords of commerce with his bizarre spiel tickled the fancy of the occasional writer. But the deception of the public was not acceptable. "Ingrid Chilberg" ended her complaint with a piece of grim wit: "At what point do we suddenly realize that the X-Files and the Matrix were documentaries?"

We have circled back to that notion of the evil deceiver, which had found expression a century and a half ago in the moral critique of Barnum's first autobiography. This new explosion of outrage recalled the force of Vance Packard's pillory of motivational research back in the 1950s. ("The work of men like Clotaire Rapaille is nothing more than a rehash of the motivational research done in the 50's," argued "Brad Clark" – and with good cause.) And, in retrospect, it foreshadowed the later outcry over the onset of a "post-truth politics" after the presidential election in 2016, where manipulation and fake news supposedly reigned over reason, evidence, and fact. The worry about the adman's dilemma and the ad-maker's sin would always revive whenever deception claimed too large a place in the practices of a community committed, if only in the ideal, to truth-telling.

5. The Ad-makers' Response: William M. O'Barr, "The Advertising Profession in the Public's Eye," 2006

What of the views of advertising professionals themselves? How did they respond to the clutter crisis Rushkoff had talked about? What did they think about their activities, their role, their impact? Well, despite the changing environment, their rhetoric was full of echoes of the past, to borrow a cliché, meaning of past stories, justifications, and explanations.

In effect they denied the substance of the image of the omnipotent Svengali that now often reoccurred in the social conversation, favouring instead a perception of themselves as highly professional specialists in the art and science of persuasion.

In 2006, when the surge of digital advertising was already apparent, the cultural anthropologist William M. O'Barr organized a series of interviews with actual ad-makers, chiefly to aid in the education of future practitioners.[76] He compiled a brief document that contained examples of descriptions, criticisms, and justifications of advertising drawn from academics, Hollywood, and the media. Most tellingly, he republished a 2005 Gallup poll which ranked a series of professionals according to the public perception of their honesty and ethics. The ad-maker was right at the bottom, just above car salesmen and telemarketers, also engaged in selling: lawyers, labour leaders, businessmen, often pilloried for lying, all did better on the ranking.[77] This document O'Barr circulated to the ad-makers. He conducted discussions in separate meetings, some collectively, with participants drawn from two top agencies, Deutsch Inc. and McCann-Erickson Worldwide. The two female executives, Linda Sawyer (CEO of Deutsch) and Nina DiSesa (chairman of McCann-Erickson New York), proved the most forceful speakers in their wide-ranging exchange. Mathew Anderson (account director), Nathan Hunt (copywriter), Karin Parin (media planner), and Alan Snitow (account planner) followed in a second joint discussion. Of this group Anderson and Hunt, classic admen it might seem, were the most opinionated and articulate. O'Barr interviewed John Heath (strategic planner), Steve Ohler (creative director), and Alan Rush (media planner) separately in one-on-one conversations.

O'Barr had gathered a fairly representative group of ad-makers.[78] Nonetheless I will supplement, more specifically juxtapose, their views with the opinions expressed in two memoirs, one by a renegade and the other by an insider, although both men had become writers of other works. *Dry* (2003) by Augusten Burroughs was a bestseller which mostly explored the author's struggles with alcoholism.[79] During the late 1980s and early 1990s, he had been a successful copywriter, or so he claimed, at a variety of New York agencies including Ogilvy & Mather, Saatchi & Saatchi, and DDB. His memoir covered only the last years of his career as an adman: it was his agency which had compelled his trip to a clinic to control his addiction. But he included sufficient information about his work, behaviour, and attitudes to "deglamorize" advertising, as a journalist from the industry publication *Adweek* (9 June 2003) put it, a bit too delicately. The book was full of wit, slashing opinions, and much cynicism, which made it an appealing read, no doubt a reason for its success. Richard Kirshenbaum's *Madboy* (2011) was a not-so-successful account of an accomplished advertising creative and executive who had co-founded and co-managed Kirshenbaum & Bond (1987–2009), a New York shop noted for its novel take on advertising.[80] Unlike *Dry*, *Madboy* was a positive treatment of the occupation and the discipline, celebrating advertising as a creative force where intelligent men and women did great work. It was also much more familiar and even dated, reminiscent of Jerry Della Femina's memoir of many years ago (Della Femina actually wrote the forward), except lacking that work's edge. Kirshenbaum presented himself as both a maverick and an innovator, and with good reason. He was one of the pioneers of the ad swarm of the 1990s and 2000s, always seeking new spaces to colonize, listing a series of firsts, such as "street-stenciling" or ads on fruit, and so his views were revealing.

O'Barr's participants were resigned to the abysmal reputation of their profession expressed in the Gallup poll. Parin was a bit surprised by the low ranking. Hunt was a bit hurt. But most were used to the public's disdain for advertising. They blamed Hollywood (the source of dismal stereotypes of the ad-maker) or the ad swarm (the internet was too much a "wild west" of advertising, according to Anderson) or the prevalence of bad advertising (four participants admitted to owning TiVo, where they might block commercials). Ohler talked of the legacy of an unfortunate history, the "lingering aura of hucksters and dishonesty," an excuse often present in the laments of adpeople in times past. Hunt feared that too much stealth marketing broke the implicit bargain with the consumer to offer a separate roster of content and commercials. Heath found that too much advertising was pushy, intrusive, leaving the impression among consumers "we've invaded their space."

What had changed, however, was the stature of the adman. It might be marketing's moment when the ad swarm seemed to colonize more and more spaces – but in practice the ordinary ad-maker was treated like a hired technician, much less an awesome magician, by many clients, whatever critics might charge or the public might occasionally fear.[81] O'Barr's subjects had little to say directly on this matter. They did agree that Hollywood's portrayal of the ad work and adpeople emphasized incorrectly the ease and the glamour of advertising. But that did not translate into power. "We can't tell our clients how to run their business," mused DiSesa. "We can suggest things to them and we do, but if we don't make money for them, then they won't stay with us. They'll go someplace else." It was Kirshenbaum who recognized the new limits.

He did so by reflecting on the way advertising and the adman was perceived by the new masters in the world of finance. Long gone were the
1950s and 1960s, when the admen might seem the key to success. Wall
Street was now where the real masters resided.

> In this environment, creative people are often looked down upon or
> ignored by most financial men (obviously, with exceptions, as I've noted
> earlier). They don't understand creativity or advertising unless it involves
> a film premiere and a hottie. They think the profession is a hobby. They
> might say: "Oh, I wish I was in a fun little business like you." I stress the word
> little or fun. "You ad guys have all the fun while we're working." Meaning:
> "I make money with real work, but I am so friggin' jealous and want to come
> on a shoot with all the models." (KL 1614–18)

Such a comment brings to mind the now-forgotten polemic of Walter
Goodman, *The Clowns of Commerce* (1957). The figure of the adman, more
properly the ad-maker, no longer loomed so large in the calculations
of corporations, where a bewildering variety of experts in marketing
worked on the business of persuasion. This was one of the messages of
Wag the Dog: the adman had rivals, persuaders like him who had adopted
his ethos and usurped his place.[82]

The result of years of a bad press and Hollywood fantasy, O'Barr's people thought, was a social conversation full of misconceptions: not even
Heath's family understood what he did. Instead, these ad-makers presumed they laboured in an institution shaped by the gospel of creativity.
The agency was full of bright people working happily to solve problems
quickly, or so DiSesa asserted. Their work was hard and difficult, often
intense, always stimulating, sometimes passionate, collaborative more
than competitive, and above all fun. That imperative of fun ran through
Kirshenbaum's memoir as well (although in an aside he did mention
he had spent some years in therapy until he decided it didn't matter
what people thought). Burroughs, on the other hand, talked of burnout
(admittedly in an interview, not directly in his book), of how he got tired
of the same damn thing day after day, how he came to loathe his dealings with corporate clients.[83] "Advertising feels like this piece of dog shit
I can't seem to scrape off my shoe" (245).

Burroughs's comment about clients highlighted a persistent difficulty
of the profession: the lack of sovereignty. Kirshenbaum "bristled" over
the need to spend large sums of money – "upward of a hundred thousand dollars" – on a Pitch to secure a significant account: architects and

interior designers didn't have to do this (KL 1793). Even so, his praise of so many of the businessmen who employed him verged on the obsequious, an attitude that was reminiscent of some of the comments by admen eighty years before, notably Theodore MacManus in *The Sword-Arm of Business* (1927). (Kirshenbaum did, nonetheless, attack Quaker Oats for the way it had squandered the cultural capital of the Snapple brand after acquisition.) Advertising was, after all, a client service business: what Wakeman years before had stigmatized as the great Fear, the loss of the account, seemed to colour Kirshenbaum's views. O'Barr's subjects were more circumspect. But their occasional comments about clients indicated their submission to the authority of the sponsor, even when the client might be wrong-headed.

The conversation of O'Barr's subjects was haunted by the ghost of the adman's dilemma, the root cause of their abysmal reputation. None of the participants confronted the issue of this affliction. Only Snitow recognized how the ad-maker played with fantasy to please and flatter – and he added that the public didn't really want realism, not in its portrayals of the body anyway, no "big fat belly on their TV screen." None of the participants countenanced the charge that advertising was one of the liars' professions. How silly and unfair, argued Hunt, was the claim that advertising was little more than "institutionalized lying." Instead of liars, "we are ridiculously truthful," much more so than, say, journalists. DiSesa denounced as "bullshit" the presumption advertising was "lies and manipulation."[84] Never had advertising been "more honest" than it was now, she claimed. Any pressure to deceive came from the client side. Besides, deception just did not work, agreed her fellow executive, Sawyer, because consumers would detect the falsehood. The ad-maker, then, belonged to the camp of the truth-tellers, a conceit that harked back to the views of the first generation of professionals in the early twentieth century. "I feel like I'm definitely part of the moral fibre of our culture," declared John Heath. Sawyer did recognize the prevalence of cynicism in the ranks of ad-makers, "but in a good spirited way," whatever that meant. These ad-makers were in denial: they could never admit, at least not publicly, that their profession employed the techniques of deception regularly, consistently, and, often, imaginatively. Nor was Kirshenbaum any more perceptive: so, for example, he said of some early work he had done for the fashion mogul Kenneth Cole that people found it "refreshing and honest" (KL 579–80).

Contrast this evasion with the admissions of Burroughs. Advertising, he concluded, was always about deception and manipulation. He opened

his account with a declaration that sometimes you were assigned the task
of making a "garbage" product seem "fantastic," absolutely essential
to the good life. That was just an extreme case, however. "Advertising
makes everything seem better than it actually is. And that's why it's such a
perfect career for me. It's an industry based on giving people false expectations. Few people know how to do that as well as I do," he observed (1).
Dry made abundantly clear that Burroughs suffered from his own version
of the adman's dilemma. He had taken up advertising at age nineteen,
ill-educated, inexperienced, but full of self-confidence and already a
master of deceit. Initially copywriting offered excitement, easy work, a
certain glamour, and a lot of money. But in time everything seemed shallow; life was hollow – a malaise which suggests the liar's plight. "Nothing
is enough, nothing is ever enough. It's like there's this pit inside of me
that can't be filled, no matter what. I'm defective" (174–5). He reflected
how his drinking buddy, an undertaker, provided society a necessary
service. "I, on the other hand, try to trick and manipulate people into
parting with their money, a disservice" (5). He sought escape: drinking
constantly and to excess was how Burroughs managed his unhappiness.
In the end, once he mastered his addiction, he found a much more
satisfying escape from his demons in the very act of writing, something
he proved he could do even better than ad work. *Dry* was, once again,
a case of the renegade speaking. There was no sign of a similar angst in
Kirshenbaum's *Madboy*.

The presumption that advertising was a corrupting force was implicit
in Burroughs's story. But it was never addressed: his was a personal memoir, not social critique. Likewise, Kirshenbaum avoided any discussion
of the ill effects of the ad swarm he promoted. Just as O'Barr's subjects
refused to recognize the adman's dilemma, so too were they no more
willing to accept the notion of the ad-maker's sin. They might admit
their profession was guilty of a few misdeeds, such as targeting children
(Anderson), especially selling expensive sneakers to inner city kids
(DiSesa). But advertising lacked the kind of power to coerce consumers
or program society assigned to it by professors and non-profits, the chief
sources of the anti-advertising conspiracy (Hunt and Anderson): advertising was no more than a "soft force" (Snitow) able only to work on consumers already in the marketplace, never able to make consumers buy
what they didn't want. According to DiSesa, it did have the power to fuel
the economy though – that motif of industry's engine – a contradiction
perhaps, but a claim that countered any charge of sin. The real culprits,
the institutions which sponsored excess or generated pollution, were the

corporations, or at least some corporations – the ad-makers were not about to blame their own clients. Besides, the ultimate cause of excess and like ills was the very materialism of American society. According to Sawyer, "great advertising is a mirror to society. It mirrors society and culture. How can advertising be held responsible for what are just the broader values in the society?" These counter-arguments were so very familiar. Ad people had responded to the motif of the ad-maker's sin in much the same way in the 1920s or the 1960s. What was new was the reference DiSesa and Ohler made to forms of social marketing, the campaigns they assisted that promoted public goods to improve the life or lot of America.[85] Call this the ad-maker's balm, a mechanism that worked to soothe any troubled conscience.

In the same way, the participants played up the motif of the consumer's friend, elaborated by Claude Hopkins and E.E. Calkins some eighty years earlier. First, advertising supported all manner of services, notably an abundance of entertainment and news media, that otherwise would be prohibitively expensive. That applied to the internet as well, claimed Snitow, where a service such as Gmail offered free email and much storage in return for "noninterruptive, hyper-relevant ads that talk about stuff that you're emailing about." Second, it was "an art form for the masses," asserted DiSesa, a declaration which evoked the theme of enchantment that had become so prevalent in the last third of the twentieth century. Advertising was a significant part of the popular culture, here a virtue instead of the lament it was in Mark Crispin Miller's critique. Third, advertising was never a "shady discipline," according to Parin, but a source of information and education, making known to Americans the brands available to enrich their lives. She added that consumers liked targeted advertisements because they spoke to the particular interests of individuals, thus making for happy shoppers – like herself. Advertising was just "a practical mechanism of communicating" information about goods and services, concluded Sawyer, both useful and innocuous.

The novel element in this defence was the claim that ad-makers were increasingly engaged in a dialogue with consumers, which recalled the wisdom of Howard Gossage. O'Barr's participants talked of becoming interactive (Rush), making connections (Heath), establishing relationships (DiSesa). Parin noted how youth, "Gen Y" in her lingo, were willing to share information about themselves to receive the kinds of messages which suited their tastes and interests. The chief means here was the internet, most especially social media (Parin mentioned myspace.com), celebrated as a mode of conversation rather than the instrument of an

ad swarm. But the notion of a new dialogue was most evident in Kirshenbaum's *Madboy*. Kirshenbaum did not deal much with the internet or
social media, even though he and his firm had sponsored digital offshoots.
He boasted of "being the precursor to advertising and branding via social
media – YouTube, Facebook, Twitter – by coproducing creative work that
engaged consumers in real dialogue, in real time." And he enthused about
a new world of marketing, where the internet effectively revitalized the old
myth of consumer sovereignty. "Consumers are controlling, commenting
on, spoofing, and creating dialogue about their favourite brands in ways
previous advertisers could never have dreamed of or controlled. Social
media is and will continue to redefine the advertising world" (KL 1873–4).
His vision of an emerging utopia where ad-makers and consumers were
joined in harmony and conversation was completely different from the
authoritarian nightmares conjured up by critics of marketing's moment.

In all, these ad-makers exhibited the symptoms of what two academics
have termed "moral myopia" and "moral muteness." In 2004 Minette E.
Drumwright and Patrick E. Murphy published the results of a series of
interviews they had conducted with a cross-section of fifty-one advertising practitioners across America in agencies large and small and active
in different fields.[86] Most subjects (thirty-eight) were male. Many (nineteen) were executives, though eleven identified as creatives. The inform-
ants reported few concerns with ethics in their work or with advertising
in general: they suffered from myopia, "a distortion of moral vision that
prevents moral issues from coming into focus," and/or simply muteness, meaning "that they rarely talk about moral issues."[87] Most interesting were the assortment of rationalizations the participants offered to
excuse their lack of concern.

Consumers are really smart, really astute.

Now I think the responsibility goes back to families and the law.

I think this is probably one of the most ethical business[es] there is. It is so
regulated.

I don't have a lot of time to sit and think about if the people who make this
thing are evil. You just don't have time to do that.

The [client] company is running a business. They can choose what they
want to convey.

Unfortunately, the solution [to ethical dilemmas] is often to do even less interesting advertising that's even more acceptable to the masses by offending no one.

When you start looking for ethical issues, they are everywhere ... You can open up a can of worms that just goes on and on.

Neither Burroughs nor Kirshenbaum worried much about the issue of ethics. Burroughs was a cynic, Kirshenbaum was oblivious. O'Barr's subjects did worry, at least a bit, given the structure of the discussion. DiSesa had avoided working on a cigarette account. Rush claimed he would refuse an assignment that conflicted with his personal beliefs. But you could easily find the sentiments expressed in the quotations above present in what O'Barr's practitioners said. Thus, from Linda Sawyer: "But at the end of the day, the consumer is in ultimate control. It's not done as trickery. Deceit and persuasion are two very different things. And I think consumers really understand the difference." Anderson observed that responsibility lay with the consumer: "If you just respond to advertising and do what it says, then you're lazy and deserve it." Roughly ninety years earlier, Helen Woodward had reflected on the peculiar moral code of her co-workers, then mostly admen. They were honest in their dealings with their fellows; they were duplicitous in their dealings with clients and the public; and they were blind to the contradiction. It was the nature of the game. The ad-maker was always the licensed deceiver, an unavoidable if sometimes unpleasant fact of life.

It could pall, however. Even Kirshenbaum felt a certain relief once he exited the life of the adman. In a revealing aside in his "Epilogue," after he and his partner had sold the firm, he expressed his glee, embodied in the fact that he used some of the new wealth to buy his wife an expensive bauble that shouted success to the world at large.

So once the final payment hit the account and I suddenly became one of the youngest chairmen in America (read: hood ornament), I did a little shopping for my ego. And you know what? It felt good to be able to do it. Because every time my wife wears the Earn Out (to match the emerald and diamond earrings I bought her ... which she also doesn't wear), I know that every glimmer and glint will make up for every ass I had to kiss, every line of copy I had to change for some boorish client, every credit someone else took for my creative idea, and the looks of every Wall Street guy who asked me if people in the ad business actually make a real living. (KL 2848–53)

Conclusion
DECEPTION AND ITS DISCONTENTS: FAREWELL "DON DRAPER," 2015

This is a story about how hard it is for him. He has a lot of admirable qualities and is basically a moral person, and he makes mistakes. His morality is conflicting. It's situational, which is the disease of the 20th century.

> – Matthew Weiner, 2010[1]

Don Draper is an icon of this time [of modernity] – freed by a negation of his past, remaking himself in pursuit of his dreams, and tortured by it all. This suffering is ours as well.

> – John Elia, 2010[2]

At the center of this constellation stands the drama's antihero, Don Draper, the firm's brilliantly talented creative director: a man, we learn, who not only sells lies, but is one.

> – Daniel Mendelsohn, 2011[3]

There's no doubt that Don Draper was – and I hope still is – a sinner. But forget the fake identity and the sleeping around, and forget all that booze: his metaphysical sin is that he created, and lived within, a web of lies called advertising. And the eternal fascination of *Mad Men* is that it captured how the whole world was ensnared by that web.

> – Owen Gleiberman, 2015[4]

It wasn't that Don couldn't see the difference between the lie and the truth – that difference consumed him – it's that he believed that the lie was more important. And he ended the show with, at the very least, a damn good lie.

> – Dave Thier, 2015[5]

Don Draper did not leave the world quietly. The airing of the last episode of *Mad Men* on 17 May 2015 generated a lot of speculation before and much commentary after in the press – and presumably in the community of fans. The finale was a ratings success: it attracted 3.3 million viewers, the third highest total of the seven seasons, of which 1.7 million were estimated to belong in AMC's "key demographic," adults aged 25 to 54.[6] Critics and viewers were eager to find out how the show's creator, Matthew Weiner, would conclude the saga of Don Draper. A few previous episodes saw Draper escape work and shed his possessions in a precipitous flight westward. What might happen next? Would a newly naked Draper or a reborn Dick Whitman (his "real" name) find peace and comfort in some place outside the matrix created by advertising? Or would Draper commit suicide, in some measure a resolution suggested by the show's animated title sequence? One especially bizarre speculation had Draper become D.B. Cooper, the notorious airplane hijacker who in 1971 got away with his heist and disappeared from sight.[7] What was not so expected, though, was that Draper would end as the consummate adman.

The last episode, entitled "Person to Person," had Draper reach a California retreat where the clients sought to find their true selves. He had only his clothes, his bag, some money. His present companion, Stephanie, the niece of Anna Draper (the wife of the man whose identity Don had stolen), disappeared to find the child she had abandoned, despite Don's advice for her to move forward. Before and at the retreat, he made troubled long-distanced calls to the three last women in his life, his daughter Sally, his dying ex-wife Betty, and his onetime pupil Peggy, to whom he wished a sad goodbye. He had an emotional encounter with another client of the retreat at a joint therapy session which revealed his own angst about a life wasted, empty, and dishonoured. In short, Don was left bereft of family, friends, job, possessions, and self-respect. (His situation seemed much worse than that of Vic Norman at the end of Wakeman's *The Hucksters*.) During the final moments of the episode, a montage of scenes wrapped up the separate tales of the main characters of the series. The last scene of the montage focused on a new Don: in a crisp, tailored white shirt, sitting lotus fashion among a group outside on a clifftop with the ocean behind them, meditating and chanting, an image of peace, harmony, new beginnings. Except that then his mouth slowly produced a slight smile, as if of enlightenment. The scene abruptly switched – what is called a "smash cut" – to end the episode with forty-five seconds of an ad, sufficient for viewers to recognize one of the most famous commercials of the twentieth century: Coca-Cola's *Hilltop*, aka *Buy the World a Coke* (1971). The smash cut left the distinct impression that an inspired Don Draper was the creator of this classic. He had translated his new-found sense of inner peace into a marvel of advertising art.[8]

Weiner and his team had neatly crafted this conclusion out of history and drama. The Coca-Cola agency was in fact McCann-Erickson. Earlier in *Mad Men*, McCann had purchased Don's agency, supposedly as an independent subsidiary, but soon the talent was absorbed into the main offices of the parent company. That unwelcome move apparently provoked, in large part, Don's flight westward. The fact McCann was at work on the Coke account was referenced in the drama. Likewise, in a clever bit of symbolic play, Don fixed a malfunctioning Coke dispenser at a motel in one of the last episodes. It was, then, reasonable to presume that Don returned from California to "fix" the Coca-Cola account at McCann-Erickson. His half-smile was, perhaps, a sign that the adman had found the "Big Idea" necessary to fashion a super commercial.

Furthermore, *Hilltop* had embodied the utopian dreams associated with sixties counter-culture, especially the so-called hippie subculture. McCann-Erickson had set out to fashion a commercial that celebrated harmony, empathy, love, peace, and happiness. It assembled a collection of attractive young people of both sexes and many nationalities, dressed in national costumes, on a hilltop outside Rome. They mouthed the lyrics to a song actually performed by a British group, the New Seekers, called "I'd Like to Teach the World to Sing (In Perfect Harmony)" – while boldly presenting bottles of Coke. In this way the commercial captured and commercialized some of the spirit that infused the brighter side of west-coast youth culture.[9] It fitted the sweet type of ideology propagated by the retreat, modelled on the Esalen Institute, where Don was cured, however briefly, of his angst.

But Don Draper was not transformed. He remained what he was, at his core: an adman, one of the master creatives. The last season, in fact, referenced the course of events shown in the much-noted title sequence of each show.[10] Recall how each one began with the dissolution of the adman's office, his fall between skyscrapers sporting ad images, to finish with the adman back in his seat of power, looking out on the world he had fashioned. In the last few episodes Don lost nearly everything, and he seemed in free fall in "Person to Person." True, we may not have witnessed his return to his seat of power. But the juxtaposition of the move from meditation to smile to *Hilltop* clip conveyed the rejuvenation of Don's fundamental self, hence influence.[11]

The finale was widely accepted as a fitting, if cynical, ending to this extended saga of the adman.[12] Supposedly audience response to "Person to Person" was overwhelmingly favourable.[13] Television critics were equally impressed, even those who thought the series had lost some of its panache in the seasons prior to the finish. According to Rotten

Tomatoes, the review aggregator, the finale scored a 92 per cent from the community of critics.[14] The Writers Guild of America gave *Mad Men*'s last season the top award in television drama series, although "Person to Person" was only nominated but did not win in the episode competition.[15]

The belief that Matthew Weiner had scored something of a triumph had much to do with the quality of the drama and the skills of the writers and actors, of course. Still, its appeal, the feeling of satisfaction over a story well told and well finished, neatly dovetailed with the mix of ideas about the figure of the adman long present in the social conversation. Now, the show promoters and apologists had often proclaimed the realism of *Mad Men*, its faithful reproduction of the way it was back in the 1960s. In one interview, Jerry Della Femina, now something of an ad legend, claimed that the show was a reasonably accurate portrayal of the life of Madison Avenue, though most of his comments focused on the quantities of sex, booze, and fashion evident then and there.[16] But what the treatment of the adman was most obviously faithful to was stereotype and cliché. According to the historian and journalist Thomas Frank, the adman, particularly in the sixties, was "one of the great evildoers of the age, the symbol of everything that people believed was wrong with American capitalism."[17] The show was, then, a realistic portrayal of a presumption. Perhaps that is one reason a series of brief interviews by ad-makers featured on the AMC website to promote *Mad Men* were so full of irony and self-mockery: the subjects knew they were talking more about expectations and impressions, more image than reality.[18] During its long run of seven seasons, the saga of Don Draper had explored many times the practices of deception, the sense of personal angst, both the liar's plight and the victim's malaise, the attractions of affluence, especially the value of money, the arrogance of creativity, the persistent search for a stable identity and the equally persistent appeal of escape, notably the elusive goal of a true romance able to counter the falsity of a world of deceit. Which is why I will conclude this cultural biography with some reflections on the extensive literature by television critics and academics that *Mad Men* and especially Don Draper inspired. The result may seem a bit bewildering.

Over the years a few prominent critics charged the makers of *Mad Men* with seeking to flatter the audience, to demonstrate how enlightened "we" now were, by emphasizing the dark side of the 1960s.[19] The episodes were full of sexism and racism, they charged, of anti-Semitism, hypocrisy, homophobia, over-drinking, and assorted kinds of irresponsibility, whether in child care or collecting trash. Was the purpose to make "us" feel smug because "we" behaved so much better? Perhaps. But more importantly, *Mad Men* constituted an extended investigation of the prevalence, sometimes the charms, of deception as well as its costs to individuals, relationships, business, and sometimes society. David Marc, a television historian, captured the mix of attributes, the special flavour, which made *Mad Men* singular on American television:

> But loyal viewing reveals a complex hybrid drawing energy from multiple sources: an oddball crime show primarily concerned with misdemeanors, in which guilt is in the eye of the beholder more often than on the books; a gothic medical sci-fi series in which a team of specialists are paid by corporations to experiment on the psyche of a nation; and an occult tale where, behind the mounds of data generated by taste tests and focus groups, dark arts rule.[20]

One common observation was just how enigmatic the character of Don Draper was. Especially in the early seasons, he was seen as a man of mystery, even portrayed as such by his colleagues on the show. "Don is one thing on the inside and another thing on the outside," explained Matt Weiner, "I think that's the American story."[21] And when Don's back story was revealed, he turned out to be a very doubled, contradictory, tormented master of creativity, an exaggeration of stereotype here. So too was his extreme masculinity, a pose which hid a fragile ego – one scholar spoke of masquerade[22] – reminiscent of the sneers James Rorty had made about the manhood of admen back in the 1930s. Likewise, Weiner's own comment that Draper was "basically a moral person" (see above) recalled the claim by Helen Woodward that admen were usually "honorable people," honest among themselves, but forced by advertising into both deception and self-deception.[23] The historian Diane Harris decided Draper was really "passing" as a bourgeois male, largely because of the suppression of his tawdry origins, the child of a prostitute mother and drunken father; but she could just as easily have reflected on his amorality, his conduct and his cynicism, which were full of transgression.[24] That brings to mind the tirade of Walter Goodman, back in 1957, when he called admen the "clowns of commerce," despite all their self-righteous rhetoric about telling the truth and improving ordinary life. But to the historian Jeremy Varon, Draper was a resigned rebel, aware of "the tyranny of the 'rules' he so resists" yet prepared to submit to enjoy the American dream.[25] And in a weird kind of logic, Thomas Frank decided Draper's keen perception that "it's all make-believe – that 'you're born alone and you die alone' and this world just drops a bunch of rules on top of you to make you forget those facts" – made him "the most upright man there is, a brave independent surrounded by stuffed shirts and yes-men."[26] We are back to enigma and ambiguity.

Nor was there agreement over the character of Draper as played by Jon Hamm. According to Mark Greif a critic and professor of literature, Draper was supposed to be "a social savant" who knew how to bend men and women to his will. Not so Hamm. "Hamm looks perpetually wimpy and underslept. His face is powdered and doughy. He lacks command. He is witless."[27] Daniel Mendelsohn (yet another author, critic, and professor of literature) found Hamm the most "remarkably vacant" of all the actors, meaning you never felt his supposed torment – but then he also found the characters "unrelentingly repellent."[28] But to the editor and writer Benjamin Schwartz, Hamm was comparable to such masculine greats as Clark Gable, Cary Grant, and Humphrey Bogart. "Here is an actor who at once projects sexual mastery and ironic intelligence, poise and vulnerability."[29] And James Meek, a British novelist and journalist, argued that Hamm as Draper, the private as well as the public person, was horribly contradictory. "His character suffers from a cartoonish spring-backability: his morals are constantly being blown to pieces, his integrity always falling off a cliff, yet each time, his essential virtue is made whole again. He helps people selflessly, yet by 1969 has two suicides on his tab. He's vindictive yet loyal, controlling yet tolerant, devious yet trustworthy; for Don, nobility is an occasional, random quality."[30] Draper, as a character and a role, appeared endlessly controversial.

Jeremy Varon went on to argue that "*Mad Men* joins a pageant of iconic representations of white masculinity in crisis and, specifically, the hazards of upper-middle-class mediocrity and ennui as experienced by men." What was unusual was how *Mad Men*, or perhaps the handsome Jon Hamm, had made this "spectacle of masculinity in crisis at once so elegant, alluring, and instructive."[31] Varon noted Sinclair Lewis's novel *Babbitt* and the films *The Graduate* and *American Beauty*, even the *Sopranos* TV series, as other representations. But he made no direct reference to the figure of the adman. In fact, though, the adman had long been treated as a tool to explore, and moralize, about the emotional and ethical troubles of the bourgeois male. That concern had been foreshadowed in H.G. Wells's *Tono-Bungay* (1909), where the young persuader George Ponderevo occasionally anguished over the nature of his business of selling patent medicines. The concern was especially obvious in the postwar surge of persuader fictions, both novels and movies. The key work here was Frederic Wakeman's *The Hucksters* (1946), whose Vic

Norman became the standard model of the male caught up in a state of angst. The theme of a crisis was also apparent, if much less intense, in such nonfiction as Martin Mayer's *Madison Avenue, USA* (1958), David Ogilvy's *Confessions of an Advertising Man* (1963), and occasionally in the collection of memoirs ad-makers wrote in the mid-twentieth century. This too had been foreshadowed even in the Claude Hopkins's classic *My Life in Advertising* (1927), though here the signs of angst were hidden beneath a gruff pose of self-assertion. Indeed, the shape of the adman's dilemma was, if only in retrospect, evident in P.T. Barnum's memoirs.

Varon had specified that the problems of mediocrity and ennui were at the root of this crisis of masculinity. But in the case of the adman the imperatives of deception and self-deception were the cause of the angst. Some critics were not impressed by the show's handling of advertising. James Meek was struck by the lack of overt criticism of advertising in *Mad Men*.[32] Thomas Frank decided "its treatment of the ad game, which is its nominal focus, is also surprisingly weak."[33] But many commentators were also impressed by the prevalence of assorted kinds of deception in the program's repertoire of issues. Varon, again, noted this feature. "Indeed, the Mad World is almost entirely devoid of ethical conduct, defined by altruism and moral awareness. Instead, the characters mostly serve as accomplices to each other's deceptions."[34] Daniel Mendelsohn, one of the show's harshest critics, pointed to "the pervasive theme of falseness and hypocrisy that the writers find not only in the advertising business itself, but in the culture of the sixties as a whole just before the advent of feminism, the civil rights movement, and the sexual liberation of the 1970s."[35] Andreja Novakovic and Tyler Whitney, two graduate students at Columbia, highlighted the comment Midge, a girlfriend, made to Draper in the first season: "You make the lie. You invent want. You're for them, not us." They also noted a specific incident of the victim's malaise: where Betty, then married to Don, got so exercised when she felt duped and embarrassed because his strategy of marketing Heineken targeted her, or rather her type, something revealed in public at her own dinner party.[36] David Marc found the root cause of Draper's difficulties in his own self-defeating conduct, which can be taken as an example of the liar's plight. "Fulfilment is difficult for him to envision, perhaps impossible to achieve, because the life he has made is an unending series of seductions: clients, mistresses, neighbors and, of course, the buying public."[37] But the film critic Owen Gleiberman enthused how *Mad Men* "was never more mesmerizing than when Don was pitching a new product, because what he revealed in those scenes was a born actor's genius for believing in a lie until it becomes the truth. Don lied with every breath in his personal life, but on the job he got respect and big money for turning lying into an art form."[38] Similarly, the English professor Jim Hansen was very impressed that Draper "recognizes identity itself as an illusion," unlike ordinary mortals. "Like any artist, he shapes an illusion in order to produce the effects he seeks. By manipulating surfaces, Don proves himself to be the master of public relations."[39] Such comments are reminiscent of the sentiments of pleasure supposedly experienced by patrons witnessing and decoding the assorted deceptions of Barnum's museum back in the mid-nineteenth century. They also speak to the persistent – and some moralist might claim perverted – appeal of any master of deceit who shaped life.

There was one tale of moral turmoil, highlighted by Michael Ross, a professor of English and cultural studies, that deserves close attention because it reveals the adman's dilemma in its starkest form. The event revolved around a Pitch near the end of an episode entitled "In Care Of," which closed season 6 in June 2013. Always the innovator, Don Draper, now an executive at Sterling Cooper & Partners, had also become increasingly troubled and erratic, prone to drunken escapes from work and life. He was tasked with preparing and presenting a proposal to Hershey, one of the largest chocolate makers in the country and a company that had hitherto never advertised nationally. Initially he performed superbly. He told his audience of agency fellows and company representatives how the campaign would build on the existing fame of the brand to position Hershey as the "currency of affection," "the childhood symbol of love." He offered one example of these "sweet tales of childhood" that would soon fill American television. He told how his father had rewarded him with a small treat after he had mowed the lawn. He could have anything he wanted at the drugstore, but he chose the Hershey bar. "And as I ripped it open, my father tousled my hair and forever his love and the chocolate were tied together." It was obviously captivating: a Hershey man called Draper "a lucky little boy." But the story was a lie. Don was never a lucky little boy, as the home audience knew by now. Then, which likely amazed onlookers, Draper suddenly decided to tell the truth. He said, he had been an unhappy and unwanted orphan brought up in a whorehouse. When he managed to thieve more than a dollar from a john, one of the women bought Don a Hershey bar. He relished the chocolate: "I would eat it alone in my room with great ceremony feeling like a normal kid." This was hardly the kind of tale to tell on American television in 1968, even if it celebrated the brand. Draper said as much. He told the stunned meeting that Hershey didn't need to advertise, and it certainly didn't need Draper to tell a boy what Hershey meant, because the boy already knew. The confession blew away any chance the agency might get the account. And it destroyed his position at the agency. His act of truth-telling was unacceptable, the last offence in a series of missteps which determined that Draper could not remain an adman. Shortly afterwards, the partners met and told Draper to accept a forced leave of absence to pull himself together.

Draper had suffered a bad case of the liar's plight. He could no longer practice the necessary deception, even when the lie had worked. He was suddenly disgusted with his own duplicity, despite having practiced deceit, and so effectively, throughout his personal and working life. He prefaced his disclosure by saying to the Hershey man, "I don't know if I'll ever see you again." He had to tell the truth now to avoid yet further and lasting moral error. But his colleagues too had to respond to what Michael Ross called Draper's "apostasy." "The 'moral' is plain: honesty and advertising are unsuitable bedfellows."[40] Indeed: writers, renegades, eventually filmmakers had been saying much the same about the indus-try and the craft since the days of Barnum. And insiders, apologists or champions, had usually denied the reality or the force of the charge. At the end of the episode, we see Draper drive his children to see the whore-house where he had grown up, now a thoroughly dilapidated building. It was a further attempt to rectify a wrong, no longer to live in his fabri-cated world but to tell the truth about his reality, however sad and sordid.

Largely missing from *Mad Men* was the narrative of justification ad-makers had employed during much of the twentieth century to legitimize their conduct. That lack might be ascribed to the prevalent cynicism of recent times. Or to the impact of the postmodern moment on the per-ception of the importance or even existence of truth. But it also reflected views previously articulated in the social conversation. Certainly some commentators seemed unconcerned by the issue of legitimacy. For exam-ple, the Teschners – Gabrielle is an artist and George a philosophy profes-sor – dismissed the charge that Draper perpetuated lies because instead, apparently, he created "truths, albeit ones that are relative and imperma-nent."[41] That comment harked back to the creed of pragmatism appar-ent in the huckster fictions early in the twentieth century. The journalist David Thier praised Don's farewell (see the quotation above) because it ended with "a damn good lie." That comment brought to mind the assorted admissions and confessions made over the years by Draper Dan-iels, David Ogilvy, or Jerry Della Femina about exaggeration, illusion, and having fun. David Pierson, a professor of media studies, was much more interested in how *Mad Men* showed Draper and the other ad-makers producing, regulating, and manipulating desire, the key to the regime of stimulation in "late capitalism."[42] That recalled the view of capitalism articulated in Naomi Klein's bestseller *No Logo*. The deceit that really mattered, according to many critics, was the one in Draper's private life: his treatment of others, notably his philandering, and his own struggles or doubts over his authenticity. When he made his *mea culpa* to Peggy on the phone, what he confessed were his personal sins:

> I broke all my vows.
> I scandalized my child.
> I took another man's name and made nothing of it.

The deceptions of ad work were presumed and accepted, a necessary evil or an allowable act to fuel the fantasies of the consumer society.

Similarly *Mad Men* did not address directly all of the motifs or draw obviously upon some of the other narratives of understanding apparent over the course of the social conversation. The ad-maker's sin was only ever in the background because, as Mendelsohn pointed out, the show presumed the adman's duplicity was a reflection of the times, not the cause of some massive dishonesty. Nowhere was the complex of contagion and immunity conspicuous, possibly because the public, hapless or otherwise, was normally off-stage. Signs of the tradition of anti-advertising were evident, but hardly in the shape of that false scold Michael Wilde of Herman Wouk's *Aurora Dawn*. Also discernable was the gospel of creativity, apparent in the awe over Draper's skill at producing an original campaign. He clearly was deemed an innovator, perhaps not a Bernbach, but of the stature of a Della Femina and a George Lois.[43] That designation, however, was linked to the chief narrative here, the chronicle of struggle, and the presiding motif of the adman's dilemma.

But *Mad Men* had explored in detail the figure of the adman which had long existed in the world of representations, the world created by novels, memoirs, movies, polemic, and the like. Here the adman became a complicated, ambiguous, and ambivalent character in the saga of modernity: a producer and a consumer, an artist and a businessman, the master of spectacle and surveillance, a person who dealt in the rational and the irrational, in science and magic, a broker who served different interests (notably the client, the public, and the agency).[44] In some ways he was a professional, but rarely in the years after 1910 self-employed.

Admen operated mostly in a corporate setting: bureaucracy, hierarchy, convention, team work, all a part of their work life. They had authority, exercising power over the social imagination – or, put another way, over life, because they created dreams and nightmares to shape ordinary behaviour. Admen and other persuaders, consequently, were biopolitical figures: they addressed populations, they created markets, they operated on desire (and fear), they were crucial to the circulation of goods and ideas. But the adman was not sovereign: he was often a servant of business, the state, or a sponsor. Admen and the other persuaders could enjoy considerable wealth, selling their souls for material gain perhaps, but rarely achieving security or tranquillity. They existed in a highly competitive environment, a place of risk and uncertainty, full of the trappings of masculinity (even after women entered the ranks of persuaders in considerable numbers). They dealt with so-called realities, whether objects or people or policies, yet they fashioned what was often regarded as a discourse of untruth. They were sometimes respected but often disdained, constantly troubled by charges of immorality or amorality, of falseness.[45]

One of the ironies of this cultural biography is that the figure of the adman, in the shape of Don Draper, won so much attention just as he was passing out of history. *Mad Men* became at the end something of a requiem. "Don Draper wouldn't recognise 75% of what we do." That declaration – and he repeated variations on it a few times – was from Sir Martin Sorrell, then master of the marketing colossus WPP and a declared fan of *Mad Men*. The money was now in what he called media, data, and digital, and the old priority of creativity was no longer central.[46] Perhaps the popularity of *Mad Men* owed something to the force of nostalgia (as Thomas Frank has suggested) for a presumed less-complicated time when the adman was in his prime, before the arrival of so many adwomen and public relations specialists and marketing experts made persuasion a much more complicated endeavour. For despite the ad swarm of the past twenty-five years, the ordinary advertising practitioner is now just one technician among many in the industry. The US Bureau of Labor Statistics, for example, listed for 2016 such occupations as "Advertising sales agents" (222,000), "Advertising and promotions managers" (67,000), "Marketing and sales managers" (1,066,000), and "Public relations and fundraising managers" (62,000). Moreover, more and more women are prominent players in advertising and marketing, as much as are admen. Again, according to the US Bureau of Labor Statistics, 45 per cent of marketing and sales managers, nearly 57 per cent of advertising and promotions managers, and 71 per cent of public relations and fund-raising managers were women in 2016.[47] Contemplating, even condemning, this licensed deceiver of times past, when he was so distinctive, had proved a way of exploring the ongoing project of truth (finding and telling) and its inevitable clash with the practices of deception (fabricating and promoting). Perhaps saying farewell to Don Draper also meant saying goodbye to the cultural significance of the figure of the adman?

Except, of course, that the equivalent figure, and often villain, is now more aptly named the persuader.

Afterword

THE TRIUMPH OF THE HUCKSTER: DONALD J. TRUMP, REPUBLICAN NOMINATION ACCEPTANCE SPEECH, 21 JULY 2016

We keep hearing from the Trump-naysayers that Trump's mouth is a problem. But where you see a loudmouth, I see candor. Where you see a lack of filter, I see transparency. Where you see a man who gaffes, I see a man who is willing to wipe the cancer of political correctness out of our society. Where you see a loose cannon, I see a man who says what he means and means what he says. Or, would we rather the typical Hollywood celebrity or establishment politician (the two are remarkably similar) who runs a statement by 20 handlers, 10 advisers, and a social-media team before making it?

– A.J. Delgado, 2015[1]

A ghost haunted the vigorous debate provoked by the extraordinary triumph of Donald Trump in the Republican primaries of 2015–16. What upset, even infuriated, critics was the absence of anything resembling the adman's dilemma. Trump should have been its victim, felled by his lies, full of remorse over his conduct. He wasn't. Voters should have been disgusted. Most Republicans weren't. Despite the best efforts of rivals and pundits, he won, and then, to the horror of much of the intelligentsia, he beat political veteran Hillary Clinton, the presumed favourite. I will focus here on that first victory in the primaries. Why tell this story? Because, in part, it is about the lack. It tells how a particular mix of character and circumstance worked to disable the yoke of the adman's dilemma. Whether that was unique, a singular assemblage, or the prototype of future acts of persuasion, political or otherwise, was not clear. Nonetheless, as we shall see, some commentators saw Trump's success as the sign of the arrival of a so-called post-truth era.

The acceptance speech Donald Trump delivered in Cleveland in the mid-summer of 2016 after he received the Republican nomination for president was remarkable in many ways.[2] As commentators noted, the lengthy address to the nation was especially angry and menacing, much more so than similar recent speeches, its dark vision of an America in crisis reminiscent of Richard Nixon's speech back in 1968 (and, it was thought, an address modelled on Nixon's effort).[3] Elsewhere on the hustings, Trump had declared the American dream dead. He now portrayed a dystopia full of violence and disorder and poverty, a nation in despair threatened by aliens at home and enemies abroad, run by a corrupt and incompetent elite of politicians, business magnates, and media bosses. One of his special targets was the wave of undocumented immigrants, especially Mexicans, who had taken jobs, suppressed wages, fostered crime, and overwhelmed public services. Another was the prospect of an influx of Muslims, potential terrorists who hated America and would maim and kill its citizens. Yet a third was the series of trade agreements, such as NAFTA, and in general the whole gospel of free trade, which had purportedly deindustrialized America, depriving its citizens of decent jobs and wages. The fourth target was a foreign policy that had failed to suppress terrorism, allowed supposed allies to freeload at American expense, had left the United States humiliated and dishonoured, and proved costly in money and lives. Overall he condemned what he termed a "rigged system," where politics and economics were designed to empower and enrich the elite at the expense of ordinary citizens. Hillary Clinton, his opponent, was of course cast as the tool of this elite.

No less startling was the way in which Trump had positioned himself as the sole saviour of America. Although he did sometimes refer to "we," meaning the Republicans, his speech was full of "I" and "me": I saw, I visited, I promise, believe me. He boasted of his past business success as proof of his ability to act: "I have made billions of dollars in business making deals – now I'm going to make our country rich again." He shouted to the forgotten and exploited people, "I am your voice." Everything would change for the better once he was in the White House: "I alone can fix it." Trump presented himself, as he had in the campaign, as the strongman a desperate America needed.

What he promised was to be the law and order president who would bring safety and security back to America by combatting gangs, crime, and terrorism vigorously and unremittingly. He would build "a great border wall" in the south to keep out illegals, drugs, and crime, a barrier he had said elsewhere that Mexico would be forced to pay for, the signature claim of his campaign over the previous year. He made reference to the need to stop the flow of Syrian refugees into the United States – elsewhere he spoke of Muslims generally – unless they could demonstrate their ideological sympathy for the American way. He would rebuild a "depleted military" and compel allies to "pay their fair share" for defence. He emphasized his intent to destroy ISIS, the so-called Islamic State whose vicious assaults had so alarmed the public. But he would also be the president of prosperity and renewal. He affirmed he would renegotiate the existing trade deals with China as well as with the members of NAFTA, pursuing an "America First" strategy. "Americanism, not globalism, will be our credo." Jobs and investment would return to the American heartland. He also promised to eliminate government waste and to reduce the tax burden, two clichés of past Republican platforms.

But Trump's remedy was, as one journalist put it, more "a kind of fortress conservatism, taking a bunkered outlook on the world and fixating on challenges to America's economic supremacy and to its character as a nation defined by the white working class."[4] One upset conservative in the *National Review* concluded that this was all no more than a plot to expand big government, casting Trump as an "old-school Democrat" and a "post-war Teamsters' boss."[5] In the words of David Brooks, a noted columnist and conservative, Trump was nothing less than a reincarnation of the "dark knight," a political version of the action hero Batman, "your muscle and your voice in a dark, corrupt and malevolent world."[6]

What also provoked comment was the very style of Trump's speech. It was so unlike his efforts in the recent past. During the campaign, at rallies and in the candidates' debates, sometimes in interviews, he had established a free-wheeling, arrogant, and aggressive mode of expression, full of quips and insults, lots of gestures, more colloquial than staged, which excited the passions of his fans and floored his rivals. Their impact was buttressed with the extensive, often unrestrained use of Twitter. He played well an elaborate game of honour – where Putin, for instance, got praise – and especially dishonour, where critics and rivals were trashed. Nobody else employed so effectively such an unconventional style, one so unlike what was expected of a candidate for president. He caused sensations, which explained why the media had given him so much free publicity. Now he delivered a much more formal address, a set piece that, according to one source, had been crafted by two speechwriters from the earlier Bush era.[7] But if so, this too was vintage Trump. The speech was actually reminiscent of the style and content of his initial foray (though less formal) when he entered the race in June 2015. Trump was a versatile and talented speaker who could employ different styles when it suited his purposes.

Trump's performance pulled in a slightly larger total of watchers (34.9 million) than did Clinton's acceptance speech (33.8 million) a week later.[8] And he did earn a slight "bounce" in support in national polls.[9] Which did not mean viewers were pleased with Trump's address: polling indicated that while a third of the sample were impressed, slightly more were hostile, Gallup claiming his effort received the lowest positive response since the organization began counting such events in 1996.[10] The finding expressed yet again just how polarizing the rise of Donald Trump had proved in the year since he had entered the race for the Republican nomination on 16 June 2015. He had increasingly won over a large proportion of the Republican base, notably non-Hispanic white males, which propelled him to victory in primary after primary until by May his success in the Republican contest was assured. That success, however, shocked the Republican establishment, who thought Trump a dangerous outsider who could never win the actual presidential election but might seriously damage the party's standing in Congress. And that success frightened a large number of people, especially among the educated public and the Hispanic and African-American minorities, who feared a Trump presidency could only produce a catastrophe. Certainly many of the reporters and pundits, including some noted conservatives, were disturbed, if not aghast, at Trump's rise. The hysteria reached a crescendo in the spring of 2016 as the incredible, the unthinkable, became a reality: a Trump nomination. There were editorials, essays, investigations, reports, and documentaries exploring who Trump was, where his support came from, why he had succeeded, and what the Trump phenomenon might signify. Nor was the excitement confined to the United States: Canada's CBC, the BBC, and its British rivals all produced documentaries about what had happened and was happening.[11]

The usual answer to "why" was a particular mix of circumstance and character. Before long, the prevailing narrative in the social conversation had focused on the emergence of what one BBC documentary called an "Angry America" brought on by demographic and economic change. Much of the so-called white middle and working class, especially those lacking an advanced education, were anxious and resentful because they found their incomes, their status, their values, and their lifestyles increasingly threatened by events, aliens at home, and enemies abroad.[12] Their concerns? Too much debt, insecure or ill-paying jobs, crime in the streets (although crime statistics were down), and horrific terrorist attacks. The much celebrated "creative classes," the very rich, banks and big business, all had benefitted from the era of globalization and high-tech development. Not so hard-working, ordinary Americans, or so it seemed. They felt neglected and even betrayed by Washington, not only by President Obama and liberal Democrats, whose promises of renewal in 2008 were never realized, but by a Congress so rife with partisan and factional division that it could not act to address significant issues, such as the ongoing problems of deindustrialization and illegal immigration. They railed against Hispanic and African Americans, against takers who lived off welfare, against businesses which took jobs outside the USA; against a Washington that would not listen, against terrorists whom no authorities seemed able to defeat. The times were ripe for a populist revolt, spiced with class, nativist, and racist animosities.[13] The Tea Party and the Occupy movements of a few years earlier were clear signs of deep discontent. Another was the surge that fuelled the challenge of Bernie Sanders in the contest for the Democratic nomination. The Republican primaries soon became the most emphatic and important means of expressing the new mood of insurgency. The many contenders for the nomination – mostly existing politicians – were a lackluster lot.[14] The outstanding exception was the great outsider, the billionaire real estate promoter and reality television celebrity, Donald J. Trump. He understood and exploited the narrative of resentment, and became the instrument in America of a populist movement that in Britain and Europe was also challenging the *status quo*.[15]

For a time, and especially in the late winter and spring of 2016, the largest volume of commentary centred on Trump's character: how he looked, what he wore, how he spoke and gestured, and above all what he said. Which was fitting, since in this case the character soon did mould the circumstances: he fashioned the "perfect political storm" which transformed the Republican race.[16] Here the narrative of the huckster prevailed, almost from the beginning. True, at first pundits deemed Trump's candidacy a joke. The *New York Daily News* greeted the event with the headline "Clown Runs for Prez."[17] He was occasionally portrayed as a new incarnation of P.T. Barnum because of his notoriety as an entertainer, an epithet common even before he entered politics.[18] He was charged with turning the race for the nomination into a form of reality game show, where arrogance and insult and cruelty excited the crowds – turning the candidates' debates into the political equivalent of the TV series *The Apprentice* (2004–15), which he had hosted and dominated.[19] Eventually, Neal Gabler blamed the media for having given so much free publicity to this "pseudo-candidate" (borrowing from the lexicon of Daniel Boorstin), because coverage meant high ratings, as a result of the public's fascination and horror over the sayings and doings of this celebrity.[20]

But the clown soon became something much worse, because his outlandish declarations and constant insults, his egomania and braggadocio and bullying manner, all resonated with the mood of the Republican base, enabling him to rise in the polls above all rivals. He was called a huckster selling deceptions and fantasies to the public, although the reference here was more to the con man and the salesman, close relatives of the adman.[21] Much effort was spent identifying and denouncing his penchant for falsehood, including outright lies. Often cited was a finding by PolitiFact, a project owned by the *Tampa Bay Times*, to test the truth of politics: "PolitiFact recently calculated that only 2 percent of the claims made by Trump are true, 7 percent are mostly true, 15 percent are half true, 15 percent are mostly false, 42 percent are false, and 18 percent are 'pants on fire.'"[22]

Soon the narrative morphed into a claim that Trump was actually a demagogue, and perhaps a fascist, because of his self-evident authoritarianism.[23] At the moment of Trump's triumph, the *New York Times* (21 July 2016) carried a story noting his antecedents: populists and nationalists such as William Randolph Hearst, Charles Lindbergh (one of whose slogans, "America First," Trump used), and George Wallace. Critics soon recalled Sinclair Lewis's *It Can't Happen Here* (1935), a novel about an American-style fascist who wins the presidency in the mid-1930s.[24] An alternate variation of the narrative deemed Trump either a sociopath or a psychopath, subject to such mental ills as Narcissistic Personality Disorder or Antisocial Personality Disorder.[25] This was the frightening observation of a much-alarmed Tony Schwartz, the purported writer of Trump's super-successful manual and memoir *The Art of the Deal* (1987), in a lengthy interview published in *The New Yorker* (25 July 2016) that garnered some attention in the social conversation.[26] Such speculations drove some pundits into a state of extreme panic over the prospect of a President Trump in control of America's nuclear arsenal. Andrew Sullivan warned of "an extinction-level event" should Trump triumph.[27]

But this narrative of the huckster, however prevalent among critics and liberals, ran counter to the equally compelling story of Donald Trump the truth-teller and plain-speaker. Plain speech, in the words of the historian Jackson Lears, presumed "a society where people said what they meant and meant what they said."[28] During the primary campaign Trump occasionally employed the tactic of avowal ("I mean, you know, you can call it what you want, but I am a truth teller, and I will tell the

truth") and disavowal (when he disavowed any link to the tainted David
Duke of KKK notoriety) to establish his credentials as a truth-teller.[29]
In his acceptance speech, he had emphasized how he only spoke the
truth: "there will be no lies. We will honor the American people with
the truth, and nothing else." Others, especially the Hillary Clinton camp
but also the media, lied. "So if you want to hear the corporate spin, the
carefully crafted lies, and the media myths – the Democrats are holding
their convention next week." Briefly in the same address he referred to
the ill of political correctness, one of his prime targets during the primaries. Then, time and again, he had sneered at political correctness
as a liberal evil which chilled debate and forestalled action. During the
campaign, his notorious comments about undocumented Mexicans as
rapists, his mockery of a disabled reporter, his angry insult to the questioning Megyn Kelly ("There was blood coming out of her eyes, blood
coming out of her wherever"), his stigmatizing of Muslims as terrorists:
these were all just evidence that "he told it like it is." Likewise his suggestion that the whole system of rule was rigged and his taste for conspiracy
theory: these too could appear as plain speech. This line of argument
seemed all the more persuasive because Trump self-financed his campaign (so he boasted) and was never dependent on the ways and whims
of donors, as were his rivals.

Which was only part of the reason Trump was unique. He had demonstrated an unmatched ability to control the news, whatever the doubts
and hostilities of reporters or columnists. He was particularly adept at the
use of Twitter to constantly excite interest, often sending out compact
tweets of abuse and invective that were retweeted by his followers and
treated as news by the mainstream media.[30] One journalist who analysed
seven months of his tweets found "a running stream of insults, slogans,
and media commentary," mostly negative.[31] Similarly he employed rallies,
press conferences, interviews, even call-ins to broadcast programs, all to
occupy the news space with his claims or ideas, starving rivals of valuable
attention.[32] And he benefitted enormously from the way his name and
his "truths" filled the news feeds of Facebook, itself infamous as a source
of fake news but a major source of information for many Americans.[33]
Consequently, the author Neal Gabler dubbed Trump "the Emperor of
Social Media," whose personality and style so suited "his technological
moment."[34] But he was not beholden to or frightened by any journalist or media outlet: despite all the free publicity, by one account worth
nearly $2 billion, he had warned reporters and commentators he would
toughen the libel laws to ensure their honesty.[35] "I think the media is

among the most dishonest groups of people I've ever met," Trump once stated. "They're terrible."[36] The press seemed to be his tool, not vice versa.

One further and especial attribute was his avoidance of the advertising man: Trump did not use much of the kind of political advertising often cast as a powerful force in American elections, sometimes considered the bane of politics, even when his Republican rivals tried fruitlessly to stem his march with advertising.[37] According to one source, he spent merely $19 million on television ads, whereas rival teams wasted huge amounts of donors' money on campaign promotions: Ben Carson at $78 million, $105 million for Marco Rubio, and a most extravagant $139 million for Jeb Bush – who secured only four delegates! During the primaries Trump had no pollster, no speechwriter, no political strategist, not even a Super PAC.[38] He was his own man, authentic and sincere, who spoke what was on his mind, not words filtered through the voice of the adman or subjected to the censor of the politically correct. How different from the slick, polished images of rivals propagated by persuaders and designed for the media. A.J. Delgado, whose comment opened this Afterword, argued the Trump phenomenon spelled the demise of "the political consultant class."[39] At the annual meeting of the American Association of Political Consultants in April 2016, according to another journalist, an unspoken but frightening question haunted the proceedings: "What if their tactics and strategies simply don't work?" Trump's triumph seemingly exposed the fact that these well-paid persuaders could no longer work their magic for their clients, if they had ever been able to realize their grand claims.[40]

"But he's onto something, because secretly everybody's getting tired of political correctness, kissing up," declared another "manly man," the famed Clint Eastwood, though he was no great fan of Donald Trump. "That's the kiss-ass generation we're in right now. We're really in a pussy generation. Everybody's walking on eggshells."[41] It seemed as though many Americans, and particularly the Republican base, were upset by what they thought was the prevalence of censored speech: one poll in the fall 2015 showed that eight in ten Republicans agreed that political correctness was a "big problem" in the United States.[42] Fighting that evil was bound to be very popular. Trump's conversational manner, his simple and blunt vocabulary, his fragmented sentences, his quips and insults, the subject of so much comment, made this accomplished promoter and proud billionaire seem one of the people.[43] Even his penchant for outrageous and offensive comments about people were allowed, approved, perhaps welcomed, by his supporters, though they might shock Republican notables. The occasional responses from his fans that appeared in the press illustrated how Trump's co-option of the plain-speech tradition had such a powerful appeal, especially when compared to his rivals:

> The brash real-estate tycoon and TV star has struck a nerve, saying things that America's political elites would never publicly admit.[44]

> "Other Republicans offer 'canned bullshit,' Rice went on. "People have got so terribly annoyed and disenchanted and disenfranchised, really, by candidates who get up there, and all their stump speeches promise everything to everyone."[45]

> "I love the fact that he wouldn't be owing anybody," Nancy Merz, a fifty-two-year-old Hampton Republican, told me.[46]

> "We have to remember he's not a politician, so he's going to make these types of mistakes," said Abel Guerrero, a nurse who immigrated with his parents to the US from Colombia. "He talks straight from the heart. And sometimes when you're telling the truth, the truth hurts."[47]

> "Donald Trump is very real and very sincere. We're tired of being cheated. The more they try to attack him, the more we love him."[48]

> "I think Hillary is a big-mouth bitch," Mr. Martin continued, when the topic turned to [the] former secretary of state. "I can't stand her. I don't like listening to her. She's a liar. She's a fraud."[49]

One might conclude that Trump set out deliberately to lie to the public to galvanize support. Or, like many a persuader before him, Trump was a beneficiary of self-deception: he believed what he said, however false, at the moment he said it. In any case his apparent sincerity, what he once termed "truthful hyperbole," worked wonders.[50] His fans did not care about his lies because they were so impressed by his blunt style and his commitment: in the words of Salena Zito, a writer and commentator, "they took Trump seriously, not literally," the opposite of so many pundits upset by his falsehoods.[51]

But Trump's style and his version of the truth was not the only reasons his brand so appealed to the Republican base. He surrounded himself with the aura of the action hero, a much-honoured figure in American fantasy, who could do what always defeated lesser men or women. A few observers detected the growth of an authoritarian mood – or was it a persona? – among a significant body of voters who clearly favoured Trump.[52] His ability to wheel and deal with the politicians promised to end the perceived crisis of governance that had too often paralysed Washington.[53] It was his proposed solutions, no matter how vague or outlandish they might seem to liberals and some conservatives, which explained in part how evangelicals could favour so flawed a candidate.[54] Commentators rightly noted both the populist and nationalist cast of his platform, even elements such as tax reform and tax reduction familiar to conservatives. But they were less conscious of the biopolitical dimension of Trump's vision of America. Understanding this angle required probing his use of the politics of disgust. Trump himself evinced a definite sense of distaste for the unclean, messy human body: he did not like to shake hands, he mocked a sweaty Marco Rubio, he sneered at Hillary Clinton's bathroom break, he found menstruation objectionable.[55] (This anxiety over the disordered body contrasted with Trump's passion for the clean, the designed, the glossy, and the finished, often with gold, with which he filled his habitats.)

That kind of disgust carried over into his public policies, mixed as well with a good dose of shame and fear: the dirty and shabby airports of a decaying America, the crime and disorder in the streets, the ugliness and violence and poverty of the inner city. What he promised was a social body protected from outside contagion by the famous wall, the ban on Muslims (replaced by an ideological test), and a strengthened military. Such schemes evoked the notion of a bounded and closed nation from which the unclean and the disordered would be banished. Similarly, he promised to end the sickness eating away at America by a war on crime and a process of massive deportation. His determination to renegotiate trade deals and discipline wayward corporations would not only produce jobs but invigorate the nation's economy. No contamination here from foreign shores and foreigners themselves.[56] Much of this might be counted "dog-whistle politics," geared to appeal to the nativism or racism supposedly endemic in the Republican base.[57] Hence "Make America Strong Again," his slogan and vision, might be translated as "make America white again." But the slogan and the proposals embodied the ideal of purity, the other side of disgust, a cleansing of the American body and soul to restore their lost splendour. According to the ethicist Jonathan Haidt and his colleagues, conservatives were more prone than liberals to building their moral universe on a psychological foundation that incorporated "purity/sanctity."[58] Perhaps so, but in 2015 and 2016 the politics of disgust had a widespread appeal to a disturbed electorate.

It might well be appropriate to call Trump one of Barnum's children, especially given his fame as an entertainer. Had he not converted the primary contest into a kind of media circus, a political version of reality TV full of sound and fury? Certainly he had proved a master of the carnivalesque: he had used mockery, insult, hype, and lies to overturn the normal political process, to defeat partisan authorities, to counter political advertising, and to awaken a feverish support among rank-and-file Republicans, most especially the less educated white Anglo males in the working and middle classes. As with Barnum, it didn't seem to matter when Trump's deceptions were exposed: publicity, good or bad, served his purpose. He relished all the attention. If he had infuriated and frightened many people even in the Republican party, he had also made politics exciting again for much of the American public. The primary contest had become a grand spectacle.

But it is even more fitting to cast him as a later-day version of the nostrum moguls, the patent medicine kings, proffering a social medicine to cure a sick society. Like them, he claimed to offer something the so-called establishment – in his case Washington – could not. Like them, he posed as a friend of the ordinary American, a plain-speaker who told the unvarnished truth. Because he was a successful entrepreneur, an unfettered billionaire and a tough negotiator, he had the proven skills to end the governance crisis that had defeated the best efforts of the politicians who were his rivals for the public's favour. His unusual proposals of a cleansing and a purifying, so simple and so novel, promised a social transformation: America would return to a state of good health. That was why he was not only a new or updated Barnum. Trump had cast himself as a social doctor.

Either label, of course, made him a huckster. Certainly Trump had demonstrated that his "truthful hyperbole" could work magic in the realm of politics as well as business and entertainment. Had the fears that underlay *Wag the Dog*, about manipulation and falsity, come to pass?[59] He embraced, like some previous admen (say, Bernbach), the plain-speech tradition, always more an enticing myth than an actual practice. His tweets in particular, so compact and so blunt, seemed like ads for a refreshing and frank person – to fans. Certainly no adman's dilemma had worked as a mechanism of restraint here. Trump had, at least temporally and partially, mastered the adman's dilemma that bedeviled and conditioned the process of persuasion, acting very much as the sovereign self who manufactured support in an increasing number of fans. Though not to all Americans: just before the convention his negative ratings, the anxiety and dislike he provoked, were very high.[60] His antics frightened much of the public. Moreover, Delgado's assertion that the Trump phenomenon marked the welcome demise of the adman in politics was premature, given the volume of political advertising in the immediately following contests for the presidency and Congress. Total political ad spending in 2016 reached almost $10 billion, a record – and this despite Trump's reluctance to sponsor television ads.[61] But it is at the very least strange how the ending of this cultural biography of the adman saw the triumph of a throwback to the first years of modern publicity.

Despite the shock and all the resulting chatter, Trump's eventual victory in the November election did not in itself mark a transformation of politics, certainly not the arrival of a "post-truth" politics or era (to borrow the Word of the Year).[62] The contest had hardly been a battle between truth and falsity, whatever the perception of some partisans. The presidential campaigns had featured two candidates with low trust ratings: many people believed Hillary Clinton was also a deceiver.[63] There may have been a large volume of lies, half-truths, fake news and such, but there had also been a proliferation of fact-checkers and truth squads, evidence of that traditional obsession with fact. Debunking, actual and false, was very much in fashion. Besides, what was really new?[64] Martin Jay has correctly reasoned that deceit has had a necessary, if rarely honoured, place in a formal democracy, despite dreams of a "transparent politics."[65] The claim and complaint that emotion outweighed reason, that deception triumphed, could have been made equally in many previous situations.[66] The public's trust in the media had fallen, but it had not been robust for many years prior to 2016.[67] Slightly over a decade earlier, the comedian Stephen Colbert had coined the word "truthiness" to indicate a "truth" that someone felt intuitively must be right, without the need for evidence or the demands of logic. That too caught on in the social conversation and was also named by dictionary powers a Word of the Year for 2005, because it appeared to suit the behaviour of so many people.

However singular Donald Trump may have been in the contests of 2015–16, he was not at all unique in the realm of politics in American history, and a series of journalists and academics had already discovered all sorts of predecessors and precedents.[68] As Melville had suggested so long ago, the confidence man was an American type. Americans had

long lived some of their time in "the suspicious society" that the alarmist Ralph Keyes had named in his book *The Post-Truth Era* (2004).[69] The
activities of the adman were one of the agents which had shaped that
kind of public sphere, where suspicion and trust must coexist. That Donald Trump secured a narrow electoral (and not popular) victory is only
one more episode in that ongoing clash between truth and deception in
the saga of modernity.

THE MORAL OF THE BIOGRAPHY

Allow me a last summation, if only to clarify why this exploration matters. *The Adman's Dilemma* is not only a cultural history but something of a moral biography of a modern sinner. I have described the dilemma as a motif, a condition or an affliction, a spectre and a social mechanism or yoke. I could also add a warning and a legacy. The various narratives of understanding spoke to the unfortunate prevalence of deception in the lifeworld and the system, to borrow from the vocabulary of Jürgen Habermas, whether you put that down to human nature, the condition of modernity, or the practice of biopolitics. Over time the figure of the adman became a significant subject in the social conversation around which all sorts of people might debate the often-unwelcome fact that truth was not enough. The marketplace certainly required usable fictions to speed the circulation of goods from producers to buyers. The public, consumers and voters, needed the exaggerations and the fantasies of advertising to guide and soothe, to reassure and excite, despite the many social costs. Thus the adman had a definite utility as a master storyteller, though that would be only grudgingly recognized. He might be rewarded with affluence or privileges, say a degree of creative freedom. He might also be cursed with insecurity and doubts. Occasionally the stories amounted to a reflection on the vicissitudes of masculinity. But outsiders rarely honoured such a figure because the adman's activities clashed with the virtues of authenticity, sincerity, and above all truth-telling that were supposed to ensure the vigour and persistence of civilization. Indeed at some moments critics strove to limit, if not banish, his deceptions to protect the understanding, if not the sanctity, of reality. It was this double nature of the adman which haunted his biography, an attribute summed up in the phrase "a necessary evil."

He, as a licensed deceiver, was a soul caught up in an inevitable and unavoidable predicament that expressed what was deemed an insoluble contradiction of the times. And this, the adman's dilemma, was his legacy to the ongoing game and business of persuasion, even as it seemed the figure of the adman was disappearing into the ranks of a myriad of persuaders.

NOTES

Introduction

1 Cited in Brad Adgate, "What 'Mad Men' Was And Wasn't," *Forbes*, 17 May 2015.

2 See Jesse McLean, *Kings of Madison Avenue: The Unofficial Guide to Mad Men* (Toronto: ECW Press, 2009).

3 See the brief but effective surveys of the early impact and influence of *Mad Men* in the introduction to Scott F. Stoddart, ed., *Analyzing Mad Men: Critical Essays on the Television Series* (Jefferson NC and London: McFarland & Company, 2011), Kindle Edition, and in Gary G. Edgerton, "The Selling of *Mad Men*: A Production History," in Edgerton, ed., *Mad Men: Dream Come True TV* (London and New York: I.B. Taurus 2011), Kindle Edition, 15–16, 19.

4 For example, the way Maureen Dowd (in "Mad Men and Mad Women," *New York Times*, 2 April 2011) used the phrase in a discussion of conservative-minded lawmakers.

5 Reported in *Ad Age Mobile*, 1 November 2010.

6 Cited in Tony Crouse, "Every Woman Is a Jackie or a Marilyn: The Problematics of Nostalgia," in Stoddart, *Analyzing Mad Men*, KL 2773. The designation KL is the abbreviation of Kindle Location, the system Kindle uses to locate text where there is no page reference (or sometimes in addition to a page reference). KL will be used in the text and in the endnotes where there is no page reference available.

7 Duke University, "The Reality of Ad Men," 20 November 2008, and Rod Carveth and James B. South, eds., *Mad Men and Philosophy: Nothing Is as It Seems* (Hoboken, NJ: John Wiley & Sons, 2010).

8 Stephanie Newman, *Mad Men on the Couch: Analyzing the Minds of the Men and Women of the Hit TV Show* (New York: St Martin's Press, 2012), Kindle Edition.

9 Daniel Mendelsohn, "The Mad Men Account," *New York Review of Books*, 24 February 2011, 4, 6, 8. That speculation may not have much substance. One might better surmise that the extraordinary presence of all kinds of marketing in daily life inspired much public curiosity in a sophisticated and stylish drama about the figure of the adman.

10 Television had occasionally carried a show that featured an advertising practitioner. The most famous was Darrin Stephens in *Bewitched* (1964–72), one of the hits of the sixties. Still, as the husband he was only a secondary character; the star of the situation comedy was Samantha, a witch and a wife, played by Elizabeth Montgomery.

11 The increasing faith in statistics as both knowledge and instrument has been analysed in Ian Hacking, *The Taming of Chance* (Cambridge and New York: Cambridge University Press, 1990).

12 One sign of this project was a speech that President Woodrow Wilson gave in 1916 to the Associated Advertising Clubs in Philadelphia. He praised the organization for its determination to promote "candor and truth" in advertising. Then he went a step further to extol the necessity of truth-telling: "The only thing that ever set any man free, the only thing that ever set any nation free, is the truth. A man that is afraid of the truth is afraid of the law of life. A man that does not love the truth is in the way of decay and of failure." Woodrow Wilson, "Address to the Associated Advertising Clubs in Philadelphia, Pennsylvania," 29 June 1916, at Gerhard Peters and John T. Woolley, The American Presidency Project, www.presidency.ucsb.edu/ ws/?pid=117734, accessed 16 March 2017.

13 "Each society has its régime of truth, its 'general politics' of truth: that is, the types of discourse which it accepts and makes function as true; the mechanisms and instances which enable one to distinguish true and false statements, the means by which each is sanctioned; the techniques and procedures accorded value in the acquisition of truth; the status of those who are charged with saying what counts as true." Michel Foucault, "Truth and Power," in *Power/Knowledge: Selected Interviews and Other Writings 1972–77*, ed. Colin Gordon (New York: Pantheon Books, 1980), 131. In that 1977 interview, Foucault did not elaborate on the details of this regime. One later useful exploration is Lorna Weir's "The Concept of Truth Regime," *Canadian Journal of Sociology* 33.2 (2008): 367–86.

14 According to Kevin Guilfoy, or so he suggested, Draper recognized that truth was irrelevant in the realm of advertising. That seems a bit of a stretch: Draper's insight was specific to the issue of cigarette advertising. See Kevin Guilfoy, "Capitalism and Freedom in the Affluent Society," in Carveth and South, *Mad Men and Philosophy*, 34.

15 Nikolas Rose, a sociologist and Foucauldian, provided a brief definition
of this ideal, and what he treated as a fiction: "coherent, bounded,
individualized, intentional, the locus of thought, action, and belief, the
origin of its own actions, the beneficiary of a unique biography." Nikolas
Rose, *Inventing Our Selves: Psychology, Power, and Personhood* (Cambridge, UK:
Cambridge University Press, 1998), 3.

16 Iain MacRury, *Advertising* (London and New York: Routledge, 2009), 37–8.

17 I have derived the notion of narratives of understanding, common and
persistent storylines which inform the ways in which individuals discuss or
imagine experience, how they make sense of their world, from works such
as Karen Halttunen, "Cultural History and the Challenge of Narrativity,"
in Victoria Bonnell and Lynn Hunt, eds., *Beyond the Cultural Turn: New
Directions in the Study of Society and Culture* (Berkeley and London: University
of California Press, 1999), 165–81.

18 This conception of narrative is based on a brief but superb analysis of the
form: Jerome Bruner, "The Narrative Construction of Reality," *Critical
Inquiry* 18.1 (Autumn 1991): 1–21.

19 The decision to call the basic storyline a "narrative" and its versions and
variants "stories" is arbitrary. I use the term "tales" to refer to pieces of a
story. Some purists have even doubted that any story can ever be retold,
which would automatically render my project unintelligible: see Barbara
Herrnstein Smith, "Narrative Versions, Narrative Theories," *Critical Inquiry*
7.1 (Autumn 1980): 213–36 and Aaron Smuts, "Story Identity and Story
Type," *Journal of Aesthetics and Art Criticism* 67.1 (February 2009): 5–13. But,
as Smuts pointed out, we commonly do recognize that stories can be retold.
My view is that particular clusters of stories do have sufficiently in common
to enable labelling these as basic narratives.

20 See J. David Velleman, "Narrative Explanation," *The Philosophical Review*
112.1 (January 2003): 1–25 for a discussion of how stories work their magic.

21 The term "cultural biography" is used elsewhere but normally refers to
the life of an actual person. See the review essay by Leonard Cassuto,
"The Silhouette and the Secret Self: Theorizing Biography in Our Times,"
American Quarterly 58.4 (January 2006): 1249–61. He calls this approach
"a narrative of the interplay between cultural currents and the individual
psyche." A fine example of the genre, though it does not claim the title,
is Natalie Zemon Davis, *Trickster Travels: A Sixteenth-Century Muslim Between
Worlds* (New York: Hill and Wang, 2006).

22 There are some models for such a cultural biography, however. In 1983,
near the end of his life, Foucault explored the story of the truth-teller in
classical Greece and Rome in a series of lectures; see Michel Foucault,

Fearless Speech (Los Angeles: Semiotext(e), 2001). Daniel Pick, working from George du Maurier's novel *Trilby*, analysed the story of the enchanter in nineteenth-century culture: see Daniel Pick, *Svengali's Web: The Alien Enchanter in Modern Culture* (New Haven, CT: Yale University Press, 2000). And closer to my kind of concerns, see Stephen Shapin's *The Scientific Life: A Moral History of a Late Modern Profession* (Chicago and London: University of Chicago Press, 2008), which explores both the idea of the scientist and the realities of a life in science.

23 For a useful and detailed assessment of the issue of retelling a story in different media, see Seymour Chatman, "What Novels Can Do That Films Can't (And Vice Versa)," *Critical Inquiry* 7.1 (Autumn 1980): 121–40. It was to this piece that Smith directed much of her attack in "Narrative Versions, Narrative Theories."

24 On the whole issue of narrative and self, see Elinor Ochs and Lisa Capps, "Narrating the Self," *Annual Review of Anthropology* 25 (1996): 19–43, and Margaret R. Somers, "The Narrative Constitution of Identity: A Relational and Network Approach," *Theory and Society* 23.5 (October 1994): 605–49.

25 George A. Dunn, "'People Want to Be Told What to Do So Badly That They'll Listen to Anyone': Mimetic Madness at Sterling Cooper," in Rod Carveth and James B. South, eds., *Mad Men and Philosophy: Nothing Is as It Seems*, 31–2. The famous quotation is from the *Communist Manifesto*.

26 The office setting is crucial, of course, because black can have a wide variety of meanings. See John Harvey, *Men in Black* (Chicago: University of Chicago Press, 1995).

Prelude: The Con Man, the Adman, and the Trickster

1 I employ the phase "the saga of modernity" to indicate that modernity is a useful fiction to capture how life has evolved during the past two centuries or so. One volume after another has been written to define such terms as "the modern," "modernity," "modernism," and "modernization." The engine of modernity is sometimes the spread of industrial and finance capitalism (Karl Marx and his successors), or the Enlightenment project writ large (Jürgen Habermas), where reason trumps tradition, or perhaps the rise of biopower (Michel Foucault), when life becomes the object of politics. "History and Progress; Truth and Freedom; Reason and Revolution; Science and Industrialism: these are the main terms of the 'grand narratives' of modernity," claimed theorist Krishan Kumar. See Jürgen Habermas, "Modernity: An Unfinished Project," in Maurizio Passerin d'Entrèves and Seyla Benhabib, eds., *Habermas and the Unfinished Project of Modernity: Critical*

Essays on The Philosophical Discourse of Modernity (Cambridge, MA: MIT Press, 1997), 38–55; Michel Foucault, *The History of Sexuality: An Introduction* (New York: Vintage Books, 1990), 143; and Krishan Kumar, *From Post-Industrial to Post-Modern Society: New Theories of the Contemporary World* (Oxford and Cambridge: Blackwell, 1995), 84. But there is no consensus on which of Kumar's narratives might work best to capture or shape the phenomenon of modernity.

2 There are many editions of this work now available. I have used Herman Melville, *The Confidence-Man* (Hazleton, PA: Pennsylvania State University, 2002), an online version available 7 January 2015, but no longer readily available in December 2017. Pages cited in the text are to this edition, which likely differ from printed works.

3 One especially entertaining example of this chaos of interpretation appeared as a published conversation between Cornel West and D. Graham Burnett, "Metaphysics, Money & the Messiah: A Conversation about Melville's *The Confidence Man*," *Daedalus* (Fall 2007): 101–14.

4 "If many of the novel's characters are only 'masks' or 'avatars' of a single 'Confidence-Man,' he must obviously be a supernatural being if he is to change his appearance so rapidly and completely." Peter J. Bellis, "Melville's Confidence-Man: An Uncharitable Interpretation," *American Literature* 59.4 (December 1987): 556.

5 See Kenneth D. Pimple, "Personal Narrative, Melville's *The Confidence-Man*, and the Problem of Deception," *Western Folklore* 51.1, in an edition entitled "The Personal Narrative in Literature" (January 1992), 33–50, for a much fuller discussion of some aspects of these stratagems.

6 See, for example, a fine piece, Philip Drew's "Appearance and Reality in Melville's The Confidence-Man," *English Literary History* 31.4 (December 1964): 418–42.

7 In 1993 Bruno Latour, known for his work in Science and Technology Studies, published an intriguing philosophical tract entitled *We Have Never Been Modern*, trans. Catherine Porter (Cambridge, MA: Harvard University Press, 1993), which upturned the whole saga of modernity. Latour's critique was supposed to reveal how what he called "moderns" (and, for that matter, "anti-moderns" and "postmoderns") had neither understood nor practised "modernity." He elaborated an extraordinarily complicated version of this modernity organized around "a double task of domination and emancipation" (10), the tyranny of a host of binaries such as Nature/Society, Politics/Science, or Human/Object, and above all the distinct but twin processes of "purification" (the much-heralded production of essences) and "translation" or "mediation" (the little-recognized production of hybrids).

There was a fundamental contradiction, indeed a set of paradoxes, at the heart of modernity: apparently "moderns" thought they were doing one thing when in truth they were doing many other things. Latour emphasized not boundaries or dichotomies but connections, the existence of a host of networks that incorporated bits of nature, society, politics, and discourse to fashion a proliferation of "quasi-objects" which orchestrated life.

Neither the details of Latour's polemic nor his proposed reformation of the supposed "Modern Constitution," however innovative and provocative, count here. What matters is how he recast the saga of modernity. It was no longer about progress or mastery or liberty. It was full of confusion, characterized by misperception, but something much more than an illusion. Strangely, Latour explicitly denied that "moderns" were caught up in a state of "false consciousness" (40). "Are they lying? Deceiving themselves? Deceiving us?" (31). No, he answered, because they had manufactured certain "constitutional guarantees" which separated Nature and Society, "purification" and "mediation." And yet, throughout, Latour charged "moderns" with duplicity: lots of denial, a wilful unseeing, talking double, "this double language" (37), or just plain pretence. What was left out of their story were the hybrids and monsters, the cyborgs and tricksters, now just about everywhere, that constituted their reality. At bottom, then, his "moderns" emerged, at the very least, as the victims of an extraordinary self-deception, a peculiar tribe of people who had concocted a system of beliefs and practices which produced not truth but error and falsehood on a massive scale. Latour's take on the saga, if unintentionally, actually served to highlight the issue of deception as a defining feature of modernity.

8 "The book's basic vision is of masks; and, underneath, masks, further masks; and under all the masks there is the chance that there is nothing at all." Paul Brodtkorb, Jr, "*The Confidence-Man*: The Con-Man as Hero," *Studies in the Novel* 1.4 (Winter 1969): 428.

9 A similar mood or ambience informs two much later novels about the confidence man, Thomas Mann's 1954 *Confessions of Felix Krull: Confidence Man* (New York: Vintage Books, 1992) and Joyce Carol Oates, *My Heart Laid Bare* (New York: Plume, 1999). The authors seem taken with the character's amorality and the freedom from convention it brings.

10 Sisella Bok's 1978 *Lying: Moral Choice in Public and Private Life* (New York: Vintage Books, 1999) was the effective start of contemporary deception studies in the realm of philosophy. Another early entry was Max Black's "The Prevalence of Humbug," in *The Prevalence of Humbug and Other Essays* (Ithaca: Cornell University Press, 1983), www.ditext.com/black/humbug. html, accessed December 2010. Later, *Social Research* 63.3 (Fall 1996)

published an excellent collection of articles under the general title "Truth-telling, Lying and Self-Deception." A few years earlier Robert Solomon had produced an intriguing and critical survey of the philosophical treatment of deception, "What a Tangled Web: Deception and Self-Deception in Philosophy," in a book largely devoted to the psychology of lying: Michael Lewis and Carolyn Saarni, eds., *Lying and Deception in Everyday Life* (New York and London: The Guilford Press, 1993), Kindle Edition. The philosopher Harry Frankfurt published a brief essay which proved a surprise bestseller, no doubt in part because of its unusual title: *On Bullshit* (Princeton and Oxford: Princeton University Press, 2005). A more recent, exhaustive survey of the field is similar in tone and intent to Bok's book: Thomas L. Carson, *Lying and Deception: Theory and Practice* (Oxford: Oxford University Press, 2010).

11 Friedrich Nietzsche, *On Truth and Untruth: Selected Writings*, trans. and ed. Taylor Carmen (New York: HarperCollins e-books, 2010), Kindle Edition, 20–2.

12 Robert W. Mitchell, "The Psychology of Human Deception," *Social Research* (Fall 1996): 819–61.

13 That is a simple definition of the phenomenon and is thus open to a variety of criticisms. For a fulsome discussion of the problem of definition, see J.E. Mahon's 2008 "The Definition of Lying and Deception" in Stanford Encyclopedia of Philosophy, at http://plato.stanford.edu/ in January 2011.

14 Supposedly, 91 per cent of respondents in one survey admitted to lying regularly; see the eccentric Right-wing polemic on human nature in a decaying America, George Serban, *Lying: Man's Second Nature* (Westport, CT, and London: Praeger, 2001), 77. In one survey a group of psychologists learned that 77 college students reported telling two small lies a day and 70 "community members," mostly adults, one per day: Bella M. DePaulo, Deborah A. Kashy, Susan E. Kirkendol, Melissa M. Wyer, and Jennifer A. Epstein, "Lying in Everyday Life," *Journal of Personality and Social Psychology* 70.5 (1996): 979–95. See also DePaulo's discussion of this and later research on the phenomenon of ordinary lying in Bella M. DePaulo, "The Many Faces of Lying," smg.media.mit.edu/library/DePaulo.ManyFacesOfLies. pdf, January 2011, and *The Hows and Whys of Lies*, Kindle Edition, 2010. Yet another study has people lying, "on average, three times during a routine ten-minute conversation with a stranger or casual acquaintance." See Maria Konnikova, "Cons," *Skeptic* 21.1 (2016): 29, an excerpt from her book *The Confidence Game*.

15 Gary D. Bond and Lassiter F. Speller, "Gray Area Messages," in Matthew S. McGlone and Mark L. Knapp, eds., *The Interplay of Truth and Deception: New Agendas in Communication* (New York and London: Routledge, 2010), 35–52.

16 Solomon offers an excellent discussion of the role of self-deception in
   ordinary life and social affairs; see Solomon, "What a Tangled Web."
17 Mary Mothersill, "Some Questions About Truthfulness and Lying," *Social
   Research* (Fall 1996): 913.
18 Michael J. Chandler and Jamie Afifi, "On Making a Virtue Out of Telling
   Lies," ibid., 731. In fact another title seems operative (this listed on the
   cover page) in the bulk of the article: "Deception as a Marker of Children's
   Developing Conceptions of Mental Life."
19 Bernard Williams, *Truth and Truthfulness: An Essay on Genealogy* (Princeton
   NJ: Princeton University Press, 2002), Kindle Edition, KL 1569.
20 The historian Martin Jay has raised some hackles by making such claims
   about political duplicity in a lecture and later a book entitled "The Virtues
   of Mendacity: On Lying in Politics." See also his talk recorded on *Book
   TV*, C-Span2, on 6 May 2010, www.c-spanvideo.org/videoLibrary/event.
   php?id=184067&timeline, and his book *The Virtues of Mendacity: On Lying
   in Politics* (Charlottesville and London: University of Virginia Press, 2010),
   Kindle Edition. John Keane took issue with this kind of argument in a
   keynote address, "Lying, Journalism, Democracy," notes for a keynote
   public lecture at the 2010 Journalism Education Association of Australia
   Conference, University of Technology, Sydney, 25 November 2010,
   ebookbrowse.com/jk-lectures-lying-journalism-democracy-pdf-d42977963.
21 Cited in Clancy Martin, "Review of Harry Frankfurt, *On Truth*," *Ethics* (July
   2007): 760.
22 Hence this ambiguous comment after a survey of findings: "the conclusion
   seems to be that lying is prevalent in that we are likely to encounter
   lies on a daily basis, but infrequent in comparison to everyday honest
   communication. In other words, most people do lie at times, but most
   people are much more honest than not." Timothy R. Levine and
   Rachel K. Kim, "Some Considerations for a New Theory of Deceptive
   Communication," in Matthew S. McGlone and Mark L. Knapp, eds., *The
   Interplay of Truth and Deception: New Agendas in Communication* (New York and
   London: Routledge, 2010), 18.
23 The resulting conundrum was explored in a very clever movie, purportedly
   about truth but even more about deception. Based on a 2003 mystery
   novel by the Argentinian mathematician Guillermo Martinez, *The Oxford
   Murders* (2007) tracked the successful efforts of a fictitious scholar, an aged
   Professor Seldom, to hide a murder committed by an old and dear friend,
   Beth, to whom he owed what he believed was a life debt. Seldom was one
   of those masters of logic who denied the possibility of truth; he declared
   that philosophy was dead, that philosophers must be silent because they

could never find one indisputable truth, not even in the abstract realm
of mathematics. (The movie opened with a striking rendition of Ludwig
Wittgenstein's supposed proof of the fruitlessness of humanity's search
for truth.) But if truth, at least absolute and certain truth, was impossible,
deception certainly was not. Seldom's denial of truth rested in part on a
comparison of the intricacies of a logical series of numbers and the crude
repetitions of serial murders. He concocted a fiction of an ongoing serial
murderer who communicated his (or was it her?) intent in the form of
cryptic symbols arranged as a logical series to predict the apparent crimes.
He claimed the murderer's purpose was to score an intellectual victory
over Seldom himself, a falsehood that Seldom managed to sell to the
police. Unfortunately his enterprise worked as well to inspire a third party
to commit a heinous act of murder, killing some helpless innocents. One
graduate student, Martin, eventually figured out what Seldom had done and
so had caused. But was that "the truth"? Well, certainly not the whole truth.
Seldom confronted the young man with the fact that Martin was the real
culprit, the person who had initiated the whole mess. For Martin's truthful
words, unintentionally of course, had inspired Beth to act to free herself
from a frightful burden of care by murdering her sick but odious mother.
The movie might thus be understood as a defence of deceit, a critique of
truth-telling, a commentary on the dangers of the lie, or an assertion of
the inevitability of paradox. No wonder the last scene showed a perplexed
Martin caught in a web of confusion.

24 Bok, *Lying*, 20. She refers to what I call the victim's malaise as "the
perspective of the deceived."

25 Williams, *Truth and Truthfulness*, Kindle Edition, KL 2177.

26 See Nicole Smith Dahmen, "Construction of the Truth and the
Destruction of *A Million Little Pieces*," *Journalism Studies* 11.1 (2010):
115–30. But, of course, other values can sometimes negate the force of the
commitment: so the sense that President Bill Clinton was the victim of a
conspiracy countered the fact of his lying during the impeachment crisis
of the late 1990s.

27 The famous science-fiction movie *The Matrix* (1999) captured this sense
of disconnection from reality. *The Matrix* was not about advertising or
propaganda. It presumed the dominion of a totally made-up world, a
massive fiction full of simulacra (the movie even referenced the work of
Jean Baudrillard) in which humanity was trapped by the rule of intelligent
machines. The movie realized the nightmares of an Alexandre Koyré ("The
Political Function of the Modern Lie," *Commentary* 8.3 [June 1945],
290–300) or a Hannah Arendt about totalitarian regimes where people

lived a lie – except they had no idea their present was totally false. In
fact *The Matrix* was only one of a small group of productions, fictional
and factual, that probed the primacy of deception around the end of the
twentieth century and the beginning of the new millennium: novels like
The Savage Girl (2001) or *Homo Zapiens* (2003), movies such as *They Live*
(1988), *Wag the Dog* (1998), or *Thank You for Smoking* (2006), Naomi Klein's
best-selling exposé *No Logo* (2000), and the PBS documentary *The Persuaders*
(2004). According to *The Matrix*, the solution was the negation of the action
hero, here called Neo, who learned how to master the code and dispel
illusion in an orgy of violence. Perhaps it is not surprising that one of the
characters, awakened to the prospect of continued deprivation and endless
war, decided to betray the cause of truth and live the lie.

28 On Kant and the harm of the lie, see Jacques Derrida, "History of the Lie:
Prolegomena," 74, and Williams, *Truth and Truthfulness*, Kindle Edition,
KL 1966.

29 Bok, *Lying*, especially 23–8.

30 Solomon, "What a Tangled Web," *Lying and Deception in Everyday Life*, Kindle
Edition, 55.

31 In a commentary on Michel de Montaigne, Max Black noted "the familiar
observation that the liar is parasitic on general, though not universal,
veracity: lying, as a species of deceit, would be futile in the absence of
general efforts to be truthful." Black, "The Prevalence of Humbug," online
edition, www.ditext.com/black/humbug.html.

32 Hannah Arendt, "Truth and Politics" (1967), in Peter Beahr, ed., *The
Portable Hannah Arendt* (New York: Penguin Books, 2000), 566.

33 Paul Ekman, "Why Don't We Catch Liars?" *Social Research* (Fall 1996): 84,
and Paul Ekman and Mark G. Frank, "Lies That Fail," in Lewis and Saarni,
Lying and Deception in Everyday Life, Kindle Edition, 194.

34 Harry Frankfurt, *On Truth* (New York: Knopf, 2006), Kindle Edition, 79. The
first part of the quotation is from the poet Adrienne Rich's *Lies, Secrets, and
Silence* (New York: W.W. Norton, 1979), 191.

35 According to Frankfurt, the philosopher Baruch Spinoza maintained that
"a person who despises or is indifferent to the truth must be a person
who despises or is indifferent to his own life." Frankfurt, *On Truth*, Kindle
Edition, 46.

36 The quotation is from John Rawls, *A Theory of Justice* (Cambridge, MA:
Harvard University Press, 1971), 440, cited in Michael P. Lynch, *True to Life:
Why Truth Matters* (Cambridge, MA, and London: MIT Press, 2004), 124.

37 Paul Ekman, "Why Don't We Catch Liars?," *Social Research* (Fall 1996),
809, 811.

38 Bernard Williams, "Truth, Politics and Self-Deception," ibid., 614.

39 Perez Zagorin, "The Historical Significance of Lying and Dissimulation," ibid., 863–912.

40 Michael Pettit, *The Science of Deception: Psychology and Commerce in America* (Chicago and London: University of Chicago Press, 2013), 4–5, 7. Pettit's fascinating book explores the interconnections between the rise of the discipline of psychology and the prevalence of deception in the consumer culture.

41 The Propaganda of the Faith, apparently, was "quite the largest, oldest, most magnificent, most unabashed, and most lucrative enterprise in sales-publicity in all Christendom." Thorstein Veblen, Note to Chapter XI, "Manufactures and Salesmanship," in *Absentee Ownership – Business Enterprise in Recent Times: The Case of America* (B.W. Heubsch, 1923), cited at larvatus. livejournal.com/187423.html, 5 February 2010. At least on the Left, Veblen was the most innovative and accomplished economist in early twentieth-century America.

42 Brooks Jackson, "Finding the Weasel Word in 'Literally True'," in McGlone and Knapp, *The Interplay of Truth and Deception*, 1–15. Jackson, a former journalist, was the director of the Annenberg Political Fact Check, at the University of Pennsylvania, and co-author with Kathleen Hall Jamieson of *unSpun: Finding Facts in a World of Disinformation*. Other articles in this book include further examples of deception in advertising.

43 Bok was responding to a claim by the TV journalist Bill Moyers about the baleful influence of advertising and the like which had made deception "the household furniture of American life." She demurred: "Very often, in fact, advertising is not deceptive. You know, there is much factual, informative advertising. We learn to look at certain activities like advertising in a very different way and to listen to what it says in a very different way, so that we develop certain kinds of protections." *The World of Ideas*, October 1988, Transcript, Public Affairs Television, Inc., 1989.

44 There is a contradiction which should be registered here. Once upon a time publicity was supposed to drive the Enlightenment project to success. Then publicity meant revelation, ensuring the triumph of reason, a way of banishing abuse and privilege, a means of making society transparent. That happy conception of the role of print and press, for example, informed the political philosophy of Jeremy Bentham, who deemed publicity an essential tool of truth. Present in his essay "Of Publicity" (c. 1789) was the motif of light and darkness: publicity acted as a method of public surveillance, working to dispel the secrecy that benefited "the malefactor," "the tyrant," and "the timid or indolent man" who were the obstacles to liberation.

"In proportion as it is desirable for improbity to shroud itself in darkness, in
the same proportion is it desirable for innocence to walk in open day." First
and foremost publicity was "a system of distrust" that the public wielded to
restrict authority. But Bentham also dreamed that "the régime of publicity,"
once fully developed as a free flow of information, would enlighten public
opinion and educate the governors. "A habit of reasoning and discussion
will penetrate all classes of society." Such notions persisted among liberals
of later generations, particularly in England and America: see, for example,
the discussion of the idea of publicity in nineteenth-century England in
Patrick Joyce, *The Rule of Freedom: Liberalism and the Modern City* (London:
Verso, 2003). The once-Marxist Jürgen Habermas, one of the outstanding
political philosophers of the late twentieth century, argued that publicity
had worked to fashion a distinct sphere of free debate and so to limit the
oppression of the state. These views were outlined in his first book, *The
Structural Transformation of the Public Sphere: An Inquiry into a Category of
Bourgeois Society* (Cambridge, MA: MIT Press, 1989). This is the English
translation (by Thomas Burger) of the 1962 German original. Much more
than Bentham, Habermas saw publicity as a system of advocacy, rather than
distrust, which acted to engender what he called "rational-critical discourse"
in the public sphere. But Habermas also recognized that the nature of
publicity had changed since those halcyon days of bourgeois modernity.
Increasingly after, say, 1900, an organized publicity had operated as a tool
of domination and deception, used by elites to discipline the minds and
conduct of the citizenry. The rest of his story of modern times was full of
lament and decline.

45 One could well start tracking this obsession with a general work by the
famed psychoanalyst of archetypes, Carl Jung: *Four Archetypes: Mother, Rebirth,
Spirit, Trickster*, trans. R.F.C. Hull (Princeton and Oxford, 1970). A more
specific treatment in the realm of anthropology, Paul Radin's *The Trickster
– A Study in American Indian Mythology* (New York: Philosophical Library,
1956), established the significance of the character in American studies.
But a very different work by a literary scholar has given the trickster a more
recent popularity: Lewis Hyde, *Trickster Makes This World: Mischief, Myth,
and Art* (New York: Farrar, Straus, & Giroux, 1998). Then there are more
severely academic works such as William J. Hynes and William G. Doty,
eds., *Mythical Trickster Figures: Contours, Contexts, and Criticisms* (Tuscaloosa:
University of Alabama Press, 1993), which looked at the trickster type in
non-Western traditions as well as in the West. The noted historian Natalie
Zemon Davis used the term to explore the life of a cross-cultural subject
in her *Trickster Travels: A Sixteenth-Century Muslim between Worlds* (New York:

Farrar, Straus and Giroux/Hill and Wang, 2006). Others have found echoes of the trickster in contemporary popular culture: Helena Bassil-Morozow, *The Trickster in Contemporary Film* (London: Routledge, 2011). It should be added that some women scholars have found examples of female tricksters; see, for example, Bei Cai, "A Trickster-Like Woman: Subversive Imagining and Narrating of Social Change," *Communication Studies* 59.4 (2008): 275–90. A search on the word "trickster" on the World Wide Web soon reveals a variety of sites which attest to the popularity of the obsession.

46 Hyde, *Trickster Makes This World,* 7.

47 William J. Hynes, "Mapping the Characteristics of Mythic Tricksters: A Heuristic Guide," in Hynes and Doty, *Mythical Trickster Figures,* 34 and 55.

48 The notion of the carnivalesque was introduced in Mikhail Bakhtin's *Rabelais and His World,* trans. Helene Islowski (Bloomington: Indiana University Press, 1984). The notion has been much discussed and refined since the first English publication of the book in 1968. See, in particular, Peter Stallybrass and Allon White, *The Politics and Poetics of Transgression* (London: Methuen, 1986).

49 Regarding the signs of the carnivalesque in advertising, see Jackson Lears, *Fables of Abundance: A Cultural History of Advertising in America,* New York: Basic Books 1994 and Paul Rutherford, *The New Icons? The Art of Television Advertising* (Toronto: University of Toronto Press, 1994). Lears argues that the carnivalesque spirit was suppressed during the course of the late nineteenth century and especially after 1900, when corporations took command of national advertising. Yet it persisted in the memory, say, the "unconscious" as well, of advertising, and might re-emerge at various times, as in the Depression. I think the triumph of television, especially colour television, which Lears does not treat, enabled and encouraged the return of the carnivalesque to promote a wide array of products, such as (if only at times) tobacco and alcohol, and had infused a variety of surreal commercials by the end of the twentieth century.

50 See Donald Meyer's 1965 study *The Positive Thinkers: Popular Religious Psychology from Mary Baker Eddy to Norman Vincent Peale and Ronald Reagan* (Middletown, CT: Wesleyan University Press, 1988), rev. ed.

51 Hyde, *Trickster Makes This World,* 8, 11, 13.

52 Barbara Ehrenreich, *Bright-Sided: How the Relentless Promotion of Positive Thinking Has Undermined America* (New York: Henry Holt, 2009), Kindle Edition, 35.

53 Foucault, *"Society must be defended": Lectures at the Collège de France 1975–1976,* trans. D. Macey (New York: Picador, 2003), 250. The other kind of biopower was referred to as anatamo-politics or more often discipline,

where individuals were arranged in enclosed spaces like prisons, barracks, workshops, or schools to produce efficient and tamed souls. The key work on discipline was his 1975 *Discipline & Punish: The Birth of the Prison*, trans. Alan Sheridan (New York: Vintage Books, 1979). Foucault had more to say about biopolitics in a later series of lectures, *Security, Territory, Population: Lectures at the Collège de France 1977–1978*, trans. G. Burchell (New York: Palgrave Macmillan, 2007). He also wrote of the philosophy and practice in his 1976 *The History of Sexuality. Volume 1: An Introduction*, trans. R. Hurley (New York: Vintage Books, 1990). For an overview, see T. Lemke, *Biopolitics: An Advanced Introduction*, trans. E.F. Trump (New York and London: New York University Press, 2011). See also Paul Rutherford and Stephanie Rutherford, "The Confusions and Exuberances of Biopolitics," *Geography Compass* 7.6 (2013): 412–22, which surveys the literature on biopolitics up to 2013.

54 For a general discussion of the nature and requirements of biopolitics, see the key article by Paul Rabinow and Nikolas Rose, "Biopower Today," *BioSocieties* 1 (2006): 195–217. Rabinow (an anthropologist) and Rose (a sociologist) are leading figures in the community of Foucault-inspired scholars. They have published extensively on a range of topics, although perhaps the most notable work in this field is Rose's *The Politics of Life Itself: Biomedicine, Power, and Subjectivity in the Twenty-First Century* (Princeton and Oxford: Princeton University Press, 2007). Here Rose delivered a general comment on biopower: "Biopower is more a perspective than a concept: it brings into view a whole range of more or less rationalized attempts to intervene upon the vital characteristics of human existence – human beings, individually and collectively, as living creatures who are born, mature, inhabit a body that can be trained and augmented, and then sicken and die" (54). By contrast, I treat biopolitics as a philosophy and strategy of governance. In actual practice biopolitical projects might often draw upon disciplinary bodies – consider the way the assault on alcohol employed propaganda, regulation, the prison, the church, and so on. But not so in the case of advertising, where the messages, the propaganda, was directed at the public or various markets, even where it sought to turn individuals into consumers.

55 Among these instruments of guidance might be listed the sanitary idea of such import in nineteenth-century England, the cult of exercise in late twentieth-century America, the books of etiquette which informed codes of behaviour in so many countries in both centuries, and the civics curricula that was used to inculcate the rules of citizenship into school children. Foucault once defined technologies of the self as "each a matrix of practical reason … which permit individuals to effect by their own means, or with the help of others, a certain number of operations on their own bodies and

souls, thoughts, conduct, and way of being, so as to transform themselves in order to attain a certain state of happiness, purity, wisdom, perfection, or immortality" (225). Michel Foucault, "Technologies of the Self," *Essential Works of Foucault 1954–1984, vol. 1: Ethics, Subjectivity and Truth*, ed. Paul Rabinow (New York: The New Press 1997), 223–51.

56 I have dealt with an aspect of this process in *A World Made Sexy: Freud to Madonna* (Toronto: University of Toronto Press, 2007). That book treats the development of the erotic sell by a series of advertising practitioners over the course of the twentieth century.

57 The phrase appears in Hyde's work, though its merit was emphasized in Margaret Atwood's review of *Trickster Makes This World* in the Los Angeles *Times*, 25 January 1998.

58 See two pieces by Turner on, among other things, what he calls liminal personae. "Betwixt and Between: The Liminal Period in *Rites de Passage*," in Turner, *The Forest of Symbols: Aspects of Ndembu Ritual* (Ithaca: Cornell University Press, 1967), 93–111, and Turner, "Process, System, and Symbol: A New Anthropological Synthesis," *Daedalus* 106.3, the edition entitled *Discoveries and Interpretations: Studies in Contemporary Scholarship* 1 (Summer 1977), 61–80.

59 The medieval historian Caroline Walker Bynum brought home this fact in an intriguing commentary, albeit about women's stories in the Middle Ages: "Women's Stories, Women's Symbols: A Critique of Victor Turner's Theory of Liminality," in her *Fragmentation and Redemption: Essays on Gender and the Human Body in Medieval Religion* (New York: Zone Books, 1992), 27–51.

60 Frankfurt, *On Truth*, Kindle Edition, 17.

61 Frankfurt, *On Bullshit*, 22.

62 Michael Schudson, *Advertising, the Uneasy Persuasion: Its Dubious Impact on American Society* (New York: Basic Book, 1984), 11. Schudson went on to call the recognition of deception "the primary fact to understand about advertising." That underpinned his claims about the limited impact of advertising. "Apologists are wrong that advertising is simply information that makes the market work more efficiently – but so too are the critics of advertising who believe in its overwhelming power to deceive and to deflect human minds to its ends. Its power is not so determinative nor its influence so clear" (11).

63 Ian Leslie, *Born Liars: Why We Can't Live Without Deceit* (Toronto: Anansi, 2011), 291.

64 The quotations are from his own listing at uk.linkedin.com/pub/ian-leslie/4/86/a48, accessed 12 June 2011. Other information about Leslie's careers is from www.guardian.co.uk, www.groundwoodbooks.com (about Anansi authors) and www.greenheaton.co.uk (literary agents).

65 "Advertisers are often accused of selling lies to the public, but advertising can be deceptive without being dishonest. It's true that, for example, no deodorant really has the power to turn adolescent boys into girl magnets. But the truth status of most advertising is like that of fiction; consumers are openly invited to suspend disbelief. Both the advertiser and the advertised-to generally understand that a little deception (or self-deception) is good for us." Leslie, *Born Liars*, 275.

1 The Huckster's Game

1 Frank Presbrey, *The History and Development of Advertising*, 1929 (New York: Greenwood Press, 1968), 298. Daniel Lord was a founder of the Lord & Thomas advertising agency. The anecdote was about his encounter on a train with a fellow persuader, though also a rival for the patronage of business.
2 "Revelations of a Showman," *Blackwood's Edinburgh Magazine* 77 (February 1855): 199.
3 Ibid., 193.
4 The first speculation appeared in a piece by Alan Farnham, "America's Original Huckster," *Fortune Magazine* 133.2 (5 February 1996) and the second is a comment in the documentary *P.T. Barnum's City of Humbug* sponsored by the *New York Times* in 2007 (video.nytimes.com/video/2007/11/08/arts/1194817116620/p-t-barnum-s-city-of-humbug.html).
5 The term cropped up in a retrospective: see Andrew Curry, "The King of Humbug," *U.S. News & World Report* 131.9 (10 September 2001).
6 Respectively, the London *Star* and *La France*, cited in "Foreign Opinions of Barnum," *New York Times*, 28 April 1891, and Professor William Lyon Phelps in 1940, cited in Irving Wallace, *The Fabulous Showman: The Life and Times of P.T. Barnum* (New York: Knopf 1959), 63.
7 The Della Femina comment appeared in an NBC television documentary entitled *Sex, Buys and Advertising* (1990).
8 That practice would continue throughout his career, even when he was primarily a circus promoter. See Michael Pettit, "'The Joy in Believing': The Cardiff Giant, Commercial Deceptions, and Styles of Observation in Gilded Age America," *Isis* 97.4 (December 2006), 659–77, and Sarah Amato, "The White Elephant in London: An Episode of Trickery, Racism and Advertising," *Journal of Social History* 43.1 (October 2009), 31–66.
9 This has been explored by, among others, Bluford Adams in his *E Pluribus Barnum: The Great Showman and the Making of U.S. Popular Culture* (Minneapolis and London: University of Minnesota Press, 1997), especially 85–7.

10 Barnum was not the first advertising practitioner, of course. There had been admen and advertisers long before in, for example, Great Britain: see Gary Hicks, *The First Adman: Thomas Bish and the Birth of Modern Advertising* (Victorian Secrets Limited, ebook, 2012). And normally the man designated the first advertising agent in America is Volney B. Palmer (1799–1864), who started the first advertising agency in Philadelphia in 1842; see Donald R. Holland, "Volney B. Palmer, 1799–1864: The Nation's First Advertising Agency Man" (Lexington, KY: The Association for Education in Journalism, 1976). But it was Barnum's doings that fascinated the public.

11 For an extensive discussion of Barnum and his legacy from the standpoint of the discipline of marketing, see Stephen Brown, "Chapter 4: Reconfiguring Marketing: The Greatest Sham on Earth," Sage Knowledge (downloaded 2013), from his 2001 book *Marketing – The Retro Revolution*.

12 This episode has been thoroughly explored in Benjamin Reiss, *The Showman and the Slave: Race, Death, and Memory in Barnum's America* (Boston: Harvard University Press, 2001).

13 There are a number of Barnum biographies and many more specialized studies of aspects of his career. The single most complete and authoritative, however, is A.H. Saxon, *P.T. Barnum: The Legend and the Man* (New York: Columbia University Press, 1989).

14 His pseudonym announced the con: "diddle" was a common term for some species of trickery. Much of *The Adventures* has been published in James W. Cook, editor, *The Colossal P.T. Barnum Reader: Nothing Else Like It in the Universe* (Urbana and Chicago: University of Illinois Press, 2005).

15 The autobiographies appeared in foreign editions, especially British, as well. Of course the number of copies in circulation can only be an estimate, and the claim that it was second only to the Bible does seem a mighty exaggeration. See, for instance, Amy Lynn Reading, "Courting Inauthenticity: Deception and Revelation in American Autobiography," unpublished PhD dissertation, Yale University, 2007, 40–1. Soon enough came a few biographies which largely repeated the material Barnum had made available in his own autobiographical project.

16 The reported cost of the publishing rights appeared in "Barnum," *Fraser's Magazine for Town and Country* 51 (February 1855): 214. The outlandish figure of five million is mentioned in Christoph Irmscher, *The Poetics of Natural History: From John Bartram to William James* (New Brunswick, NJ: Rutgers University Press, 1999), 121. Irmscher quotes Barnum asserting this in October 1955.

17 This was a friendly lampoon, likely based on drafts of *The Life* but written by another (George Thompson), *The Autobiography of Petite Bunkum* (New York: P.F. Harris, 1855).

18 Such as a front-page ad in the *New York Daily Tribune*, 23 December 1854.

19 Saxon, *Barnum*, 3, 9.

20 On the notion of an autobiographical contract, see Sidonie Smith and Julia Watson, *Reading Autobiography: A Guide for Interpreting Life Narratives* (Minneapolis and London: University of Minnesota Press, 2001) and Linda Anderson, *Autobiography*, 2nd ed. (London and New York: Routledge, 2011).

21 P.T. Barnum, *The Life of P.T. Barnum* (New York: Redfield, 1855), iv. Hereafter page references to this edition are cited in the text.

22 All of these quotations are taken from the *Tribune* ad, which was repeated in other newspapers. Were these fair quotations? I suspect so, even if they were very selective. I was only able to check one of them, that from the *New York Times* – "A very amusing Book, which every one will read, half the world will abuse, and nobody can help laughing at and with" – which was accurate, though the whole review was less sympathetic. At least one critical review presumed the Albany *Knickerbocker* wrote what was claimed, and that provoked shock and horror: [W.H. Hurlbut] "Barnum's and Greeley's Biographies," *Christian Examiner* 58 (March 1855), 258.

23 See G. Thomas Couser, "Prose and Cons: The Autobiographies of P.T. Barnum," *Altered Egos: Authority in American Autobiography* (New York and Oxford: Oxford University Press, 1989), 54–5.

24 Hence the comments of Terence Whelan in his "Introduction" to the 2000 edition of *The Life*, published by the University of Illinois Press, xxxiii.

25 This in a general discussion of early satire: Todd Nathan Thompson, "Modest Proposals: American Satire and Political Change from Franklin to Lincoln," unpublished PhD dissertation, Chicago: University of Illinois, 2008, 175–83.

26 Reading, "Courting Inauthenticity." Reading positions Barnum's autobiographical project as the first in a stream of American life narratives that extended into the late twentieth century.

27 And at least according to another scholar, Franklin's autobiography boasted some attributes that were apparent in *The Life*: certainly self-fashioning, a utilitarian view of morality and religion, the mastery of rhetoric, even the use of deception. This is my gloss on what Daniel Walker Howe said about the Franklin volumes in *Making the American Self: Jonathan Edwards to Abraham Lincoln* (Oxford and New York: Oxford University Press, 2009). Howe, however, admitted that he explicitly excluded "charlatans or tricksters" from his survey.

28 Jackson Lears, *Fables of Abundance: A Cultural History of Advertising in America* (New York: Basic Books, 1994). Lears's study, like Marchand's *Advertising the American Dream*, is a stellar work in the field of advertising and cultural history,

though more informed by theory than Marchand's study. Lears dealt at length with the origins and the character of the carnivalesque and its impact on the style and imagery of early American advertising, especially in Part I, "The Reconfiguration of Wealth: From Fecund Earth to Efficient Factory," 17–133. Barnum also figures in Lears's work, albeit briefly, in a passage which emphasized his doubled and contentious approach to promotion (265–7).

29 The expression is properly ascribed to a rival showman. See Saxon, *Barnum*, 334–7.

30 The quotation is from the *Nashville Union and American*, 15 December 1854. Other early reviews are from the *Hudson Register*, 13 December 1854; the *Bangor Daily Whig and Courier*, 13 December 1854; Lewis Gaylord Clark, "Literary Notices," *Knickerbocker* 45 (January 1855), 80–3; *The Church of England Quarterly Review* 38.3 (January 1855), 241. Whelan (xv) quotes from the *Springfield Republican* (unfortunately undated), which actually thought the book offered a hidden moral lesson, "that mere humbugs and deceptions generally fail," an astonishing misreading of *The Life*.

31 Horace Greeley was the crusading proprietor of the *New York Tribune*. The other book was James Parton, *The Life of Horace Greeley, Editor of the New York Tribune* (New York: Mason Bros., n.d.).

32 This review was reprinted much later in *Writings of Severn Teackle Wallis (1896)*, vol. 2: *Critical and Political* (Baltimore: John Murphy & Co., 1896), 69–84.

33 The reference was to Henry David Thoreau's later famous work, *Walden; or, a Life in the Woods* (1854).

34 This comment on the need to censor appeared in the review of a work by a different scoundrel, whom the writer deemed a lesser follower of Barnum. "American Literature: Burnham's History of the Hen Fever," *Putnam's Monthly Magazine of American Literature, Science and Art* (May 1855): 550.

35 The *London Times* went a step further. It suggested Barnum's villainy was inherited, that he was likely "of Hebrew extraction," thus drawing on the tradition of anti-Semitism.

36 In fact that spirit was much more pronounced in Barnum's first, semi-fictional autobiography, *The Adventures of Barnaby Diddledum*, though the reviewers were apparently not aware of this work. But witness this declaration from the *Adventures*: "Studying character, and playing upon the folly and credulity of mankind, I have always made it a point to see how far humbug can possibly be carried, and I have been a little astonished sometimes at my own success." Cook, *The Colossal P.T. Barnum Reader*, 31.

37 The reference here is to two rogues, the first a fictional character of sixteenth-century Spanish literature and the second a legendary adventurer and sometime occultist of the eighteenth century.

38 Benjamin Brandreth was a maker and heavy advertiser of patent medicines.

39 This aspect of biopolitics has been explored at length by the philosopher Roberto Esposito: see *Bíos: biopolitics and philosophy*, trans. T. Campbell (Minneapolis and London: University of Minnesota Press, 2008) and *Immunitas: The Protection and Negation of Life*, trans. Z. Hanafi (Cambridge, UK, and Malden, MA: Polity Press, 2011), first published in Italian in 2002. The urge to purify, of course, had its sinister side: it found expression in forms of state racism, notably directed against the Jews in the case of Nazi Germany. Esposito covered this dimension in his work. So too, much more briefly, did Foucault: in the final lecture of his 1975–6 course at the Collège de France, "Society Must Be Defended." See Foucault, *"Society must be defended": Lectures at the Collège de France 1975–1976*, trans. D. Macey (New York: Picador, 2003), 239–64.

40 Quoted in Whelan, "Introduction," xxix, and Saxon, *Barnum*, 16.

41 Quoted in Saxon, *Barnum*, 3.

42 Herbert Fingarette, *Self-Deception* (Berkeley and London: University of California Press, 1969) Kindle Edition, KL 1502.

43 P.T. Barnum, *The Humbugs of the World. An Account of Humbugs, Delusions, Impositions, Quackeries, Deceits and Deceivers Generally, in All Ages* (New York: Carleton, 1866), Gutenberg Project eBook, 2008.

44 This argument was put forward in Richard Herskowitz, "P.T. Barnum's Double Bind," *Social Text* 2.2 (Summer 1979), 133–41.

45 He made this brief comment about the first version of his memoirs in his new autobiography: "Having an extensive sale, they were, however, very hastily, and, therefore, imperfectly, prepared. These are not only out of print, but the plates have been destroyed." P.T. Barnum, *Struggles and Triumphs, or Forty Years' Recollections by P.T. Barnum* (Buffalo: Warren, Johnson & Co., 1872), vi.

46 Ibid., 125–6.

47 Ibid., 499.

48 From the Barnum obituary, 8 April 1891, reprinted in Cook, *The Colossal P.T. Barnum Reader*, 239.

49 Wallace, *The Fabulous Showman*.

50 Neil Harris, *Humbug: The Art of P.T. Barnum* (Boston and Toronto: Little, Brown and Company, 1973).

51 James W. Cook, *The Arts of Deception*.

52 Walter A. McDougall, *Throes of Democracy: The American Civil War Era 1829–1877*, HarperCollins eBook, 2009.

53 Ibid., 160.

54 These phrases are taken from Michael Saler, "Modernity and Enchantment: A Historiographical Review," *American Historical Review* 111.3 (June 2006), 692–716. Saler makes the case for a "modern enchantment" which took hold especially in the realm of mass culture. Although he sees advertising as part of that culture, his survey does not pay much attention to advertising or its deceptions, whether they too "delight but do not delude."

55 Presbrey, *The History and Development of Advertising*, 1929 (New York: Greenwood Press, 1968, 297–8. But Presbrey also recognized how Barnum had established the lasting commercial benefits of aggressive advertising.

56 "Modern high-pressure advertising was Barnum's most lamentable contribution to history." Wallace, 63.

57 Charles Baxter, "Hatching Monsters," *Lapham's Quarterly Online*, captured 31 August 2011. This was in an archive of "Reconsiderations" originally published on 27 December 2010.

58 What might this 75 million mean if translated into current dollars? It is impossible to provide an exact equivalent. We can use the Consumer Price Index, though this only dates back to 1913, to give an indication of the present buying power of that 75 million. $1 in 1913 had the same buying power as $23 in 2012. Recognizing that the Adams figure dates from 1905, the amount Americans invested in patent medicines was the equivalent of at least $1.725 billion.

59 The editions differed, since later ones contained more material. I have used an edition that included both series and some extra material. Samuel Hopkins Adams, *The Great American Fraud* – with articles on the "Nostrum Evil and Quacks" from *Collier's Weekly* – (Chicago: American Medical Association & P.F. Collier & Son, 1907), 4th ed., hereafter *Fraud* (with page references in the text or endnotes in parentheses).

60 The fear of social harm, of course, was embedded in the moral criticism of *The Life of P.T. Barnum*. But the critics never elaborated that fear in sufficient detail and depth to fashion a full-blown narrative.

61 Although the nostrums were commonly referred to as patent medicines, strictly speaking they were nothing of the sort, since they did not have a patent. They were proprietary remedies whose actual formulas were usually closely guarded secrets. On the overall story of patent medicines, see James Harvey Young, *The Toadstool Millionaires: A Social History of Patent Medicines in America before Federal Regulation* (Princeton, NJ: Princeton University Press, 1961), online edition, www.quackwatch.com/13Hx/MM/00p.html, captured 4 March 2011.

62 Cited in Peggy M. Baker, "Patent Medicine: Cures & Quacks," at the Pilgrim Hall Museum website, www.pilgrimhallmuseum.org/pdf/Patent_Medicine.

pdf, accessed 17 April 2017. Baker was the director and librarian of the museum.

63 But see Sarah Stage's chapter "The Poisoning Century" in *Female Complaints: Lydia Pinkham and the Business of Women's Medicine* (New York: W.W. Norton, 1979). Calomel is a mercury compound, thus potentially toxic, which was in wide use in the nineteenth century to "cure" an assortment of ailments, especially as a diuretic or purgative.

64 It was a risky business, though, given all the competition. The adman George Rowell, an agency owner of the time, who also dabbled in the patent medicine business, noted in his autobiography that a few entrepreneurs did very well. "Forty years ago it was frequently said that the time for great profits from the sales of patent medicines had passed and would never come again; but since then Dr. R.V. Pierce has made a great success financially; so, too, has Brent Good, with Carter's Little Liver Pills; Dr. Kilmer, with his Swamp Root; Dr. Hartman, with P-e-r-u-n-a; Lydia Pinkham, with her Female Compound; and many others might be named. Dr. J.C. Ayer, of Lowell, had established his trademarks at an earlier date, and his success has never been equaled by any other, although Dr. Hostetter, with his Bitters, was a close second. The chances of success, however, are now so remote that he is either a bold or an imprudent man who ventures at the present day upon the introduction of a new remedy by means of advertising." George P. Rowell, *Forty Years an Advertising Agent 1865–1905* (New York: Printers' Ink Publishing, 1906), 399.

65 Claude C. Hopkins, *My Life in Advertising* (New York: Harper Bros., 1927), 73. Hopkins himself made a lot of money out of one patent medicine, Liquozone, in which he had a part interest. It was during his later career at Lord & Thomas, though, where he achieved fame as a master of what was then considered "modern" and "scientific" advertising.

66 See his chapter XXX, "Cleaning Up the Patent-Medicine and Other Evils," in his autobiography *The Americanization of Edward Bok: The Autobiography of a Dutch Boy Fifty Years After* (New York: C. Scribner's Sons, 1923, Gutenberg Project eBook, 2002).

67 Roosevelt spoke out on 14 April 1906 when laying the cornerstone of a new government building. He was upset by the negative and sensational character of the various assaults, which he feared could well foster cynicism if not revolution. He drew on Bunyan's *Pilgrim's Progress*, employing "the description of the Man with the Muckrake, the man who could look no way but downward ... who would neither look up nor regard the crown he was offered, but continued to rake to himself the filth of the floor." See the

reprint of the speech in Herbert Shapiro, ed., *The Muckrakers and American Society* (Boston: D.C. Heath, 1968), 3–8.

68 Reported in Bok's memoirs. See also Mark Sullivan, *The Education of an American* (New York: Doubleday, Doran, 1938), 183–91. In fact there was a Mrs. Pinkham, a daughter-in-law, though the women's letters were likely answered by a correspondence bureau. The company, of course, denied any attempt to deceive, though it seems for a time sales suffered because of the exposé. See Stage, *Female Complaints*, 163.

69 This discussion of Adams is drawn from Samuel V. Kennedy's biography, *Samuel Hopkins Adams and the Business of Writing* (Syracuse: Syracuse University Press, 1999).

70 Young, *Toadstool Millionaires*, 147.

71 The issue carried photographs of a car race and earthquakes in Italy, a continuing story on the reclamation of dry lands in the West, editorial comment on an insurance scandal, and a short story, along with numerous ads.

72 The bill was also speeded through Congress by the outrage resulting from the revelations in Upton Sinclair's *The Jungle*. The act specified that certain dangerous substances, such as alcohol or opiates, had to be publicized. If the healer listed other ingredients, then that listing had to be accurate.

73 Young (*Toadstool Millionaires*) suggests roughly 500,000; Adams thought 400,000 (Kennedy, *Adams*, 52).

74 "The fighting of public health legislation is the primary object and chief activity, the very raison d'etre, of the Proprietary Association" (129).

75 Commenting on headache remedies, "In the 'ethical' field the harm done by this class of proprietaries is perhaps as great as in the open field, for many of those which are supposed to be sold only in proscriptions are as freely distributed to the laity as Peruna. And their advertising is hardly different" (37–8).

76 "He exploits himself as a member of the Ohio and Kentucky State Medical Societies, which he is not, and Surgeon for the Inter-Urban Railway Company of Cincinnati, which writes me that he is not in their employ; also examining physician for the New York Mutual Life Insurance Company, the Massachusetts Mutual Life Insurance Company, the Prudential Life Insurance Company, and other similar organizations. His commission with the latter company was terminated in 1897, the New York Mutual got rid of him as soon as the nature of his business became known to them, and the Massachusetts Mutual informs me that he hasn't done any work for them for nearly ten years" (78).

77 "Where the money is already paid, most people are too inert to undertake
    the effort of getting it back. It is the easy American way of accepting a
    swindle as a sort of joke" (59).
78 For a fascinating discussion of the use of testimonials, and much else,
    by the healers, see Daniel J. Robinson, "Mail-Order Doctors and Market
    Research, 1890–1930," in Philip Scranton, Uwe Spiekermann, and Hartmut
    Berghoff, eds., *The Rise of Marketing and Market Research* (New York: Palgrave
    Macmillan, 2012), 73–93.
79 Young, who interviewed Adams, claimed that Hartman welcomed Adams,
    telling him "everything, even after being warned that the planned article
    was bound to be critical."
80 "'It can be used any length of time without acquiring a drug habit,' declared
    the Peruna book, and therein, I regret to say, lies specifically and directly.
    The lie is ingeniously backed up by Dr. Hartman's argument that 'nobody
    could get drunk on the prescribed doses of Peruna'" (13).
81 One nostrum maker, Lydia Pinkham, was deemed an exception. Faced
    by a collapse of family fortunes, she and her sons began marketing her
    home remedy as the Vegetable Compound in 1875. It quickly proved very
    successful because of heavy advertising. That advertising promised women
    a panacea: it was, so an ad in 1881 claimed, "a positive cure" for problems
    of the uterus, the change of life, depression, exhaustion, nervousness,
    cravings, sleeplessness – and the kidney troubles of either sex. Pinkham
    occasionally employed a "pain and agony" style which highlighted the
    plight of neglect, the horrors of illness, and the transforming effects of her
    remedy.
      Nonetheless later writers judged her a sincere and authentic advocate
    of women's health, so they often excused the excesses of her advertising.
    She dosed her own family members with her remedy when they fell ill. She
    advised those correspondents who were sick to adopt a new regimen of
    health, irrespective of the virtues of her Vegetable Compound or any other
    nostrum she might recommend. Her health guides helped to educate
    women about their particular nature and the necessary means to ensure
    well-being. In short, she really did care. "A helpful daughter, an inspiring
    companion, an ideal wife, a loving mother, a thinker, a worker, a healer,
    a friend – Lydia E. Pinkham takes her place by divine right among the
    foremost of America's Great Women" (30). These were the final words of a
    kind of extended advertisement written by the popular philosopher Ebert
    Hubbard.
      See, respectively, Elbert Hubbard, *Lydia E. Pinkham: being a sketch of her
    life and times* (East Aurora, NY: The Roycrofters, 1915); Robert Collyer

Washburn, *The Life and Times of Lydia E. Pinkham* (New York and London: G.P. Putnam's Sons, 1931); and Jean Burton, *Lydia Pinkham is Her Name* (New York: Farrah Straus and Company, 1949). Academic treatments of Pinkham, of course, were more measured: see Sarah Stage, *Female Complaints: Lydia Pinkham and the Business of Women's Medicine* (New York: W.W. Norton, 1979) and Susan Strasser, "Commodifying Lydia Pinkham: A Woman, a Medicine, and a Company in a Developing Consumer Culture," Working Paper no. 32, *Cultures of Consumption, and ESRC-AHRC Research Programme* (London, UK: Birkbeck College, 2007).

82 On thanatopolitics, a form of slaughter, see Michel Foucault, "The Political Technology of Individuals," in *Essential Works of Foucault 1954–1984*, vol. 3: *Power*, ed. James D. Faubion, trans. Robert Hurley et al. (New York: The New Press, 2000), 416.

83 See, for instance, Eric Jamieson, *The Natural History of Quackery* (Springfield, IL: Charles C. Thomas, 1961).

84 In a Wikipedia essay dated 25 March 2012.

85 For a discussion of the economic vision expressed in the novel, see William Kupinse, "Wasted Value: The Serial Logic of H.G. Wells's 'Tono-Bungay,'" *NOVEL: A Forum on Fiction* 33.1 (Autumn 1999), 51–72. Michael Ross has an extended treatment of the way Wells treats advertising and the Ponderevos in *Designing Fictions: Literature Confronts Advertising* (Montreal and Kingston: McGill-Queen's University Press, 2015), 32–55.

86 Earnest Elmo Calkins, *Business the Civilizer* (Boston: Little, Brown, and Company, 1928), 2.

87 David A. Zimmerman, "Novels of American Business, Industry, and Consumerism," *The Cambridge History of the American Novel*, ed. Leonard Cassuto, Clare Virginia Eby, and Benjamin Reiss (Cambridge and New York: Cambridge University Press, 2011), 409.

88 My neglect of this famous novel does not mean I doubt its influence, only that it does not deal with the figure of the adman. By contrast, Simone Weil Davis has paid much more attention to *Babbitt* in her account of advertising in the 1920s, largely in a comparison with the advertising practitioner Bruce Barton; see *Living Up to the Ads: Gender Fictions of the 1920s* (Durham and London: Duke University Press, 2000).

89 Butler was a prolific author, most famous for his short story "Pigs Is Pigs" (1905), a satire of bureaucracy. Katherine Harper chronicled his endeavours in "The Man from Muscatine: A Bio-Bibliography of Ellis Parker Butler," unpublished PhD dissertation, Bowling Green University, 2000.

90 Ellis Parker Butler, *Perkins of Portland: Perkins the Great* (Boston: Herbert B. Turner & Co., 1906), 14.

91 The novel is briefly outlined in a discussion of Lefèvre's stories of financiers in Todd Douglas Doyle, "Artists and Financiers in Wall Street Fiction," unpublished PhD dissertation, University of Toledo, 2001.

92 Edwin Lefèvre, *H.R.* (New York and London: Harper & Brothers, 1915), Gutenberg.Project eBook, 2010.

93 In one written version of the play, the authors emphasize that the statistics were real: Roi Cooper Megrue and William Hackett, *It Pays to Advertise; a farcical fact in three acts* (New York: Samuel French, c. 1917), 4.

94 Roi Cooper Megrue and William Hackett, *It Pays to Advertise*, novelized by Samuel Field (New York: Duffield & Co., 1915). Much of the novel incorporated the playscript, often verbatim. Field added material, however, for example about adman Peale's sad domestic arrangements, which actually served to slow down the pace of the story.

95 Tuttle's movie contained much from the original play – but some scenes were added or altered, especially to include a touch of slapstick humour, one of Tuttle's signatures. Movie versions of the play were also produced in Sweden and France. The play was occasionally revived later on, notably in 2009 by the Metropolitan Playhouse in New York, presumably because of the interest in advertising fostered by the success of the TV series *Mad Men*.

96 Aaron Hoffman, *Nothing But Lies: A Farce in Three Acts* (New York and London: Samuel French, 1923). It only played on Broadway, at the Longacre Theatre, from October 1918 through February 1919. It too was made into a silent movie (1920) and later a movie in France, "Rien que des mensonges" (1933), produced by Paramount.

97 This first appeared in a newspaper. Christopher Morley, *The Story of Ginger Cubes* (New York Evening Post, 1922). Morley wrote two other novels, *The Haunted Bookshop* (1919) and *Thunder on the Left* (1925), which dealt with promotion. These are analysed in Ross, *Designing Fictions*, 58–65.

98 William E. Woodward, *Bunk* (New York and London: Harper & Brothers), 1923.

99 Harford Powel Jr, *The Virgin Queene* (Boston: Little, Brown, & Co., 1928).

100 Hereafter I use in-text citations for the various quotations where the page reference refers to a source already mentioned.

101 The phrase is actually a steal from a mystery novel about art theft: Iain Pears, *The Immaculate Deception*, 1999 (London: HarperCollins, 2007).

102 The notion of the hapless public, however, had appeared in the social conversation long before, as evident in the moral assault on Barnum's autobiography.

103 For an extensive and excellent discussion of the birth and character of pragmatism, see Louis Menand's study of American philosophers of the

time, *The Metaphysical Club: A Story of Ideas in America* (New York: Farrar, Straus and Giroux, 2001).

104 William James, *Pragmatism: A New Name for Some Old Ways of Thinking*, 1907. All references are to the 2004 Kindle Edition.

105 But he was aware of that kind of criticism of pragmatism. Witness these comments in his lecture: "A favorite formula for describing Mr. Schiller's doctrines and mine is that we are persons who think that by saying whatever you find it pleasant to say and calling it truth you fulfil every pragmatistic requirement" (KL 1606–7). "Schiller says the true is that which 'works.' Thereupon he is treated as one who limits verification to the lowest material utilities. Dewey says truth is what gives 'satisfaction.' He is treated as one who believes in calling everything true which, if it were true, would be pleasant" (KL 1613–15).

106 Roy was one of the beatniks with whom Draper was briefly acquainted through his girlfriend of the moment.

2 The Rise of the Advertising Agent

1 S.N. Behrman, "The Advertising Man," *New Republic* (20 August 1919): 84, 86. The last sentence was actually a response to some criticisms that an advertising practitioner had made of the American scene. It was also the final sentence in this humorous but critical portrayal of the figure of the adman.

2 Behrman, "The Advertising Man," 85.

3 Hilaire Belloc, *The Contrast* (London: J.W. Arrowsmith, 1923), 55.

4 Georges Duhamel, *America the Menace: Scenes from the Life of the Future* (New York: Arno Press, 1974), 128.

5 Stephen Fox, *The Mirror Makers: A History of American Advertising and Its Creators* (New York: Vintage Books, 1985), 39, 118.

6 See Ellen Gruber Garvey, *The Adman in the Parlor: Magazines and the Gendering of Consumer Culture, 1880s to 1910s* (New York: Oxford University Press, 1996) for an intriguing discussion of how the newly popular magazines trained readers to consume advertisements. Another dimension of this form of "education," occurring later, has been assessed in Lisa Jacobson, *Raising Consumers: Children and the American Mass Market in the Early Twentieth Century* (New York: Columbia University Press, 2004).

7 The actual history of advertising in this period has already been told in a series of excellent studies, notably Fox, *The Mirror Makers*; Jackson Lears, *Fables of Abundance: A Cultural History of Advertising in America* (New York: Basic Books, 1994); Stuart Ewen, *Captains of Consciousness: Advertising and the Social Roots of the Consumer Culture* (New York: McGraw-Hill, 1976); Roland

358 Notes to page 77

Marchand, *Advertising the American Dream: Making Way for Modernity 1920–1940* (Berkeley: University of California Press, 1985); William Leach, *Land of Desire: Merchants, Power, and the Rise of a New American Culture* (New York: Vintage Books, 1994); Sussan Strasser, *Satisfaction Guaranteed: The Making of the American Mass Market* (New York: Pantheon, 1989); Pamela Walker Laird, *Advertising Progress: American Business and the Rise of Consumer Marketing* (Baltimore and London: Johns Hopkins University Press, 1998); and Richard Ohmann, *Selling Culture: Magazines, Markets, and Class at the Turn of the Century* (London and New York: Verso, 1996). Juliann Sivulka's survey history, *Soap, Sex, and Cigarettes: A Cultural History of American Advertising* (Belmont CA: Wadsworth Publishing Company, 1998), has two chapters on the period (99–191) where she explores the impact of advertising on American lifestyles. In one chapter of his survey, Gary Cross explores the birth of the consumer society early in the twentieth century; see *An All-Consuming Century: Why Commercialism Won in Modern America* (New York: Columbia University Press 2000), 17–65.

These works concentrated on innovations and changes in advertising and marketing. But the ways, the styles, and the ethos of the huckster persisted after 1900 in smaller agencies outside New York, in fields such as the selling of books and patent medicines, investments, some direct mail campaigns, even (to a degree) the famed Wrigley's chewing gum advertisements. One can find the persistence of, say, the carnivalesque or of "duping delight" in the cycle of huckster fictions. There were a few memoirs by advertising practitioners that recalled the pleasures of huckstering as well: Helen Woodward, *Through Many Windows* (New York and London: Harper & Brothers, 1926); Harden Bryant Leachman, *The Early Advertising Scene* (Story Book Press, 1949); or Maxwell Sackheim, *My First Sixty-five Years in Advertising* (New York: Prentice Hall, 1970).

8 US Census, *Bicentennial Edition: Historical Statistics of the United States, Colonial Times to 1970*, Part 1, Chapter D, "Labor," 142.

9 Cited in Marchand, *Advertising the American Dream*, 33 and 371n23.

10 Lorna Weir has outlined at some length the different kinds of truth that coexist in the modern regimes of power: thus, not only science but symbolic (especially religious), governmental, and mundane. See her "The Concept of Truth Regime," *Canadian Journal of Sociology* 33.2 (2008): 367–86.

11 Michel Foucault, "Truth and Power" (1977 interview), in *Power/Knowledge: Selected Interviews and Other Writings 1972–77*, ed. Colin Gordon (New York: Pantheon Books, 1980), 132. Foucault did not elaborate on the concept of a regime of truth, but he did speak and write a lot about truth before his death in 1984, and I have drawn on this material to fill out the aspects of

this concept appropriate to my study. See also a later collection of essays, Michel Foucault, *The Politics of Truth*, ed. Sylvère Lotringer, trans. Lysa Hochroth and Catherine Porter (Los Angeles: Semiotext(e), 2007).

12 "'Truth' is to be understood as a system of ordered procedures for the production, regulation, distribution, circulation and operation of statements." "'Truth' is linked in a circular relation with systems of power which produce and sustain it, and to effects of power which it induces and which extend it. A régime of truth." Foucault, "Truth and Power," 133.

13 Foucault placed science at the heart of the modern regime of truth. But otherwise, because I think his emphasis neglected the multiplicity of truth discourses, his outline of the political economy of truth is compelling: "'Truth' is centred on the form of scientific discourse and the institutions which produce it; it is subject to constant economic and political excitement (the demand for truth, as much for economic production as for political power); it is the object, under diverse forms, of immense diffusion and consumption (circulating through apparatuses of education and information whose extent is relatively broad in the social body, notwithstanding certain strict limitations); it is produced and transmitted under the control, dominant if not exclusive, of a few great political and economic apparatuses (university, army, writing, media); lastly, it is the issue of a whole political debate and social confrontation ('ideological' struggles)." "Truth and Power," 131–2.

14 On truth games, see Michel Foucault, "The Ethics of the Concern of the Self as a Practice of Freedom" (1984 interview), in *Essential Works of Foucault 1954–1984*, v.1: *Ethics, Subjectivity and Truth*, ed. Paul Rabinow, trans. Robert Hurley et al. (New York: The New Press, 1997), 280–301.

15 Michel Foucault, *Fearless Speech*, ed. Joseph Pearson (Los Angeles: Semiotext(e), 2001), 169. This set of lectures explored at length a rigorous kind of truth-telling in ancient Greece called *parrhesia*. During the last years of his life, Foucault provided one of the most elaborate philosophical treatments of the virtues of the truth-teller. That exercise was one aspect of his so-called turn to ethics and his "journey to Greece," when he slowly retreated from his earlier fascination with the implacable forces of biopower and governmentality to discover how the subject might manage the condition and the fashioning of his own life. Foucault's analysis of the truth-teller occurred mostly in his lectures, not his books, and these lectures have only recently been published in English. See *The Hermeneutics of the Subject: Lectures at the Collège de France 1981–1982*, ed. Frédéric Gros, trans. Graham Burchell (New York: Picador, 2005); *The Government of Self and Others: Lectures at the Collège de France 1982–1983*, ed. Frédéric Gros, trans.

Graham Burchell (New York: Palgrave Macmillan, 2010); *The Courage of
the Truth (The Government of Self and Others II): Lectures at the Collège de France
1983–1984*, ed. Frédéric Gros, trans. Graham Burchell (Houndmills, UK,
and New York: Palgrave Macmillan 2011); and in particular *Fearless Speech*,
a transcript of Foucault's lectures delivered in English late in 1983 at the
University of California, Berkeley.

His focus was on the evolution of the "parrhesiastes," the free speaker
who spoke and lived the truth, in Greco-Roman history. He, for the person
was almost always a man, was undeniably a moral figure, often at risk
because he spoke truth to power. Exile, if not death, was an ever-present
menace should the parrhesiast offend the masses or the authorities. The
discourse of that persona was full of virtue: it was complete, exact, sincere,
transparent, personal, and courageous. "The one who uses parrhesia, the
parrhesiastes, is someone who says everything he has in mind: he does not
hide anything, but opens his heart and mind completely to other people
through his discourse" (Foucault, *Fearless Speech*, 12). That process Foucault
contrasted with the flattery and persuasion of the sophist or the rhetorician
who twisted or masked or denied the truth. Initially the parrhesiast came to
fame as an honoured person (and sometimes an irritant) in the practice of
Athenian democracy, later as a necessary adviser to the Hellenic and Roman
monarchs who ruled the ancient world. In the Imperial era, moreover, the
parrhesiast also acted as a personal adviser to members of the Roman elite,
telling them the truths of their life and guiding them in the care of the self.
Foucault's final 1984 lectures at the Collège de France explored how one
extreme brand of parrhesiast, the Cynics, sought to live an unvarnished and
even scandalous life; in short, to live their kind of truth.

More generally, Foucault ascribed to the activities of the parrhesiast the
roots of the critical tradition in the West. You can see modern echoes of
this type in the celebration of the "pure" (but not applied?) scientist or the
bureaucratic and corporate whistle-blowers. Here, in short, was another
version, a much older version, of that contrast of artifice versus authenticity
around which modern writers would organize the adman's dilemma. I am
left with the impression that the parrhesiast of the Greco-Roman era played
a contrary role to that of our modern adman. In other words, that the
modern persuader is the conflicted successor, mostly the rhetorician, rarely
the truth-teller.

16 The truth-in-advertising campaign has been treated in a number of works.
One of the most useful early studies, though very biased, is a celebration by
H.J. Kenner, himself a leader, entitled *The Fight for Truth in Advertising* (New
York: Round Table Press, 1936). A second, much shorter contemporary

account is found in Herbert W. Hess, "History and Present Status of the 'Truth-in-Advertising' Movement," *Annals of the American Academy of Political and Social Science* 101 (May 1922): 211–20. Then there are works by scholars: Richard S. Tedlow, "From Competitor to Consumer: The Changing Focus of Federal Regulation of Advertising," *Business History Review* 55.1 (Spring 1981): 35–58; D.G. Brian Jones, Alan J. Richardson, and Teri Shearer, "Truth and the Evolution of the Professions: A Comparative Study of 'Truth in Advertising' and 'True and Fair' Financial Statements in North America during the Progressive Era," *Journal of Macromarketing* 20.1 (June 2000): 23–35; Zeynep K. Hansen and Marc T. Law, "The Political Economy of Truth-in-Advertising Regulation during the Progressive Era," *Journal of Law and Economics* 51 (May 2008): 251–69; Ross D. Petty, "The Historic Development of Modern US Advertising Regulation," *Journal of Historical Research in Marketing* 7.4 (2015): 524–48. Laird also has two chapters on "legitimating the advertising profession" (in *Advertising Progress*, 304–61) that examine more broadly ideas and events in the community of ad-makers.

Truth-in-advertising would persist as a cry and a cause well after the 1920s. It would also appear in the promotions of the industry outside the United States. It expressed an ideal of the professional that could never be achieved because it denied one aspect of advertising: its reliance on deception. Its appeal waned after the gospel of creativity took hold of the craft after 1960 because the adman-as-innovator might find comfort or esteem as a kind of artist and enchanter. But it did not disappear. In 2015, for example, Advertising Standards Canada, an industry group that sought to build and strengthen public trust in advertising, mounted a clever truth-in-advertising campaign using print, radio, and television ads. At www.adstandards.com/en/psa/site/index.html, accessed April 2017.

17 Joseph H. Appel, "Introduction: Some Truths About Advertising," in H.J. Kenner, *The Fight for Truth in Advertising*, xvii.

18 Kenner, *The Fight for Truth in Advertising*, 33–4.

19 See David M. Kennedy, *Over Here: The First World War and American Society*, 25th Anniversary Edition, (Oxford and New York: Oxford University Press, 2004) for a superb analysis of the condition of America prior to the onset of war and the concerns that it provoked in political circles. For the actual career of the CPI, see James R. Mock and Cedric Larson, *Words That Won the War: The Story of the Committee on Public Information 1917–1919* (Princeton: Princeton University Press, 1939); Stephen Vaughn, *Holding Fast the Inner Lines: Democracy, Nationalism, and the Committee on Public Information* (Chapel

Hill: University of North Carolina Press, 1980); and Stewart Ewen, *PR! A Social History of Spin* (New York: Basic Books, 1996), 102–27.

20 George Creel, *How We Advertised America: The First Telling of the Amazing Story of the Committee on Public Information that Carried the Gospel of Americanism to Every Corner of the Globe* (New York and London: Harper & Brothers, 1920). Creel had also submitted a more formal report to the government and the Congress.

21 Ewen, *PR!*, 111. Apparently Creel appropriated that pleasing phrase from a description of the onetime home of Walter Lippmann, where Progressive intellectuals in Washington had gathered. Creel used the term in a paper published in July 1918, "Public Opinion in War Time," in the *Annals of the American Academy of Political and Social Science.*

22 Cited in Kennedy, *Over Here*, 90.

23 The term "professional-managerial class" was introduced by the Ehrenreichs back in the late 1970s; they defined this class in the context of popular politics and Marxist theory because they were seeking to understand the fate of the Left, its past and its future. See Barbara and John Ehrenreich, "The Professional-Managerial Class," *Radical America* 11.2 (March–April 1977): 7–31, and "The New Left and the Professional-Managerial Class," *Radical America* 11.3 (May–June 1977): 7–22. They later published "The Professional-Managerial Class" in Pat Walker, ed., *Between Labor and Capital* (Boston: South End Press, 1979), where a succession of other activists and academics discussed the virtues and defects (mostly the latter) of their theory. Their argument has been updated in their "Death of a Yuppie Dream: The Rise and Fall of the Professional-Managerial Class" (Rosa Luxemburg Stiftung, New York Office, February 2013), 2–16.

24 No doubt such a comment may appear a bit fuzzy. Personally, I think the PMC was only a possible or emerging class, united to some extent by function, culture, and ethos, as the Ehrenreichs pointed out, but whose boundaries were never firm, whose cohesion was riven by separate interests, and so never able to crystallize as a full-fledged class, certainly not after 1930, when the Progressive movement subsided. Consequently, while I use the Ehrenreichs' terminology, I have put their label in quotation marks to indicate the doubt.

25 Sometimes this group or elements of it has been called "the new middle class" or even just the "new class." From the beginning there was much discussion among various kinds of Marxists (see *Between Labor and Capital*) as to whether or not the PMC really constitutes an identifiable class or merely a series of clusters that never could find a social identity. William Leach (in *Land of Desire*) preferred the term "brokering class" to describe

those intermediaries who aided the course of business. Still, Richard
Ohmann has made a compelling case for the vigour and coherence of the
PMC in America between roughly 1890 and 1910, specifically in chapter 7
of *Selling Culture* (118–74). The Ehrenreichs themselves pointed out that the
issue of whether the PMC was a class or a stratum did not matter too much.
See Barbara and John Ehrenreich, "Rejoinder," *Between Labor and Capital*,
especially 321–9.

26 Ehrenreichs, "The Professional-Managerial Class," *Between Labor and Capital*,
18. These statistics, however, are only rough estimates. The Ehrenreichs
counted engineers, manufacturing managers (but not for 1900), social
and recreation and religious workers (but not for 1900), college faculty,
accountants and auditors, government officials and administrators and
inspectors, and editors and reporters.

27 Persons employed, aged 16 or older, as of April 1930. *Historical
Statistics*, 127.

28 The classic discussion of the inherent rivalry between managers and
capitalists remains James Burnham, *The Managerial Revolution* (New York:
John Day Co., 1941). On the wider issue of the ideals and values of the
PMC, see Michael Schudson, "Review Article: A Discussion of Magali
Sarfatti Larson's *The Rise of Professionalism: A Sociological Analysis*" (Berkeley:
University of California Press, 1977), in *Theory and Society* 9.1, Special Issue
on Work and the Working Class (January 1980): 215–29; Stewart Clegg, Paul
Boreham, and Geoff Dow, "The Professional-Managerial Class," in *Class,
Politics and the Economy*, 1986 (New York: Routledge, 2013), 158–70, who
doubt whether the PMC really ever emerged as a class; and Steven Brint
and Kristopher Proctor, "Middle-Class Respectability in Twenty-First-Century
America: Work and Lifestyle in the Professional-Managerial Stratum," in
*Thrift and Thriving in America: Capitalism and Moral Order from the Puritans to
the Present*, ed. Joshua J. Yates and James Davison Hunter (Oxford and New
York: Oxford University Press, 2011).

29 Michael Augspurger, "Sinclair Lewis' Primers for the Professional
Managerial Class: 'Babbitt,' 'Arrowsmith,' and 'Dodsworth,'" *The Journal of
the Midwest Modern Language Association* 34.2 (Spring 2001): 73–97.

30 On the problems of advertising practitioners in influencing the course of
professional instruction, see Quentin J. Schultze, "'An Honorable Place':
The Quest for Professional Advertising Education, 1900–1917," *Business
History Review* 56.1 (Spring 1982): 16–32.

31 Cited in Laird, *Advertising Progress*, 361.

32 And not without reason. Roland Marchand, one of the masters of
advertising history in the United States, called the advertising agents

of the 1920s no less than "the most modern of men" (*Advertising the American Dream*, 1). Why? Well, first of all, because that was the self-conceit of these agents and creators of the buoyant advertising of the day: they saw themselves as "the apostles of modernity," in Marchand's words, meaning the missionaries of the new and improved, the heralds of progress. They worked in the hectic milieu of cities and metropolises, amidst the skyscrapers and the crowds, the very places where the economic destiny of the nation was determined. They employed the most advanced technology and institutions of mass communication to reach out to the masses and provide the information and persuasion necessary to maintain the pace of consumption. They urged innovation on business and on consumers, seeking always to speed the circulation of goods, in a word of novelty, throughout the land. Never before were there so many admen, and so crucial to the course of events, to furthering (writes Marchand) "the processes of efficiency, specialization, and rationalization" (2) in the marketplace.

33 Similar commentaries appeared on the margins of the social conversation, in trade periodicals such as *Printers' Ink* and *Advertising & Selling*. See Stephen Shapiro, "The Big Sell – Attitudes of Advertising Writers about Their Craft in the 1920s and 1930s," unpublished PhD dissertation, University of Wisconsin, 1969.

34 Christine Frederick, *Selling Mrs. Consumer* (New York: The Business Bourse, 1929), 336–7.

35 See Liz McFall, "What About the Old Cultural Intermediaries? An Historical Review of Advertising Producers," *Cultural Studies* 16.4 (2002): 532–52, for a general and critical discussion of the culture/economy separation.

36 "Agency work is not a commodity; it is a creative service. That creative service is what the advertising agency sells. It is intangible, if you like, as imponderable as the knowledge which enables a doctor to diagnose and prescribe, a lawyer to give an opinion or to try a case, an artist to paint a picture, or a scientist to invent a new formula." Roy S. Durstine, *This Advertising Business* (New York and London: Charles Scribner's Sons, 1928), 100–1.

37 In his second autobiography, Calkins sought to highlight the virtues of his own story by making a slightly disparaging remark about Hopkins: "If your taste runs to success stories, you might read Claude Hopkins *How I Made $1,000,000 in Advertising*." What is peculiar here is that Hopkins did not write that book, at least not with that title. See E.E. Calkins, *"And Hearing Not –": Annals of an Adman* (New York: Charles Scribner's Sons, 1946), 245. There is some further evidence of animosity cited in Rob Schorman,

"Claude Hopkins, Earnest Calkins, Bissell Carpet Sweepers and the Birth of Modern Advertising," *Journal of the Gilded Age and Progressive Era* 7.2 (April 2008), 184n9.

38 Claude C. Hopkins. *My Life in Advertising* (New York and London: Harper & Brothers, 1927), 168. That translates roughly into 2016 figures as either $2.20 million in purchasing power or $38.6 million in "economic power," meaning "relative to the total output of the economy." These figures were obtained from the calculator of Measuring Worth (www.measuringworth. com) on 8 October 2017.

39 The Schorman article cited earlier claims that Hopkins, along with Calkins (though Calkins's involvement with Bissell was slight), laid the foundations of modern advertising in this endeavour. On Hopkins's career, see Stephen Fox, *The Mirror Makers*, 52–7, and Tommy Smith, "Claude C. Hopkins," in Edd Applegate, ed., *The Ad Men and Women: A Biographical Dictionary of Advertising* (Westport, CT, and London: Greenwood Press, 1994), 195–9.

40 Samuel Hopkins Adams, *The Great American Fraud*, 25.

41 Hopkins himself did not employ the term USP, or unique selling proposition. That was coined by a star of the 1950s, Rosser Reeves, who acknowledged his debt to the ways and claims of Hopkins and another hard-sell advocate of the early twentieth century, John E. Kennedy. See Tommy Smith, "Rosser Reeves," *The Ad Men and Women*, 256–61.

42 Tim Wu, *The Attention Merchants: The Epic Scramble to Get Inside Our Heads* (Alfred A. Knopf, 2016), Kindle Edition, 24. Wu's book contains a fine discussion of Hopkins's personality and career.

43 Ibid., 53–7.

44 On Lasker, see Jeffrey L. Cruikshank and Arthur W. Schultz, *The Man Who Sold America: The Amazing (but True!) Story of Albert D. Lasker and the Creation of the Advertising Century* (Harvard Business Press), Kindle Edition, 2012. That biography contains a great deal of information on Hopkins.

45 Hopkins, *My Life*, 269–70.

46 Edd Applegate, "Albert D. Lasker," in *Ad Men and Women*, 209.

47 Hopkins, *My Life*, 270.

48 Ibid., unpaginated preface.

49 Ibid., 199.

50 The award was established by Edward Bok, longtime editor of the *Ladies Home Journal*, in 1923 and administered by the Harvard School of Business. E.E. Calkins, *"And Hearing Not –,"* 268–9. Calkins received the award for the year 1925, according to *Time*, 8 March 1926.

51 Theodore MacManus, *The Sword-Arm of Business* (New York: The Devin-Adair Company, 1927), vii.

52 Earnest Elmo Calkins, *"Louder Please!": The Autobiography of a Deaf Man* (Boston: The Atlantic Monthly Press, 1924), 157.

53 Scholars have credited Calkins with a leading role in harnessing art, design, and style to the needs of marketing: see Stuart Ewen, *All Consuming Images: The Politics of Style in Contemporary Culture* (New York: Basic Books, 1988), 45–52, and Michele H. Bogart, *Advertising, Artists, and the Borders of Art* (Chicago and London: The University of Chicago Press, 1995), 207–12.

54 Tim Wu, *The Attention Merchants*, 57–9. Wu, however, does not deal with Calkins but focuses on his contemporary, Theodore MacManus.

55 Cited in Arthur J. Kaul, "Earnest Elmo Calkins," *Ad Men and Women*, 93–8.

56 Listed here, aside from the two autobiographies cited previously, are the works employed in this study: *Modern Advertising* (New York and London: D. Appleton & Co., 1916); *The Business of Advertising* (New York and London: D. Appleton and Co., 1915); *The Advertising Man* (New York: Charles Scribner's Sons, 1922); *Business the Civilizer* (Boston: Little, Brown, and Company, 1928); "Beauty the New Business Tool,". *Atlantic Monthly*, August 1927 (at www.theatlantic.com/magazine/archive/1927/08/beauty-the-new-business-tool/376227/ in December 2017); and "What Consumer Engineering Really Is," in Roy Sheldon and Egmont Arens, *Consumer Engineering: A New Technique for Prosperity* (New York and London: Harper, 1932), 1–14.

57 "It was Barnum, more than any other man, who created the idea that advertising is a yell and a lie. It was he who said that 'the American public loves to be humbugged,' and did most to brand advertising as a mere catch-penny device." Herbert N. Casson, *Ads and Sales: A Study of Advertising and Selling from the Standpoint of the New Principles of Scientific Management* (Chicago: L.C. McClurg, 1911), 51–2.

58 Frank Presbrey, *The History and Development of Advertising* (Garden City NY: Doubleday, Doran & Co., 1929).

59 Calkins, *The Advertising Man*, 10, 9.

60 Hopkins, *My Life*, 74, 73.

61 The record was full of stories of the ill repute of the advertising man. Thus F.W. Ayer, eventually a leading ad-maker, was in his early years upset when a person he respected claimed, in disgust, that an agent was "Nothing but a drummer, and he never will be anything else!" This is told in Ralph M. Hower, *The History of an Advertising Agency: N.W. Ayer & Son at Work 1869–1949* (Cambridge, MA: Harvard University Press, 1949), 55. Hower's book is an excellent treatment of one of the most prominent of the first wave of major advertising agencies.

62 George Presbury Rowell, *Forty Years an Advertising Agent 1865–1905* (New York: Printers' Ink Publishing, 1906).

63 The popular philosopher Elbert Hubbard, in an account of the virtues of advertising, simply defined science as "the effective way of doing things." Hubbard, *The Book of Business* (East Aurora, NY: The Roycrofters, 1913), 95. One of the leading proponents of science in advertising was Stanley Resor, master of the J. Walter Thompson agency. See Peggy J. Kreschel, "The 'Culture' of J.W. Thompson, 1915–1925," *Public Relations Review* 16.3 (Fall 1990): 80–93.

64 The book proved so popular it soon went through a number of editions. See Walter Dill Scott, *The Psychology of Advertising: A Simple Exposition of The Principles of Psychology In Their Relation to Successful Advertising*, 5th ed. (Boston: Small, Maynard & Company, 1913). Scott had been producing articles and books in this field since 1903. But there were soon competitors by other psychologists: Harry L. Hollingworth, *Advertising and Selling: Principles of Appeal and Response* (New York and London: D. Appleton & Co., 1920), published for the Advertising Men's League of New York (copyright 1913); Daniel Starch, *Advertising: Its Principles, Practice, and Technique* (Chicago and New York: Scott, Foresman & Co., 1914); Henry Foster Adams, *Advertising and Its Mental Laws* (New York: Macmillan, 1920; copyright 1916). For an overview, see Ellen Mazur Thomson, "'The Science of Publicity': An American Advertising Theory, 1900–1920." *Journal of Design History* 9.4 (1996), 253–72.

65 See, in addition to the works by Calkins and Hopkins, Truman A. DeWeese, *The Principles of Practical Publicity: Being a Treatise on The Art of Advertising* (Philadelphia: George W. Jacobs, 1908); George French, *The Art and Science of Advertising* (Boston: Sherman, French & Company, 1909); Casson, *Ads and Sales*, 1911; Paul Terry Cherington, *Advertising as a Business Force: A Compilation of Experience Records* (Doubleday, Page & Co, 1913), published for the Associated Advertising Clubs of America; John Lee Mahin, *Advertising: Selling the Consumer* (Doubleday, Page & Co., 1914), published for the Associated Advertising Clubs of the World; Herbert Hess, *Productive Advertising* (Philadelphia and London: Lippincott, 1915); Frederick J. Allen, *Advertising as a Vocation* (New York: Macmillan, 1919); Frank LeRoy Blanchard, *The Essentials of Advertising* (New York: McGraw-Hill Book Company, Inc., 1921); S. Roland Hall, *The Advertising Handbook: A Reference Work Covering the Principles and Practice of Advertising* (New York: McGraw-Hill, 1921); Harry Tipper, Harry L. Hollingworth, George Burton Hotchkiss, and Frank Alvah Parsons, *Advertising: Its Principles and Practice*, 1915 (New York: Ronald Press, 1921),

2nd ed.; and Wilbur D. Nesbit, *First Principles of Advertising* (New York: Gregg Publishing, 1922).

66 MacManus, *The Sword-Arm of Business*, 160–88. This kind of self-advertising had actually been pioneered much earlier by Charles Austin Bates in his *Good Advertising and Where It Is Made* (New York: Bates [1905?]).

67 Hopkins, *Scientific Advertising* (New York: McGraw-Hill, 1966), Kindle Edition, 213.

68 Hopkins, *My Life*, 121.

69 Calkins, *The Business of Advertising*, 57.

70 Calkins and Holden, *Modern Advertising*, 62.

71 Calkins, *The Advertising Man*, 26.

72 Calkins, *The Business of Advertising*, 334.

73 Calkins, "Beauty the New Business Tool."

74 Calkins, *The Advertising Man*, 21.

75 Calkins, *Business the Civilizer*, 121.

76 Calkins, *The Business of Advertising*, 335–6. He deemed this so important that he repeated the comment in *The Advertising Man*, 161.

77 Hopkins, *Scientific Advertising*, 250. Similarly in *My Life*, 112: "But when we make specific and definite claims, when we state actual figures or facts, we indicate weighed and measured expressions. We are telling either the truth or a lie. People do not expect big concerns to lie. They know that we cannot lie in the best mediums. So we get full credit for those claims."

78 MacManus, *The Sword-Arm of Business*, 144, 46.

79 Durstine, *This Advertising Business*. 44–5. BDO, or Barton Durstine & Osborn, would shortly become BBDO when the firm merged with the Batten Co. in 1928. The paid testimonial was a favoured technique of BDO's powerful rival, the J. Walter Thompson agency.

80 One exception was George F. French, a trade journalist who wrote for advertising periodicals: "It [Advertising] is permeated with a subtle dishonesty that is difficult to characterize and more difficult to eradicate. There is in too large a proportion of current advertising a percentage of untruth that does not harmonize with the exalted office the profession is performing for the benefit of the best ends of civilization – untruths of reservation as well as of statement." French, *Advertising: The Social and Economic Problem* (New York: The Ronald Press Co., 1915), 42. Later apologists of the 1920s were not willing to admit that so wide a domain of untruth remained in the world of advertising.

81 Hopkins, *My Life*, 118–19.

82 Calkins, *Business the Civilizer*, 120.

83 Calkins, *"Louder Please!,"* 237.

84 "I have never had a friend as a client. I have never had the sympathy of an advertiser in my life. Still, I respect them for their position. They desire to exploit their accomplishments, just as I do. But they represent the seller's side. I must represent the consumer. And those conceptions are usually as far apart as the poles." Hopkins, *My Life*, 101.

85 "New habits are created by general education. They are created largely by writers who occupy free space. I have never known of a line where individual advertisers could profitably change habits." Hopkins, *My Life*, 148.

86 Calkins, *Business the Civilizer*, 242.

87 Hopkins, *My Life*, 218.

88 Ibid., 116, 185. Here is the continuation of the sheep analogy: "They [people] cannot judge values, nor can you and I. We judge things largely by others' impressions, by popular favor. We go with the crowd. So the most effective thing I have ever found in advertising is the trend of the crowd."

89 Calkins, *Business the Civilizer*, 209.

90 Calkins, *The Business of Advertising*, 9.

91 Witness these comments from that philosopher of free enterprise, Elbert Hubbard, in a chapter he wrote for *The Book of Business*: "Business is the science of human service. Commerce is eminently a divine calling" (99). "Advertising is the proper education of the public as to where the thing can be found, and therefore it is a necessity" (116). Paul T. Cherington referred to "the modern conception of advertising as a public service" in his foreword to Frederick J. Allen, *Advertising as a Vocation* (vi), a notion he had elaborated in Paul Terry Cherington, *The Advertising Book 1916* (Doubleday, Page, 1916). George French, in *Advertising: The Social and Economic Problem*, claimed that "the only good advertising is that which works for the good of the people who are to read and be influenced by it" (20).

92 "Advertising reflects the crudeness, vulgarity, and materialism of the age" (Calkins, *Business the Civilizer*, 20). "When we say that this is an industrial, a capitalistic, or a materialistic age, we have indeed said something which, as the saying is, 'cramps our style' from the cradle to the grave. About the only thing most of us can do is to try and render the process as decent as possible" (MacManus, *The Sword-Arm of Business*, 33).

93 Presbrey, *Advertising*, 609–10. The journalist was William Allen White.

94 This kind of warning had been made earlier by Casson. "It [advertising] prevents laziness and stagnation. It makes us hustle and produce more wealth. Cut off all advertising for one year, and there would be a sensational decrease in our output. At once the pace would slacken, the energy would diminish, and the fate that threatens all moving things would be upon us." Herbert Casson, *Ads and Sales*, 54–5.

95 "It [advertising] is the method by which the desire is created for better
   things. When that once exists, new ambition is developed for the creation
   and use of wealth. The uncivilized make little progress because they have
   few desires. The inhabitants of our country are stimulated to new wants
   in all directions. In order to satisfy their constantly increasing desires
   they necessarily expand their productive power. They create more wealth
   because it is only by that method that they can satisfy their wants. It is
   this constantly enlarging circle that represents the increasing progress of
   civilization." President Calvin Coolidge, "Address Before the American
   Association of Advertising Agencies," Washington, D.C., 27 October 1926,
   www.presidency.ucsb.edu, accessed 2 July 2011.

96 Simone Weil Davis claimed that the ad-makers had a particular problem
   here, namely how to regender "influence" as "persuasion" so as to shed
   the practice of its feminine connotations derived from nineteenth-century
   views of uplift. Davis, *Living Up to the Ads: Gender Fictions in the 1920s*
   (Durham and London: Duke University Press, 2000). That interpretation,
   however appealing, neglects the significance of rhetoric as a manly art of
   persuasion that has its origins in Greco-Roman times. See also Marchand's
   chapter, "Men of the People," in *Advertising the American Dream*, 25–51, on
   the ideas and types of ad-makers in the 1920s.

97 Frederick Allen, in *Advertising as a Vocation*, listed sixteen separate qualities
   (120–1). George French, in *Advertising: The Social and Economic Problem*,
   devoted six pages to showing how the adman ought to be broadminded,
   accomplished, a student of psychology and sociology, an observer and a
   doer, sociable, philosophic, the generalist, a leader; in short, an admirable
   man (145–50). Wilbur Nesbit, vice-president of an agency, claimed the
   adman must have a "conscience," "clarity of vision," an understanding of
   human nature, and "a selling sense." Nesbit, *First Principles of Advertising*,
   11. A quartet of authors argued the advertising practitioner must
   have "a breadth of training" in business, psychology, writing, and art,
   as demanding as in any other profession; see Tipper, Hollingworth,
   Hotchkiss, and Parsons, *Advertising: Its Principles and Practice*, 401.

98 Calkins, *Business the Civilizer*, 51.

.99 Hopkins, *My Life*, 8. See also Hopkins, *Scientific Advertising*, 220–1.

100 Calkins and Holden, *Modern Advertising*, 3.

101 Hopkins, *Scientific Advertising*, 276.

102 That emphasis, of course, was commonplace. "The advertising man is a
    mental worker. His mind is the instrument which he uses in his work"
    (Adams, *Advertising and Its Mental Laws*, 20). Casson believed the proper
    model for the adman was the engineer: "He, too, has to deal with opposing

forces. He has to measure and calculate and construct. And he is none the less a builder, because the structure he creates is made of Public Opinion, instead of wood and steel" (Casson, *Ads and Sales*, 56).

103 Hopkins did mention this problem in his autobiography. I will deal more broadly with the issue of independence and subservience later in the book.

104 Cited in Larry Tye, *The Father of Spin: Edward L. Bernays and the Birth of Public Relations*, 1998 (New York: Henry Holt, 2012), Kindle Edition, 60. $100,000 translates into roughly $1.6 million in 2016 dollars (according to the converter at www.measuringworth.com, accessed 29 November 2017). I have drawn much of the detail in this paragraph from Tye's account. But see also Stuart Ewen, *PR! The Social History of Spin*, on Bernays and his ways.

105 In the text these books are abbreviated as CPO and P.

106 This awareness is apparent in Bernays's personal papers, according to one of his biographers. See Tye, *The Father of Spin*, especially 46.

107 For a discussion of how the argument played out in the pages of *Printers' Ink*, the main industry newspaper, see Merle Curti, "The Changing Concept of 'Human Nature' in the Literature of American Advertising," *Business History Review* 41.4 (Winter 1967): 335–57. Curti claimed there was a progression from the assumption of rationality to the presumption of irrationality, which was informed by psychology, between roughly the 1880s and the 1950s, except for a brief reversal during part of the Depression.

108 See his *The Structural Transformation of the Public Sphere: An Inquiry into a Category of Bourgeois Society*, 1962 (Cambridge, UK: Polity, 1989).

109 Much of this discussion grows out of the various works of Dr Robert Heath, a British practitioner turned scholar. See "Low Involvement Processing – A New Model of Brand Communication," *Journal of Marketing Communications* 7 (2001): 27–33; Heath and Paul Feldwick, "Fifty Years Using the Wrong Model of Advertising," *International Journal of Market Research* 50.1 (2007): 29–59; and Heath, *Seducing the Subconscious: The Psychology of Emotional Influence in Advertising* (Malden, MA, and Oxford, UK, 2012). Heath, however, is a champion of an alternative psychological tradition.

110 On Watson, see Kerry W. Buckley, *Mechanical Man: John Broadus Watson and the Beginnings of Behaviorism* (New York and London: Guilford Press, 1989).

111 These views of the human subject rest on such general works as Antonio R. Damasio, *Descartes' Error: Emotion, Reason and the Human Brain* (New York: Avon Books, 1994) and Joseph LeDoux, *Synaptic Self: How Our Brains Become Who We Are* (Harmondsworth, UK: Viking Penguin, 2002). See also John O'Shaughnessy and Nicholas Jackson O'Shaughnassy, *Persuasion in Advertising* (London and New York: Routledge, 2004).

112 Much the same kind of dispute about the nature of the consumer, his and her subjectivity, existed in Great Britain. Peter Miller and Nikolas Rose explored the issue in one essay on the work the Tavistock Institute of Human Relations produced on consumption and the consumer during the post–Second World War era. They found at least three sets of views, which they termed the psychoanalytical, the social psychological, and the rational. See "Mobilizing the Consumer: Assembling the Subject of Consumption," in *Governing the Present: Administering Economic, Social and Personal Life* (Cambridge, UK, and Malden, MA: Polity, 2008), Kindle Edition.

113 Bruce Barton, *The Man Nobody Knows: A Discovery of the Real Jesus* (Indianapolis: Bobbs-Merrill Co., 1925). Hereafter *The Man*.

114 Richard M. Fried, *The Man Everybody Knew: Bruce Barton and the Making of Modern America* (Chicago: Ivan R. Dee, 2005), 102.

115 See Stephen Prothero, *American Jesus: How the Son of God Became a National Icon* (New York: Farrar, Straus and Giroux, 2003).

116 This line of argument is developed at length in Andrew M. McKinnon, "Jesus, the American Advertising Man: Bruce Barton, The Man Nobody Knows, and Faith in Consumer Capitalism," unpublished PhD dissertation, University of Toronto, 2006, 173–219.

117 An extensive survey of these letters concludes they came mostly from members of the Protestant middle class. See McKinnon, "Jesus, the American Advertising Man," 104–6.

118 "Tellingly," declared the historian Stephen Prothero, "the letters ignore almost entirely Barton's depiction of Jesus as a successful executive." Prothero, *American Jesus*, 104. The views of correspondents have also been summarized in Edrene S. Montgomery, "Bruce Barton's The Man Nobody Knows: A Popular Advertising Illusion," *Journal of Popular Culture* 19.3 (Winter 1985), 21–33.

119 "What the hundreds of carefully catalogued letters from readers to Barton demonstrate is that ordinary believers read differently than intellectuals and theologians, that they found in Barton's work not second-rate theology but, instead, a pragmatic, lived religion that helped them make sense of modernity and their place within it." Erin A. Smith, "'Jesus, My Pal': Reading and Religion in Middlebrow America," *Canadian Review of American Studies* 37.2 (2007): 150.

120 Barton did not praise all businessmen, just those with vision. He treated Judas as a narrow-minded accountant – "he had the virtues and the weaknesses of the small bore business man" (177–8) – who could never understand the splendour of Jesus's mission.

121 The comment appeared in Charles Francis Potter, "Present Day Portraits of Jesus," *The Bookman* (July 1925): 590. There were, of course, some complimentary reviews: see the brief mention of these in Fried, *The Man Everybody Knew*, 96–7. See also Leo P. Ribuffo, "Jesus Christ as Business Statesman: Bruce Barton and the Selling of Corporate Capitalism," *American Quarterly* 33.2 (Summer 1981): 221–2.

122 James L. Dwyer, "Review," *The Commonweal* (1 July 1925): 214.

123 One writer in a religious periodical concluded, "Jesus, under Mr. Barton's hand, is in fact reduced to moral proportions which make him a kind of sublimated Babbitt." "Booming Religion as a Business Proposition," *The Christian Century* (21 May 1925): 658.

124 Gilbert Seldes, "The Living Christ," *The New Republic* (24 June 1925): 327.

125 [Reinhold Niebuhr] "Jesus as Efficiency Expert," *The Christian Century* (2 July 1925): 851.

126 James Rorty, *Our Master's Voice: Advertising* (New York: John Day Co., 1934), 329. Rorty devoted a whole chapter, entitled "The Carpenter Re-Carpentered," to Barton and his book.

127 MacManus, *The Sword-Arm of Business*, 35–6. MacManus did not actually name Barton, but simply referred to the writer as "a young man."

128 Respectively, Steven Biel, "The Book Case: The Boardroom Christ," *CommonWealth* (January 1998): 76; Roland Marchand, *Creating the Corporate Soul*, 130; Susan Jacoby, "The Man Nobody Knows," "On Faith Blog," *Washington Post*, 9 May 2007; and Fox, *The Mirror Makers*, 108.

129 Fried, *The Man Everybody Knew*, 96.

130 For treatments of this dimension of *The Man*, see Wayne Elzey, "Jesus the Salesman: A Reassessment of *The Man Nobody Knows*," *Journal of the American Academy of Religion* 46.2, Supplement (June 1978), 152–77; Ribuffo, "Jesus Christ as Business Statesman"; Davis, *Living Up to the Ads*, 46–79, where she juxtaposes a close analysis of *The Man* and Lewis's *Babbitt*; McKinnon, "Jesus, the Advertising Man"; and John Ramage, *Twentieth-Century American Success Rhetoric: How to Construct a Suitable Self* (Carbondale: Southern Illinois University Press, 2005), 63–98.

131 The phrase was coined by an official of General Electric: Marchand, *Creating the Corporate Soul*, 134. Rorty later claimed that Barton's "syndicated sermonettes were published in hundreds of newspapers": *Our Master's Voice*, 316. Marchand has a full chapter on Barton's campaigns (130–63), as does McKinnon (216–63).

132 *Printers' Ink*, 3 November 1927, 192.

133 He expressed these doubts in a letter he wrote in 1926. See Fox, *The Mirror Makers*, 108–9.

134 Stephen Brown, *Marketing – The Retro Revolution*, London: Sage 2001, 43. Although he championed marriage, family, and fidelity, Barton was later involved in a messy court case arising out of an affair he had with a colleague. Brown, however, considered all marketers members of a "duplicitous breed."

135 "Printed columns are the modern thoroughfares; published advertisements are the cross-roads where the sellers and the buyers meet" (139). "He [Christ] would be a national advertiser today, I am sure, as he was the great advertiser of his own day" (140).

136 This from an obituary in the Manchester *Guardian*. Cited in Warren I. Susman, chapter 8, "Culture Heroes: Ford, Barton, Ruth," in *Culture as History: The Transformation of American Society in the Twentieth Century* (New York: Pantheon Books, 1984), 127.

137 Ramage, *Twentieth-Century American Success Rhetoric*, 88–90.

138 Niebuhr, "Jesus as Efficiency Expert," 851.

139 Dwyer, "Review," 214.

140 "As his right arm rose and fell, striking blows with that little whip, the sleeve dropped back to reveal muscles hard as iron. No one who watched him in action had any doubt that he was fully capable of taking care of himself. No flabby priest or money-changer cared to try conclusions with that arm" (37). Christ's enemies were often described as flabby or fat.

141 Rorty, *Our Master's Voice*, 326.

142 Seldes, "The Living Christ," 127.

143 Fried, *The Man Everybody Knew*, 212–13. Fried notes that by early 1959 the publisher estimated sales in twelve different versions of nearly 800,000 copies. In fact total sales in all editions, including translations, may have been well over a million copies.

144 Walter B. Pitkin, *The Consumer: His Nature and His Changing Habits* (New York and London: McGraw Hill, 1932), v. Pitkin was most famous for his book *Life Begins at Thirty* (1932). The quotation, albeit slightly modified, was repeated in one adman's memoir, suggesting that it stung: see Harden Bryant Leachman, *The Early Advertising Scene* (Story Book Press, 1949), 9.

145 The distrust of the consumer society has been ably chronicled in Daniel Horowitz, *The Morality of Spending: Attitudes Towards the Consumer Society in America, 1875–1940* (Chicago: Ivan R. Dee, 1992).

146 Max Lerner asserted: "Veblen is the most creative mind American social thought has produced." Cited in T.J. Jackson Lears, "Beyond Veblen: Remapping Consumer Culture in Twentieth Century America," apparently a 1985 paper for a conference, CHARM, 456 (at www.charmassociation.org/CHARM%20 proceedings/Proceedings%20Vol.%202.htm in March 2018). Jackson Lears's chief concern was to combat Veblen's impact on the understanding of

consumer society. There is an extensive treatment of Veblen's unhappiness with consumption in Charles McGovern, *Sold American: Consumption and Citizenship, 1920–1945* (Chapel Hill: University of North Carolina Press, 2006), 138–49. McGovern's book is yet another fine piece of scholarship in the field of advertising studies: he deals at length with the industry's struggles to meet challenges, enhance its reputation, and justify its existence.

147 "The Propaganda of the Faith is quite the largest, oldest, most magnificent, most unabashed, and most lucrative enterprise in sales-publicity in all Christendom." Veblen, *Absentee Ownership and Business Enterprise in Recent Times: The Case of America* (New York: B.W. Huebsch, 1923), 319. In his 1904 *The Theory of Business Enterprise* (New York: Charles Scribner's Sons, 1915), 385–90, Veblen had dealt with advertising's sad impact on the press. In *The Vested Interests and the State of the Industrial Arts* (New York: B.W. Huebsch, 1919), he thought advertising no more than "waste motion," and feared more effort was spent boosting "the consumption of goods than on their production" (36). In *The Engineers and the Price System* (New York: B.W. Huebsch, 1921), he claimed that "salesmanship is the most conspicuous, and perhaps the gravest, of these wasteful and industrially futile practices that are involved in the businesslike conduct of industry" (50).

148 Veblen, *Absentee Ownership*, 307n12; 306n12; 312n19.

149 Ibid., 306.

150 Chase was not quite the first to do so, though. A bit earlier, Ralph Borsodi (1886–1977) had dealt at length with the harms of national advertising, always "a species of charlatanism" (298), in *National Advertising vs Prosperity: A Study of the Economic Consequences of National Advertising* (New York: The Acadia Press, 1923). The book did not generate much interest, however. Borsodi went on later to win fame as a critic of "the ugly civilization" (the title of one of his books) of modernity and an advocate of an agrarian order and a simpler life.

151 Robert B. Westbrook. "Tribune of the Technostructure: The Popular Economics of Stuart Chase," *American Quarterly* 32.4 (Autumn 1980): 387–408. McGovern also has an extensive treatment of Chase in *Sold American*.

152 Stuart Chase and F.J. Schlink, *Your Money's Worth: A Study in the Waste of the Consumer's Dollar* (New York: Macmillan, 1936), 166, Many years later, the English Marxist Raymond Williams would elaborate at length on the similarities of magic and advertising in what became a classic study in the history of advertising, "Advertising: the Magic System," in *Problems in Materialism and Culture* (London: Verso, 1980), 170–95.

153 Stuart Chase, *The Tragedy of Waste* (New York: Macmillan, 1927), 42.

154 Chase, *The Tragedy of Waste*, 125.

155 Chase and Schlink, *Your Money's Worth*, 9. "The ultimate consumer is buried under tons of advertising matter" (25).

156 Ibid., 260.

157 Ibid., 2.

158 "The authors of this book have no quarrel with the technique of advertising as such. It is a magnificent technique. Sanely applied it would remake the world. Think of what might be done with applied psychology in a great publicity campaign for public health, for better housing, for cleaning up the slums, for honest and timely information about goods." Chase and Schlink, *Your Money's Worth*, 42.

159 Calkins, *Business the Civilizer*, 3–29, where Calkins used *The Tragedy of Waste* to launch a defence of advertising; Durstine, *This Advertising Business*, especially 292–303; and Barton, "The Creed of an Advertising Man," 4–6 and 189–90. There is a broader survey of the response, favourable and critical, to *Your Money's Worth* in McGovern, *Sold American*, 178–82.

160 Chase was not an opponent of the consumer society, not at least to the extent of Veblen. Yes, his work did suggest a certain nostalgia for a more innocent past where customers knew their local merchants and supposedly the merits of commodities. But he wanted to empower consumers by providing them with objective knowledge about brands to ensure better living.

161 Calkins, *Business the Civilizer*, 4.

162 Chase and Schlink, *Your Money's Worth*, 69.

163 Sharon Brock, "Helen Rosen Woodward," *The Ad Men and Women*, 344–53, and Juliann Sivulka, *Ad Women: How They Impact What We Need, Want, and Buy* (New York: Prometheus Books, 2009), Kindle Edition, KL 1112–64.

164 Helen Woodward, *Through Many Windows* (New York and London: Harper & Brothers, 1926), 289.

165 Ibid., 386.

166 Woodward took a second look at advertising twelve years later, where she did find it produced some social benefits, although in the end she concluded the work remained "flimsy" and "trivial." Woodward, *It's an Art* (New York: Harcourt, Brace and Company, 1938). The characters in a novel she wrote about advertising expressed similar sentiments; see her *Queen's in the Parlor* (Indianapolis: The Bobbs-Merrill Company, 1933).

167 Cited in Kathy Newman, *Radio Active: Advertising and Consumer Activism, 1935–1947* (Berkeley and Los Angeles: University of California Press, 2004), 59.

168 James Rorty was the father of philosopher Richard Rorty. The best description of James's early career and personality is in a chapter of Neil Gross's *Richard Rorty: The Making of an American Philosopher* (Chicago and London: University of Chicago Press, 2008), 29–62.

169 Rorty, *Our Master's Voice*, n.p. Page references in the text are to this book.
170 On the Tugwell bill and its fate, as well as the struggles of the consumer movement, see Inger L. Stole, *Advertising on Trial: Consumer Activism and Corporate Public Relations in the 1930s* (Urbana and Chicago: University of Illinois Press, 2005).
171 Roughly at that moment, the Marxist Antonio Gramsci was elaborating hegemony theory in an Italian prison. See, for example, the assortment of entries on hegemony in Gramsci, *Selections from Cultural Writings*, ed. David Forgacs and Geoffey Nowell-Smith, trans. William Boelhower (Cambridge, MA: Harvard University Press, 1985) and *Further Selections from the Prison Notebooks*, ed. and trans. Derek Boothman (Minneapolis: University of Minnesota Press, 1995). The theory would not win attention in America, however, until the late 1960s and 1970s.

   That said, the concept of hegemony would come to influence later studies of advertising in ways that would have been familiar to Rorty: see, for instance, Robert Goldman's *Reading Ads Socially* (London and New York: Routledge, 1992), which analyses over a decade of advertisements from the United States. Likewise, Rorty's notion of a "pseudoculture" propagated by advertising would be resurrected in scholarly books such as Andrew Wernick's *Promotional Culture: Advertising, Ideology and Symbolic Expression* (London: Sage, 1991): he was concerned with showing how advertising in its broadest sense "had come to shape not only that [meaning 'our'] culture's symbolic and ideological contents, but also its ethos, texture, and constitution as a whole" (vii).
172 "I venture to predict that when a formidable Fascist movement develops in America, the ad-men will be right up in front; that the American versions of Minister of Propaganda and Enlightenment Goebels [*sic*] (the man whom wry-lipped Germans have Christened 'Wotan's Mickey Mouse') will be both numerous and powerful." Rorty, *Our Master's Voice*, 394.
173 Fox, *The Mirror Makers*, 124.
174 Rorty eventually shed much of his radicalism, becoming a fervent anti-communist. Instead he worked to promote reforms in the realms of public health, nutrition, co-operative enterprise, and social ecology. See John Michael Boles, "James Rorty's Social Ecology: Technology, Culture, and the Economic Base of an Environmentally Sustainable Society," *Organization & Environment* 11.2 (June 1998): 155–79.
175 The movie was much changed from the play. In particular Hecht substituted Plunkett for another character in the original play, Earnest Friedman, who was an art dealer.

176 The magazine was launched in 1931. See Margaret McFadden,
    "'WARNING – Do not risk federal arrest by looking glum!': *Ballyhoo*
    Magazine and the Cultural Politics of Early 1930s Humor," *Journal of
    American Culture* 26.1 (March 2003): 124–33.

177 Cited in the *New York Times*, 11 November 1934. Larrabee was the managing
    editor of *Printers' Ink*, the oldest of advertising journals. He was speaking to
    a convention of one group of the Advertising Federation of America. He
    hoped to persuade his listeners of the wisdom of cleansing advertising of
    liars and crooks to forestall regulation. Their activities, he claimed, did more
    to discredit advertising than "Jim Rorty and the entire Communist party."

178 Jodie T. Allen, "How a Different America Responded to the Great
    Depression," Pew Research Center (at www.pewresearch.org/2010/12/14/
    how-a-different-america-responded-to-the-great-depression/ in April 2013).
    Of course such public opinion surveys were still in their infancy, and the
    results were skewed towards the views of educated white males.

179 See Inger L. Stole, *Advertising at War: Business, Consumers, and Government
    in the 1940s* (Urbana, Chicago, and Springfield: University of Illinois Press,
    2012) for a closely reasoned account of the advertising industry's efforts
    during the war to "cement" its place in American society.

180 I have used the much later 2009 Kindle Edition, which includes the
    introduction that Wouk prepared for an illustrated edition.

181 There is a fine description and analysis of Wouk's novel in Ross, *Designing
    Fictions*, 93–103.

182 Erik L. Olson, "How Magazine Articles Portrayed Advertising from 1900 to
    1940," *Journal of Advertising* 24.3 (Autumn 1995): 41–54. The author himself
    pointed out that ninety-two articles over forty years was hardly evidence of a
    vigorous debate. He also admitted the coding techniques he employed might
    well have exaggerated the positive spin. Even so, Olson's finding does fit the
    conclusion that a kind of double vision persisted in the social conversation.

183 See, in particular, McGovern, *Sold American*, 261–5, for an extended
    treatment of the creed and the project to ensure it prevailed.

3 The Chronicle of Struggle

1 There were 508 items in *Time* on advertising practitioners in the twenty-five
  years between January 1946 and December 1970. Between July 1927 and
  June 2013 there were a total of 927 items. But that figure should be kept in
  perspective: over a slightly longer period, from March 1923 to September
  2013, there were over 26,000 items on doctors, nearly the same amount on
  lawyers, and 3,501 on, of all people, philosophers.

2 Lizabeth Cohen, *A Consumers' Republic: The Politics of Mass Consumption in Postwar America* (New York: Alfred A. Knopf, 2003), 7. Cohen's masterful account includes much material on advertising and advertising practitioners, although neither the industry nor the profession is a major focus of her work.

   There were precedents for this kind of political enterprise. Frank Trentmann has argued the significance of a prewar "civic consumerism" which "grafted consumer desire and accumulation onto the civic ideal of the propertied, active citizen." He found the origins of this creed in Herbert Hoover's conception of the American dream and American democracy, especially his book *American Individualism* (1922). See Trentmann, *Empire of Things: How We Became a World of Consumers, from the Fifteenth Century to the Twenty-first* (London: Allen Lane and Penguin, 2017), Kindle Edition, KL 4740–81.

3 David Potter, *People of Plenty: Economic Abundance and the American Character* (Chicago and London: University of Chicago Press, 1954).

4 Figures from Ken Ohlemeyer, Jr, "History: 1950s," and J. Douglas Tripley, "History: 1970s," *The Advertising Age Encyclopedia of Advertising*, vol. 2, ed. John McDonough and Karen Egolf (New York and London: Fitzroy Dearborn, 2003), 782, 791.

5 See Nancy Bowman, "Philip Morris Companies," *The Advertising Age Encyclopedia of Advertising*, vol. 3, especially 1228.

6 See, for instance, "Advertising: Odious Sizzle" (2 December 1946); "Advertising: Wherever We Are" (23 December 1957); "Television: Diet for Commercials" (23 November 1959); "Advertising: Moment of Truth" (25 January 1960); "Advertising: A Matter of Taste" (16 February 1970); and "Advertising: The Elusive Truth" (4 September 1972).

7 "A recent survey of admen published in *Advertising Age*," reported *Time* (12 October 1962), "revealed that only 8% of those polled considered their fellow admen to be 'honest.'"

8 The Cardinal edition used here, complete with a new preface, was from Pocket Books, Inc., dated 1959. Much later Mayer would write a sequel, *Whatever Happened To Madison Avenue?* (1991), which tracked the declining economic and cultural significance of advertising. This account was not nearly so popular as his first effort.

9 *The Reporter* (3 April 1958): 47–8.

10 The Ehrenreichs have estimated that by 1972, 24 per cent of American jobs were in PMC occupations. Cited in Barbara and John Ehrenreich, "The Real Story Behind the Crash and Burn of America's Managerial Class," www.alternet.org, accessed 20 March 2017. The essay was posted from the Rosa Luxemburg Stiftung, New York Office, 19 February 2013.

11 *Time* (13 October 1952) offered a small article full of examples of this lingo.

12 *Time* thought the age was sixty-one. *Time*, 12 October 1962.

13 "The advertising business has never been known for its serenity," *Time* claimed in another story (16 February 1968). "Faces in the front offices change with nervous rapidity."

14 Daniel Horowitz, *The Anxieties of Affluence: Critiques of American Consumer Culture, 1939–1979* (Amherst and Boston: University of Massachusetts Press, 2004). Horowitz focused his attention more on intellectuals than on novelists or film directors.

15 Frederic Wakeman, *The Hucksters* (New York and Toronto: Rinehart & Company, 1946). The novel has received a certain amount of attention from scholars interested in the history of radio. See Alan Havig, "Frederic Wakeman's *The Hucksters* and the Postwar Debate Over Commercial Radio," *Journal of Broadcasting* 28.2 (Spring 1984): 187–99; Kathy M. Newman, *Radio Active: Advertising and Consumer Activism, 1935–1947* (Berkeley and London: University of California Press, 2004); and Cynthia Barbara Meyers, "Admen and the Shaping of American Commercial Broadcasting, 1926–1950," unpublished PhD dissertation, University of Texas at Austin, 2005. There is also a chapter on the novel in Jessica McKelvie Kemp's study of literature: "Soliciting Desire: The Ad-Man as Narrative Negotiation between Art, Desire, and Consumer Capitalism in Twentieth-Century Novels," unpublished PhD dissertation, University of Rochester, 2007. Michael Ross has a very interesting discussion of *The Hucksters* in *Designing Fictions: Literature Confronts Advertising* (Montreal and Kingston: McGill-Queen's University Press, 2015), 80–93. The term "social melodrama," in the words of John G. Cawelti, indicates something of a hybrid, a mix of the intensified effects and the moral freight of melodrama with "a detailed, intimate, and realistic analysis of major social or historical phenomena." Cawelti, *Adventure, Mystery, and Romance: Formula Stories as Art and Popular Culture* (Chicago and London: University of Chicago Press, 1976), 261.

16 "Love Those Hucksters' Airy Froth," *Variety* 163.7 (24 July 1946): 34.

17 Paul F. Lazarsfeld and Patricia L. Kendall, *Radio Listening in America: The People Look at Radio – Again* (New York: Prentice-Hall, 1948), 75–80.

18 "Huckster – that was a good name for an advertising man. A high class huckster who had a station wagon instead of a pushcart." Wakeman, *The Hucksters*, 45.

19 Fairfax M. Cone, *With All Its Faults: A Candid Account of Forty Years in Advertising* (Boston and Toronto: Little, Brown, 1969), 163.

20 Michael Ross argued that Norman's anxiety over his masculinity was inspired by his failure to serve in active duty in the war. "The psychological

mainspring of Wakeman's narrative is Vic Norman's need to redeem his manhood, called in doubt by his noncombatant war status; Evans provides him with a formidable Axis-style autocrat to take on, and vanquish, in single combat." Michael Ross, *Designing Fictions*, 91. On my reading, though, the anxiety was rooted in the demands the work of the adman placed on his sense of masculine honour.

21 This was purportedly based on a real incident: George Washington Hill had removed his dental bridge in a meeting with the account manager Raymond Rubicam as part of an explanation of how to engage the public. Cited in Andrew Cracknell, *The Real Mad Men: The Renegades of Madison Avenue and the Golden Age of Advertising* (Philadelphia: Running Press Book Publishers, 2011), Kindle Edition, 2012, KL 311–14.

22 That was not the whole story, added Seldes. The real culprit was the fact that network radio had fallen "into the hands of men who use programs for a secondary purpose: to sell commodities." Gilbert Seldes, "The Man with the Cigar," *Hollywood Quarterly* 2.1 (October 1946), 105.

23 "'Hucksters' Satirizes Air Advertising," *Broadcasting, Telecasting* 30.21 (27 May 1946), 24.

24 These fictions were first identified and discussed by Stephen Fox in *The Mirror Makers: A History of American Advertising and Its Creators* (New York: Vintage Books, 1985), 199–210, who placed them firmly in the tradition of anti-advertising. More recently, Susan Smulyan, in "Advertising Novels as Cultural Critique," chapter 4 of her *Popular Ideologies: Mass Culture at Mid-Century* (Philadelphia: University of Pennsylvania Press, 2007), 116–55, argued that the novels were vehicles of social criticism. Jack Boozer, in his *Career Movies: American Business and the Success Mystique* (Austin: University of Texas Press, 2002), 146–98, analysed a selection of these and later movies to show how Hollywood understood the world of promotion. The list of titles has been drawn as well from a much wider selection of sources, especially assorted sites on the World Wide Web. It is likely not complete.

25 "Estranged from community and society in a context of distrust and manipulation; alienated from work and, on the personality market, from self; expropriated of individual rationality, and politically apathetic – these are the new little people, the unwilling vanguard of modern society." C. Wright Mills, *White Collar: The American Middle Classes*, 1951 (London and New York: Oxford University Press, 1969), xviii.

26 Lizabeth Cohen included a brief but fine description and analysis of Schneider's *The Golden Kazoo*. She put this in two contexts: the way the techniques of advertising were shaping politics and the fact Schneider's worries

about massification were soon to be dated because the industry was turning towards market segmentation. Cohen, *A Consumers' Republic*, 334–6, 343.

27 The sales figure from "Wilson, Sloan: The Man in the Gray Flannel Suit," at 20th Century American Bestsellers website, bestsellers.lib.virginia.edu/submissions/182, accessed 17 April 2017. Ten years later, almost 270,000 copies had been sold.

28 See, for example, Shepherd Mead's 1954, *The Big Ball of Wax: A Novel of Tomorrow's Happy World*, Kindle Edition, Edward Shepherd Mead Estate, 2012, or Edward Hannibal, *Chocolate Days, Popsicle Weeks* (Boston: Houghton Mifflin, 1970), Kindle Edition, 2012. But for a different view of the significance of the social criticism in the persuader fictions, see Smulyan, *Popular Ideologies*, 116–55.

29 Herman Wouk, *Aurora Dawn*, 1947 (New York: Hachette Book Group, 2009), Kindle Edition, KL 71. The later preface was published in 1956.

30 Galbraith, "Onward and Upward with the Admen," *The Reporter* (2 May 1957): 47.

31 Spectorsky, "SR Runs Six Up the Flagpole," *Saturday Review*, 8 November 1958, 14. In the course of the review, he also referred to the novels as "business westerns" full of "good guys and bad guys."

32 Galbraith, "Onward and Upward with the Admen," 48.

33 In an earlier novel by Arkady Leokum (1946), though much less successful than Hodgins's book, there are far more reflections on initially the joys but eventually the miseries of writing ads. Thus: "He lay in bed, thinking. What a business! What a fantastic mess. A never-never world. Distorted characters. Weird lives. Unsubstantial, without plan or purpose. Without belief." Leokum, *Please Send Me, Absolutely Free...: A Novel* (New York and London: Harper & Brothers 1946), 136.

34 Eric Hodgins, *Blandings' Way* (New York: Simon and Schuster, 1950), 25.

35 That phrase appeared in the comments of Bill Cole, Blandings's longtime friend, who added that "the economic world in which he lives seems willing to pay him a lot of money for it, so that his wife can wear clothes of expensive simplicity, and his two daughters can have the best of everything. What is wrong with that?" Ibid., 284.

36 Sloan Wilson, *The Man in the Gray Flannel Suit*, 1955 (New York: Four Walls Eight Windows, 2002), Kindle Edition, KL 2867. The rest of the references are in the text and designated by the Kindle system of location.

37 At this point in the story Tom had not only impressed the network executive, he had also secured his inheritance.

38 William Bear, ed., *Elia Kazan: Interviews* (Jackson: University Press of Mississippi, 2000), 114. In another interview Kazan pointed out the novel

drew on people and incidents in his own life, though he admitted its main character was not himself. Jeff Young, *Kazan on Film: The Master Director Discusses His Films – Interviews With Elia Kazan* (New York: Newmarket Press, 1999), 291.

39 It beat out novels by Thornton Wilder, Irving Wallace, and Leon Uris, as well as Ira Levin's *Rosemary's Baby* and William Styron's *The Confessions of Nat Turner*. *The Arrangement* sold a purported 215,000 copies in stores and many more via book clubs, the Literary Guild, and the Dollar Book Club. See Candice Cloos, "Kazan, Elia, The Arrangement," *20th-Century American Bestsellers* at bestsellers.lib.virginia.edu/decade/1960, accessed March 2018. That source summarizes a range of criticisms. One review by the noted literary critic Granville Hicks found the novel well-meaning but too familiar and superficial: Hicks, "Literary Horizons: What a Man Might Be," *Saturday Review*, 4 March 1967, 30.

40 For instance Vincent Canby, the reviewer for the *New York Times* (19 November 1969), thought *The Arrangement* Kazan's worst effort as film writer and director.

41 Elia Kazan, *The Arrangement* (London: Sphere Books, 1973), 250. Further page references are in the text.

42 Young, *Kazan on Film*, 291, 293.

43 The discussion of the crucial role and appeal of confession appears in Foucault, *The History of Sexuality*, vol. 1: *An Introduction*, trans. Robert Hurley (New York: Pantheon Books 1978), especially 58–63.

44 Ibid., 62.

45 Ibid., 59.

46 Spectorsky, "SR Runs Six Up the Flagpole," 15.

47 Galbraith, "Onward and Upward with the Admen," 48.

48 The history of actual women in American advertising has been surveyed in Juliann Sivulka, *Ad Women: How They Impact What We Need, Want, and Buy* (New York: Prometheus Books, 2009), Kindle Edition, where she makes a case for their role in the shaping of both advertising and the consumer society. She uses a series of linked biographies of prominent individuals, such as Mathilde C. Weil, who started an agency in 1880; Helen Woodward, of course; Helen Lansdowne Resor (1886–1964), who was a major force as a celebrated copywriter at J. Walter Thompson (run by her husband Stanley); and Shirley Polykoff (1908–98), another copywriter who created a famous campaign for Clairol in the 1950s and 1960s. Despite the achievements of these ad-makers, however, advertising remained largely a male domain where men dominated executive and creative positions. That was obvious in postwar America. This situation

would only change late in the twentieth century, though even then the masculine imprint on the ethos of the industry and the profession remained.

49 There is an intriguing discussion of Hudson's masquerade and his mix of styles – virginal, homosexual, and impotent – in Tamar Jeffers McDonald, "'Very Little Wrist Movement': Rock Hudson Acts Out Sexual Heterodoxy," *Canadian Journal of Communication* 31.4 (2006): 843–58.

50 See the discussion of the movie in Frank Krutnik, "The Enterprise of Seduction: Sex and Selling in Lover Come Back," *Journal of Popular Film & Television* 22.4 (Winter 1995): 180–91, and of Doris Day's roles in Dennis Bingham, "'Before She Was a Virgin ...': Doris Day and the Decline of Female Film Comedy in the 1950s and 1960s," *Cinema Journal* 45.3 (Spring 2006): 3–31, especially 24.

51 Consider for instance the arguments in Jack Boozer, *Career Movies: American Business and the Success Mystique* (Austin: University of Texas Press, 2002), especially 51.

52 Anne Tolstoi Wallach, *Women's Work: A Novel* (New York and Scarborough: New American Library of Canada Limited, 1981), 305. Wallach was herself an experienced advertising woman.

53 E. Evalyn Grumbine, *Patsy Breaks Into Advertising* (New York: Dodd, Mead & Company, 1939), 251.

54 Nancy Griffin, "FILM; Diane Keaton Meets Both Her Matches," *New York Times*, 14 December 2003.

55 This program was available as openmind_ep1025 through the Internet Archive in 2011.

56 The nickname served as the title of a later biography by Kenneth Roman, *The King of Madison Avenue: David Ogilvy and the Making of Modern Advertising* (New York: Palgrave Macmillan, 2009).

57 This is from the first Dell edition of October 1964. The quotation appeared on the back cover and purportedly came from *Best Sellers*.

58 The page references are to David Ogilvy, *Confessions of an Advertising Man* (New York: Dell, 1964).

59 Jane Maas, *Mad Women: The Other Side of Life on Madison Avenue in the '60s and Beyond* (New York: Thomas Dunne Books, 2012), Kindle Edition, 151.

60 The ad-maker was George Lois. Cited in Maas, *Mad Women*, 148.

61 See Jackson Lears, *Fables of Abundance*, for a discussion of the plain speech tradition and advertising.

62 For a discussion of this notion of the ideal self, see Nikolas Rose, *Inventing Our Selves: Psychology, Power, and Personhood* (Cambridge, UK: Cambridge University Press, 1998).

63 See Daniel Walker Howe, *Making the American Self: Jonathan Edwards to Abraham Lincoln* (New York: Oxford University Press, 2009), Kindle Edition, 13. Howe deals at some length with Franklin, life-writing, and notions of self.

64 "Where would advertising be if we told the truth? Ogilvy, for instance, makes a big deal out of telling facts. But do you really think the loudest sound in my Rolls-Royce is the sound of the electric clock?" Finnegan was Eddie Anderson's boss. Elia Kazan, *The Arrangement*, 304.

4 A Worrisome Dominion

1 Frederik Pohl and C.M. Kornbluth, *The Space Merchants* (New York: Ballantine Books 1953), 44. Initially published as *Gravy Planet* and as a serial in *Galaxy Science Fiction* in 1952.

2 Ibid., 10.

3 The book was translated into twenty-five languages, according to Pohl. It was reprinted as a classic by the Library of America in 2012. Andrew Liptak, "Frederik Pohl and C.M. Kornbluth, Space Merchants," *Kirkus*, 6 September 2013, www.kirkusreviews.com, accessed 24 March 2017.

4 Cited in "Advertising: The Mammoth Mirror," *Time*, 12 October 1962. The quotation was widely available on the World Wide Web in different collections in June 2014. It also appears in Eric Clark, *The Want Makers* (London: Hodder & Stoughton, 1988), 371. But what was not made clear anywhere was the source of this quotation.

5 Cited in Eugene Davidson, *Reflections on a Disruptive Decade: Essays from the Sixties* (Columbia: University of Missouri Press, 2000), 29. There was as well an earlier British tradition of anti-advertising: see, for example, Denys Thompson, *Voice of Civilization, An Enquiry into Advertising* (London: F. Muller, 1943).

6 Cited in "Advertising: The Real Enemy," *Time*, 22 September 1961.

7 Erik Barnouw, *Tube of Plenty: The Evolution of American Television* (London, Oxford, New York: Oxford University Press, 1975), 198. In fact, however, already a diversified pattern of viewing had emerged, where some homes watched a lot more than the average, some much less, and viewing frequency varied by age, gender, and education.

8 This, of course, was before the remote control device, the mute button, the VCR, or TiVo made avoidance much easier. Surveys by the 1960s discovered that people left the room to go to the bathroom or kitchen or took up other activities when a cluster of commercials came on the little screen.

9 "National output of goods and services doubled between 1946 and 1956, and would double again by 1970, with private consumption expenditures holding steady at two-thirds of [the] gross national product (GNP, the total market value of final goods and services produced by the nation's economy) over the era." Lizabeth Cohen, *A Consumers' Republic: The Politics of Mass Consumption in Postwar America* (New York: Alfred A. Knopf, 2003), 121.

10 This observation is merely a restatement of an argument put forward by Michel Foucault, notably in "The Subject and Power," in *Power*, ed. James D. Faubion, trans. Robert Hurley et al., *Essential Works of Foucault 1954–1984* (New York: New Press, 2000), 326–48. Which is one reason why I haven't employed the term "hegemony" here, although in some ways it may seem more fitting than "dominion." Hegemony is a Marxist notion of rule derived from the work of Antonio Grasmci and much elaborated by later theorists. It refers to a situation in which the ideas and interests of the ruling class have been accepted, as Raymond Williams put it, "as 'normal reality' or 'commonsense' by those in practice subordinated to it" (Williams, *Keywords: A Vocabulary of Culture and Society* [London: Fontana Press 1976], 145). A successful hegemony operates through the control of language and culture to produce general consent, though it may also involve negotiation and accommodations with other blocs in society, such as the "professional-managerial class." See Terry Eagleton, *Ideology: An Introduction* (London and New York: Verso, 1991, 112–17). But the fury of anti-advertising indicated that the ideas and the vision that informed the project of the consumers' republic were hardly uncontested, hardly commonsense. At least at this stage, in the thirty years after the Second World War, it was not "hegemonic." There was resistance at both the intellectual and the popular levels of society, the latter evident in the findings of public opinion surveys discussed at the end of this chapter.

11 In her Prologue, and throughout her book, Cohen argued that a variety of definitions of the citizen emerged in the United States, pre– and post–Second World War: "citizen consumers," "purchaser consumer," and the amalgam "purchaser as citizen." *A Consumers' Republic*, 8. For the record, Cohen does not employ the term, nor then the theory, of biopolitics in her seminal history. Foucault is not referenced in her index. The application of the label "biopolitical" consequently is my gloss on her account of the making of the consumers' republic. It suits because the project she described involved the conduct of conduct, an effort to administer life, a discourse of truth (in this case economics, especially Keynesianism), a coalition of authoritative spokespeople, and operations to work on the desires (and fears) of populations, such as advertising.

12 The page references in the text are to the book under discussion in each paragraph.

13 One of his biographers claims the book sold "no more than a few hundred copies," although it did earn "respectful reviews." Philip Marchand, *Marshall McLuhan: The Medium and the Messenger* (Toronto: Random House, 1989), 110.

14 The edition used here is McLuhan, *The Mechanical Bride: Folklore of Industrial Man* (Boston: Beacon Press, 1969). I have also discussed this book at greater length in *A World Made Sexy*, 128–33.

McLuhan's effort to decode advertising in ways that would show how the adman appropriated and shaped the culture would intrigue succeeding generations of scholars. Much of this work was itself structured by the techniques of semiotic analysis influenced by the pioneering efforts of the French theorist Roland Barthes, notably his "Rhetoric of the Image," on one Panzani food ad, a 1964 essay reprinted in his *Image-Music-Text*, trans. Stephen Heath (New York: Hill and Wang, 1994), 32–51. One outstanding later example is Judith Williamson's *Decoding Advertisements: Ideology and Meaning in Advertising* (London and New York: Marion Boyars, 1978), which uses both psychology and semiotics to decipher ads – and to arm readers against their artifice.

15 David M. Potter, *People of Plenty: Economic Abundance and the American Character*, Phoenix Edition (Chicago and London: University of Chicago Press, 1958). There is a chapter on Potter and *People of Plenty* in Daniel Horowitz's *Anxieties of Affluence*. The alarm over the way advertising had pervaded and shaped communications would persist. See, for example, one such update, a comprehensive work by Leo Bogart, a renowned media scholar, published forty years later, entitled *Commercial Culture: The Media System and the Public Interest* (New York and Oxford: Oxford University Press, 1995).

16 Walter Goodman, *The Clowns of Commerce* (New York: Sagamore Press, 1957). There appears to be some confusion about the initial date of publication, WorldCat, for example listing an edition from 1954, while other sources and reviews in 1957 suggest otherwise. That said, the copyright notice indicates some of the essays date from 1954. Goodman himself went on to a distinguished career as a reporter, editor, TV critic, and the author of eight other books, including an exposé of the House Committee on Un-American activities. See his obituary in the *New York Times*, 7 March 2002.

17 Packard has been the subject of a first-rate biography by Daniel Horowitz, *Vance Packard & American Social Criticism* (Chapel Hill and London:

University of North Carolina Press, 1994). The statistics are taken from Horowitz's discussion at 133–5.

18 Jackson Lears, review of Daniel Horowitz, *Vance Packard and American Social Criticism*, in *The New Republic*, 3 October, 1994, 33.

19 This is from Vance Packard, *The Hidden Persuaders* 1957 and 1980 (New York: Ig Publishing, 2007), Kindle Edition. The pages of this edition are not the same as in earlier ones.

20 Horowitz, *Vance Packard*, 162. Such was the opinion of at least one reviewer: "I strongly suspect that the fame and sales volume of *The Hidden Persuaders* was due less to its effect as a moralistic tocsin than to the chance it gave the reader to share vicariously in the satanic fun of mass persuasion." Lloyd Barenblatt in *The Public Opinion Quarterly* 22.4 (Winter 1958–9): 579.

21 Freudian psychoanalysis was at the height of its influence in America in the 1950s. The Russian physiologist Ivan Pavlov was famous for his work on conditioning, which fostered the fear that psychological techniques could embed a conditioned reflex in the human mind. In 1950, the sociologist David Riesman had published *The Lonely Crowd*, which depicted the rise of a new type of personality, the other-directed individual, who was especially susceptible to persuasion. The actual history of MR has been told in Lawrence R. Samuel, *Freud on Madison Avenue: Motivation Research and Subliminal Advertising in America* (Philadelphia: University of Pennsylvania Press, 2010).

22 Packard used the Freudian term "unconscious" and the more common psychological term (at least in America) "subconscious" almost interchangeably.

23 The edition I have used is Vance Packard, *The Status Seekers: An Exploration of Class Behaviour in America* (London: Longmans, 1959).

24 Read Bill McKibben's introduction to the Kindle edition of the book: Packard, *The Waste Makers* 1960 (Brooklyn NY: Ig Publishing, 2011), Kindle Edition. The page references in the text are to this edition.

25 Mark Crispin Miller makes a similar point about Packard's significance in the introduction to the Kindle edition of *The Hidden Persuaders*.

26 See Horowitz's chapter, "The Crack in the Picture Window: The Response of Critics to the Trilogy," in *Vance Packard*, 179–205.

27 A.C. Spectorsky, "Motivation Research as Big Brother: The Hidden Persuaders by Vance Packard," *ETC.: A Review of General Semantics* 14.5 (Spring 1957): 222–4. Spectorsky, a well-known journalist of the day, wrote a number of nonfiction works, notably *The Exurbanites*. He was then editor of *Playboy* and was tasked to bring some intellectual distinction to the magazine.

28 Samm Sinclair Baker, *The Permissible Lie: The Inside Truth About Advertising* (Cleveland and New York: World Publishing, 1968), 4. Baker admitted he had employed this permissible lie when he worked as a copywriter, though he claimed he did not recognize the deception until he left the profession. Unlike Goodman before him, however, Baker did not consider admen the primary agents, only puppets ruled by their clients. He painted a picture of an angst-ridden profession very similar to that spelled out earlier by Mayer and *Time.*

29 I have used the fortieth anniversary edition of *The Affluent Society* (Boston and New York: Houghton Mifflin, 1998), which was the basis for the Kindle edition.

30 John Chamberlain, "Papa Knows Best," *The Freeman/Ideas on Liberty*, August 1958, 62.

31 About ten years later, Galbraith added to his critique of advertising (though he did not use the term "the dependence effect") in *The New Industrial State* (1967). Many commentators, then and later, noted how Galbraith accorded advertising a central place in the management of the affluent society. But he never actually proved this argument with any detailed analysis. His was a work of assertion, which was one reason critics discounted the so-called Galbraithian system. See, for example, Cyril A. Zebot, "Economics of Affluence," *Review of Social Economy* 17.2 (September 1959): 112–25; Robert M. Solow, "The New Industrial State, or Son of Affluence," *National Affairs* 9 (Fall 1967), 100–8; J.R. Stanfield, "'The Affluent Society' after Twenty-Five Years," *Journal of Economic Issues* 17.3 (September 1983): 589–607; and Douglas J. Lamdin, "Galbraith on Advertising, Credit, and Consumption: A Retrospective and Empirical Investigation with Policy Implications," *Review of Political Economy* 20.4 (October 2008): 595–611.

32 Daniel J. Boorstin, *The Image: A Guide to Pseudo-Events in America*, 1961 (New York: Vintage Books, 1992).

33 The preface was available on Rushkoff's blog at www.rushkoff.com/my-preface-to-boorstins-the-image/, accessed March 2018.

34 For some interesting later appraisals, see Stephen J. Whitfield, "The Image: The Lost World of Daniel Boorstin," *Reviews in American History* 19.2 (June 1991): 302–12, and Michael Orth, "Twenty-First Century Reflections: A Theoretical Dialectic of Daniel Boorstin's The Image," *Forum*, 2011, digitalcommons.calpoly.edu/cgi/viewcontent. cgi?article=1088&context=forum. Boorstin's work was, of course, a precursor to the famous speculations by Jean Baudrillard over the triumph of "hyperreality": see *Simulacra and Simulation*, 1981, trans. Sheila Faria Glaser (Ann Arbor: University of Michigan Press, 1994). Baudrillard

devoted even more time and effort to assessing the impact of advertising on the perception of reality: see his early work, *The System of Objects*, 1968, trans. James Benedict (London and New York: Verso, 1996).

35 Betty Friedan, *The Feminine Mystique*, 1963 (New York and London: W.W. Norton, 2001), 7. Friedan made the statement about the lie in her introduction to the tenth anniversary edition in 1973.

36 One of the ironies of her polemic was that its research was based on the generosity of Ernest Dichter, identified only as "this most helpful of hidden persuaders" (208) and by name briefly in the footnotes, who allowed Friedan access to his abundant files on women's yearnings.

37 This is taken from an unpaginated version on the web: Aldous Huxley, *Brave New World Revisited*, 1958, www.huxley.net/, accessed 26 June 2014.

38 Hence this comment on the kind of statements that formed part of what he called "a language of total administration": "They have in common a telescoping and abridgment of syntax which cuts off development of meaning by creating fixed images which impose themselves with an overwhelming and petrified concreteness. It is the well-known technique of the advertisement industry, where it is methodically used for 'establishing an image' which sticks to the mind and to the product, and helps to sell the men and the goods. Speech and writing are grouped around 'impact lines' and 'audience rousers' which convey the image. This image may be 'freedom' or 'peace,' or the 'nice guy' or the 'communist' or 'Miss Rheingold.' The reader or listener is expected to associate (and does associate) with them a fixated structure of institutions, attitudes, aspirations, and he is expected to react in a fixated, specific manner." Herbert Marcuse, *One-Dimensional Man: Studies in the Ideology of Advanced Industrial Society* (Boston: Beacon Press 1964), 73–4.

39 John Berger, *Ways of Seeing* (London: BBC and Penguin, 1972), 129. Among the devices he mentioned were atmosphere, settings, pleasures, objects, poses, symbols of prestige, gestures, signs of love. Berger's book and documentary were an effort to show how gender and class biases were embedded in art and advertising. The two works proved extremely popular with academics in North America, where they were often used in classroom instruction.

40 *Killing Us Softly: Advertising's Image of Women* (1979) was widely shown in university classrooms and periodically updated in new editions. During the 1970s a much more scholarly, if much less popular, analysis of the gender bias of advertising was written by a leading sociologist, Erving Goffman: *Gender Advertisements* (London: Macmillan, 1976). Kilbourne eventually

wrote *Deadly Persuasion: Why Women and Girls Must Fight the Addictive Power of Advertising* (1999).

41 Wilson Bryan Key, *Subliminal Seduction: Ad Media's Manipulation of a Not So Innocent America* (SS in the text) (Englewood Cliffs, NJ: Prentice-Hall, 1973) and *Media Sexploitation* (MS in the text) (Scarborough, ON: New American Library of Canada, 1977).

42 Cited in Eric J. Zanot, J. David Pincus, and E. Joseph Lamp, "Public Perceptions of Subliminal Advertising," *Journal of Advertising* 12.1 (1983): 40. And a decade or so later, after yet another book, the estimate of his sales rose above two million copies. Cited in Martha Rogers and Kirk H. Smith, "Public Perceptions of Subliminal Advertising: Why Practitioners Shouldn't Ignore This Issue," *Journal of Advertising Research* 33.2 (March–April 1993): 10.

43 The subliminal scare has been ably described and its significance assessed by Charles Acland in *Swift Viewing: The Popular Life of Subliminal Influence* (Durham and London: Duke University Press, 2012), Kindle Edition. Acland does analyse Key's books. Acland, however, is much more interested in the late 1950s furor.

44 Witness this comment: "Ultimately, the particulars of Key's texts are less important than this self-help mission. Even if no one actually read Key's book, people turned the hunt for ad manipulation into a parlor game. Lessons in subliminal advertising became common at civic groups and schools, where the uninitiated were taught how to spot embeds. (Many of us who were in middle school in the late 1970s can remember classroom exercises devoted to finding skulls in liquor ads and deconstructing fashion spreads.) This practice supposedly made people more discriminating, critical media consumers." Carrie McLaren, "Subliminal Seduction," *Stay Free! Magazine* 22 (Spring 2004), at www.stayfreemagazine.org/archives/22/subliminal-advertising.html, accessed June 2014.

45 This from *Killing Us Softly* (1979). She moderated the charge in a 1987 remake of the documentary and her 1999 book.

46 Christopher Lasch, *The Culture of Narcissism: American Life in an Age of Diminishing Expectations,* 1979 (New York and London: W.W. Norton, 1991).

47 See Horowitz, *The Anxieties of Affluence,* 225–44, for a discussion of the whole strange affair.

48 Respectively, Jacques Ellul, *Propaganda: The Formation of Men's Attitudes,* 1962, trans. Konrad Kellen and Jean Lerner (New York: Vintage Books, 1973) and Guy Debord, *The Society of the Spectacle,* 1967, trans. Donald Nicholson-Smith (New York: Zone Books, 1995). Both books enjoyed considerable influence in America, though among academics and intellectuals rather than the public. Ellul posited a world saturated with propaganda where freedom

was deeply imperilled. Debord described a West overcome with spectacle, images crafted by capitalism and its agents to administer life. Both of these diatribes, however different in their objects and their claims, were about deception.

49 The version I used was a later edition, which did incorporate a few changes from the original. Jerry Kirkpatrick, *In Defense of Advertising: Arguments from Reason, Ethical Egotism, and Laissez-Faire Capitalism* (Claremont, CA: TLJ Books, 2007), eBook edition.

50 Which is not meant as a dismissal. The work was reductionist perhaps, certainly no fair or objective assessment of anti-advertising, but it was nonetheless imaginative.

51 Harry Lewis Bird, *This Fascinating Advertising Business* (Indianapolis and New York: Bobbs-Merrill Company, 1947), 24. Bird seems to have been a journalist, presumably engaged at some point in the industry's print media.

52 Fred Manchee, *The Huckster's Revenge: The Truth about Life on Madison Avenue* (New York: Thomas Nelson & Sons 1959), ix.

53 Bernice Fitz-Gibbon, *Macy's, Gimbel's, and Me* (New York: Simon & Schuster, 1951); John Gunther, *Taken at the Flood: The Story of Albert D. Lasker* (New York: Harper & Brothers, 1960); Milton Biow, *Butting In: An Adman Speaks Out* (Garden City, NY: Doubleday, 1964); Jim Ellis, *Billboards to Buicks: Advertising as I Lived It* (New York: Abelard-Schuman, 1968); Fairfax M. Cone, *With All Its Faults: A Candid Account of Forty Years in Advertising* (Boston: Little, Brown, 1969); Maxwell Sackheim, *My First Sixty-five Years in Advertising* (New York: Prentice Hall, 1970); Draper Daniels, *Giants, Pygmies, and Other Advertising People* (Chicago: Crain Publications, 1974); and Shirley Polykoff, *Does She … or Doesn't She?: And How She Did It* (Garden City, NY: Doubleday, 1975). This list is not exhaustive: there were other works both during the period and later, especially by women such as Jane Maas (1986 and 2012) and the famed Mary Wells Lawrence (2002).

54 On the obeisance to and misreading of Borden, see Vincent P. Norris, "Advertising History – According to the Textbooks," *Journal of Advertising* 9.3 (January 1980): 3–11.

55 "The pact does not promise, much less guarantee, factual truth on every level; rather, it affirms the author's identity with the work's narrator and protagonist. Thus the genre has an identity claim at its core: by definition, a memoir or autobiography purports to represent its author and the extra-textual world more or less directly, in a way that fiction, no matter how historical or autobiographical, does not claim to do." G. Thomas Couser, *Memoir: An Introduction* (New York: Oxford University Press, 2012), Kindle Edition, 81.

56 This comment from one study of the genre of autobiography: "But they are also performing several rhetorical acts: justifying their own perceptions, upholding their reputations, disputing the accounts of others, settling scores, conveying cultural information, and inventing desirable futures among others." Sidonie Smith and Julia Watson, *Reading Autobiography: A Guide for Interpreting Life Narratives* (Minneapolis and London: University of Minnesota Press, 2001), Kindle Edition, 10.

57 See the description of this complicated affair in John McDonough, "Biow Company, Inc.," in *The Advertising Age Encyclopedia of Advertising*, vol. 1, ed. John McDonough and Karen Egolf (New York and London: Fitzroy Dearborn, 2003), 178–80. At the time of the scandal in 1953, Biow was the eighth largest agency in the country, with billings of $50 million. It suffered a hemorrhaging of accounts and closed its doors in 1956.

58 Wirsig, a journalist attached to the industry periodical *Printers' Ink*, wrote the foreword to Walter Weir's *Truth in Advertising and Other Heresies* (New York: McGraw-Hill, 1963).

59 Later, however, Shirley Polykoff revealed to Jane Maas her sense of grievance over the way she had been underpaid despite her success. "'Get the money before they screw you, darling,' she said. 'Before they screw you the way they screwed me.'" Jane Maas, *Mad Women: The Other Side of Life on Madison Avenue in the '60s and Beyond* (New York: Thomas Dunne Books, 2012), Kindle Edition, 52.

60 Edward L. Bernays, *Crystallizing Public Opinion* (New York: Liveright, 1961), xxxii.

61 Dichter, *Handbook of Consumer Motivations: The Psychology of the World of Objects* (New York: McGraw-Hill, 1964).

62 Cohen, *A Consumers' Republic*, 307. See her chapter 7, "Culture: Segmenting the Mass" (292–344), for an extended discussion of this significant shift in the structure and goals of persuasion.

63 Note this comment from James Webb Young: "Talked with one of the elder statesmen of advertising about the post-war world and the future of our private enterprise system. He said he couldn't worry too much about it, believing that under any kind of system persuasion would be needed, and that there would be some place for the man who had made an art of it" (26–7).

64 Raymond A. Bauer and Stephen A. Greyser, *Advertising in America: The Consumer View* (Boston: Harvard, 1968).

65 Ralph M. Hower, *The History of an Advertising Agency: N.W. Ayer & Son at Work 1869–1949* (Cambridge, MA: Harvard University Press, 1949) and Neil H. Borden, *The Economic Effects of Advertising* (Chicago: Richard D. Irwin, 1942).

66 Raymond A. Bauer, "Limits of Persuasion," *Harvard Business Review* 36.5 (September/October 1958): 105–10, and "The Obstinate Audience," *American Psychologist* 19.5 (May 1964): 319–28.

67 "The point here is that the issue of advertising's persuasive powers – whether they be real or mythical – is part of the folklore that affects Americans' attitudes toward advertising" (Bauer and Greyser, 15).

68 The respondents were asked which three or four topics they had "the strongest opinions about." Only 7 per cent said advertising. Contrast this with religion (52 per cent), education (33 per cent), the federal government (32 per cent), and labour unions (18 per cent). Professional sports earned 11 per cent, higher than big business (8 per cent). Bauer and Greyser, 454.

69 Ibid., 166. That finding did not altogether please the sponsors, since it suggested that the public was oblivious to most ads – hardly the kind of fact helpful to an ad-maker trying to sell his or her services to a client.

70 "The data of the present study reinforce what the student of communication and advertising already knows: *The consumer is no helpless passive target of communication.* He is an active defender of his time, energy, attention, and interests." Ibid., 357.

71 He had been involved with the project on the Academic Review Committee.

72 Ibid., 463, 466, 460.

73 This amalgamates the sums of "generally" and "partially" agree in the tables. Ibid., 458, 459.

74 Ibid., 473.

75 Robin A. Coulter, Gerald Zaltman, Keith S. Coulter. "Interpreting Consumer Perceptions of Advertising: An Application of the Zaltman Metaphor Elicitation Technique," *Journal of Advertising* 30.4 (Winter 2001): 14.

76 See, for instance, Richard Pollay and Banwari Mittal, "Here's the Beef: Factors, Determinants, and Segments in Consumer Criticism of Advertising," *Journal of Marketing* 57 (July 1993): 99–114.

77 There eventually arose a small academic industry devoted to considering how consumers felt about advertising, publicity, and marketing, an industry that soon probed attitudes in other parts of the world. Aside from the crucial Pollay/Mittal and Coulter/Zaltman/Coulter articles, here are some other entries over the years: H.G. Schutz and Marianne Casey, "Consumer Perceptions of Advertising as Misleading," *Journal of Consumer Affairs* 15.2 (December 1981), 340–57; James R. Wills and John K. Ryans, "Attitudes toward Advertising: A Multinational Study," *Journal of International Business Studies* (Winter 1982), 121–9; John E. Calfee and Debra Jones Ringold, "The 70% Majority: Enduring Consumer Beliefs about Advertising," *Journal of Public Policy & Marketing* 13.2 (October 1994): 228–38; Sharon Shavitt, Pamela Lowrey,

and James Haefner, "Public Attitudes toward Advertising: More Favorable than You Might Think," *Journal of Advertising Research* 38.4 (July/August 1998), online at Academic OneFile; Stephanie O'Donohoe, "Living with Ambivalence: Attitudes to Advertising in Postmodern Times," *Marketing Theory* 1.1 (March 2001): 91–108; Hristo Katrandjiev, "Public Attitudes towards Advertising: An Empirical Iinvestigation," *Economic Alternatives* 1.17 (2007), 17–28.

78 Eric J. Zanot, J. David Pincus, E. Joseph Lamp, "Public Perceptions of Subliminal Advertising," *Journal of Advertising* 12.1 (January 1983): 39–44, and Martha Rogers and Kirk H. Smith, "Public Perceptions of Subliminal Advertising: Why Practitioners Shouldn't Ignore This Issue," *Journal of Advertising Research* 33.2 (March–April 1993): 10–18.

5 The Gospel of Creativity

1 Andrew Cracknell, *The Real Mad Men: The Renegades of Madison Avenue and the Golden Age of Advertising* (London: Elwin Street Productions, 2011), Kindle Edition, KL 1028.

2 Jane Maas, *Mad Women: The Other Side of Life on Madison Avenue in the '60s and Beyond* (New York: Thomas Dunne Books, 2012), Kindle Edition, 137.

3 Gernot Grabher, "The Project Ecology of Advertising: Tasks, Talents and Teams," *Regional Studies* 36.3 (May 2002): 245–62. Grabher argued that the account planner, the advertising employee who used research results to represent the consumer perspective, embodied the "scientific logic of advertising" (248).

4 Cited in Sean Nixon, *Advertising Cultures: Gender, Commerce, Creativity* (London: Sage, 2003), 144.

5 On the creativity boom, see Dean Keith Simonton, "The Psychology of Creativity: A Historical Perspective," a paper presented at the Green College Lecture Series on The Nature of Creativity: History, Biology, and Socio-Cultural Dimensions, University of British Columbia, 2001, simonton.faculty. ucdavis.edu/wp-content/uploads/sites/243/2015/08/HistoryCreativity.pdf; Thomas Osborne, "Against 'Creativity': A Philistine Rant," *Economy and Society* 32.4 (November 2003): 507–25, a critical account; or Beth A. Hennessey and Teresa M. Amabile, "Creativity," *Annual Review of Psychology* 61 (2010), 569–98, among many other essays, articles, and books.

6 See, for example, Charles Altieri, "Poetics as 'Untruth': Revising Modern Claims for Literary Truths," *New Literary History* 29.2, Revisionism (Spring 1998): 305–28. Hence this kind of comment in a discussion of *Heart of Darkness*: "Conrad, as so often, shows a truth and celebrates the courage of truthfulness." Bernard Williams, *Truth and Truthfulness: An Essay on Genealogy* (Princeton, NJ: Princeton University Press, 2002), Kindle Edition, KL 4779.

7 See, for example, John Hollander, "The Shadow of a Lie: Poetry, Lying, and the Truth of Fictions," *Social Research* (Fall 1996): 643–61.

8 His essay took the form of a fictional discussion between two opinionated souls. Oscar Wilde, "The Decay of Lying: a Dialogue," in *The Nineteenth Century: A Monthly Review* 25 (January–June 1889): 35–56.

9 Nietzsche, *On Truth and Untruth*, Kindle Edition, 150.

10 "Since about 1800, there has been a tendency to heroize the artist, to see in his or her life the essence of the human condition, and to venerate him or her as a seer, the creator of cultural values." Charles Taylor, *The Ethics of Authenticity* (Cambridge, MA: Harvard University Press, 2008), 62.

11 Witness this comment from one philosopher on irony. "The point is that irony is not merely distinct from deceit, but that an ironical assertion is not an assertion; if someone says of an embarrassing attempt at wit, 'That was very amusing,' he has not asserted that it was amusing (since he did not mean what he said), nor that it was not amusing (since he has merely implied it)." Williams, *Truth and Truthfulness*, Kindle Edition, KL 1369.

12 David Bazelon, "The Paths of Deception," *Times Literary Supplement*, 11 August 1978, 907–8. Bok (*Lying: Moral Choice in Public and Private Life*) took a hard line on lying, as had St Augustine and Immanuel Kant. She saw deceit, like violence, as a form of coercion that endangered the individual. She feared that a plague of lies threatened to fatally undermine the sense of trust that was the bedrock of life and politics. She urged the wisdom of a renewed commitment to truth-telling, and she proposed a variety of techniques people might use to determine how to find an ethical alternative to lying. Bazelon did not care for her moral thrust or her faith in moral command: the case for abstention was just hopelessly naive. But he was actually more distressed by what he thought was her narrow focus on lying, which consequently missed the ubiquity of deception. "Deception – in all its myriad formations, from faked silence through calculated bumbling to shrewd miscomprehension and careful mis-statements, all the way to the intense and indignant sincerity of the principled highroller – is the major form of modern power." The result was that we lived not in a world of truth but in "a made-up world."

13 In short, the virtues of truth-seeking, especially sincerity, may well be trumped by the pursuit of authenticity. That I take as the perhaps unintended observation of Bernard Williams, particularly the last paragraph of his intriguing chapter "From Sincerity to Authenticity." Williams, *Truth and Truthfulness*, Kindle Edition, especially KL 3680.

14 In fact Barnum did not make the "sucker" claim, although he was infamous as the author of the statement. Its author was a rival, David Hannum.

15 Cited in Stephen Fox, *The Mirror Makers: A History of American Advertising and Its Creators* (New York: Vintage Books, 1985), 333.

16 For brief biographies of Bernbach, see Sammy R. Danna, "William Bernbach" in Edd Applegate, ed., *The Ad Men and Women*, 56–62, and Deborah K. Morrison, "Bernbach, William," in John McDonough and Karen Egolf, *The Advertising Age Encyclopedia of Advertising*, vol.1 (New York and London: Fitzroy Dearborn, 2003), 165–7. Doris Willens has also published a sometimes-critical biography, *Nobody's Perfect: Bill Bernbach and the Golden Age of Advertising* (CreateSpace, 2009).

17 According to Willens (50), the report was actually inspired by Bernbach. A striking DDB ad for Ohrbach's had captured the fancy of Madison Avenue, and *Time* (17 March 1958) noted how it had become the talk of the town. But that report failed to mention Bernbach, instead singling out an employee. The new report was by way of correction, emphasizing that Bernbach was the creative engine of DDB.

18 Witness these two quotations. "I'm not the pompous or important guy or the huckster they [clients] expect to find as the president of the agency" (65). "I feel that if the agency makes an ad and the client doesn't like it, the client ought to run it anyway" (67). Mayer was very much impressed by how plain Bernbach's clothes and office were. Martin Mayer, *Madison Avenue, U.S.A.*, 1958 (New York: Pocket Books, 1959).

19 Noted in "The Old Soft Sell," *New York Magazine*, 15 May 1972, 85.

20 Jerry Della Femina, *From Those Wonderful Folks Who Gave You Pearl Harbor: Front Line Dispatches from the Advertising War*, 1970 (New York and Toronto: Simon & Schuster, 2010), and George Lois with Bill Pitts, *George, Be Careful: A Greek Florist's Kid in the Roughhouse World of Advertising* (New York: Saturday Review Press, 1972).

21 Larry Dobrow, *When Advertising Tried Harder. The Sixties: The Golden Age of American Advertising* (New York: Friendly Press, 1984); Bob Levenson, *Bill Bernbach's Book: A History of the Advertising That Changed the History of Advertising* (New York: Villard Books, 1987); Mary Wells Lawrence, *A Big Life in Advertising* (New York: Alfred A. Knopf, 2002); Dominik Imseng, *Think Small: The Story of the World's Greatest Ad* (Full Stop Press, 2014), Kindle Edition, KL 309–10; Lee Clow, "Advertising at the End of the Twentieth Century" in Jackie Merri Meyer, ed., *Mad Ave: Award-Winning Advertising of the 20th Century* (New York: The Art Directors Club, 2000), 231; Andrew Cracknell, *The Real Mad Men*, KL 3088 and KL 248–9; Thomas Frank, *The Conquest of Cool: Business Culture, Counterculture, and the Rise of Hip Consumerism* (Chicago and London: University of Chicago Press, 1997), 55.

Thomas Frank's book was an imaginative and substantial treatment of advertising in the 1960s that explored in detail how the adman transformed the content and style of advertising to suit the times, especially following the impact of television and the arrival of the "counterculture." He argued that the adman's Creative Revolution both predated and co-opted the counterculture, or at least some aspects of that disparate phenomenon, in order to ensure and accelerate mass consumption. Bernbach figured as a visionary in the assault on the dullness and uniformities supposedly attendant on the reign of the mass culture in the 1950s. Here, however, he was only acting out an attribute built into the capitalism of America. "Consumer capitalism did not demand conformity or homogeneity; rather it thrived on the doctrine of liberation and continual transgression that is still familiar today" (20). "What happened in the sixties is that hip became central to the way American capitalism understood itself and explained itself to the public" (26). Frank's interpretation at times seems a sophisticated expression of the ideas evident in the narrative of anti-advertising. It also appears to draw on the notions about power that were evident in hegemony theory.

22 On the dominion of the information processing model, see Robert Heath and Paul Feldwick, "Fifty Years of Using the Wrong Model of Advertising," *International Journal of Market Research* 50.1 (2008): 29–59. The caricature of postwar advertising is featured in some of the works referenced earlier by Dobrow, Levenson, Frank, Imseng, and Cracknell. See also Lawrence R. Samuel, "Thinking Smaller: Bill Bernbach and the Creative Revolution in Advertising of the 1950s," *Advertising & Society Review* 13.3 (2012), online edition, muse.jhu.edu/issue/26422. For a discussion of the supposed best of television commercials in that era, see Paul Rutherford, *The New Icons?*, 10–37.

23 Listed here are the sources of Bernbach's maxims. On art: Dobrow, *When Advertising Tried Harder*, 20. On rules: "Bill Bernbach," *Advertising Age* (29 March 1999). On emotion: *Bill Bernbach Said* (1989, 1), cited in Robert Heath, *Seducing the Subconscious: The Psychology of Emotional Influence in Advertising* (Chichester, UK: Wiley-Blackwell, 2012), 179. On notice, on style, on warm persuasion, on logic, on instinct, on poets: DDB Worldwide website. Some of these quotations from the DDB website, of course, appeared in printed sources. Furthermore, Bernbach said similar kinds of things in a 1977 interview for the archives of the American Association of Advertising Agencies (AAAA), where he spoke to then AAAA President John Crichton; the interview was available on YouTube on 8 March 2010.

24 See Antonio Damasio, *Descartes' Error*, and Joseph LeDoux, *Synaptic Self.*

25 On sincerity: DDB Worldwide website. Lawrence, *A Big Life*, 4. Della Femina, *From Those Wonderful Folks*, 29. Imseng, *Think Small*, KL 619–21.

26 Cited in Levenson, *Bill Bernbach's Book*, 194.

27 Which is a gloss on observations in Cracknell, *The Real Mad Men*, KL 1028–9, 1040–1, 1072–4.

28 See stills from the commercials in Levenson, *Bill Bernbach's Book*, 46–50. These and other commercials are available in other forms, sometimes online, and in a collection of ads and films produced by DDB itself.

29 Randall Rothenberg, *Where the Suckers Moon: An Advertising Story* (New York: Alfred A. Knopf, 1994), 65. Rothenberg goes on to quote Levenson himself from a private interview: "'We didn't tell lies,' Bob Levenson, a copywriter who followed Julian Koenig on the account and thereafter became its creative director, said in 1992. 'Our mission was to sell merchandise, not to reveal big truths'" (66). Or, put another way, some deception was inevitable and acceptable to sell the goods.

30 The innovator was a type that fitted well Raymond Williams's famous description of the system of advertising as magic: "it is clear that we have a cultural pattern in which the objects are not enough but must be validated, if only in fantasy, by association with social and personal meanings which in a different cultural pattern might be more directly available. The short description of the pattern we have is *magic*: a highly organized and professional system of magical inducements and satisfactions, functionally very similar to magical systems in simpler societies, but rather strangely co-existent with a highly developed scientific technology" (335). Available at xroads.virginia.edu/~DRBR2/rwilliams. pdf, accessed 26 March 2017. Sometimes the description of a leading ad-maker will employ such terms as "magician," "wizard," or "alchemist" to suggest how the individual used creativity to transform the mundane into the extraordinary. Obviously, in the end, what is "magicked" is not the product but the consumer of the ad and/or the brand. Which may suggest, as some critics have (like Packard when contemplating Motivational Research) that advertising is more akin to hypnosis than to magic. But, of course, Williams's reference is not to a "real" form of magic that actually worked, say transmuted lead into gold, but to a system of thought that worked on beholders in times past.

31 So described in Wikipedia, among other sources, in his biographical entry of 13 May 2015.

32 Howard Luck Gossage, *Is There Any Hope for Advertising?*, ed. Kim Rotzoll, Jarlath Graham, and Barrows Mussey (Urbana and Chicago: University of Illinois Press, 1986).

33 This quotation is cited (4) in the new introduction Della Femina wrote for the reissue of his memoir, noted below.

34 Jerry Della Femina, *From Those Wonderful Folks*. The extraordinary success of the fictional series *Mad Men* brought a renewal of interest in Della Femina's memoir.

35 George Lois with Bill Pitts, *George, Be Careful.* Lois would later write a series of other books about advertising and graphic design.

36 But perhaps this "denial" is only a part of the legend. Other sources claim her resignation from Jack Tinker was a result of a contract dispute. See Laurie Freeman, "Lawrence, Mary Wells 1928–," in *The Advertising Age Encyclopaedia of Advertising*, vol. 2, ed. John McDonough and Karen Egolf (New York and London: Fitzroy Dearborn, 2003), 922.

37 Lawrence, *A Big Life in Advertising*, 46.

38 Marilyn Much, "Ad Exec Mary Wells Lawrence Had A Midas Touch," *Investors' Business Daily*, 20 June 2003.

39 Richard Stengal in *Time*, 27 May 2002.

40 The salary cited in Bruce Horovitz, "Queen of Advertising Tells All," *USA Today*, 2 May 2002. It should be noted that WRG returned to private hands later in the 1970s.

41 The phrase appears in a retrospective essay on her memoirs entitled *A Big Life (in Advertising)* at Agency-review.com, accessed 20 May 2015.

42 "Lifetime Achievement: Mary Wells," *Adweek*, 20 May 2011.

43 Mary Wells suffered breast and then uterine cancer in 1980 and 1984 respectively. See the entry on Wells Lawrence at www.britannica.com, accessed 21 May 2015.

44 Agency-review.com, accessed 20 May 2015.

45 That last, overly harsh criticism appeared in a review by David Rakoff in the Baltimore *Sun*, 16 June 2002. The comparison of the book to "one long chat" appeared in the review of the Pittsburgh *Post-Gazette*, 19 May 2002.

46 "Mary Wells Uncle Tommed it to the top," cited in Ariel Levy, *Female Chauvinist Pigs: Women and the Rise of Raunchy Culture* (New York: Simon & Schuster, 2005), 111.

47 Della Femina offered as evidence one of May Wells's campaigns for Love cosmetics. "Do you think an establishment agency could have produced a campaign for Love cosmetics the way Mary Wells did? It is a brilliant campaign and the packaging of the cosmetics themselves is phenomenal. The kids like the bottles so much they keep them after they've run out of lotion. The campaign is talking to kids the way they like being talked to. The kids they've used in the ads and the commercials are hippie-looking. They're also very good looking, and all they talk about is

love ... The cosmetics business is a terrific jungle. But the fact that Love is selling means that they've got good advertising." Della Femina, *From Those Wonderful Folks*, 161.

48 These comments are drawn from later discussions: Jed Perl, "Arrivederci MoMA," *The New Republic*, 6 February 2006; Steven Heller, "When Low Got High," www.printmag.com, 20 November 2012; William S. Smith, "Overview: Between the High and the Low," *Art in America*, 1 September 2015.

49 The assorted complaints are drawn from many different sources, in addition to the essays cited in the text: P. Plagens, "MoMA Takes the Low Road," *Newsweek*, 10 October 1990; Kay Larson, "Pop Goes the Easel," *New York Magazine*, 15 October 1990, 93–4; Michael Kimmelman, "High and Low' Misses the Ins and Outs,' *New York Times*, 21 October 1990, a less vitriolic appraisal; Hilton Kramer, "The Varnedoe Debacle: MOMA's New 'Low,'" *The New Criterion*, December 1990, a fiercely conservative attack; Philip Berger, "Pop Goes the Art World," *Chicago Reader*, 21 March 1991; Rosalind Krauss, "Introduction," *October* 56 High/Low: Art and Mass Culture (Spring 1991): 3–5, a postmodern critique; Suzanne Muchnic, "Highs and Lows of Kirk Varnedoe," Los Angeles *Times*, 23 June 1991; Ivan Karp, "High and Low Revisited," *American Art* 5.3 (Summer 1991): 12–17; Graham Bader, "High & Low: Graham Bader on Soft-core," *Artforum International* 43.2 (October 2004), 109–12, which recalled many of the charges of Left critics.

50 The quoted term is from Stephen C. Dubin's *Arresting Images: Impolitic Art and Uncivil Actions* (London and New York: Routledge, 1992). Dubin, a professor of sociology, explored various artistic controversies, though not the exhibition in question here.

51 Here is a sample of the articles about Varnedoe: William Grimes, "Kirk Varnedoe Is in the Hot Seat as MOMA's Boy," *New York Times Magazine*, 11 March 1990; John Russell, "The Modern Charts Its Course Step by Step," *New York Times*, 13 May 1990; Karen Wilkin, "Making Sport of Modern Art," *The New Criterion*, November 1990; Calvin Tomkins, "The Modernist: Kirk Varnedoe, the Museum of Modern Art, and the Tradition of the New," *The New Yorker*, 5 November 2001, a particularly interesting retrospective.

52 The two key texts were Greenberg's "Avant-Garde and Kitsch," first published in *The Partisan Review* in 1939, and Macdonald's "A Theory of Mass Culture," first published in *Diogenes* in 1953. Both were collected in Bernard Rosenberg and David Manning White, eds., *Mass Culture: The Popular Arts in America* (New York: The Free Press, 1957). Others played a part in the creation of the narrative, such as Alfred H. Barr Jr, the art historian who controlled the fortunes of MoMA for many years.

53 The page reference in this section is to Kirk Varnedoe and Adam Gopnik, *High & Low: Modern Art and Popular Culture* (New York: Museum of Modern Art, 1990).

54 See the comment in Adam Lehner, "Early Decision," *Artforum International* (1 January 2002): 32, occasioned by Varnedoe's retirement as director due to illness. A bit later, Varnedoe's obituary in the *New York Times* (15 August 2003) noted, "With time, the breakdown of traditional artistic hierarchies and the book that came out of the exhibition have been increasingly accepted and influential."

55 But not always. In an aside, Gopnik did reference "the manipulative language of advertising" and suggest a distaste for "a disposable culture of manufactured lies" (390). Varnedoe did occasionally summarize the views expressed in the tradition of anti-advertising. In a brief reference to Vance Packard, though, he made this suggestive complaint: "Not for the first time, people who thought they practiced witchcraft brought forth people disposed to hunt witches: wishful thinking about irresistible power on the part of advertisers found a match in a muckraking effort to convince the public it was prey to a plot" (317).

56 They were accompanied by Sasha Newman, a critic and historian, identified in the credits as the writer and consultant. Note that this self-declared "film essay" was only a partial record – much of its thirty-one minutes was filled with comments from artists and videos of popular culture. Michael Blackwood, Producer and Director, *Art in an Age of Mass Culture*, Michael Blackwood Productions, 1991. In addition, MoMA put online a series of black-and-white installation photographs of the exhibition: www.moma. org/calendar/exhibitions/1764?/locale=en#installation-images, accessed 3 October 2016.

57 In *Art in an Age of Mass Culture*, Gopnik offered a kind of justification when speaking about Jasper Johns, namely, that the kinds of items and thus the culture the exhibition favoured depended on the artists and what sparked their interest – and apparently that was not television.

58 This approach was well described in Kirk Varnedoe, "High & Low: Modern Art & Popular Culture: Three Comparisons," *MoMA* 2.6 (Autumn 1990): 9–15.

59 A kind of catalogue composed of illustrated essays was published under the general direction of Nicole Ouvrard: *Art & Pub: Art & Publicité 1890–1990* (Paris: Éditions du Centre Pompidou, 1990).

60 *The Art of Persuasion* was published in conjunction with an exhibition organized by the International Museum of Photography at George Eastman House in Rochester, New York.

61 The recent history of such institutions is surveyed in Anamaria Tomuic, "Mediated Histories of Advertising, Museum Exhibitions and Digital Archives," *Journal of Media Research* 8.1 (2015): 3–18.

62 See Joan Gibbons, *Art and Advertising* (London and New York: I.B. Taurus, 2005), for an extended survey of the intersections of what is now termed "contemporary art" and advertising, roughly after 1980.

63 The publicity can be sampled on the film's website at www.artandcopyfilm. org, accessed 24 May 2015.

64 See www.oneclub.org/oc/hall-of-fame/, accessed 24 May 2015.

65 Ibid.

66 That has been argued, admittedly from a distinctly Left perspective, in Barbara Ehrenreich and John Ehrenreich, "Death of a Yuppie Dream: The Rise and Fall of the Professional-Managerial Class," Rosa Luxemburg Stiftung, New York Office, February 2013, 2–16. But see also Steven Brint and Kristopher Proctor, "Middle-Class Respectability in Twenty-First-Century America: Work and Lifestyle in the Professional-Managerial Stratum," in *Thrift and Thriving in America: Capitalism and Moral Order from the Puritans to the Present*, ed. Joshua J. Yates and James Davison Hunter (Oxford and New York: Oxford University Press, 2011) and Randy Martin, "Coming Up Short: Knowledge Limits and the Decomposition of the Professional Managerial Class," *International Critical Thought* 5.1 (2015): 95–110.

67 "Floyd T. McBee III," 14 August 2013, on the Amazon.com webpage for the documentary. Accessed 27 May 2015.

68 Jerry Goodis, *Have I Ever Lied to You Before?* (Toronto and Montreal: McClelland and Stewart, 1972). John Spotton (director), *Have I Ever Lied to You Before?*, National Film Board of Canada, 1976. Francis Welch (director) and Peter York (writer), *The Rise and Fall of the Ad Man* (UK: BBC Bristol, 2008). Pablo Larraín (director), *No* (Chile: Fabula, 2012).

69 H.C. Potter, director, based on the 1946 novel of the same name by Eric Hodgins.

70 Frederic Wakeman, *The Hucksters* (New York and Toronto: Rinehart & Company, 1946), and Rosser Reeves, *Reality in Advertising* (New York: Alfred A. Knopf, 1970).

71 James Webb Young, *The Diary of an Adman: The War Years June 1, 1942– December 31, 1943* (Chicago: Advertising Publications Inc., 1944); Eric Hodgins, *Blandings' Way* (New York: Simon and Schuster, 1950); and David Ogilvy, *Confessions of an Advertising Man* (New York: Dell, 1963).

72 James Webb Young, *A Technique for Producing Ideas* (New York: McGraw-Hill, 2003). The edition was based on an earlier work appearing in 1965 and published in McGraw-Hill's series of "advertising classics." I used a Kindle edition.

73 Alex Osborn, *Unlocking Your Creative Power: How to Use Your Imagination to Brighten Life, to Get Ahead* (New York: Hamilton Books, 2009), 120. This was a revised and abridged version of the original book.

74 See his biography in the institute's house organ, *The Journal of Creative Behavior* (18 February 2004): 70–2.

75 There were claims that the dyad was pioneered earlier, in the 1930s, by others: see Jay Chiat, "Depression Era Advertising: In the Face of Economic Devastation," in Meyer, ed., *Mad Ave.* But the accepted view credited Bernbach.

76 George Lois, "The Sixties: Madison Avenue's Creative Revolution" in Meyer, ed., *Mad Ave.*

77 Nina DiSesa, *Seducing the Boys Club: Uncensored Tactics from a Woman at the Top* (New York: Ballantine Books, 2008), Kindle Edition, 25.

78 There were, of course, variations on this model. William O'Barr presumed the creative team was really a foursome: the copywriter and the art director, but also the account manager, representing the client, and the account planner, the specialist on the consumer and the audience. William M. O'Barr, "Creativity in Advertising," *Advertising and Society Review* 11.4 (2011), online, muse.jhu.edu/issue/21795.

79 Michael J. Arlen, *Thirty Seconds* (New York: Penguin Books, 1980).

80 Brian Moeran, "The Organization of Creativity in Japanese Advertising Production," *Human Relations* 62.7 (2009): 963–85.

81 Matt Seidel, "Gone in Thirty Seconds: On Michael J. Arlen's Advertising Drama," *The Millions* (online literary magazine), 2 February 2015, themillions.com/2015/02/gone-in-thirty-seconds-on-michael-j-arlens-advertising-drama.html, accessed March 2015. Obviously a retrospective review.

82 Sean Nixon, *Advertising Cultures: Gender, Commerce, Creativity* (London: Sage, 2003); Charlotte McLeod, Stephanie O'Donohoe, and Barbara Townley, "Pot Noodles, Placements and Peer Regard: Creative Career Trajectories and Communities of Practice in the British Advertising Industry," *British Journal of Management* 22 (2011): 114–31; Karen Malia, "Rare Birds: Why So Few Women Become Ad Agency Creative Directors," *Advertising & Society Review* 10.3 (2009), muse.jhu.edu/issue/16993; Jean Grow, David Roca, and Sheri J. Broyles, "Vanishing Acts: Creative Women in Spain and the United States," *International Journal of Advertising* 31.3 (January 2012): 657–79.

83 Nina DiSesa, *Seducing the Boys Club*, 53.

84 In addition to previous sources, see also Sheri J. Broyles and Jean M. Grow, "Creative Women in Advertising Agencies: Why So Few 'Babes in Boyland'?" *Journal of Consumer Marketing* 25.1 (January 2008): 4–6, and Michele Rene

Gregory, "Inside the Locker Room: Male Homosociability in the Advertising Industry," *Gender, Work and Organization* 16.3 (May 2009): 323–47.

85 See, for example, Chris Hackley and Arthur J. Kover, "The Trouble with Creatives: Negotiating Creative Identity in Advertising Agencies," *International Journal of Advertising* 26.1 (February 2007): 63–78.

86 Rothenberg devoted one chapter to the filming of a particular commercial; see *Where the Suckers Moon*, 235–54. He did observe, however, that ad-making was an agency's medium, presumably giving auteur significance to the creatives.

87 Nixon, *Advertising Cultures*, 77.

88 The quotations are from Ebert's review, dated 11 April 1990, at rogertebert.com, accessed 18 February 2016.

89 *New York Times*, 11 April 1990.

90 For a discussion of these and other works of fiction, see William M. O'Barr, "High Culture/Low Culture: Advertising in Literature, Art, Film, and Popular Culture," *Advertising & Society Review* 7.1 (September 2006), at muse.jhu.edu/journals/asr/v007/7.1unit04.html, accessed 10 April 2010.

91 Christopher Campbell, "Don Draper Has Nothing on the Late-'60s Mad Men of 'Putney Swope,'" 10 July 2014, at filmschoolrejects.com/features/putney-swope-at-45.php, accessed 23 August 2014.

92 This bare outline, however, leaves the false impression that the movie boasted a coherent storyline. It also masks much of the comedy and excess. Actually, the story was more a loose frame for a wealth of jokes and gags, most especially towards the end, where the cynical message got lost. Now some of the weird characters, such as the "A-rab," were both well-chosen and funny. The fake commercials were effective satires of that lesser art. But all too many other comedy sketches seemed a bit forced or overly long and merely gratuitous, adding little to the plot. Too often Downey tried to excite interest with some usually crude sexual innuendo. Furthermore, the movie was full of bits of racism, misogyny, and vulgarity that often detracted from the satire. Was it really necessary to have a Nazi type declare, with a giggle, "Throw another Jew on the fire"? Or to present the president and his wife as corrupt circus dwarves, dominated by that same Nazi? "Visual graffiti of this order don't [*sic*] merit public exposure," asserted one acerbic contemporary critic (David Wilson, "Putney Swope," *Monthly Film Bulletin* [1 January 1970], 247).

93 On the decay of mass society theory and its stories see, for example, Andrew Ross, *No Respect: Intellectuals & Popular Culture* (New York and London, 1989) and Thomas Frank, *The Conquest of Cool: Business Culture, Counterculture, and the Rise of Hip Consumerism* (Chicago and London: University of Chicago Press, 1997).

94 Michael Schudson, *Advertising, the Uneasy Persuasion: Its Dubious Impact on American Society* (New York: Basic Books, 1984), 209–33. Schudson's description is much more elaborate than Dee's summary. It was soon widely accepted in scholarly circles as an excellent analysis of the nature of American advertising. By the way, it also turned up in Varnedoe and Gopnik's *High & Low*, 305. The interpretation is open to criticism because it can seem too reductionist if you actually view, say, a selection of the annual Clios or Cannes award-winning commercials, where there is so much variety in style, tone, character, intensity, and focus. But it remains a useful description of at least some of the television advertising in the mid- and late twentieth century. Schudson's superb book dealt with much more than this issue. In particular he questioned whether advertising had much cultural power. *Advertising, the Uneasy Persuasion* remains a classic in the field of advertising studies.

95 See Rutherford, *The New Icons?*, for a historical discussion of the character of award-winning commercials from around the world.

96 The page references in this section are to Jonathan Dee, *Palladio: A Novel* (New York: Vintage Books, 2002).

97 The reviewer of the *New York Times*, for example, considered the novel "a good failure. Better a large, messy, brainy novel that doesn't entirely succeed than a sterile, perfectly cohesive bit of nothing." Claire Dederer, "Art for Marketing's Sake," *New York Times*, 13 January 2002. For other views, see James Marcus in *The Atlantic Monthly*, 12 February 2002; Joy Press, "A Hard Sell," *Village Voice*, 29 January 2002; Richard W. Strachan's blog richardwstrachan.com/2011/03/04/book-review-palladio-by-jonathan-dee/, accessed 25 October 2015; or Francesca Mari, "The Plot Against Irony: On Jonathan Dee," *Idiom*, 2 July 2011, at idiommag. com/2011, accessed 25 October 2015. The novel was rereleased in 2011.

98 At least some of these were recognizable, drawn from real life, though none were footnoted.

99 Page references in the text are to the 2003 First Vintage Contemporaries Edition of *Palladio*.

100 Philip Roth wrote a bestselling novel, *Everyman* (New York: Vintage Books, 2006), where the elusive goal of art that so attracted the adman also proved in practice an impossible dream. His protagonist was a retired art director who had become an adman to ensure a good living but had always dreamed of painting, apparently like "thousands and thousands of other art directors working in ad agencies" (102). But what he discovered when he could devote himself to art was that he had nothing worthwhile to say. "It was as though painting had been an exorcism. But designed to expel what malignancy? The oldest of his self-delusions. Or had he run to painting to

attempt to deliver himself from the knowledge that you are born to live and you die instead? Suddenly he was lost in nothing" (103). Roth's novel was not really about advertising or the adman, as it was focused on the troubles, the sense of loss, and the regrets of old age of a once-successful man. But the story also seems to reflect on the adman's dilemma, as it spoke to the hollowing out of the self of a man who for too long had laboured in the field of advertising, something which had stunted his soul.

101 Robin Clifford at www.reelingreviews.com/thankyouforsmoking.htm, accessed 29 February 2016.

102 Internet Movie Database estimated the budget at $6.5 million, and the box office in the USA at nearly $25 million. Accessed 2 March 2016.

103 Witness this comment: "Intent on avoiding anything like an actual point of view, *Thank You for Smoking* instead opts for an air of condescending, holier-than-thou snarkiness, looking down with equal disdain at every one of its soulless, avaricious characters." *Slant Magazine*, 23 February 2006.

104 Lexi Feinberg at www.cinemablend.com/reviews/, accessed 29 February 2016.

105 The authors tell the story that a public relations practitioner actually proposed the title "Smoking Is Good for You," which they rejected because it was too close to that of Christopher Buckley's novel. John C. Stauber and Sheldon Rampton, *Toxic Sludge Is Good for You: Lies, Damn Lies, and the Public Relations Industry* (Monroe, ME: Common Courage Press, 1995).

106 Peter Bradshaw in *The Guardian*, 13 October 2012.

107 Jeremy Kay, "Morgan Spurlock for Sale. Buy, Buy, Buy," *The Guardian*, 24 January 2011.

108 See David Carr, "Financing the Hand That Slaps (or Nibbles) You," *New York Times*, 15 April 2011.

109 Jesse Cataldo in *Slant Magazine*, 17 April 2011.

110 Hence this comment: "It's an amusing, shallow film with some serious contributions from the likes of Noam Chomsky, Ralph Nader and various academic students of advertising and opinion making, but it is short on historical perspective and he doesn't consider the Pentagon's placement of soldiers and military hardware over the years." Philip French in *The Guardian*, 15 October 2011.

111 Cited at www.boxofficemojo.com/movies/?id=greatestmovieeversold.htm, accessed 3 March 2016.

112 Regarding the critics, respectively Paul Moore, see blog.spout. com/2009/01/20/art-and-copy-review-sundance-2009/, accessed 21 February 2009; Walter Addiego, San Francisco *Chronicle*, 13 November 2009; Moren at about.com, accessed 21 October 2009; Rabin at avclub. com, accessed 1 October 2014; and Paul Moore, ibid.

6 A Tyranny of Signs

1 Randall Rothenberg, *Where the Suckers Moon*, 42.

2 Joshua Ferris, *Then We Came to the End: A Novel* (New York: Little, Brown and Company, 2007), Kindle Edition, 234. This brag came from the narrator of the novel, an anonymous ad-maker, who was enjoying a moment of hubris.

3 The documentary was produced and directed by Rhonda Schwartz and hosted by Deborah Norville. Both Schwartz and Norville received writing credits.

4 That was in 1995, well before the web had become so important. Donald McCloskey and Arjo Klamer, "One Quarter of GDP Is Persuasion," *The American Economic Review* 85.2 (May 1995): 191–5. A number of studies have probed the increasing significance of marketing in America and other affluent countries, especially since 2000. See Gilles Marion, "Marketing Ideology and Criticism: Legitimacy and Legitimization," *Marketing Theory* 6.2, 2006: 245–62; Adam Arvidsson, *Brands: Meaning and Value in Media Culture* (London and New York: Routledge, 2006); Per Skålén, Mark Fellesson, and Martin Fougère, *Marketing Discourse: A Critical Perspective* (London: Routledge, 2008); the essays in Mats Alvesson and Hugh Willmott, eds., *Studying Management Critically* (London: Sage, 2003) as well as Detlev Zwick and Julien Cayla, eds., *Inside Marketing: Practices, Ideologies, Devices*, published at Oxford Scholarship Online: May 2011, www.oxfordscholarship.com. Many of these works employ notions of power drawn from both Marx and Foucault, including his conception of biopolitics. The result can sometimes seem confusing or outlandish (thus Arvidsson labels brands "immaterial" and Skålén et al. muddle Foucault's concepts of biopower and pastoral power), but these critical marketing studies, as they are sometimes called, are also both imaginative and provocative.

5 The general significance of emotion would soon be emphasized by the publication and acclaim of Antonio Damasio's *Descartes' Error* in 1994. In the next decade, the academic Robert Heath would apply such notions particularly to advertising: see Robert Heath, *Seducing the Subconscious: The Psychology of Emotional Influence in Advertising* (Chichester, UK: Wiley-Blackwell, 2012).

6 One newspaper critic was not at all amused: Howard Rosenberg of the *Los Angeles Times* (32 July 1990) decided the self-styled news special was really an extended commercial for Deborah Norville. Norville had recently arrived as co-host of NBC's *Today*, which was slumping in the ratings. Rosenberg also took the opportunity to slam NBC for its shoddy advertising practices.

7 *Forbes*, 14 September 2016.

8 Tim Wu, *The Attention Merchants: The Epic Scramble to Get Inside Our Heads* (New York: Alfred A. Knopf, 2016).

9 Put another way, precious few public or private species were free of advertising, so that much time was now colonized by marketing. That was the reason Wu advocated, as one reviewer noted, "a kind of zoning that declares certain times and spaces off-limits to commercial messages" to protect "our mental space." (Jacob Weisberg, "They've Got You, Wherever You Are," *New York Review of Books*, 27 October 2016, 16.) Wu even detected signs of a user revolt, as evidenced by the increasing recourse to ad-blockers to defeat sponsored media on the web. All of which sounded much like the lament, the recommendations, and the hopes of generations of critics of the adman and his messages.

10 Mara Einstein, *Black Ops Advertising: Native Ads, Content Marketing, and the Covert World of the Digital Sell* (New York and London: O/R Books, 2016). Aside from an excessive title and a wildly alarmist final chapter, Einstein's book was a closely reasoned and carefully substantiated exploration of stealth marketing. Missing, though, was much data on how people actually felt about the ad swarm, apparently because researchers had not yet collected such information.

11 The world of marketing's moment, however, can be read a different way. Terry O'Reilly and Mike Tennant, two veteran admen from Canada, have produced a marvellous collection of anecdotes of success and failure about advertising and promotion over the years and around the world, though especially in the past forty years or so and particularly in America: see *The Age of Persuasion: How Marketing Ate Our Culture* (Toronto: Vintage Canada, 2011). Previously these admen had created a popular radio series (of the same title) for the Canadian Broadcasting Corporation, the country's public broadcaster. They were "insiders," not "renegades," to use my book's terminology. They, too, recognized the ad clutter, calling advertising "the most conspicuous, ubiquitous force in modern culture" (xii). Yet, though critical of aspects of advertising, their account is full of stories of the wonder and humour of a world fashioned by ad-makers, marketers, and their promotions – billboards, reason-why campaigns, viral advertising, guerilla marketing, sensory advertising, parody ads, ad lingo, the YouTube scene, and so on. As one of the book's blurbs declared, it was both "entertaining and enlightening," and much more positive than Miller's comment or Wu's worries.

12 A survey of meanings available on the internet and carried out in November 2015 revealed a range of variations: "To 'wag the dog' means to purposely divert attention from what would otherwise be of greater importance, to something else of lesser significance" [usingenglish.com];

"When something of secondary importance improperly takes on the role of something of primary importance" [urbandictionary.com]; or "The less important or subsidiary factor, person, or thing dominates a situation; the usual roles are reversed: the financing system is becoming the tail that wags the dog" [oxforddictionaries.com].

13 The amounts were taken from the Internet Movie Database on 13 November 2015.

14 Ebert's review was accessed in November 2015 at rogerebert.com.

15 This paragraph rests on material in "The Line Between Truth and Fiction" and "From Washington to Hollywood and Back" on the New Line Entertainment DVD of *Wag the Dog;* Tom Stempel, "The Collaborative Dog: *Wag the Dog* (1997)," *Film & History: An Interdisciplinary Journal of Film and Television Studies* 35.1 (Fall 2005): 60–4; and Eleftheria Thanouli, *Wag the Dog: A Study on Film and Reality in the Digital Age* (New York and London: Bloomsbury, 2013).

16 Cited in "Wag the Dog: About The Production," at filmscouts.com, accessed 9 November 2015.

17 Ibid.

18 The Myers comment was on the documentary "From Washington to Hollywood and Back."

19 Notably "The Precession of Simulacra" (1981) and other essays in Jean Baudrillard, *Simulacra and Simulation*, trans. Sheila Faria Glaser (Ann Arbor: University of Michigan Press, 1994).

20 Thanouli put forward in her analysis of the movie the argument about autopoiesis, linking this to the work of Niklas Luhmann and adding some reflections on how the movie also suited the ideas of Actor-Network Theory elaborated by Bruno Latour. Thanouli, *Wag the Dog*, 123–4.

21 Kalle Lasn, one of the founders, eventually produced a mix of memoir, polemic, and manifesto entitled *Culture Jam: The Uncooling of America* (New York: William Morrow, 1999).

22 "As an exposé about large-scale advertising, it takes its place next to such works as Stuart Chase's *Tragedy of Waste* (1929), Vance Packard's *The Hidden Persuaders* (1957), and more recently Juliet Schor's *Born to Buy* (2004)." Matthew P. McCallister, "*No Logo* Legacy," *Women's Studies Quarterly* 38.3–4 (Fall/Winter 2010): 287.

23 Naomi Klein's website (July 2015) mentions over a million copies in print, and translation into twenty-five languages. There is also the claim that *Time* called the book one of the one hundred most important non-fiction works published since 1923. The essays were entitled *Fences & Windows*. The documentary bore the title *No Logo*, though with the subtitle "Brands,

Globalization and Resistance," and was sponsored by the Media Education Foundation, a Left group headed by Sut Jhally. One of the most revealing interviews she gave was to the filmmakers of *The Persuaders* (2004), a PBS documentary on advertising and marketing: this interview was published on the show's website.

24 I use the Canadian edition, *No Logo: Taking Aim at the Brand Bullies* (Toronto: Alfred A. Knopf Canada, 2000).

25 The phrase actually refers to a shift in the humanities and social sciences back in the 1970s to centre the role of culture in the scholarly conversation. The phrase was applied to capitalism not by Klein but by Adam Arvidsson in *Brands*, 51ff.

26 Juliet Schor, "Combatting Consumerism and Capitalism: A Decade of *No Logo*," *Women's Studies Quarterly* 38.3–4 (Fall/Winter 2010): 299–30.

27 The interview occurred in the course of the PBS documentary *The Persuaders* (2004).

28 See the excerpt published in *The Guardian* on 16 January 2010.

29 Mayer was especially concerned that monies once funneled into advertising were going into other kinds of marketing. Martin Mayer, *Whatever Happened to Madison Avenue? Advertising in the '90s* (Boston, Toronto, London: Little, Brown, 1991). This book was not nearly so successful as its predecessor. In fact the growing importance of finance in the affairs of business as well as the further sophistication of public relations did mean that the adman was no longer deemed so crucial to the success of many companies, as in times past.

30 See the online chart at www.galbithink.org/ad-spending.htm. Note that the rate of growth and the index soon fell back in the new millennium: the index was only 2.0 per cent of GDP in 2007. These figures reflect a particular table of the history of the total ad spend in the United States between 1919 and 2007. This table was based on an earlier collection of figures long ago assembled by Robert J. Coen of McCann-Erickson and more recently compiled by Dr Douglas A. Galbi of the Federal Communications Commission. (See the discussion in Mercedes Esteban-Bravo, José M. Vidal-Sanz, and Gökhan Yildirim, "Expenditure Trends in US Advertising: Long-Term Effects and Structural Changes with New Media Introductions," Working Paper 15, Business Economic Series 06, June 2012 (corrected July 2013) Universidad Carlos III de Madrid.)

31 In fact there was a misprint in the text, "Rothberg" appearing instead of Rothenberg. The reference was to his book *Where the Suckers Moon: An Advertising Story* (New York: Alfred A. Knopf, 1994). There Rothenberg had explored in depth the campaign created by Wieden & Kennedy to rejuvenate the Subaru car company.

32 *The Guardian*, 16 January 2010.

33 Russell Belk, "The Naomi Klein Brand," *Women's Studies Quarterly* 38.3–4 (Fall/Winter 2010): 293–8.

34 *The Guardian*, 16 January 2010.

35 In the book Klein was actually talking about the people's situation post-9/11. "Without a story, we are, as many of us were after September 11, intensely vulnerable to those people who are ready to take advantage of the chaos for their own ends. As soon as we have a new narrative that offers a perspective on the shocking events, we become re-oriented and the world begins to make sense once again." *The Shock Doctrine: The Rise of Disaster Capitalism* (New York: Metropolitan Books/Henry Holt, 2008).

36 *The Rebel Sell: Why the Culture Can't Be Jammed* (Toronto: Harper Perennial, 2005), paperback edition with a new afterword, 346.

37 Respectively, Kim Sawchuk, *Canadian Journal of Communications* 25.4 (2000); Paul S. Segerstrom, "Naomi Klein and the Anti-Globalization Movement," Stockholm School of Economics, 2010; James Ledbetter "Brand Names," *New York Times*, 23 April 2000; Walden Bello, *Yes Magazine*, 30 September 2001; anonymous, davostoseattle.wordpress.com, 13 July 2008; Chris Willmore, May 2000, The Keep.org; Juliet Schor, "Combatting Consumerism and Capitalism: A Decade of *No Logo*," *Women's Studies Quarterly* 38.3–4 (Fall/Winter 2010) 299–301.

38 See in particular William Leach, *Land of Desire: Merchants, Power and the Rise of a New American Culture* (New York: Vintage Books, 1993).

39 See Richard Ohmann, *Selling Culture: Magazines, Markets, and Class at the Turn of the Century* (London and New York: Verso, 1996) on the ways advertising nourished brands before and after 1900.

40 Jackson Lears, *Fables of Abundance: A Cultural History of Advertising in America* (New York: Basic Books, 1994) and Thomas Frank, *The Conquest of Cool: Business Culture, Counterculture, and the Rise of Hip Consumerism* (Chicago and London: University of Chicago Press, 1997).

41 Roland Marchand, *Advertising the American Dream: Making Way for Modernity, 1920–1940* (Berkeley and London: University of California Press, 1985) and *Creating the Corporate Soul: The Rise of Public Relations and Corporate Imagery in American Big Business* (Berkeley and London: University of California Press, 1998).

42 Thus Stuart Ewen, *All Consuming Images: The Politics of Style in Contemporary Culture* (New York: Basic Books, 1988) and Rutherford, *The New Icons?*

43 He argued this not in his own publication but in what was ostensibly a review of *Fences & Windows* published in *Prospect Magazine* (February 2003).

44 Respectively, bar two, Osbourne in Jonathan Dee's *Palladio* (2002), Lacouture the head of a coolhunting/trendsetting company in Alex

Shakar's *The Savage Girl* (2001), and Gardner the super-villain in John Beck's potboiler *The Overton Window* (2010); Marshall in Nancy Meyer, *What Women Want* (2000) and Nayler in Jason Reitman, *Thank You for Smoking* (2006). Rapaille, an unusual market researcher, appeared in Rachel Dretzin and Barak Goodman, *The Persuaders* (2004); Bernays was the star villain in Adam Curtis, *The Century of the Self* (2002), a widely known BBC production; the two Republican consultants were the subjects of biographical documentaries: Stefan Forbes, *Boogie Man: The Lee Atwater Story* (2008) and Michael Kirk, *Karl Rove: The Architect* (2005); the progressive Carville and his firm of Greenberg Carville Schrum were the key agents in Rachel Boynton's *Our Brand Is Crisis* (2006), about the fixing of the presidential campaign in Bolivia in 2002, much later the basis of a not very successful 2015 movie of the same name.

45 For example, Tim Padgett, "What's Next After That Odd Chicken?" 3 October 2004, www.time.com, accessed 27 February 2011; Danielle Sacks, "Can Alex Bogusky Help Microsoft Beat Apple?" 9 May 2008, www. fastcompany.com, accessed 27 February 2011; Danielle Sacks, "Alex Bogusky Tells All: He Left the World's Hottest Agency to Find His Soul," 1 September 2010, www.fastcompany.com/1676890/alex-bogusky-tells-all-he-left-worlds-hottest-agency-find-his-soul, accessed 27 February 2011; Simon Houpt, "A Former Rock Star of the Ad World Explains Why He Doesn't Watch Commercials," *Toronto Globe and Mail*, 4 March 2011; Avi Dan, "Alex Bogusky, on the Next 510 Years in Advertising," 11 November 2012, Forbes/ CMO Network, accessed 3 December 2015.

46 *Pattern Recognition* (New York: Berkley Books, 2003); *Spook Country* (New York: Berkley Books, 2007); and *Zero History* (New York: G.P. Putnam's Sons, 2010). These books are abbreviated in the text, respectively, as PR, SC, and ZH.

47 For example, Lisa Zeidner in the *New York Times* (19 January 2003) said the hero's travels around the globe gave *Pattern Recognition* "its exultant, James Bond-ish edge."

48 On the signals of postmodernity, utopia, and dystopia, see Fredric Jamieson, *Archeologies of the Future: The Desire Called Utopia and Other Science Fictions* (London and New York: Verso, 2005), especially 384–92; Tom Henthorne, *William Gibson: A Literary Companion* (McFarland, 2011); Janine Tobeck, "The Man in the Klein Blue Suit: Searching for Agency in William Gibson's Bigend Trilogy," in *Blast, Corrupt, Dismantle, Erase: Contemporary North American Dystopian Literature*, ed. Brett Josef Grubisic, Gisèle M. Baxter, and Tara Lee (Waterloo: Wilfrid Laurier University Press, 2014); Esko Suoranta, "Agents or Pawns? Power Relations in William Gibson's Bigend Trilogy," *Fafnir – Nordic Journal of Science Fiction and Fantasy Research* 1.1 (2014): 19–30.

Regarding Gibson's dissent, see the interview by David Wallace-Wells in *The Paris Review* (2011) at www.theparisreview.org/interviews/6089/william-gibson-the-art-of-fiction-no-211-william-gibson, accessed 30 November 2015.

49 James Urquhart in the *Financial Times* (FT.com), 29 July 2011.

50 So Gibson asserted in an interview with Vice: "William Gibson," 3 September 2010, by Jesse Pearson, www.vice.com/read/william-gibson.

51 Tobeck argued Bigend appears both "supernatural" and "mundane" in the stories – it is in the first persona that he becomes an "advertising deity." Tobeck, "The Man in the Klein Blue Suit."

52 Alex Link, "Global War, Global Capital, and the Work of Art in William Gibson's Pattern Recognition," *Contemporary Literature* 49.2 (Summer 2008): 213. Tom Cruise had played the vampire Lestat in the movie version of Anne Rice's novel *Interview with the Vampire* (1994).

53 In one interview Gibson suggested that Bigend was himself a victim of self-deception: "I've always had a sense of Bigend as someone who presents himself as though he knows what's going on, but who in fact doesn't. It's just my sense of the subtext of the character: he's bullshitting himself, at the same time as he's bullshitting all of us. He's not sure: he thinks that possibly it works the way he says it works. I think that when he's feeling good, he doesn't care. He just needs to say something that sounds Bigendish." "Maximus Clarke Talks with William Gibson about His 'Speculative Novels of Last Wednesday,'" 22 September 2010, at maudnewton.com/blog, accessed 29 November 2015.

54 There is an excellent exploration of the Svengali stereotype in Daniel Pick, *Svengali's Web: The Alien Enchanter in Modern Culture* (New Haven, CT: Yale University Press, 2000).

55 This attribute has been noticed by others. See Christopher Turner's mention of Dichter's "Svengali-like techniques" in a general discussion of Freud, psychoanalysis, and advertising: "The Hidden Persuader: Ernest Dichter, the 'Freud of Madison Avenue,'" *Cabinet Magazine* 44 (Winter 2011/12), online at http://daily-struggles.tumblr.com/post/72163030562/the-hidden-persuader-by-christopher-turner, accessed 6 December 2015. On Dichter, see Lawrence Samuel, *Freud on Madison Avenue: Motivation Research and Subliminal Advertising in America* (Philadelphia and Oxford: University of Pennsylvania, 2010). On mass media and the fear of mass hypnosis at and after mid-century, see Charles Acland, *Swift Viewing: The Popular Life of Subliminal Influence* (Durham and London: Duke University Press, 2012).

56 "Rove was particularly wary of the media because they frequently caricatured him as the Svengali of the White House, a diabolical genius who pulled the strings of a puppet president." Bill Sammon, "Rove Regards

Svengali Reputation as Politically Convenient Myth," *Washington Examiner*, 14 August 2007.

57 As part of that same documentary, however, Bob Garfield, a longtime columnist at *Advertising Age*, specifically denounced the Svengali myth. Here he conformed to the standard practice of industry apologists. In the interview, he said: "There's this idea that advertising people and marketers are these Svengalis who not only know everything about us but can manipulate us to act out their will. Well, they can't. They've never been able to. They're no better at it now than they ever were before. It's really, really hard to make anybody buy anything." The interview was at www.pbs.org/wgbh/pages/frontline/shows/persuaders/interviews/garfield.html, accessed 6 December 2015.

58 This line of argument was also evident in the earlier work of Stuart Ewen, *PR!: A Social History of Spin* (New York: Basic Books, 1996). In a review of Ewen's work, Mark Dery described Bernays as "a larger-than-life Svengali": "The Hidden Persuaders," *Salon*, 11 November 1996.

59 Other critics have noted how Bigend is not quite a villain. See Tom Henthorne, *William Gibson: A Literary Companion* (Jefferson, NC: McFarland, 2011), 25. Also Tobeck, "The Man in the Klein Blue Suit."

60 Christian DuChateau, "Sci-fi Prophet Wraps High-tech Trilogy," CNN, 31 July 2011.

61 Douglas Gorney, "William Gibson and the Future of the Future," *Atlantic*, 14 September 2010. Gibson added: "The closest thing that might ever have existed, however briefly, was when [Sex Pistols manager] Malcolm McLaren was hired by the Polish government to "rebrand Poland." I think the very idea of that having happened was part of the original inspiration for Bigend."

62 For instance, this comment from Sorrell cited in *Adweek*, 25 March 2016: "The definition of creativity needs to change. We're not in the advertising business anymore."

63 See, for example, his comments in Deborah Bothun and Daniel Gross, "Thought Leader Interview: Sir Martin Sorrell," in *Strategy & Business* Special Report, Global Entertainment and Media Outlook 2016–2020: A World of Differences, www.strategy-business.com/outlook, accessed 4 August 2016.

64 Hence these thoughts about Hilfiger from Pollard: "This stuff is simulacra of simulacra of simulacra. A diluted tincture of Ralph Lauren, who had himself diluted the glory days of Brooks Brothers, who themselves had stepped on the product of Jermyn Street and Savile Row, flavoring their ready-to-wear with liberal lashings of polo kit and regimental stripes. But Tommy is the null point, the black hole" (PC 17).

65 The concepts of contagion and immunity are derived from a reading of
    works on biopolitics, in particular those of Roberto Esposito: *Bíos: Biopolitics
    and Philosophy* and *Immunitas: The Protection and Negation of Life.*

    As an aside, there has been a much more favourable view of contagion,
    although not so styled, in Malcolm Gladwell's well-known book *The Tipping
    Point: How Little Things Can Make a Big Difference* (New York and Boston:
    Black Bay Books, 2001). There, for example, he described how the Lambe-
    sis agency fashioned a campaign that boomed Airwalk shoes. "Lambesis, in
    other words, was piggy-backing on social epidemics, associating Airwalk with
    each new trend wave that swept through youth culture" (211). "They took
    the cultural cues from the Innovators – cues that the mainstream kids may
    have seen but not been able to make sense of – and leveled, sharpened, and
    assimilated them into a more coherent form. They gave these cues a specific
    meaning that they did not have previously and packaged that new sensibil-
    ity in the form of a pair of shoes" (213). What was missing from *The Tipping
    Point* was any sense of the need for immunity. Instead Gladwell wrote about
    the importance of imitation, which seemed, in his view of life in a world of
    brands, a virtue.

66 The website was www.pbs.org/wgbh/pages/frontline/shows/persuaders,
    accessed 7 December 2015.

67 The responses were accessed on 16 March 2009.

68 Dretzin and Rushkoff would collaborate later to make another *Frontline*
    documentary entitled *Digital Nation* (2010), but that one did not delve into
    advertising. Rushkoff, however, returned to the concerns of *The Merchants
    of Cool* (2001) when, with another filmmaker, he fashioned *Generation Like*
    (2014), also for *Frontline*. Rushkoff was the author of books on the media,
    communications, and culture.

69 "Consumers are like roaches. You spray them and spray them, and after a
    while, it doesn't work anymore. We develop immunities."

70 "They [the public] said it again and again: 'Be clear with us. Be straight
    with us. Common sense; clarity; down the road, look us straight in the eye.'
    That's exactly what I do. I help them do that."

71 Where possible I include the name of the correspondent in quotation marks.
    I have also edited the quotations to remove errors in spelling or grammar.

72 Thus this comment from "Steve Schachter": "Choice is Freedom. I contend
    that America is a better place because of these choices and one small
    price we pay for these freedoms is to enable marketers who ultimately are
    a source for our continued increase in the American standard of living
    to convey their messages in the most effective and efficient manners they
    choose."

73 For example, "Lyle Schemer," a copywriter, asserted, "Thing is, Rushkoff portrayed advertising as far more nefarious and powerful than it actually is. John Philip Jones, an aging ad luminary, used to comment on how weak, indeed, advertising is as a force. He'd say, 'Can you remember the last 5 ads you saw?'"

74 This anonymous individual expressed his views in the "producer's chat," where he wondered whether his ambivalence was widespread. Dretzin thought it was.

75 Michael Pettit, *The Science of Deception*, 8.

76 William M. O'Barr, "The Advertising Profession in the Public's Eye," *Advertising & Society Review* 7.1 (September 2006), at muse.jhu.edu/journals/advertising_and_society_review/v007/7.1unit05.html. O'Barr had written and taught on advertising.

77 Specifically, advertising practitioners rated 11 per cent (very high/high), 50 per cent (average), and 35 per cent (low/very low) on the scale. At the top were members of the medical professions.

78 The one significant specialty missing was art director.

79 Augusten Burroughs, *Dry* (New York: St Martin's Press, 2003), Kindle Edition. Burroughs made clear that this memoir was not wholly a work of fact: "This memoir is based on my experiences over a ten-year period. Names have been changed, characters combined, and events compressed. Certain episodes are imaginative re-creation, and those episodes are not intended to portray actual events." Furthermore, in an interview appearing in *Salon* (8 July 2003), Burroughs claimed it began life as a rehab exercise, only later taking on the shape of a memoir, eventually listed as no. 2 in what had become a trilogy of memoirs. See also Julia Felsenthal, "Augusten Burroughs on Writing Memoir and Falling in Love with His Agent," *Vogue* (30 March 2016).

80 Richard Kirshenbaum, *Madboy. Beyond Mad Men: Tales from the Mad, Mad World of Advertising* (New York: Open Road Integrated Media, 2011). The agency had been sold to the MDC partners network, becoming Kirshenbaum Bond Senecal + Partners or kbs+p, in 2009. Kirshenbaum stayed on for a time but moved on to new enterprises and won some fame as a writer.

81 But there were important exceptions: the stars of the industry. The documentary *The Persuaders* clearly positioned Andy Spade (of the airline Song fame) and Clotaire Rapaille (the market researcher) as wizards deemed such by their eager sponsors.

82 The declining significance of Madison Avenue, for example, was one of the themes in Al Ries and Laura Ries, *The Fall of Advertising & the Rise of PR* (New York: HarperCollins, 2004). The authors, and Al Ries was a noted marketing expert and bestselling writer, were rivals of the adman, with their own marketing and consulting enterprise.

83 *Adweek*, 9 June 2003. The distaste for clients, especially the need to kowtow
to these corporate types, was abundantly clear in his memoir, however.

84 Likewise the comment by O'Reilly and Tennant (who wrote as one author):
"I doubt that any discipline this side of national politics is subject to more
rigorous checks and balances than advertising – not by governments or
industry regulators (who tend to constrict the honest brokers and leave
loopholes for transgressors) but by the advertiser's competition. Rival
brands watch one another constantly – as Heinz watched Campbell's –
tracking their opponents' every move and ready to pounce on anyone
foolish enough to cut corners or make a false claim." *The Age of Persuasion*,
265. They even republished, with approval, a "manifesto" of sorts produced
by Bob Levenson (of Doyle Dane Bernbach) in the late 1960s for a *Time*
contest where agencies designed "an ad in the public interest" (272). In
that manifesto stood this maxim: "And above all, the messages we put on
those pages and on those television screens must be the truth. For if we play
tricks with the truth, we die" (273).

85 I have dealt with the history of this kind of advertising in *Endless Propaganda:
The Advertising of Public Goods* (Toronto: University of Toronto Press, 2000).

86 Minette E. Drumwright and Patrick E. Murphy, "How Advertising
Practitioners View Ethics: Moral Muteness, Moral Myopia, and Moral
Imagination," *Journal of Advertising* 33.2 (Summer 2004): 7–24.

87 Ibid., 7. But some of the respondents did demonstrate what the authors
called a "moral imagination," a readiness to see and talk about ethical
concerns. It was not clear how many were so inclined, however.

Conclusion: Deception and Its Discontents

1 Dave Itzkoff, "Matthew Weiner Closes the Books on Season 4 of 'Mad Men',"
Arts Beat – *New York Times* Blog, 17 October 2010. The quotation indicated
how Weiner regarded Don Draper as a representative of the classic American
male of the twentieth century, beset with moral difficulties but determined to
move forward. This epigraph opens a series of comments which demonstrate
how Draper took on a variety of meanings important to the times, what I
have called elsewhere "marketing's moment."

2 John Elia, "Don Draper, on How to Make Oneself (Whole Again)," in Rod
Carveth and James B. South, *Mad Men and Philosophy: Nothing Is as It Seems*
(Hoboken, NJ: John Wiley & Sons, 2010), 183. Elia, an academic, went
a step further than Weiner in the previous quotation. Draper was also
representative of the human plight in modern times, cut free from the past,
always caught up in self-fashioning, and always in a state of angst.

3 Daniel Mendelsohn, "The Mad Men Account," *New York Review of Books*, 24 February 2011, 4. The writer and critic Mendelsohn here pointed out that whatever else one might say of Draper, the crucial aspect of this character was his public and private role as a deceiver.

4 Owen Gleiberman, "Mad Men: The Final Verdict," bbc.com, accessed 20 May 2015. The film critic Gleiberman added to Mendelsohn's observation by presenting Don the deceiver as a victim as well, once again making Draper a representative of everyone in an era so polluted with advertising.

5 Dave Thier, "How the Last 10 Seconds of the Mad Men Finale Saved Don Draper," forbes.com, accessed 17 May 2015. The final entry in this list of epigraphs, the comment by the freelance writer Thier, suggested not just sympathy but admiration, the respect for the person who can deceive so well. That too seemed a common response to the show's finale, to Draper himself, and occasionally to the figure of the adman.

6 Jethro Nededog, "'Mad Men' Series Finale Nabs Highest Ratings Ever," businessinsider.com, accessed 19 May 2015.

7 See "Did This Woman Predict 'Mad Men's' Ending Two Years Ago?" by *The Daily Beast*, thedailybeast.com, accessed 6 May 2015.

8 Like the series in general, "Person to Person" was about a lot more than just Don Draper. Much of the airtime was devoted to ending the stories of the other principal characters.

9 The commercial was one entry in a long-running campaign McCann-Erickson designed for Coca-Cola between 1969 and 1982. I have discussed the campaign, and briefly the commercial, in *The New Icons?*, 44–50.

10 Technically this was part 2 of season 7, entitled "The End of an Era."

11 Which was apparently Weiner's intent: see Ashley Lee, "'Mad Men' Series Finale: Matthew Weiner Explains, Character Surprises and What's Next," hollywoodreporter.com, accessed 20 May 2015.

12 See, for instance, James Poniewozik, "Review of Mad Men Series finale, 'Person to Person,'" time.com, accessed 18 May 2015, and Alan Sepinwall, "Series Finale Review: 'Mad Men' – 'Person to Person': I'd like to buy the world a Coke?," m.hitfix.com, accessed 18 May 2015.

13 Cited by Neela Debnath in "Showbiz & TV," express.co.uk, accessed 22 May 2015, though it is not clear how that conclusion was reached.

14 "Mad Men: Season Seven (2014–2015)," rottentomatoes.com, accessed 19 June 2016.

15 Dave McNary, "WGA Honors 'Big Short,' 'Spotlight,' 'Mad Men' at 68th Awards," *Variety*, 13 February 2016.

16 "Veteran Ad Exec Says 'Mad Men' Really About Sex, Booze," *USA Today*, 31 August 2009, www.usatoday.com, accessed 13 April 2010.

17 Thomas Frank, "Ad Absurdum and the Conquest of Cool: Canned Flattery for Corporate America," *Salon*, 22 December 2013, accessed 4 June 2014.

18 Della Femina was one of those featured. "AMC Presents: Ad Legends," amctv.com, accessed 14 March 2014.

19 See, for instance, Mark Greif, "You'll Love the Way It Makes You Feel," *London Review of Books* 30.20 (23 October 2008): 15–16; Benjamin Schwarz, "Mad About Mad Men," *The Atlantic*, 25 September 2009; Mendelsohn, "The *Mad Men* Account"; and James Meek, "The Shock of the Pretty," *London Review of Books* 37.7 (9 April 2015), online, accessed 11 April 2015.

20 David Marc, "Mad Men: A Roots Tale of the Information Age," in Gary R. Edgerton, ed., *Mad Men: Dream Come True TV* (London and New York: I.B. Taurus, 2011), Kindle Edition, 227.

21 From an interview in 2009, cited in ibid., KL 451.

22 Linda Kaganovsky, "'Maidenform': Masculinity as Masquerade," in Lauren M.E. Goodlad, Lilya Kaganovsky, Robert A. Rushing, eds., *Mad Men, Mad World: Sex, Politics, Style, and the 1960s* (Durham and London: Duke University Press, 2013), Kindle Edition, 238–56.

23 Helen Woodward, *It's an Art* (New York: Harcourt, Brace and Company, 1938), 22. See also her earlier memoir, Helen Woodward, *Through Many Windows* (New York and London: Harper and Brothers, 1926), 366–7. Woodward was referring here to a trade mostly made up of men.

24 Diane Harris, "Mad Space," in *Mad Men, Mad World*, 69.

25 "Don combines nuclear-age nihilism with an oddly stoic "Be Here Now" spiritualism of the coming 1960s." Jeremy Varon, "History Gets in Your Eyes: *Mad Men*, Misrecognition, and the Masculine Mystique," in *Mad Men, Mad World*, 261.

26 Thomas Frank, "Ad Absurdum and the Conquest of Cool." The cited quotation is drawn from what Draper once said.

27 Greif, "You'll Love the Way It Makes You Feel," 16.

28 Mendelsohn, "The Mad Man Account," 6, 4.

29 Schwarz, "Mad About Mad Men."

30 Meek, "The Shock of the Pretty."

31 Varon, "History Gets in Your Eyes," 262.

32 Meek, "The Shock of the Pretty."

33 Frank, "Ad Absurdum and the Conquest of Cool."

34 Varon, "History Gets in Your Eyes," 272.

35 Mendelsohn, "The Mad Men Account," 4.

36 Andreja Novakovic and Tyler Whitney, "'In on It': Honesty, Respect, and the Ethics of Advertising," in *Mad Men and Philosophy*, 118, 113. The Midge comment came from "The Hobo Code" in the first season. Supposedly

Betty's distress and fury contributed to the eventual dissolution of the marriage. The tale was part of an episode in the second season entitled "A Night to Remember."

37 David Marc, "Mad Men: A Roots Tale of the Information Age," 231.

38 Owen Gleiberman, "Mad Men: The Final Verdict," bbc.com, accessed 20 May 2015.

39 Jim Hansen, "Mod Men," in *Mad Men, Mad World*, 146.

40 Michael L. Ross, *Designing Fictions: Literature Confronts Advertising* (Montreal and Kingston: McGill-Queen's University Press, 2015), 163.

41 George Teschner and Gabrielle Teschner, "Creating the Need for the New: 'It's Not the Wheel. It's the Carousel,'" *Mad Men and Philosophy*, 128.

42 David P. Pierson, "Unleashing a Flow of Desire: Sterling Cooper, Desiring-Production, and the Tenets of Late Capitalism," in Scott F. Stoddart, ed., *Analyzing Mad Men: Critical Essays on the Television Series* (Jefferson, NC, and London: McFarland & Company, 2011), Kindle Edition.

43 One of the games critics and fans liked to play was to guess which real advertising practitioner was the proper model for Don Draper. Aaron Taube in "Meet The Real-Life Mad Men Who Inspired Don Draper," businessinsider.com, accessed 9 May 2014, found four possible candidates: Draper Daniels, Albert Lasker, Emerson Foote, and George Lois. Apparently the latter was not so convinced: he thought Draper a "talentless bum."

44 The ambivalence and the confusions surrounding the adman were hardly unique: in some ways they manifested what was deemed the serious unsettling of the modern soul. Some scholars talked of the divided soul of the moderns. "Modern individuals are faced with the paradoxical task of living against themselves and experiencing their lives in certain important ways as being 'impossible.' From the mid-19th century on, moderns have become accustomed to the claim that our experience of the world leaves us divided – whether we characterize this division as one of misrecognition (Hegel), alienation (Marx), ressentiment (Nietzsche), neurosis (Freud), or bad faith (Sartre), the division is present, is variously constitutive of individuals, and is on many accounts what impels moderns towards political and ethical responsibility." Nancy Luxon, "Ethics and Subjectivity: Practices of Self-Governance in the Late Lectures of Michel Foucault," *Political Theory* 36.3 (June 2008): 377–8.

Others imagined the tyranny of a double bind whereby the individual was much troubled, sometimes rendered impotent, sometimes inspired to innovate, by contradictory commands originating from the different sources of authority in modern society. John Grumley, "Negotiating the 'Double Bind': Heller's Theory of Modernity," *European Journal of Social Theory* 3.4 (2000): 429–47.

Let me explore the claims about this burdened individual made by one of the most prominent of the theorists of modernity, the sociologist Anthony Giddens, in his *Modernity and Self-Identity: Self and Society in the Late Modern Age* (Cambridge, UK: Polity Press, 1991). His focus was chiefly on the situation in the last decades of the twentieth century. And to be fair he took great pains to discuss female as well as male subjects, even if the masculine norm of mastery over self and others seemed to lurk beneath his account. Giddens argued that the modern person was constantly engaged in a process of self-fashioning, or what he liked to call the "reflexive project of the self." We lived in an unavoidable situation of surveillance, watched by ourselves and by others, where we monitored our own conduct and surroundings and, in turn, our behaviour was recorded by numerous institutions. We constructed a life narrative that affirmed and manifested our authenticity as a person according to a series of directives emanating from institutions, experts, our surroundings, the media, and so on. Such a biography amounted to a work of self-justification, and a way to ensure our own coherence and identity. We had agency, but we also suffered anxiety and sometimes much shame, especially when our answers to the questions "Who am I?" and "How have I lived?" rang false. Authenticity, being true to oneself: that was a recurring problem of modernity. (Some scholars argued that authenticity was a peculiarly modern invention, born in the eighteenth century.) Nothing was certain, and all around us persisted risks that we must calculate and manage to ensure our security and our progress. Little wonder that the modern self was beset by a series of predicaments, notably about coherence and over autonomy, as well as by the spectre of meaninglessness. The chapter aptly entitled "Tribulations of the Self" posits four main dilemmas of the modern self: "unification versus fragmentation," "powerlessness versus appropriation," "authority versus uncertainty," and "personalized versus commodified experience." The binary structure of modernity, and the consequent sense of paradox and contest, was stamped upon the soul of the modern self.

Perhaps it needs to be said that Giddens's treatment of the modern self is hardly the first or last word on this enormously complicated subject. See the excellent overview by Jerrold Seigel, "Problematizing the Self," in Victoria Bonnell and Lynn Hunt, eds., *Beyond the Cultural Turn: New Directions in the Study of Society and Culture* (Berkeley, Los Angeles, and London: University of California Press, 1999), 281–314.

45 The mixture of camaraderie, competition, and hierarchy in the milieu of the adman was nicely captured in a sombre comedy about office life by Joshua Ferris entitled *Then We Came to the End* (New York: Little, Brown, 2007, Kindle Edition). The novel told the story of work life at a Chicago advertising agency

in crisis around 2000. An economic downturn threatened the survival of the agency: there were fewer clients and so less billings. The story concentrated on a group of copywriters and art directors who were fearful of losing their well-paying jobs. Over the course of a year or so, one after another of these creatives was terminated because the agency needed to save money. That produced a persistent atmosphere of anxiety. The ad-makers operated in an environment structured by various specialties, different rankings and kinds of status, and strict lines of authority. One of the participants, Joe Pope, had an anomalous status, both creative and management, because he had the favour of the section's director, Lynn Mason (who was actually dying of cancer). He became the target of much suspicion, even hatred, since he seemed protected from the plight and fears of others. The creative staff did form a little community bound together by work, rumour, complaint, and desire. Much time was spent on talking, sharing stories, speculating, making jokes, having fun. They oscillated between relishing their jobs, proud of their artistry, and bored by the routine of work or upset by the problems of dealing with other sections of the agency and the wishes of clients. Sometimes they seemed conscious of their supposed power to shape the habits or views of consumers, sometimes they seemed frustrated by their inability to fashion the necessary tools of persuasion. On occasion the ad-makers did work as a team, collaborating to produce, in one case, a pro bono campaign for a cancer association. But they also competed vigorously to win the approval of Mason, an accomplished woman and a partner, who stood above the fray. "Nobody talks about it, nobody says a word, but the real engine running the place is the primal desire to kill," claimed the narrator. "To be the best ad person in the building, to inspire jealousy, to defeat all the rest. The threat of layoffs just made it a more efficient machine" (109). In the end only two admen escaped, one to launch a successful landscaping firm and the other to get killed in Afghanistan.

46 Rachel Savage, "WPP Boss Martin Sorrell: 'Don Draper wouldn't recognise 75% of what we do,' *Management Today*, 12 June 2014, updated 25 April 2016. See also Tanya Dua, "What's on Martin Sorrell's Mind: 'We need to rename advertising,'" *Digiday*, 1 October 2015; Eric Reguly, "Beyond Don Draper: The Tireless Tycoon at the Helm of the World's Largest Ad Group," Toronto *Globe and Mail*, 27 March 2015; Deborah Bothun and Daniel Gross, "Thought Leader Interview: Sir Martin Sorrell," in *Strategy & Business* Special Report, Global Entertainment and Media Outlook 2016–2020: A World of Differences, www.strategy-business.com/outlook, accessed 4 August 2016.

47 Bureau of Labor Statistics, "Employed Persons by Detailed Occupation …," 2016, www.bls.gov/cps/cpsaat11.pdf, accessed 17 April 2017.

Afterword: The Triumph of the Huckster

1 A.J. Delgado is a self-declared conservative columnist, a Hispanic American, the daughter of Cuban immigrants. Her gender, her ethnic background, and even her political views made her unusual among the sympathizers of Donald J. Trump. See her "Reasons Why It Should Be Donald Trump in 2016," www.breitbart.com, 22 October 2015, accessed 9 August 2016.

2 The speech was widely available on the web, including YouTube, as was a printed version. One version, complete with a barrage of footnotes to prove Trump's claims, was at assets.donaldjtrump.com/DJT_Acceptance_Speech.pdf, accessed 19 August 2016.

3 David Smith, "Trump's Republican Convention Speech: What He Said and What He Meant," *The Guardian*, 22 July 2016, www.theguardian.com/us-news/ng-interactive/2016/jul/22/donald-trump-republican-convention-speech-transcript-annotated, accessed 20 August 2016; "FACT CHECK: Donald Trump's Republican Convention Speech, Annotated," NPR, 21 July 2016, www.npr.org/2016/07/21/486883610/fact-check-donald-trumps-republican-convention-speech-annotated, accessed 20 August 2016; John Cassidy, "Donald Trump's Dark, Dark Convention Speech," *The New Yorker*, 22 July 2016, www.newyorker.com/news/john-cassidy/donald-trumps-dark-dark-convention-speech, accessed 20 August 2016.

4 Alexander Burns, "Donald Trump May Break the Mold, but He Fits a Pattern, Too," *New York Times*, 21 July 2016, www.nytimes.com/2016/07/21/us/politics/donald-trump-presidential-race.html, accessed 20 August 2016.

5 David French, "Trump's Speech Makes It Official: It's Democrat v. Democrat in 2016," *National Review*, 22 July 2016, www.nationalreview.com/article/438234/donald-trump-convention-speech-small-government-conservatism-dead, accessed 20 August 2016.

6 David Brooks, "The Dark Knight," *New York Times*, 22 July 2016, www.nytimes.com/2016/07/22/opinion/campaign-stops/the-dark-knight.html, accessed 19 August 2016. Brooks's comment alluded to the character of Batman, who had warred to save a corrupted Gotham city in a very popular series of movies.

7 Sam Leith, "Donald Trump's Convention Speech Dissected," *Financial Times*, 22 July 2016, www.ft.com/content/38e84758-5566-11e6-9664-e0bdc13c3bef, accessed 20 August 2016.

8 Brian Stelter, "Trump Prevails over Clinton in Convention Speech Ratings Race," CNNmoney, 30 July 2016, money.cnn.com/2016/07/29/media/democratic-convention-night-four-ratings/, accessed 18 April 2017.

9 Jennifer Agiesta, "Donald Trump Bounces into the Lead," CNN, 25 July 2016, www.cnn.com/2016/07/25/politics/donald-trump-hillary-clinton-poll/index.html, accessed 20 August 2016.

10 Ben Mathis-Lilley, "Trump's Convention Speech Most Poorly Received since 1996, Poll Finds," *Slate*, 27 July 2016, www.slate.com/blogs/the_slatest/2016/07/27/gallup_trump_rnc_speech_least_liked_since_company_began_collecting_data.html, accessed 20 August 2016, and "More People Watched Donald Trump's Convention Speech than Hillary Clinton's – and Hated It," *Washington Post*, 1 August 2016, www.washingtonpost.com/news/the-fix/wp/2016/08/01/more-people-watched-donald-trumps-convention-speech-than-hillary-clintons-and-hated-it/?utm_term=.02d28072ad06, accessed 20 August 2016.

11 *CBC Fifth Estate*, "The Rise and Rage of Donald Trump: The Fire Breather," 11 March 2016; *Sky News*, "Trump: America's Next President?" 17 March 2016; *Channel 4 (UK)* "The Mad World of Donald Trump," 27 March 2016; or *BBC Panorama* "Angry America," 20 July 2016.

12 Aside from the previously mentioned BBC documentary, which focused on Bakersfield California, two other essays were especially good explorations of the causes and the mood: Thomas Frank, "Millions of Ordinary Americans Support Donald Trump. Here's Why," *The Guardian*, 8 March 2016, www.theguardian.com/commentisfree/www.theguardian.com/commentisfree/, accessed 9 August 2016, and Arlie Russell Hochschild, "No Country for White Men," *Mother Jones*, October 2016, 20–9.

13 "Fear trumps hope," *The Economist*, 7 May 2016, www.economist.com/news/briefing/21698252-donald-trump-going-be-republican-candidate-presidency-terrible-news, accessed 19 August 2016; Julian Baggini, "How Rising Trump and Sanders Parallel Rising Populism in Europe," *New Perspectives Quarterly* 33.2 (May 2016): 22–5; Martin Eiermann, "How Donald Trump Fits into the History of American Populism," *New Perspectives Quarterly* 33 (May 2016): 29–34.

14 That observation owes much to a marvellous essay on Trump's rivals by Eliot Weinberger, "They Could Have Picked …," *London Review of Books*, 28 July 2016, Kindle Edition.

15 In addition to the essays mentioned above, see John Kenneth White, "Donald Trump and the Scourge of Populism," *The Forum* 14.3 (October 2016): 265–79, and Edward G. Carmines, Michael J. Ensley, and Michael W. Wagner, "Ideological Heterogeneity and the Rise of Donald Trump," *The Forum* 14.4 (December 2016): 385–97.

16 The phrase comes from a documentary, *CBC Fifth Estate*, "The Rise and Rage of Donald Trump: The Fire Breather," 11 March 2016.

17 Cited in *CBC Fifth Estate*, "The Rise and Rage of Donald Trump."

18 "He indeed was the P.T. Barnum of his time – in Atlantic City, flashy, gaudy," said Robin Leach, the famed host of *Lifestyles of the Rich and Famous*: from an interview in The History Channel, "The Making of Trump," 1 March 2016. See also Evan Osnos, "The Fearful and the Frustrated: Donald Trump's Nationalist Coalition Takes Shape – For Now," *The New Yorker*, 31 August 2015, www.newyorker.com/magazine/2015/08/31/the-fearful-and-the-frustrated, accessed 9 August 2016.

19 This was an interpretation argued strongly in an online version of the academic journal *Television & New Media*, online June 2016. The claim had been made much earlier by a journalist, Jessica Yellin, "Trump's Playing Politics by Reality Show Rules," *The Daily Beast*, 16 September 2015.

20 Neal Gabler, "We All Enabled Donald Trump: Our Deeply Unserious Media and Reality-TV Culture Made This Horror Inevitable," *Salon*, 14 March 2016, www.salon.com/2016/03/14/we_all_enabled_donald_trump_our_deeply_unserious_media_and_reality_tv_culture_made_this_horror_inevitable/, accessed 6 August 2016.

21 This too was nothing new when it came to Trump's reputation: see Richard Cohen, "Donald Trump: The Comeback Huckster," *Washington Post*, 18 April 2011, www.washingtonpost.com/opinions/donald-trump-the-comeback-huckster/2011/04/18/AFtvej0D_story.html?utm_term=.b7a09ae6d708, accessed 16 August 2016. But see also David Vognar, "Trump the Huckster," *Huffington Post*, 25 May 2016, www.huffingtonpost.com/david-vognar/trump-the-huckster_b_10131478.html, accessed 16 August 2016; Helaine Olen, "The Huckster-in-Chief," *Slate*, June 2016, www.slate.com/articles/business/moneybox/2016/06/what_the_trump_university_playbooks_really_teach_us.html, accessed 16 August 2016; or Robert Reich, "The Huckster Populist," www.facebook.com/RBReich/posts/ (later robertreich.org/post/146997952550), accessed 16 August 2016 (which appeared also on the website of the Daily Kos and SFGate, 8 July 2016).

22 Dan P. McAdams. "The Mind of Donald Trump," *The Atlantic*, June 2016, www.theatlantic.com/magazine/archive/2016/06/the-mind-of-donald-trump/480771/, accessed 16 August 2016.

23 Joe Pompeo, "Dowd on Trump's Transformation from 'Huckster' to 'Hitler," *Politico*, 12 March 2016, www.politico.com/blogs/on-media/2016/03/dowd-on-trumps-transformation-from-huckster-to-hitler-220678, accessed 16 March 2016. See also Christian Salmon, "Trump, Fascism, and the Construction of 'the People': An Interview with Judith Butler," *Mediapart*, 29 December 2016, www.versobooks.com/blogs/3025-trump-fascism-and-the-construction-of-the-people-an-interview-with-judith-butler, accessed 8 April

2017, and William E. Connolly, "Trump, the Working Class, and Fascist Rhetoric," *Theory & Event* 20.1 (January 2017), Supplement, 23–37.

24 Malcolm Harris, "It Really Can Happen Here: The Novel that Foreshadowed Donald Trump's Authoritarian Appeal," *Salon*, 29 September 2015, www.salon.com/2015/09/29/it_really_can_happen_here_the_novel_ that_foreshadowed_donald_trumps_authoritarian_appeal/, accessed 9 August 2016. And there were similarities between the promises and the style of Senator Windrip, Lewis' villain, and those of Donald Trump. Others noticed the similarities to the scenario outlined in Philip Roth's more recent novel *The Plot against America* (2004): David Denby, "The Plot Against America: Donald Trump's Rhetoric," *The New Yorker*, 15 December 2015.

25 See M. David, "Harvard Psychologist Explains Trump Is 'Dangerous' Because He's Literally a Narcissistic Psychopath," *Counter Current News*, 27 February 2016, countercurrentnews.com, accessed 15 August 2016; James Hamblin, "Donald Trump: Sociopath?," *The Atlantic*, 20 July 2016, www. theatlantic.com/health/archive/2016/07/trump-and-sociopathy/491966/, accessed 15 August 2016; Daniel Berger, "Donald Trump: Profile of a Sociopath," *Huffington Post*, 3 August 2016, www.huffingtonpost.com/ daniel-berger/trump-profile-of-a-sociopath_b_11318128.html, accessed 15 August 2016; and Anton Ashcroft, "Donald Trump: Narcissist, Psychopath or Representative of the People?" *Psychotherapy and Politics International* 14.3 (October 2016): 217–22.

26 The actual report was by Jane Mayer, variously entitled "Trump's Boswell Speaks" (in print) and "Donald Trump's Ghostwriter Tells All" (online). Here Schwartz was cast as the real author of the hit book, now contrite because he had made Trump so famous. He claimed he would retitle the bestseller "The Sociopath."

27 Andrew Sullivan, "America Has Never Been So Ripe for Tyranny," *New York Magazine*, 1 May 2016, nymag.com/daily/intelligencer/2016/04/america-tyranny-donald-trump.html, accessed 8 September 2016. Or Kim Bellware, "Donald Trump Is 'A Unique Threat to American Democracy: *Washington Post*," 24 July 2016, www.huffingtonpost.ca/entry/donald-trump-washington-post-threat_us_579502a9e4b0d3568f8397e1, accessed 26 August 2016. Sullivan's essay was a particularly fine discussion of Trump's character and rise, if from the perspective of a libertarian.

28 In my account of the phenomenon, I draw on Jackson Lears, "Beyond Veblen: Rethinking Consumer Culture in America," in Simon J. Bronner, ed., *Consuming Visions: Accumulation and Display of Goods in America 1880–1920*, published for The Henry Francis du Pont Winterthur Museum (New York and London: W.W. Norton, 1989), 75–6.

29 This is discussed in an intriguing piece by the Foucault scholar Bernard E. Harcourt: "Questions on Avowal, Subjectivity, and Truth," 6 March 2016, http://blogs.law.columbia.edu/foucault1313/2016/03/06/three-questions-on-avowal-subjectivity-and-truth/, accessed 19 August 2016.

30 In June 2015 Trump had nearly three million followers, a number that rapidly escalated to 12.8 million before the election and reached twenty million just before he was inaugurated as president. Of course many of the accounts were dormant. See Kevin Drum, "Raw Data: Donald Trump's Twitter Followers," *Mother Jones*, 22 December 2016, www.motherjones.com/kevin-drum/2016/12/raw-data-donald-trumps-twitter-followers, accessed 6 April 2017; Angeli Kakade, "Here's How Many Fake Twitter Followers Trump Has," www.aol.com/article/news/2017/02/08/heres-how-many-fake-twitter-followers-trump-has/21710754/, accessed 6 April 2017; and Rob Salkowitz, "Trump's 20 Million Twitter Followers Get Smaller under the Microscope," www.forbes.com/sites/robsalkowitz/2017/01/17/trumps-20-million-twitter-followers-get-smaller-under-the-microscope/#7f43b72c4407, accessed 6 April 2017.

31 Zachary Crockett, "What I Learned Analyzing 7 Months of Donald Trump's Tweets," 16 May 2016, www.vox.com/2016/5/16/11603854/donald-trump-twitter, accessed 31 March 2017. On the strengths and weaknesses of Twitter as a tool of political discourse, as well as Trump's success, see also Andreas Jungherr, "Twitter Use in Election Campaigns: A Systematic Literature Review," *Journal of Information Technology & Politics* 13.1 (January 2016): 72–91, and Brian L. Ott, "The Age of Twitter: Donald J. Trump and the Politics of Debasement," *Critical Studies in Media Communication* 34.1 (January 2017): 59–68.

32 Chris Wells, Dhavan V. Shah, Jon C. Pevehouse, Junghwan Yang, Ayellet Pelled, Frederick Boehm, Josephine Lukito, Shreenita Ghosh, and Jessica L. Schmidt, "How Trump Drove Coverage to the Nomination: Hybrid Media Campaigning," *Political Communication* 33.4 (October 2016): 669–76. One professor of English and a media scholar, Richard A. Grusin, later compared Trump to a form of algae which chocked the media space: "Donald Trump's Evil Mediation," *Theory & Event* 20.1 (January 2017), Supplement, 86–99. See also Julia R. Azari, "How the News Media Helped to Nominate Trump," *Political Communication* 33.4 (October 2016): 677–80.

33 The Pew Research Center claimed 44 per cent of Americans got news from Facebook. Cited in Olivia Solon, "Facebook's Failure: Did Fake News and Polarized Politics Get Trump Elected?" *The Guardian*, 10 November 2016, www.theguardian.com/technology/2016/nov/10/facebook-fake-news-election-conspiracy-theories, accessed 31 March 2017. The article went on

to explore the prevalence and problems of fake news on Facebook. Another essay at NYMag.com summarized the ill: "All throughout the election, these fake stories, sometimes papered over with flimsy 'parody site' disclosures somewhere in small type, circulated throughout Facebook: The Pope endorses Trump. Hillary Clinton bought $137 million in illegal arms. The Clintons bought a $200 million house in the Maldives. Many got hundreds of thousands, if not millions, of shares, likes, and comments; enough people clicked through to the posts to generate significant profits for their creators. The valiant efforts of Snopes and other debunking organizations were insufficient; Facebook's labyrinthine sharing and privacy settings mean that fact-checks get lost in the shuffle. Often, no one would even need to click on and read the story for the headline itself to become a widely distributed talking point, repeated elsewhere online, or, sometimes, in real life. (Here's an in-the-wild sighting of a man telling a woman that Clinton and her longtime aide Huma Abedin are lovers, based on 'material that appeared to have been printed off the internet.')" At nymag.com/selectall/2016/11/donald-trump-won-because-of-facebook.html, accessed 2 April 2017.

34 Neal Gabler, "Donald Trump, the Emperor of Social Media," 29 April 2016, billmoyers.com/story/donald-trump-the-emperor-of-social-media/, accessed 31 March 2017.

35 The figure of nearly $2 billion from Mark Andrejevic, "The Jouissance of Trump," *Television & New Media* 17.5 (June 2016): 3, online at journals. sagepub.com/doi/abs/10.1177/1527476416652694. By the time he won the election, that estimate had ballooned to $5 billion: Grusin, "Donald Trump's Evil Mediation," S-92.

36 "Trump Promises Harsh Media Criticism of Him Will Be ILLEGAL If He's President," Counter Current News, 27 February 2016, countercurrentnews. com, accessed 18 August 2016.

37 On political advertising, for example, see the classic history, if now dated, by Edwin Diamond and Stephen Bates, *The Spot: The Rise of Political Advertising on Television* (Cambridge, MA, and London: MIT Press, 1984).

38 A Super PAC is a supposedly independent group tasked with raising massive amounts of monies from corporations, unions, or individuals, much of which gets spent on political advertising. The material on Trump and his rivals came from Molly Ball, "'There's Nothing Better Than a Scared, Rich Candidate.' How Political Consulting Works – or Doesn't," *The Atlantic*, October 2016, www.theatlantic.com/magazine/archive/2016/10/theres-nothing-better-than-a-scared-rich-candidate/497522/, accessed 4 October 2016.

39 "… there is the political consultant class, whose entire cushy livelihoods are threatened by Trump's rise. Why? He's shown you can make it without

their useless input and advice. The pointless wizard behind the curtain is
revealed – uh-oh. Standing up for Trump is also standing up against these
Pharisees."

40 Ball, "'There's Nothing Better Than a Scared, Rich Candidate.'" She
went on to cite a raft of academics who had tested and questioned the
effectiveness of political advertising in past contests as well. Things changed
somewhat during the months of the actual presidential campaign. Although
Clinton spent much more on television ads, the Trump team made greater
use of targeted digital ads, so much so that afterwards there arose a claim
these ads were crucial to his narrow victory in key states. See "The Candidate
Ad Spending Race," Associated Press, 15 November 2016, elections.
ap.org/content/ad-spending, accessed 31 March 2017; Rebecca Stewart,
"US Political Ad Spend Hit Record High in 2016 but TV Lost Momentum
Thanks to Donald Trump," www.thedrum.com/news/2017/01/04/
us-political-ad-spend-hit-record-high-2016-tv-lost-momentum-thanks-donald-
trump, 4 January 2017, accessed 31 March 2017; Hannes Grassegger and
Mikael Krogerus, "The Data That Turned the World Upside Down," 28
January 2017, motherboard.vice.com/en_us/article/mg9vvn/how-our-
likes-helped-trump-win, accessed 2 April 2017; "How the Trump Campaign
Built an Identity Database and Used Facebook Ads to Win the Election,"
medium.com/startup-grind/how-the-trump-campaign-built-an-identity-
database-and-used-facebook-ads-to-win-the-election-4ff7d24269ac, accessed
2 April 2017; but from this sceptic, Dave Karpf, "Will the Real Psychometric
Targeters Please Stand Up," civichall.org/civicist/will-the-real-psychometric-
targeters-please-stand-up/, 1 February 2017, accessed 7 April 2017.

41 Cited in Michael Hainey, "Clint and Scott Eastwood: No Holds Barred in
Their First Interview Together," *Esquire*, 3 August 2016, www.esquire.com/
entertainment/a46893/double-trouble-clint-and-scott-eastwood, accessed 5
August 2016.

42 Neil Macdonald, "Trump's War on Political Correctness Redefining U.S.
Race," *CBC News*, 30 March 2016, www.cbc.ca/news/politics/, accessed
5 August 2016. So too did 62 per cent of Democrats and 68 per cent of
Independents.

43 David Denby, "The Plot Against America: Donald Trump's Rhetoric," *The
New Yorker*, 15 December 2015, www.newyorker.com/culture/cultural-
comment/plot-america-donald-trumps-rhetoric, accessed 9 August 2016;
Serina Sandhu, "Donald Trump's Use of Grammar 'Typical of Children
Aged 11 and Under'," *The Independent*, 17 March 2016, www.independent.
co.uk/news/world/americas/us-elections/donald-trump-uses-language-
typical-of-children-under-11-a6936256.html, accessed 9 August 2016;

George Will, "Is There a Method to Trump's Madness?" 3 August 2016, *National Review* Archive, www.nationalreview.com/article/438649/donald-trumps-method-his-madness, accessed 9 August 2016; Claire Cain Miller, "Measuring Trump's Language: Bluster but Also Words That Appeal to Women," *New York Times*, 14 March 2016, https://www.nytimes.com/2016/03/15/upshot/donald-trump-is-among-the-most-feminine-sounding-candidates.html, accessed 9 August 2016; John McWhorter, "Trump Is Extremely Articulate – That's Why He's So Dangerous," *Time*, 14 March 2016, time.com, accessed 9 August 2016.

44 David Paulin, "Donald Trump Raises Uncomfortable Truths," American Thinker, www.americanthinker.com/articles/2015/07/, 10 July 2015, accessed 9 August 2016.

45 Fred Rice, identified as a "Republican state representative," in Osnos, "The Fearful and the Frustrated."

46 Ibid.

47 Anthony Zurcher, "Fear and Anger in Trump-land," www.bbc.com/news, 11 August 2016, accessed 12 August 2016.

48 Sandra Stone, Florida, March 2016: "US Election: 50 Trump Supporters Explain Why," *BBC*, 13 June 2016, www.bbc.com/news/, accessed 9 August 2016.

49 Zurcher, "Fear and Anger."

50 "Trump takes an expansive view of reality. 'I play to people's fantasies,' he writes in 'The Art of the Deal,' his 1987 memoir. 'I call it truthful hyperbole. It's an innocent form of exaggeration – and a very effective form of promotion.'" Jane Mayer, "Trump's Boswell Speaks," 23.

51 Salena Zito, "Taking Trump Seriously, Not Literally," *The Atlantic*, 23 September 2016, www.theatlantic.com/politics/archive/2016/09/trump-makes-his-case-in-pittsburgh/501335/, accessed 8 April 2017.

52 See, for example, Amanda Taub, "The Rise of American Authoritarianism," 1 March 2016, www.vox.com/2016/3/1/11127424/trump-authoritarianism, accessed 6 April 2017. "People who score high in authoritarianism, when they feel threatened, look for strong leaders who promise to take whatever action necessary to protect them from outsiders and prevent the changes they fear." "What he [Andrew McWilliams, a PhD student] found was astonishing: Not only did authoritarianism correlate, but it seemed to predict support for Trump more reliably than virtually any other indicator." And as Taub reported, other scholars were also finding the growth of authoritarianism.

53 "Lots of Americans are thus strongly attracted by the prospect of a man – or woman – on horseback: a bold, decisive individual who will sweep

away all the quibblers and naysayers, the obstructionists and the special interests, and just get something done. The persona Trump cultivated in 'The Apprentice,' a show that was on prime-time television for 11 years, was a perfect fit for this kind of appeal. Every week showcased Trump in a position of apparently complete authority, dispensing advice, subjecting the contestants to a severe grilling, and, of course, summarily 'firing' anyone who did not meet his high standards." William G. Mayer, "Why Trump – and How Far Can He Go?," *The Forum* 13.4 (2015): 545.

54 Hence this comment from a self-declared Christian perspective: "But the main reason I call him 'a good candidate with flaws' is that I think most of the policies he supports are those that will do the most good for the nation." Wayne Grudem, "Why Voting for Donald Trump Is a Morally Good Choice," 28 July 2016, townhall.com/columnists/waynegrudem/, accessed 9 August 2016.

55 See Frank Bruni, "Blood, Sweat and Trump," *New York Times*, 23 December 2015, www.nytimes.com/2015/12/23/opinion/blood-sweat-and-trump. html, accessed 19 August 2016, and Thomas B. Edsall, "Purity, Disgust and Donald Trump," *New York Times*, 6 January 2016, www.nytimes. com/2016/01/06/opinion/campaign-stops/purity-disgust-and-donald- trump.html, accessed 16 August 2016.

56 Some of the biopolitical angle was outlined, though not in name, by Alexander Hurst, "Donald Trump and the Politics of Disgust," *New Republic*, 31 December 2015, newrepublic.com, accessed 19 August 2016 and McAdams, "The Mind of Donald Trump."

57 Hence this critique: "There is, similarly, no reason to suppose he is racist, as many have. But a significant minority of his supporters are – 17% of them consider ethnic diversity bad for America, a strikingly high number – and Mr. Trump's dog-whistling on immigration seems at least partly designed to appeal to them. No wonder 86% of African-Americans and 80% of Hispanics have a negative view of him. Through a conscious effort to spread discord he regularly transgresses moral lines that no decent American public figure ever should." "Fear Trumps Hope," *The Economist*, 7 May 2016.

58 Jesse Graham, Jonathan Haidt, and Brian A. Nosek, "Liberals and Conservatives Rely on Different Sets of Moral Foundations," *Journal of Personality and Social Psychology* 96.5 (May 2009): 1029–46. See also Yoel Inbar, David Pizarro, Ravi Iyer, and Jonathan Haidt, "Disgust Sensitivity, Political Conservatism, and Voting," *Social Psychological and Personality Science* 3.5 (September 2012): 537–54 and Haidt, "What Makes People Vote Republican?" *Edge* website, www.edge.org/conversation/jonathan_haidt- what-makes-people-vote-republican, accessed 18 August 2016.

59 On 9 November, right after the election, David Remnick, editor of *The New Yorker*, published a particularly dismal response to Trump's victory that expressed the shock of many public intellectuals. In his widely read essay "An American Tragedy" he declared, "That the electorate has, in its plurality, decided to live in Trump's world of vanity, hate, arrogance, untruth, and recklessness, his disdain for democratic norms, is a fact that will lead, inevitably, to all manner of national decline and suffering." At www.newyorker.com/news/news-desk/an-american-tragedy-2, accessed 9 April 2017.

60 A poll organized by the *Washington Post* and ABC News found seven in ten Americans viewed him unfavourably, and over 50 per cent felt "strongly" about that opinion. Scott Clement, "Negative Views of Donald Trump Just Hit a New Campaign High: 7 in 10 Americans," *Washington Post*, 15 June 2016.

61 Sean J. Miller, "Digital Ad Spending Tops Estimates," www. campaignsandelections.com/campaign-insider/digital-ad-spending-tops-estimates, 4 January 2017, accessed 31 March 2017.

62 In mid-November 2016, Oxford Dictionaries had declared "post-truth" the Word of the Year: an adjective "relating to or denoting circumstances in which objective facts are less influential in shaping public opinion than appeals to emotion and personal belief" (www.oxforddictionaries.com/press/news/2016/12/11/WOTY-16, accessed 9 April 2017). Oxford had noted how the adjective, coined as early as 1992, had come into common use because of the Brexit referendum in the UK and the presidential race in the US. A year earlier the communications scholar Jayson Harsin had already proclaimed there was a shift in "multiple societies" from regimes of truth to "regimes of posttruth": "Regimes of Posttruth, Postpolitics, and Attention Economies," *Communication, Culture & Critique* 8.2 (June 2015): 327–33.

63 CNN and CBS polls in the summer of 2016 found two-thirds of respondents thought Clinton dishonest. Cited in Aaron Blake, "4 Brutal Numbers that Greet Hillary Clinton at the Democratic National Convention," *Washington Post*, 25 July 2016, at washingtonpost.com, accessed 9 April 2017. The CNN poll found only 30 per cent deemed her "honest and trustworthy," whereas 43 per cent thought that way about Trump.

64 One amusing reflection on post-truth as a staple of history, and not just modernity, was ascribed to a poem by Geoffrey Chaucer: see Eleanor Parker, "Chaucer's Post-Truth World," posted 9 February 2017, *History Today*, www.historytoday.com, accessed 30 March 2017.

65 Martin Jay, *The Virtues of Mendacity: On Lying in Politics* (Charlottesville and London: University of Virginia Press, 2010), Kindle Edition.

66 This, of course, was widely recognized by critics of the post-truth argument.
The columnist Barton Swain in the *Washington Post* (5 January 2017) directly
addressed the arrival of post-truth politics. "The latter event, particularly as
embodied by Trump's campaign, was said to be uniquely bereft of respect
for factual truth. Well, maybe; but surely we aren't prepared to say that
American culture pre-Trump was characterized by reverence for truth. Long
before Trump got here, our political debates teemed with disinformation of
every variety: gross hyperbole, calculated non sequiturs, culpable omissions,
unfalsifiable accusations, deliberate vagueness, outright lies. It seems wrong
to associate only Trump with this alleged new era of untruth; thousands
before him did their part." At washingtonpost.com, accessed 9 April 2017.
In support of such claims, consider the evidence of negative advertising
in this book of twenty-five years earlier: Kathleen Hall Jamieson, *Dirty
Politics: Deception, Distraction, and Democracy* (New York and Oxford: Oxford
University Press, 1992).

67 The Gallup polling agency has carried on for years a survey of "confidence
in institutions." In early June 2016 the combined ranking of "a great deal"
and "quite a lot" stood at 21 per cent for television news and 20 per cent for
newspapers (the military were at the top at 73 per cent). Only 19 per cent had
as much confidence in Internet news. Compare this to 46 per cent (1993) and
then 35 per cent (1994) for television news (the first years it was surveyed) and
42 per cent (1973), 30 per cent (1990), or 12 per cent (2008) for newspapers.

68 This involved identifying other politicians noted for duplicity or
mendacity, such as Lyndon Johnson, Richard Nixon, or Bill Clinton, and
finding potential demagogues such as William Randolph Hearst, Charles
Lindbergh, or George Wallace. It also meant tracking down the history of
the assorted ideas Trump expressed during the course of the campaigns.
One especially imaginative and useful result was a series of Trump syllabi,
reading lists for a possible course, launched initially by *The Chronicle of
Higher Education* (19 June 2016) and available on the web: the first Trump
Syllabus (www.chronicle.com/article/Trump-Syllabus/236824), soon after
Trump Syllabus 2.0 (www.publicbooks.org/trump-syllabus-2-0/), and in
January 2017, from Nyron Crawford and Matt Wray, Trump Syllabus 3.0
(www.publicbooks.org/trump-syllabus-3-0/), all accessed 6 April 2017.

69 Ralph Keyes, *The Post-Truth Era: Dishonesty and Deception in Contemporary Life*,
New York: St Martin's Press, 2004. Keyes's target was really the spread and
the frequency of casual lying, though he did have some very interesting
descriptions of lying in many domains. He did not consider advertising at all.
    Before Keyes, there had been other works on the frequency and the im-
port of deception in the public sphere of America, even treatments of what

we now call fake news: see, for instance, Cynthia Crossen's *Tainted Truth: The Manipulation of Fact in America,* 1994 (New York: Simon & Schuster, 1996), which exposed what she considered the massive amount of biased and dubious research about all sorts of public issues which was published and circulated in America. And then there were attacks on the apparent surge of propaganda, such as Anthony R. Pratkanis and Elliot Aronson's *Age of Propaganda: The Everyday Use and Abuse of Persuasion* (New York: W.H. Freeman, 1992), which sought to combat the ill-effects of all the mass persuasion, meaning advertising, spin, and outright propaganda. Suspicion, it had long appeared, was as necessary as trust to living an effective life in America, however contradictory that might sound.

The more recent controversy over the selling of the war on Iraq back in 2003 surely demonstrated the need for an aware, thus suspicious, citizenry. Among the many studies occasioned by that war, I will cite only Sheldon Rampton and John Stauber's *Weapons of Mass Deception: The Uses of Propaganda in Bush's War on Iraq* (New York: Tarcher/Penguin, 2003) and my own *Weapons of Mass Persuasion, Marketing the War Against Iraq* (Toronto: University of Toronto Press, 2004). That book drew on the literature about "the propaganda state," particularly the work of Noam Chomsky, to argue that "democracy was overwhelmed by a torrent of lies, half-truths, infotainment, and marketing" (193). The deceptions involved in the ongoing War on Terror, in a similar fashion, generated a spate of documentaries, American and foreign, on marketing and deceit in wartime, with such titles as *War Is Sell* (2004), *Spinning Terror* (2006), *There You Go Again: Orwell Comes to America. Propaganda Then and Now* (2007), *The Lies That Led To War* (2007), *Militainment, Inc.: Militarism & Pop Culture* (2007), or *War Made Easy: How Presidents & Pundits Keep Spinning Us to Death* (2008).

The alarms raised over the post-truth politics in the aftermath of Brexit and Trump, in short, were yet another entry in an ongoing narrative of outrage over the danger to democracy of deception in its many forms. These stories might just as well be cited as evidence that a regime of truth persists, sufficient to provoke analysis and outcry, as evidence that artifice and propaganda are everywhere. At the time of writing, it is not at all clear whether the operations of the Trump presidency will mark a permanent change in what appears to be a long-lasting but often-shifting balance between truth and deception in the game of politics.

CONCEPT INDEX

NAME INDEX

Parenthetical designations indicate either the role of a person or source in this cultural biography or the title of the work in which a fictional character appears. Fictional characters are listed by their first name, wherever that name is available.